Intercultural Communication: A Reader

Seventh Edition

LARRY A. SAMOVAR
San Diego State University

RICHARD E. PORTER
California State University, Long Beach

Wadsworth Publishing Company
Belmont, California
A Division of Wadsworth, Inc.

Communication Editor: Holly Allen
Editorial Assistant: Joshua King
Production: Mary Douglas/Myrna Engler
Print Buyer: Barbara Britton
Permissions Editor: Robert Kauser
Copy Editor: Lura S. Harrison
Compositor: TypeLink, Inc.
Cover Design: Craig Hanson
Cover Photograph: Adventure Photo
Printer: Malloy Lithographing, Inc.

I(T)P ™

International Thomson Publishing
The trademark ITP is used under license

© 1994 by Wadsworth, Inc.

Printed in the United States of America
1 2 3 4 5 6 7 8 9 10—98 97 96 95 94

Library of Congress Cataloging in Publication Data

Intercultural communication: a reader / [edited by]
    Larry A. Samovar, Richard E. Porter. — 7th ed.
        p. cm.
    Includes bibliographical references and index.
    ISBN 0-534-20832-0
    1. Intercultural communication.   I. Samovar,
Larry A.   II. Porter, Richard E.
HM258.I52   1993
303.48′2 — dc20   93-22761
                                                          CIP

Contents

Chapter 3 Co-Cultures: Living in Two Cultures   125

PART THREE
INTERCULTURAL INTERACTION:
TAKING PART IN INTERCULTURAL COMMUNICATION   173

Chapter 4 Verbal Processes: Thinking and Speaking   176

**PART FOUR
INTERCULTURAL COMMUNICATION:
SEEKING IMPROVEMENT   333**

Chapter 8 Ethical Considerations: Prospects for the Future 406

Index 445

Preface

The occasion of this seventh edition of our book has been one of excitement. The fact that we have been received with the popularity to warrant a new addition is exciting and obviously pleasing. Yet as we proceeded, we wanted to be cautious enough to preserve the basic framework and philosophy that has sustained us through six previous editions. It would have been imprudent of us to abandon an orientation to intercultural communication that has found wide acceptance for over two decades. The field as well as the authors, however, have continued to evolve; we knew, therefore, that some reshaping was necessary. This latest edition grants us the opportunity to combine these two complementary positions. First, it reflects our continued belief that the basic core of the field should not be changed for the sake of simply being novel. This type of change would rob the book of those concepts that have been infused into all the other editions. Second, we believe that as our intercultural contacts change both in number and intensity, there is a need to present essays that mirror that change. We have always perceived each new edition as an opportunity to examine that change and to stake out new territory for the field — territory that takes into account the complexities of communicating in the 1990s.

As the field of intercultural communication has grown, we have attempted in each new edition to grow with the field and to fuse the old with the new. In 1972, the first edition contained 34 articles and essays. The sixth edition contained 45; now there are 42 articles in our collection of readings. Some of these have appeared in all previous editions. In this seventh edition, we have 19 new essays, 13 of which were prepared especially for this volume.

APPROACH

The basic motivation driving this book has remained the same since both authors became interested in the topic of intercultural communication some 25 years ago. It is our sincere belief that the ability to communicate effectively with people from diverse cultures and co-cultures benefits each of us as individuals, and has potential to benefit the other 5.5 billion people with whom we share this planet. We have intentionally selected materials that will assist you in understanding those intercultural communication principles that are instrumental to the achievement of success when interacting with people from diverse cultures.

Fundamental to our approach is the conviction that communication is a social activity; it is something people do with and to each other. While the activity might begin in our heads, it is manifested in our behaviors—be they verbal or nonverbal. In both explicit and implicit ways, the information and the advice contained in this book is usable; the ideas presented can be translated into action.

USE

As in the past, we intend this anthology to be for the general reader. We have, consequently, selected materials that are broadly based, comprehensive, and suitable for both undergraduate and graduate students. Although the level of difficulty varies from article to article, we have not gone beyond the level found in most textbooks aimed at college and university students.

Intercultural Communication: A Reader is designed to meet three specific needs. The first comes from a canon that maintains that successful intercultural communication is a matter of highest importance if humankind and society are to survive. Events during the last 20 years have created a world that sees us linked together in a multitude of ways. From pollution to economics to health care, what happens to one culture has the potential to happen to all cultures. This book, then, is designed to serve as a *basic anthology* for courses concerned with the issues associated with human interaction. Our intention is to make this book theoretical and practical so that the issues associated with intercultural communication can be first understood and then acted upon.

Second, the book may be used as a *supplementary text* in existing service and basic communication skills courses and interpersonal communication courses. The rationale is a simple one: Understanding other cultures is indispensable in this age of cross-cultural contact. It matters very little if that contact is face to face or on the public platform.

Third, the book provides *resource material* for courses in communication theory, small group communication, organizational and business communication, and mass communication, as well as for courses in anthropology, sociology, social psychology, social welfare, social policy, business, and international relations. The long list of possible uses only serves to underscore the increased level of intercultural interaction that is characteristic of what is often called the "global village."

ORGANIZATION

The book is organized into four closely related parts. In Part One, "Intercultural Communication: An Introduction," our purpose is twofold: We hope to acquaint you with the basic concepts of intercultural communication while at the same time arousing your interest in the topic. Hence, the essays in this part are both theoretical and philosophical. The selections explain what intercultural communication is and why it is important.

Part Two, "Socio-Cultural Backgrounds: What We Bring to Intercultural Communication," has two chapters that both serve the same goal: They seek to examine the influence of socio-cultural forces on human interaction. Chapter Two deals with how these forces direct the communication patterns of people from international cultures. To make this point, we have selected cultures from the Arab world, East Asia, India, and Greece. While many cultures have been left out, you will still be able to get an appreciation of the link between culture and behavior.

Chapter Three moves us from the international arena to co-cultures that operate within the United States. Here again, space constraints have limited the total number of co-cultures we could scrutinize. Yet, we believe that by having selected groups such as Latinos, African Americans, the disabled, gays and lesbians, and women, you will get an image of the cultural diversity found in those groups that most of you come in contact with on a regular basis. Many of these same co-cultures, and others, are so very important to the study of intercultural communication that we will return to them in later chapters.

In Part Three, "Intercultural Interaction: Taking Part in Intercultural Communication," our analysis focuses on the verbal and nonverbal symbols used in intercultural communication as well as the context in which they occur. In Chapter Four, we offer readings that will introduce you to some of the difficulties you might encounter when your intercultural partner employs a different language system. We will look at how these verbal idiosyncrasies and distinctions influence problem-solving, speaking, perception, translation, interpeting, and understanding.

Chapter Five, which is also concerned with symbols, explains some of the ways in which cultural diversity in nonverbal messages can influence the entire transaction. Differences in movement, facial expressions, eye contact, silence, space, time, and the like are detailed so that you might have a better appreciation of how culture and communication work in tandem.

Chapter Six continues with the theme of how culture modifies interaction. This time, however, the interaction is examined in a specific context. The assumption is that there are culturally diverse rules that influence how members of a culture behave in certain settings. To clarify this important issue we have selected seven "places" where cultures often follow rules that differ from those found in North America. More specifically, we will look at settings related to business, groups, negotiations, counseling, education, and health care.

Part Four, "Intercultural Communication: Seeking Improvement," contains two chapters concerned with improving intercultural communication. The readings offered in Chapter Seven are intended to provide you with knowledge and suggestions for improving intercultural communication. Each essay presents some type of practical recommendations.

The eighth and final chapter probes the ethical and future dimensions of intercultural communication. Essays that deal with moral issues and the future directions and challenges of intercultural communication are at the center of this chapter. It is the intent of this chapter to ask you not to conclude your study of intercultural communication with the reading of a single book or the completion of one course. We believe that the study of intercultural communication should be a lifetime endeavor. Each time we want to share an idea or feeling with someone from another culture we face a new and exhilarating learning experience. We urge everyone to seek out as many of these experiences as possible. A philosopher once wrote, "Tomorrow, when I know more, I'll recall that piece of knowledge and use it better."

ASSISTANCE

As in the past, a number of people have helped us rethink and reshape this project. We are especially thankful for the energy and friendship provided by Ed McDaniel and Susan Hellweg. We also want to express appreciation to our editors Holly Allen and Peggy Randall. And, of course, Rebecca Hayden, who had enough courage and insight some 20 years ago to decide that intercultural communication should and would become a viable discipline. All three of these editors were stern enough to keep us in check while at the same time allowing us the flexibility to move in new directions.

In a culture that values change, this collection would not have survived for over 20 years if we had not been fortunate enough to have so many scholars willing to contribute original essays to each of the editions. Here in the seventh edition we want to acknowledge the work of June Ock Yum, Nemi C. Jain, Ellen D. Kussman, Lisa Skow, Edith A. Folb, Dawn O. Braithwaite, Julia T. Wood, Randall E. Majors, Susan A. Hellweg, Janis F. Andersen, Robert Powell, Devorah A. Lieberman, Robert Shuter, Shirley N. Weber, Peter Andersen, La Ray M. Barna, Brian H. Spitzberg, Young Yun Kim, David W. Kale, Mary Jane Collier, Dolores and Robert Cathcart, Anne and

Robert Pedersen, Stella Ting-Toomey, Derald Wing Sue, Stephen and Anna Banks, Carol Dolphin, Sidney Ribeau, John Baldwin, Michael Hecht, Patricia Geist, and Wen-Shu Lee. We thank all of you for letting us expose your work to thousands of other people who share your commitment to intercultural matters.

Gary Evans, Eastern Michigan University; Alberto Gonzalez, Bowling Green University; and Lawrence Israel, Western Michigan University were among the instructors who reviewed the manuscript and made many helpful suggestions.

Finally we express our gratitude to the countless users of prior editions who have allowed us to "talk to them" about intercultural communication. While it may have been a rather intangible connection, we have greatly appreciated it.

Larry A. Samovar
Richard E. Porter

PART ONE

Intercultural Communication: An Introduction

Precision of communication is important, more important than ever, in our era of hair-trigger balances, when a false or misunderstood word may create as much disaster as a sudden thoughtless act.

—James Thurber

Intercultural communication, as we might rightly suspect, is not new; it has existed as long as people from different cultures have been encountering one another. What is new, however, is the systematic study of exactly what happens when intercultural contacts and interactions take place—when the communication process involves culturally diverse people.

Perhaps the initial impetus for the study of intercultural communication was the knowledge that technology has produced the means of our own self-destruction. Historically, intercultural communication, more often than not, has employed a rhetoric of force rather than reason. But, with the forces of change sweeping the world, perhaps we are now seeking forms of communication other than traditional force. The reason for this new study is also pragmatic. Our mobility, increased contact among cultures, a global economy and marketplace, and the emergence of multicultural organizations and work forces require that we develop communication skills and abilities appropriate to a multicultural society and to life in a global village.

Traditionally, intercultural communication took place only among an extremely small proportion of the world populace. Ministers of state and government, certain merchants, missionaries, explorers, and a few tourists were primarily the travelers and visitors to foreign lands. Until rather recently, we Americans had little contact with other cultures, even within our own country. Members of nonwhite races were segregated. Only in recent years have laws changed to foster integrated schools, work forces, and, to some extent, neighborhoods.

1

In addition, those who made up the vast white middle Euro-America remained at home, rarely leaving their own county. This situation, of course, has changed markedly; we are now a mobile society among ever-increasing mobile societies.

This increased contact with other cultures and domestic co-cultures makes it imperative for us to make a concerted effort to understand and to get along with people who may be vastly different from ourselves. The ability, through increased awareness and understanding, to coexist peacefully with people who do not necessarily share our background, views, beliefs, values, customs, habits, or life styles cannot only benefit us in our own neighborhoods but can also be a decisive factor in forestalling international conflict.

At the outset of our inquiry, there is a need to specify the nature of intercultural communication and to recognize that various viewpoints see it somewhat differently. From what we have already said, you should suspect that there are a variety of ways in which the topic of intercultural communication can be explored. There are perspectives that look at intercultural communication from a mass media point of view. Scholars who follow this approach are concerned with such issues as international broadcasting, worldwide freedom of expression, Western domination of information, and the use of modern electronic technologies for instantaneous worldwide transmission of information. Other groups investigate international communication. Here the emphasis is on communication between nations and between governments. It is the communication of diplomacy and propaganda. Still others are interested in the communication inherent in international business which includes such diverse concerns as negotiations and communication within multicultural organizations.

Our concern is with the more personal aspects of communication—what happens when people from different cultures interact face to face. Hence, we identify our approach as one that examines the interpersonal dimensions of intercultural communication as it occurs in a variety of contexts. For this reason, we have selected articles for this collection because they focus on those variables of both culture and communication that come into play *during the communication encounter*—that time when participants from different cultures are trying to share ideas, information, and feelings.

Inquiry into the nature of intercultural communication has raised many questions, but it has produced few theories and far fewer answers. Most of the inquiry has been associated with fields other than communication, primarily: anthropology, international relations, social psychology, and socio- and psycholinguistics. Although the direction of research has been diverse, the knowledge has not been coordinated. Much that has emerged has been more a reaction to current socio-racial-ethnic concerns rather than an attempt to define and explain intercultural communication. But, it is quite clear that knowledge of intercultural communication can aid in solving communication problems before they arise. School counselors who understand some of the reasons why the poor perceive school as they do might be better able to treat young truants. Those who know that Native Americans and Hispanics use eye contact in ways that differ from other Americans may be able to avert misunderstanding. And, perhaps, those who realize that some people treat illness as a curse may be better able to deliver necessary health care. In essence, what we are saying is that many problems can be avoided by understanding the components of intercultural communication

1

Approaches: Understanding Intercultural Communication

This exploration of intercultural communication begins with a series of diverse articles that (1) introduce the philosophy that underlies our concept of intercultural communication, (2) provide a general orientation and overview of intercultural communication, (3) theorize about the analysis of intercultural transactions, (4) provide insight into cultural differences, and (5) demonstrate the relationships between culture and perception. Our purpose at this point is to give you a sufficient introduction to the many wide and diverse dimensions of intercultural communication so that you will be able to approach the remainder of this volume with an appropriate frame of reference to make your further inquiry interesting, informative, and useful.

We begin with "An Introduction to Intercultural Communication" in order to introduce some of the specific topics and issues associated with the study of intercultural communication and to present in rather broad terms what it involves. We start by defining and explaining the role of human communication. We then turn our attention to the specific areas of culture and communication and show how they interrelate to form the field of intercultural communication. By examining the major variables that affect intercultural communication, we better understand how it operates. By knowing at the outset of the book what the study of intercultural communication entails, you should have a greater appreciation for the selections that follow.

Dean C. Barnlund in "Communication in a Global Village" traces communication and transportation developments that have led to the apparent shrinking of the contemporary world and the emergence of the global community. He points out the ramifications of the global village in terms of the forms and kinds of interactions that necessarily accompany such a new community of people. Barnlund considers problems of meaning associated with cultural differences, interpersonal encounters, intercultural encounters, and the role of the "collective unconscious" in intercultural interactions.

We then turn our attention to how people come to identify with the various general and specific cultures in which they have membership. Mary Jane Collier, in her article "Cultural Identity and Intercultural Communication," begins with an introduction to the notion of culture by considering symbols and meanings, cultural norms, cultural history, types of cultures based on national and ethnic considerations as well as gender, profession, geographic location, organizations, and physical ability or disability. She shows how each of these factors contributes to the identification of culture across a general–specific dimension. After having shown the range of cultures available to individuals, Collier discusses cultural identification showing the diverse mechanisms by which individuals come to the particular cultural identification they hold.

Inherent in intercultural communication is the problem that arises whenever diverse cultural patterns are used as the basis of communication. In the next article, Donal Carbaugh in "Toward a Perspective on Cultural Communication and Intercultural Contact," reveals these problems through a series of cases where diverse cultural patterns have led to confusion. He demonstrates quite vividly the perplexities that can arise when differing cultural patterns about norms for classroom interaction, standards for public debate, or premises for feelings come into contact with one another.

The final article in this chapter underscores the importance of culture in human interaction. Edward T. Hall in his selection "Context and Meaning" discusses the grand connection between culture and human communicative behaviors by demonstrating how culture provides a highly selective screen between people and their outside worlds. This cultural filter effectively designates what people attend to as well as what they choose to ignore. This link between culture and behavior is further illustrated through Hall's discussion of high- and low-context communication, in which he shows how people from different cultural backgrounds learn to concentrate on the unique aspects of their environments.

An Introduction to Intercultural Communication

RICHARD E. PORTER
LARRY A. SAMOVAR

"The times, they are a changin'" proclaimed Bob Dylan in his popular folk song of the 1960s. Dylan was right, the times were changing, but not necessarily in the manner envisioned by the folk singers of three decades ago. Several important events have caused major changes to occur, both worldwide and locally. These changes have transformed the world into the global village forecast by Marshall McLuhan in the 1960s. Among the events leading to the development of the global village were (1) improvements in transportation technology, (2) developments in communication technology, (3) globalization of the economy, and (4) changes in immigration patterns. These changes have created major changes in both worldwide and local patterns of communication and interaction and are of primary concern to the study of intercultural communication.

Improvements in transportation technology have helped to shrink the earth figuratively to a global village by providing the means for people to travel almost anywhere in the world within less than a day's time. (Future aircraft now in the design stage will increase travel speeds so that the travel time between China and the United States, for instance, will come to be measured in durations of minutes rather than hours.)

Developments in communication technology paralleled those in travel technology and provided further movement toward the global village. It is now possible for people to have instantaneous vocal, graphic, and textual communication with most parts of the world. Indeed, with a few hundred dollars worth of battery-powered equipment in the form of a facsimile machine and a cellular telephone, it is possible to be in instant oral and print communication with others in almost any place in the world while driving interstate highways in the United States.

Although these improvements in communication technology have produced many effects, three are significant to intercultural communication. First, new communication technology has created an almost free flow of news and information throughout the world and has become so important in the everyday conduct of commerce and government that it cannot be set aside. These changes have made it virtually impossible to keep communication capabilities out of the hands of common citizens. Government attempts to censor the free flow of ideas, opinions, and information have been frustrated. In China, for instance, during the Tiananmen Square demonstrations of mid-1983, the Chinese government attempted to ban foreign correspondents from reporting observed incidents, cutting their access to telephone and television broadcast facilities. American television viewers, however, were shown many incidents by reporters using their cellular telephones to call the United States via a communications satellite. By the time the Chinese government reacted to this technology, the story and all information had long since been disseminated to the world. In other parts of the world, similar incidents have occurred; for example, the widespread and multiple changes that took place in the old Soviet Union are due in part to the availability of news and information. And, because of today's communication technology, the ongoing events in Bosnia-Herzegovina and Croatia as well as Somalia cannot escape world scrutiny.

Second, communication technology also has dissolved our isolation. Not more than a half-century ago it was virtually impossible for the average citizen to have an informed awareness of what was happening outside his or her city, let alone be informed about the world. People had to wait for reports to arrive by mail or appear in newspapers, where the news could be up to several months old. Although transcoastal and transoceanic telegraph and telephone services and the development of radio permitted essentially instantaneous contact, those channels of communication were quite easy to control in terms of who might use them and what information they might contain. Today is quite different. With existing communication technology we can sit in our living rooms and watch events anywhere on earth, or, indeed, in space orbiting the earth, as these events are actually happening. Only a scant few years ago we had to wait hours, days, and even weeks to learn who won gold medals in the Olympic Games. Today, we can witness these events in our living rooms as they occur.

Third, the immediacy of this new communication technology has impacted us in another manner: In the past when news and information reception was delayed and we learned of events days, perhaps weeks, after they occurred, it was difficult to develop strong feelings about what might have happened thousands of miles away. But, consider the difference in the impact between *reading* in a newspaper that the police had beaten someone while making an arrest and actually *seeing* videotape of the Rodney King beating. Similarly, television coverage of the Reginald Denny beating *as it occurred* at the outset of the 1992 riots in Los Angeles could not help but move us. The ability to deny the cruelty of these acts is virtually reduced to zero.

Globalization of the economy has further brought people together. At the end of World War II, the United States was the only military and economic superpower. Most of the rest of the world's economy was in disarray. Most industries had been destroyed and few banks were functioning.

Because the United States escaped World War II with its industry and its banking system intact, we were the dominant economic force in the world.

Only 5 percent of American businesses faced international competition. In the 1990s, however, 75 percent of American industries face international competition. This leads to interdependence among national economies and to intercultural contact in arenas of both politics and business.

As the economy has internationalized, the U.S. presence overseas has increased dramatically. Today, over 8,000 U.S. companies have international operations in foreign countries. American holdings total over $309 billion with some $3.5 billion committed to more than 600 joint ventures with China. IBM has worked with Japan to build a plant there to produce advanced versions of computer memory chips. Additionally, 1 million Americans apply for business passports each year, with more than 2.5 million Americans now working abroad.

Simultaneously, foreign presence in the United States has increased; over 5,000 foreign firms operate in the United States. Foreigners have invested more than $300 billion and own nearly $1.5 trillion in U.S. assets, a 200% increase since 1980. In 1990, overseas concerns controlled over 13% of American industrial assets, causing companies such as AT&T to prepare thousands of its annual stockholder reports in foreign languages. Foreign investors own more than 1 million acres of U.S. farmland and 64% of the commercial property in downtown Los Angeles. It is obvious that the strength of our economy depends on communication with and among other cultures such as Japan, Germany, Great Britain, the Netherlands, Korea, Italy, France, Canada, Saudi Arabia, as well as many smaller nations.

Changes in immigration patterns have also contributed to the development of the global village. Although transportation improvements, communication technology, and globalization of the economy have figuratively shrunk the world, recent immigration patterns have physically shifted segments of the world population. Contacts with new cultures or with cultures that previously appeared unfamiliar, alien, and at times mysterious are becoming a normal part of our day-to-day routine. People from Vietnam, Cambodia, Laos, Cuba, Haiti, Columbia, Nicaragua, El Salvador, and Ecuador, among others, have entered the United States to become our neighbors and add to the cultural diversity of our society. As these people adjust their lives to this culture, we will have increasing intercultural contacts in our daily lives. Adaptation to this new cultural diversity by American businesses was demonstrated recently when some telephone companies advertised in the Chinese language to remind the Chinese community to call home during the Chinese New Year holiday.

While this global phenomenon involving transportation, communication, an international economy, and migration was taking place, change was also taking place within our own boundaries. Domestic events made us focus our attention on often demanding co-cultures. African Americans, Asians, Hispanics, Native Americans, women, homosexuals, the poor, the disabled, the homeless, and countless other groups became visible and vocal as they cried out for recognition and their rightful place in our community.

This attention on co-cultures made us realize that although intercultural contact is inevitable, it is not always successful. The communicative behavior of the co-cultures frequently disturbed many of us. Their behavior seemed strange, at times even bizarre, and frequently it failed to meet our normal expectations. We discovered, in short, that intercultural communication is difficult. Even when the natural barrier of a foreign language is dissolved, we can still fail to understand and to be understood.

These communication difficulties, both in the international arena and on the domestic scene, give rise to a major premise: *The difficulty with being thrust into a global village is that we do not yet know how to live like villagers; there are too many of us who do not want to live with "them."* Ours is a culture in which racism and ethnocentrism run deep below the surface. Although there has been a lessening of overt racial violence since the 1960s, the enduring racist-ethnocentric belief system has not been appreciably affected. In many respects, racism and ethnocentrism have become institutionalized and are practiced unconsciously. The result is a structured domination of people of color by the white Anglo power structure. Until this deep-seated antagonism is eliminated, we will not be able to assume our proper place in a global village community.

Our inability to yet behave as good citizens in the global village is cause for major concern because we have not learned to respect and accept one another; we have not learned to communicate with one another effectively, to understand one another, because our cultures are different. Thus, even if we have the strongest desire to communicate, we are faced with the difficulties imposed upon us by cultural diversity and its impact on the communication process.

Concern with the difficulties cultural diversity poses for effective communication have given rise to the marriage of culture and communication and to the recognition of intercultural communication as a field of study. Inherent in this fusion is the idea that *intercultural communication entails the investigation of those elements of culture that most influence interaction when members of two different cultures come together in an interpersonal setting*.

To help us understand what is involved in intercultural communication we will begin with a fundamental definition: **Intercultural communication** occurs whenever a message produced in one culture must be processed in another culture. The rest of this article will deal with intercultural communication and point out the relationships between communication, culture, intercultural communication, and cultural context.

COMMUNICATION

To understand intercultural interaction, we must first understand human communication. Understanding human communication means knowing something about what happens when people interact, why it happens, the effects of what happens, and finally what we can do to influence and maximize the results of that event.

Understanding and Defining Communication

We begin with a basic assumption that communication is a form of human behavior that is derived from a need to connect and interact with other human beings. Almost everyone desires social contact with other people, and this need is met through the act of communication, which unites otherwise isolated individuals. Our behaviors become messages to which other people may respond. When we talk, we are obviously behaving, but when we wave, smile, frown, walk, shake our heads, or gesture, we also are behaving. These behaviors frequently become messages; they communicate something to someone else.

Before behaviors can become messages, however, they must meet two requirements: First, they must be observed by someone, and second, they must elicit a response. In other words, any behavior that elicits a response is a *message*. If we examine this last statement, we can see several implications.

The first implication is that the word *any* tells us that both verbal and nonverbal behaviors may function as messages. Verbal messages consist of spoken or written words (speaking and writing are word-producing behaviors) while nonverbal messages consist of the entire remaining behavioral repertory.

Second, behavior may be either conscious or unconscious. We frequently do things without being aware of them. This is especially true of nonverbal behavior involving such habits such as fingernail biting, toe tapping, leg jiggling, head shaking, staring, and smiling. Even such things as slouching in a chair, chewing gum, or adjusting glasses are frequently unconscious behaviors. Since a message consists of behaviors to which people may respond, we must thus acknowledge the possibility of producing messages unknowingly.

A third implication of the behavior-message linkage is that we frequently behave unintentionally, in some cases uncontrollably. For instance, if we are embarrassed we may blush or speak with vocal disfluencies; we do not intend to blush or to stammer, but we do so anyway. Again, these unintentional behaviors can become messages if someone perceives them and responds to them.

This concept of conscious-unconscious, intentional-unintentional behavioral relationships gives us a basis to formulate a clearer definition of communication. **Communication** may be defined as that which happens whenever someone responds to the behavior or the residue of the behavior of another person. When someone perceives our behavior or its residue and attributes meaning to it, communication has taken place regardless of whether our behavior was conscious or unconscious, intentional or unintentional. If we think about this for a moment, we must realize that it is impossible for us not to behave. Being necessitates behavior. If behavior has communication potential, then it is also impossible for us not to communicate. In other words, we cannot not communicate.

Behavioral **residue** (just mentioned in our definition) refers to those things that remain as a record of our actions. For instance, this article that you are reading is a behavioral residue—it resulted from certain behaviors. As the authors we had to engage in a number of behaviors; we had to research, think, and use our word processors. Another example of behavioral residue might be the odor of cigar smoke lingering in an elevator after the cigar smoker has departed. Smoking the cigar in the elevator was the behavior; the odor is the residue. The response you have to that odor is a reflection of your past experiences and attitudes toward cigars, smoking, smoking in public places, and, perhaps, people who smoke cigars.

Our approach to communication has focused on the behavior of one individual causing or provoking a response from another by the attribution of meaning to behavior. **Attribution** means that we draw upon our past experiences and give meaning to the behavior that we observe. We might imagine that somewhere in each of our brains is a meaning reservoir in which are stored all of the experience-derived meanings we possess. These various meanings have developed throughout our lifetimes as a result of our culture acting upon us as well as the result of our individual experiences within that culture. Meaning is relative to each of us because each of us is a unique human being with a unique background and a unique set of experiences. When we encounter a behavior in our environment each of us dips into our individual, unique meaning reservoirs and selects the meaning we believe is most likely to be appropriate for the behavior encountered and the social context in which it occurred.

If someone walks up to us and says: "If you've got a few minutes, let's get a cup of coffee," we observe this behavior and respond to it by giving it meaning. The meaning we give it is drawn from our experience with language and word meaning and also from our experience with this person and the social context. Our response could vary significantly depending upon prior experiences and the circumstances. If the person is a friend, we may interpret the behavior as an invitation to sit and chat for a few minutes. On the other hand, if the behavior comes from someone with whom we have had differences, the response may be one of attributing conciliatory goodwill to the message and an invitation to try to settle past differences. Yet another example could be a situation in which the person is someone you have seen in a class but do not know. Then your ability to respond is lessened because you may not be able to guess fully the other person's intention. Perhaps this is someone who wants to talk about the class; perhaps it is someone who only wants social company until the next class; or perhaps, if gender differences are involved, it may be someone attempting to "hit" on you. Your response to the observed behavior is dependent upon knowledge, experience, and social context.

Usually this works quite well, but at other times it fails and we misinterpret a message; we attribute the wrong meaning to the behavior we have observed. This may be brought about by inappropriate behavior where someone does or says something not intended. Or it could be brought about by the experiential backgrounds of people being sufficiently different that behavior is misinterpreted.

The Ingredients of Communication

Next, we examine the *ingredients* of communication, the various components that fit together to form what we call communication. Since our purpose in studying intercultural communication is to develop communication skills to apply with conscious intent, our working definition of communication will specify *intentional* communication. We further define *communication* as: *a dynamic transactional behavior-affecting process in which people behave intentionally to induce or elicit a particular response from another person*. Communication is complete only when the intended behavior is perceived by the intended receiver and that person responds to and is affected by the behavior. These transactions must include all conscious or unconscious, intentional or unintentional, verbal, nonverbal, and contextual stimuli that act as cues about the quality and credibility of the message. The cues must be clear to both the behavioral source of the transaction and the processor of that behavior.

This definition allows us to identify eight specific ingredients of communication within the framework of intentional communication. First is a *behavioral source*. This is a person with both a need and a desire to communicate. The need may be a social desire to be recognized as an individual, to share information with others, or to influence the attitudes and behaviors of one or more others. The source's wish to communicate indicates a desire to share his or her internal state of being with another human being. Communication, then, is really concerned with the connecting of individuals and the sharing of internal states with varying degrees of intention to influence the information, attitudes, and behaviors of others.

Internal states of being cannot be shared directly; we must rely on symbolic representations of our internal states. This brings us to the second ingredient, *encoding*. **Encoding** is an internal activity in which verbal and nonverbal behaviors are selected and arranged to create a message in accordance with the contextual rules that govern the interaction and the rules of grammar and syntax applicable to the language being used.

The result of encoding is expressive behavior that serves as a *message*, the third ingredient, to represent the internal state that is to be shared. A **message** is a set of verbal and or nonverbal symbols that represent a person's particular state of being at a particular moment in time and space. Although en-

coding is an internal act that produces a message, a message is external to the source; it is the behavior or behavioral residue that must connect a source and a responder across time and space.

Messages must have a means by which they move from source to responder, so the fourth communication ingredient is the *channel*, which provides a connection between a source and a responder. A **channel** is the physical means by which a message moves between people.

The fifth ingredient is the *responder*. **Responders** observe a source's behavior or its residue and, as a consequence, become linked to the message source. Responders may be those intended by the source to receive the message or they may be others who, by whatever circumstance, intercept and perceive the behavior once it has entered a channel. Responders have problems with messages, not unlike the problems sources have with internal states of being. Messages usually impinge on people in the form of light or sound energy, although they may be in forms that stimulate any of the senses. Whatever the form of sensory stimulation, people must convert these energies into meaningful experiences.

Converting external energies into a meaningful experience is called **decoding**, the sixth ingredient of communication. Decoding is akin to a source's act of encoding, because it also is an internal activity. Through this internal processing of a message, meaning is attributed to a source's behaviors that represents his or her internal state of being.

Response — what a person decides to do about a message — is the seventh ingredient. Response may vary from as little as a decision to do nothing to an immediate overt physical act of violence. If communication has been somewhat successful, the response of the message recipient will resemble to some degree that desired by the source who created the response-eliciting behavior.

The final ingredient of communication is **feedback**, information available to a source that permits him or her to make qualitative judgments about communication effectiveness. Through the interpretation of feedback, one may adjust and adapt his or her behavior to an ongoing situation. Although feedback and response are not the same thing, they are clearly related. Response is what a person decides to do about a message, and feedback is information about the effectiveness of communication. They are related because a message recipient's behavior is the normal source of feedback.

These eight ingredients of communication make up only a partial list of the factors that function during a communication event. In addition to these elements, when we conceive of communication as a process there are several characteristics that help us understand how communication actually works.

First, communication is *dynamic*: It is an ongoing, ever-changing activity. As participants in communication, we constantly are affected by each other's messages and, as a consequence, we undergo continual change. Each of us in our daily lives meets and interacts with people who exert some influence over us. Each time we are influenced we are changed in some way, which means that as we go through life we do so as continually changing, or dynamic, individuals.

A second characteristic of communication is that it is *interactive*. Communication must take place between people. This implies two or more people who bring to a communication event their own unique backgrounds and experiences that serve as a backdrop for communicative interaction. Interaction also implies a reciprocal situation in which each party attempts to influence the other — that is, each party simultaneously creates messages designed to elicit specific responses from the other.

Third, communication is *irreversible*. Once we have said something and someone has received and decoded the message, we cannot retrieve it. This circumstance sometimes results in what is called "putting your foot in your mouth." The source may send other messages in attempts to modify the effect, but it cannot be eliminated. This is frequently a problem when we unconsciously or unintentionally send a message to someone. We may affect them adversely and not even know it; then during future interactions we may wonder why that person is reacting to us in what we perceive to be an unusual manner.

Fourth, communication takes place in both a *physical* and *social context*; both establish the rules that govern the interaction. When we interact with someone, it is not in isolation but within specific physical surroundings and under a set of specific social dynamics. Physical surroundings include specific physical objects such as furniture, window coverings, floor coverings, lighting, vegetation, or the presence or absence of physical clutter; noise levels; and acoustics; as well as competing messages. Many aspects of the physical environment can and do affect communication: The comfort or discomfort of a chair, the color of the walls, or the total atmosphere of a room are but a few.

The symbolic meaning behind physical surroundings, a kind of nonverbal communication, also governs communication. Social context defines the social relationships that exist between people as well as the rules that govern the interaction. In our culture in the United States, we tend to be somewhat cavalier toward social hierarchies and to pay much less attention to them than do people in other cultures. Nevertheless, such differences as teacher-student, employer-employee, parent-child, admiral-seaman, senator-citizen, physician-patient, and judge-attorney establish rules that specify expected behavior, and thus affect the communication process.

Quite frequently, physical surroundings actually define the social context. An employer may sit behind a desk while an employee stands before the desk to receive an admonition. In a courtroom, the judge sits elevated facing the courtroom, jurors, and attorneys, indicating the social superiority of the judge relative to the other officers of the court. Attorneys sit side by side, indicating a social equality between accuser and accused until such time as the jury of peers renders a verdict. No matter what the social context, it will have some effect on communication. The form of language used, the respect or lack of respect shown one another, the time of day, personal moods, who speaks to whom and in what order, and the degree of nervousness or confidence people express are but a few of the ways in which the social context can affect communication.

At this point, we should see clearly that human communication does not take place in a social vacuum. Rather, communication is an intricate matrix of interacting social acts that occur in a complex social environment that reflects the way people live and how they come to interact with and get along in their world. This social environment is culture, and if we truly are to understand communication, we must also understand culture.

CULTURE

The Basic Function of Culture

Culture is a complex, abstract, and pervasive matrix of social elements which functions as an all-encompassing form or pattern for living by laying out a predictable world in which an individual is firmly oriented. Culture enables us to make sense of our surroundings, aiding the transition from the womb to this new life.

From the instant of birth, a child is formally and informally taught how to behave. Children, regardless of their culture, quickly learn how to behave in a manner that is acceptable to adults. Within each culture, therefore, there is no need to expend energy deciding what an event means or how to respond to it. The assumption is that people who share a common culture can usually be counted on to behave "correctly" and predictably. Hence, culture reduces the chances of surprises by shielding people from the unknown. Try to imagine a single day in your life without having access to the guidelines your culture provides. Without the rules that govern your actions, you would soon feel helpless. From how to greet strangers to how to spend our time, culture provides us with structure. To lack culture is to lack structure. We might even go so far as to say that "our primary mode of biological adaptation is culture, not anatomy."[1]

Definition of Culture

We have already indicated that culture is a complex matrix of interacting elements. Culture is ubiqui-tous, multidimensional, complex, and all-pervasive. Because it is so broad, there is not a single definition or central theory of what it is. Definitions of culture run the gamut from "an all-encompassing phenomenon" to descriptions listing nearly all human activity. For our purposes, we define **culture** as: the deposit of knowledge, experience, beliefs, values, attitudes, meanings, hierarchies, religion, notions of time, roles, spatial relations, concepts of the universe, and material objects and possessions acquired by a group of people in the course of generations through individual and group striving.

The Ingredients of Culture

Although scholars may lack a definitive ingredient list for culture most agree that any description should include the three categories submitted by Almaney and Alwan. They contend that

cultures may be classified by three large categories of elements: artifacts (which include items ranging from arrowheads to hydrogen bombs, magic charms to antibiotics, torches to electric lights, and chariots to jet planes); concepts (which include such beliefs or value systems as right or wrong, God and man, ethics, and the general meaning of life); and behaviors (which refer to the actual practice of concepts or beliefs).[2]

These authors provide an excellent example of how these three aspects might be reflected within a culture: "Whereas money is considered an artifact, the value placed upon it is a concept, but the actual spending and saving of money is behavior."[3]

Other inventories provide additional listings of the content of culture. Some of these additional ingredients of particular interest to intercultural communication include cultural history, cultural personality, material culture, role relationships, art, language, cultural stability, cultural beliefs, ethnocentrism, nonverbal behavior, spatial relations, time, recognition and reward, and thought patterns.[4]

The Characteristics of Culture

Six characteristics of culture are of special importance to intercultural communication: (1) culture is learned; (2) culture is transmissible; (3) culture is dynamic; (4) culture is selective; (5) the facets of culture are interrelated; and (6) culture is ethnocentric.

Culture Is Not Innate; It Is Learned. From infancy on, members of a culture learn their patterns of behavior and ways of thinking until they have become internalized. The power and influence of these behaviors and perceptions can be seen in the ways in which we acquire culture. Our culture-learning proceeds through interaction, observation, and imitation. A little boy in North America whose father tells him to shake hands when he is introduced to a friend of the family is learning culture. The Arab baby who is read the Koran when he or she is one day old is learning culture. The Hindu child who lives in a home where the women eat after the men is learning culture. The Jewish child who helps conduct the Passover celebration is learning culture.

All of this learning occurs as conscious or unconscious conditioning that leads one toward competence in a particular culture.[5] This activity is frequently called **enculturation**, denoting the total activity of learning one's culture.

Culture Is Transmissible. The symbols of a culture are what enable us to pass on the content and patterns of a culture. We can spread our culture through the spoken word as when the recorded voice of radio actor Brace Beemer brings us the voice of the Lone Ranger from the 1940s or when the recorded voice of President Franklin Roosevelt tells us that December 7, 1941 will live as a day in infamy. We can use the written word as a symbol and let others read about the War of Independence, learn about Abraham Lincoln through reading the Gettysburg Address, or even learn cultural strategies of persuasion by reading Aristotle's *Rhetoric*.

We also can use nonverbal actions as symbols, for example, showing others that we usually shake hands to greet one another. National flags symbolize our claim to territory or demonstrate our loyalty. Rolls Royce automobiles and Rolex watches evidence our success and status. A cross speaks of our love for God. The use of symbols is at the core of culture.

The portability of symbols allows us to package and store them as well as transmit them. The mind, books, pictures, films, videos, and the like enable a culture to preserve what it deems to be important and worthy of transmission. Each individual, regardless of his or her generation, is heir to a massive "library" of information that has been collected in anticipation of his or her entry into the culture.

Culture Is Dynamic. As with communication, culture is ongoing and subject to fluctuation; they seldom remain constant. As ideas and products evolve within a culture, they can produce change through the mechanisms of invention and diffusion.

Invention is usually defined as the discovery of new practices, tools, or concepts that most members of the culture eventually accept. In North America, the civil rights movement and the invention of television are two good examples of how ideas and products reshaped a culture.

Diffusion, or borrowing from another culture, is another way in which change occurs. The assimilation of what is borrowed accelerates as cultures come into direct contact with each other. For example, as Japan and North America share more commerce, we see Americans assimilating Japanese business management practices and the Japanese incorporating American marketing tactics.

In addition to invention and diffusion, other factors foster cultural change. The concept of *cultural calamity* illustrates how cultures change. Consider for a moment the effects of war or revolution. The calamity of Vietnam brought changes to both Vietnam and the United States. Not only did it create a new population of refugees, but it also forced us to reevaluate some cultural assumptions concerning global influence and military power. Currently, many cultural changes are taking place in Eastern Europe and the old Soviet Union. The elimination of the Berlin Wall, the unification of East and West Germany, the dissolution of the Soviet Union into numerous smaller states, and the problems of adjustment to new economies and governments are producing enormous changes in the affected cultures.

Although cultures do change, most change only affects the surface structure of the culture. The deep structure resists major alterations. Changes in dress, food, transportation, housing, and the like while visible are simply attached to the existing cultural value system. Elements associated with the deep structure of a culture such as values, ethics and morals, work and leisure, definitions of freedom, the importance of the past, religious practices, the pace of life, and attitudes toward gender and age are so very deep in the structure of a culture that they tend to persist generation after generation. Even the demands for more liberal governments in China and Russia have their roots in the histories of those countries. In the United States, studies conducted on American values show that most of the central values of the 1990s are similar to the values of the past 200 years. When analyzing cultural change we cannot be fooled because downtown Tokyo looks much like Paris, London, or New York. Most of what is important in a culture is below the surface. It is like the moon—we observe the front, which appears flat and one-dimensional, but there is another side and dimensions that we cannot see.

Culture Is Selective. Every culture represents a limited choice of behavior patterns from the infinite patterns of human experience. This selection, whether it be what shoes to wear or how to reach God, is made according to the basic assumptions and values that are meaningful to each culture. Because each individual has only these limited cultural experiences, what we know is but an abstraction of what there is to know. In other words, culture also defines the *boundaries* of different groups.[6]

This characteristic is important to all students of intercultural communication for two reasons. First, it reminds us that what a culture selects to tell each succeeding generation is a reflection of what that culture deems important. In the United States for example, being healthy is highly valued, and therefore messages related to that idea are selected. Sec-

ond, the notion of selectivity also suggests that cultures tend to separate one group from another. If one culture selects work as an end (Japan) while another emphasizes work as a means to an end (Mexico), we have a cultural separation.

Facets of Culture Are Interrelated. This characteristic serves to inform us that culture is like a complex system. As Hall clearly states: "You touch a culture in one place and everything else is affected."[7] The women's movement in the United States may serve as an example of this. They may be but two simple words, but the phenomenon has been like a large stone cast into a pond. The women's movement has brought about changes in gender roles, sexual practices, educational opportunities, the legal system, career opportunities, and even female-male interaction.

Culture Is Ethnocentric. Ethnocentrism, centeredness on one's own group, might well be the characteristic that most directly relates to intercultural communication. The important tie between ethnocentrism and communication can be seen in the definition of the word itself. Keesing notes that ethnocentrism is a "universal tendency for any people to put its own culture and society in a central position of priority and worth."[8] Ethnocentrism, therefore, becomes the perceptual window through which a culture interprets and judges all other cultures. Ethnocentrism leads to a subjective evaluation of how another culture conducts its daily business. That this evaluation can only be negative is clear if you realize that a logical extension of ethnocentrism is the position that "our way is the right way." Most discussions of ethnocentrism even enlarge the concept to include feelings of superiority. Keesing notes: "Nearly always the folklore of a people includes myths of origin which give priority to themselves, and place the stamp of supernatural approval on their particular customs."[9]

As we have seen, culture is extremely complex and influences every aspect of our lives. There are, however, specific aspects of culture that are of particular interest in the study of intercultural communication. For the sake of simplicity and to put some limitation on our discussion, we will examine three major elements: *perceptual processes, verbal processes,* and *nonverbal processes.*

These three interacting cultural elements are the constituent elements of intercultural communication. When we combine them, as we do when we communicate, they are like the components of a quadriphonic stereo system—each one relates to and needs the other to function properly. In our discussion, we separate these elements to identify and discuss them, but in actuality they do not exist in isolation nor do they function alone.

Perception

In its simplest sense, **perception** is the internal process by which we select, evaluate, and organize stimuli from the external environment. In other words, perception is the conversion of the physical energies of our environment into meaningful experience. A number of corollary issues arising out of this definition help explain the relationship between perception and culture. A basic belief is that people behave as they do because of the ways in which they perceive the world and that these behaviors are learned as part of their cultural experience. Whether in judging beauty or describing snow, we respond to stimuli as we do primarily because our culture has taught us to do so. We tend to notice, reflect on, and respond to those elements in our environment that are important to us. We in the United States might respond principally to a thing's size and cost, while in Japan color might be the important criterion.

Social Perception. Social perception is the process by which we construct our unique social realities by attributing meaning to the social objects and events we encounter in our environments. It is an extremely important aspect of communication. Culture conditions and structures our perceptual processes so that we develop culturally inspired perceptual sets. These sets not only help determine which external stimuli reach our awareness, but more important, they significantly influence the so-cial aspect of perception—the social construction of reality—by the attribution of meaning to these stimuli. The difficulties in communication caused by this perceptual variability can best be lowered by knowing about and understanding the cultural elements that are subject to diversity, coupled with an honest and sincere desire to communicate successfully across cultural boundaries.

There are three major socio-cultural elements that have a direct and major influence on the meanings we develop for our perceptions. These elements are our *belief/value/attitude systems, world view,* and *social organization.* When these three elements influence our perceptions and the meanings we develop for them, they are affecting our individual, subjective aspects of meanings. We all may see the same social entity and agree upon what it is in objective terms, but what the object or event means to us individually may differ considerably. Both an American and a Chinese might agree in an objective sense that a particular object is a young dog, but they might disagree completely in their interpretation of the dog. The American might see it as a cute, fluffy, loving, protective pet. The Chinese, on the other hand, might see the dog as something especially fit for the Sunday barbecue. You see, it is an American's cultural background that interprets the dog as a pet, and it is the Chinese cultural background that regards dog meat as a delicacy.

Belief/Value/Attitude Systems. **Beliefs**, in a general sense, can be viewed as individually held subjective probabilities that some object or event possesses certain characteristics. A belief involves a link between the belief object and the characteristics that distinguish it. The degree to which we believe that an event or an object possesses certain characteristics reflects the level of our subjective probability and, consequently, the depth or intensity of our belief. That is, the more certain we are in a belief, the greater is the intensity of that belief.

Culture plays an important role in belief formation. Whether we accept the *New York Times,* the Bible, the entrails of a goat, tea leaves, the visions induced by peyote, or the changes specified in the

Taoist *I Ching* as sources of knowledge and belief depends on our cultural backgrounds and experiences. In matters of intercultural communication, there are no rights or wrongs as far as beliefs are concerned. If someone believes that voices in the wind can guide one's behavior along the proper path, we cannot throw up our hands and declare the belief wrong (even if we believe it to be wrong); we must be able to recognize and to deal with that belief if we wish to obtain satisfactory and successful communication.

Values are the valuative aspect of our belief/value/attitude systems. Valuative dimensions include qualities such as usefulness, goodness, aesthetics, need satisfaction, and pleasure. Although each of us has a unique set of personal values, there also are values called *cultural values* that tend to permeate a culture. **Cultural values** are a set of organized rules for making choices, reducing uncertainty, and reducing conflicts within a given society. They are usually derived from the larger philosophical issues inherent in a culture. These values are generally normative in that they inform a member of a culture what is good and bad, right and wrong, true and false, positive and negative, and so on. Cultural values define what is worth dying for, what is worth protecting, what frightens people, what are considered to be proper subjects for study or ridicule, and what types of events lead individuals to group solidarity. Cultural values also specify which behaviors are important and which should be avoided within a culture.

Values express themselves within a culture as rules that prescribe the behaviors that members of the culture are expected to perform. These are called **normative values**. Thus, Catholics are supposed to attend Mass, motorists are supposed to stop at stop signs, and workers in our culture are supposed to arrive at work at the designated time. Most people follow normative behaviors; a few do not. Failure to do so may be met with either informal or codified sanctions. The Catholic who avoids Mass may receive a visit from a priest; the driver who runs a stop sign may receive a fine; and the employee who is tardy too frequently may be discharged.

Normative values also extend into everyday communicative behavior by specifying how people are to behave in specific communication contexts. This extension acts as a guide to individual and group behavior that minimizes or prevents harm to individual sensitivities within cultures.

Beliefs and values contribute to the development and content of *attitudes*. An **attitude** may be defined formally as a learned tendency to respond in a consistent manner to a given object of orientation. This means that we tend to avoid those things we dislike and to embrace those we like. Attitudes are learned within a cultural context. Whatever cultural environment surrounds us helps shape and form our attitudes — our readiness to respond — and ultimately our behavior.

World View. This cultural element, though somewhat abstract, is one of the most important elements found in the perceptual aspects of intercultural communication. World view deals with a culture's orientation toward such philosophical issues as God, humanity, nature, the universe, and others that are concerned with the concept of being. In short, our world view helps us locate our place and rank in the universe. Because world view is so complex, it is often difficult to isolate during an intercultural interaction. In this examination, we seek to understand its substance and its elusiveness.

World view issues are timeless and represent the most fundamental bases of a culture. A Catholic has a different world view than a Moslem, Hindu, Jew, Taoist, or an atheist. The way in which Native Americans view the individual's place in nature differs sharply from the Euro-American's view. Native Americans see themselves as one with nature; they perceive a balanced relationship between humankind and the environment, a partnership of equality and respect. Euro-Americans, on the other hand, see a human-centered world in which humans are supreme and are apart from nature. They may treat the universe as theirs — a place to carry out their desires and wishes through the power of science and technology.

World view influences a culture at very profound levels. Its effects are often quite subtle and not revealed in such obvious and often superficial ways as dress, gestures, and vocabulary. We can think of a world view as analogous to a pebble tossed into a pond. Just as the pebble causes ripples that spread and reverberate over the entire surface of the pond, world view likewise spreads itself over a culture and permeates every facet of it. World view influences beliefs, values, attitudes, uses of time, and many other aspects of culture. In its subtle way, it is a powerful influence in intercultural communication because as a member of a culture, each communicator's world view is so deeply imbedded in the psyche that it is taken for granted, and each communicator tends to assume automatically that everyone else views the world as he or she does.

Social Organization. The manner in which a culture organizes itself and its institutions also affects how members of the culture perceive the world, and how they communicate. It might be helpful to look directly at two of the dominant social units found in a culture.

The *family*, although it is the smallest social organization in a culture, is one of the most influential. The family sets the stage for a child's development during the formative periods of life, presents the child with a wide range of cultural influences that affect almost everything from his or her first attitudes to the selection of toys, and guides the child's acquisition of language and the amount of emphasis placed on it. Skills from vocabulary building to developing dialects are the purview of the family. The family also offers and withholds approval, support, rewards, and punishments, having a marked effect on the values children develop and the goals they pursue. If, for example, children learn by observation and communication that silence is paramount in their culture, as Japanese children do, they will reflect that aspect of culture in their behavior and bring it to intercultural settings.

The *school* is another social organization that is important. By definition and history, schools are endowed with a major portion of the responsibility for passing on and maintaining a culture. They are a community's basic link with its past as well as its taskmaster for the future. Schools maintain culture by relating to new members what has happened, what is important, and what one as a member of the culture must know. Schools may teach geography or wood carving, mathematics or nature lore; they may stress revolution based on peace or predicated on violence, or they may relate a particular culturally accepted version of history. But whatever is taught in a school is determined by the culture in which that school exists.

Verbal Processes

Verbal processes include not only how we talk to each other but also the internal activities of thinking and meaning development for the words we use. These processes, verbal language and patterns of thought, are vitally related to perception and the attachment and expression of meaning.

Verbal Language. Any discussion of language in intercultural settings must include an investigation of language issues in general before dealing with specific problems of foreign language, language translation, and the argot and vernacular of co-cultures. Here, in our introduction to the various dimensions of culture, we will look at verbal language as it relates to our understanding of culture.

In the most basic sense, **language** is an organized, generally agreed upon, learned symbol system used to represent human experiences within a geographic or cultural community. Each culture places its own individual imprint on word symbols. Objects, events, experiences, and feelings have a particular label or name solely because a community of people has arbitrarily decided to so name them. Thus, because language is an inexact system of symbolically representing reality, the meanings for words are subject to a wide variety of interpretations.

Language is the primary vehicle by which a culture transmits its beliefs, values, norms, and world view. Language gives people a means of connecting and interacting with other members of their culture and a means of thinking. Language thus serves both as a mechanism for communication and as a guide to social reality. Language influences perceptions, transmits meaning, and helps mold patterns of thought.

Patterns of Thought. The mental processes, forms of reasoning, and approaches to problem solution prevalent in a community make up another major component of culture. Unless they have had experiences with people from other cultures who follow different patterns of thought, most people assume everyone thinks and solves problems in much the same way. We must be aware, however, that there are cultural differences in aspects of thinking and knowing. This diversity can be clarified and related to intercultural communication by making a general comparison between Western and Eastern patterns of thought. In most Western thought there is an assumption of a direct relationship between mental concepts and the concrete world of reality. This orientation places great stock in logical considerations and rationality. There is a belief that truth is out there somewhere and that it can be discovered by following correct logical sequences — one need only turn over the right rocks in the right order and truth will be there. The Eastern view, best illustrated by Taoist thought, holds that problems are solved quite differently. To begin with, people are not granted instant rationality; truth is not found by active searching and the application of Aristotelian modes of reasoning. On the contrary, individuals must prepare themselves to receive truth and then wait. If truth is to be known, it will make itself apparent. The major difference in these two views is in the area of activity: To the Western mind, human activity is paramount and ultimately will lead to the discovery of truth; in the Taoist tradition, truth is the active agent, and if it is to be known, it will be through the activity of truth making itself apparent.

A culture's thought patterns affect the way individuals in that culture communicate, which in turn affects the way each person responds to individuals from another culture. We cannot expect everyone to employ the same patterns of thinking, but understanding that many patterns exist and learning to accommodate them will facilitate our intercultural communication.

Nonverbal Processes

Verbal processes are the primary means for the exchange of thoughts and ideas, but closely related nonverbal processes often can overshadow them. Most authorities agree that the realm of nonverbal processes comprises the following topics: gestures, facial expressions, eye contact and gaze, posture and movement, touching, dress, objects and artifacts, silence, space, time, and paralanguage. As we turn to the cultural nonverbal processes relevant to intercultural communication, we will consider three aspects: *nonverbal behavior* that functions as a silent form of language, the *concept of time*, and the *use* and *organization of space*.

Nonverbal Behavior. It would be foolish for us to try to examine all of the elements that constitute nonverbal behavior because of the tremendous range of activity included in this form of human activity. An example or two will enable us to visualize how nonverbal issues fit into the overall scheme of intercultural understanding. For example, touch as a form of communication can demonstrate how nonverbal communication is a product of culture. German women as well as men shake hands at the outset of every social encounter; in the United States, women are less likely to shake hands. Vietnamese men do not shake hands with women or elders unless the woman or the elder offers the hand first. In Thailand, people do not touch in public, and to touch someone on the head is a major social transgression. You can imagine the problems that would arise if one did not understand some of these differences.

Another example of nonverbal communication is eye contact. In the United States we are encouraged to maintain good eye contact when we communicate. In Japan and other Asian countries, however, eye contact often is not important, and among

Native Americans, children are taught that eye contact with an adult is a sign of disrespect.

The eyes can also be used to express feelings. For instance, widening the eyes may note surprise for an Anglo, but the feelings denoted by eye widening are culturally diverse. Widened eyes may also indicate anger by a Chinese, a request for help or assistance by a Hispanic, the issuance of a challenge by a French person, and a rhetorical or persuasive effect by an African American.

As a component of culture, nonverbal expression has much in common with language: Both are coding systems that we learn and pass on as part of the cultural experience. Just as we learn that the word *stop* can mean to halt or cease, we also learn that an arm held up in the air with the palm facing another person frequently means the same thing. Because most nonverbal communication is culturally based, what it symbolizes often is a case of what a culture has transmitted to its members. The nonverbal symbol for suicide, for example, varies among cultures. In the United States it is usually a finger pointed at the temple or drawn across the throat. In Japan, it is a hand thrust onto the stomach, and in New Guinea it is a hand placed on the neck. Both nonverbal symbols and the responses they generate are part of cultural experience, what is passed from generation to generation. Every symbol takes on significance because of one's past experience with it. Even such simple acts as waving the hand can produce culturally diverse responses. In the United States, we tend to wave goodbye by placing the hand out with the palm down and moving the hand up and down; in India and in parts of Africa and South America, this is a beckoning gesture. We should also be aware that what may be a polite or friendly gesture in one culture may be an impolite and obscene gesture in another. Culture influences and directs those experiences, and is, therefore, a major contributor to how we send, receive, and respond to nonverbal symbols.

The Concept of Time. A culture's concept of time is its philosophy toward the past, present, and future and the importance or lack of importance it places on time. Most Western cultures think of time in lineal-spatial terms; we are time bound and well aware of the past, present, and future. In contrast, the Hopi Indians pay very little attention to time. They believe that each object — whether a person or plant, or an animal — has its own time system.

Even within the dominant mainstream of American culture, we find groups that have learned to perceive time in ways that appear strange to many outsiders. Hispanics frequently refer to Mexican or Latino time when their timing differs from the predominant Anglo concept, and African Americans often use what is referred to as BPT (black people's time) or hang loose time — maintaining that priority belongs to what is happening at that instant.

Use of Space. The way in which people use space as a part of interpersonal communication is called **proxemics**. It involves not only the distance between people engaged in conversation but also their physical orientation. Arabs and Latinos, for example, tend to interact physically closer together than do North American Anglos. What is important is to realize that people of different cultures have different ways in which they relate to one another spatially. When talking to someone from another culture, therefore, we must realize that what would be a violation of our personal space in our culture is not so intended by the other person. We may experience feelings that are difficult to handle; we may believe that the other person is overbearing, boorish, or even making inappropriate, unacceptable sexual advances when indeed the other person's movements are only manifestations of his or her cultural learning about how to use space.

Physical orientation is also culturally influenced, and it helps to define social relationships. North Americans prefer to sit where they are face to face or at right angles to one another. We seldom seek side-by-side arrangements. Chinese, on the other hand, often prefer a side-by-side arrangement and may feel uncomfortable when placed in a face-to-face situation.

We also tend to define social hierarchies through our nonverbal use of space. Sitting behind a desk while speaking with someone who is standing is usually a sign of a superior-subordinate relationship, with the socially superior person seated. Misunderstandings can easily occur in intercultural settings when two people, each acting according to the dictates of his or her culture, violate each other's expectations. If we were to remain seated when expected to rise, for example, we could easily violate a cultural norm and unknowingly insult our host or guest.

Room furnishings and size can also be an indication of social status. In corporate America, status within the corporation is often measured by desk size, office size, whether one has carpet on the office floor, and whether the carpet is wall to wall or a mere rug.

How we organize space also is a function of our culture. Our homes, for instance, preserve nonverbally our cultural beliefs and values. South American house designs are extremely private, with only one door opening onto the street and everything else behind walls. North Americans are used to large unwalled front yards with windows looking into the house, allowing passersby to see what goes on inside. In South America, a North American is liable to feel excluded and wonder about what goes on behind all those closed doors.

INTERCULTURAL COMMUNICATION

The link between culture and communication is crucial to understanding intercultural communication because it is through the influence of culture that people learn to communicate. A Korean, an Egyptian, or an American learns to communicate like other Koreans, Egyptians, or Americans. Their behavior conveys meaning because it is learned and shared; it is cultural. People view their world through categories, concepts, and labels that are products of their culture.

Cultural similarity in perception makes the sharing of meaning possible. The ways in which we communicate, the circumstances of our communication, the language and language style we use, and our nonverbal behaviors are primarily all a response to

and a function of our culture. And, as cultures differ from one another, the communication practices and behaviors of individuals reared in those cultures will also be different.

Our contention is that intercultural communication can best be understood as cultural diversity in the perception of social objects and events. A central tenet of this position is that minor communication problems are often exaggerated by perceptual diversity. To understand others' worlds and actions, we must try to understand their perceptual frames of reference; we must learn to understand how they perceive the world. In the ideal intercultural encounter, we would hope for many overlapping experiences and a commonality of perceptions. Cultural diversity, however, tends to introduce us to dissimilar experiences and, hence, to varied and frequently strange and unfamiliar perceptions of the external world.

In all respects, everything so far said about communication and culture applies to intercultural communication. The functions and relationships between the components of communication obviously apply, but what especially characterizes intercultural communication is that sources and responders come from different cultures. This alone is sufficient to identify a unique form of communicative interaction that must take into account the role and function of culture in the communication process.

In this section, intercultural communication will first be defined and then discussed through the perspective of a model. Finally, then its various forms will be shown.

Intercultural Communication Model

Intercultural communication occurs whenever a message that must be understood is produced by a member of one culture for consumption by a member of another culture. This circumstance can be problematic because, as we have already seen, culture forges and shapes the individual communicator. Culture is largely responsible for the

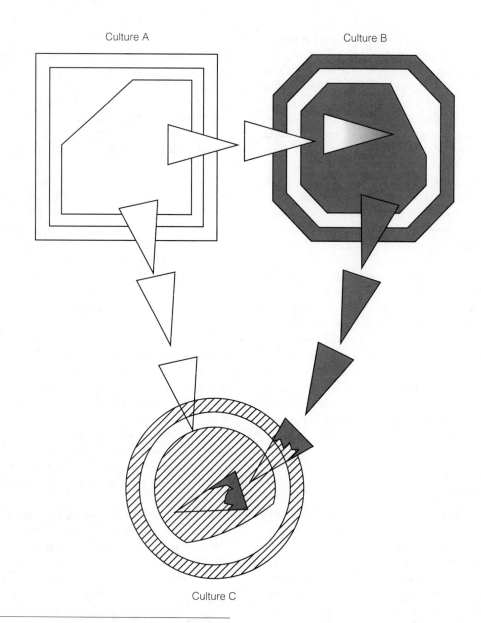

Figure 1 Model of Intercultural Communication

construction of our individual social realities and for our individual repertoires of communicative behaviors and meanings. The communication repertories people possess can vary significantly from culture to culture, which can lead to all sorts of difficulties. Through the study and understanding of intercultural communication, however, these difficulties at the least can be reduced and at best nearly eliminated.

Cultural influence on individuals and the problems inherent in the production and interpretation of messages between cultures are illustrated in Figure 1. Here, three cultures are represented by three distinct geometric shapes. Cultures A and B are purposefully similar to one another and are represented by a square and an irregular octagon that resembles a square. Culture C is intended to be quite different from Cultures A and B. It is represented both by its circular shape and its physical distance from Cultures A and B. Within each represented culture is another form similar to the shape of the influencing parent culture. This form represents a person who has been molded by his or her culture. The shape representing the person, however, is somewhat different from that of the parent culture. This difference suggests two things: First, there are other influences besides culture that affect and help mold the individual, and, second, although culture is the dominant shaping force on an individual, people vary to some extent from each other within any culture.

Message production, transmission, and interpretation across cultures is illustrated by the series of arrows connecting them. When a message leaves the culture in which it was encoded, it carries the content intended by its producer. This is represented by the arrows leaving a culture having the same pattern as that within the message producer. When a message reaches the culture where it is to be interpreted, it undergoes a transformation because the culture in which the message is decoded influences the message interpretation and hence its meaning. The content of the original message changes during that interpretation phase of intercultural communication because the culturally different repertories of social reality, communicative behaviors, and meanings possessed by the interpreter do not coincide with those possessed by the message producer.

The degree of influence culture has on intercultural communication is a function of the dissimilarity between the cultures. This also is indicated in the model by the degree of pattern change that occurs in the message arrows. The change that occurs between Cultures A and B is much less than the change between Cultures A and C and between Cultures B and C. This is because there is greater similarity between Cultures A and B. Hence, the rep-

ertories of social reality, communicative behaviors, and meanings are similar and the interpretation effort produces results more nearly like the content intended in the original message. Since Culture C is represented as being quite different from Cultures A and B, the interpreted message is considerably different and more nearly represents the pattern of Culture C.

The model suggests that there can be wide variability in cultural differences during intercultural communication, due in part to circumstances or forms. Intercultural communication occurs in a wide variety of situations that range from interactions between people for whom cultural differences are extreme to interactions between people who are members of the same dominant culture and whose differences are reflected in the values and perceptions of co-cultures existing within the dominant culture. If we imagine differences varying along a minimum-maximum dimension (see Figure 2), the degree of difference between two cultural groups depends on their relative social uniqueness. Although this scale is unrefined, it allows us to examine intercultural communication acts and gain insight into the effect cultural differences have on communication. To see how this dimensional scale helps us understand intercultural communication, we can look at some examples of cultural differences positioned along the scale.

The first example represents a case of maximum differences — those found between Asian and Western cultures. This may be typified as an interaction between two farmers, one who works on a communal farm on the outskirts of Beijing in China and the other who operates a large mechanized and automated wheat, corn, and dairy farm in Michigan. In this situation, we would expect to find the greatest number of diverse cultural factors. Physical appearance, religion, philosophy, economic systems, social attitudes, language, heritage, basic conceptualizations of self and the universe, and degree of technological development are cultural factors that differ sharply. We must recognize, however, that these two farmers also share the commonality of farming, with its rural life style and love of land. In some respects, they may be more closely related than they are to

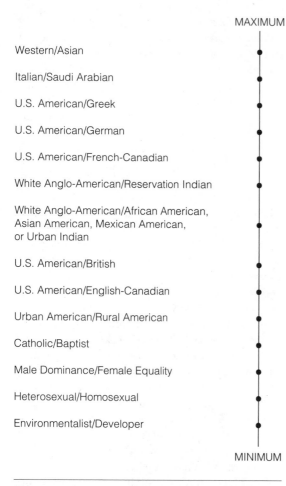

MAXIMUM

Western/Asian

Italian/Saudi Arabian

U.S. American/Greek

U.S. American/German

U.S. American/French-Canadian

White Anglo-American/Reservation Indian

White Anglo-American/African American,
Asian American, Mexican American,
or Urban Indian

U.S. American/British

U.S. American/English-Canadian

Urban American/Rural American

Catholic/Baptist

Male Dominance/Female Equality

Heterosexual/Homosexual

Environmentalist/Developer

MINIMUM

Figure 2 Arrangement of Compared Cultures, Subcultures, and Subgroups Along a Scale of Minimum to Maximum Socio-cultural Differences

members of their own cultures who live in large urban settings. In other words, across some cultural dimensions, the Michigan farmer may have more in common with the Chinese farmer than with a Wall Street securities broker.

Another example nearer the center of the scale is the difference between American culture and German culture. Less variation is found: Physical characteristics are similar, and the English language is derived in part from German and its ancestor languages. The roots of both German and American philosophy are found in ancient Greece, and most

Americans and Germans share some form of the Judeo-Christian tradition. Yet there are some significant differences. Germans have political and economic systems that are different from those found in the United States. German society tends toward formality while in the United States we tend toward informality. Germans have memories of local warfare and the destruction of their cities and economy, of having been a defeated nation on more than one occasion. The United States has never lost a war on its own territory.

Examples near the minimal end of the dimension can be characterized in two ways. First are variations found between members of separate but similar cultures — for instance, between U.S. Americans and English-Canadians. The differences are less than those found between American and German cultures, between American and Greek cultures, between American and British cultures, or even between American and French-Canadian cultures, but greater than generally found within a single culture. Second, minimal differences also may be seen in the variation between co-cultures, within the same dominant culture. Socio-cultural differences may be found between members of the Catholic church and the Baptist church; environmentalists and advocates of further development of Alaskan oil resources; middle-class Americans and the urban poor; mainstream Americans and the gay and lesbian community; the able and the disabled; or male dominance advocates and female equality advocates.

In both of these categorizations, members of each cultural group have much more in common than in the examples found in the middle or at the maximum end of the scale. They probably speak the same language, share the same general religion, attend the same schools, and live in the same neighborhoods. Yet, these groups to some extent are culturally different; they do not fully share the experiences, nor do they share the same perception. They see their worlds differently.

COMMUNICATION CONTEXT

Any communicative interactions takes place within some social and physical context. When people are communicating within their culture, they are usually aware of the context and it does little to hinder the communication. When people are engaged in intercultural communication, however, the context in which that communication takes place can have a strong impact. Unless both parties to intercultural communication are aware of how their culture affects the contextual element of communication, they can be in for some surprising communication difficulty.

Context and Communication

We begin with the assumption that communicative behavior is governed by **rules**, principles or regulations that govern conduct and procedure. Communication rules act as a system of expected behavior patterns that organize interaction between individuals. Communication rules are both culturally and contextually bound. Although the social setting and situation may determine the type of rules that are appropriate, the culture determines the rules. In Iraq, for instance, a contextual rule prohibits females from having unfamiliar males visit them at home; in the United States, however, it is not considered socially inappropriate for unknown males to visit females at home. Rules dictate behavior by establishing appropriate responses to stimuli for a particular communication context.

Communication rules include both verbal and nonverbal components; the rules determine not only what should be said but how it should be said. Nonverbal rules apply to proper gestures, facial expressions, eye contact, proxemics, vocal tone, and body movements.

Unless one is prepared to function in the contextual environment of another culture, he or she may be in for a disappointing experience. The intercultural situation can be one of high stress, both physically and mentally. The effects of this stress are called *culture shock*. In order to avoid culture shock, it is necessary to have a full understanding of communication context and how it differs culturally. We must remember that cultural contexts are neither right nor wrong, better nor worse; they are just different.

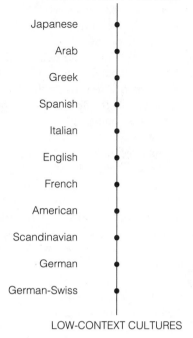

Figure 3 High- and Low-Context Cultures

Having determined that cultures develop rules that govern human interaction in specific contexts, we need now to gain some insight into a general concept of context. Anthropologist Edward T. Hall has written extensively about context.[10] Although he categorizes cultures as being either high-context or low-context, context really is a cultural dimension that ranges from high to low. An example of various cultures placed along that dimension can be seen in Figure 3.[11]

In high-context cultures most of the information is either in the physical context or is internalized in the people who are a part of the interaction. Very little information is actually coded in the verbal message. In low-context cultures, however, most of the information is contained in the verbal message and very little is embedded in the context or within the participants. In high-context cultures such as those of Japan, Korea, and Taiwan, people tend to be more aware of their surroundings and their environment and do not rely on verbal communication as their main information source. The Korean language contains the word *nunchi* that literally means being able to communicate through your eyes. In high-context cultures, the belief is that so much information is available in the environment that it is unnecessary to state verbally that which is obvious. Oral statements of affection, for instance, are very rare; when the context says "I love you," it is not necessary to state it orally.

There are four major differences in how high- and low-context cultures affect the setting. First, verbal messages are extremely important in low-context cultures. It is in the verbal message that the information to be shared is coded; it is not readily available from the environment because people in low-context cultures tend not to learn how to perceive information from the environment. Second, low-context people who rely primarily on verbal messages for information are perceived as less attractive and less credible by people in high-context cultures. Third, people in high-context cultures are more adept at reading nonverbal behavior and reading the environment. Fourth, people in high-context cultures have an expectation that others are also able to understand the unarticulated communication; hence, they do not speak as much as people from low-context cultures.

SUMMARY

In many respects the relationship between culture and communication is reciprocal; each affects and influences the other. What we talk about; how we talk about it; what we see, attend to, or ignore; how we think; and what we think about are influenced by our culture. In turn, what we talk about, how we talk about it, and what we see help shape, define, and perpetuate our culture. Culture cannot exist without communication; one cannot change without causing change in the other.

We suggested that the chief problem associated with intercultural communication is error in social perception brought about by the cultural diversity that affects the perceptual process. The attribution of meaning to messages is in many respects influenced by the culture of the person responding to the message behavior. When the message being interpreted is encoded in another culture, the cultural influences and experiences that produced the message may have been entirely different from the cultural influences and experiences that are being drawn on to interpret and respond to the message. Consequently, unintended errors in meaning attribution may arise because people with entirely different backgrounds are unable to understand one another accurately.

We discussed several socio-cultural variables that are major sources of communication difficulty. Although they were discussed in isolation, we cannot permit ourselves to conclude that they are unrelated; they are all related in a matrix of cultural complexities. For successful intercultural communication, we must be aware of these cultural factors affecting communication in both our own culture and in the culture of the other party. We need to understand not only cultural differences, which will help us determine sources of potential problems, but also cultural similarities, which will help us become closer to one another.

The approach we have taken is also based on a fundamental assumption: *The parties to intercultural communication must have an honest and sincere desire to communicate and to seek mutual understanding*. This assumption requires favorable attitudes about intercultural communication and an elimination of superior-inferior relationships based on membership in particular cultures, races, religions, or ethnic groups. Unless this basic assumption has been satisfied, our theory of cultural diversity in social perception will not produce improvement in intercultural communication.

At the beginning of this article we mentioned how changes in transportation and communication technology had brought us to the brink of the global village. We also suggested that we, as a people, do not yet know how to live as global villagers. We want to return to this point as we finish and leave you with some thoughts about it.

The prevailing direction in the United States today seems to be toward a pluralistic, multicultural society. An underlying assumption of this position, one that is seldom expressed or perhaps seldom realized, is that this requires that we as a society be accepting of the views, values, and behaviors of other cultures. This means that we must be willing to "live and let live." We do not seem able or willing to do this, however, nor are we sure that it is proper to do so in all circumstances. But if we are to get along with one another, we must develop toleration for others' culturally diverse customs and behaviors — a task that will be difficult.

Even within the dominant mainstream culture, we are unable to accept diversity; for example, we find ourselves deeply divided over such issues as right to life versus freedom of choice. When we must cope with the diversity of customs, values, views, and behaviors inherent in a multicultural society, we find ourselves in much greater states of frustration and peril. Three closely timed events covered extensively in the news media serve as examples of our difficulty. Cable News Network (CNN) carried a story on March 2, 1990 about fundamentalist Christians in a southern community who were demanding the removal of a statue of Buddha from the front of an Asian restaurant because "It is the idol of a false god; it's in the New Testament." Also, news media carried a story about a judge who dismissed wife-beating charges against an Asian man because this behavior was appropriate and acceptable in the man's culture. The action by the judge was immediately assailed by the feminist movement even though the judge had admonished the man that he could not persist in this behavior in the future because it is not acceptable in this society and further charges would not be dropped. The final event was a series of news reports in the Los Angeles print media relating to the disappearance of young dogs and puppies in portions of the Los Angeles area where there had been an influx of Southeast Asian immigrants. The speculation was that these animals were ending up on barbecue spits, as dog meat is considered a delicacy by these immigrants.

This series of events has led us to conclude that there are some major obstacles we must overcome if we are to become proper members of the global village. Perhaps the greatest challenge is in determining what rules will govern the global village, and perhaps more importantly, who will generate those rules. We want to raise this issue here because it is important and worthy of much consideration. We do not have the answers, but we can formulate the questions and provide some guidelines for thinking about the answers.

We believe it is necessary to start from an assumptive position: *Cultural diversity is desirable and we elect to embrace and become a multicultural society.* We realize that our question about who writes the rules has a pragmatic answer: the dominant culture. But, ours is an axiological concern: What ought to be the rules that govern interaction in a truly culturally diverse multicultural society? And, who ought to be determining these rules?

What we may really be asking is how much cultural diversity in the major aspects of social behavior can our society permit and still find ourselves cohesive as a society? Ought we or can we permit wife beating among co-cultures if wife beating is a part of that co-culture's heritage? When we go out on our patios on Sunday afternoon and place a piece of dead steer on our barbecues ought we or can we permit our Southeast Asian neighbor to place a dead puppy on his or her barbecue spit if eating dog meat is a part of that cultural heritage? Ought we or can we permit Samoan adults to discipline their children by harsh beatings if that behavior is a part of the Samoan cultural tradition? Ought we or can we permit Asian parents to treat their children's illnesses by *coining* where the child is rubbed with a coin that leaves long bruises on the back and arms in order to drive out the evil that is causing the child to be sick?

As our society continues to accept immigrants and refugees, we will find a continuing increase in cultural diversity. If we continue to assert actively the value of cultural diversity and claim to embrace and accept a multicultural global village orientation, we must be prepared to accept and tolerate the inherent diversity. A culturally diverse society can exist if and only if diversity is permitted to flourish.

We cannot solve the problem here, but we hope that you will continue to think about these issues because the time is upon us when we must adopt ourselves to the multicultural society that goes with the global village. And, it will be through the manner in which we can adopt to the changing population that will in large measure determine how these problems are solved. We hope that your thinking about these issues now will better prepare you for life in the global village.

NOTES

1. Marvin Harris, *Cows, Pigs, Wars, and Witches: The Riddles of Culture* (New York: Random House, 1974), p. 84.

2. A. J. Almaney and A. J. Alwan, *Communicating with the Arabs* (Prospect Heights, IL: Waveland Press, 1982), p. 5.

3. Ibid., p. 5.

4. Carley H. Dodd, *Dynamics of Intercultural Communication*, 2d ed. (Dubuque, IA: Wm. C. Brown, 1987), pp. 40–49.

5. E. Adamson Hoebel and Everett L. Frost, *Cultural and Social Anthropology* (New York: McGraw-Hill, 1974), p. 58.

6. Edward T. Hall, *Beyond Culture* (Garden City, NY: Anchor, Doubleday, 1977), pp. 13–14.

7. Ibid.

8. Felix M. Keesing, *Cultural Anthropology: The Science of Custom* (New York: Holt, Rinehart, and Winston, 1965), p. 46.

9. Ibid.

10. Hall.

11. L. Copeland and L. Griggs, Going International: *How to Make Friends and Deal Effectively in the Global Marketplace* (New York: Random House, 1985).

Communication in a Global Village

DEAN C. BARNLUND

Nearing Autumn's close.
My neighbor—
How does he live, I wonder?

—Bashō

These lines, written by one of the most cherished of *haiku* poets, express a timeless and universal curiosity in one's fellow man. When they were written, nearly three hundred years ago, the word "neighbor" referred to people very much like one's self— similar in dress, in diet, in custom, in language— who happened to live next door. Today relatively few people are surrounded by neighbors who are cultural replicas of themselves. Tomorrow we can expect to spend most of our lives in the company of neighbors who will speak in a different tongue, seek different values, move at a different pace, and interact according to a different script. Within no longer than a decade or two the probability of spending part of one's life in a foreign culture will exceed the probability a hundred years ago of ever leaving the town in which one was born. As our world is transformed our neighbors increasingly will be people whose life styles contrast sharply with our own.

The technological feasibility of such a global village is no longer in doubt. Only the precise date of its attainment is uncertain. The means already exist: in telecommunication systems linking the world by

---

From Dean C. Barnlund, *Public and Private Self in Japan and the United States* (Tokyo: Simul Press, Inc., 1975), pp. 3–24. Reprinted by permission of the publisher. Professor Barnlund taught at San Francisco State University. Footnotes deleted.

satellite, in aircraft capable of moving people faster than the speed of sound, in computers which can disgorge facts more rapidly than men can formulate their questions. The methods for bringing people closer physically and electronically are clearly at hand. What is in doubt is whether the erosion of cultural boundaries through technology will bring the realization of a dream or a nightmare. Will a global village be a mere collection or a true community of men? Will its residents be neighbors capable of respecting and utilizing their differences, or clusters of strangers living in ghettos and united only in their antipathies for others?

Can we generate the new cultural attitudes required by our technological virtuosity? History is not very reassuring here. It has taken centuries to learn how to live harmoniously in the family, the tribe, the city state, and the nation. Each new stretching of human sensitivity and loyalty has taken generations to become firmly assimilated in the human psyche. And now we are forced into a quantum leap from the mutual suspicion and hostility that have marked the past relations between peoples into a world in which mutual respect and comprehension are requisite.

Even events of recent decades provide little basis for optimism. Increasing physical proximity has brought no millennium in human relations. If anything, it has appeared to intensify the divisions among people rather than to create a broader intimacy. Every new reduction in physical distance has made us more painfully aware of the psychic distance that divides people and has increased alarm over real or imagined differences. If today people occasionally choke on what seem to be indigestible differences between rich and poor, male and female, specialist and nonspecialist within cultures, what will happen tomorrow when people must assimilate and cope with still greater contrasts in life styles? Wider access to more people will be a doubtful victory if human beings find they have nothing to say to one another or cannot stand to listen to each other.

Time and space have long cushioned intercultural encounters, confining them to touristic ex-

changes. But this insulation is rapidly wearing thin. In the world of tomorrow we can expect to live—not merely vacation—in societies which seek different values and abide by different codes. There we will be surrounded by foreigners for long periods of time, working with others in the closest possible relationships. If people currently show little tolerance or talent for encounters with alien cultures, how can they learn to deal with constant and inescapable coexistence?

The temptation is to retreat to some pious hope or talismanic formula to carry us into the new age. "Meanwhile," as Edwin Reischauer reminds us, "we fail to do what we ourselves must do if 'one world' is ever to be achieved, and that is to develop the education, the skills and the attitudes that men must have if they are to build and maintain such a world. The time is short, and the needs are great. The task faces all men. But it is on the shoulders of people living in the strong countries of the world, such as Japan and the United States, that this burden falls with special weight and urgency."

Anyone who has truly struggled to comprehend another person—even those closest and most like himself—will appreciate the immensity of the challenge of intercultural communication. A greater exchange of people between nations, needed as that may be, carries with it no guarantee of increased cultural empathy; experience in other lands often does little but aggravate existing prejudices. Studying guidebooks or memorizing polite phrases similarly fails to explain differences in cultural perspectives. Programs of cultural enrichment, while they contribute to curiosity about other ways of life, do not cultivate the skills to function effectively in the cultures studied. Even concentrated exposure to a foreign language, valuable as it is, provides access to only one of the many codes that regulate daily affairs; human understanding is by no means guaranteed because conversants share the same dictionary. (Within the United States, where people inhabit a common territory and possess a common language, mutuality of meaning among Mexican-Americans, White Americans, Black-Americans, Indian-Americans—to say nothing of old and young, poor and rich, pro-establishment and anti-establishment cultures—is a sporadic and unreliable occurrence.) Useful as all these measures are for enlarging appreciation of diverse cultures, they fall short of what is needed for a global village to survive.

What seems most critical is to find ways of gaining entrance into the assumptive world of another culture, to identify the norms that govern face-to-face relations, and to equip people to function within a social system that is foreign but no longer incomprehensible. Without this kind of insight people are condemned to remain outsiders no matter how long they live in another country. Its institutions and its customs will be interpreted inevitably from the premises and through the medium of their own culture. Whether they notice something or overlook it, respect or ridicule it, express or conceal their reaction will be dictated by the logic of their own rather than the alien culture.

There are, of course, shelves and shelves of books on the cultures of the world. They cover the history, religion, political thought, music, sculpture, and industry of many nations. And they make fascinating and provocative reading. But only in the vaguest way do they suggest what it is that really distinguishes the behavior of a Samoan, a Congolese, a Japanese, or an American. Rarely do the descriptions of a political structure or religious faith explain precisely when and why certain topics are avoided or why specific gestures carry such radically different meanings according to the context in which they appear.

When former President Nixon and former Premier Sato met to discuss a growing problem concerning trade in textiles between Japan and the United States, Premier Sato announced that since they were on such good terms with each other the deliberations would be "three parts talk and seven parts 'haragei.'" Translated literally, "haragei" means to communicate through the belly, that is to feel out intuitively rather than verbally state the precise position of each person.

Subscribing to this strategy—one that governs many interpersonal exchanges in his culture—Premier Sato conveyed without verbal elaboration his comprehension of the plight of American textile firms threatened by accelerating exports of Japanese fabrics to the United States. President Nixon—similarly abiding by norms that govern interaction within his culture—took this comprehension of the American position to mean that new export quotas would be forthcoming shortly.

During the next few weeks both were shocked at the consequences of their meeting: Nixon was infuriated to learn that the new policies he expected were not forthcoming, and Sato was upset to find that he had unwittingly triggered a new wave of hostility toward his country. If prominent officials, surrounded by foreign advisers, can commit such grievous communicative blunders, the plight of the ordinary citizen may be suggested. Such intercultural collisions, forced upon the public consciousness by the grave consequences they carry and the extensive publicity they receive, only hint at the wider and more frequent confusions and hostilities that disrupt the negotiations of lesser officials, business executives, professionals and even visitors in foreign countries.

Every culture expresses its purpose and conducts its affairs through the medium of communication. Cultures exist primarily to create and preserve common systems of symbols by which their members can assign and exchange meanings. Unhappily, the distinctive rules that govern these symbol systems are far from obvious. About some of these codes, such as language, we have extensive knowledge. About others, such as gestures and facial codes, we have only rudimentary knowledge. On many others—rules governing topical appropriateness, customs regulating physical contact, time and space codes, strategies for the management of conflict—we have almost no systematic knowledge. To crash another culture with only the vaguest notion of its underlying dynamics reflects not only a provincial naïvete but a dangerous form of cultural arrogance.

It is differences in meaning, far more than mere differences in vocabulary, that isolate cultures, and that cause them to regard each other as strange or even barbaric. It is not too surprising that many cultures refer to themselves as "The People," relegating all other human beings to a subhuman form of life.

To the person who drinks blood, the eating of meat is repulsive. Someone who conveys respect by standing is upset by someone who conveys it by sitting down; both may regard kneeling as absurd. Burying the dead may prompt tears in one society, smiles in another, and dancing in a third. If spitting on the street makes sense to some, it will appear bizarre that others carry their spit in their pocket; neither may quite appreciate someone who spits to express gratitude. The bullfight that constitutes an almost religious ritual for some seems a cruel and inhumane way of destroying a defenseless animal to others. Although staring is acceptable social behavior in some cultures, in others it is a thoughtless invasion of privacy. Privacy, itself, is without universal meaning.

Note that none of these acts involves an insurmountable linguistic challenge. The words that describe these acts—eating, spitting, showing respect, fighting, burying, and staring—are quite translatable into most languages. The issue is more conceptual than linguistic; each society places events in its own cultural frame and it is these frames that bestow the unique meaning and differentiated response they produce.

As we move or are driven toward a global village and increasingly frequent cultural contact, we need more than simply greater factual knowledge of each other. We need, more specifically, to identify what might be called the "rulebooks of meaning" that distinguish one culture from another. For to grasp the way in which other cultures perceive the world, and the assumptions and values that are the foundation of these perceptions, is to gain access to the experience of other human beings. Access to the world view and the communicative style of other cultures may not only enlarge our own way of experiencing the world but enable us to maintain constructive relationships with societies that operate according to a different logic than our own.

SOURCES OF MEANING

To survive, psychologically as well as physically, human beings must inhabit a world that is relatively free of ambiguity and is reasonably predictable. Some sort of structure must be placed upon the endless profusion of incoming signals. The infant, born into a world of flashing, hissing, moving images, soon learns to adapt by resolving this chaos into toys and tables, dogs and parents. Even adults who have had their vision or hearing restored through surgery describe the world as a frightening and sometimes unbearable experience; only after days of effort are they able to transform blurs and noises into meaningful and therefore manageable experiences.

It is commonplace to talk as if the world "has" meaning, to ask what "is" the meaning of a phrase, a gesture, a painting, a contract. Yet when thought about, it is clear that events are devoid of meaning until someone assigns it to them. There is no appropriate response to a bow or a handshake, a shout or a whisper, until it is interpreted. A drop of water and the color red have no meaning, they simply exist. The aim of human perception is to make the world intelligible so that it can be managed successfully; the attribution of meaning is a prerequisite to and preparation for action.

People are never passive receivers, merely absorbing events of obvious significance, but are active in assigning meaning to sensation. What any event acquires in the way of meaning appears to reflect a transaction between what is there to be seen or heard, and what the interpreter brings to it in the way of past experience and prevailing motive. Thus the attribution of meanings is always a creative process by which the raw data of sensation are transformed to fit the aims of the observer.

The diversity of reactions that can be triggered by a single experience—meeting a stranger, negotiating a contract, attending a textile conference—is immense. Each observer is forced to see it through his own eyes, interpret it in the light of his own values, fit it to the requirements of his own circumstances. As a consequence, every object and message is seen by every observer from a somewhat different perspective. Each person will note some features and neglect others. Each will accept some relations among the facts and deny others. Each will arrive at some conclusion, tentative or certain, as the sounds and forms resolve into a "temple" or "barn," a "compliment" or "insult."

Provide a group of people with a set of photographs, even quite simple and ordinary photographs, and note how diverse are the meanings they provoke. Afterward they will recall and forget different pictures, they will also assign quite distinctive meanings to those they do remember. Some will recall the mood of a picture, others the actions; some the appearance and others the attitudes of persons portrayed. Often the observers cannot agree upon even the most "objective" details—the number of people, the precise location and identity of simple objects. A difference in frame of mind—fatigue, hunger, excitement, anger—will change dramatically what they report they have "seen."

It should not be surprising that people raised in different families, exposed to different events, praised and punished for different reasons, should come to view the world so differently. As George Kelly has noted, people see the world through templates which force them to construe events in unique ways. These patterns or grids which we fit over the realities of the world are cut from our own experience and values, and they predispose us to certain interpretations. Industrialist and farmer do not see the "same" land; husband and wife do not plan for the "same" child; doctor and patient do not discuss the "same" disease; borrower and creditor do not negotiate the "same" mortgage; daughter and daughter-in-law do not react to the "same" mother.

The world each person creates for himself is a distinctive world, not the same world others occupy. Each fashions from every incident whatever meanings fit his own private biases. These biases, taken together, constitute what has been called the "assumptive world of the individual." The world each person gets inside his head is the only world he knows. And it is this symbolic world, not the real world, that he talks about, argues about, laughs about, fights about.

Interpersonal Encounters

Every communication, interpersonal or intercultural, is a transaction between these private worlds. As people talk they search for symbols that will enable them to share their experience and converge upon a common meaning. This process, often long and sometimes painful, makes it possible finally to reconcile apparent or real differences between them. Various words are used to describe this moment. When it involves an integration of facts or ideas, it is usually called an "agreement"; when it involves sharing a mood or feeling, it is referred to as "empathy" or "rapport." But "understanding" is a broad enough term to cover both possibilities; in either case it identifies the achievement of a common meaning.

If understanding is a measure of communicative success, a simple formula—which might be called the *Interpersonal Equation*—may clarify the major factors that contribute to its achievement.

Interpersonal Understanding = f (Similarity of Perceptual Orientations, Similarity of Belief Systems, Similarity of Communicative Styles)

That is, "Interpersonal Understanding" is a function of or dependent upon the degree of "Similarity of Perceptual Orientations," "Similarity of Systems of Belief," and "Similarity of Communicative Styles." Each of these terms requires some elaboration.

"Similarity in Perceptual Orientations" refers to a person's prevailing approach to reality and the degree of flexibility he manifests in organizing it. Some people can scan the world broadly, searching for diversity of experience, preferring the novel and unpredictable. They may be drawn to new foods, new music, new ways of thinking. Others seem to scan the world more narrowly, searching to confirm past experience, preferring the known and predictable. They secure satisfaction from old friends, traditional art forms, familiar life styles. The former have a high tolerance for novelty; the latter a low tolerance for novelty.

It is a balance between these tendencies, of course, that characterizes most people. Within the same person attraction to the unfamiliar and the familiar coexist. Which prevails at any given moment is at least partly a matter of circumstance: when secure, people may widen their perceptual field, accommodate new ideas or actions; when they feel insecure they may narrow their perceptual field to protect existing assumptions from the threat of new beliefs or life styles. The balance may be struck in still other ways: some people like to live in a stable physical setting with everything in its proper place, but welcome new emotional or intellectual challenges; others enjoy living in a chaotic and disordered environment but would rather avoid exposing themselves to novel or challenging ideas.

People differ also in the degree to which their perceptions are flexible or rigid. Some react with curiosity and delight to unpredictable and uncategorizable events. Others are disturbed or uncomfortable in the presence of the confusing and complex. There are people who show a high degree of tolerance for ambiguity; others manifest a low tolerance for ambiguity. When confronted with the complications and confusions that surround many daily events, the former tend to avoid immediate closure and delay judgment while the latter seek immediate closure and evaluation. Those with little tolerance for ambiguity tend to respond categorically, that is, by reference to the class names for things (businessmen, radicals, hippies, foreigners) rather than to their unique and differentiating features.

It would be reasonable to expect that individuals who approach reality similarly might understand each other easily, and laboratory research confirms this conclusion: people with similar perceptual styles attract one another, understand each other better, work more efficiently together and with greater satisfaction than those whose perceptual orientations differ.

"Similarity in Systems of Belief" refers not to the way people view the world, but to the conclusions they draw from their experience. Everyone develops a variety of opinions toward divorce, poverty, religion, television, sex, and social customs. When belief and disbelief systems coincide, people are likely to understand and appreciate each other better. Research done by Donn Byrne and replicated by the author demonstrates how powerfully human beings are drawn to those who hold the same beliefs and how sharply they are repelled by those who do not.

Subjects in these experiments were given questionnaires requesting their opinions on twenty-six topics. After completing the forms, each was asked to rank the thirteen most important and least important topics. Later each person was given four forms, ostensibly filled out by people in another group but actually filled out to show varying degrees of agreement with their own answers, and invited to choose among them with regard to their attractiveness as associates. The results were clear: people most preferred to talk with those whose attitudes duplicated their own exactly, next chose those who agreed with them on all important issues, next chose those with similar views on unimportant issues, and finally and reluctantly chose those who disagreed with them completely. It appears that most people most of the time find satisfying relationships easiest to achieve with someone who shares their own hierarchy of beliefs. This, of course, converts many human encounters into rituals of ratification, each person looking to the other only to obtain endorsement and applause for his own beliefs. It is, however, what is often meant by "interpersonal understanding."

Does the same principle hold true for "Similarity of Communicative Styles"? To a large extent, yes. But not completely. By "communicative style" is meant the topics people prefer to discuss, their favorite forms of interaction—ritual, repartee, argument, self-disclosure—and the depth of involvement they demand of each other. It includes the extent to which communicants rely upon the same channels—vocal, verbal, physical—for conveying information, and the extent to which they are tuned to the same level of meaning, that is, to the factual or emotional content of messages. The use of a common vocabulary and even preference for similar metaphors may help people to understand each other.

But some complementarity in conversational style may also help. Talkative people may prefer quiet partners, the more aggressive may enjoy the less aggressive, those who seek affection may be drawn to the more affection-giving, simply because both can find the greatest mutual satisfaction when interpersonal styles mesh. Even this sort of complementarity, however, may reflect a case of similarity in definitions of each other's conversational role.

This hypothesis, too, has drawn the interest of communicologists. One investigator found that people paired to work on common tasks were much more effective if their communicative styles were similar than if they were dissimilar. Another social scientist found that teachers tended to give higher grades on tests to students whose verbal styles matched their own than to students who gave equally valid answers but did not phrase them as their instructors might. To establish common meanings seems to require that conversants share a common vocabulary and compatible ways of expressing ideas and feelings.

It must be emphasized that perceptual orientations, systems of belief, and communicative styles do not exist or operate independently. They overlap and affect each other. They combine in complex ways to determine behavior. What a person says is influenced by what he believes and what he believes, in turn, by what he sees. His perceptions and beliefs are themselves partly a product of his manner of communicating with others. The terms that compose the Interpersonal Equation constitute not three isolated but three interdependent variables. They provide three perspectives to use in the analysis of communicative acts.

The Interpersonal Equation suggests there is an underlying narcissistic bias in human societies that draws similar people together. Each seeks to find in the other a reflection of himself, someone who views the world as he does, who interprets it as he does, and who expresses himself in a similar way. It is not surprising, then, that artists should be drawn to artists, radicals to radicals, Jews to Jews—or Japanese to Japanese and Americans to Americans.

The opposite seems equally true: people tend to avoid those who challenge their assumptions, who dismiss their beliefs, and who communicate in strange and unintelligible ways. When one reviews history, whether he examines crises within or between cultures, he finds people have consistently shielded themselves, segregated themselves, even fortified themselves, against wide differences in modes of perception or expression (in many cases, indeed, have persecuted and conquered the infidel

and afterwards substituted their own cultural ways for the offending ones). Intercultural defensiveness appears to be only a counterpart of interpersonal defensiveness in the face of uncomprehended or incomprehensible differences.

INTERCULTURAL ENCOUNTERS

Every culture attempts to create a "universe of discourse" for its members, a way in which people can interpret their experience and convey it to one another. Without a common system of codifying sensations, life would be absurd and all efforts to share meanings doomed to failure. This universe of discourse—one of the most precious of all cultural legacies—is transmitted to each generation in part consciously and in part unconsciously. Parents and teachers give explicit instruction in it by praising or criticizing certain ways of dressing, of thinking, of gesturing, of responding to the acts of others. But the most significant aspect of any cultural code may be conveyed implicitly, not by rule or lesson but through modelling behavior. The child is surrounded by others who, through the mere consistency of their actions as males and females, mothers and fathers, salesclerks and policemen, display what is appropriate behavior. Thus the grammar of any culture is sent and received largely unconsciously, making one's own cultural assumptions and biases difficult to recognize. They seem so obviously right that they require no explanation.

In *The Open and Closed Mind*, Milton Rokeach poses the problem of cultural understanding in its simplest form, but one that can readily demonstrate the complications of communication between cultures. It is called the "Denny Doodlebug Problem." Readers are given all the rules that govern his culture: Denny is an animal that always faces North, and can move only by jumping; he can jump large distances or small distances, but can change direction only after jumping four times in any direction; he can jump North, South, East or West, but not diagonally. Upon concluding a jump his master places some food three feet directly West of him. Surveying the situation, Denny concludes he must jump four times to reach the food. No more or less. And he is right. All the reader has to do is explain the circumstances that make his conclusion correct.

The large majority of people who attempt this problem fail to solve it, despite the fact that they are given all the rules that control behavior in this culture. If there is difficulty in getting inside the simplistic world of Denny Doodlebug—where the cultural code has already been broken and handed to us—imagine the complexity of comprehending behavior in societies where codes have not yet been deciphered. And where even those who obey these codes are only vaguely aware and can rarely describe the underlying sources of their own actions.

If two people, both of whom spring from a single culture, must often shout to be heard across the void that separates their private worlds, one can begin to appreciate the distance to be overcome when people of different cultural identities attempt to talk. Even with the most patient dedication to seeking a common terminology, it is surprising that people of alien cultures are able to hear each other at all. And the peoples of Japan and the United States would appear to constitute a particularly dramatic test of the ability to cross an intercultural divide. Consider the disparity between them.

Here is Japan, a tiny isolated nation with a minimum of resources, buffeted by periodic disasters, overcrowded with people, isolated by physical fact and cultural choice, nurtured in Shinto and Buddhist religions, permeated by a deep respect for nature, nonmaterialist in philosophy, intuitive in thought, hierarchical in social structure. Eschewing the explicit, the monumental, the bold and boisterous, it expresses its sensuality in the form of impeccable gardens, simple rural temples, asymmetrical flower arrangements, a theater unparalleled for containment of feeling, an art and literature remarkable for their delicacy, and crafts noted for their honest and earthy character. Its people, among the most homogeneous of men, are modest and apologetic in manner, communicate in an ambiguous and evocative language, are engrossed in interpersonal rituals and prefer inner serenity to influencing others. They occupy unpretentious buildings of wood and paper and live in cities laid out as casually as farm villages. Suddenly from these rice paddies emerges an industrial giant, surpassing rival nations with decades of industrial experience, greater resources, and a larger reserve of technicians. Its labor, working longer, harder and more frantically than any in the world, builds the earth's largest city, constructs some of its ugliest buildings, promotes the most garish and insistent advertising anywhere, and pollutes its air and water beyond the imagination.

And here is the United States, an immense country, sparsely settled, richly endowed, tied through waves of immigrants to the heritage of Europe, yet forced to subdue nature and find fresh solutions to the problems of survival. Steeped in the Judeo-Christian tradition, schooled in European abstract and analytic thought, it is materialist and experimental in outlook, philosophically pragmatic, politically equalitarian, economically competitive, its raw individualism sometimes tempered by a humanitarian concern for others. Its cities are studies in geometry along whose avenues rise shafts of steel and glass subdivided into separate cubicles for separate activities and separate people. Its popular arts are characterized by the hugeness of Cinemascope, the spontaneity of jazz, the earthy loudness of rock; in its fine arts the experimental, striking, and monumental often stifle the more subtle revelation. The people, a smorgasbord of races, religions, dialects, and nationalities, are turned expressively outward, impatient with rituals and rules, casual and flippant, gifted in logic and argument, approachable and direct yet given to flamboyant and exaggerated assertion. They are curious about one another, open and helpful, yet display a missionary zeal for changing one another. Suddenly this nation whose power and confidence have placed it in a dominant position in the world intellectually and politically, whose style of life has permeated the planet, finds itself uncertain of its direction, doubts its own premises and values, questions its motives and materialism, and engages in an orgy of self criticism.

It is when people nurtured in such different psychological worlds meet that differences in cultural perspectives and communicative codes may sabotage efforts to understand one another. Repeated collisions between a foreigner and the members of a contrasting culture often produce what is called "culture shock." It is a feeling of helplessness, even of terror or anger, that accompanies working in an alien society. One feels trapped in an absurd and indecipherable nightmare.

It is as if some hostile leprechaun had gotten into the works and as a cosmic caper rewired the connections that hold society together. Not only do the actions of others no longer make sense, but it is impossible even to express one's own intentions clearly. "Yes" comes out meaning "No." A wave of the hand means "come," or it may mean "go." Formality may be regarded as childish, or as a devious form of flattery. Statements of fact may be heard as statements of conceit. Arriving early, or arriving late, embarrasses or impresses. "Suggestions" may be treated as "ultimatums," or precisely the opposite. Failure to stand at the proper moment, or failure to sit, may be insulting. The compliment intended to express gratitude instead conveys a sense of distance. A smile signifies disappointment rather than pleasure.

If the crises that follow such intercultural encounters are sufficiently dramatic or the communicants unusually sensitive, they may recognize the source of their trouble. If there is patience and constructive intention the confusion can sometimes be clarified. But more often the foreigner, without knowing it, leaves behind him a trail of frustration, mistrust, and even hatred *of which he is totally unaware*. Neither he nor his associates recognize that their difficulty springs from sources deep within the rhetoric of their own societies. Each sees himself as acting in ways that are thoroughly sensible, honest and considerate. And—given the rules governing his own universe of discourse—each is. Unfortunately, there are few cultural universals, and the degree of overlap in communicative codes is always less than perfect. Experience can be transmitted with fidelity only when the unique properties of each code are recognized and respected, or where the motivation and means exist to bring them into some sort of alignment.

THE COLLECTIVE UNCONSCIOUS

Among the greatest insights of this modern age are two that bear a curious affinity to each other. The first, evolving from the efforts of psychologists, particularly Sigmund Freud, revealed the existence of an "individual unconscious." The acts of human beings were found to spring from motives of which they were often vaguely or completely unaware. Their unique perceptions of events arose not from the facts outside their skins but from unrecognized assumptions inside them. When, through intensive analysis, they obtained some insight into these assumptions, they became free to develop other ways of seeing and acting which contributed to their greater flexibility in coping with reality.

The second of these generative ideas, flowing from the work of anthropologists, particularly Margaret Mead and Ruth Benedict, postulated a parallel idea in the existence of a "cultural unconscious." Students of primitive cultures began to see that there was nothing divine or absolute about cultural norms. Every society had its own way of viewing the universe, and each developed from its premises a coherent set of rules of behavior. Each tended to be blindly committed to its own style of life and regarded all others as evil. The fortunate person who was able to master the art of living in foreign cultures often learned that his own mode of life was only one among many. With this insight he became free to choose from among cultural values those that seemed to best fit his peculiar circumstances.

Cultural norms so completely surround people, so permeate thought and action, that few ever recognize the assumptions on which their lives and their sanity rest. As one observer put it, if birds were suddenly endowed with scientific curiosity they might examine many things, but the sky itself would be overlooked as a suitable subject; if fish were to become curious about the world, it would never occur to them to begin by investigating water. For birds and fish would take the sky and sea for granted, unaware of their profound influence because they comprise the medium for every act. Human beings, in a similar way, occupy a symbolic universe governed by codes that are unconsciously acquired and automatically employed. So much so that they rarely notice that the ways they interpret and talk about events are distinctively different from the ways people conduct their affairs in other cultures.

As long as people remain blind to the sources of their meanings, they are imprisoned within them. These cultural frames of reference are no less confining simply because they cannot be seen or touched. Whether it is an individual neurosis that keeps an individual out of contact with his neighbors, or a collective neurosis that separates neighbors of different cultures, both are forms of blindness that limit what can be experienced and what can be learned from others.

It would seem that everywhere people would desire to break out of the boundaries of their own experiential worlds. Their ability to react sensitively to a wider spectrum of events and peoples requires an overcoming of such cultural parochialism. But, in fact, few attain this broader vision. Some, of course, have little opportunity for wider cultural experience, though this condition should change as the movement of people accelerates. Others do not try to widen their experience because they prefer the old and familiar, seek from their affairs only further confirmation of the correctness of their own values. Still others recoil from such experiences because they feel it dangerous to probe too deeply into the personal or cultural unconscious. Exposure may reveal how tenuous and arbitrary many cultural norms are; such exposure might force people to acquire new bases for interpreting events. And even for the many who do seek actively to enlarge the variety of human beings with whom they are capable of communicating there are still difficulties.

Cultural myopia persists not merely because of inertia and habit, but chiefly because it is so difficult to overcome. One acquires a personality and a cul-

ture in childhood, long before he is capable of comprehending either of them. To survive, each person masters the perceptual orientations, cognitive biases, and communicative habits of his own culture. But once mastered, objective assessment of these same processes is awkward since the same mechanisms that are being evaluated must be used in making the evaluations. Once a child learns Japanese or English or Navaho, the categories and grammar of each language predispose him to perceive and think in certain ways, and discourage him from doing so in other ways. When he attempts to discover why he sees or thinks as he does, he uses the same techniques he is trying to identify. Once one becomes an Indian, an Ibo, or a Frenchman—or even a priest or scientist—it is difficult to extricate oneself from that mooring long enough to find out what one truly is or wants.

Fortunately, there may be a way around this paradox. Or promise of a way around it. It is to expose the culturally distinctive ways various peoples construe events and seek to identify the conventions that connect what is seen with what is thought with what is said. Once this cultural grammar is assimilated and the rules that govern the exchange of meanings are known, they can be shared and learned by those who choose to work and live in alien cultures.

When people within a culture face an insurmountable problem they turn to friends, neighbors, associates, for help. To them they explain their predicament, often in distinctive personal ways. Through talking it out, however, there often emerge new ways of looking at the problem, fresh incentive to attack it, and alternative solutions to it. This sort of interpersonal exploration is often successful within a culture for people share at least the same communicative style even if they do not agree completely in their perceptions or beliefs.

When people communicate between cultures, where communicative rules as well as the substance of experience differs, the problems multiply. But so, too, do the number of interpretations and alternatives. If it is true that the more people differ the harder it is for them to understand each other, it is equally true that the more they differ the more they have to teach and learn from each other. To do so, of course, there must be mutual respect and sufficient curiosity to overcome the frustrations that occur as they flounder from one misunderstanding to another. Yet the task of coming to grips with differences in communicative styles—between or within cultures—is prerequisite to all other types of mutuality.

Cultural Identity and Intercultural Communication

MARY JANE COLLIER

Several useful approaches that can help you understand and improve the quality of your intercultural communication encounters are included in this book. One option you have for understanding why you and others behave in particular ways and learning what you can do to increase the appropriateness and effectiveness of your communication is to view communication from the perspective of cultural identity enactment.

This article presents an approach to culture that focuses on how individuals enact or take on one or more cultural identities. Questions that are answered here include the following: (1) What is a cultural identity? (2) How are multiple cultural identities created and negotiated with others? (3) How can knowledge of the cultural identity approach help you become more competent when dealing with persons who are taking on an identity different from yours? (4) What are the benefits of such an approach to intercultural communication research, training, and practice?

CULTURE

We approach culture here in a very specific way. **Culture** is defined as a historically transmitted system of symbols, meanings, and norms (Collier & Thomas, 1988; Geertz, 1983; and Schneider, 1976).

This original article appears here in print for the first time. All rights reserved. Permission to reprint must be obtained from the publisher and the author. Mary Jane Collier teaches at Oregon State University.

Notice the emphasis placed on the communication process in the definition. Notice also, that culture is *systemic*, meaning it comprises many complex components that are interdependent and related; they form a type of permeable boundary.

Symbols and Meanings

The components of the system are the patterned symbols such as verbal messages, nonverbal cues, emblems, and icons, as well as their interpretations or assigned meanings. Culture is what groups of people say and do and think and feel. Culture is not the people but the communication that links them together. Culture is not only speaking a language and using symbols but interpreting those symbols consistently; for example, traffic lights in South Africa are called "robots" and in England elevators are called "lifts." In urban areas, gang members change the items of clothing that denote gang membership periodically so that only in-group members know who is "in" and who is "out."

Norms

Another major component of the system of culture is normative conduct. **Norms** here are patterns of appropriate ways of communicating. It is important not only to speak with symbols that are understood, or to use nonverbal gestures or modes of dress so that the cues will be understood consistently, but also to use the symbols at acceptable times, with the appropriate people, with the fitting intensity. Japanese Americans may send their children to Japanese school and speak Japanese at home, but they may speak English at work and use direct and assertive forms of communication in business or educational settings. Malay women may wear traditional Muslim dress and show respectful silence to elders in the family, but they may be assertive and use a louder tone of voice among women in social settings.

History

The cultural system of communication is historically transmitted and handed down to new members of the group. Groups with histories include corporations, support groups, national groups, or civil rights groups. History is handed down when new employees are trained, "ground rules" are explained to new members of groups such as Alcoholics Anonymous, or dominant beliefs and the value of democracy are taught to U.S. American children in school.

We learn to become members of groups by learning about past members of the group, heroes, important precepts, rituals, values, and expectations for conduct. We are taught how to follow the norms of the group. In this way we perpetuate the cultural system. When a person becomes a college professor and joins a particular academic institution, she or he is taught about the mission of the institution, past academic heroes (faculty who have won awards, published prestigious works), the importance of "publish or perish" versus the importance placed on effective instruction, the role of sports or liberal arts in the institution, commitment to multiculturalism, and so on. The symbols and norms change over the life of the system, but there is enough consistency in what is handed down to be able to define the boundaries between systems (universities) and distinguish cultural members of one system from members of another.

Types of Cultures

Many groups (though not all) form cultural systems. Examples of many types of groups have already been included. In some cases, shared history or geography provides commonality of world view or life style which helps create and reinforce a cultural system of communication.

To create a culture groups must first define themselves as a group. This definition may be made on the basis of nationality, ethnicity, gender, profession, geography, organization, physical ability or disability, community, or type of relationship, among others. We will discuss many of these groups later.

Once the group defines itself as a unit, a cultural system may develop. For instance, U.S. Americans define themselves as a group based on use of English as a shared code; reinforcement of democracy through political discussion and action; individual rights and freedoms of speech, press, religion, and assembly being explicitly described in the Bill of Rights and enforced in the courts; and so forth. Attorneys or sales clerks or homemakers may be linked by similarities in daily activities and standard of living. Friends may see their group as including persons who like the same activities and support one another.

National and Ethnic Cultures. To better understand the many different types of cultures, we can categorize them from the more general and more common, to those that are more specific. National and ethnic cultures are fairly general. These kinds of groups base membership on heritage and history that has been handed down among several generations. Their history is based on traditions, rituals, codes of language, and norms.

Persons who share the same nationality were born in a particular country and spent a significant number of years and a period of socialization in that country. Such socialization promotes and reinforces particular values, beliefs, and norms. Because many people contribute to the creation of a national culture's symbols, meanings, and norms, "national culture" is fairly abstract so predictions about language use and what symbols mean can only be generalized. Japanese national culture, for instance, has been described as collectivistic, high context, high on power distance, and other-face oriented (Gudykunst & Ting-Toomey, 1988). Yet, not all Japanese people follow these norms in every situation. But, when comparing Japanese to Germans, the Japanese, as a group, are more group oriented and emphasize status hierarchies more than the Germans as an overall group (Hofstede, 1980).

Ethnicity is a bit different — ethnic groups share a sense of heritage and history, and origin from an area outside of or preceding the creation of their present nation-state of residence (Banks, 1984). Ethnic groups, in most but not all cases, share racial characteristics and many have a specific history of having experienced discrimination. In the United States, ethnic group members include African Americans, Asian Americans (Japanese Americans, Chinese Americans, Vietnamese Americans, Korean Americans, and so on), Mexican Americans, Polish Americans, Irish Americans, Native American Indians, and Jewish Americans, just to name a few examples.

Remember that national and ethnic cultures are the *communication systems* that are created by persons who share the same nationality or ethnicity. From this perspective, culture is the process of creating a perceived commonality and community of thought and action. Culture is based on what people say and do and think and feel *as a result* of their common history and origins.

Gender. Many subcategories of gender cultures exist. Groups create, reinforce, and teach what is interpreted as feminine or masculine. Groups also reinforce what is appropriate or inappropriate for a good husband, wife, feminist, chauvinist, heterosexual, gay, or lesbian. Mothers and fathers, religious leaders, teachers, and the media all provide information about how to be a member of a particular gender culture.

Profession. Politicians, physicians, field workers, sales personnel, maintenance crews, bankers, and consultants share common ways of spending time, earning money, communicating with others, and learning norms about how to be a member of their profession. Health care professionals probably share a commitment to health, to helping others, and to improving others' quality of life. They also share educational background, knowledge about their aspect of health care, and standards of practicing their profession.

Geographical Area. Geographical area sometimes acts as a boundary, contributing to the formation of a cultural group. In South Africa, the area surrounding Cape Town has it's own version of spoken Afrikaans, has a higher population of Coloreds (those of mixed race), and is viewed by many as the most cosmopolitan area in South Africa. The South in the United States has its own traditions, historical orientation, and southern drawl. Rural communities sometimes differ from urban communities in political views, values, life style, and norms.

Organization. Large corporations such as IBM, Nike, or Xerox create the most common type of organizational culture. In this culture members are taught the corporate symbols, myths, heroes, and legends, and what it means to be an employee. The proper chain of command, procedures and policies, and schedules are also taught. Finally, they learn the norms in the corporation—who to talk to, about what, at which particular moment. Some corporations value "team players" while others value "individual initiative." Some corporations have mottos like "Never say no to an assignment" or "Never be afraid to speak up if you don't have what you need."

Support groups have their own version of organizational culture. Alcoholics Anonymous, Overeaters Anonymous, and therapy and support groups, among others, form their own sets of symbols, interpretations, and norms. "Let go and let God" is an important requirement in the Anonymous groups; relinquishing individual control to a higher power is a tool in managing one's addictions. Social living groups, such as sororities and fraternities, international dormitories, and the like, often create their own cultures as well.

Physical Ability or Disability. Groups form a culture based upon shared physical ability or disability. Professional athletic teams teach rookies how to behave and what to do to be an accepted member of the team. Persons who have physical handicaps share critical life experiences and groups teach them how to accept and overcome their disability, as well as how to communicate more effectively with those who do not have the disability (Braithwaite, 1991).

CULTURAL IDENTIFICATION AS A PROCESS

Each individual, then, has a range of cultures to which she or he belongs in a constantly changing environment. Everyone may concurrently or simultaneously participate in several different cultural systems each day, week, and year. All cultures that are created are influenced by a host of social, psychological, and environmental factors as well as institutions and context.

Consider African Americans in the United States. In the last 30 years, myriad factors have all affected what it means to be African American in the United States including: civil rights marches, leaders such as Martin Luther King, Jr., affirmative action, racism, the resurgence of the Ku Klux Klan, television shows such as "Roots" and "Cosby," films by Spike Lee, Anita Hill's testimony in the hearing of Supreme Court nominee Clarence Thomas, and the riots among African Americans and Hispanics in South Central Los Angeles following the Rodney King verdict.

Cultures are affected not only by changing socioeconomic and environmental conditions, but by other cultures as well. A person who is a member of a support group for single mothers in her community is influenced by other cultural groups such as feminists, conservative religious groups, or the Republican party members who made family values and two-parent families an important issue in the 1992 presidential campaign. The important questions from a cultural identity approach may be things like, "What does it mean to be a single mother who is Euro-American, Catholic, out of work, and living in a large city in the Midwest? How does that identity come to be and how is it communicated to others? How does it change across different contexts and relationships?"

CULTURAL IDENTITY

Diverse groups can create a cultural system of symbols used, meanings assigned to the symbols, and ideas of what is considered appropriate and inappropriate. When the groups also have a history and begin to hand down the symbols and norms to new members, then the groups take on a *cultural identity*. **Cultural identity** is the particular character of the group communication system that emerges in the particular situation.

A Communication Perspective

Cultural identities are negotiated, co-created, reinforced, and challenged through communication; therefore we approach identity from a communication perspective. *Social psychological perspectives* view identity as a characteristic of the person and personality, and self as centered in social roles and social practices. A *communication perspective* views identity as something that emerges when messages are exchanged between persons. Thus, **identity** is defined as an enactment of cultural communication (Hecht, Collier, & Ribeau, 1993).

Identities are *emergent*; they come to be in communication contexts. Since you are being asked to emphasize a communication perspective, what you study and try to describe and explain are identity patterns as they occur among persons in contact with one another. Although we have noted that such factors as media, literature, and art influence identity, our focus is directed at the interaction between people. Identities are co-created in relationship to others. Who we are and how we are differs and emerges depending upon who we are with, the cultural identities that are important to us and the others, the context, the topic of conversation, and our interpretations and attributions.

Properties of Cultural Identity

As students and researchers in intercultural communication, we can apply our knowledge about how cultural identities are enacted and developed in order to explain and improve our understanding of others' conduct. We outline the properties or characteristics of cultural identities and then compare the properties across different cultural groups. These comparisons ultimately help us build theories of cultural and intercultural identity communication.

The first property we outlined is self-perception; this addresses both avowal by the individual and ascription by others. Second, we note modes of expressing identity. Identities are expressed through core symbols, labels, and norms. The third property focuses on the scope of the identity, and whether the identity takes an individual, a relational, or a communal form. A fourth property examines the enduring, yet dynamic, quality of cultural identity. Fifth, affective, cognitive, and behavioral components of identity provide us with a means of contrasting what groups think, feel, say, and do. Sixth, we describe the content and relationship levels of interpretation in messages revealing cultural identity. Content and relationship interpretations allow us to understand when power and control issues contribute to conflict or when friendships and trust can be developed. Seventh, salience and variations in intensities characterize identity in new or unusual settings. Being the one who stands out in an otherwise homogeneous group causes us to be conscious of and perhaps alter the intensity with which we claim our identity.

Avowal and Ascription Processes. Each individual may enact various cultural identities over the course of a lifetime as well as over the course of a day. Identities are enacted in interpersonal contexts through avowal and ascription processes. **Avowal** is the self an individual portrays, analogous to the face or image she or he shows to others. Avowal is the individual saying, "This is who I am."

Ascription is the process by which others attribute identities to an individual. Stereotypes and attributions communicated are examples of ascriptions. In part, identity is shaped by others' communicated views of us. For example, a black Zulu female's cultural identities in South Africa are not only shaped by her definition and image of what it means to be a black Zulu female but also by the white Afrikaners for whom she works, her Zulu family and relatives, the township in which she lives in poverty, her white teachers who speak Afrikaans and English, and so forth.

Another way of thinking about this is to say that cultural identities have both subjective and ascribed meanings. In Japan, a philosophy and practice known as *amae* is common. **Amae** signifies an other-orientation or group-orientation, and a sense of obligation to the group. An individual is expected to sacrifice individual needs and give to others; others are expected to reciprocate, thereby maintaining the harmony and cohesiveness of the group (Doi, 1989; Goldman, 1992).

Amae represents the interdependence of subjective and ascribed meanings in relationships. The meanings may not be shared across cultural groups, however. To many Japanese, such a complex, long-term, obligatory relationship with members of ingroups is a functional and revered system of relational maintenance. To U.S. Americans, such rules and obligations to others may appear to be unnecessary, threaten individuality and choice, and therefore be unacceptable.

Information about avowal and ascription can be useful in understanding the role others play in developing your own cultural identities. If a particular group has low self-esteem or a high need for status, those aspects of identity may be influenced by the stereotypes or conceptions held and communicated by other groups.

Modes of Expression: Core Symbols, Labels, and Norms. Cultural identities are expressed in core symbols, labels, and norms. **Core symbols** tell us about the definitions, premises, and propositions regarding the universe and the place of humans in the universe that are held by members of the cultural group. They are expressions of cultural beliefs about the management of nature and technology and such institutions as marriage, education, and politics. The symbols point us to the central ideas and concepts and the everyday behaviors that characterize membership in that cultural group.

Sometimes these core symbols can be summarized into a set of fundamental beliefs; sometimes a particular mode of dress, gesture, or phrase captures the essence of a cultural identity. Carbaugh (1989) analyzed transcripts of the popular television talk show, "Donahue." After doing a content analysis of the comments made by audience members, he proposed *self-expression* as a core symbol of mainstream U.S. identity.

Authenticity, powerlessness, and expressiveness were identified as three core symbols among Afri-

can Americans (Hecht, Ribeau, & Alberts, 1989; Hecht, Larkey, Johnson, & Reinard, 1991). These core symbols were posited after African Americans were asked to describe recent satisfying and dissatisfying conversations with other African Americans and with Euro-Americans, and to describe strategies for conversational improvement. African Americans talked about the need for persons to be authentic, honest, and real, described the negative impact of feeling powerless, and outlined a need to be expressive in their conduct.

Labels are a category of core symbols. The same label may vary widely in its interpretation. The term *American* is perceived as acceptable and common by many residents of the United States and as ethnocentric and self-centered by residents of Central America and Canada, and is associated with a group that is privileged, wealthy, and powerful by some countries that are not industrialized. *Hispanic* is a general term many social scientists use to describe "persons of Mexican, Puerto Rican, Cuban, Central or South American, or other Spanish culture of origin, regardless of race" (Marin & Marin, 1991, p. 23).

Persons may choose to describe their own ethnicity with a much more specific label such as *Mexican-American* or *Chicano* or *Chicana*. Chicano and Chicana individuals may have their own ideas about what it means to be a member of that culture. Whether the label was created by members of the group or members of another group provides useful information about what the label means and how it is interpreted.

Cultural groups create and reinforce standards for "performing the culture" appropriately and effectively. Norms for conduct are based upon core symbols and *how they are interpreted*. Defining who you are tells you what you should be doing. Norms of appropriate and acceptable behavior, moral standards, expectations for conduct, and criteria to decide to what degree another is behaving in a competent manner form the prescriptive or evaluative aspect of cultural identity. An individual is successful at enacting identity when one is accepted as a competent member of the group. Immigrants, for example, are judged to be competent and accepted by members of the U.S. American culture when they speak English, use appropriate greetings, demonstrate respect for the individual rights of their neighbors to privacy, and so forth.

Attention to the property of shared norms gives us the ability to determine what is appropriate from the point of view of the group members. Comparing norms of conduct across groups and identifying norms in intercultural conversations is helpful in figuring out how to improve our own individual effectiveness as a communicator. Finally, identification of norms in this way provides valid information for trainers, teachers, and practitioners as they develop their training programs.

Individual, Relational, and Communal Forms of Identity. Identities have individual, relational, and communal properties. As researchers of culture, we can study culture from the point of view of individuals. Each person has individual interpretations of what it means to be U.S. American or Austrian or Indian, and each person enacts his or her cultural identities slightly differently. If we want to understand why an individual behaves in a particular way, we can ask him or her to talk about that cultural identity and experience as a group member.

When we study culture from a relational point of view we observe the interaction between people, friends, coworkers, or family members, who identify themselves as members of the same or different groups. Then we can identify the themes in their talk such as trust or power.

Collier (1989) found that Mexican-American friends emphasized the importance of their relationship by meeting frequently and spending a significant portion of time together. They also described the most important characteristics of friendship as support, trust, intimacy, and commitment to the relationship. In contrast, when Mexican Americans and Anglo Americans talked about their friendships with one another, they described common activities, goals, and respect for family.

When we study culture in terms of its communal properties we observe the public communication contexts and activities in communities and neighborhoods that establish cultural identity. Rituals, rites of passage, and holiday celebrations are other sources of information about how persons use cultural membership to establish community with one another.

Enduring and Changing Property of Identity. Cultural identities are both enduring and changing. As already mentioned, cultures have a history that is transmitted to new members over time. Cultural identities change because of economic, political, social, psychological, and contextual factors, not to mention the influence of other cultural identities.

Enacting the cultural identity of being gay or lesbian in the 1990s has certain things in common with being gay in the 1980s and 1970s. Individuals who "come out of the closet" encounter similar stereotypes and ascriptions to those in earlier centuries. However, the political climate in some areas of the country in which ballot initiatives were proposed to limit the rights of gays or link gays with other groups such as sadomasochists, affect the cultural identity of the group. Sometimes context changes how one manifests identity and how intensely one avows an identity. Announcing your affiliation and pride as a member of the Right to Life, anti-abortion coalition, at a rally of pro-abortion supporters is different from attending a Right to Life meeting and avowing your identity in that context.

Affective, Cognitive, and Behavioral Components of Identity. Identities have affective, cognitive, and behavioral components. Persons have emotions and feelings attached to identities. Such emotions change depending upon the situation. Sometimes, a particularly strong or violent avowal of an identity is a signal of the importance of that identity and the degree to which it is perceived to be threatened. Perhaps this knowledge can help us interpret why rioting occurred in South Central Los Angeles after the Rodney King verdict.

The cognitive component of identity relates to the beliefs we have about that identity. Persons hold a range of beliefs about each culture group to which they belong, but certain similarities in beliefs become evident when you ask people to talk about what it means to be U.S. American or Thai or a member of Earth First!, an environmentalist group. Members of Earth First! share beliefs in the value of ancient forests, distrust of executives who run the logging companies, politicians who support the lumber industry, and the view that spiking trees and sabotaging logging equipment is sometimes necessary as a form of protest. Such beliefs can be summarized into a core symbol, here the name of the organization, *Earth First!*

The behavioral component of cultural identity focuses on the verbal and nonverbal actions taken by group members. We come to be members of a group through our actions with one another and our reactions to one another. These verbal and nonverbal actions can be studied, and patterns described. The dimensions of cultural variability described by Hofstede (1980) such as collectivism and individualism are patterns of communicative conduct evident when particular cultural identities are enacted. Comparing what groups say and do allows us as researchers to begin to understand why some groups experience frequent misunderstandings or conflict.

Content and Relationship. Identities comprise both content and relationship levels of interpretation. When persons communicate with each other, messages carry information as well as implications for who is in control, how close the conversational partners feel to each other or conversely how hostile they feel toward each other, how much they trust each other, or the degree of inclusion or exclusion they feel.

Sometimes persons use their in-group language to reinforce their in-group status and establish distance from the out-group (Giles, Coupland, & Coupland, 1991). At other times they may use the language of the out-group in order to adapt and align with the out-group. Mexican Americans may speak Spanish when in neighborhood communities to preserve their history and roots and to reinforce their identification and bond as a people. The same persons may speak English at school or at work because the supervisor and executives of the company demand it.

Salience and Intensity Differences. Identities differ in their salience in particular contexts, and identities are enacted with different intensities at different times. The intensities provide markers of strong involvement, and investment in the identity. As a white U.S. American female professor visiting South Africa there were times in which I was most aware of being a white minority among the black majority, times when I was aware of being a U.S. American who was stereotyped somewhat negatively, and times when I was most aware of being a college professor. But, when I learned that female employees in South Africa do not receive maternity leave and receive a lower housing allowance than males, my feminist identity became more salient, causing me to adopt a stronger tone and assert my views about equal pay for equal work in a more direct manner when talking with male executives in corporations.

CULTURAL IDENTITY AND COMMUNICATION COMPETENCE

Using cultural identity as an approach can help us better analyze others' conduct and decide how to do what is mutually competent. Spitzberg and Cupach (1984) point out that communication competence requires motivation and knowledge, as well as skills to demonstrate what behavior is appropriate and effective.

Cultural competence is the demonstrated ability to enact a cultural identity in a mutually appropriate and effective manner. Intercultural competence becomes a bit more complex. **Intercultural competence** is the reinforcement of culturally different identities that are salient in the particular situation. Intercultural competence occurs when the avowed identity matches the identity ascribed. For example, if you avow the identity of an assertive, outspoken U.S. American and your conversational partner avows himself or herself to be a respectful, nonassertive Vietnamese, then each must ascribe the corresponding identity to the conversational partner. You must jointly negotiate what kind of relationship will be mutually satisfying. Some degree of adjustment and accommodation is usually necessary.

A common problem in intercultural communication occurs when persons who describe themselves as the same nationality or ethnicity do not share ideas about how to enact their identity and disagree about the norms for interaction. Chicanos in the United States may differ from second- and third-generation Mexican Americans about the need to speak Spanish or call attention to their heritage. Nonetheless, understanding the identity being avowed and ascribed and noting the intensity with which the identity is avowed, enables us to understand why a particular cultural identity emerges salient in particular situations and therefore what contextual, social, or psychological factors are operating in the situation.

Some benefits of the cultural identity approach in intercultural communication situations include the following: We can acknowledge that all individuals have many potential cultural identities which may emerge in a particular situation. Remembering that identities change from situation to situation can be helpful in overcoming the tendency to treat others as stereotypical representatives of a particular group. Asking for information about what is appropriate for their cultural identity is an effective tool in becoming interculturally competent. Explaining what your own cultural identity norms are and why you behaved in a particular way can also be a useful way to increase the other person's understanding and can help develop relational trust.

Researchers, trainers, and practitioners can utilize the cultural identity approach to identify similarities and differences in behaviors, in interpretations, or in norms. It is possible to begin to explain why group members behave as they do or feel as they do in their conduct with others from the same and different groups. Trainers and teachers can compare group symbols, interpretations, and norms as well as teach others to develop analytical skills to use in their own situations.

Cultural identity as an approach to the study of culture and intercultural communication is only one of many approaches. Ongoing research, critique, and application will test the merit of the approach. Hopefully, the approach has sparked the beginning of a dialogue that will continue throughout all of our lifetimes.

REFERENCES

Banks, J. (1984). *Teaching Strategies for Ethnic Studies* (3rd ed.) Boston, MA: Allyn & Bacon.

Braithwaite, D. (1991). "Just How Much Did That Wheelchair Cost?": Management of Privacy Boundaries by Persons with Disabilities. *Western Journal of Speech Communication, 55*, 254–274.

Carbaugh, D. (1989). *Talking American: Cultural Discourses on Donohue*. Norwood, NJ: Ablex Publishing.

Collier, M. J. (1989). Cultural and Intercultural Communication Competence: Current Approaches and Directions for Future Research. *International Journal of Intercultural Relations, 13*, 287–302.

Collier, M. J., and Thomas, M. (1988). Cultural Identity: An Interpretive Perspective. In Y. Y. Kim and W. Gudykunst, (Eds.), *Theories in Intercultural Communication*. Newbury Park, CA: Sage Publications: 99–122.

Doi, T. (1989). *The Anatomy of Dependence*. Tokyo, Japan: Kodansha Publishers.

Geertz, C. (1983). *Local Knowledge*. New York: Basic Books.

Giles, H., Coupland, N., and Coupland, J. (1991). Accommodation Theory: Communication, Contexts and Consequences. In J. Giles, N. Coupland, and J. Coupland (Eds.), *Contexts of Accommodation: Developments in Applied Sociolinguistics*. Cambridge, England: Cambridge University Press.

Goldman, A. (1992). "The Centrality of "Ningensei" to Japanese Negotiating and Interpersonal Relationships: Implications for U.S.-Japanese Communication." Paper presented at Speech Communication Association Conference, Chicago, Illinois.

Gudykunst, W., and Ting-Toomey, S. (1988). *Culture and Interpersonal Communication*. Newbury Park, CA: Sage Publications.

Hecht, M., Collier, M. J., and Ribeau, S. (1993). *African-American Communication*. Newbury Park, CA: Sage Publications.

Hecht, M., Larkey, L. K., Johnson, J. N., and Reinard, J. C. (1991). "A Model of Interethnic Effectiveness." Paper presented at the International Communication Association Conference, Chicago, Illinois.

Hecht, M., Ribeau, S., and Alberts, J. K. (1989). An Afro-American Perspective on Interethnic Communication. *Communication Monographs, 56*, 385–410.

Hofstede, G. (1980). *Culture's Consequences*. Newbury Park, CA: Sage Publications.

Marin, G., and Marin, B. V. (1991). *Research with Hispanic Populations*. Newbury Park, CA: Sage Publications.

Schneider, D. (1976). Notes Toward a Theory of Culture. In K. Basso and H. Selby (Eds.), *Meaning in Anthropology*. Albuquerque: University of New Mexico Press.

Spitzberg, B. H., and Cupach, W. R. (1984). *Interpersonal Communication Competence*. Newbury Park, CA: Sage Publications.

Toward a Perspective on Cultural Communication and Intercultural Contact

DONAL CARBAUGH

Consider three examples of situated communication conduct. Each demonstrates poignant moments where communication is culturally tailored from different social fabrics, with each moment set in motion by different classes of persons, each conducted through indigenous forms, and each felt deeply to be the appropriate conduct to perform. Each example also demonstrates how such action is problematic, at least to one participant in each scene, making immediate coordination of action and meaning difficult if not impossible.[1]

Case 1: An instructor of psychology at a university in America's heartland designs a course on race and ethnic relations. In it, he asks members of self-identified ethnic groups — including Native Americans such as the Osage — to sit together, in groups, and discuss "matters concerning cultural heritage." Participants in each group are advanced undergraduate and graduate students, all knowledgeable about the topic. Yet, despite the prodding of the instructor most students do not participate verbally in the groups. Moreover, those who do are the least informed, while those most informed make comments like "I don't know, what do you think?" and "Yeah, I guess that sounds okay to me."

Case 2: A recent episode of "60 Minutes" took correspondent Morley Safer to Antigua, a Caribbean island community. Investigating his topic — was it

From *Semiotica*, volume 80½, (1990) pp. 15–35. Reprinted by permission of Mouton de Gruyter, A Division of Walter de Gruyter & Co. Donal Carbaugh teaches at the University of Massachusetts.

real estate investment and its influences on Antiguan society? — took him eventually to an Antiguan public gathering. The gathering was set up for the viewer, by Safer, as a kind of colonial town meeting where issues relating to the controversial topic would be addressed and progress toward rational conciliation made. What transpired, however, was quite different. Safer asked his first question of the Antiguans, precipitating what appeared to be a heated exchange with several participants. Standing almost nose to nose, each talked noisily, independently, and simultaneously. Safer tried to interrupt several times but was unsuccessful. The participants continued, giving each other no sign of impropriety. The bewildered Safer was unable to continue any further. He turned to the camera, shrugged his shoulders, and concluded his interview while several Antiguans continued "conversing" in the background.

Case 3: On the atoll of Ifaluk in the Western Pacific, an American sits outside the house of a sick person whom she has come to visit. During a pause in a chat with a woman next to her, a small girl about four years old approaches. Coming closer, she performs a little dance, makes a funny face, then waits. Thinking she is cute, the American woman smiles at her antics. The Ifaluk woman sitting next to the American woman observes her smile, then reprimands her, saying, "Don't smile at her — she'll think that you're not justifiably angry."

The cases sketched here demonstrate the kinds of problems confronted in this essay — the use of cultural patterns to communicate, and deep perplexities that are sometimes generated when cultural patterns of communication contact one another, such as Osage and Anglo norms for classroom interaction, Antiguan and Anglo standards for public debate, and Ifaluk and Anglo premises for what to feel. Each case also raises more general questions: what cultural types of person are being cued in these exchanges? What types of cueing are enabled? In what form is communication conducted? What range of feelings are salient, given that personhood is thus symbolized? communication so shaped?

I will raise these issues, and return to the cases above, as I propose some elements in a cultural perspective on communication. What I hope to achieve is a kind of stock-taking of some recent ethnography of communication research, mainly as it addresses the classic problem of meaning — form variation through ethnotheoretical models of personhood, communication itself, and feelings. What I suggest is an approach to communication in which these three predominantly linguistic phenomena can be investigated through both properties of culturally communicated meanings and indigenous communicative forms. By the end, I hope to have shown how this kind of problem can be addressed through folk models of personhood, communication, and emotions. My point is not of course that all three phenomena must be addressed in all cultural studies, but that each can provide a fruitful avenue for the cultural study of communication, especially as a way of addressing cultural variations in communicative meanings and forms.

The perspective I argue for has diverse predecessors. In communication studies, Carey (1975) has prodded researchers beyond a "transmission model" of communication, toward a "ritual model" which interprets communication as a "sacred ceremony," as "the maintenance of society in time" (1975: 6). Philipsen (1987) advances a conceptual framework for cultural communication study in which moments of shared identity are performed and transformed through ritual, myth, and social drama. Similar approaches have been put forward by others, most notably those interested in the ways communication shapes meaningful action in human institutions (Pacanowsky & O'Donnell-Trujillo, 1983; Putnam & Pacanowsky, 1983), and its role in performing culture (Fine, 1984).

The Cultural Studies school(s) addresses issues of culture and communication through at least three distinct models: production studies, textual analyses, and community studies (Johnson, 1986–87). The approach presumes generally that culture is meaning-making, a process intimately linked with social relations of struggle and ideological battle. The dynamics of the process are typically explored through levels of discursive organization, themselves organized according to the relations between those forms and meanings that are dominant and those in opposition (Hall, 1980; Fiske, 1987).

In performance studies, Bauman (1986) has continued to put forward an ethnographic approach to oral forms, especially by examining moments when persons perform narratives. He explores both the structure of these oral stories and the structure of events so narrated. His main interests revolve around the meanings, forms, and functions of these "culturally defined scenes." Bauman traces his performance approach to Goffman (1959), Goffman of course being a central figure in the management of social identities in fact-to-face interactions, exploring routine performances of radio shows, telephone conversations, lectures, and so on.

Hymes (1962, 1972) is often credited with founding such ethnographic study of communication as investigates the diverse verbal resources available in particular human communities. While his own empirical work has focused upon Native-American ethnopoetics (primarily the inscribing of devices which preserve speech performance and cue cultural themes), the general ethnographic program he initiated spans a rich spectrum of theoretical concerns, from various communicative forms such as joking and wailing to the social classes using each, to the cultural meanings expressed, to their contextual use, and so on, with each such interest grounded in at least one cultural field (Hymes, 1981; Philipsen & Carbaugh, 1986). Sherzer (1987) has recently proposed a related discourse-oriented approach, making "a level or component of language use" the main datum of study, especially as it expresses relations between language and culture. Sherzer's program focuses primarily upon texts of verbal art and playfulness through which, he argues, language–culture relations are most fully activated. Both Hymes and Sherzer acknowledge deep debts to the earlier works of Sapir (1921).

Each of these approaches suggests a way of responding to the relationship between communication and culture. Each also has its own preferred objects and methods of analysis. But all share certain fundamental commitments: (1) the nexus of culture and communication warrant serious investigations; (2) such investigation treats some product or property of communication performance as situated in particular social and cultural fields; (3) an understanding of such performance requires attention to levels of discursive form(s), their meaning(s) and social use. Building on what I take to be these common themes, I propose one development of the third commitment: a response to the form–meaning problem which brings cultural models of persons, communication, and feeling into play, both as a way to understand particular social and cultural fields and as a way to theorize at the nexus of communication and culture. I do not propose a full-blown theory of communication, nor of culture. What I aim to do is move toward those general goals. To do so, I will ground the essay in several assumptions about communication and culture. This enables a movement beyond the irritating tautology "communication is culture," or vice versa. Next, I will propose a tensional base for a cultural approach to communication. Then I will discuss the cultural communication of personhood, speaking, and emotion, with each responding to variations of cultural meanings, forms, and social use. I will conclude by considering the use of the proposed framework in other current and future studies.

COMMUNICATION AND CULTURE

The view of communication put forth here builds on three basic assumptions: (1) *Communication is the primary social process*. This is to say that social persons, relations, and institutions (be they political, economic, or whatever) can be approached as media and outcomes of communication. Any human creation, from the concepts and actions of "physicians," "friends," or "France," can be explored as resources in, and of, particular communication systems. As Sapir (1931: 78) put it: "Society is only apparently a static sum of social institutions; actually it is being reanimated or creatively reaffirmed day to day by particular acts of a communicative nature which obtain among individuals participating in it." Communication thus is the primary social process through which social life is created, maintained, and transformed. (2) *Communication involves structures and processes of meaning-making*. Coupled with the above, communication is constituent of so-cial life, since it involves the human effort to render the world meaningful, or intelligible. Thus, the foundation laid here suggests not that communication is constitutive of the world, but that communication constitutes *meanings* that are in, of, and about the world. Sometimes the structures and processes of sense-making are held in common, persons act as if they share a common sense; such a sense also may be imperfectly shared or contested. Thus, that communication is meaning-making does not necessarily involve a "likeness of minds," but it does involve malleable structures and processes of meanings. (3) *Communication is situated action, involving particular forms and multiple functions.* The three parts of this assumption point to communication (a) as situated in contexts, occurring in physical space, between particular (classes of) persons, about identifiable topics; (b) as enacted through particular forms, identifiable devices, acts and act sequences; and (c) as accomplishing multiple functions, from uniting and dividing to stratifying, from directing to proposing. All things persons do with their words are included (Hymes, 1962, 1972). Following the above, communication is the primary and situated social process of meaning-making, which occurs in particular forms and yields multiple outcomes.

Culture can be understood on the bases of four assumptions.

1. *Culture is a system of symbols, symbolic forms, and meanings* (Schneider, 1976; Geertz, 1973). The assumption derives from Kenneth Burke's (1986: 445) dramatistic approach, by exploring symbolic action as "a teministic center from which many related considerations can be shown to radiate." The approach to "human relations and human motives is via a methodical inquiry into cycles or clusters of terms and their functions" (Burke, 1986: 445; see also Geertz, 1973: 453). Rather than words and meanings, it is particular *systems* or clusters of symbols, symbolic forms and meanings that can be called a culture. Like Burke, Schneider, Geertz, and others use the symbol concept broadly, to point not only to 'terms', but also to nonverbal and material symbols. Further, the use goes beyond mere representations of the natural world, to the constitutive role of symbols in social life.

2. *Culture systems have integrative and transformative potential.* The culture system enables a kind of regnance, a placing of "disparate parts . . . into a meaningful whole" (Schneider, 1976: 204). Systems of symbols and meanings may be invoked, thus showing how parts fit together into a whole. For example, one irony of the contemporary American culture system, and perhaps postmodernism generally, is that the whole seems somehow to fit together in part because its symbol system says *collectively* "that there is no such thing as a whole, it is illusory." What results is an integration through symbols of nonintegration (Carbaugh, 1988b). The culture system also enables transformation and change. New forms of action and meaning, if created efficaciously, must be created through an existing system, thus moving the culture in some directions rather than others.

3. *The culture system is mutually intelligible, commonly accessible, and deeply felt.* Particular systems of symbols and meanings, or patterns of culture, resonate with the native view. This does not mean that they replicate it (Geertz, 1976; and see the issues raised in Clifford and Marcus, 1986). What it means is that symbol systems and patterns can be identified which people commonly orient to when acting in, or reporting about, socio-cultural life. Such symbols and patterns are abstracted and/or used—by analysts and/or actors—*as if* they expressed a common sense. Through such a system, the world is made to appear coherent and mutually intelligible, if not agreeable. By commonly accessible, I point to those codes to which persons have access—not necessarily access in the sense that they are performable by them (e.g., not everyone can perform reprimands or weddings), but access in the sense that the code is contacted by them, coordinatable with them. Schutz (1977: 229) has put it this way: "We, the actors on the social scene, experience the world we live in as a world both of nature and of culture, not as a private but as an intersubjective one, that is, as a world common to all of us, either actually given or potentially accessible to everyone; and this involves intercommunication and language." Finally, the systems of codes, the discourses of culture, are deeply felt. They suggest that about which feeling is appropriate; the range of things it is sensible to feel, in what degree, with what reaction (Scruton, 1979). In these senses, the culture system is mutually intelligible, widely accessible, and deeply felt (Carbaugh, 1988a).

4. *Culture is historically grounded.* As Geertz (1973: 84) has put it, culture is "an historically transmitted pattern of meanings embodied in symbols, a system of inherited conceptions expressed in symbolic forms by means of which men communicate, perpetuate and develop their knowledge about and attitudes towards life." The culture system is grounded, as highly particular meanings are being projected from a very particular past. Similar symbols and forms may occur in various societies, but the sense which they speak, the system of which they are a part, is of a particular place and time. In this sense, culture is not the history of a symbol, or form, but grounded in historical *systems* of symbols, symbolic forms, *and their meanings*. In sum: culture is a potentially integrative and changeable system of symbols, symbolic forms, and meanings that is mutually intelligible, commonly accessible, deeply felt, and historically grounded.

The above assumptions help distinguish communication from culture, such that not all communication is culture (in its strong sense), and not all culture is communication. Such a distinction is pertinent especially when confronted with moments of intercultural contact. For example, there are moments of communication, moments of situated meaning-making, which involve codes that are not mutually intelligible, nor deeply felt, but may in principle at least be accessible to participants. Consider the three cases that introduce this essay. The Osage student when speaking with the Anglo teacher, the Antiguan when speaking with the American reporter, and the Ifaluk woman when speaking with the fieldworker all clearly involve communication—that is, they involve socially situated processes of meaning-making, in particular forms, for particular purposes. And each involves performances of culture; particular systems of symbols and meanings are displayed. But on each occasion, no one uses codes that are, among all participants, mutually intelligible and deeply felt. The social process lacks full qualities of mutual intelligibility and feeling. In this specific sense, there is communication, or socially situated meaning-making, but not culture, if culture involves mutual intelligibility and sentiment. Each person presents culture, but the social process—between them—of communication, while acted through distinctive culture systems, is not itself culture. Further, if communicative processes of repair were initiated by the teacher, Mr. Safer, or the American woman, if additional aspects of each culture system were invoked to offer an account, then perhaps further perplexities would result, such as a deepening of noncoordinated meanings and further misalignment of actions. In such cases, culture systems are involved, but they are not the same as the communication process (although an understanding of them would be essential in order to understand the process).

There are less complex examples. Within any society, moments occur (such as some contemporary family discussions about religion) when persons care little about the ideas, and are not confident as to what they mean. Communication—socially situated meaning-making—has taken place, but culture (in its strong and fullest sense) seems little involved. Again, there is communication, but not a deep sense of culture.

On the other side, there may be culture without communication. Consider the view of culture presented by David Schneider (1980: 127), for example, the concepts and premises of American kinship. From this view, "the study of culture" is *an abstraction*; it involves "how [people] define and understand what they are doing," but does not necessarily address how culture affects social action, nor how it is "articulated in social action." As an abstraction, the culture system is distinguished from communication; there can be culture, abstracted systems of symbols and meanings, considered outside of communication contexts, away from socially situated meaning-making. Thus, not all communication is culture, fully, nor is all culture communication.[2]

Note that the approach presented here is one not of concentric circles (communication in the context of culture, or vice versa), but one of intersecting circles. The argument could be summarized: communication and culture are distinctive, but non-exclusive. Above, I pointed to the non-overlapping parts of the circles. Now I wish to discuss their intersection, which is the major concern of the essay (see Figure 1).

I refer to the intersection of the circles, following Philipsen (1987), as cultural communication. Cultural communication highlights the aspects of socially situated meaning-making that are mutually intelligible, deeply felt, and accessible to persons. Brought into view are properties of communication that are cultural, and in turn, properties of culture that are communicated. Central to cultural communication are the twin accomplishments of mutual intelligibility and shared identity, common meaning and membership. Charles Taylor (1977: 122) summarizes the accomplishment:

Common meanings are the basis of community. Intersubjective meaning gives a people a common language to talk about social reality and a common understanding of certain norms, but only with common meanings does this common reference world contain significant common actions, celebrations, and feelings. These are objects in the world that everybody shares. This is what makes community.

The properties of communication that are so expressed, commonly understood and powerfully felt, are part and parcel of the culture system. When performed, they demonstrate a common sense and shared identity, membership in community, in one group or groups rather than others. Thus, as cultural codes animate communication, there is — at some level — mutual intelligibility and depth of feeling.

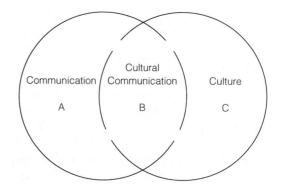

Figure 1 Communication, Culture, and Cultural Communication

These of course are only moments, and sometimes fleeting at that. Nonetheless, communication does involve, at times, the realization of culture in conversation, the display of a penetrating significance. What is expressed? Not only common meanings, but membership; not only coherence, but community (Carbaugh, 1988b).

A TENSIONAL BASE OF CULTURAL COMMUNICATION: CREATIVE EVOCATIVENESS

Several questions are often raised about a cultural approach to communication: when you say culture pattern of communication, are you saying that people conform to rules? that they are governed by their history? that they follow the standards of a community? that they, in so many words, blindly reproduce already established patterns of action and meaning? I respond to these questions by pointing to a set of tensions in cultural communication. I label the set, collectively, a creative evocativeness, a quality intrinsic in communication which necessitates an equivocal "yes and no" response to the questions.

The cultural voice of communication *enables and constrains*. Any situated form of saying, such as Israeli griping (Katriel, 1985), enables some themes, such as imperfections, while constraining others, such as praise. More generally, discourses of science enable claims of validity and truth, but constrain tales of mystery. Any system of cultural communication, or what Burke (1965) has called "an orientation" or "terministic screen," is always, in principle, a partial perspective, legitimizing some meanings and actions while disattending to others, enabling some sayings while constraining others (see Giddens, 1984: 25).

Cultural communication swings along moments on a *past–present–future dimension*. As Gadamer (1977) has argued, all persons are born into traditions, historical communication systems, where each has its own "prejudices," its own standards of morality. The cultural voice, then, always stands in relation to what has been said previously, but always may influence creatively what may be said consequently. Any such saying both draws from and contributes to the historical conditions of its production.

But tradition is not merely an impersonal voice from a past; it is continually reactivated, and potentially transformed, in situated performances. Richard Bauman (1986: 4) puts the dynamic this way: "the individual and the creative are brought up to parity with tradition in a dialectic played out within a context of situated action, a kind of praxis." His performance-centered approach to folklore infuses traditional genres of a folk's lore with "the creative individuality of the performer's accomplishment" (1986: 8). Thus, cultural communications can express varying degrees of an *individual–communal* voice. Philipsen (1987) has argued similarly that cultural performance addresses a fundamental tension between individual impulses for freedom and the constraints of communal life. Bakhtin (1987: 89) summarizes the tension when he writes about cultural communication and its "varying degrees of otherness or varying degrees of our-own-ness." In all these cases, cultural forms of communication are animated with a voice both individual and communal. The degrees of each may of course vary with each performance, but all cultural communication may express such an individual–communal voice.

Finally, moments of cultural communication *produce and reproduce* their own forms for action, their own patterns of meanings (Giddens, 1984). All such communication reproduces some resources, but may also create others. Cultural communication does not require a simple reproduction of templates and schemes, although some moments may be acted as such. What it may also involve is contexted and creative play—a productive addition to, or even a creative transformation of, the cultural voice reproduced.

In sum: the cultural voice is evocative, it does call forth deep feeling from the past, reproducing a communal lore, constraining those present. But it can do more than that. It can ground the recognition of presence, of individual and social creativity, enabling new directions, producing better outcomes. This is the dialectical nature of the cultural voice. It is collective and communal, yes, but it is also particular and personal. It reproduces, yes, but it can also transform. Cultural communication as conceived here embraces such a tensional base, moments where forms for action and patterns of meaning are evoked and creatively played, where persons are engaged socially in a creative evocativeness.

CULTURAL MODELS OF PERSONHOOD, COMMUNICATION, AND EMOTION

What version of social life is being creatively evoked as persons speak, and how can it be understood? My response to this question suggests looking at three structural elements in cultural communication systems, especially personhood, communication, and emotion, as they demonstrate indigenous forms and their meanings.[3]

Consider once again the case that introduces the essay, the Osage who were asked by an Anglo teacher to discuss in small groups, with other Osage, ideas of their cultural heritage (Wieder and Pratt, forthcoming). This classroom scene has designed into it two Angelicized cultural imperatives for communicating: (1) it is good to gather in small groups to talk; and (2) talk about one's personal and social circumstances, or cultural heritage, should be readily forthcoming because each person is an individual with the right and freedom to speak (Carbaugh, 1988b). These rather innocently assumed imperatives are problematic for the Osage who wants to display "cultural heritage." The main reason for the problem is that if the Anglo imperatives for talk were fully followed by an Osage, the resulting performance would be assessed, from the standpoint of Osage imperatives, as falling short of the "real Osage Indian" identity. The two cultural counter-premises that are used interactionally to evaluate such an identity are: (1) if one wants to display a "real Indian" identity, and one is with other Indians whom one does not know, or with some others of asymmetrical status such as teachers or elders, it is preferable that one be silent; and (2) the semantics of such silence are associated with harmony, modesty, and respect. When in the context with other Osage, as in this classroom, it is preferable for Osage to display their cultural identity. By doing so, they remain silent, or produce appropriately inane comments about their cultural heritage like "I don't know, what do you think?" This display of cultural identity is important especially because Osage see, hear, and evaluate among themselves different levels of "Indianness." Some are said to be "more Indian" than others, with assessments being made solely on the basis of routine and continuous communicative performance. The Osage's communication, then, if it is to be evaluated as "real Indian" by peers, must demonstrate the proper cultural forms and meanings of Osage practice, especially in contexts where their "cultural heritage" is being presented as the topic of discussion. The irony of this case is that the classroom context was created to celebrate cultural heritage, but the common bases used to motivate and evaluate the dominant forms of action (the Anglo) tend to undercut or subvert the cultural tradition of another (the Osage).

Note how this case of intercultural contact involves the display of cultural models of personhood (the Anglo and Osage) through culturally identifia-

ble *forms* (open discussion and silence) and *meanings* (freedom, independence, and expressiveness for the former; harmony, modesty, and respect for the latter).[4] During all such cultural enactments, one can be heard to cue a shared identity deemed important to at least some members. It is this cueing, and the subsequent process of enabling the identity, or suppressing it, that in part animates this Osage-Anglo communication. All such moments may be unravelled by listening to the models of personhood rendered appropriate to the context, the forms available for expressing them, and the meanings of the performance to members and their interlocutors.

Similar intercultural dynamics of the classroom are discussed by Boggs (1985) among Hawaiian students, by Chick (1985) among Zulu and other South Africans, by Michaels (1981) among black and white children, and by Scollon and Scollon (1981) among Athabaskans and Anglo Alaskans. The communicative role of cultural identities, forms, and meanings is demonstrated further by examining the Teamster male and his use of silence and indirection (Philipsen, 1975), Malagasy men and women and their different use of an ideal non-confrontational verbal style (Keenan, 1974), black churchgoers and the call–response form (Daniel & Smitherman, 1976), and Israelis' use of griping and a style of direct, straight talk (Katriel, 1985, 1986), to list just a few. In all of these empirical studies, the interactional cueing and management of cultural identity occurs through such particular communication forms, with local meanings. By discovering such cultural features as these in communication, we can better understand how personhood is a cultural and interactional accomplishment, and how intercultural contacts involve, at least in part, the display and management of cultural identities.

Consider a second case, the Antiguan "discussion" broadcast on the popular American television program "60 Minutes." The reporter, Morley Safer, entered the public building, which looked a lot like a New England Town Hall, and witnessed not deliberative argument, but a kind of intense "conversation" with several participants speaking at once, noisily, giving no sign that the activity was abnormal or a turn away from business as usual. What is interesting about this case, for our purposes, is that Safer's expectations for appropriate communication—along with many viewers—were violated. As symbolic of a typical American viewer, Safer was obviously surprised, expecting such a scene to yield kinds of communication one might call "public speaking" or "debate." Such forms are typically structured, for Americans, so that one issue is addressed at a time, with interruptions dispreferred, turns at talk taken one at a time, turns exchanged at designated points, and some standard forms of logic used—for example, propositions, syllogisms, and analogy. But what Safer found himself immersed in was a different *form* of talk, a form identified and valued by Antiguans as "making noise" (Reisman, 1974). Such talk involves repetition of themes, lack of a strong norm against interruption, acceptance of two or more voices talking at once, a pattern of entry into the "noise" by "knocking" several times, and various personal and expressive associations (Reisman, 1974: 124). This Antiguan cultural form enables a performance fraught with *meanings* of unconvention, antagonism, and non-rationality. That such a form is so diametrically opposed to what many Americans would expect is quite remarkable.

The juxtaposition of the Antiguan and American cases demonstrates how persons use one sub-system of culture (its terms for talk) to identify and evaluate contextual uses of speech (interactional accomplishments in sequences). In this intercultural situation, the occasion is identified by one actor as appropriate for "public speaking" or "debate," but performed by others as "making noise." Each uses such terms to say something about talk, to identify its patterning in action and meaning, to describe its formative place in society (Philipsen, 1976).

Cultural terms for talk enable actors to mark off some sequences as instances of a kind of intelligible action that is unlike other kinds of action. Such identification operates within a society (for example, identifying the form of communication in an academic course as "lecture" rather than "discussion") as much as between societies (for example, "de-bate" and "making noise"). Discovering how actors order their talk, through their own words for it, provides points of access into the cultural modeling of communication itself. Where terms such as "being a man" or "a real Indian" express a class of person that is elaborated through cultural forms and meanings, so too do terms for talk such as "making noise" identify cultural patterns of communication as instances of a cultural form and its meanings.

Several recent works have demonstrated the power of such a focus in cultural studies of communication, including Abrahams and Bauman's (1971) study of seventeen St. Vincentian terms for acts of speech, Sherzer's (1983) description of at least ten Kuna communication patterns that are named indigenously, Rosaldo's (1973, 1982) studies of seven Ilongot terms for talk, Brenneis's (1978, 1984) studies of four Fiji folk genres of speech, Katriel's (1985, 1986) studies of two prominent verbal forms identified and enacted by some Israelis, and two studies of so-called mainstream American terms for talk (Carbaugh, 1988b; Katriel & Philipsen, 1981). Further, three recent works have comparatively analyzed indigenously identified sequences of talk in order to advance hypotheses about the cross-cultural principles of ceremonial dialogues, especially relations among the cyclical form, contexts of its use, and its socio-cultural functions (Urban, 1986), to develop a conceptual framework for distinguishing types of such terms and their message functions (Carbaugh, 1989), and to propose a semantic metalanguage for the cultural interpretation and comparative study of such speech acts and genres (Wierzbicka, 1985). Such work demonstrates how studies of cultural terms for talk yield indigenous models of communication, can help unravel complexities in intercultural communication, and can provide empirical groundwork for cross-cultural hypotheses about communication.

Consider finally the situation on the atoll of Ifaluk in which the American woman smiles after an approaching small girl performs a dance and makes a funny face. The American woman expressed a degree of delight and happiness at seeing the child's public play, a kind of emotion expression typical in similar American scenes. But after seeing the American woman smile, the Ifaluk woman sitting next to her reprimanded her by saying, "Don't smile at her — she'll think you're not justifiably angry" (Lutz, 1987: 290). The Ifaluk woman thus evaluated the American woman's emotion expression as inappropriate, and further instructed her that expressions of 'justifiable anger' should be forthcoming. Why should this be the case? For the Ifaluk woman, the sequence has unfolded in this way. The child was heard to express the emotion "ker," or happiness/excitement, a potential disruption in this Ifaluk situation. Such expression by a child signifies, for the Ifaluk, an act of misbehavior. When one witnesses misbehavior, it is required that one express "song," or justifiable anger. Since the American woman did not express "song," the emotion most appropriate after "ker," she was reprimanded. After this reprimand, both women can and should express the justifiable anger, "song," so that the child will feel and express "metagu," or fear and anxiety, which symbolizes for the girl that she recognizes the error in her ways. The girl's expression of fear is, in this case, a positive expression, for it displays that the girl is developing the proper moral awareness (see Lutz, 1987).

Displayed in this situation are parts of two cultural systems. With one, the expression of happiness by a child leads to an expression of happiness by an adult; with the other, the expression of happiness by a child leads to an expression of justifiable anger by an adult, leading to a proper fear or anxiety in the child. Any cultural communication system can be understood in part by tracing how expressions of emotion are linked to both situated acts and events, and how emotion expression is ordered sequentially, if so. The approach leads to discovering the range of emotions it is sensible to feel, how and when they should be expressed, and with what intensity. Such an understanding advances knowledge about emotion as culturally situated expression, and how it comes to play in situations of intercultural contact.

Several recent studies have explored emotion from a cultural perspective; for example, as has al-

ready been mentioned, Lutz (1987) has explored Ifaluk emotion theory, as well as a set of tensions that run through the Western cultural conception of emotion (1986). Lakoff and Kovecses (1987) elaborate the emotion of anger in American English through its metaphorical structure. Bailey (1983) explores how "passion," in several American scenes, is an ominous and sensible force in the negotiation of — among other things — person identities and group decisions. R. Rosaldo (1984) has examined the cultural force of emotions through the grief and rage of the Ilongot. Related studies of Ilongot emotion and its link to Ilongot notions of personhood appear in M. Rosaldo (1982, 1985).[5] These studies are highly suggestive for a cultural communication theory of emotion. They provide empirical instantiation of emotion expression from the standpoint of various culture systems, demonstrating ways to develop cultural communication theory of emotion through further ethnographic and comparative study.

Each of the above phenomena can be made distinct analytically, but all are intimately related. Reflect again on the Osage in the Anglo classroom. "Being a real Indian" is inseparable from the communicative form of silence that is used to constitute "real Indianness." A model of personhood is linked intimately to a communicative form. Elsewhere, the Osage cultural identity is expressed rather differently, especially in some contexts of symmetrical relationships, when a cultural form of "razzing," a kind of ritual insulting, is performed. A cultural identity fraught with meaning and morality is thus identified culturally through the "real Indian" phrase, is linked intimately to cultural models for communicating such as silence and "razzing," is expected to act differently in different social contexts, and is evaluated on the basis of such performance. We have available to us neither the vocabulary and expression of emotion available to this class of person, nor a sense of its role in the above communicative patterns, if indeed it is relevant. But the general point is that in cultural communication, the common structures of personhood, communication, and emotion are identified and evaluated, and the interrelations among them form a powerful vocabulary of motives for communal action.

These three interactional accomplishments are productive for cultural communication study. Most of the studies presented above focus on one of these phenomena, and that is often a major task. Several recent pieces have explored relations between the phenomena—for example, the Ilongot model of personhood and their indigenous conceptions of communication (M. Rosaldo, 1982), the Ilongot personhood and feeling (M. Rosaldo, 1985), and the Israeli Sabra identity and cultural style of speaking, "dugri" (Katriel, 1986). Others have been investigating the American case, searching for relations between American discourses on personhood such as "being an individual" and "having a self," and folk frames for speaking such as "being honest" and "sharing" (Carbaugh, 1988b), as well as between cultural codes of honor and dignity and their attendant models of speaker and speaking (Philipsen, 1986). Regarding the American case, it is interesting to explore how persons, as "individuals with a self," communicate, by "sharing inner feelings," with emotions that are greatly varied since they are "natural" and linked to "the individual" organism's experience (Carbaugh, 1988b; Lutz, 1986). How communication constructs and reveals social life through such cultural enactments of personhood, communication itself, and emotion warrants our continuing serious study.

SOME PROBES FOR THE CULTURAL ANALYSIS OF COMMUNICATION

This paper has presented an assumptive base for inquiry into cultural communication, discussed a dialectical tension of creative evocativeness, and presented three structural elements whose forms and meanings provide access to spoken culture systems. In developing the latter, several recent empirical studies were reviewed. Each demonstrates to varying degrees how local standards of coherence are both media and outcome of specific communication practices, and further, how such standards,

when applied, give voice to a shared identity in community. Thus, my exposition rests not only on the logic of an assumptive statement, but on the empirical grounds where persons talk. Moreover, if such cultural voices are to be heard and understood, we must position ourselves at a conceptual place that enables us to hear.

Studies of cultural communication must attend to local standards of coherence as they are used communally. This kind of attention can be piqued through three classes of probes: (1) the cultural communication of personhood (what classes of persons are cued? through what verbal forms? with what meanings? which cueings are enabled? by whom? which constrained? how so?); (2) the cultural communication of communication (what sequences of action are identified culturally by participants? what verbal resources are available for discussing communicative actions? through what forms are such acts and sequences performed? what are the meanings of these to participants? how do these folk labelings and enactments of communication relate to classes of persons? social relations? distribution of resources?); and (3) the cultural communication of emotion (what emotions are expressed routinely? through what forms? with what meanings? with what intensity? in what sequences?). Probes such as these provide starting points for inquiry, raising certain moments of communication to the foreground so that we may understand better not only what persons are saying, but also what they are saying about themselves, the kinds of persons they speak to, the way they talk, their acts and sequences, and what they feel. Addressing such concerns can throw a cultural conversation into some light, making otherwise inscrutable ways more available for scrutiny.

One especially useful kind of study would, like Bauman's (1986) of narratives, give the voices of tension—if audible—an audible voice. Given a cultural communicative practice, what does it enable? What does it constrain? What from the past is evoked? What from the future is portended? To what degree is action animated by egocentric impulses? By sociocentric constraints? To what extent is there reproduction of structures and resources? To what extent is there production, perhaps even transformation? The tensional forces in situated cultural discourses need to be unravelled, when and if they operate.

There is much work to be done. As noted already, there are several current exemplary empirical pieces. I mention empirical pieces since it is my firm belief that general theorizing, while useful for purposes of conceptual organization, direction, and review, should take a seat within the carefully driven empirical car, the one traversing the roads of cultural communication, navigating the geography of speech, trying intensively to chart the discursive terrain. Such an approach gives theory a grounding it cannot have otherwise.

Several stops along the way now should be easier. First, the description and interpretation of communication as it creatively reveals cultural models of persons, communication, and emotion is warranted. Such inquiry—whether focused on one, more, or another of these communicative structures—will provide a record of aspects of cultural systems as they are accomplished interactionally, coherently, communally. Let us understand culture in communication. Second, such study places cultural analysts in a position to understand better moments where culture systems contact one another. Given a grounded understanding, for example, of the "real Indian" person for the Osage, "noisy" communication for the Antiguan, or "justifiable anger" for the Ifaluk, we are better able to describe and explain their use and consequences when played against a university professor, an investigative journalist, and a female fieldworker, respectively. Let us understand cultures in communication. Third, a level of generality is to be gained by juxtaposing cultural communication systems. Such gains are evident in celebrated comparative work like Brown and Levinson's (1978) theory of politeness, or Basso's (1970) theory of silence. In fact, several authors are working comparatively to understand cultural models of personhood (Dumont, 1970, 1985; Shweder & Bourne, 1984), communication (Carbaugh, 1989), and emotion (Wierzbicka, 1985). While these stud-

ies vary in their contribution to cultural communication study, they do demonstrate cultural phenomena ready to be studied from such a perspective, and the procedures and benefits of such comparative study. Let us understand communication across cultures.

NOTES

1. The first story is reported in Wieder and Pratt (forthcoming); the second is a report of my own, but is given Antiguan cultural force by Reisman (1974); the latter story is reported and analyzed in Lutz (1987: 290).

2. Note, however, that culture can always be retrieved from communication contexts. At some level, a system of symbols, forms, and meanings is operative, even if it is not, for example, deeply felt in the immediate communicative situation. Suggested here is a distinction between—for lack of better terms—"amplified culture," which is explicitly coded into interactional encounters and retrievable by participants, and "muted culture," which is more implicitly coded and less retrievable by them. "Amplified" and "muted," as used here, refer to the degree to which the structures are common *and* public in communication, not to actional forces. For example, for some Americans, persons (are said to) "have" a "self" which is unique and relatively independent from others. This illustrates an amplified structure of culture which is commonly intelligible, immediately accessible, and deeply felt. But that the category "self" is itself grounded historically, and provides a social role of conformity for persons, is counter to the "strong culture" and thus holds a "muted" quality which is less intelligible, accessible, and felt (Carbaugh, 1988b). This is a crucial distinction precisely because some "muted" elements of culture carry powerful actional consequences. Put visually, and in terms of Figure 1, one can always get from A to C, with the links sometimes unveiling powerful, if (for example) less intelligible, actional forces.

3. Once again, the reader should be alerted to my intended multivocal use of the term *communication*: it refers at different times to the general perspective of inquiry (the Cultural Communication Perspective), to communication principles that span diverse culture systems (in this paper, cultural communication structures, such as personhood, communication, and emotion), and to particular communication practices within a culture (cultural communication practices,

such as "being a man" in Teamsterville, "sharing feel-ings" on "Donahue," expressing the feeling of "lek" in Bali). As William James pointed out, communication is a "double-barrelled" term; it both is a practice and affords a perspective on practices. We must try to distin-guish the one from the other, placing ourselves in posi-tions better to assess communication perspectives, principles, and practices.

By discussing personhood, communication, and emotion, and the tension of creative evocativeness in-troduced above, I intend to develop Philipsen's (1987) general approach by adding three structural phenom-ena, and dialectical bases, respectively.

4. The interpretations of these two cases derive from more elaborate accounts (Wieder and Pratt, forthcom-ing; Carbaugh, 1987, 1988b).

5. A philosophical argument that common culture di-rects persons as to what to feel, models of how to feel, and with what intensity, as well as specific and general objects of feeling, has also been advanced (Scruton, 1979).

REFERENCES

Abrahams, R. and Bauman, R. (1971). Sense and non-sense in St. Vincent: Speech behavior and deco-rum in a Caribbean community. *American An-thropologist* 73, 762–772.

Bailey, F. G. (1983). *The Tactical Uses of Passion: An Essay on Power, Reason, and Reality*. Ithaca, NY: Cornell University Press.

Bakhtin, M. (1987). *Speech Genres and Other Essays*, trans. by V. McGee. Austin: University of Texas Press.

Basso, K. (1970). To give up on words: Silence in Western Apache culture. *Southwestern Journal of Anthropology* 26, 213–230.

Bauman, R. (1986). *Story, Performance, and Event: Contextual Studies of Oral Narrative*. Cam-bridge: Cambridge University Press.

Boggs, S. (1985). *Speaking, Relating, and Learning: A Study of Hawaiian Children at Home and at School*. Norwood, NJ: Ablex.

Brenneis, D. (1978). The matter of talk: Political per-formances in Bhatgaon. *Language in Society* 7, 159–170.

— (1984). Grog and gossip in Bhatgaon: Style and substance in Fiji Indian conversation. *American Ethnologist* 11, 487–506.

Brown, P. and Levinson, S. (1978). Universals in language usage: Politeness phenomena. In *Ques-tions and Politeness: Strategies in Social Inter-action*, E. Goody (ed.). Cambridge: Cambridge University Press.

Burke, K. (1965). *Permanence and Change*. India-napolis: Bobbs-Merrill.

— (1986). Dramatism. *International Encyclopedia of the Social Sciences* 7, 445–452.

Carbaugh, D. (1987). Communication rules in *Do-nahue* discourse. *Research on Language and So-cial Interaction* 21, 31–61.

— (1988a). Comments on "culture" in communica-tion inquiry. *Communication Reports* 1, 38–41.

— (1988b). *Talking American: Cultural Discourses on* Donahue. Norwood, NJ: Ablex.

— (1989). Fifty terms for talk: A cross-cultural study. *International and Intercultural Communica-tion Annual* 13, 93–120.

Carey, J. (1975). A cultural approach to communica-tion. *Communication* 2, 1–22.

Chick, K. (1985). The interactional accomplishment of discrimination in South Africa. *Language in Society* 14, 299–326.

Clifford, J. and Marcus, G. (eds.) (1986). *Writing Eth-nography: The Poetics and Politics of Ethnogra-phy*. Berkeley: University of California Press.

Daniel, J. and Smitherman, G. (1976). How I got over: Communication dynamics in the Black commu-nity. *Quarterly Journal of Speech* 62, 26–39.

Dumont, L. (1970). *Homo hierarchicus*, trans. by M. Sainsbury. Chicago: University of Chicago Press.

— (1985). A modified view of our origins: The Chris-tian beginnings of modern individualism. In *The Category of the Person*, M. Carrithers, S. Collins, and S. Lukes (eds.). New York: Columbia Univer-sity Press.

Fine, E. (1984). *The Folklore Text*. Bloomington: In-diana University Press.

Fiske, J. (1987). British cultural studies and televi-sion. In *Channels of Discourse*, R. Allen (ed.). Chapel Hill: University of North Carolina Press.

Gadamer, H. (1977). *Philosophical Hermeneutics*. Berkeley: University of California Press.

Geertz, C. (1973). *The Interpretation of Cultures*. New York: Basic Books.

—(1976). From the native's point-of-view: On the nature of anthropological understanding. In *Meaning in Anthropology*, K. Basso and H. Selby (eds.). Albuquerque: University of New Mexico Press.

Giddens, A. (1984). *The Constitution of Society*. Cambridge: Polity Press.

Goffman, E. (1959). *The Presentation of Self in Everyday Life*. Garden City, NY: Doubleday Anchor.

Hall, S. (1980). Cultural studies: Two paradigms. *Media, Culture and Society* 2, 57–72.

Hymes, D. (1962). The ethnography of speaking. In *Anthropology and Human Behavior*, T. Gladwin and W. Sturtevant (eds.). Washington, DC: Anthropological Society of Washington.

—(1972). Models of the interaction of language and social life. In *Directions in Sociolinguistics: The Ethnography of Communication*, J. Gumperz and D. Hymes (eds.). New York: Holt, Rinehart, and Winston.

—(1981). *In Vain I Tried to Tell You*. Philadelphia: University of Pennsylvania Press.

Johnson, R. (1986–1987). What is cultural studies anyway? *Social Text* 16, 38–80.

Katriel, T. (1985). "Griping" as a verbal ritual in some Israeli discourse. In *Dialogue: An Interdisciplinary Approach*, M. Dascal (ed.). Amsterdam: John Benjamins.

—(1986). *Talking Straight: "Dugri" Speech in Israeli Sabra Culture*. Cambridge: Cambridge University Press.

Katriel, T. and Philipsen, G. (1981). "What we need is communication": "Communication" as a cultural category in some American speech. *Communication Monographs* 48, 302–317.

Keenan, E. O. (1974). Norm-makers, norm-breakers: Uses of speech by men and women in a Malagasy community. In *Explorations in the Ethnography of Speaking*, R. Bauman and J. Sherzer (eds.). Cambridge: Cambridge University Press.

Lakoff, G. and Kovecses, Z. (1987). The cognitive model of anger inherent in American English. In *Cultural Models in Language and Thought*, D. Holland and N. Quinn (eds.). Cambridge: Cambridge University Press.

Lutz, C. (1986). Emotion, thought, and estrangement: Emotion as a cultural category. *Cultural Anthropology* 1, 287–309.

—(1987). Goals, events, and understanding in Ifaluk emotion theory. In *Cultural Models in Language and Thought*, D. Holland and N. Quinn (eds.). Cambridge: Cambridge University Press.

Michaels, S. (1981). "Sharing time": Children's narrative styles and differential access to literacy. *Language in Society* 10, 423–442.

Pacanowsky, M. and O'Donnell-Trujillo, N. (1983). Organizational communication as cultural performances. *Communication Monographs* 50, 126–147.

Philipsen, G. (1975). Speaking "like a man" in Teamsterville: Culture patterns of male role enactment in an urban neighborhood. *Quarterly Journal of Speech* 61, 13–22.

—(1976). Places for speaking in Teamsterville. *Quarterly Journal of Speech* 62, 15–25.

—(1986). Mayor Daley's council speech: A cultural analysis. *Quarterly Journal of Speech* 72, 247–260.

—(1987). The prospect for cultural communication. In *Communication Theory: Eastern and Western Perspectives*, L. Kincaid (ed.), 245–254. New York: Academic Press.

Philipsen, G. and Carbaugh, D. (1986). A bibliography of fieldwork in the ethnography of communication. *Language in Society* 15, 387–398.

Putnam, L. and Pacanowsky, M. (1983). *Communication and Organizations*. Beverly Hills, CA: Sage.

Reisman, K. (1974). Contrapuntal conversations in an Antiguan village. In *Explorations in the Ethnography of Speaking*, R. Bauman and J. Sherzer (eds.). Cambridge: Cambridge University Press.

Rosaldo, M. Z. (1973). I have nothing to hide: The language of Ilongot oratory. *Language in Society* 2, 193–223.

—(1982). The things we do with words: Ilongot speech acts and speech act theory in philosophy. *Language in Society* 11, 203–237.

—(1985). Toward an anthropology of self and feeling. In *Culture Theory: Essays on Mind, Self, and*

Emotion, R. Shweder and R. Levine (eds.). Cambridge: Cambridge University Press.

Rosaldo, R. (1984). Grief and a headhunter's rage: On the cultural force of emotions. In *Text, Play, and Story: The Construction and Reconstruction of Self and Society*, E. Bruner (ed.). Washington, DC: American Ethnological Society.

Sapir, E. (1921). *Language*. New York: Harcourt, Brace, and World.

—(1931). Communication. In *Encyclopedia of the Social Sciences*, vol. 4, 78–81. New York: Macmillan.

Schneider, D. (1976). Notes toward a theory of culture. In *Meaning in Anthropology*, K. Basso and H. Selby (eds.). Albuquerque: University of New Mexico Press.

—(1980). *American Kinship*. Chicago: University of Chicago Press.

Schutz, A. (1977). Concept and theory formation in the social sciences. In *Understanding and Social Inquiry*, F. Dallmayr and T. McCarthy (eds.). Notre Dame, IN: University of Notre Dame Press.

Scollon, R. and Scollon, S. (1981). *Narrative, Literacy and Face in Interethnic Communication*. Norwood, NJ: Ablex.

Scruton, R. (1979). The significance of common culture. *Philosophy* 54, 51–70.

Sherzer, J. (1983). *Kuna Ways of Speaking: An Ethnographic Perspective*. Austin: University of Texas Press.

—(1987). A discourse-centered approach to language and culture. *American Anthropologist* 89, 295–309.

Shweder, R. and Bourne, E. (1984). Does the concept of the person vary cross-culturally? In *Culture Theory: Essays on Mind, Self, and Emotion*, R. Shweder and R. Levine (eds.). Cambridge: Cambridge University Press.

Taylor, C. (1977). Interpretation and the sciences of man. In *Understanding and Social Inquiry*, F. Dallmayr and T. McCarthy (eds.). Notre Dame, IN: University of Notre Dame Press.

Urban, G. (1986). Ceremonial dialogues in South Africa. *American Anthropologist* 88, 371–386.

Wieder, D. L. and Pratt, S. (forthcoming). On being a recognizable Indian among Indians. In *Cultural Communication and Intercultural Contact*, D. Carbaugh (ed.). Hillsdale, NJ: Lawrence Erlbaum.

Wierzbicka, A. (1985). A semantic metalanguage for a crosscultural comparison of speech acts and genres. *Language in Society* 14, 491–514.

Context and Meaning

EDWARD T. HALL

One of the functions of culture is to provide a highly selective screen between man and the outside world. In its many forms, culture therefore designates what we pay attention to and what we ignore.[1] This screening function provides structure for the world and protects the nervous system from "information overload."[2] Information overload is a technical term applied to information processing systems. It describes a situation in which the system breaks down when it cannot properly handle the huge volume of information to which it is subjected. Any mother who is trying to cope with the demands of small children, run a house, enjoy her husband, and carry on even a modest social life knows that there are times when everything happens at once and the world seems to be closing in on her. She is experiencing the same information overload that afflicts business managers, administrators, physicians, attorneys, and air controllers. Institutions such as stock exchanges, libraries, and telephone systems also go through times when the demands on the system (inputs) exceed capacity. People can handle the crunch through delegating and establishing priorities; while institutional solutions are less obvious, the high-context rule seems to apply. That is, the only way to increase information-handling capacity without increasing the mass and complexity of the system is to program the memory of the system so that less information is required to activate the system, i.e., make it more like the couple that

has been married for thirty-five years. The solution to the problem of coping with increased complexity and greater demands on the system seems to lie in the preprogramming of the individual or organization. This is done by means of the "contexting" process. . . .

The importance of the role of context is widely recognized in the communication fields, yet the process is rarely described adequately, or if it is, the insights gained are not acted upon. Before dealing with context as a way of handling information overload, let me describe how I envisage the contexting process, which is an emergent function; i.e., we are just discovering what it is and how it works. Closely related to the high–low-context continuum is the degree to which one is aware of the selective screen that one places between himself and the outside world.[3] As one moves from the low to the high side of the scale, awareness of the selective process increases. Therefore, what one pays attention to, context, and information overload are all functionally related.

In the fifties, the United States government spent millions of dollars developing systems for machine translation of Russian and other languages. After years of effort on the part of some of the most talented linguists in the country, it was finally concluded that the only reliable, and ultimately the fastest, translator is a human being deeply conversant not only with the language but with the subject as well. The computers could spew out yards of printout but they meant very little. The words and some of the grammar were all there, but the sense was distorted. That the project failed was not due to lack of application, time, money, or talent, but for other reasons, which are central to the theme of this [article].

The problem lies not in the linguistic code but in the context, which carries varying proportions of the meaning. Without context, the code is incomplete since it encompasses only part of the message. This should become clear if one remembers that the spoken language is an abstraction of an event that happened, might have happened, or is being planned. As any writer knows, an event is usually infinitely more complex and rich than the language

From Edward T. Hall, *Beyond Culture* (Garden City, N.Y.: Doubleday & Company, 1976), pp. 85–103. Copyright © 1976, 1981 by Edward T. Hall. Reprinted by permission of Doubleday and The Lescher Agency. Professor Hall is affiliated with Northwestern University.

used to describe it. Moreover, the writing system is an abstraction of the spoken system and is in effect a reminder system of what somebody said or could have said. In the process of abstracting, as contrasted with measuring, people take in some things and unconsciously ignore others. This is what intelligence is: paying attention to the right things. The linear quality of a language inevitably results in accentuating some things at the expense of others. Two languages provide interesting contrasts. In English, when a man says, "It rained last night," there is no way of knowing how he arrived at that conclusion, or if he is even telling the truth, whereas a Hopi cannot talk about rain at all without signifying the nature of his relatedness to the event—firsthand experience, inference, or hearsay. This is a point made by the linguist Whorf[4] thirty years ago. However, selective attention and emphasis are not restricted to language but are characteristic of the rest of culture as well.

The rules governing what one perceives and [what one] is blind to in the course of living are not simple; at least five sets of disparate categories of events must be taken into account. These are: the subject or activity, the situation, one's status in a social system, past experience, and culture. The patterns governing juggling these five dimensions are learned early in life and are mostly taken for granted. The "subject" or topic one is engaged in has a great deal to do with what one does and does not attend. People working in the "hard" sciences, chemistry and physics, which deal with the physical world, are able to attend and integrate a considerably higher proportion of significant events observed than scientists working with living systems. The physical scientist has fewer variables to deal with; his abstractions are closer to the real events; and context is of less importance. This characterization is, of course, oversimplified. But it is important to remember that the laws governing the physical world, while relatively simple compared to those governing human behavior, may seem complex to the layman, while the complexity of language appears simple to the physicist, who, like everyone else, has been talking all his life. In these terms it is all too easy for the person who is in full command of

a particular behaviorial system, such as language, to confuse what he can *do* with a given system, with the unstated rules governing the way the system operates. The conceptual model I am using takes into account not only what one takes in and screens out but what one does not know about a given system even though one has mastered that system. The two are *not* the same. Michael Polanyi[5] stated this principle quite elegantly when he said, "The structure of a machine cannot be defined in terms of the laws which it harnesses."

What man chooses to take in, either consciously or unconsciously, is what gives structure and meaning to his world. Furthermore, what he perceives is "what he intends to do about it." Setting aside the other four dimensions (situation, status, past experience, and culture), theoretically it would be possible to arrange all of man's activities along a continuum ranging from those in which a very high proportion of the events influencing the outcome were consciously considered to those in which a much smaller number were considered. In the United States, interpersonal relations are frequently at the low end of the scale. Everyone has had the experience of thinking that he was making a good impression only to learn later that he was not. At times like these, we are paying attention to the wrong things or screening out behavior we should be observing. A common fault of teachers and professors is that they pay more attention to their subject matter than they do to the students, who frequently pay too much attention to the professor and not enough to the subject.

The "situation" also determines what one consciously takes in and leaves out. In an American court of law, the attorneys, the judge, and the jury are compelled by custom and legal practice to pay attention only to what is legally part of the record. Context, by design, carries very little weight. Contrast this with a situation in which an employee is trying to decipher the boss's behavior—whether he is pleased or not, and if he is going to grant a raise. Every little clue is a story in itself, as is the employee's knowledge of behavior in the past.

One's status in a social system also affects what must be attended. People at the top pay attention to different things from those at the middle or the bottom of the system. In order to survive, all organizations, whatever their size, have to develop techniques not only for replacing their leader but for switching the new leader's perceptions from the internal concerns he focused on when he was at the lower and middle levels to a type of global view that enables the head man or woman to chart the course for the institution.

The far-reaching consequences of what is attended can be illustrated by a characteristic fault in Western thinking that dates back to the philosophers of ancient Greece. Our way of thinking is quite arbitrary and causes us to look at ideas rather than events—a most serious shortcoming. Also, linearity can get in the way of mutual understanding and divert people needlessly along irrelevant tangents. The processes I am describing are particularly common in the social sciences; although the younger scientists in these fields are gradually beginning to accept the fact that when someone is talking about events on one level this does not mean that he has failed to take into account the many other events on different levels. It is just that one can talk about only a single aspect of something at any moment (illustrating the linear characteristic of language).

The results of this syndrome (of having to take multiple levels into account when using a single-level system) are reflected in a remark made by one of our most brilliant and least appreciated thinkers in modern psychiatry, H. S. Sullivan,[6] when he observed that as he composed his articles, lectures, and books the person he was writing to (whom he projected in his mind's eye) was a cross between an imbecile and a bitterly paranoid critic. What a waste. And so confusing to the reader who wants to find out what the man is really trying to say.

In less complex and fast-moving times, the problem of mutual understanding was not as difficult, because most transactions were conducted with people well known to the speaker or writer, people with similar backgrounds. It is important for conversationalists in any situation—regardless of the area of discourse (love, business, science)—to get to know each other well enough so that they realize what each person is and is not taking into account. This is crucial. Yet few are willing to make the very real effort—life simply moves too fast—which may explain some of the alienation one sees in the world today.

Programming of the sort I am alluding to takes place in all normal human transactions as well as those of many higher mammals. It constitutes the unmeasurable part of communication. This brings us to the point where it is possible to discuss context in relation to meaning, because what one pays attention to or does not attend is largely a matter of context. Remember, contexting is also an important way of handling the very great complexity of human transactions so that the system does not bog down in information overload.

Like a number of my colleagues, I have observed that meaning and context are inextricably bound up with each other. While a linguistic code can be analyzed on some levels independent of context (which is what the machine translation project tried to accomplish), *in real life the code, the context, and the meaning can only be seen as different aspects of a single event*. What is unfeasible is to measure one side of the equation and not the others.[7]

Earlier, I said that high-context messages are placed at one end and low-context messages at the other end of a continuum. A high-context (HC) communication or message is one in which most of the information is either in the physical context or internalized in the person, while very little is in the coded, explicit, transmitted part of the message. A low-context (LC) communication is just the opposite; i.e., the mass of the information is vested in the explicit code. Twins who have grown up together can and do communicate more economically (HC) than two lawyers in a courtroom during a trial (LC), a mathematician programming a computer, two politicians drafting legislation, two administrators writing a regulation, or a child trying to explain to his mother why he got into a fight.

Although no culture exists exclusively at one end of the scale, some are high while others are low. American culture, while not on the bottom, is toward the lower end of the scale. We are still considerably above the German-Swiss, the Germans, and the Scandinavians in the amount of contexting needed in everyday life. While complex, multi-institutional cultures (those that are technologically advanced) might be thought of as inevitably LC, this is not always true. China, the possessor of a great and complex culture, is on the high-context end of the scale.

One notices this particularly in the written language of China, which is thirty-five hundred years old and has changed very little in the past three thousand years. This common written language is a unifying force tying together half a billion Chinese, Koreans, Japanese, and even some of the Vietnamese who speak Chinese. The need for context is experienced when looking up words in a Chinese dictionary. To use a Chinese dictionary, the reader must know the significance of 214 radicals (there are no counterparts for radicals in the Indo-European languages). For example, to find the word for star one must know that it appears under the sun radical. To be literate in Chinese, one has to be conversant with Chinese history. In addition, the spoken pronunciation system must be known, because there are four tones and a change of tone means a change of meaning; whereas in English, French, German, Spanish, Italian, etc., the reader need not know how to pronounce the language in order to read it. Another interesting sidelight on the Chinese orthography is that it is also an art form.[8] To my knowledge, no low-context communication system has ever been an art form. Good art is always high-context; bad art, low-context. This is one reason why good art persists and art that releases its message all at once does not.

The level of context determines everything about the nature of the communication and is the foundation on which all subsequent behavior rests (including symbolic behavior). Recent studies in sociolinguistics have demonstrated how context-dependent the language code really is. There is an excellent example of this in the work of the linguist Bernstein,[9] who has identified what he terms "restricted" (HC) and "elaborated" (LC) codes in which vocab-

ulary, syntax, and sounds are all altered: In the restricted code of intimacy in the home, words and sentences collapse and are shortened. This even applies to the phonemic structure of the language. The individual sounds begin to merge, as does the vocabulary, whereas in the highly articulated, highly specific, elaborated code of the classroom, law, or diplomacy, more accurate distinctions are made on all levels. Furthermore, the code that one uses signals and is consistent with the situation. A shifting of code signals a shift in everything else that is to follow. "Talking down" to someone is low-contexting him—telling him more than he needs to know. This can be done quite subtly simply by shifting from the restricted end of the code toward the elaborated forms of discourse.

From the practical viewpoint of communications strategy, one must decide how much time to invest in contexting another person. A certain amount of this is always necessary, so that the information that makes up the explicit portions of the message is neither inadequate nor excessive. One reason most bureaucrats are so difficult to deal with is that they write for each other and are insensitive to the contexting needs of the public. The written regulations are usually highly technical on the one hand, while providing little information on the other. That is, they are a mixture of different codes or else there is incongruity between the code and the people to whom it is addressed. Modern management methods, for which management consultants are largely responsible, are less successful than they should be, because in an attempt to make everything explicit (low-contexting again) they frequently fail in their recommendations to take into account what people already know. This is a common fault of the consultant, because few consultants take the time (and few clients will pay for the time) to become completely contexted in the many complexities of the business.

There is a relationship between the worldwide activism of the sixties and where a given culture is situated on the context scale, because some are more vulnerable than others. HC actions are by definition rooted in the past, slow to change, and highly stable. Commenting on the need for the stabilizing effect of the past, anthropologist Loren Eiseley[10] takes an anti-activist position and points out how vulnerable our own culture is:

Their world (the world of the activist), therefore, becomes increasingly the violent, unpredictable world of the first men simply because, in lacking faith in the past, one is inevitably forsaking all that enables man to be a planning animal. For man's story,[11] in brief, is essentially that of a creature who has abandoned instinct and replaced it with cultural tradition and the hard-won increments of contemplative thought. The lessons of the past have been found to be a reasonably secure construction for proceeding against an unknown future.[12]

Actually, activism is possible at any point in the HC–LC continuum, but it seems to have less direction or focus and becomes less predictable and more threatening to institutions in LC systems. Most HC systems, however, can absorb activism without being shaken to their foundations.

In LC systems, demonstrations are viewed as the last, most desperate act in a series of escalating events. Riots and demonstrations in the United States, particularly those involving blacks,[13] are a message, a plea, a scream of anguish and anger for the larger society to *do something*. In China (an HC culture), the Red Guard riots apparently had an entirely different significance. They were promulgated from the top of the social order, not the bottom. They were also a communication from top to bottom: first, to produce a show of strength by Mao Tse-tung; second, to give pause to the opposition and shake things up at the middle levels—a way of mobilizing society, not destroying it. Chinese friends with whom I have spoken about these riots took them much less seriously than I did. I was, of course, looking at them from the point of view of one reared in a low-context culture, where such riots can have disastrous effects on the society at large.

Wherever one looks, the influence of the subtle hand of contexting can be detected. We have just spoken of the effects of riots on high- and low-context political systems, but what about day-to-day matters of perception? On the physiological level of color perception, one sees the power of the brain's need to perceive and adjust everything in terms of context. As any interior designer knows, a powerful painting, print, or wall hanging can change the perceived color of the furnishings around it. The color psychologist Faber Birren[14] demonstrated experimentally that the perceived shade of a color depends upon the color context in which it occurs. He did this by systematically varying the color of the background surrounding different color samples.

Some of the most impressive demonstrations of the brain's ability to supply the missing information—the function of contexting—are the experiments of Edwin Land, inventor of the Land camera. Working in color photography using a single red filter, he developed a process that is simple, but the explanation for it is not. Until Land's experiments, it was believed that color prints could be made only by superimposing transparent images of three separate photographs made with the primary colors—red, blue, and yellow. Land made his color photographs with two images: a black-and-white image to give light and shadow, and a single, *red* filter for color. When these two images were projected, superimposed on a screen, even though red was the only color, they were perceived in full color with all the shades, and gradations of a three-color photograph![15] Even more remarkable is the fact that the objects used were deliberately chosen to provide no cues as to their color. To be sure that his viewers didn't unconsciously project color, Land photographed spools of plastic and wood and geometric objects whose color would be unknown to the viewer. How the eye and the visual centers of the brain function to achieve this remarkable feat of internal contexting is still only partially understood. But the actual stimulus does only part of the job.

Contexting probably involves at least two entirely different but interrelated processes—one inside the organism and the other outside. The first takes place in the brain and is a function of either past experience (programmed, internalized contexting) or the structure of the nervous system (innate contexting), or both. External contexting comprises the situation and/or setting in which an event occurs (situational and/or environmental contexting).[16]

One example of the growing interest in the relationship of external context to behavior is the widespread interest and concern about our public-housing disasters. Pruitt-Igoe Homes in St. Louis is only one example. This $26-million fiasco imposed on poor blacks is now almost completely abandoned. All but a few buildings have been dynamited, because nobody wants to live there.

Objections and defects in high-rise public housing for poor families are legion: Mothers can't supervise their children; there are usually no community service agencies nearby and no stores or markets; and quite often there is no access to any public transportation system. There are no recreation centers for teenagers and few places for young children to play. In any budget crunch, the first thing to be cut is maintenance and then the disintegration process starts; elevators and hallways turn into death traps. The case against high-rise housing for low-income families is complex and underscores the growing recognition that environments are not behaviorally neutral.

Although situational and environmental context has only recently been systematically studied, environmental effects have been known to be a factor in behavior for years. Such men as the industrialist Pullman[17] made statements that sounded very advanced at the time. He believed that if workers were supplied with clean, airy, well-built homes in pleasant surroundings, this would exert a positive influence on their health and general sense of well-being and would make them more productive as well. Pullman was not wrong in his analysis. He simply did not live up to his stated ideals. The main street of his company town, where supervisors lived, was everything he talked about. But his workers were still poorly housed. Being isolated in a company town in close proximity to the plush homes of managers made their inadequate living conditions more obvious by way of contrast, and the workers finally embarked on a violent strike. There were many other human, economic, and political needs, which Pullman had not taken into account, that led to worker dissatisfaction. Pullman's professed idealism backfired. Few were aware of the conditions under which his laborers actually lived and worked, so that the damage done to the budding but fragile environmentalist position was incalculable and gave ammunition to the "hard-nosed," "practical" types whose minds were focused on the bottom-line figures of profit and loss.

Quite often, the influence of either programmed contexting (experience) or innate contexting (which is built in) is brushed aside. Consider the individual's spatial needs and his feelings about certain spaces. For example, I have known women who needed a room to be alone in, whose husbands did not share this particular need, and they brushed aside their wives' feelings, dismissing them as childish. Women who have this experience should not let my talking about it raise their blood pressure. For it is very hard for someone who does not share an unstated, informal need with another person to experience that need as tangible and valid. Among people of northern European heritage, the only generally accepted proxemic needs are those associated with status. However, status is linked to the ego. Therefore, while people accept that the person at the top gets a large office, whenever the subject of spatial needs surfaces it is likely to be treated as a form of narcissism. The status and organizational aspects are recognized while internal needs are not.

Yet, people have spatial needs independent of status. Some people can't work unless they are in the midst of a lot of hubbub. Others can't work unless they are behind closed doors, cut off from auditory and visual distractions. Some are extraordinarily sensitive to their environments, as though they had tentacles from the body reaching out and touching everything. Others are impervious to environmental impact. It is these differences, when and if they are understood at all, that cause trouble for architects. Their primary concern is with aesthetics, and what I am talking about lies underneath aesthetics, at a much more basic level.

As often happens, today's problems are being solved in terms of yesterday's understanding. With few exceptions, most thinking on the man-environment relationship fails to make the man-environment (M-E) transaction specific, to say nothing of taking it into account. The sophisticated architect pays lip service to the M-E relationship and then goes right on with what he was going to do anyway, demonstrating once more that people's needs, cultural as well as individual—needing a room of one's own—are not seen as real. Only the building is real! (This is extension transference again.)

Of course, the process is much more complex than most people think. Until quite recently, this whole relationship had been unexplored.[18] Perhaps those who eschewed it did so because they unconsciously and intuitively recognized its complexity. Besides, it is much easier to deal with such simple facts as a balance sheet or the exterior design of a building. Anyone who begins to investigate context and contexting soon discovers that much of what is examined, even though it occurs before his eyes, is altered in its significance by many hidden factors. Support for research into these matters is picayune. What has to be studied is not only very subtle but is thought to be too fine-grained, or even trivial, to warrant serious consideration.

One hospital administrator once threw me out of his office because I wanted to study the effects of space on patients in his hospital. Not only was he not interested in the literature, which was then considerable, but he thought I was a nut to even suggest such a study. To complicate things further, proxemics research requires an inordinate amount of time. For every distance that people use, there are at least five major categories of variables that influence what is perceived as either correct or improper. Take the matter of "intrusion distance" (the distance one has to maintain from two people who are already talking in order to get attention but not intrude). How great this distance is and how long one must wait before moving in depends on: what is going on (activity), your status, your relationship in a social system (husband and wife or boss and subordinate), the emotional state of the parties, the urgency of the needs of the individual who must intrude, etc.

Despite this new information, research in the social and biological sciences has turned away from context. In fact, attempts are often made to consciously exclude context. Fortunately, there are a few exceptions, men and women who have been willing to swim against the main currents of psychological thought.

One of these is Roger Barker, who summarized twenty-five years of observations in a small Kansas town in his book *Ecological Psychology.*[19] Starting a generation ago, Barker and his students moved into the town and recorded the behavior of the citizens in a wide variety of situations and settings such as classrooms, drugstores, Sunday-school classes, basketball games, baseball games, club meetings, business offices, bars, and hangouts. Barker discovered that much of people's behavior is situation-dependent (under control of the setting), to a much greater degree than had been supposed. In fact, as a psychologist, he challenged many of the central and important tenets of his own field. In his words:

The view is not uncommon among psychologists that the environment of behavior is a relatively unstructured, passive, probabilistic arena of objects and events upon which man behaves in accordance with the programming he carries about within himself. . . . When we look at the environment of behavior as a phenomenon worthy of investigation for itself, and not as an instrument for unraveling the behavior-relevant programming within persons, the situation is quite different. From this viewpoint the environment is seen to consist of highly structured, improbable arrangements of objects and events which coerce behavior in accordance with their own dynamic patterning. . . . We found . . . that we could predict some aspects of children's behavior more adequately from knowledge of the behavior characteristics of the drugstores, arithmetic classes, and basketball games they inhabited than from knowledge of the behavior tendencies of particular children. . . . (emphasis added) (p. 4)

Later Barker states,

The theory and data support the view that the environment in terms of behavior settings is much more than a source of random inputs to its inhabitants, or of inputs arranged in fixed array and flow patterns. They indicate, rather, that the envi-

ronment provides inputs with controls that regulate the inputs in accordance with the systemic requirements of the environment, on the one hand, and in accordance with the behavior attributes of its human components, on the other. This means that the same environmental unit provides different inputs to different persons, and different inputs to the same person if his behavior changes; and it means, further, that the whole program of the environment's inputs changes if its own ecological properties change; if it becomes more or less populous, for example. (p. 205)[20]

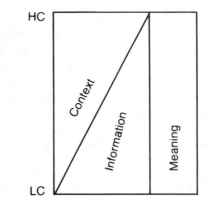

Figure 1

Barker demonstrates that in studying man *it is impossible to separate the individual from the environment in which he functions.* Much of the work of the transactional psychologists Ames, Ittelson, and Kilpatrick,[21] as well as my earlier work,[22] leads to the same conclusion.

In summary, regardless of where one looks, one discovers that a universal feature of information systems is that meaning (what the receiver is expected to do) is made up of: the communication, the background and preprogrammed responses of the recipient, and the situation. (We call these last two the internal and external context.)

Therefore, what the receiver actually perceives is important in understanding the nature of context. Remember that what an organism perceives is influenced in four ways—by status, activity, setting, and experience. But in man one must add another crucial dimension: *culture.*

Any transaction can be characterized as high-, low-, or middle-context [Figure 1]. HC transactions feature preprogrammed information that is in the receiver and in the setting, with only minimal information in the transmitted message. LC transactions are the reverse. Most of the information must be in the transmitted message in order to make up for what is missing in the context (both internal and external).

In general, HC communication, in contrast to LC, is economical, fast, efficient, and satisfying; however, time must be devoted to programming. If this programming does not take place, the communication is incomplete.

HC communications are frequently used as art forms. They act as a unifying, cohesive force, are long-lived, and are slow to change. LC communications do not unify; however, they can be changed easily and rapidly. This is why evolution by extension is so incredibly fast; extensions in their initial stages of development are low-context. To qualify this statement somewhat, some extension systems are higher on the context scale than others. A system of defense rocketry can be out of date before it is in place and is therefore very low-context. Church architecture, however, was for hundreds of years firmly rooted in the past and was the material focus for preserving religious beliefs and ideas. Even today, most churches are still quite traditional in design. One wonders if it is possible to develop strategies for balancing two apparently contradictory needs: the need to adapt and change (by moving in the low-context direction) and the need for stability (high-context). History is replete with examples of nations and institutions that failed to adapt by holding on to high-context modes too long. The instability of low-context systems, however, on the present-day scale is quite new to mankind. And furthermore, there is no reservoir of experience to show us how to deal with changes at this rate.

Extensions that now make up most of man's world are for the most part low-context. The question is, how long can man stand the tension between himself and his extensions? This is what *Future*

Shock[23] and *Understanding Media*[24] are all about. Take a single example, the automobile, which completely altered the American scene in all its dimensions—exploded communities, shredded the fabric of relationships, switched the rural-urban balance, changed our sex mores and churchgoing habits, altered our cities, crime, education, warfare, health, funerals. (One undertaker recently experimented with drive-in viewing of the corpse!) In summary:

The screens that one imposes between oneself and reality constitute one of the ways in which reality is structured.

Awareness of that structure is necessary if one is to control behavior with any semblance of rationality. Such awareness is associated with the low-context end of the scale.

Yet there is a price that must be paid for awareness—instability; obsolescence, and change at a rate that may become impossible to handle and result in information overload.

Therefore, as things become more complex, as they inevitably must with fast-evolving, low-context systems, it eventually becomes necessary to turn life and institutions around and move toward the greater stability of the high-context part of the scale as a way of dealing with information overload.

NOTES

1. *The Hidden Dimension* discusses this quality of culture in more detail.

2. Meier (1963)

3. Man also imposes a selective screen between the conscious part of his mind and the unconscious part. Sullivan (1947) and Freud (1933)

4. Whorf (1956)

5. Polanyi (1968)

6. Sullivan (1947)

7. The linguist Noam Chomsky (1968) and his followers have tried to deal with the contexting feature of language by eliminating context and going to so-called "deep structure." The results are interesting but end up evading the main issues of communication and to an even greater extent stress ideas at the expense of what is actually going on.

8. For further information on Chinese, see Wang (1973).

9. Bernstein (1964)

10. Eiseley (1969)

11. I do not agree with Eiseley's generalizing about all of mankind, because activism, like everything else, has to be taken in context. As we will see, LC cultures appear to be more vulnerable to violent perturbations than HC cultures.

12. Saul Bellow's (1974) article on the role of literature in a setting of changing times is also relevant to this discussion. Bellow makes the point that for some time now there has been a conscious effort on the part of avant-garde Western intellectuals to obliterate the past. "Karl Marx felt in history the tradition of all dead generations weighing like a nightmare on the brain of the living. Nietzsche speaks movingly of 'it was', and Joyce's Stephen Daedalus also defines history as a 'nightmare from which we are trying to awaken.'" Bellow points out, however, that there is a paradox that must be met, for to do away with history is to destroy one's own part in the historical process. It is reasonably certain, however, that what these men were trying to do was to redefine context in order to reduce its influence on men's actions. Simply to do away with the past would lead to an incredibly unstable society, as we shall see.

13. Black culture is much higher on the context scale than white culture, and one would assume from our model that riots do not have the same meaning for blacks as they do to the white society in which the blacks are imbedded.

14. Birren (1961)

15. For further details on this fascinating set of experiments, see Land (1959).

16. These distinctions are completely arbitrary and are for the convenience of the writer and the reader. They do not necessarily occur in nature. The inside-outside dichotomy has been struck down many times, not only by the perceptual transactionalists (Kilpatrick, 1961) following in Dewey's footsteps but in my own writings as well. Within the brain, experience (culture) acts on the structure of the brain to produce mind. It makes little difference *how* the brain is modified; what is important is that modification does take place and is apparently continuous.

17. Buder (1967)

18. See Hall (1966) for a comprehensive treatment of man's relationship to the spaces he builds as well as a bibliography on the subject.

19. Barker (1968) and Barker and Schoggen (1973)

20. The interested reader will find it worthwhile to consult Barker's works directly.

21. Kilpatrick (1961)

22. Hall (1966)

23. Toffler (1970)

24. McLuhan (1964)

BIBLIOGRAPHY

Barker, Roger G. *Ecological Psychology*. Stanford, Calif.: Stanford University Press, 1968.

————, and Schoggen, Phil. *Qualities of Community Life*. San Francisco: Jossey-Bass, 1973.

Bellow, Saul. "Machines and Story Books," *Harper's Magazine*, Vol. 249, pp. 48–54, August 1974.

Bernstein, Basil. "Elaborated and Restricted Codes: Their Social Origins and Some Consequences." In John J. Gumperz and Dell Hymes (eds.). The Ethnography of Communication, *American Anthropologist*, Vol. 66, No. 6, Part II, pp. 55–69, 1964.

Birren, Faber. *Color, Form and Space*. New York: Reinhold, 1961.

Buder, Stanley. "The Model Town of Pullman: Town Planning and Social Control in the Gilded Age," *Journal of the American Institute of Planners*, Vol. 33, No. 1, pp. 2–10, January 1967.

Chomsky, Noam. *Language and Mind*. New York: Harcourt, Brace & World, Inc., 1968.

Eiseley, L. "Activism and the Rejection of History," *Science*, Vol. 165, p. 129, July 11, 1969.

Freud, Sigmund. *New Introductory Lectures on Psychoanalysis*. New York: W. W. Norton & Company, Inc., 1933.

Hall, Edward T. "Art, Space and the Human Experience." In Gyorgy Kepes (ed.). *Arts of the Environment*. New York: George Braziller, Inc., 1972.

————. *The Hidden Dimension*. Garden City, N.Y.: Doubleday, 1966.

————. "Human Needs and Inhuman Cities." In *The Fitness of Man's Environment, Smithsonian Annual II*. Washington, D.C.: Smithsonian Institution Press, 1968. Reprinted in *Ekistics*, Vol. 27, No. 160, March 1969.

Kilpatrick, F. P. *Explorations in Transactional Psychology* (contains articles by Adelbert Ames, Hadley Cantril, William Ittelson, and F. P. Kilpatrick). New York: New York University Press, 1961.

McLuhan, Marshall. *Understanding Media*. New York: McGraw-Hill, 1964.

Meier, Richard. "Information Input Overload: Features of Growth in Communications-Oriented Institutions," *Libri* (Copenhagen), Vol. 13, No. 1, pp. 1–44, 1963.

Polanyi, M. "Life's Irreducible Structure," *Science*, Vol. 160, pp. 1308–12, June 21, 1968.

Sullivan, Harry Stack. *Conceptions of Modern Psychiatry*. New York: William Alanson White Psychiatric Foundation, 1947.

Toffler, Alvin. *Future Shock*. New York: Bantam Books, 1970.

Wang, William. "The Chinese Language," *Scientific American*, Vol. 228, No. 2, February 1973.

Whorf, Benjamin Lee. *Language, Thought, and Reality*. New York: The Technology Press of M.I.T. and John Wiley, 1956.

CONCEPTS AND QUESTIONS
FOR CHAPTER 1

1. What is intercultural communication?

2. In what ways are intercultural communication and communication alike? In what ways are they different?

3. What is meant by the term cultural value? How are these values manifested within a given culture?

4. What is meant by social perception, and how does it relate to intercultural communication?

5. What is the relationship between culture and perception?

6. How does one's world view contribute to how she or he perceives the world. What are the major cultural influences that form and shape one's world view?

7. How does the concept of a global village affect your view of international relations and your ability to relate to world events?

8. Porter and Samovar have asserted that people are not yet prepared for life in a global village. What is meant by that statement? Do you agree or disagree with the assertion? Why?

9. What does Barnlund mean by the "collective unconscious," and how does it relate to intercultural communication?

10. How does Collier classify cultures?

11. According to Collier, in what ways do we express our cultural identities?

12. What does Carbaugh mean when he says that "Communication is the primary social process?"

13. How does Carbaugh's concept of personhood help in understanding the dynamics inherent in intercultural communication?

14. How does Hall's discussion of high- and low-context communication relate to some of the underlying premises about intercultural communication?

15. How would someone from an extremely different cultural background respond on a first visit to your city? To your home?

16. As the United States emerges into a pluralistic, multicultural society, what contributions can you make in preparing for this society?

PART TWO

Socio-Cultural Backgrounds: What We Bring to Intercultural Communication

All persons are puzzles until at last we find in some word or act the key to the man, to the woman; straightway all their past words and actions lie in light before us.

— Emerson

One of the most important aspects of human communication is the fact that the experiential backgrounds participants bring to a communication experience will affect their behavior during the encounter. Psychologists A. H. Hastorf and H. Cantril underscore this issue when they note that each person acts according to the personal uniqueness he or she brings to the occasion. Think about those countless situations when you and some friends shared an experience and found that there were major differences in your reactions. What you deemed dull your companions found exciting; what you considered pointless they found meaningful. The messages received were the same for all participants; yet, because each of you has a unique personality and background, you experienced a variety of feelings, sensations, and responses. Each of you brought different backgrounds to the event and as a result attributed individual meanings to the shared experience. In short, the event meant what it did to you because of your own unique past history.

We contend that to understand any communication encounter you must appreciate the idea that there is much more to communication than the mere analysis of messages. Messages and the responses you make to them are products of your unique past experiences. And it is this uniqueness of experience that greatly contributes to the "immutable barriers in nature" between each individual's thoughts.

Individual past experience takes on added significance when we introduce the many dimensions of culture. Individuals are influenced not only by personal experiences but more importantly by their culture as well. As we detailed in Part One, culture refers to those cumulative deposits of knowledge, beliefs, views, values, and behaviors acquired by a large group of people and passed on from one generation to the next. In this sense, culture, in both conscious and unconscious ways, not only teaches you how to think and what to think about, it also dictates such values as what is attractive and what is ugly, what is good and what is evil, and what is appropriate and what is not. In short, your culture tells you how to see and interpret your world. Furthermore, culture teaches you such things as how close to stand next to strangers, how to greet friends, when to speak and when to remain silent, and even the various ways in which you can properly display your anger. When you are interacting with others and become disturbed by their actions you can, for instance, cry, become physically violent, shout, or remain silent. Each of these behaviors is a manifestation of what you have learned; it is largely influenced by your culture.

These cultural influences affect your ways of perceiving and acting; they contain the societal experiences and values that are passed from generation to generation. Because these behaviors are so much a part of your persona, there is a danger that you might forget they are culturally diverse. This is why a person from Japan, for example, might remain silent if disturbed by someone's actions while an Israeli or an Italian would more likely verbalize such displeasure.

Whatever the culture, you can better understand your behavior and the reactions of others if you realize that what you are hearing and seeing is a reflection of that culture. As you might predict, this understanding is greatly facilitated when your cultural experiences are similar to those of the people with whom you are interacting. Conversely, when different and diverse backgrounds are brought to a communication encounter, it is often difficult to share internal states and feelings. In this section we focus on those difficulties by examining some of the experiences and perceptual backgrounds found in a variety of international cultures as well as those found in a number of American co-cultures.

2

International Cultures: Understanding Diversity

Communication among members of international cultures poses one of the most perplexing intercultural communication problems. How we are to understand others when they come from different sections of the global village is a most difficult question. We need only to look around the world at any particular moment in time to find disagreement, strife, and fighting — the locations may change, but the problems persist. Nations become prominent in the news, and what happens within them and between them directly affects the entire world. Although few of us at present are directly involved with these countries, we may be in contact with their students who are studying in the United States; they may be our classmates or our students.

To help us better understand people from international cultures, we must learn to appreciate their diversity. This means that we must pass through a state of toleration for that which is different and develop true appreciation of that diversity, from which will come a perspective to help us learn how to interact with those people with whom we do come in contact. This chapter offers articles that will introduce us to diversity in cultural values as well as in specific international cultures.

Understanding how people in other cultures view their world is crucial to successful intercultural communication. World view establishes how people view themselves, each other, and their places in the universe and serves as an underlying pattern for interaction within a culture. You interact with others according to how you view one another.

Perhaps one of the greatest cultural dichotomies in interaction patterns is found between North Americans and East Asians. In her article "The Impact of Confucianism on Interpersonal Relationships and Communication Patterns in East Asia," June Ock Yum paints for us an intriguing picture of Confucianism's effect on how people view and interact with one another. She traces the various major components of Confucian philosophy and how they tend to determine East Asian patterns of interaction. As a counterpoint to her discussion, Yum makes continuous comparisons to prevalent North American interaction patterns so you can easily understand the differences between the two cultures.

Continuing with East Asian cultures, Akbar Javidi and Manoochehr Javidi, in "Cross-Cultural Analysis of Interpersonal Bonding: A Look at East and West," argue for a new approach to cross-cultural bonding. They believe that the final decade of the twentieth century and of the second millennium A.D. "should be a time in which members of both Eastern and Western societies set aside their ethnocentrism in an attempt to approach each other for the purpose of peaceful coexistence, which requires intercultural bonding." To aid us in achieving this goal, they examine the interpersonal communication process in Western and Eastern cultures. This analysis includes an examination of each culture's values concerning interpersonal bonding by giving attention to (1) self-concept versus group-concept, (2) doing versus being, (3) equality versus inequality, (4) formality versus informality, (5) uncertainty versus certainty, and (6) acceptance based upon common interest versus acceptance of the whole person.

Nemi C. Jain and Ellen D. Kussman then shift our attention to the Indian subcontinent as they provide a glimpse of Hindu culture in their article "Dominant Cultural Patterns of Hindus in India." Jain and Kussman demonstrate how the Hindu world view, belief in reincarnation, concept of *karma,* aims of human life, paths to salvation, concept of *dharma,* Indian caste system, and spirit of tolerance, which have persisted over thousands of years, permeate Indian culture. This provides a basis for the perceptual frames of reference common to much of India and a feeling for what it is to be Hindu.

We turn next to an examination of the Arabic culture. Janice Walker Anderson's article "A Comparison of Arab and American Conceptions of 'Effective' Persuasion" details Arabic orientations toward discourse. She shows the differences between Arabic and American concepts of persuasion and the cultural diversity in persuasive strategies.

In the final article, we turn our attention to the Greek culture. In "*Palevome*: Foundations of Struggle and Conflict in Greek Interpersonal Communication," Benjamin J. Broome demonstrates how a sense of contest and struggle permeates everyday life in Greece and that it is an essential dynamic of Greek interpersonal communication. He uses the Greek verb *palevome* (we are struggling) to illustrate the Greek perspective on conflict and its role in everyday interaction.

The Impact of Confucianism on Interpersonal Relationships and Communication Patterns in East Asia

JUNE OCK YUM

INTRODUCTION

New communication technology has removed many of the physical barriers against communication between the East and the West, but there remain philosophical and cultural barriers, which are not well understood. The increased opportunity for interaction between different cultural groups, however, has sensitized some scholars to the need to study Eastern perspectives on communication.

Most cross-cultural studies of communication simply describe foreign communication patterns and then compare them to those of North America, rarely going beneath the surface to explore the source of such differences. This paper goes beyond these limitations and explores the philosophical roots of the communication patterns in East Asian countries, before comparing them to those of North America. The assumption here is that communication is a basic social process and that, as such, it is influenced by the philosophical foundations and value systems of the society in which it is found.

There is always a danger in generalizing certain cultural patterns to large geographical areas. Even though we often refer to "Eastern" or "Asian" perspectives, there are many patterns, sometimes contradictory, within the region. For instance, the popular notion that Asians are more spiritual than Westerners might apply to India but not to China, Korea, or Japan. Nakamura (1964) has maintained that the Chinese and the Japanese are much more nonmetaphysical than Westerners. For this reason, this paper is limited to the East Asian countries of China, Korea, and Japan, those that have been most influenced by Confucian philosophical principles. Other countries that have been influenced by Confucianism are expected to have similar characteristics. For instance, Vietnam, the only country in Southeast Asia to have been influenced more by China than India, also exhibits the strong emphasis on social relationships and devotion to the hierarchical family relations that are the essence of Confucian doctrines (Luce & Summer, 1969).

SOCIAL RELATIONSHIPS VERSUS INDIVIDUALISM

If one has to select the main difference between East Asian and North American perspectives on communication, it would be the East Asian emphasis on social relationships as opposed to the North American emphasis on individualism. According to Hofstede (1980), individualism-collectivism is one of the main dimensions that differentiate cultures. He defined individualism as the emotional independence of individual persons from groups, organizations, or other collectivities. Parsons, Shils, and Olds (1951) have suggested that self-orientation versus collectivity orientation is one of the five basic pattern variables that determine human action. Self-orientation occurs when a person gives "priority in a given situation to his own private interests, independently of their bearings on the interests or values of a given collectivity" (Parsons, Shils, & Olds, 1951, p. 81), as opposed to taking directly into account the values and interests of the collectivity before acting.

The individualism-collectivism dichotomy, however, is not identical to the difference between the East Asian emphasis on social relationships and

This essay appeared first in the sixth edition and has been revised for this edition. All rights reserved. Permission to reprint must be obtained from the author and publisher. Professor Yum teaches at Towson State University, Towson, Maryland.

North American emphasis on individualism. In East Asia, the emphasis is on proper social relationships and their maintenance rather than any abstract concern for a general collective body. In a sense, it is a collectivism only among those bound by social networks. For example, a recent study on the Chinese value system found that the Confucian value of reciprocity and proper relationships was not correlated with Hofstede's individualism-collectivism dimension (Chinese Culture Connection, 1987). Hui and Triandis (1986) have recommended that collectivism be treated in two different ways: (1) as a concern for a certain subset of people and (2) as a concern for a generalized collectivity of people.

In the 1830s, the French social philosopher Alexis de Tocqueville coined the term *individualism* to describe the most notable characteristic of American people. Bellah, Madsen, Sullivan, Swidler, and Tipton (1985, pp. vii, 142) agree that individualism lies at the very core of American culture, contending that "individualism . . . has marched inexorably through our history" and that "we believe in the dignity, indeed the sacredness, of the individual. Anything that would violate our right to think for ourselves, judge for ourselves, make our own decision, live our lives as we see fit, is not only morally wrong, it is sacrilegious." According to Varenne (1977), there is but one system of principles regulating interpersonal relationships in America and that is individualism.

Even though many Americans feel they must get involved, they are also committed to individualism, including the desire to cut free from the past and define one's own self. Thus, the primary mode of American involvement is choosing organizations that one can voluntarily join or voluntarily withdraw from. Varenne (1977, p. 53) said that Americans perceive social structure "not as a system made up of different groups considered to be in a symbiotic relationship, but rather of different individuals who come together to do something."

Considering this cultural orientation, it is not surprising that the dominant paradigm of communication is an individualistic one. Each communicator is perceived to be a separate individual engaging in diverse communicative activities to maximize his or her own self-interest.

In contrast, the most notable characteristic in East Asia is the emphasis on social relationships. Hall and Beadsley (1965) have maintained that, compared to East Asian countries, North America is in the Stone Age when it comes to social relationships. This East Asian preoccupation with social relationships stems from the doctrines of Confucianism.

CONFUCIANISM

In the philosophical and cultural history of East Asia, Confucianism has endured as the basic social and political value system for over 1,000 years. One reason (and indication) that Confucianism has had such a profound impact is that it was adopted as the official philosophy of the Yi dynasty for 500 years in Korea, of the Tokugawa shogunate in Japan for 250 years, and of many dynasties in China.

Confucianism was institutionalized and propagated both through the formal curricula of the educational system and through the selection process of government officials. Confucian classics were required textbooks in the school systems throughout the history of China, Korea, and Japan before modern educational curricula were implemented. Government officials used to be selected through national exams that mostly examined the knowledge and the level of understanding of Confucian philosophy.

Another reason why Confucianism has exerted a much stronger impact than the other religious, philosophical systems of East Asia (such as Buddhism and Taoism) is that it is a pragmatic and present-oriented philosophy. When a student named Tzu-lu asked Confucius about serving spirits, Confucius said, "If one cannot yet serve men, how can he serve the spirits?" Asked about death, Confucius replied, "If you do not understand life, how can you understand death?" (McNaughton, 1974, p. 145). Max Weber commented, "Confucianism is extremely rationalistic since it is bereft of any form of metaphysics and in the sense that it lacks traces of nearly any religious basis. . . . At the same time, it is more realistic than any other system in the sense that it lacks and excludes all measures which are not utilitarian" (quoted by Nakamura, 1964, p. 16).

Confucianism is a philosophy of human nature that considers proper human relationships as the basis of society. In studying human nature and motivation, Confucianism sets forth four principles from which right conduct arises: *jen* (humanism), *i* (faithfulness), *li* (propriety), and *chih* (wisdom or a liberal education).

The cardinal principle, *jen* (humanism), almost defies translation since it sums up the core of Confucianism. Fundamentally it means warm human feelings between people. *Jen* is like a seed from which spring all the qualities that make up the ideal man. In addition, *jen* refers to the possession of all these qualities to a high degree. The actual practice or embodiment of *jen* in our daily lives is closely related to the concept of reciprocity. Confucius said that practicing *jen* is not to do to another man what you yourself don't want. In his own words: "If there's something that you don't like in the person to your right, don't pass it on to the person on your left. If there's something you don't like in the person to your left, don't pass it on to the person on your right" (McNaughton, 1974, p. 29).

It is suggested that Confucius himself once picked out reciprocity (*shu*) as the core of his thought. Confucius said, "There has never been a case where a man who did not understand reciprocity was able to communicate to others whatever treasures he might have had stored in himself" (McNaughton, 1974, p. 28). Therefore, practicing *jen* implies the practice of *shu*, which in turn means to know how it would feel to be the other person, to become like-hearted, and to be able to empathize with others.

The second principle of Confucianism is *i*, meaning faithfulness, loyalty, or justice. As the definition suggests, this principle also has strong implications for social relationships. Like *jen*, *i* is a difficult concept to translate. It may be easier to understand *i* through its opposite concept, which is personal or individual interest and profit. *I* is thus that part of human nature that allows us to look beyond personal, immediate profit and to elevate ourselves to

the original goodness of human nature that bridges ourselves to other people (Yum, 1987). According to the principle of *i*, human relationships are not based on individual profit but rather on the betterment of the common good.

If *jen* and *i* are the contents of the Confucian ethical system, *li* (propriety, rite, respect for social forms) is its outward form. As an objective criterion of social decorum, *li* was perceived as the fundamental regulatory etiquette of human behavior. Mencius suggested that *li* originated from deference to others and reservation of oneself. Confucius said that *li* follows from *jen*, that is, from being considerate to others. Only when people overcome themselves and so return to propriety can they reach humanness. On the other hand, propriety without humanness was perceived to be empty and useless.

THE IMPACT OF CONFUCIANISM ON INTERPERSONAL RELATIONSHIP PATTERNS

At least three of the four principles of Confucianism deal directly with social relationships. Under such a strong influence, East Asian countries have developed interpersonal relationship patterns that are quite different from the individualistic pattern of North America. Table 1 illustrates these five differences.

Particularistic Versus Universalistic Relationships

Human relationships under Confucianism are not universalistic but particularistic. As we described earlier, the warm human feelings of *jen* are exercised according to one's relationship with another person. Ethics in Confucian thought, therefore, are based on relationships and situations rather than on some absolute and abstract good. Instead of applying the same rule to everybody with whom they interact, East Asians differentially grade and regulate relationships according to the level of intimacy, the

Table 1 Comparison Between the North American and the East Asian Orientations
to Interpersonal Relationship Patterns

East Asian Orientations	North American Orientations
1. Particularistic	Universalistic
Particular rules and interaction patterns are applied depending upon the relationship and context	General and objective rules are applied across diverse relationships and context
2. Long-term and asymmetrical reciprocity	Short-term and symmetrical reciprocity or contractual reciprocity
3. Sharp distinction between in-group and out-group members	In-group and out-group distinction is not as sharp
4. Informal intermediaries	Contractual intermediaries
Personally known intermediaries Frequently utilized for diverse relationships	Professional intermediaries Utilized only for specific purposes
5. Personal and public relationships often overlap	Personal and public relationships are often separate

status of the persons involved, and the particular context. The East Asian countries have developed elaborate social interaction patterns for those whose social position and relationship to oneself is known, but there are few universal patterns that can be applied to someone who is not known.

From a North American point of view, applying different rules to different people and situations may seem to violate the sacred code of fairness and equality that accompanies the individualistic values. In North America, human relationships are not particularized. Rather, one is supposed to treat each person as an integral individual and apply general and objective rules. For instance, it is quite common in America for people to say "Hi" or "Good morning" to anybody they encounter during their morning walk, or to strike up a conversation with another person waiting in line. If you said "Hello" or "Good morning" to a stranger in Korea, you would be looked upon as a rather odd person.

The East Asian approach suggests that it is more humanitarian to consider the particular context and the persons involved in understanding the action and behavior rather than evaluate them according to generalized rules which to a certain extent are impersonal.

Long-Term Asymmetrical Reciprocity Versus Short-Term Symmetrical or Contractual Reciprocity

Reciprocity as an embodiment of *jen* is the core concept in Confucianism, just as individualism is the core concept of the North American culture. While people may voluntarily join together for specific purposes in North America, each individual remains equal and independent; thus people join or drop out of clubs without any serious group sanctions. Commitments and obligations are often perceived as threats to one's autonomy or freedom of action. Relations are symmetrical-obligatory—that is, as nearly "paid off" as possible at any given moment—or else contractual—the obligation is to an institution or to a professional with whom one has established some contractual base (Condon & Yousef, 1975).

In contrast, Confucian philosophy views relationships as complementary or asymmetrical and reciprocally obligatory. In a sense, a person is forever indebted to others, who in turn are constrained by other debts. Dependence is not looked down upon. Rather, dependency is accepted as a necessary part of human relationships. Under this system of reciprocity, the individual does not calculate what he or she gives and receives. To calculate would be to think about immediate personal profits, which is the opposite of the principle of mutual faithfulness, *i*. It is somewhat unusual in Korea, for example, for a group of friends, colleagues, or superior and subordinates to go "Dutch" and split the bill for dinner or drinks. Rather, each person takes turns and pays for the whole group. In North America, people generally insist on "paying their own way." The practice of basing relationships on complementary obligations creates warm, lasting human relationships but also the necessity to accept the obligations accompanying such relationships.

In-group/Out-group Distinction

North American culture does not distinguish as strongly between in-group members and out-group members as East Asian countries do. Allegiance to a group and mobility among groups are purely voluntary, so that the longevity of membership in and loyalty to a particular group are both limited.

Mutual dependence as prescribed by the Confucian principle of *i*, however, requires that one be affiliated and identify with relatively small and tightly knit groups of people over long periods of time. These long-term relationships work because each group member expects the others to reciprocate and also because group members believe that sooner or later they will have to depend on the others. People enmeshed in this kind of network make clear distinctions between in-group and out-group members. For example, linguistic codes for in-group members are often different from those for out-group members. What is inside the group and what is outside it have drastically different meanings.

Informal Intermediaries Versus Contractual Intermediaries

Because the distinctions between in-group and out-group members are so strict, it is imperative to have an intermediary to help one initiate a new relationship in East Asia. Confucian emphasis on propriety *(li)* also dictates that one has to follow proper rituals in establishing a new relationship, and an intermediary is part of such rituals. The intermediary has an in-group relationship with both parties and so can connect them. One strategy is for the intermediary to bring up an existing relationship that links the two parties, for example, explaining that "you are both graduates of so-and-so college" or "you are both from province A." Alternatively, the intermediary can use his or her own connections with them to create an indirect sense of in-groupness, for example, explaining that one is "my junior from high school" and the other "works in the same department as I do."

Intermediaries in the United States, however, are mostly professional or contractual in nature: lawyers, negotiators, marriage counselors, and the like. The intermediary is an objective third person who does not have any knowledge of the parties' characteristics other than those directly related to the issue at hand. Also, the intermediary deals with each party as a separate, independent individual. Using personal connections to attain a desired goal does occur in the United States, but such a practice may be frowned on as nepotism and may also be perceived as giving up one's own individual freedom.

Overlap of Personal and Public Relationships

The Confucian concept of *i* leads to a strong distaste for a purely business transaction, carried out on a calculated and contractual basis. Therefore, in East

Table 2 Comparison Between the North American and the East Asian Orientations to Communication Patterns

East Asian Orientations	North American Orientations
1. Process orientation	Outcome orientation
Communication is perceived as a process of infinite interpretation	Communication is perceived as the transference of messages
2. Differentiated linguistic codes	Less differentiated linguistic codes
Different linguistics codes are used depending upon persons involved and situations	Linguistic codes are not as extensively differentiated as East Asia
3. Indirect communication emphasis	Direct communication emphasis
The use of indirect communication is prevalent and accepted as normative	Direct communication is a norm despite the extensive use of indirect communication
4. Receiver centered	Sender centered
Meaning is in the interpretation	Meaning is in the messages created by the sender
Emphasis is on listening, sensitivity, and removal of preconception	Emphasis is on how to formulate the best messages, how to improve source credibility, and how to improve delivery skills

Asian countries there is a tendency to mix personal with public relationships. Even though the obvious purpose of a meeting is for business, both parties feel more comfortable if the transaction occurs on a more personal, human level. According to the principles of social reciprocity, there are several steps to follow if you want to develop an effective business relationship in Korea (Lee, 1983): (1) have frequent contacts over a relatively lengthy period of time, (2) establish a personal and human relationship, (3) if possible, create some common experiences such as sports, drinking, or travel, (4) foster mutual understanding in terms of personality, personal situations, and the like, and (5) develop a certain level of trust and a favorable attitude. The goal is to diminish the clear distinction between a personal relationship and a public relationship. It is implied that if one develops a warm personal relationship, a good public relationship will follow, because it is based on trust and mutual reciprocity. Such qualities are expected to endure rather than be limited to the business deal of the moment.

In the United States, there is a rather sharp dichotomy between private and public life. Since the primary task of the individual is to achieve a high level of autonomous self-reliance, there is an effort to separate the two lives as much as possible. Since the notion of "organizational man" is contradictory to the self-reliant individual, there is a certain level of anxiety about becoming an organizational man (Bellah et al., 1985). Some also perceive private life as a haven from the pressure of individualistic, competitive public life, and as such it must be protected.

THE IMPACT OF CONFUCIANISM ON COMMUNICATION PATTERNS

Confucianism's primary concern with social relationships has strongly influenced communication patterns in East Asia. In general, it has strengthened patterns that help to build and maintain proper human relationships. Table 2 compares East Asia and North America in terms of communication patterns.

Process- Versus Outcome-Oriented Communication

Since the main function of communication under Confucian philosophy is to initiate, develop, and maintain social relationships, there is a strong emphasis on the kind of communication that promotes such relationships. For instance, it is very important in East Asia to engage in small talk before initiating business and to communicate personalized information, especially information that would help place each person in the proper context. Communication is perceived to be an infinite interpretive process (Cheng, 1987), which cannot be compartmentalized into sender, message, channel, and receiver. It presumes that each partner is engaged in an ongoing process and that the relationship is in flux.

In contrast, when the main function of communication is to actualize autonomy and self-fulfillment, as in North America, the outcome of the communication is more important than the process. With short-term, discontinuous relationships, communication is perceived to be an action that is terminated after a certain duration and then replaced by a new communication. Tangible outcomes in terms of friends gained, opponents defeated, and self-fulfillment achieved become the primary function of communication.

Differentiated Versus Less Differentiated Linguistic Codes

East Asian languages are very complex and are differentiated according to social status, the degree of intimacy, age, sex, and the level of formality. There are also extensive and elaborate honorific linguistic systems in East Asian languages (Brown & Levinson, 1978; Ogino, Misono, & Fukushima, 1985). These differentiations are manifested not only in referential terms but also in verbs, pronouns, and nouns. They result from Confucian ethical rules that place the highest value on proper human relationships (*i*) and on propriety (*li*). McBrian (1978) has argued that language forms an integral component of social stratification systems, and the hierarchical Confu-

cian society is well represented by the highly stratified linguistic codes in Korea.

Martin (1964) has proposed that one of the main differences between English, Japanese, and Korean is the levels of speech. In both Korean and Japanese, there are two axes of distinction: the axis of address and the axis of reference. The axis of address is divided into plain, polite, and honorific while the axis of reference is divided into humble and neutral (Martin, 1964). An honorific form is used to refer to the receiver's action, while a humble form is used to refer to the sender's action—the reverse would not be appropriate. The most deferential form of speech combines the honorific address form for receiver and the humble form of self-reference.

The English language also employs different codes depending upon intimacy and status difference between the speaker and listener. In general, however, English forms of address are reasonably well described by a single binary contrast: first name (FN) versus title plus last name (TLN) (Brown & Ford, 1964). Certain European languages also contrast the familiar and formal forms, such as *tu* and *vous* in French. The use of FN or TLN can either be reciprocal (both sides use the same form of address) or nonreciprocal (one side uses FN and the other side uses TLN). Status and intimacy also play a role in greetings. For example, "Hi" is more common to intimates and to subordinates while "Good morning" is for distant acquaintances and superiors (Brown & Ford, 1964). In contrast, Ogino, Misono, and Fukushima (1985), working in Japan, found 210 different word forms, through 8 address situations, which can be put into 20 different categories. Moreover, in modern American English practice, the distance between the mutual FN and mutual TLN represents only a very small increment of intimacy, sometimes as small as five minutes of conversation. In East Asian communication situations, the distance between very honorific languages and very informal ones is quite large and more often than not cannot be altered even after a long acquaintance.

In English, the speech level is defined mainly by address forms, while in Korean or Japanese, pronouns, verbs, and nouns all have different levels. Thus, in English "to eat" is "to eat" regardless of the person addressed. In the Korean language, however, there are three different ways of saying "to eat": *muk-da* (plain), *du-shin-da* (polite), and *chap-soo-shin-da* (honorific). Different levels of a verb are often accompanied by different levels of a noun: Rice may be *bap* (plain), *shik-sa* (polite), or *jin-ji* (honorific).

In English, the pronoun "you" is used to refer alike to the old and young, to the president of the country, and to the child next door. In East Asian languages, there are different words for "you" depending upon the level of politeness and upon the relationship. There is also the compulsory or preferential use of a term of address instead of the pronoun, as when one says: *Jeh sh Wang.Shin.shen.de shu .ma*? (Literally, "Is this Mr. Wang's book?") instead of "Is this your book?" (Chao, 1956, p. 218). Actual role terms, such as professor, aunt, student, and so forth, are used in place of the pronoun "you" even in two-partner communication because they clarify and accentuate the relationships between the two communicators better than the simple second person reference. Since Confucianism dictates that one should observe the proprieties prescribed by a social relationship, the generalized "you" does not seem to be appropriate in most communication situations in East Asian countries.

This differentiation of linguistic codes in East Asian cultures bears out the familiar psycholinguistic principle that for language communities the degree of lexical differentiation of a referent field increases with the importance of that field to the community (Brown & Ford, 1964). The importance of social relationships in Confucian societies has therefore promoted the differentiation of linguistic codes to accommodate highly differentiated relationships.

Emphasis on Indirect Communication Versus Emphasis on Direct Communication

Most cultures have both direct and indirect modes of communication. Metaphor, insinuations, innuendos, hints, and irony are only a few examples of the kinds of indirect communication that can be found in most linguistic communities. According to Searle (1969), indirect speech acts occur when the speaker communicates to the hearer more than he or she actually says by referring to some mutually shared background information and by relying on the hearer's powers of rationality and inference. Brown and Levinson (1978) have suggested that indirect speech acts are universal because they perform a basic service in strategies of politeness.

Even though the indirect mode of communication seems to be universal, however, the degree to which it is elaborated varies from culture to culture. For instance, the Malagasy speech community values an indirect style (Keenan, 1974), while certain Sabra culture prefers a straight-talking (*dugri*) style (Katriel, 1986). Rosaldo (1973) maintained that the Euro-American association of direct talk with a scientific and democratic attitude may not hold true in different cultural contexts. In Ilongot society, for example, direct talk is perceived as authoritarian and exclusionary while indirect language is perceived as accommodating and sensitive to individual wishes.

Brown and Levinson (1978) have suggested that politeness phenomena in language (indirectness is just one of them) derive from the notion of "face," the public self-image that every member wants to claim for himself or herself. According to Katriel (1986), indirect speech acts are the result of predominant concern for the other person's face. The Confucian legacy of consideration for others and concern for proper human relationships has led to the development of communication patterns that preserve one another's face. Indirect communication helps to prevent the embarrassment of rejection by the other person or disagreement among partners, leaving the relationship and each other's face intact. Lebra (1976) suggested that "defending face" is one of the main factors influencing Japanese behavior. She listed a number of concrete mechanisms for defending face, such as mediated communication (asking someone else to transmit the message), refracted communication (talking to a third person in the presence of the hearer), and acting as a delegate (conveying one's message as being from someone else), which are all indirect forms of communication.

The use of the indirect mode of communication in East Asia is pervasive and often deliberate. In comparing Japanese and American organizations, it has been noted that American employees strive to communicate with each other in a clear, precise, and explicit manner, while Japanese often deliberately communicate in a vague and indirect manner (Hirokawa, 1987; Pascale & Athos, 1981). The extensive nature of indirect communication is exemplified by the fact that there are sixteen evasive "maneuvers" that can be employed by the Japanese to avoid saying no (Imai, 1981).

It has also been suggested that there is a significant difference in the level of indirectness between North American and East Asian communication patterns. An American might say "The door is open" as in indirect way of asking the hearer to shut the door, while in Japan, instead of saying "The door is open," one often says "It is somewhat cold today." This is even more indirect, because no words refer to the door (Okabe, 1987). Operating at a still higher level of indirection, one Japanese wife communicated to her husband her discord with her mother-in-law by slight irregularities in her flower arrangements (Lebra, 1976).

One of Grice's maxims for cooperative conversation is "manner," which suggests that the speaker should avoid obscurity of expression and ambiguity (Grice, 1975). This direct communication is a norm in North America, despite the extensive use of indirect communication. Grice's principle would not be accepted as a norm, however, in East Asia. Okabe (1987) has shown that in Japan, the traditional rule of communication, which prescribes not to demand, reject, assert yourself, or criticize the listener straightforwardly, is a much more dominant principle than Grice's maxim of manner.

Reischauer (1977, p. 136) concluded that "the Japanese have a genuine mistrust of verbal skills, thinking that these tend to show superficiality in contrast to inner, less articulate feelings that are communicated by innuendo or by nonverbal means." Thus, even though both North American and East Asian communication communities em-ploy indirect communication, its use is much more prevalent and accepted as normative in the former than the latter.

Receiver Versus Sender Centeredness

North American communication very often centers on the sender, and until recently the linear, one-way model from sender to receiver was the prevailing model of communication. Much emphasis has been placed on how senders can formulate better messages, improve source credibility, polish their delivery skills, and so forth. In contrast, the emphasis in East Asia has always been on listening and interpretation.

Cheng (1987) has identified infinite interpretation as one of the main principles of Chinese communication. The process presumes that the emphasis is on the receiver and listening rather than the sender or speech making. According to Lebra (1976, p. 123), "anticipatory communication" is common in Japan, in which, instead of the speaker's having to tell or ask for what he or she wants specifically, others guess and accommodate his or her needs, sparing him or her embarrassment in case the verbally expressed request cannot be met. In such cases, the burden of communication falls not on the message sender but on the message receiver. A person who "hears one and understands ten" is regarded as an intelligent communicator. To catch on quickly and to adjust oneself to another's position before his or her position is clearly revealed is regarded as an important communication skill. One of the common puzzles expressed by foreign students from East Asia is why they are constantly being asked what they want when they are visiting in American homes. In their own countries, the host or hostess is supposed to know what is needed and serve accordingly. The difference occurs because in North America it is important to provide individual freedom of choice; in East Asia, it is important to practice anticipatory communication and to accommodate accordingly.

With the emphasis on indirect communication, the receiver's sensitivity and ability to capture the under-the-surface meaning and to understand implicit meaning becomes critical. In North America, an effort has been made to improve the effectiveness of senders through such formal training as debate and public speech, whereas in East Asia, the effort has been on improving the receiver's sensitivity. The highest sensitivity is reached when one empties the mind of one's preconceptions and makes it as clear as a mirror (Yuji, 1984).

Recently, there has been increased interest in listening in the United States as well. Both communication scholars and practitioners recognize that listening is not only necessary from the instrumental aspect of communication (comprehension) but, more importantly, for the affective aspect (satisfaction of being listened to).

DISCUSSION

This paper compared the East Asian emphasis on social relationships with the North American emphasis on individualism. These two emphases produce very different patterns of interpersonal relationships and communication. The conclusions drawn in this paper are not absolute, however. Each culture contains both orientations to some degree. It is simply more probable that East Asians would exhibit certain patterns of communication, such as indirect communication, more often than North Americans, and vice versa.

The North American preoccupation with individualism and related concepts, such as equality, fairness, and justice, and its far-reaching influences on the whole fiber of society are well documented. On the other hand, the importance of social relationships as a key to the East Asian countries has been recognized only recently. For instance, investigations of Japanese management styles have found that one of the fundamental differences between Japanese and American management is the personalized, interdependent relationships among employees and between managers and employees in Japan. These human relationships are related to loyalty and high productivity. It is not uncommon to explain such relationships away as merely a result of other organizational practices, such as life-long employment. If one looks under the surface, however, one realizes that it is derived from a thousand-year-old Confucian legacy, and that similar human relationship patterns are found outside of large organizations. Consequently, attempts to transplant such a management style to North America with its philosophical and cultural orientation of individualism cannot be entirely satisfactory. The culture itself would have to be modified first.

There has been increasing concern in North America about the pursuit of individualism at the expense of commitment to larger entities such as the community, civic groups, and other organizations. It has been suggested that modern individualism has progressed to such an extent that most Americans are trapped by the language of individualism itself and have lost the ability to articulate their own need to get involved (Bellah et al., 1985). Although individualism has its own strength as a value, individualism that is not accompanied by commitments to large entities eventually forces people into a state of isolation, where life itself becomes meaningless.

If human beings are fundamentally social animals, it is necessary to balance the cultural belief system of individualism with the need to get involved with others. Americans have joined voluntary associations and civic organizations more than any other citizens of the industrialized world. However, such recent phenomena as the "me" generation and young stockbrokers who pursue only personal gain at the expense of their own organizations or the society as a whole can be perceived as pathological symptoms of individualism driven to its extreme. Bellah et al. (1985, p. 284) have maintained that "social ecology is damaged not only by war, genocide, and political repression. It is also damaged by the destruction of the subtle ties that bind human beings to one another, leaving them frightened and alone." They strongly argue that we need to restore social ecology by making people aware of our intricate connectedness and interdependence.

The emphasis of Confucianism on social relationships is conducive to cooperation, warm relaxed human relations, consideration of others, and group harmony, but it has costs as well. Under such social constraints, individual initiative and innovation are slow to appear, and some individuals feel that their individuality is being suffocated. Because of the sharp distinction between in-groups and out-groups, factionalism may be inevitable. Within such well-defined sets of social relationships, people have a well-developed sense of obligation but a weak sense of duty to impersonal social entities.

Ironically, the solution for both the North American problems of excessive individualism and the excessive adherence to in-groupness in East Asia is the same: to be receptive to others. For the North Americans, this means accepting the limitations of self-reliance, becoming committed to a group, and putting the common good ahead of personal wants. For the East Asians, this means making their group boundaries more flexible and accepting outsiders with humanness and commitment to the common good.

There have been substantial changes in the East Asian societies since World War II. There has been an irrepressible influx of Western values; imported films and television programs are ubiquitous. However, it is not easy to change several hundred years of Confucian legacy. In Japan, for example, a greater proportion of young people than old expressed a preference for a boss endowed with the virtues of humanness and sympathy over a more efficient boss who would not ask for extra devotion (Dore, 1973). A similar finding was reported in Korea. When Korean workers, mostly in manufacturing plants, were asked their reasons for changing jobs, those who answered "a better human relationship and more humane treatment" still outnumbered those who answered "better payment" (Kim, 1984).

It seems inevitable, however, that the East Asian countries will see an increasing number of people who do not have traditional, binding relationships as the society moves further toward industrialization and higher mobility. The task will be to find a way for such people to cope with life without the protection of close in-group memberships and to learn to find satisfaction in expressing individual freedom and self-reliance.

REFERENCES

Bellah, R., Madsen, R., Sullivan, W., Swidler, A., and Tipton, S. (1985). *Habits of the Heart: Individualism and Commitment in American Life*. New York: Harper & Row.

Brown, R. W., and Ford, M. (1964). "Address in American English." In D. Hymes (Ed.), *Language in Culture and Society*. New York: Harper & Row.

Brown, R., and Levinson, S. (1978). "Universals in Language Usage: Politeness Phenomena." In E. Goody (Ed.), *Questions and Politeness*. Cambridge: Cambridge University Press.

Chao, Y. R. (1956). "Chinese Terms of Address." *Language*, *32*, 217–241.

Cheng, C. Y. (1987). "Chinese Philosophy and Contemporary Communication Theory." In D. L. Kincaid (Ed.), *Communication Theory: Eastern and Western Perspectives*. New York: Academic Press.

Chinese Culture Connection. (1987). "Chinese Values and the Search for Culture-Free Dimensions of Culture." *Journal of Cross-Cultural Psychology*, *18*, 143–164.

Condon, J., and Yousef, F. (1975). *An Introduction to Intercultural Communication*. New York: Bobbs-Merrill.

Dore, R. (1973). *British Factory, Japanese Factory: The Origins of National Diversity in Industrial Relations*. Berkeley and Los Angeles: University of California Press.

Grice, P. H. (1975). "Logic and Conversation." In P. Cole and J. L. Morgan (Eds.), *Studies in Syntax*. Vol. 3. New York: Academic Press.

Hall, J., and Beadsley, R. (1965). *Twelve Doors to Japan*. New York: McGraw-Hill.

Hirokawa, R. (1987). "Communication Within the Japanese Business Organization." In D. L. Kincaid (Ed.), *Communication Theory: Eastern and Western Perspectives*. New York: Academic Press.

Hofstede, G. (1980). *Culture's Consequences*. Newbury Park, Calif.: Sage.

Hui, C. H., and Triandis, H. C. (1986). "Individualism-Collectivism: A Study of Cross-Cultural Research." *Journal of Cross-Cultural Psychology*, *17*, 225–248.

Imai, M. (1981). *Sixteen Ways to Avoid Saying No*. Tokyo: Nihon Keizai Shimbun.

Katriel, T. (1986). *Talking Straight: Dugri Speech in Israeli Sabra Culture*. Cambridge: Cambridge University Press.

Keenan, E. (1974). "Norm Makers, Norm Breakers: Uses of Speech by Men and Women in a Malagasy Community." In R. Bauman and J. Sherzer (Eds.), *Explorations in the Ethnography of Speaking*. Cambridge: Cambridge University Press.

Kim, S. U. (1984). *"Kong-jang no-dong-ja-ye ee-jik iyu"* ("Reasons for Changing Jobs Among Factory Workers"). Hankook Daily Newspaper, May 2 (in Korean).

Lebra, T. S. (1976). *Japanese Patterns of Behavior*. Honolulu: The University Press of Hawaii.

Lee, K. T. (1983). *Hankook-in ye u-shik koo-jo* (Cognitive Patterns of Korean People). Seoul, Korea: Shin-Won Moon-Wha Sa (in Korean).

Luce, D., and Sommer, J. (1969). *Viet Nam—the Unheard Voices*. Ithaca, N.Y.: Cornell University Press.

McBrian, C. (1978). "Language and Social Stratification: The Case of a Confucian Society." *Anthropological Linguistics*, *2*, 320–326.

McNaughton, W. (1974). *The Confucian Vision*. Ann Arbor: University of Michigan Press.

Martin, S. E. (1964). "Speech Levels in Japan and Korea." In D. Hymes (Ed.), *Language in Culture and Society*. New York: Harper & Row.

Nakamura, H. (1964). *Ways of Thinking of Eastern Peoples*. Honolulu: East-West Center Press.

Ogino, T., Misono, Y., and Fukushima, C. (1985). "Diversity of Honorific Usage in Tokyo: A Sociolinguistic Approach Based on a Field Survey." *International Journal of Sociology of Language*, *55*, 23–39.

Okabe, K. (1987). "Indirect Speech Acts of the Japanese." In D. L. Kincaid (Ed.), *Communication Theory: Eastern and Western Perspectives*. New York: Academic Press.

Parsons, T., Shils, E., and Olds, J. (1951). "Categories of the Orientation and Organization of Action." In T. Parsons and E. A. Shils (Eds.), *Toward a General Theory of Action*. Cambridge, Mass.: Harvard University Press.

Pascale, R., and Athos, A. (1981). *The Art of Japanese Management: Application for American Executives*. New York: Warner Communications.

Reischauer, E. (1977). *The Japanese*. Cambridge, Mass.: Harvard University Press.

Rosaldo, M. (1973). "I Have Nothing to Hide: The Language of Ilongot Oratory." *Language in Society*, *11*, 193–223.

Searle, J. R. (1969). *Speech Acts*. Cambridge: Cambridge University Press.

Varenne, H. (1977). *Americans Together: Structured Diversity in a Midwestern Town*. New York and London: Teachers College Press.

Yuji, A. (Trans. N. Chung). (1984). *Ilbon-in ye usik koo-jo* (Japanese Thought Patterns). Seoul, Korea: Baik Yang Publishing Co. (in Korean).

Yum, J. O. (1987). Korean Philosophy and Communication. In D. L. Kincaid (Ed.), *Communication Theory: Eastern and Western Perspectives*. New York: Academic Press.

Cross-Cultural Analysis of Interpersonal Bonding: A Look at East and West

AKBAR JAVIDI
MANOOCHEHR JAVIDI

Intimacy is the gift that bonds us to one another. We understand our likenesses and can acknowledge our differences in this process of sharing ourselves. We can see how similar our fears and our hurts are, and in seeing we gain strength.

— *Casey & Vanceburg, 1983*

The final decade of the twentieth century and of the second millennium A.D. should be a time in which members of both Eastern and Western societies set aside their ethnocentrism in an attempt to approach each other for the purpose of peaceful coexistence, which requires intercultural bonding (Boechner, 1984; Gudykunst & Kim, 1984; Gudykunst, Ting-Toomey, & Chua, 1988; Servaes, 1988). Forming intercultural bonds is difficult because of inadequate mutual understanding of cultural differences. Servaes (1988), discussing cultural identities in Eastern and Western societies, suggests that "each culture operates out of its own logical structure. . . . [I]ntercultural communications are only successful when these logical foundations are understood and accepted as equal by the people concerned" (p. 58). For example, Eastern cultures, often viewed as homogeneous and collectivistic, contrast with Western

cultures, viewed as heterogeneous and individualistic (see also Gudykunst, Ting-Toomey, & Chua, 1988; Okabe, 1983). Thus, these differences influence how individuals from these cultures relate to one another and, more importantly, how they develop interpersonal bonds.

Boechner (1984, p. 544) refers to interpersonal bonding as "the process of forming individualized relationships — affinities that are close, deep, personal, and intimate." Because the development of relationships from the acquaintance level to the bonded level is an integral aspect of human life, the process by which this occurs has been of interest to social psychologists.

In 1983, Altman and Taylor proposed a model of relationship development that they termed "social penetration," the process by which people come to know each other. The process is orderly, with interpersonal communication progressing from superficial, nonintimate topics to intimate ones as relationships develop. People allow others to know them gradually. They assess the reward and cost (satisfaction/dissatisfaction) they gain from interaction with others. The development depends upon the quantity and nature of the reward and cost balance of an ongoing exchange to predict the outcomes of future interactions. If the predictions are favorable, people move successively to more intimate levels of encounters (Reardon, 1987, p. 165). With their social penetration theory, Altman and Taylor (1983) propose four stages of relational development: (a) orientation, (b) exploration, (c) affective exchange, and (d) stable exchange.

In 1987, Knapp expanded the social penetration theory and posited five stages of interpersonal relationship development: (a) initiating, (b) experimenting, (c) intensifying, (d) integrating, and (e) bonding. Culture and interpersonal communication are important functions in the development of interpersonal bondings. Although the applicability of stages of interpersonal relationship development suggested by Altman and Taylor (1973) and Knapp (1987) can be generalized to both Western and Eastern cultures (Gudykunst & Kim, 1984; Gudykunst, Ting-Toomey, & Chua, 1988; Klopf, 1987), the direction of interpersonal communication in the process

From *The Howard Journal of Communications*, Vol. 3, Nos. 1 & 2 (Summer/Fall 1991), pp. 129–138. Reprinted by permission of the publisher. Akbar Javidi teaches at the University of Nebraska. Manoochehr Javidi teaches at North Carolina State University.

of forming interpersonal bondings is distinctly unique in each of these two cultures.

The direction of interpersonal communication in most Western cultures, occurs on the horizontal axis, while, in most Eastern cultures, it occurs on the vertical axis (Gudykunst, Ting-Toomey, & Chua, 1988). In addition, each culture, with distinctly differing social stratifications, has its own unique cultural values concerning approaches taken during the process of interpersonal bonding development. Consequently, while the ends of states of bonding development are similar in each culture, the values concerning approaches to these ends vary because of diverse cultural stratifications. These approaches are discussed under six categories of cultural values: (a) self-concept versus group-concept, (b) doing versus being, (c) equality versus inequality, (d) informality versus formality, (e) uncertainty reduction, and (f) acceptance of a person based on an area of common interest versus acceptance of the whole person. Understanding these values will help to develop solid and effective interpersonal bonds and friendships.

EASTERN AND WESTERN CULTURES' VALUES CONCERNING APPROACHES TO FORMING INTERPERSONAL BONDINGS

Values Concerning Self-Concept Versus Group-Concept

Self-concept plays a more significant role in the process of interpersonal bonding development in most Western cultures, where the emphasis is on self-maintenance, than it does in Eastern cultures. For example, the United States is classified as a horizontal, individualistic culture in which, as Klopf (1987) states, people are assumed to be independent; hence, they are aware of who they are, what they should do, and what they want to be or to become. Their interpersonal communication behaviors are determined mainly by perception of self. In other words, according to Samovar, Porter, and Jain (1981), Americans tend to emphasize their self-concept in terms of self-awareness, self-image, self-esteem, self-identity, self-reliance, self-assistance, self-actualization, self-expression, and self-determination. Stewart (1972) states that the development of relationships with Americans hinges on the ability to evoke their self-interest and participation. Therefore, if Americans are to be influenced, messages designed to affect them should be translated into the language of the self (Klopf, 1987).

In contrast to Western cultures, in most Eastern cultures that are classified as vertical cultures, self-concept plays a less significant role in the process of interpersonal bonding development. People in these cultures are interested mainly in maintaining their groups (for example, immediate family and extended family) rather than maintenance of self. Similarly, Klopf (1987) points out that the group is the primary social identity in most of these cultures. In addition, Gudykunst and Kim (1984) state that people in these cultures are interdependent and obligated to conform to their groups' norms and values. In the same vein, Klopf (1987) claims that throughout East and Southeast Asia, in varying degrees, the self is not a person's primary concern. The predominant value is congeniality in social interactions based upon relationships among people rather than on the self. In most of these cultures, people's behaviors are directed first to maintaining affiliation in the groups and upholding congenial social relations. Goals that would be personally rewarding, enhancing the self, are of secondary importance in these cultures.

Values Concerning Doing Versus Being

Maruyama (1961) states that in vertical societies (for example, Japan) an individual's birth, family background, age, and rank tend to be more important than his or her later achievements (Okabe, 1983). In other words, "who a person is" is much more important than "what a person does" in vertical cultures. Maruyama classifies Western cultures as *doing* cultures and Eastern cultures as *being* cultures. For instance, in a *doing* culture such as the United States, people seem to be oriented toward instant results. In most interpersonal relations, they expect events to occur at a rapid pace. For them, a mind set of "who a person is" or "what type of people he or she comes from" is far less important than that person's ability to produce. In contrast, time may be interpreted differently in most Eastern cultures. People in these cultures take time to explore others' backgrounds prior to forming close relationships with them. In the process of bonding development, individuals from Eastern cultures are more interested in *who people are* rather than in *what they do*.

Values Concerning Equality Versus Inequality

Condon (1977) provides the differences between horizontal and vertical relationships in terms of symmetrical and complementary relationships:

Symmetrical relationships maximize similarity of age, sex, role, or status and serve to encourage the apparent differences of each individual as an individual. Complementary relationships maximize differences in age, sex, role, or status and serve to encourage the mutuality of the relationship, the interdependence. (pp. 53–54)

In horizontal cultures, people are presumed to be equal or egalitarian and symmetrical in their relationships (Okabe, 1983). Klopf (1987) points out that in horizontal cultures, such as the United States, people believe that humans are created equal; therefore, running through American interpersonal relationships is this theme of equality.

In sharp contrast, people of vertical cultures are assumed to be unequal or unegalitarian and complementary in their relationships. People in such cultures are divided into numerous groupings, each structured along multiple status levels (Okabe, 1983); hence, people tend to shape their interpersonal relations in accordance with the various levels of hierarchy. Most Eastern cultures are characterized as vertical cultures in which interpersonal relationships take place on hierarchical levels that supply individuals with guidelines concerning how to be-

have. Interpersonal communication rules in these cultures give individuals direction regarding whom to talk to, when, and how. In addition, interpersonal communication in these cultures is structured according to status; hence, it is relatively predictable (Klopf, 1987). In Asian, African, and Middle Eastern cultures, age is a predictor of status (Dodd, 1983, p. 221). For example, in most Eastern cultures, respect and loyalty toward older people is absolute (Klopf, 1987). Especially in immediate and extended family contexts, younger individuals show honor and courtesy to older ones in ways not usually practiced by members of most Western cultures, such as the United States. In addition, differences in sex, status, and rank are maximized between participants in interpersonal communication situations in most Eastern cultures (Klopf, 1987).

Consequently, age and gender are key factors in friendship development in these cultures. In Japan, for instance, few close relationships develop if there is an age disparity. The closest relationships seem to be between those of almost identical age, and the partners are usually the same sex (Klopf, 1987). Same sex friendship in Eastern cultures is supported by a proposition from Cronen and Shulter (1983, p. 112), "the more vertically oriented a culture is, the more the individuals are attracted to same sex friendships."

Values Concerning Formality Versus Informality

Interpersonal communication style also plays an important role in the course of relationship development. In horizontal cultures, for example, communicators frequently are informal because of the complementary relationships among people, whereas they are formal in vertical cultures because of symmetrical relationships among people. Okabe (1983) points out that in a horizontal culture such as North America, people tend to treat others with informality and directness. They avoid the use of formal codes of conduct, titles, honorifics, and ritualistic manners in their interactions with others. They may prefer a first-name basis and direct address. They endeavor to equalize their language in their interpersonal relations regardless of differences in age, sex, status, and rank. In sharp contrast, in a hierarchical culture, such as Japan, people believe that formality in interpersonal relations is essential. The value of formality in verbal and nonverbal styles allows for a smooth and predictable interaction for the Japanese. They cannot communicate unless they know the status of the other person, because both verbal and nonverbal communication styles depend upon the status of the other person (Okabe, 1983; Stewart, 1972).

Relationships between students and teachers are formal in most Eastern cultures. Feig and Blair (1975), for instance, state that in Iran and Turkey when the teacher enters a classroom, all the students stand. When the students meet a teacher, they bow. Iranian teachers who allow their students to treat them without respect are not taken seriously by the students. Moreover, Iranian students lose respect for teachers who are too friendly and common with them.

Values Concerning Uncertainty Reduction

The process of uncertainty reduction plays an important role in developing and expanding interpersonal relationships. The function of interpersonal communication is to reduce uncertainty and to increase predictability of communication interactants' behaviors (Berger & Calabrese, 1975). The amount of uncertainty reduced affects the nature of the communication that occurs. For example, a decrease in uncertainty brings about an increase in communication and interpersonal attraction. If the amount of uncertainty in initial interaction is not reduced, further communication will be difficult and the relationship may not continue (Gudykunst & Kim, 1984; Gudykunst, Ting-Toomey, & Chua, 1988). The reward of uncertainty reduction is security within the individual communication interactants and the desire to continue the relationship.

Hall (1976) uses low- and high-context schema to illustrate differences in uncertainty reduction processes in horizontal cultures versus vertical cultures. He characterizes horizontal cultures as *low-context* cultures and vertical cultures as *high-context* cultures. Therefore, Hall (1976) draws a distinction between high-context and low-context communication by suggesting that:

A high-context communication or message is one in which most of the information is either in physical context or is internalized in the person, while very little is in the coded, transmitted, explicit part of the message. A low-context communication is just the opposite, i.e., the mass of information is vested in explicit codes. (p. 79)

Low-context cultures are heterogeneous in terms of norms and values, and are classified as individualistic cultures in which people may disagree upon specific norms and values. High-context cultures are homogeneous in terms of norms and values, in many aspects of daily life, and in consciousness, and are classified as collectivistic. Such cultures demand individuals to conform to cultural norms and values and to identify with the groups to which they belong.

Triandis (1989) goes further still and classifies high-context cultures and low-context cultures as *tight* cultures and *loose* cultures:

Tight cultures have norms that are reliably imposed. Little deviation from normative behavior is tolerated, and severe sanctions are administered to those who deviate. Loose cultures either have unclear norms about most social situations or tolerate deviance from the norm. (p. 511)

Thus, it can be generalized that in high-context cultures characterized as vertical, homogeneous, collectivistic, and tight, high-context communication is more likely to occur. Whereas, in low-context cultures classified as horizontal, heterogeneous, individualistic, and loose, low-context communication is more likely to occur. Therefore, because of these unique cultural characteristics, in the course of relationship development, high- and low-context cultures value and utilize distinctly differing types of uncertainty reduction strategies, which fall into three categories: (a) verbal versus nonverbal means, (b) background versus attitude information, and (c) high versus low rate of self-disclosure.

Oral Versus Nonoral Means. In the process of relationship development, members of high-context cultures reduce their uncertainties by utilizing relatively fewer oral means and more nonoral means than do members of low-context cultures, and they have a relatively higher level of accuracy in predicting others' behaviors, because information is internalized by the members or resides in the context (Gudykunst & Kim, 1984). Consequently, in high-context cultures people expect their fellow interactants to know what is on their minds (Hall, 1976).

The United States is characterized as a low-context culture because of its cultural diversity and heterogeneity, which make oral uncertainty reduction strategies more necessary and, therefore, more highly prized. Conversely, most non-Western cultures (for example, China, Korea, Japan, and Taiwan) are classified as high-context cultures because of their cultural homogeneity and collectivity, which encourage fewer oral than nonoral strategies (Okabe, 1983; Gudykunst & Nishida, 1984). For instance, Gudykunst and Nishida (1984) report that people in Japan display more nonoral affiliative expressiveness and express more confidence in predicting others' behaviors in the process of relationship development than do people in the United States, who use more interactive uncertainty reduction strategies, such as oral self-disclosure and interrogation.

Background Versus Attitude Information. In the process of relationship development, members of high-context cultures and low-context cultures seek distinctly different types of information for the purposes of uncertainty reduction and prediction of others' future behaviors. Members of high-context cultures, such as most non-Western cultures, are interested in gathering background (demographic) information, such as what high school or university a person attended, his or her hometown, the company for which he or she works, the father's occupa-

tion, and the religious background (Gudykunst & Kim, 1984; Nakane, 1984). In these cultures, most of the information is internalized in the members or in the physical contexts (Hall, 1976) and people are able to reduce uncertainty and obtain a high level of accuracy in predicting others' future behaviors by making a rich array of dependable inference from these types of information (Alexander, Cronen, Kang, Tsou, & Banks, 1980; Gudykunst, 1983; Gudykunst, Ting-Toomey, & Chua, 1988). Therefore, it is the background information that allows people in high-context cultures to determine whether or not a person is indeed unknown (Nakane, 1984). Perhaps this is the major reason why members of these cultures are often reluctant to provide this type of information in certain communication situations.

By contrast, in low-context cultures, such as the United States, people are not able to reduce uncertainty to the same degree by using background information. They seek information on others' attitudes and values, such as: What kind of food do you like? or, What kinds of books do you read? or, What movies do you watch? They, perhaps, make relatively fewer inferences from this type of information (Alexander, Cronen, Kang, Tsou, & Banks, 1980; Gudykunst, 1983).

High Versus Low Rate of Self-Disclosure. People of low-context, horizontal cultures value self-disclosure more than people of high-context, vertical cultures in the course of relationship development. For instance, Americans tend to maximize their "public selves," that is, they disclose more about themselves than do the Japanese, who are apt to keep their "private selves" to a maximum in their interpersonal interactions (Barnlund, 1974; Okabe, 1983; Condon, 1977). As regards the significant difference in the rate of self-disclosure of Americans and Japanese, Barnlund (1989) states:

While American image suggests substantial disclosure to close acquaintances because of an equal status, an emphasis on verbal expression, and greater social spontaneity, the Japanese image

*suggests somewhat less disclosure due to more for-
mal relationships, the higher value placed on harmony, and the lesser importance attached to
purely verbal forms of disclosure. (p. 108)*

For example, Japanese friendship rarely involves
self-disclosure (Barnlund, 1989), while Americans
tend to disclose about themselves at a higher rate
(D'Honnau, 1979; Plog, 1968; Strassberg & Anchor,
1975). Moreover, the results of a comparison study
on rate of self-disclosure in nine Eastern cultures
conducted by Melikan (1962) showed no significant
differences in low self-disclosure rates among these
cultures.

Values concerning low self-disclosure rates in
Eastern cultures versus Western cultures can be attributed to the complementary characteristic of interpersonal relationships in these cultures, where
people have been conditioned to conceal their
thoughts, feelings, and emotions for the purpose of
retaining harmonious interpersonal relationships
with those around them, especially with members
of their immediate and extended families.

Values Concerning a
Common Interest Versus
Acceptance

In the United States, which is heterogeneous and
technological, relationships are formed primarily
around activities, such as work, children's schools,
charities, political activities, leisure, and various occasions for sharing food and drink (Gudykunst &
Kim, 1984). In addition, because of the individualistic nature of American society, people tend to limit
relationships to an area of common interest (Stewart,
1972). That is, relationships are compartmentalized
(Klopf, 1987) and centered around a specific activity
(Feig, 1980).

From early childhood, Americans are raised not
to expect all things from one person. Consequently,
as Feig (1980) mentions, Americans apportion their
personalities to some degree, and they view others
as composites of distinct accomplishments and interests. For instance, they may have a friend for playing bridge, another for socialization, and a third for

playing tennis. Consequently, their friendships are
not expected to be profound (Glenn, 1966). Hence,
they have different friends for different activities.

This activity-oriented nature of friendship reflects the U.S. value concerning the importance of
each individual and the maximizing of fulfillment of
individual needs. For Americans, a relationship is
considered healthy to the extent that it serves the
expected activity for each of the involved parties.
This activity-oriented nature, coupled with great social mobility, contributes to the relatively unstable
and impermanent nature of interpersonal relationships in the United States and other technologically
advanced Western cultures. As people move from
one residence or job to another, few friends are retained in lasting relationships. Instead, people look
forward to establishing a new circle of friends with
whom they can share mutually helpful and satisfying
social functions and activities (Gudykunst & Kim,
1984). According to Stewart (1972), older, middle-
class, conservative Americans avoid personal commitments to others and are reluctant to get involved
in an obligatory manner.

In contrast to the United States, in most non-
Western cultures that are homogeneous and less
technological, relationships are imposed according
to birth, schooling, work, and residence. Intimate
relationships tend to develop as a consequence of
prolonged affiliations rather than by actively seeking them out. The primary basis for many interpersonal relationships in non-Western cultures does
not depend so much upon specific activities that
people do with or for each other, as on mutual liking and affection for each other's disposition and
temperament. Their emphasis is on a more generalized acceptance of the whole person. Once a relationship has developed into an intimate one, it often
is expected to last throughout life (Gudykunst &
Kim, 1984).

For instance, the importance of friendship for
members of most Islamic cultures, such as Iran and
Saudi Arabia, is seen in terms of brotherhood and
sisterhood, embracing the whole person. Most
friendships are formed in this manner. When friendship becomes more intimate, it is often extended
over a few generations.

In sum, while in most Western cultures (for example, the United States) people tend to limit friendship to an area of common interest, people in most non-Western cultures tend to be more person-oriented, embracing the whole person as a friend (Stewart, 1972).

CONCLUSION

Today, people from diverse cultural groups interact at a more accelerated rate than in any previous era, which undoubtedly will increase by the twenty-first century. During such interaction, however, communicators may have previously established negative attitudes about one another. As a result, each attempts to employ values and interpersonal communication skills that have been acquired within the respective culture. Under these conditions, however, literature on bonding suggests that the interaction will not be effective, and that interpersonal communication bonds will not be developed.

Relying heavily on the literature reviewed in this paper, several pragmatic suggestions can be made to enhance attempts to develop effective interpersonal bonds across cultures. First, communicators must realize that cultural diversities are valuable resources that should be preserved and extended. Second, the communicators should replace their ethnocentric prejudicial attitudes with positive ones. Third, they should accept, respect, and be willing to interact with one another. Fourth, they should strive to understand each other's cultural similarities and dissimilarities, including interpersonal communication approaches. Fifth, they should be flexible enough to adjust to the others' dissimilarities, so that they can predict and respond appropriately to the others' behavior. Finally, they must realize that mutual awareness of distinctive cultural approaches to bonding development is beneficial to bonding development, and be receptive to alternative cultural approaches (Gudykunst, Ting-Toomey, & Chua, 1988).

Although, individuals of the cultures discussed herein might perceive the opposite culture's communication approaches as an incomprehensible, complex maze, adequate information serves as a roadmap through it (Servaes, 1988). The desire to remove the barriers to intercultural communication is nearly universal as we move toward the ideal of a global community (Gudykunst & Kim, 1984; Gudykunst, Ting-Toomey, & Chua, 1988; Servaes, 1988). Members of Eastern and Western cultures need to understand the complexity of developing intercultural bonds to enhance intercultural friendship.

NOTE

Both authors wish to thank William J. Starosta and Melbourne S. Cummings for their insightful comments and suggestions.

REFERENCES

Alexander, A., Cronen, V. E., Kang, W. K., Tsou, B., & Banks, J. (1980). *Pattern of topic sequencing and information gain: A comparative study of relationship development in Chinese and American cultures*. Paper presented at the Speech Communication Association Convention, New York.

Altman, I., & Taylor, D. A. (1983). *Social penetration: The development of interpersonal relationships*. New York: Holt, Rinehart, Winston.

Barnlund, D. S. (1974). The public self and the private self in Japan and the United States. In J. C. Condon & M. Saito (Eds.), *Intercultural encounters with Japan: Communication-contact and conflict*. Tokyo: Simul Press.

Barnlund, D. S. (1989). *Communication style of Japanese and Americans: Images and reality*. Belmont, CA: Wadsworth.

Berger, C., & Calabrese, R. (1975). Some exploration in initial interaction and beyond. *Human Communication Research*, 1, 99–112.

Boechner, P. A. (1984). The functions of human communication in interpersonal bonding. In C. C. Arnold & J. W. Bowers (Eds.), *Handbook of rhetorical and communication theory* (pp. 554–621). Boston: Allyn and Bacon.

Casey, K., & Vanceburg, C. (1983). *The promise of a new day*. New York: Harper & Row.

Condon, C. J. (1977). *Interpersonal communication*. New York: Macmillan.

Cronen, V. E., & Shulter, R. (1983). Forming intercultural bonds. In W. B. Gudykunst (Ed.), *Intercultural communication theory* (pp. 89–118). Beverly Hills: Sage.

D'Honnau, M. (1979). Question of the week: Do you have many Japanese friends? *Japan Times*, 30 September.

Dodd, H. C. (1983). *Dynamics of intercultural communication*. Dubuque, IA: Wm. C. Brown.

Feig, J. (1980). *Thais and North Americans*. Chicago, IL: International Press.

Feig, J., & Blair, J. (1975). *There is a difference*. Washington, DC: Meridien.

Glenn, E. (1966). Meaning and behavior. *Journal of Communication*, 16, 29–36.

Gudykunst, W. (1983). Uncertainty reduction and predictability of behavior in low- and high-context cultures: An exploratory study. *Communication Quarterly*, 31, 49–55.

Gudykunst, W. B., & Kim, Y. Y. (1984). *Communicating with strangers: An approach to intercultural communication*. Palo Alto, CA: Addison-Wesley.

Gudykunst, W., & Nishida, T. (1984). Social penetration in close friendships in Japan and the United States. In R. Bastrom (Ed.), *Communication Yearbook*, 7, Beverly Hills, CA: Sage.

Gudykunst, W. B., & Ting-Toomey, S., with Chua, E. (1988). *Culture and interpersonal communication*. Newbury Park, CA: Sage.

Hall, E. T. (1976). *Beyond culture*. New York: Anchor.

Jourard, S. (1961). Self-disclosure patterns in British and American college formats. *Journal of Social Psychology*, 54, 315–320.

Klopf, W. D. (1987). *Intercultural encounters: The fundamentals of intercultural communication*. Inglewood, CA: Morton.

Knapp, M. L. (1987). *Social intercourse: From greeting to goodbye*. Boston, MA: Allyn and Bacon.

Maruyama, M. (1961). *The intellectual traditions in Japan*. Tokyo: Jeuanami Shoten.

Melikan, L. (1962). Self-disclosure among university students in the Middle East. *Journal of Social Psychology*, 57, 257–263.

Nakane, C. (1984). The social system reflected in interpersonal communication. In J. Condon & M. Saito (Eds.), *Intercultural encounters with Japan*. Tokyo: Simul Press.

Okabe, R. (1983). Cultural assumptions of East and West. In W. B. Gudykunst (Ed.), *Intercultural communication theory* (pp. 21–44). Beverly Hills: Sage.

Plog, S. (1968). The disclosure of self in the United States and Germany. *Journal of Social Psychology*, 65, 193–203.

Reardon, K. K. (1987). *Intercultural communication: Where minds meet*. Belmont, CA: Wadsworth.

Samovar, L. A., Porter, R. E., & Jain, N. C. (1981). *Understanding intercultural communication*. Belmont, CA: Wadsworth.

Servaes, J. (1988). Cultural identity in East and West. *The Howard Journal of Communications*, 1, 58–71.

Stewart, E. C. (1972). *American cultural patterns: A cross-cultural perspective*. Washington, DC: Society of Intercultural Education, Training, and Research.

Strassberg, D., & Anchor, K. (1975). Rating intimacy of self-disclosure. *Psychology Reports*, 37, 562.

Triandis, C. H. (1989). The self and social behavior in differing cultural contexts. *Psychology Review*, 96, 506–517.

Dominant Cultural Patterns of Hindus in India

NEMI C. JAIN
ELLEN D. KUSSMAN

For more than 3000 years, the peoples of the Indian subcontinent have sought the deepest truths in order to transform limited and imperfect human life into potential greatness. Their insights and discoveries have shaped what many consider one of the world's richest and most long-lived cultures.

India has been the cradle of several religions: Hinduism, Jainism, Buddhism, and Sikhism. The great majority of her people follow Hinduism, which can be taken to mean simply "the religion of India" (Ellwood, 1992). During the last 1200 years, India has also been influenced by Islam, Christianity, and Judaism, and thus has become one of the most culturally pluralistic societies in the world. Like any other culture, Indian culture is complex and consists of many interrelated beliefs, values, norms, social systems, and artifacts. In spite of its multiethnic, multilingual, and highly stratified nature, India is united by a set of cultural patterns that is widely shared among the Hindus living in India and abroad. The term *cultural patterns* refers to "the systematic and often repetitive nature of human behavior, interaction, and organization . . . human behavior is channeled and constrained by underlying systems that impose regularity and rules on what otherwise might be random activity" (Damen, 1987, p. 110).

Hinduism is an amorphous body of beliefs, philosophies, worship practices, and code of conduct. In its present form, Hinduism embraces many often contradictory beliefs and practices. Its essential spirit, however, seems to be "live and let live." The very nature of Hinduism leads to a great tolerance of other religions as followers tend to believe that the highest divine powers complement one another for the well-being of humanity and the universe. Hinduism, because of its resilience, absorption, and respect for alternative ways of reaching the same goals, has maintained vitality since its inception. As a dominant force, it influences the cultural patterns and communication behavior of over a half billion Hindus in India and abroad.

India is a most suitable culture for study because of her preeminence in Asia, her leadership role among developing nations, and her increasing participation in international affairs. In addition, Indian culture provides an instructive contrast to American cultural patterns. The purpose of this article is to discuss briefly (1) the Hindu world view; (2) belief in reincarnation; (3) the concept of *karma*; (4) the aims of human life; (5) paths to salvation; (6) the concept of *dharma*; (7) the Indian caste system, and (8) the spirit of tolerance.

Each of these cultural patterns includes numerous assumptions, beliefs, values, and norms that are overlapping and closely interrelated. Within the same culture, variations of cultural patterns normally occur. In fact, contradictions among cultural patterns are probably universal throughout societies. At times we may simplify and make firm generalizations to avoid constant use of qualifiers. Despite internal variations and contradictions, we believe these eight cultural patterns provide a useful description of Hindu Indian culture.

WORLD VIEW

World view refers to a set of interrelated assumptions and beliefs about the nature of reality, the organization of the universe, the purposes of human

This article was prepared especially for this edition. All rights reserved. Permission to reprint must be obtained from the authors and the publisher. Professor Jain teaches in the Department of Communication and is a Research Fellow in the Center for Asian Studies at Arizona State University. Ellen Kussman is a doctoral candidate in Intercultural Communication at Arizona State University.

life, God, and other philosophical issues concerned with the concept of being (Samovar & Porter, 1991). India's great sages and philosophers have sought to understand the deepest level of reality and to satisfy the deep human longing for spiritual fulfillment. The quest generated the basic Indian wisdom that the fundamental energizing power of the cosmos and the spiritual energy of human beings are one and the same. Because of our participation in the ultimate energy and power of reality, it is possible to transform our superficial, suffering, and limited existence into a free and boundless one. This spiritual transformation has constituted the ultimate aim in life for most Indian people over the ages (Koller, 1982).

The origins and development of the Hindu world view can best be understood in terms of the following concepts: (1) undivided wholeness and ultimate reality; (2) levels of reality; and (3) the normative dimension of reality.

Undivided Wholeness and Ultimate Reality

According to Hinduism, the world of distinct and separate objects and processes is a manifestation of a more fundamental reality that is undivided and unconditional. This undivided wholeness constituting the ultimate level of reality is known by various names: *Brahman, Ātman, Puruṣa, Jīva, Allah*, and Lord. What is especially important about this belief is that, first, the ultimate reality is not seen as separate and apart from ordinary things and events, but is the inner being and energizing force of everyday existence. Initially developed in the sacred ancient Hindu scriptures, the Vedas and Upaniṣads, this belief is an integral part of Hinduism, Jainism, Buddhism, and Yoga (Koller, 1982).

Second, existence at the deepest level is boundless in the sense that all possibilities may coexist without excluding or comprising one another. Time, space, the number of gods and goddesses, and so on are endless. Indian mythology especially celebrates the idea that opposites not only exist together but enrich one another with all of their differences arising simultaneously in an unrestricted universe of infinite freedom.

Third, the ultimate reality is so profound that reason is incapable of apprehending it. Human reason is an effective faculty for guiding our investigations of the empirical world and for understanding the rules of our practical and theoretical activities. Since it operates by differentiating and comparing, however, it is incapable of comprehending the deepest dimensions of reality that are beyond all divisions and differences. This profound nature of reality underlies Indian mysticism and encourages the emphasis upon Yoga and meditation (Koller, 1982).

Finally, the ultimate reality has no form and no name. What can be given a name and form is not the ultimate. From ancient Vedic times to the present, however, the ultimate reality has been symbolized by unlimited numbers of gods and goddesses who participate partially in the higher reality that they symbolize, pointing to the fullness of that reality. This is why a Hindu can say in the same breath that there are millions of gods, only one god, and no gods. The last two statements mean, respectively, that all gods symbolize the one ultimate reality and that this reality cannot be captured entirely by one symbol. But that a deity is not the ultimate reality does not mean it is unreal. On the contrary, because the deity as symbol participates in the deeper levels of reality, its reality is greater than that of our ordinary existence. Through rituals and devotion to gods and goddesses, it is believed that one can achieve a spiritual transformation of life.

Levels of Reality

Within the undivided wholeness of the totality of existence, there are various levels of reality. These range from nonexistence to empirical existence limited by space and time, to consciousness limited only by conditions of awareness, to an indescribable level beyond all conditions and limits whatsoever. The deeper the level of reality, the more fully one participates in the truth of being. One of the clearest examples of the tendency to distinguish between levels of reality occurs in the Taittirīya Upaniṣad, where five different levels of reality composing the "Self" are identified:

At the lowest level the Self is material and identified with food. At the next level the Self is identified with life: "Different from and within that which consists of the essence of food is the Self consisting of life." Identifying a still higher level of reality, the text goes on to say, "Different from and within that which consists of the essence of life is the Self which consists of mind (rudimentary forms of awareness that humans share with other animals)." Next, a fourth level of reality is recognized. Here is a still deeper source of consciousness and existence: the Self said to be of the nature of understanding (Vijñāna). *Finally, the Self is identified with joy as the fifth and ultimate level of reality. Joy* (ānanda) *or bliss is regarded as the root or source of all existence, the foundation of higher consciousness, lower consciousness, life, and matter (Koller, 1982, p. 101).*

Normative Dimension of Reality

The deepest level of reality is normative. According to Hinduism, norms for right living are an integral part of the fabric of human existence — they are not derived from human reason and are not imposed on life from the outside. The foundation of norms is much deeper than reason; it emanates from the very nature and expression of reality at its deepest level. Human reason only interprets and applies the norms of true or right living.

In the West, norms are usually conceived as rationally derived to fulfill human needs and aspirations. In India, it is generally recognized that a person who is true to the inner norms of existence has incredible power. Human existence is regarded as a manifestation and expression of a deeper reality. The fundamental norm of the universe is the orderly coursing of this deeper reality in its central being. Moral and social rules are partial expressions of this highest norm. The normative dimensions of the interconnected reality refer to the Hindu concept of *dharma*.

BELIEF IN REINCARNATION

In Hinduism, the Supreme Being is the impersonal *Brahman*, the ultimate level of reality, a philosophical absolute, serenely blissful, beyond all ethical or metaphysical limitations. The basic Hindu view of God involves infinite being, infinite consciousness and infinite bliss. *Brahmā* is conceived of as the Supreme Soul of the universe. Every living soul is a part, a particular manifestation, of the *Brahmā*. Individual souls seem to change from generation to generation, but actually only the unimportant, outer details change — a body, a face, a name, a different condition or status in life. The *Brahmā*, however, veiled behind these deceptive "realities," is continuous and indestructible. This hidden self or *ātman* is a reservoir of being that never dies, is never exhausted, and is without limit in awareness and bliss. *Ātman*, the ultimate level of reality at the individual level, is the infinite center of every life. Body, personality, and *ātman* together make up a human being (Smith, 1958).

The eternal *ātman* is usually buried under the almost impenetrable mass of distractions, false ideas, illusions, and self-regarding impulses that compose one's surface being. Life is ordinarily lived at a relatively superficial level, a level at which the ultimate reality is experienced only in fragmented and limited forms. These fragmented and partial forms of existence are actually forms of bondage, restricting access to the full power or energy of life flowing from the deepest level of reality. The aim of life is to cleanse the impurity from one's being to the point where its infinite center, the eternal *ātman*, will be fully manifest.

The Hindu belief in reincarnation affirms that individual souls enter the world and pass through a sequence of bodies or life cycles. On the subhuman level, the passage is through a series of increasingly complex bodies until at last a human one is attained. Up to this point, the soul's growth is virtually automatic. With the soul's graduation into a human body, this automatic, escalator mode of ascent comes to an end. The soul's assignment to this exalted habitation is evidence that it has reached self-consciousness, and with this state comes freedom, responsibility, and effort. Now the individual soul, as a human being, is fully responsible for its behavior through the doctrine of *karma* — the moral law of cause and effect. The present condition of each individual life is a product of what one did in the previous life; and one's present acts, thoughts, and decisions determine one's future states (Smith, 1958).

CONCEPT OF *KARMA*

Karma means basically action or activity. Actions always imply cause and effect, for nothing in this world acts or moves without an impelling cause. *Karma*, therefore, also refers to that chain of cause and effect, set in motion by one's deeds in the world. Sooner or later, through inexorable laws of justice built into *dharma*, they rebound to affect one's own future. As one sows, so one reaps (Ellwood, 1992, p. 64).

The concept of *karma* and the completely moral universe it implies carries two important psychological corollaries. First, it commits the Hindu who understands it to complete personal responsibility. Each individual is wholly responsible for his or her present condition and will have exactly the future he or she is now creating. Conversely, the idea of a moral universe closes the door to all appeals to chance or accident. In this world, there is no chance or accident. *Karma* decrees that every decision must have its determinate consequences, but the decisions themselves are, in the last analysis, freely arrived at. Or, to approach the matter from another direction, the consequences of a person's past decisions condition his or her present lot, as a card player is dealt a particular hand but is left free to play that hand in a number of ways. This means that the general conditions of life — rank, station, position — are predetermined by one's past *karma*. However, individual humans as carriers of a soul are free to determine actions independently of the soul (Smith, 1958).

According to Hinduism, the ultimate aim of life is to free oneself progressively from the exclusive identification with the lower levels of the self in or-

der to realize the most profound level of existence. Since at this deepest level, the self is identical with ultimate reality — the *Brahman* — once this identity has been realized, there is nothing that can defeat or destroy the self. Thus, the soul puts an end to the process of reincarnation and merges with the *Brahman*, from whence it originated in the first place. This state for an individual soul is called *moksha, mukti, nirvāna* or liberation.

AIMS OF HUMAN LIFE

What do human beings want? What are the aims of human life? Hindu saints and philosophers have pondered these questions for a long time and have provided some interesting insights into human needs, wants, desires, motivations, and values. According to Hinduism, all people have four legitimate basic aims of human life: (1) *kāma*, pleasure or enjoyment; (2) *artha*, wealth or success; (3) *dharma*, righteousness, faithful duty or code of conduct; and (4) *moksha*, liberation or salvation. These four aims have constituted the basis of Indian values. Indian literature concerned with moral and social life accepts these four aims as fundamental in life. Taken together, these aims define the good life for a Hindu, giving a sense of direction to guide a person to what he or she may and may not aim at in life (Jain, 1991).

Hinduism recognizes the importance of enjoyment or *kāma* in human life. This is natural because we are all born with built-in pleasure-pain reactors and human senses. The concept of *kāma* is used in two ways in Indian literature. In the narrower sense, *kāma* is sexual desire and is symbolized by *Kāma*, the love god. *Kāma Sūtra*, along with a number of other texts, provides instructions on how to obtain the greatest sexual pleasures. As a basic human aim, however, *kāma* goes beyond this narrower sense of sexual pleasure to include all forms of enjoyment, including that of fame, fortune, and power.

A common stereotype of Indian people as so single-mindedly intent on religious salvation that there is no room for laughter, fun, or games is incorrect. Traditionally and currently, Hindus value stories, games, festivals, and parties filled with music, laughter, and fun! As a basic aim in life, *kāma* legitimizes the human pursuit of pleasure and recognizes that wealth and various goods are to be enjoyed as a way of fulfilling human nature.

India, however, has not taken pleasure as life's highest value. Hindus believe that the world holds immense possibilities for enjoyment through our senses. Moreover, there are other worlds above this one where pleasures mount by a factor of a million at each successive round; we shall experience these worlds too at later stages in our becoming (Smith, 1958). *Dharma* regulates the pursuit of pleasure at the various stages of life; for example, sexual activity is to be restricted to one's spouse and drugs and intoxicating beverages are regarded as wrong and sinful because of the injury they do. But, as long as the basic rules of morality are observed, one is free to seek all the pleasure one wishes.

The second aim of life is *artha* or worldly success (wealth, success, power, fame, and so on). Hinduism recognizes that worldly success is a worthy goal to be neither scorned nor condemned. Moreover, its satisfactions last longer than sensual pleasures. Unlike *kāma*, worldly success is a social achievement with implications for one's life, as well for one's family, relatives, caste group, and society. In this respect, it is a higher value than sensual pleasure. Although much of the Western world regards Indians as deliberately choosing poverty as a way of life, this is not true. The *Pañctantra*, a popular collection of Indian wisdom states: "Wealth gives constant vigor, confidence, and power. Poverty is a curse worse than death. Virtue without wealth is of no consequence. The lack of money is the root of all evil" (Koller, 1982, p. 65).

A certain limited amount of wealth is indispensable for one's living, for upkeeping a household, raising a family, and discharging civic duties. Beyond this minimum, worldly achievements bring to many a sense of dignity and self-respect. In the end, however, these too are found wanting. Like pleasure, rewards of wealth or worldly success are transient and short-lived. Humans seek the higher goals of *dharma* and *moksha* which are more lasting and fulfilling.

Dharma, the third aim of life, refers to the faithful performance of one's duties. Hinduism abounds in directives to men and women for performing their social roles and responsibilities. It sets forth in elaborate detail the duties that go with age, stages of life, gender, disposition, caste, and social status. Like the other two aims of human life, *dharma* also yields notable rewards but fails to satisfy the human heart completely. Faithful performance of duty brings the praise and appreciation of peers. More gratifying than this, however, is the self-respect that comes from having done one's part, of having contributed to society. In the end, even this realization cannot provide joy adequate to human spirit. The final aim of human life must still lie elsewhere (Smith, 1958).

According to Hinduism, the first three aims of life — pleasure, worldly success, and faithful duty — are never ultimate goals of human life. At best they are means that we assume will take us in the direction of what we really seek. First, we want being. Everyone wants "to be" rather than "not to be." Second, we want to know, to be aware. Third, human beings seek joy, a resolution of feelings in which the basic motifs are the opposite of frustration, futility, and boredom. Not only are these the things we want, we want each in infinite degree. To state the full truth, according to Hinduism, we must then say that what humans really want is infinite being, infinite knowledge, and infinite joy. To gather them together in a single word, what human beings really want is liberation or *moksha* (or *mukti*) — complete release from the countless limitations that press so closely upon present existence (Smith, 1958).

As the ultimate aim of human life, *moksha* guides one's efforts to realize identity with the *Brahman* but does not repudiate the other aims. Indeed, it calls for fulfilling these aims as a preparation for achieving complete freedom and fulfillment. Even when the distinction between worldly and spiritual existence becomes prominent, the tendency is to see the distinction in terms of higher and lower levels of the same reality than to postulate two different and opposing realities (Smith, 1958).

Thus, pleasure, worldly success, responsible discharge of duty, and liberation are the four aims of human life. These are what humans think they want, what they really want. What human beings most want, however, are infinite being, infinite awareness, and infinite joy. According to Hinduism, they are all within one's reach and can be attained through multiple paths to salvation (Smith, 1958).

PATHS TO SALVATION

Hinduism recognizes four different types of people: "Some are basically reflective. Others are primarily emotional. Still others are essentially active. Finally, some are most accurately characterized as experimental" (Smith, 1958, p. 35). A distinct path, or *yoga*, is suitable to a person's disposition and capacity for achieving salvation or *moksha*. The four paths are: (1) *jñāna yoga*, the path of knowledge; (2) *bhakti yoga*, the path of devotion; (3) *karma yoga*, the path of work; and (4) *rāja yoga*, the path of meditation.

Jñāna yoga, intended for individuals who have philosophical and intellectual orientations, attempts to overcome ignorance through the powers of knowledge and differentiation. Through logic and reflection, individuals strive to distinguish between the surface self and the larger Self that lies behind it. *Jñāna yoga* is the shortest but steepest path to salvation, and few people have the rare combination of rationality and spirituality required for it.

Jñāna yoga consists of three steps. The first, hearing, includes the study of scriptures and other philosophical writings in order to acquaint oneself with the concepts of self, the ultimate reality, and eternal being. The second step, thinking, encompasses intensive reflection and contemplation about the distinction between the self and Self. "If the *yogi* is able and diligent, such reflections will in due time build up a lively sense of the abiding Self that underlies his phenomenal personality" (Smith, 1953, p. 38). The third step, shifting self-identification from the passing to the eternal part of being, occurs through a variety of means, such as profound reflecting and thinking of one's finite self in the third person. The latter involves observing one's activities with calm detachment from a distance.

The second path to salvation, *bhakti yoga*, relies more on emotion than reason. The most powerful and pervasive emotion is love. "People tend to become like that which they love, with the name thereof progressively written on their brows. The aim of *bhakti yoga* is to direct toward God the geyser of love that lies at the base of every heart" (Smith, 1958, p. 39).

In contrast to *jñāna yoga*, *bhakti yoga* relies on religious worship and rituals through which people attempt to achieve the virtues of gods and goddesses. Hindus cherish gods' human incarnations, such as *Rāma* and *Krishna*, because they feel that gods can be loved most readily in human form. This is the most popular path currently followed in India.

Karma yoga, the third path to salvation, is intended for action-oriented people:

Work can be a vehicle for self-transcendence. Every deed a person does for the sake of his or her own private welfare adds another coating to the ego and in thus thickening it insulates it further from God within or without. Correlatively, every act done without thought of self diminishes self-centeredness until finally no barrier remains to cloud one from the divine (Smith, 1958, p. 45).

Depending on their dispositions, followers of *karma yoga* may choose to practice under the mode of *jñāna yoga* (knowledge) or *bhakti yoga* (devotion). For example, a *karma yogi* with an intellectual bent would engage in such activities as producing, disseminating, and utilizing knowledge. On the other hand, a *karma yogi* with a devotional outlook would be involved in activities such as social worship, religious festivals, and the construction of temples.

The final path of salvation, *rāja yoga*, is considered the royal way to salvation. Followers of *rāja yoga* are experimental in nature and believe that affairs of the spirit can be approached empirically. This path is based on the belief that ". . . our true selves are vastly more wonderful than we now realize and [on] a passion for direct experience of their full reach" (Smith, 1958, p. 51). Followers engage in physical, mental, and spiritual exercises through which they reach their inner spirits.

The four paths to salvation are not exclusive, because no person is solely of one disposition — either reflective, emotional, active, or experimental. "While most persons will, on the whole, find travel on one road more satisfactory than on others and will consequently tend to keep close to it, Hinduism encourages people to test all four and combine them as best suits their needs" (Smith, 1958, pp. 60–61). Each path of salvation, however, is guided by its appropriate *dharma*.

CONCEPT OF DHARMA

Dharma defines a code of conduct that guides the life of a person both as an individual and as a member of society. It is the law of right living, the observance of which secures the double objectives of happiness on earth and *moksha*. The life of a Hindu is regulated in a very detailed manner. Personal habits, social and family ties, fasts and feasts, religious rituals, obligations of justice and morality, and even rules of personal hygiene and food preparation are all conditioned by *dharma*.

Dharma, as a social value with a strong sense of morality, accounts for the cohesion in Hindu society. Harmony is achieved when everyone follows his or her own *dharma*. It is the system of norms supported by the general opinion, conscience, or spirit of the people. *Dharma* does not force people into virtue but trains them for it. It is not a fixed code of mechanical rules but a living spirit that grows and moves in response to the development of society (Koller, 1982).

The individual and social dimensions of *dharma* are interdependent. The conscience of the individual requires a guide, and one must be taught the way to realize one's aims of life and to live according to spirit and not senses. *Dharma*, at the social level, holds all living beings in a harmonious order. Virtue is conduct contributing to social welfare, and vice is opposite (Radhakrishnan, 1979).

Dharma is usually classified according to the requirements of one's state in life and one's position in society, for these two factors determine one's own specific *dharma*. Thus, at the individual level, *āśrama dharma* refers to duties attending one's particular stage in life. According to Hindu philosophy, human life consists of four stages or *āśramas*: student, householder, retiree, and renunciator (Jain, 1991, pp. 84–85). Specifically, the students' *dharma* includes obligations of sobriety, chastity, and social service. The householder stage requires marriage, raising a family, producing the goods necessary for society according to one's occupation, giving to the needy, and serving the social and political needs of the community. In the retiree stage, the individual is required to control his or her attachment to worldly possessions; it is the time for working out a philosophy for oneself, the time of transcending the senses to find and dwell at one with the timeless reality that underlies the dream of life in this world. Finally, the renunciator is a disinterested servant of humanity who finds peace in the strength of spirit and attempts to fulfill the ultimate aim of human life, *moksha* or liberation. This is also the stage of complete renunciation of worldly objects and desires.

Varṇa dharma, on the other hand, refers to the duties attending one's caste, social class, or position. The Hindu caste system and its relationship with *dharma* are discussed in more detail later.

Hinduism recognizes a *universal dharma* that applies to any person regardless of caste, social class, or stage in life. For example, telling the truth, avoiding unnecessary injury to others, not cheating, and so on are common *dharmas* that all human beings share. Other *dharmas* are determined by particular circumstances and therefore cannot be specified in advance. The rules for determining specific requirements of action in unusual and unpredictable situations is that the higher *dharmas* and values should always prevail. Noninjury and compassion are basic moral principles in deciding cases of conflicting moral duties, and one must never engage in behavior that is detrimental to spiritual progress (Koller, 1982).

CASTE SYSTEM

The caste system is a unique feature of Indian culture. No Indian social institution has attracted as much attention from foreign observers, nor has any other Indian institution been so grossly misunderstood, misrepresented, or maligned. Even the word *caste*, which is derived from the Portuguese *casta* (color), is a misnomer connoting some specious notion of color difference as the foundation of the system. It is a curious fact of intellectual history that caste has figured so prominently in Western thought.

The caste system began in India about 3000 years ago. During the second millenium B.C., a host of Aryans possessing a different language and culture and different physical characteristics (tall, fair-skinned, blue-eyed, straight-haired) migrated to India. The class of differences that followed eventually established the caste system because the Aryans took for themselves the kinds of work thought to be desirable: They became the rulers, the religious leaders, the teachers, and the traders. The other people were forced to become servants for the Aryans and to do less pleasing kinds of work. The outcome of this social classification and differentiation was a society clearly divided into four castes, hierarchically, from higher to lower:

1. *Brahmins* — seers or priests who perform such duties as teaching, preaching, assisting in the sacrificial processes, giving alms, and receiving gifts;

2. *Kashtryās* — administrators or rulers responsible for protecting life and treasures;

3. *Vaiśyas* — traders, business people, farmers, and herders;

4. *Śūdras* — artisans such as carpenters, blacksmiths, and laborers.

In the course of time, a fifth group developed that was ranked so low as to be considered outside and beneath the caste system itself. The members of this fifth "casteless" group are variously referred to as "untouchables," "outcastes," "scheduled castes," or (by Mahatma Gandhi) *Harijans* — "children of God." People in this group inherit the kinds of work that in India are considered least desirable, such as scavenging, slaughtering animals, leather tanning, and sweeping the streets (Chopra, 1977, pp. 27–29).

The caste system began as a straightforward, functional division of Hindu society. It was later misinterpreted by priests to be as permanent and as immutable as the word of God. Accordingly, the caste system was justified in terms of the "immutable and inborn" qualities of individuals, the unchangeable result of "actions in previous incarnations," and the unalterable basis of Hindu religion.

The caste system applies only to the Hindu segment of Indian society. The particular caste a person belongs to is determined by birth — one is born into the caste of his or her parents. Each caste has its appropriate status, rights, duties, and *dharma*. Detailed rules regulate communication and contact among people of different castes. A caste has considerable influence on the way of life of its members; the most important relationships of life, above all marriage, usually take place within the caste.

The merit of the caste system lay in its contribution to social stability and social security. Everyone has a known role to play and a group with whom to belong. The lower castes and outcastes are not necessarily happy with their role in the system as evidenced by the numbers who converted to other religions, especially Buddhism, Islam, and Christianity — all of which allowed them to escape from caste restrictions (Terpstra, 1978).

After India's independence in 1947, discrimination based on caste was outlawed. India has launched a massive social reform movement against "untouchability." There are numerous forms of affirmative action programs and quota systems aimed at promoting the welfare of "untouchables" and lower castes. These programs have produced many benefits for disadvantaged groups in the fields of education, employment, politics, and government. Unfortunately, there is still considerable prejudice and discrimination against untouchables, especially in the rural areas which comprise approximately 75% of India's population (Jain, 1992).

As any American knows, legislation is not always effective in bringing about immediate changes in social behavior. Sudden changes will not occur rapidly in India either, especially with a behavior pattern sanctioned by religion and 3000 years of tradition. In urban areas, it is more common for one to cross caste lines in choosing occupation and in marrying. In rural areas, on the other hand, caste remains a major influence in one's life.

The implications of the caste system for communication and economy are quite obvious and quite negative. To the degree that the caste system is rigidly followed, it limits communication between caste groups and hinders free flow of information. It becomes difficult to allocate human resources efficiently. If birth and caste determine work assignments, rather than ability and performance, the output of the economy suffers. Coordination and integration of the work force and management can also be hindered by caste restrictions. Occupational caste assignments derived centuries ago in an agrarian society are not likely to mesh with today's technological, urban, industrial society.

THE SPIRIT OF TOLERANCE

An outstanding feature of Indian culture is its tradition of tolerance. According to Hinduism, the reality or existence at the deepest level is boundless. No description, formula, or symbol can adequately convey the entire truth about anything. Each perspective provides a partial glimpse of reality, but none provides a complete view. Different partial–even opposing—viewpoints are regarded as complementing each other, each contributing something to a fuller understanding of reality.

Traditionally, Indian thinkers have been willing to adopt new perspectives and new positions without, however, abandoning old positions and perspectives. The new is simply added to the old, providing another dimension to one's knowledge. The new dimension may render the old less dominant or important, but it does not require the latter's rejection. The traditional storehouse of Indian ideas is like a four-thousand-year-old attic to which things were added every year but which was never once cleaned out (Koller, 1982).

Hindu culture believes in universal tolerance and accepts all religions as true. It is believed that the highest truth is too profound to allow anyone to get an exclusive grasp on it. When no beliefs can be said to be absolutely true, no beliefs can be declared absolutely false. Hindu culture is comprehensive and suits the needs of everyone, irrespective of caste, creed, color, or gender — it has universal appeal and makes room for all.

In Jainism, an offshot of Hinduism, the theory of *syādvāda*, or "may be," has further developed India's spirit of tolerance. According to this theory, no absolute affirmation or denial is possible. As all knowledge is probable and relative, another person's point of view is as true as one's own. In other words, one must show restraint in making judgments—a very healthy principle. One must know that one's judgments are only partially true and can by no means be regarded as true in absolute terms. This understanding and spirit of tolerance have contributed to the advancement of Indian culture, helping to bring together the divergent groups with different languages and religious persuasions under a common culture (Murthy & Kamath, 1973).

SUMMARY

This article has discussed eight dominant cultural patterns of Hindus in India: world view, belief in reincarnation, the concept of *karma*, the aims of human life, the reincarnation to salvation, the concept of *dharma*, the caste system, and the spirit of tolerance. These patterns have been integral parts of Hinduism and Indian culture for the last 3000 years. They have a significant influence on the personality, values, beliefs, and attitudes of Hindus in India and abroad. An understanding of Hindu cultural patterns and their influence on communication behavior will improve the quality of intercultural communication between people of India and other cultures.

REFERENCES

Chopra, S. N. (1977). *India: An Area Study*. New Delhi: Vikas Publishing House.

Damen, L. (1987). *Culture-learning: The Fifth Dimension in the Language Classroom*. Reading, MA: Addison-Wesley.

Ellwood, R. S. (1992). *Many Peoples, Many Faiths*. 4th ed. Englewood Cliffs, NJ: Prentice-Hall.

Jain, N. C. (1991). "World View and Cultural Patterns of India." In L. A. Samovar and R. E. Porter (Eds.), *Intercultural Communication: A Reader*, (pp. 78–87). 6th ed. Belmont, CA: Wadsworth.

Jain, N. C. (February, 1992). "Teaching About Communicative Life in India." Paper presented at the annual meeting of the Western Speech Communication Association, Boise, Idaho.

Koller, J. M. (1982). *The Indian Way*. New York: Macmillan.

Murthy, H. V. S., and Kamath, S. U. (1973). *Studies in Indian Culture*. Bombay: Asia Publishing House.

Radhakrishnan, S. (1979). *Indian Religions*. New Delhi: Vision Books.

Samovar, L. A., and Porter, R. E. (1991). *Communication Between Cultures*. Belmont, CA: Wadsworth.

Smith, H. (1958). *The Religions of Man*. New York: Harper & Row.

Terpstra, V. (1978). *Cultural Environments of International Business*. Cincinnati, OH: South-Western.

A Comparison of Arab and American Conceptions of "Effective" Persuasion

JANICE WALKER ANDERSON

This rhetorical analysis will illustrate that Americans and Saudis have different "rules" for political debate. "The rhetoric used in the Western world to describe the Arab-Israeli conflict is a prime example of the use of language, not as a means of illuminating reality," Abdel-Wahab El-Messiri (quoted by D. Ray Heisey, 1970) asserted, "but as a way of evading issues and complex historical totalities" (p. 12). In our modern global village, different conceptions of persuasion meet through the mass communication process.

Although mass media reports on events in the Middle East translate the words used by Arab leaders, the reports seldom explain the different cultural standards in Arab societies for evaluating reasonableness. "We can say that what is 'reasonable,'" intercultural communication scholars Condon and Yousef (1975) explain, "is not fully separable from cultural assumptions" (p. 213). This analysis indicates some of the differences between Arab and American cultural orientations toward what constitutes "effective" persuasion.

As Richard Barton (1982) argued in "Message Analysis in International Mass Communication Research," "the study of international media processes

From *The Howard Journal of Communications*, Vol. 2, No. 1 (Winter 1989–90), pp. 81–114. Reprinted by permission of the publisher. Janice Walker Anderson is in the Communication Department, College at New Paltz, State University of New York.

lags behind the general trend in mass communication study of systematically investigating the formal qualities of media discourse" (p. 82). This study is intended as a first step toward addressing a gap in current research on international mass communications.

This paper compares the rhetorical tactics in a Saudi government advocacy advertisement, or paid editorial, with those in a Mobil Oil Corporation advocacy advertisement. . . . Advocacy advertisements promote ideas rather than products and usually argue one side of a controversial social or political issue.[1] Both paid editorials examined in this study explain to the American public the rationale behind the Arab's oil boycott in 1973. The two advocacy ads employ radically different rhetorical tactics to accomplish similar objectives.

First, the analysis will provide a brief overview of some essential aspects of Arab orientations toward discourse. Then, it will briefly set the historical context for the ads. Finally, it will compare the rhetorical tactics in the two advocacy advertisements and summarize the different basic assumptions about persuasion implicit in each artifact.

ARAB ORIENTATIONS TOWARD DISCOURSE

Before beginning the analysis, it is first necessary to acquaint American readers with some of the basics of Arab and Moslem orientations toward argumentation. "While only a small percentage (about 10%) of present-day Arabs are Bedouins," Gudykunst and Kim explain in *Communicating with Strangers*, "contemporary Arab culture holds the Bedouin ethos as an ideal to which, in theory at least, it would like to measure up" (p. 50). While values such as materialism, success, activity, progress, and rationality are featured in American culture, Arab societies revolve around the core values of "hospitality, generosity, courage, honor, and self-respect" (p. 50).

As H. Samuel Hamod indicated in "Arab and Moslem Rhetorical Theory and Practice," storytellers performed a vital function for the Bedouin tribes because few people could read or write: "[T]heir tribal storytellers functioned as historians and moralists in recounting battles and instances of outstanding bravery and cunning" (p. 97). These storytellers, or what we today might call poets, performed important political functions by establishing a means for interpreting and directing action. As A. J. Almaney and A. J. Alwan (1982) explained, a poet's poems "might arouse a tribe to action in the same manner as . . . [a politician] in a modern political campaign. . . . He was both a molder and agent of public opinion" (p. 79). Some attributed magical powers to these storytellers because they controlled the power of language which could act upon the human emotions and rouse the people to action.

To this day, poets are held in the highest esteem in Arab societies. As a result, many educated Arabs will attempt to write poetry at some time in their careers. In 1983, for example, Sheik Mani Said al-Otaiba, an oil minister from the United Arab Emirates, wrote a poem about OPEC's (Organization of Petroleum Exporting Companies) troubles maintaining oil production quotas. The *New York Times* reported that this poem "seemed to cause more hard feelings among his colleagues than the discord over prices" (Lewis, p. 6).

The reporter, Paul Lewis, discounted the importance of the Sheik's poem, asserting that his most important contribution was a passage in his dissertation "which marked him as one of the first Arabs to say publicly that it was the Nixon Administration that encouraged [OPEC] to quadruple world oil prices in 1973 by suggesting the West had few, if any, alternatives" (p. 6). In this instance, Lewis underestimated the importance that Arabs ascribe to poetry. It frequently functions in a political context to motivate action, and, as such, it is accorded as much weight as a scholarly dissertation.

In addition, Arab cultures connect inspired language and religion. Arabic plays an important religious role in Islamic societies. All Muslims, regardless of their nationality, must use Arabic in their daily prayers. The language of the Quran is considered a miracle in itself because it was produced by the Prophet Mohammed, who was illiterate. Consequently, Muslims believe that the Quran cannot be faithfully translated into other languages (Almaney & Alwan, p. 79).

The power of words lay not in their ability to reflect human experience, but in their ability to transcend it, to reach toward that which lay beyond human experience — the divine. To this day, the Quran stands as the ultimate book of style and grammar for Arabs. The cultural equivalent in the West would be using the King James Version of the Bible as our style manual.

The Arab's appreciation for the persuasive power of the rhythm and sound of words leads to a style that relies heavily on devices that heighten the emotional impact of a message. Certain words are used in speaking that have no denotative meaning. "These are 'firm' words because the audience knows the purpose behind their use, and the words are taken as a seal of definiteness and sincerity on the part of the speaker" (Hamod, p. 100). Other forms of assertion, such as repetition and antithesis, are also quite frequent. Emphatic assertions are expected, Almaney and Alwan explain: "If an Arab says exactly what he means without the expected assertion, other Arabs may still think he means the opposite" (p. 84).

Hamod explains the reasoning behind the Arab's emphasis on stylistic concerns. "He who speaks well is well educated; he who is well educated is more qualified to render judgments and it is his advice we should follow. Eloquence and effectiveness were equated" (p. 98). An Arab writer establishes credibility by displaying ability and artistry with the language.

SETTING THE
HISTORICAL CONTEXT

Both advocacy ads faced a potentially hostile American audience in presenting their views about the Middle East. The advocacy ads appeared in 1973, the year of the first oil crisis. "The press at the time," Anthony Sampson (1975), oil industry analyst, explained, "were sympathetic to the Israelis" (p. 100).

Mobil's ad, "The U.S. Stake in Middle East Peace: I," appeared in June of 1973 when another war was brewing in the Middle East. "This ad turned out to be one of the most controversial messages we've ever run," Herbert Schmertz (1986), Mobil's vice president for public affairs explained:

The issue at hand was simply the future of America's oil supply, which boiled down to the need for recognizing the strategic importance of Saudi Arabia. Our critics accused us of running this ad at the behest of the Saudis, but there was no truth to this charge (p. 168).

The *New York Times* editorial board was so concerned about the content of Mobil's ad that they did not allow it to appear in Mobil's normal position on the op-ed page. Instead, the ad was buried in the second section of the newspaper, where it was more likely to be obscured by product ads.

The Saudi ad, entitled, "An Open Letter to the American People," appeared six months later. The Saudi ad ran in the *Washington Post* two months after the 1973 war in the Middle East began.[2] The ad appeared on New Year's Day just as the consequences of the oil boycott were beginning to be felt within the United States.

Although the Saudi ad was attributed to Mr. Omar Sakkaf, Saudi minister of state for foreign affairs, he was not necessarily the sole author. In a telephone interview, Dr. Mohammed Al-Zafer, a former Saudi diplomat to the United States and now deputy director of King Khaled University in Saudi Arabia, explained that Mr. Sakkaf had died about five years before. In describing the generation of the ad, Dr. Al-Zafer stated that diplomats stationed in the United States speak fluent English. However, they would not prepare statements for publication without "having them checked ahead of time." By attributing the ad to the minister of state of foreign affairs, the Saudis indicated that it was an accurate reflection of their perspective on events in the Middle East. It is not unreasonable to assume the author(s) of the ad were probably educated, cosmopolitan Saudi officials familiar with both English and Arabic.

COMPARISON OF
RHETORICAL STRATEGIES

The two ads demonstrated quite different responses to the hostile audience that they faced. Most immediately, the ads employed different strategies for framing their arguments. In addition, they used contrasting organizing principles. Finally, the ads provided different kinds of justifications for action.

Framing the Argument

Mobil's ad, "The U.S. Stake in Middle East Peace: I," employed an inductive opening. Instead of launching immediately into a discussion of foreign affairs, the author(s) first defined a domestic problem immediate to their readers. The opening five paragraphs of the ad documented the growing gap between domestic oil production and trends in energy consumption.

Because oil and natural gas supplied over three-quarters of the United States' energy, the author(s) asserted: "Our society cannot live without adequate oil supplies . . . much less continue as an industrial society." Although domestic consumption was increasing, domestic production was declining so that foreign oil already provided one third of the United States' energy needs. "In another seven years, or less," Mobil author(s) predicted, "we will be relying on foreign sources for more than half of our oil."

Our need for increased energy supplies provided the rationale for Mobil's discussion of the Middle East. Because only the Middle East had sufficient oil reserves to meet U.S. demand, the ad concluded: "Like it or not, the United States is dependent on the Middle East even just to maintain our present living standards in the years immediately ahead."

In framing its argument, the Mobil author(s) demonstrated a typically American tendency to assume that "the world is rational in the sense that . . . events . . . can be explained and the reasons for particular occurrences can be determined" (Stewart, 1972, p. 35). Statistics described the "objective" reality of energy demand. These rational "facts" created

the necessity for action. "For Americans," Stewart explains, "the world is composed of facts — not ideas. Their process of thinking is generally inductive, beginning with facts and then proceeding to ideas" (p. 22).

The introduction of the Saudi ad, in contrast, was not concerned with the facts of energy supply and demand. It focused on competing perspectives. This "Open Letter to the American People" obliquely addressed the concerns of five distinct audiences: the American people, the American press, the "American friends of Israel," other Arab nations, and the "world in general." The first five paragraphs of the ad acknowledged the subgroups whose competing perspectives created the complexity of the political dynamics of the Middle East.

This complexity was reflected through the use of parallel structure to express contrasting ideas:

We, the Arabs, wish you a Happy New Year. Your holiday season might have been marred by the hardships of the energy crisis. Ours is haunted by the threat of death and continued aggression.

The antithesis highlighted the contrast in perspectives between the American people and the Arab people. It implicitly addressed the contrast between American materialistic values and Arab values of honor and self-respect. On the broad level of justice between nations of the world, economic hardships such as gas lines paled in comparison to displacement from a homeland.

The language structure of the opening appealed to a human tendency to respond to the rhythm of language, to enjoy, as Kenneth Burke pointed out, seeing the completion of a "form." Although American readers might not understand the content of the antithesis, they would unconsciously respond to the rhythm. The Saudi author(s) employed parallel structure to draw readers into their interpretation of the world. The literacy device illustrated the author(s)' sophistication with the language, thereby establishing their credibility through traditional means within Arab cultures.

By emphasizing the contrast between American and Arab perspectives, the opening simultaneously minimized the contrast between the Arab countries of Syria, Egypt, Jordan, and Saudi Arabia. "We, the Arabs" imposed a unitary perspective based on linguistic, religious, and cultural commonalities, not on national boundaries. "North Americans value individual centeredness and self-reliance," Gudykunst and Kim explain, "the Arabic attitude is one of mutual dependence" (p. 126). The Saudi author(s) would not perceive distinctions between individual Arab nations as particularly salient in the way that North Americans would.

But it is not in bitterness that we address this message to you and it is our hope that there will be no bitterness in you as you read it.

As though acknowledging that the American public might read the initial literary flourish as a stark exaggeration, the author(s) followed one verbal flourish with another designed to soften the impact of the first. This parallel structure emphasized commonalities. It indicated that the assertion in the opening was not intended to offend the American people. Overstatement simply indicated the sincerity of the author(s)' intentions and the seriousness of the topic. "To Arabs," Gudykunst and Kim explain, ". . . a soft tone implies weakness or even deviousness" (p. 161).

We have been under continuous attack from the American Press—with notable exceptions—for two decades, and we must confess we are unable to understand the reasoning behind this overwhelming hostility. We lived in Palestine for two thousand years, and when we resisted displacement by a foreign state, the Americans branded us aggressors.

The parallel structure was broken as this paragraph introduced two additional contrasting perspectives: the American media's portrayal of Arabs as aggressors versus the Arabs' view of themselves as victims. This paragraph employed a cultural commonplace meaningful within the Arab community. The two-thousand-year context the Saudi author(s) established and the use of the name "Palestine" emphasized the Israelis' role as interlopers. In this paragraph, the Saudi author(s) echoed the comments of Abdel-Wahab El-Messiri, arguing that the American media did not excel in describing "complex historical totalities."

"But let that pass," the fourth paragraph continued, once again backing away from the emotional tone that had been established, again indicating to the American audience that statements of Arab beliefs were not intended to initiate a hostile reaction. This single-sentence paragraph signaled a transition to a new topic:

In the past year, we have made considerable concessions, given up much of what is rightfully ours, for the sole purpose of promoting peace in the Middle East and the world in general. These concessions appear to have had no effect whatsoever on the American attitude. Indeed, wild accusations against the Arabs are increasing in volume and intensity, and all of them are so baseless that we have begun to wonder if the American people really know what the Arabs want.

The Saudi author(s) asserted the Arabs' bewilderment at the reaction of Americans toward Arabs and repeated the question that prompted the letter: "Do the American people know what we are asking for?"

The opening of the Saudi ad alluded to a range of subgroups implicit in the international mass media audience. The introduction played upon the theme of competing perspectives on events in the Middle East. Parallel structure highlighted the contrasts. A break in the rhythm indicated a redefinition offered to the American people; Arabs were victims of displacement by a foreign state, not aggressors as the American media portrayed them. While the Saudi author(s) made an effort to accommodate Americans who might not know how to interpret the assertions offered, the primary focus of the introduction was on establishing a perspective for interpretation, on naming the victims and aggressors in the region rather than on explaining principles of supply and demand.

Organizing Principles

As a result, the Saudi author(s) were not concerned with the linear development of factual premises.

The organizing principle of the Saudi ad was on the implicit level of metaphoric association, not on the level of explicit meaning. The unifying thread through the opening of the Saudi ad was the portrayal of the Arabs as victims. The unifying theme in the next section of the ad was the portrayal of the Israelis as aggressors.

Rather than mention the most recent conflict in 1973, the ad turned back to the 1967 Six-Day War. The Saudi author(s) did not provide historical explanations of the conflicts in the region. Instead, the ad simply quoted UN Resolution 242, which called for a "just and lasting peace in the Middle East based on the 'withdrawal of Israel Armed Forces from territories occupied in the recent conflict' and 'termination of all claims or states of belligerency.'" The term "recent" was used equivocally. Did it refer to the last few months or to the last five years?

"This is what we are asking for," the next paragraph of the ad explained. The simple language structure of this statement reinforced the impression that the Arabs' demands were similarly uncomplicated. By quoting an official UN resolution that the United States had approved, the ad implied that world opinion sided with the Arabs. Yet, the equivocal language in the ad made it vague in terms of the Arabs' specific demands.

The next paragraph documented that United States officials had previously criticized Israeli expansionism in the region: "President Lyndon Johnson stated in September, 1968, that 'boundaries cannot and should not reflect the weight of conquest.'" The subsequent paragraph continued the parallel structure that had been established in this section: "This is what we are asking for, and we want nothing more."

Parallel structure and repetition were employed quite consistently in the next two paragraphs: "Israel says it wants peace. So do we. Israel says it wants security. So do we." The problem was that Israel wanted peace and the Arab lands it occupied in 1967: "Israel wants peace and *lebensraum*, security and Arab land, and Israel cannot have both," the ad explained. "Leben" is a traditional drink among Arabs that consists of coagulated sour milk. If viewed as a *double entendre*, between German and Arabic, Israel wanted the milk of Arab land as well as peace. An American might translate the phrase as Israel wanted to have its cake and eat it too.

The ad consistently alternated between long, complicated paragraphs and short, single-sentence paragraphs. The variety between complexity and simplicity combined with parallel structure and repetition made the ad quite rhythmic. One result of this method of organization, however, was that an American reader needed a broad knowledge of the conflicts in the region. Those who did not share the author(s)' historical perspective would have to read between the lines.

Americans are accustomed to greater explicitness in message design, while Arabs are more accustomed to reading implicit meanings. Intercultural communication scholars use the term "contexting" to "describe the perceptual process of recognizing, giving significance to, and incorporating contextual cues in interpreting the total meaning of any stimulus in a particular communication transaction" (Gudykunst & Kim, p. 120). American culture (low context) places greatest emphasis on explicit meaning. Arab cultures (high context), on the other hand, make greater use of subtle, contextual clues in interpreting messages. In explaining what the Arabs wanted, the Saudi author(s) demonstrated a cultural tendency to rely on an implicit understanding of the history of conflicts in the region.

In comparison to the Saudi ad, Mobil's argument marched forward with the precision of a military parade. The ad operated almost exclusively in the realm of explicit meaning. Each paragraph advanced the argument one step further, and there was little variety in the length of these paragraphs. Establishing a rhythm was less important than supporting premises with factual references and statistics. By using such a structure, the Mobil author(s) consistently narrowed the range of feasible options for dealing with the situation.

The opening five paragraphs of Mobil's ad established the "facts" of America's energy needs. The next section of the ad documented the "facts" about oil supplies. After dismissing other possible oil sources such as Venezuela, the North Sea, and Mexico, the author(s) concentrated on Saudi Arabia because this country had more oil than any other nation in the world. Its "reserves can support an increase in production from the present level of about 8 million barrels a day to 20 million barrels daily," the author(s) explained. Saudi Arabia's huge oil reserves made it central to America's future economic growth.

Mobil's position as the major oil company with the smallest domestic reserves and the largest reliance on Saudi oil meant that Mobil's continued economic health depended on the Saudis (Sampson, p. 202). The "fact" of Mobil's significant self-interest in Middle Eastern oil was not mentioned. Instead, the Mobil author(s) attempted to generalize the company's concerns to the oil industry and to the nation as a whole. The lockstep logic of Mobil's argument obscured the company's unique constraints that made it particularly vulnerable to a boycott of Middle Eastern oil.

Overall, Mobil's argument was quite linear in its organization. Increased oil supplies were necessary for continued economic growth. Only the Middle East had sufficient reserves to meet increased energy needs in the United States. We needed Middle Eastern oil more than they needed our money. Therefore, we could no longer ignore Arab political concerns. Each premise was supported with statistics or examples. The step-by-step progression foreclosed from consideration alternatives such as conservation, alternative energies, or non-Middle Eastern sources of oil.

In organizing their argument, the Mobil authors reflected the cause-effect thinking that Stewart asserts is typical of Americans. As he explains, "In the ideal form, the world is seen as a unilateral connection of causes and effects projecting into the future. Since the American focuses on the future rather than the present or the past, the isolation of the critical cause becomes paramount" (p. 35). The critical cause for the Mobil author(s) was access to supplies of Saudi Arabian oil.

The majority of the Mobil ad operated in the realm of explicit meaning. Implicit meaning and stylistic devices were only employed in the ending call-to-action. This ending was cast in general terms to avoid specifically mentioning either the Israelis or the Palestinians:

So we say: It is time now for the world to insist on a settlement in the Middle East. . . . A settlement that will bring justice and security to all the peoples and all the states in that region. Nobody can afford another war in the Middle East. Nobody. Nobody.

The repetition in this section emphasized the seriousness of Mobil's concern. Who could object to a call for peace and justice for all peoples in the region? Only those who read between the lines and recognized that such a general statement might include the Palestinians.

Types of Justifications

Mobil's ad conspicuously avoided discussing the political implications of economic decisions until after its detailed delineation of oil supplies and demand. "If our country's relations with the Arab world . . . continue to deteriorate," the author(s) warned, "Saudi Arabia may conclude it is not in its interest to look favorably on U.S. requests for increased petroleum supplies." Mobil executives were concerned because "we will need the oil more than Saudi Arabia will need the money."

Without specifying what political concerns might motivate Saudi Arabia, Mobil concentrated on examining the Saudi's economic constraints. Development programs in Saudi Arabia could proceed without increased production because of the country's small population and large foreign reserves already over three billion dollars, the ad explained. Since the Saudis had no financial incentive to increase oil production, the Mobil author(s) concluded: "It is therefore time for the American people to begin adapting to a new energy age, to a vastly changed world situation, to the realities with which we will have to learn to live."

Rather than deal in the treacherous realm of political affairs, the Mobil author(s) chose the terra firma of economic concerns. Throughout the ad, Mobil offered eminently practical justifications that revolved around economic necessities. The ad twice reminded Americans that they needed to act in order to preserve their current lifestyles. Americans, Stewart asserts, assume that "the things worthy of effort are material" (p. 35).

Similarly, in explaining the Saudis' motivations, the Mobil author(s) did not concentrate on the Arabs' political concerns. Instead, Mobil executives outlined the economic resources of Saudi Arabia that allowed it to enforce its political views. Mobil's practical, economic justification did not allow room for considering abstract concepts such as justice or honor.

Justice and national honor, however, were central concerns in the Saudi ad. The Arabs initiated the boycott, the ad explained, because "our national interests demanded it." The use of the personal pronoun "our" once again reinforced the identity among all Arab nations. "In the Arab world honorable behavior is that 'which is conducive to group cohesion.' . . . [S]hameful behavior is that which tends to disrupt, endanger, impair, or weaken the social aggregate" (Patai quote by Gudykunst & Kim, p. 51).

The United States had used economic boycotts in the past, the Saudi ad reminded readers. The Arabs had been provoked into a boycott when the United States, "which had repeatedly assured us of our rights to our lands, made massive arms deliveries to the Israelis to help them remain in our lands." Although the Arabs wanted peace, they could not allow Israel to take their lands. "Nor would any just people anywhere in the world expect us to do so." The ad concluded: "We are asking the American people, especially the American friends of Israel, to understand this and to help us attain the peace we are after."

Throughout the ad, the Saudi author(s) offered justifications based on national honor and self-respect. The ad briefly acknowledged but did not discuss the economic consequences of the oil boycott, which tripled oil prices in the space of a few months and triggered one of the largest transfers of wealth in the century. In the face of displacement from a homeland, pragmatic, economic concerns such as the price of oil were secondary.

The Saudis' abstract justifications for their actions were predicated upon the past. Previous grievances against the Arabs constrained the present and limited the future. A past orientation was central to the Saudis' explanation of the boycott. The purpose of the boycott was "not to impose a change in U.S. policy in the Middle East but to demand the *implementation* of U.S. policy in the Middle East, as it has been repeatedly defined." The distinction between imposing a change in U.S. policy and asking for an existing policy to be implemented was a fine one, but it grounded the Saudis' statement that the oil boycott was not an attempt to "blackmail" the American people.

In demanding that past policies be implemented, the Saudis attributed their own orientation to the Americans, neglecting the fact that each new American political administration established new foreign policy priorities. Richard Nixon would not necessarily be constrained by the comments of Lyndon Johnson. The Saudis did not acknowledge that Americans lacked a historical memory similar to their own.

While the Saudis were concerned with the past, Mobil concentrated on the future. Mobil's ad frequently referred to "the coming years" or the "years immediately ahead." The primary motivation for action for the Mobil author(s) was future supplies of oil. In contrast, the Arabs, Stewart explains, believe "it is insane to attempt to predict future events; only God knows what the future will bring" (p. 88).

Interestingly, each ad assumed the other culture's orientation was synonymous with its own. Mobil talked about the Saudis' future economic motives, while the Saudis turned to the United States' previous foreign policy statements and appealed to Americans' sense of national honor and justice. Each ad demonstrated rhetorical ethnocentrism in attributing its orientation to the other culture.

CONCLUSION

As this analysis has indicated, the differences between these two ads go far beyond superficial contrasts between a florid style and a plain style (Glenn,

Witmeyer, & Stevenson, 1977). While Mobil imposed a unitary perspective based on "objective facts," the Saudi ad concentrated on illustrating competing interpretations of reality. Images that clarified an emotional climate were most important for the Saudi author(s); statistics clarifying "objective" reality were most important in the Mobil ad. Mobil's author(s) concentrated on practical, economic justifications predicated on future events; the Saudi author(s) emphasized abstract justifications that focused on the past. In sum, the ads were mirror images of each other in terms of their selections of rhetorical tactics.

These different rhetorical tactics implied different conceptions about the nature of reality. The Mobil author(s), employing traditional Neo-Aristotelian conceptions of argumentation, assumed an objective reality that could be accurately known and verified by systematic observation. The author(s) attempted to muster factual data and logical proof to support their argument that Arab concerns should be accorded a greater role in American foreign policy. "Reasonableness" was determined by the argument's consistency in replicating the structure of objective reality. The goal of Mobil's argument was to explain how the world of energy supply and demand worked. The advocacy advertisement's reliance on linear progression, practical justifications, and a focus on the future as an extension of the present sprang from the assumption of an objective reality.

The Saudi ad, on the other hand, focused not on objective reality, but on reality as apprehended and mediated through the intensifying and distorting prism of language. The Saudi author(s) assumed that reality could not be separated from the structure of language through which we understand reality. Consequently, they focused on naming the victims and aggressors in the region. Establishing the Arab's perspective for interpretation was more important than explaining principles of oil supply and demand. "Effectiveness" in this case was determined by the author(s)' ability to employ the rhythm and sounds of the language to advance an evaluative perspective, thereby controlling the prism through

which reality was viewed.[3] Considered in such a light, the Saudi author(s) were remarkably effective.

Despite these different orientations toward the role of discourse in society, the ads were similar in their use of strategic ambiguity. The Saudis ignored the economic consequences of the oil boycott, while Mobil was obscure when it came to discussing its self-interest in the region and in considering the feasibility of other alternatives, such as conservation. The Saudis projected an image of Arabs as a unified group rather than competing nations and ignored their contributions to aggression in the region. Each ad concealed "facts" that it did not wish to emphasize. The ads were equally cognizant of the ability of language to conceal as well as to reveal. In this sense, both ads were equally self-serving.

While the Saudi author(s) made efforts to accommodate American readers, these attempts at adaptation were likely to go unrecognized by American readers lacking an understanding of different cultural rules for political debate. A Neo-Aristotelian would argue that the Saudi ad was sloppy at best, devious at worst. Arguable premises were introduced but not developed. The ad circled around issues rather than proceeding in a linear fashion from one topic to the next. Americans, with their preference for "rational," cause-effect arguments, were likely to view such an approach as deliberately deceptive.

Arabs, on the other hand, criticized Americans because they lacked the sense of historical perspective that motivated Arabs. An Arab would view Americans' insistence on a unitary perspective based on "objective" facts as deliberately deceptive in neglecting the broader historical context behind the immediate issues. It is this American lack of a sense of "historical totalities" that contributes to Arab complaints that American portrayals are arrogant, one-sided, and simplistic.

In the end, this analysis illustrates in specific detail how "the truism of one nation becomes an argument for another" (Starosta, 1984, p. 231). Each approach to political debate makes legitimate assumptions about the nature of persuasive power. Yet, given the vastly different assumptions about the role of persuasion in society, it is not surprising that misunderstandings occur between Americans and Arabs, even when the same "language" is used. Communicating across a cultural gap requires more than just a knowledge of respective vocabularies. It also requires an understanding of the different cultural rules for what constitutes "reasonable" political debate.

NOTES

1. In the United States, advocacy advertisements mushroomed in the early seventies, as executives complained about media bias against business. By purchasing their own space, business representatives circumvented the typical editorial process, taking their case directly to the public through their own editorials. Advocacy advertising became a frequent adjunct to more traditional forms of political lobbying, offering executives total control over the final message. For a more detailed discussion of the genre, see Sethi's *Advocacy Advertising and Large Corporations* or Heath and Nelson's *Issues Management: Corporate Public Policy Making in an Information Society*.

2. The territory in the Middle East that Israel now occupies was originally called Palestine, a name taken from the Philistines who occupied the coastal part of the country in the twelfth century B.C. A Hebrew kingdom established in 1000 B.C. was subsequently controlled by Assyrians, Babylonians, Egyptians, Persians, Macedonians, Romans, and Byzantines. The Arabs took control of Palestine from the Byzantine Empire in A.D. 634–40. The Arabs maintained control until the twentieth century, when Britain captured Jerusalem in 1917.

Jewish immigration to the area increased throughout Britain's time of control, as British Foreign Secretary Arthur Balfour promised support for a Jewish state in Palestine. Discussions on partitioning the area were tabled during World War II. In 1946, the Jewish population in the region numbered 678,000 compared to 1,269,000 Arabs. Unable to resolve the problem, Britain turned it over to the United Nations in 1947, which voted for partition in the face of strong Arab opposition.

War began with the founding of the State of Israel in 1948. A cease-fire was negotiated in 1949, which increased Israeli territory by fifty percent. The simmering conflict erupted again in 1956 with the Suez crisis and in 1967, when Israel increased its territory two hundred percent by occupying the Golan Heights, the West Bank of the Jordan river, the Old City of Jerusalem, and parts of the Sinai Peninsula. These occupied territories provided the impetus for the 1973 war, which began on October sixth, Yom Kippur, the Israelis' holiest day of the year. Initial Arab gains were reversed, and a cease-fire was negotiated two weeks later.

3. This dichotomy in metaphysical first principles has been identified and discussed in detail by a variety of theorists. Walter J. Ong (1980), for example, contrasted the linear conventions of a written culture with the holistic perspective of an oral culture. Jacqueline De Romilly (1975), in *Magic and Rhetoric in Ancient Greece*, argued that these different formulations of the wellspring of symbolic power coexisted in ancient Greece. John Poulakos (1984) in *Rhetoric, the Sophists and the Possible* provides an excellent contrast between the perspective offered by Aristotelian and sophistic rhetoric. He examines the basic assumptions of each rhetoric in light of modern philosophers such as Nietzsche, Heidegger, and Foucault. What has not typically been done, however, is to illustrate how different basic assumptions about the nature of rhetoric and reality play themselves out in actual discourse.

REFERENCES

Al-Zafer, Mohammed. (1985, Dec.). Telephone interview with author.

Almaney, A. J., & Alwan, A. J. (1982). *Communicating with the Arabs: A handbook for the business executive*. Prospect Heights, IL: Waveland Press.

Barton, R. L. (1982). Message analysis in international mass communication research. In M. Mander (Ed.), *Communication in transition* (pp. 81–101). New York: Praeger.

Condon, J., & Yousef, F. (1975). *An introduction to intercultural communication*. New York: Bobbs-Merrill.

De Romilly, J. (1975). *Magic and rhetoric in ancient Greece*. Cambridge, MA: Harvard University Press.

Glenn, E. A., Witmeyer, D., & Stevenson, K. A. (1977). Cultural styles of persuasion. *International Journal of Intercultural Relations*, **1**(3), 52–66.

Gudykunst, W., & Kim, Y. (1984). *Communicating with strangers: An approach to intercultural communication*. Reading, MA: Addison-Wesley.

Hamod, H. S. (1963). Arab and Moslem rhetorical theory. *Central States Speech Journal*, **14**, 97–102.

Heisey, R. D. (1970). The rhetoric of the Arab-Israeli conflict. *Quarterly Journal of Speech,* **46**, 12–21.

Lewis, P. (1983, March 20). An oil minister's poem stole the show. *New York Times*, Sec. 6, p. 6.

The Mobil Oil Corporation. (1973, June 30). The U.S. Stake in Middle East peace: I. *New York Times*, Sec. 2, p. 30.

Ong, W. J. (1980). Literacy and orality in our times. *Journal of Communication, 30*, 197–204.

Poulakos, J. (1984). Rhetoric, the sophists and the possible. *Communication Monographs, 51*, 215–226.

Sakkaf, O. (1973, Dec. 31). Open letter to the American people. *Washington Post*, Sec. 1, p. 9.

Sampson, A. (1975). *The seven sisters*. New York: Viking Press.

Schmertz, H. with Novak, W. (1986). *Good-bye to the low profile: The art of creative confrontation*. Boston: Little, Brown.

Sethi, S. P. (1977). *Advocacy advertising and large corporations*. Lexington, MA: Lexington Books.

Starosta, W. (1984). On intercultural rhetoric. In W. Gudykunst & Y. Y. Kim (Eds.), *Methods for intercultural communication research*. (pp. 229–238). Beverly Hills: Sage.

Stewart, E. (1972). *American cultural patterns: A cross-cultural perspective*. Yarmouth, ME: Intercultural Press.

Palevome: Foundations of Struggle and Conflict in Greek Interpersonal Communication

BENJAMIN J. BROOME

Conflict is most often defined as a struggle between parties who are linked in an interdependent manner over incompatible goals, interests, or resources. In Western societies the term *conflict* usually elicits negative images; it is associated with intensity of feelings, damaged relationships, and inefficient use of time and energy. Cooperation, friendly relations, and smooth transactions are put forth as ideals. Conflict signals that something is wrong and needs to be corrected. Much of the literature on conflict management and conflict resolution, published primarily in the United States, reflects this negative image of conflict (Coser, 1956; Fink, 1968; Freud, 1949; Pruitt & Lewis, 1977; Roloff, 1976).

This view of conflict is however, culture-bound. Even though many researchers recognize the possibility of productive uses of conflict (Deutsch, 1973; Folger & Poole, 1984; Kilmann & Thomas, 1977; Putman & Wilson, 1982), the existence of conflict in a relationship is usually discussed as an irregularity; relationships in conflict are "out of balance" and

From the *Southern Communication Journal*, Vol. 55 No. 2 (Spring, 1990), pp. 260–275. Reprinted by permission of the Southern States Communication Association. Benjamin J. Broome teaches at George Mason University in Fairfax, Virginia.

need to be restored to normalcy. In contrast to this view of conflict as an abnormality, other cultural groups view struggles between parties as a way of life. This is particularly true of both traditional and contemporary Hellas, better known to English language users as the country of Greece.[1]

Permeating almost every facet of everyday life in Greece is a sense of contest. To the Western mind,[2] Greece appears to be a "maddening mobile, elusive, paradoxical world, where there seems nothing solid enough to grasp save splinters, yet where no part is less than the mystical whole and where past and present, body and soul, ideal and reality blend and struggle and blend again with each other so that the most delicate scalpel can scarcely dissect them" (Holden, 1972, p. 34). However, for Greeks, this struggle can bring with it feelings of stimulation, excitement, and genuine human contact. Even the painful feelings that are often the result of conflict are not viewed as aberrations, but rather are seen as part of the natural course of human relations. In Greece, conflict is an aspect of everyday transactions that is unavoidable.

This paper discusses the Greek approach to conflict in interpersonal communication, exploring the traditional foundations of struggle as a way of life. The views presented here are based on anthropological, sociological, linguistic, and communication literature about Greece and the author's research in Greece during 1980 to 1989.

STRUGGLE AS THE ESSENCE OF LIFE: TRADITIONAL GREEK CULTURE AND ORIENTATIONS TOWARD INTERPERSONAL CONFLICT

Ernestine Friedl (1962), in describing life in a traditional Greek village at that time, reports that when one walks through the fields and inquires about how the work is going, the people generally respond with "palevome" or "we are struggling." The villagers' use of the verb *palevo* expresses the difficult conditions confronting farmers trying to make a living from the predominately rocky soil and mountainous terrain. At the same time, it reflects the predominate worldview and orientation toward interpersonal relations characteristic of Greek reality. Triandis (1972) reports that even a positive term such as *success* is linked by Greeks with struggle, whereas for North Americans it is linked with careful planning and hard work. Nickolas Gage, author of the best-selling book *Eleni* (Gage, 1983), describes Greece as a place with "joy and tragedy straight out of Aeschylus, Sophocles, and Euripides, and it is expressed with the same classic gestures. . . . the same tendency to use strong words and violent gestures; . . . the same warm heart, the disdain for time, and the delight in life lived fully, with all the senses awake" (Gage, 1987, p. 24).

While Greece is a land of unparalleled scenic beauty, it is also a land of contrasts. Physically, the mountains and the sea meet each other throughout the country, often resulting in dramatic settings. Culturally, there are contrasts between the island inhabitants and the mountain villagers (Sanders, 1962). Historically, the Greek character has always fought over the opposing poles of a more feminine Ionian makeup and a more masculine Dorian outlook. Geographically, Greece sits between the Near East and Europe and has been invaded and occupied by forces from both, resulting in cultural influences from East and West. In politics there have been both military dictatorships and socialist governments, although the dictatorships were not the choice of the people. These contrasts and the resulting struggle between opposites are deeply embedded in the nature of Greek reality:

. . . Greek identity as a whole (is) best seen as a constant oscillation between just such opposites as these. The spirit and the flesh, ideal and reality, triumph and despair — you name them and the Greeks suffer or enjoy them as the constant poles of their being, swinging repeatedly from one to the other and back again, often contriving to embrace both poles simultaneously, but above all never reconciled, never contented, never still. This perennial sense of tension between diametrically

opposed forces is the essence of their existence — *the one absolutely consistent feature of their identity since Greek history began. In the phrase of the Cretan novelist, Kazantzakis, they are truly double-born souls. (Holden, 1972, p. 27–28, emphasis added)*

Tension and struggle in interpersonal relations are contextually embedded in several aspects of Greek history and social reality. Traditionally, Greece has revolved around village culture, even though from pre-classical times Greeks have traveled all over the world to both satisfy their curiosity and to search for new resources. Hundreds of villages have always dotted the mostly mountainous countryside and the island ports, with relatively few urban centers.

Today the situation has changed, with the majority of the population living in three or four major cities and 40% of the population residing in Athens. However, in many cases the suburbs of these urban centers resemble villages. The majority of the population of Athens are migrants from the villages and small towns of the countryside and the islands, and most residents of the capital were not born in that city (Campbell, 1983). More importantly, the majority of city residents remain closely tied to their traditional villages, often maintaining a village house and returning to the village for important religious occasions. Even with voting, most Greeks prefer to keep their registration in their villages rather than move it to their city of residence, maintaining their ties and status within remote villages. Thus, while externally many Greeks conform to more contemporary Western life-styles, they are psychologically and socially bound to a traditional culture that influences their lives in a myriad of ways (Triandis, 1986).

In order to understand the Greek approach to conflict and struggle as a way of life, it is necessary to explore two aspects of traditional Greek culture that have a strong influence on contemporary Greek thought and actions. The following section will discuss (a) the distinction between ''ingroup'' and ''outgroup'' in Greek society, and (b) the influence of ''philotimo'' on interpersonal relations.

THE CONTEXTUAL FOUNDATIONS OF INTERPERSONAL STRUGGLE

Ingroup-Outgroup Distinctions

Traditional Greek culture is more collectivist than individualistic in nature (Doumanis, 1983) and emphasizes distinctions between ingroup and outgroup to a much larger extent than do Western societies. The major differences between ingroup behavior and outgroup behavior have been extensively examined by Triandis (1972), who describes the Greek as defining his universe in terms of the triumphs of the ingroup over the outgroup. Social behavior is strongly dependent on whether the other person is a member of the ingroup or the outgroup. This affects relations with people in a wide variety of situations, such as interaction with authority figures and with persons with whom one is in conflict.

The definition of the ingroup in traditional Greek society includes family, relatives, friends, and even friends of friends. Guest and other people who are perceived as showing appropriate warmth, acceptance, and assistance quickly become friends and thus part of the ingroup. Outgroup members include those in the community outside the immediate family, the extended family, and the network of ingroup affiliations. While a traditional village community is sharply divided into subgroups on the basis of these affiliations, the structure is not entirely rigid; people who are at one point outgroup members could become ingroup members through marriage or by establishing links of cooperative interdependence (Doumanis, 1983). An individual is attached to these different groupings with varying degrees of intimacy, ranging from total identification to outward hostility.

A great deal of commitment exists between ingroup members, requiring intimacy, concern, and good conduct. It is required that an individual behave toward members of his or her ingroup with self-sacrifice, as the well-being of the ingroup is more important than that of the individual. In the context of a highly competitive social world, the ingroup provides protection and help for its members. Feelings of trust, support, cooperation, sympathy, and admiration are exchanged frequently among members of the ingroup.

Relations with outgroup members are characterized by a great deal of suspicion and mistrust. Influence and pressure from the outgroup is rejected. The relationship between authority figures and subordinates is also dependent on ingroup/outgroup considerations. For example, in larger organizations, managers, who are usually viewed by employees in Greece as part of the outgroup, are treated with avoidance and hostility. On the other hand, managers who are identified as part of the employees' ingroup are usually given submissive acceptance and warmth.

Concealment and deception play important roles in relations with the outgroup. They serve as important means for upholding ingroup honor and prestige. In a world where ingroup honor must be protected and competition is a way of life, deception becomes a useful means of fulfilling one's duties. The phrase is often heard "You can't live without lies." For Greeks, however, the word for lies, *psemata*, does not carry with it the negative connotations assigned by most Westerners. It is used more freely and with less emotional intensity (Friedl, 1959). It does not have the overtones of morality found in English, and it is sometimes even justified on religious grounds by declaring it the desire of God (du Boulay, 1976). In fact, villagers are not humiliated because someone tries to deceive them, although they become angry if the deception succeeds (Friedl, 1962).

The suspicion and mistrust of outgroup members lead to a general lack of helpfulness toward those not part of the ingroup. This is illustrated in a study reported by Triandis (1986). Comparisons were made between how people in the United States, Europe, and Greece behave toward foreign strangers and toward strangers who are fellow nationals.[5] A number of situations were used in which either a fellow national or a foreigner interacted with a sample of local people. In one situation, where the stranger asks for help from a local person, approximately 50 percent of those asked in Europe and the United States provided the assistance, regardless as to whether the request came from a foreigner or a fellow national. However, in Greece, this degree of help was only provided to the foreigner (a potential ingroup member) requesting assistance. Only 10 percent of locals agreed to help a fellow Greek whom they did not know, as this person was clearly an outgroup member.

Even cheating, while it is completely unacceptable with the ingroup, is acceptable when it is directed toward members of the outgroup. When it occurs with the outgroup, cheating is treated in the context of competition, where it is required that the outgroup member be taken advantage of if he or she is weak. The outgroup member is expected to be on guard against cheating.

The ingroup-outgroup distinction leads to a continuous struggle between members of the two groups. Actions that are inappropriate within the ingroup are applied without hesitation to relations with the outgroup. The distinction provides for the support and safety necessary to carry on the struggle, and at the same time it provides the focus for the struggle itself. Loyalty to the ingroup and feelings ranging from mild disregard to intense animosity for the outgroup provide the background upon which many conflicts are staged.

Philotimo: The Essence of Ingroup Behavior

Perhaps the most cherished term for a Greek is *eleftheria*, which means freedom. For much of its long and sometimes glorious history, Greece has been under foreign domination. For example, the Ottoman Empire ruled Greece for 400 years, and during the Second World War it suffered tremendously under German occupation. Despite this history of domination by external forces, Greeks have always maintained a strong sense of personal freedom that transcends the circumstances. Much of this can be attributed to a central aspect of Greek self-concept called *philotimo*.

Philotimo is not translatable with a single English word; it is a concept that refers to several aspects of Greek character and social relations. First, it refers to a sense of responsibility and obligation to the ingroup, particularly to the family. The most important social unit in Greece is the family, and Greeks take their family obligations seriously. They are obliged to uphold the family honor and to provide assistance to family members. This extends in various ways to other members of the ingroup. Lee (1959) says that loyalty can only be evoked in personal relations, with the result that Greeks cannot be impartial in distributing resources that are at their disposal, whether those resources are jobs or material goods. It is one's duty to take care of family and friends first, irrespective of merit or order of priority.

Second, philotimo refers to appropriate behavior within the ingroup. As Triandis (1972) indicates, a person who is considered "philotimos" behaves toward members of his ingroup in a way that is "polite, virtuous, reliable, proud, . . . truthful, generous, self-sacrificing, tactful, respectful, and grateful" (pp. 308–309). The principle of philotimo requires a person to sacrifice himself or herself to help ingroup members and to avoid doing or saying things that reflect negatively on family or friends. Appropriate ingroup behavior should be seen and felt not only by the ingroup but by the outgroup as well, thus increasing prestige for the ingroup in the eyes of the outgroup.

Third, philotimo is strongly related to a person's sense of personal honor and self-esteem. As Lee (1959) stated: "Foremost in the Greek's view of the self is his self-esteem. It is impossible to have good relations with Greeks unless one is aware of this, the Greek philotimo. It is important to pay tribute to it, and to avoid offending it, or as the Greeks say, "molesting it" (p. 141). The Greek philotimo is easily bruised, and there is constant emphasis on both protecting the philotimo and enhancing it. Protecting one's philotimo leads to a concern with losing face, with shielding the inner core of the self from ridicule, and with avoiding actions that would cause loss of respect. There is constant guard against being outsmarted by the outgroup, and it is seldom that Greeks put themselves in a position of being in less than full control of their senses in order to avoid personal abuse and damage to the ingroup.

Offense against one's philotimo brings retaliation rather than feelings of self-criticism of self-blame. As Friedl (1962) relates, the avoidance of self-blame does not have the connotation of irresponsibility, because it is a necessary part of the maintenance of self-esteem. In the same vein, philotimo is not related to feelings of remorse or guilt, and it is not strongly tied to notions of ethical morality (Holden, 1972). If actions are taken in defense of philotimo that bring harm to outgroup members, responsibility is not accepted for what occurs following the actions. If the demands of philotimo have been satisfied, the person taking action against others is entitled to reject any blame for subsequent misfortune.

Safeguarding of philotimo promotes a sense of equality between individuals, and thus it is seldom that a Greek feels inferior to another. Even differences in status levels and role responsibilities are not cast in terms of superiority or inferiority in Greece. However, the philotimo of the Greek is very different from the notion of pride. The philotimo of the Greek is promoted by actions that bring honor and respect to the family and the ingroup, not simply to the individual. Lee (1959) points out that the expression of pride carries with it the connotation of arrogance, which is detested by the Greeks. A common proverb states that "the clever (proud) bird is caught by the nose."

In many ways, interpersonal struggle is driven by concerns of philotimo. Philotimo is the key to behavior within the ingroup, and it frames much of one's behavior toward the outgroup. Requirements of philotimo lead to actions that enhance the position of the ingroup, and at the same time trigger actions in defense of the ingroup. Many conflicts occur because of the demands of philotimo. Perhaps it is because of the Greek's strong sense of philotimo that conflicts can continue over long periods of time and at a high level of intensity without feelings of guilt or remorse.

INTERPERSONAL STRUGGLE IN SOCIAL TRANSACTIONS

Greek social life has been described by du Boulay (1976) as a type of "see-saw," continuously in motion. Friedl (1962) used the word *tension* to capture the feelings of Greek villagers toward each other and the world, saying that a large number of social encounters feature a "sense of contest, of struggle, of agony, of a kind of pushing and pulling" (Friedl, 1962, p. 76). She used the metaphor of a "battle" to describe Greek social life in the village, arguing that the Greek search for identity in a culture that seeks so strongly to preserve ingroup honor and integrity is carried out to a large extent by pitting oneself against another. It is through contrast, with others that one learns to know oneself, and this leads to the necessity of maintaining differences and emphasizing contrasts. She says that "contrasts, and the tension contrasts create, become expected and desired" (Friedl, 1962, p. 76). Struggle and contrasts are evident in several related aspects of Greek social reality: (a) conversation style, (b) competitive nature of social relationships, and (c) process nature of relational struggle.

Conversation Style and the Role of Couvenda

The conversation style of Greeks has been described as "contrapuntal virtuosity, incisive, combative, loud" (Lee, 1959, p. 146). To the unaccustomed ear, every conversation appears to be an argument, and gentleness seems to play no part in dialogue. The substance of conversation is less important than the style because it is the process that counts (Holden, 1972). Discussion can be described as "a battle of personal opinion, and its end is neither to reach the truth nor to reach a conclusion; its end is sheer enjoyment of vigorous speech" (Lee, 1959, p. 146). Indeed, the Western visitor to Greece is immediately struck by the intensity of the conversation:

A city neighborhood or a village can be compared to a stage, and friends, neighbors, and kin to a Greek chorus commenting on unfolding marriages, hospitality, or sexual infidelity. No one can remain solely in the audience; however, neutrality is impossible to maintain. No one can expect to receive support of his or her reputation unless he or she defends that of allies. Manipulation of opinion depends on gossip, which in turn depends on the breaking of confidences, amusement derived from ridicule, and malicious attempts to exploit the situation. (Greece: A Country Study, 1985, p. 145).

Challenges, insults and attacks are, within appropriate limits, almost synonymous with conversing. Friedl (1962) says that conversation "has some of the quality of an arena in which each man displays himself as an individual and waits for an audience response. People talk at each other rather than with each other" (p. 83). It is not unusual for several monologues to be going on simultaneously at a table as different individuals struggle to hold center stage and assert their personalities.

Couvenda, or conversation, is extremely important in Greek society. As Triandis (1972) puts it, "Greeks love to discuss, to argue, and to match their wits with other debaters" (p. 323). Gage (1987) reports a conversation with a ship owner who believes that "to exercise the tongue and provoke the mind is the most fulfilling pastime of all" (p. 30). Davenport (1978) describes Athens as a city where social activity — eating out, drinking, dancing, singing and, above all, conversing — permeates everyday life to an extraordinary degree. From childhood, everyone receives a great deal of verbal stimulation, for conversation is a skill that no one can live without.

Couvenda plays a number of important functions in Greek society. First, it is through conversation that personal relationships are developed and maintained. Hirschon (1978) says that "company with others has an intrinsic value, solitude is abhorred and the personality type most approved is that of the open and warm individual, while someone described as closed is also seen as cold" (p. 77). Isolation and withdrawal, she says, are equivalent to social death; to engage in intense verbal exchange is thus a recognition of the other's existence.

Moreover, many Greeks feel degrees of obligation toward others, even non-relatives, from their native village or surrounding area (Gage, 1987).

When two strangers meet they will immediately try to discover if they share any common roots. More often than not they find they have common acquaintances or that one of their relatives is married to one of the other's relatives. Establishing this social bond through such a ritual allows each of them to place the other at least tentatively within the ingroup, thus promoting warmer feelings and a greater degree of trust.

Second, couvenda serves as a means of asserting a sense of equality in encounters with others. This equality is not necessarily related to status, education, or economic level, but rather refers to equality as a human being. As Friedl (1962) emphasizes: "The right to a certain give-and-take underlies all relationships and serves to keep each situation unique and each relationship one of equality on at least some level" (p. 83). This sense of equality is demanded by one's philotimo, and it is through couvenda that it is established and maintained. This may even lead one to present strong views on a topic with which she or he is unfamiliar and then to stubbornly defend these views even in the face of clear evidence against them. To lose an argument on the basis of the facts or logic presented by the other would show weakness and would put the person in an inferior position. Asserting one's personality by providing strong opinions and engaging in sometimes heated argument is a common means of elevating the philotimo on an individual level.

Third, couvenda provides a source of entertainment. Traditional village life is quite routine and repetitive, and especially before the advent of television it was through conversation that freshness and uniqueness were brought to commonplace events. Variation and uncertainty are imposed on aspects of life that otherwise have no intrinsically adventurous elements. Entertainment is enhanced by the rich oral tradition of the Greeks, whose language allows a precision of expression that promotes unsurpassed storytelling.

Gage (1987) shows how everyday language is rich in proverbs, myths, legends, and humor. He says that "even the most uneducated Greek sprinkles his speech liberally with proverbs, many of them reflecting the wry cynicism of a people who

have become accustomed to hardship, yet have managed to retain their spiritual strength and sense of humor" (pp. 59–60). Holden (1972) shows how boasting sometimes takes the form of "apparently harmless rhetorical embroidery to make actual situations seem grander, more significant and more self-flattering than they really are" (p. 94).

Finally, couvenda is important in asserting one's personality and maintaining self-esteem. Hirschon (1978) points out that social life is vital, because prestige and reputation, which depend on the opinion of others, are the measure of both the individual's merit and that of his or her family. Friedl (1962) considers couvenda as the way men and women boast of their own and their family's achievements and as the vehicle for men to display their political knowledge and engage in political argument. Boasting is socially acceptable, and Davenport (1978) believes that it is a means of promoting philotimo.

Despite the high level of intensity reflected in couvenda, arguments, debates, and other verbal disputes are not viewed as aberrations, and they do not necessarily affect relationships negatively or lead to negative feelings within relationships. Rather, they are viewed as integral aspects of daily existence. Couvenda, while it *reflects* the interpersonal struggle that is the essence of Greek reality, functions on center stage in full view of any audience. Behind the scenes lies relational struggle in which rivalry and *competition* play key roles.

Competition and Relational Struggle

Holden (1972) writes about the "deep current of rivalry and suspicion" running between Greeks. He says that relationships are in a constant state of flux because of the competitive nature of the Greek's social orientation. Greeks tend to believe that "the friend of my enemy is my enemy, and the enemy of my enemy is my friend," so they are constantly making, dissolving, and remaking coalitions as different "enemies" appear on the scene. From Holden's (1972) viewpoint, "the prospect of life without an enemy generally seems intolerable" (p. 89), so new relational struggles are constantly developing.

The ongoing struggles in Greek social life are fueled by a competitive orientation that is different from that found in most Western societies. It is often noted that whereas in Europe and the United States people compete with each other by trying to "run faster" to get ahead of the other, the Greeks compete with each other by grabbing onto their competitor to "hold them back," thus keeping them from getting ahead. The tendency to compete by bringing down one's foe signals a very different approach to conflict that can significantly affect the manner in which conflicts are managed.

The approach to competition in Greece reflects the collectivist nature of traditional Greek culture. Whereas in individualistic cultures such as the United States and most of Europe competition is between individuals, Greek competition is primarily between the ingroup and the outgroup (Triandis, 1986). The requirements of philotimo that the Greek feels toward the ingroup help prevent forms of competition that would damage the basic ties holding the ingroup together. However, the need to defend the ingroup against harm from outside can lead to intense conflicts between the ingroup and the outgroup. Doumanis (1983) states that in traditional Greek communities "social relationships were either positive or negative, with no room for neutral gradation in between. Families were either co-operating with one another, closely and intimately, or were competing aggressively, cunningly and sometimes fiercely" (p. 28).

Process Focus of Relational Struggle

Despite the competitive nature of relations with the outgroup, the interpersonal struggle characteristic of Greek relationships is not totally focused on *outcome* but rather tends to center on *process*. Heard often is the phrase "Perazmena Ksehazmena" or "What is past is forgotten." Applying not only to unpleasant events but equally to success, it points to the short-lived nature of victory and defeat. Without a competitor, life would not be very stimulating, so new relational struggles are constantly taking shape.

It can be argued that interpersonal battles provide a great deal of personal and social satisfaction to Greeks. Friedl (1962) says that it is the continuing *aghonia* (anxiety or agony) that provides for the Greek a feeling of being alive. Holden (1972) describes conflict as "generating the leaping spark of tension that is the only certain characteristic of Greekness. Tension, movement, change, process; these are the essence of Greek life" (p. 33).

Not only do struggles provide some degree of stimulation and satisfaction for Greeks, they also play an important role in strengthening ingroup solidarity. The hostility and opposition directed toward the outgroup serves as a complement to the cooperation necessary within the ingroup. Through competition with the outgroup, ingroup members attest to their allegiance with the ingroup. As Doumanis (1983) states: "The values of prestige and honor so central in the traditional Greek culture rested on the attention and opinion of friends *and* enemies, on the concerned interest of kin *and* the grudging acceptance of competitors" (p. 29, emphasis added).

In many ways, interpersonal communication and relationships in Greece mirror a description of the contrasts in the physical world. Just as the Greek countryside is dominated by mountainous and often rough terrain, conversations and relationships are characterized by transactions that seem to the outsider harsh and rocky. Physical, spiritual, and social struggles are built into the Greek landscape, psyche, and relationships in ways that are difficult for the Western European mind to comprehend. Although these struggles would exhaust the Westerner, they seem to invigorate the Greek. Differences such as these make the current Western notion of what constitutes conflict incomplete and perhaps inappropriate in describing cultures such as those in traditional and contemporary Hellas.

IMPLICATIONS FOR FUTURE RESEARCH

Greece is a society in transition, moving rapidly from a traditional village and island culture to a more westernized and cosmopolitan environment. While the traditional Greek cultural milieu exerts extensive influence on the communication patterns of contemporary urban Greeks, there are only a few reported studies that examine the urban environment (Campbell, 1983; Doumanis, 1983; Hirschon, 1983; Triandis, 1986).

The need exists to conduct additional field studies and empirical investigations of communication patterns in contemporary Greece. While this study has concentrated on *palevome* and its implications for interpersonal conflict in Greece, there are other cultural factors that impact on interpersonal communication. The time is ripe for studies examining phenomena such as time orientation, male and female role distinctions, and influence of religious worldviews in the context of contemporary Greece.

Research also needs to be conducted that examines the impact of Greek interpersonal communication on relations between Greeks and Western Europeans, North Americans, and other Westerners. While it is beyond the scope of this paper to explore such applications, the consequences for intercultural interaction are numerous. A concept like palevome can be instructive to both Western Europeans, North Americans, and Greeks as improved interpersonal relations are sought.

Finally, this examination points to a deficiency in the literature on conflict and conflict management. Much of the theoretical and research literature on conflict published in the United States must be reexamined and broadened. The culture-bound paradigm of conflict represented in the literature limits the extent to which the nature of this important phenomenon can be understood. While calls have been made for culture-specific research on communication processes (Broome, 1986), there are few reported studies in the communication literature that examine communication patterns in societies other than the United States (Shuter, 1990). Only through culture-specific research conducted in a culturally sensitive manner can we gain insight into the nature of a conflict and culture from a global perspective.

NOTES

1. The name "Greece" comes from the Latin term given by the Romans during their occupation of Greece. Greeks refer to their country as "Hellas" or "Ellada."

2. While Greece is part of the European Economic Community and is usually included geographically as part of Europe, the culture blends the traditions of both West and East in a unique way (see Woodhouse, 1983). Geographically, it sits between the west of Europe and the east of Turkey.

3. In Greece a foreign stranger is a potential ingroup member because of the emphasis the culture places on "philoxenia," or "kindness to strangers."

REFERENCES

Area handbook for Greece. (1970). Washington, DC: American University.

Barnlund, D. C. (1975). *Public and private self in Japan and the United States*. Tokyo: Simul Press.

Broome, B. J. (1986). A context-based approach to teaching intercultural communication. *Communication Education, 35*(3), 296–306.

Campbell, J. K. (1964). *Honor, family and patronage*. Oxford: Clarendon Press.

Campbell, J. K. (1983). Traditional values and continuities in Greek society. In R. Clogg (Ed.), *Greece in the 1980's*. St. Martin's Press, 184–207.

Coser, L. (1956). *The functions of conflict*. New York: Free Press.

Crimes of honor still the pattern in rural Greece. *New York Times*, Sect. 1, February 10, 1980, 22.

Davenport, W. W. (1978). *Athens*. New York: Time-Life Books.

Deutsch, M. (1973). *The resolution of conflict*. New Haven: Yale University Press.

Doumanis, M. (1983). *Mothering in Greece: From collectivism to individualism*. London: Academic Press.

de Boulay, J. (1976). Lies, mockery and family integrity. In J. G. Peristiany (Ed.), *Mediterranean Family Structure*. Cambridge University Press, 389–406.

Fink, C. F. (1968). Some conceptual difficulties in the theory of social conflict. *Journal of Conflict Resolution, 12*, 412–460.

Folger, J. P., and Poole, M. S. (1984). *Working through conflict: A communication perspective*. Glenview, IL: Scott, Foresman.

Freud, S. (1949). *An outline of psychoanalysis* (J. Strachey, trans.). New York: Norton.

Friedl, E. (1962). *Vasilika: A village in Modern Greece*. New York: Holt, Rinehart & Winston.

Gage, N. (1987). *Hellas: A portrait of Greece*. Athens: Efstathiadis Group.

Gage, N. (1983). *Eleni*. New York: Random House.

Greece: A Country Study. (1985). Washington, DC: American University.

Hirschon, R. B. (1978). Open Body/Closed Space: The Transformation of Female Sexuality. In Shirley Ardener (Ed.), *Defining Females: The Nature of Women in Society*. London: Croom Helm, 66–87.

Hirschon, R. B. (1983). Under one roof: Marriage, dowry, and family relations in Piraeus. In Michael Kenny and David I. Kertzer (Eds.), *Urban life in Mediterranean Europe: Anthropological perspectives*. Urbana: University of Illinois Press, 299–323.

Hirschon, R. B., and Gold, J. R. (1982). Territoriality and the home environment in a Greek urban community. *Anthropological Quarterly, 55*(2), 63–73.

Holden, D. (1972). *Greece without columns: The making of the modern Greeks*. Philadelphia: J. B. Lippincott, 1–36.

Kilmann, R. H., and Thomas, K. W. (1977). Developing a forced choice measure of conflict-handling behavior: The MODE instrument. *Educational and Psychological Measurement*, 309–325.

Lee, D. (1959). *Freedom and culture*. Englewood Cliffs, NJ: Prentice-Hall, Inc.

Pruitt, D., and Lewis, S. (1977). The psychology of interactive bargaining. In D. Druckman (Ed.), *Negotiations*. Beverly Hills: Sage.

Putman, L., and Wilson, D. E. (1982). Development of an organizational communication conflict instrument. In M. Burgoon (Ed.), *Communication Yearbook* (Vol. 6). Beverly Hills: Sage.

Roloff, M. E. (1976). Communication strategies, relationships, and relational changes. In G. R. Miller (Ed.), *Explorations in interpersonal communication*. Beverly Hills: Sage.

Sanders, I. T. (1962). *Rainbow in the rock*. Cambridge, MA: Harvard University Press.

Shuter, R. (Spring, 1990). The Centrality of Culture. *The Southern Communication Journal*, 55, 237–249.

Triandis, H. C. (1986). *Education of Greek-Americans for a pluralistic society*. Keynote address to the Conference on the Education of Greek Americans, New York, May.

Triandis, H. C. (1972). A comparative analysis of subjective culture. From *The Analysis of Subjective Culture*. New York: John Wiley & Sons, 299–335.

Woodhouse, C. M. (1983). Greece and Europe. In R. Clogg (Ed.), *Greece in the 1980's*. St. Martin's Press, 1–8.

CONCEPTS AND QUESTIONS
FOR CHAPTER 2

1. In what ways does a social relationship orientation affect communication behavior differently than does an individualism orientation?

2. What are the four Confucian principles of right conduct? How do they contribute to communicative behavior?

3. How do East Asian concepts of in-group–out-group differ from those of North Americans? How might these differences affect intercultural communication?

4. How does Confucianism affect linguistic codes?

5. What are the major differences in the ways in which interpersonal bonding takes place in Eastern and Western cultures?

6. How do Eastern values concerning equality differ from Western values?

7. How does the rate of self-disclosure differ in Eastern and Western cultures?

8. What unique perspectives of world view are inherent in the Hindu culture of India?

9. How might the Hindu perspective of the universe and of humankind's role in the universe affect intercultural communication between Indians and North Americans?

10. To what do Jain and Kussman refer when they discuss the Hindu spirit of tolerance? How might this spirit affect social perception and human interaction?

11. How do Arab concepts of advocacy differ from those of North Americans?

12. How do North American and Arab rhetorical strategies differ? How might these differences affect business negotiations?

13. What significant role does conflict play in Greek interaction?

14. What are the major differences between Greek and American cultures in the relationship to and the utilization of conflict?

15. Describe the conversational style of Greek interaction.

3

Co-Cultures:
Living in Two Cultures

In Chapter 2, we focused on international cultures, that is, cultures that exist beyond the immediate borders of the United States. However, numerous domestic co-cultures composed of various religious, economic, ethnic, age, gender, sexual preference, and racial groups exist within U.S. society itself. These diverse co-cultures have the potential to bring new experiences to a communication encounter, but because these co-cultures exist all around us, the dominant Euro-American culture often takes their presence for granted. Yet, if you are not aware of and do not understand the unique experiences of these co-cultures, you can experience serious communication problems. The articles in this chapter have been selected to introduce you to a number of U.S. co-cultures and to examine some of the cultural experiences and dynamics inherent in them. Admittedly, there are many more co-cultures than we have included here. Our selection was based on three considerations. First, limited space and the necessity for efficiency prohibited a long list of co-cultures. Second, we wanted to include some social communities that are frequently in conflict with the dominant culture. And third, we wanted to emphasize the co-cultures with which you are most likely to interact. To this end, we selected a representation of the major co-cultures resident in the United States.

As the United States continues its development into a pluralistic and multicultural society, there is an increased need and opportunity for effective communication between the dominant culture and the co-cultures as well as among the co-cultures themselves. Effective communication can only come about with the removal of prejudice and stereotypes and the development of an understanding of what each culture is really like. Frequently, prejudices and stereotypes lead to assumptions about members of co-cultures that are false, hurtful, and insulting.

We begin this chapter with the article "Diversity and Its Discontents," by Arturo Madrid in which he discusses some of the negative aspects of being a member of a co-culture, living alongside the dominant Euro-American culture. Madrid addresses the constant misperceptions and false assumptions that members of co-cultures must deal with and the resentment they feel about being continuously perceived as the *other*. Madrid assails the ignorance people have about Hispanic culture, pointing out how he is frequently assumed to be an immigrant although his ancestors' presence in what is now the United States predates Plymouth Rock.

In "Who's Got the Room at the Top?" Edith A. Folb discusses the concept of *intracultural* communication, where members of the same dominant culture hold slightly different values. Folb sees the crucial characteristics of this form of communication as the interrelationships of power, dominance, and nondominance as they are manifested in the particular cultures. She carefully examines these variables as they apply to African Americans, Native Americans, Mexican Americans, women, the aged, the physically challenged, and other groups that have been "caste marked and more often negatively identified when it comes to issues of power, dominance, and social control."

The next article leads us to an examination of communication involving the African-American co-culture. In "An African-American Communication Perspective," Sidney A. Ribeau, John R. Baldwin, and Michael L. Hecht examine the communicative style of the African American. They are particularly concerned with identifying satisfying and dissatisfying conversational themes, conversational strategies, and communication effectiveness from an intercultural communication perspective. They identify seven issues — negative stereotypes, acceptance, personal expressiveness, authenticity, understanding, goal attainment, and power dynamics — that impact intercultural communication. They then offer several strategies for improving intercultural communication between the African-American community and the dominant culture.

In recent years it has become apparent that disabled persons are a co-culture in our society. While there are approximately 11 million disabled Americans between the ages of 16 and 64, they often find themselves either cut off from or misunderstood by the dominant culture. The next article by Dawn O. Braithwaite looks at some of the reasons for this isolation in "Viewing Persons with Disabilities as a Culture." Specifically, she examines how disabled persons view their communication relationships with ablebodied persons. Braithwaite interviewed 57 physically disabled adults, and learned that they go through a process of redefinition. She found that redefinition involves four steps: (1) redefinition of the disabled as members of a "new" culture; (2) redefinition of self by the disabled; (3) redefinition of disability for the disabled; and (4) redefinition of disability for the dominant culture. By becoming familiar with these steps, we can improve our communication with members of the disabled co-culture.

Recently there has been much attention focused on a social community previously taken for granted by many segments of American society. Because women are so much a part of one's perceptual field, and hence part of one's daily life, it was seldom perceived that the experience of being female was a viable area of investigation. Events such as the Clarence Thomas confirmation hearings, charges of sexual harassment against prominent members of Congress, and successful campaigns for local, state, and national political office by women in unprecedented numbers have resulted in the recognition that a co-culture of women does indeed exist and that society must give serious consideration to this feminine culture and how it differs from the masculine culture.

One of the major differences between the feminine and masculine communities is their communicative behaviors. These differences, and some of the reasons behind them, are the major concern of the Julia T. Wood's article "Gender, Communication, and Culture." Wood points out the conceptual differences between sex and gender, explains how communication contributes to the social-symbolic construction of gender, and shows how gender differences are formed very early in life and thereby constrict gender cultures. She then provides examples of men and women in conversation demonstrating how gender differences in communicative

rules and purposes lead to frequent misunderstandings. She ends by providing excellent advice
on how to achieve effective communication between gender cultures.

In our final article, Randall E. Majors in "Discovering Gay Culture in America," offers innumerable
insights into the cultural experience of gays and
lesbians. There can be little doubt that in recent
years the gay culture has emerged as one of the
most vocal and visible groups on the American
scene. It employs, as do most co-cultures, special
functions and patterns of communication. Majors
investigates the dimensions of these patterns as
they relate to the gay neighborhood, gay social institutions, gay publications, and gay political
power. From this communicative behavior perspective, we can gain immeasurable insight into
the gay co-culture.

Diversity and Its Discontents

ARTURO MADRID

My name is Arturo Madrid. I am a citizen of the
United States, as are my parents and as were my
grandparents, and my great-grandparents. My ancestors' presence in what is now the United States
antedates Plymouth Rock, even without taking into
account any American Indian heritage I might have.

I do not, however, fit those mental sets that define America and Americans. My physical appearance, my speech patterns, my name, my profession
(a professor of Spanish) create a text that confuses
the reader. My normal experience is to be asked:
And where are YOU from?

My response depends on my mood. Passive-
aggressive I answer: "From here." Aggressive-pas-
sive I ask: "Do you mean where am I originally
from?" But ultimately my answer to those follow-up
questions that will ask about origins will be that we
have always been from here.

Overcoming my resentment I will try to educate,
knowing that nine times out of ten my words fall on
inattentive ears. I have spent most of my adult life
explaining who I am not.

I am, however, very clearly the *other*, if only your
everyday, garden-variety, domestic *other*. I've always known that I was the *other*, even before I knew

From *Black Issues in Higher Education*, Vol. 5, No. 4, May
1988, pp. 10–11, 16. Reprinted by permission of the publisher,
Cox, Matthews & Associates, Inc. Arturo Madrid is President of
the Tomas Rivera Center, Claremont Graduate School. This
article was excerpted from the Fourth Annual Tomas Rivera
Lecture at the 1988 National Conference of the American Association of Higher Education, Washington, D.C.

the vocabulary or understood the significance of otherness.

I grew up in an isolated and historically marginal part of the United States, a small mountain village in the state of New Mexico, the eldest child of parents native to that region and whose ancestors had always lived there. In those vast and empty spaces people who look like me, speak as I do, and have names like mine predominate. But the *americanos* lived among us: the descendants of those nineteenth century immigrants who dispossessed us of our lands; missionaries who came to convert us and stayed to live among us; artists who became enchanted with our land and humanscape; refugees from unhealthy climes, crowded spaces, unpleasant circumstances; and of course, the inhabitants of Los Alamos. More importantly, however, they—*los americanos*—were omnipresent in newspapers, newsmagazines, books, on radio, in movies and ultimately, on television.

Despite the operating myth of the day, school did not erase my *otherness*. It did try to deny it, and in doing so only accentuated it. To this day what takes place in schools is more socialization than education, but when I was in elementary school and given where I was, socialization was everything. School was where one became an American. Because there was a pervasive and systematic denial by the society that surrounded us that we were Americans. That denial was both explicit and implicit. I remember the implicit denial, our absence from the larger cultural, economic, and social spaces; the one that reminded us constantly that we were the *other*. And school was where we felt it most acutely.

Quite beyond saluting the flag and pledging allegiance to it, becoming American was learning English . . . and its corollary: not speaking Spanish. I do not argue that learning English was not appropriate. On the contrary. Like it or not, and we had no basis to make any judgments on that matter, we were Americans by virtue of having been born Americans, and English was the common language of Americans. And there was a myth, a pervasive myth, to the effect that if we only learned to speak English well and particularly without an accent—we would be welcomed into the American fellowship.

The official English movement folks notwithstanding, the true test was not our speech, but rather our names and our appearance, for we would always have an accent, however perfect our pronunciation, however excellent our enunication, however divine our diction. That accent would be heard in our pigmentation, our physiognomy, our names. We were, in short, the *other*.

Being the *other* is feeling different; it is awareness of being distinct; it is consciousness of being dissimilar. Otherness results in feeling excluded, closed out, precluded, even disdained and scorned.

Being the *other* involves a contradictory phenomenon. On the one hand being the *other* frequently means being invisible. On the other hand, being the *other* sometimes involves sticking out like a sore thumb. What is she/he doing here?

If one is the *other*, one will inevitably be seen stereotypically; will be defined and limited by mental sets that may not bear much relation to existing realities.

There is sometimes a darker side to otherness as well. The *other* disturbs, disquiets, discomforts. It provokes distrust and suspicion. The *other* frightens, scares.

For some of us being the *other* is only annoying; for others it is debilitating; for still others it is damning. For the majority otherness is permanently sealed by physical appearance. For the rest otherness is betrayed by ways of being, speaking, or of doing.

The first half of my life I spent down-playing the significance and consequences of otherness. The second half has seen me wrestling to understand its complex and deeply ingrained realities; striving to fathom why otherness denies us a voice or visibility or validity in American society and its institutions; struggling to make otherness familiar, reasonable, even normal to my fellow Americans.

Yet I also have experienced another phenomenon; that of being a missing person. Growing up in Northern New Mexico I had only a slight sense of us being missing persons. Hispanos, as we called (and call) ourselves in New Mexico, were very much a part of the fabric of the society and there were Hispano professionals everywhere about me: doctors, lawyers, schoolteachers, and administrators. My people owned businesses, ran organizations, and were both appointed and elected public officials.

My awareness of our absence from the larger institutional life of the society became sharper when I went off to college, but even then it was attenuated by the circumstances of history and geography. The demography of Albuquerque still strongly reflected its historical and cultural origins, despite the influx of Midwesterners and Easterners. Moreover, many of my classmates at the University of New Mexico were Hispanos, and even some of my professors. I thought that would also be true at U.C.L.A., where I began graduate studies in 1960. Los Angeles already had a very large Mexican population, and that population was visible even in and around Westwood and on the campus. But Mexican American students were few and mostly invisible and I do not recall seeing or knowing a single Mexican American (or for that matter Black, Asian, or American Indian) professional on the staff or faculty of that institution during the five years I was there.

Needless to say persons like me were not present in any capacity at Dartmouth College, the site of my first teaching appointment, and of course were not even part of the institutional or individual mindset. I knew then that we — a we that had come to encompass American Indians, Asian Americans, Black Americans, Puerto Ricans, and Women — were truly missing persons in American institutional life.

Over the past three decades the *de jure* and *de facto* segregation that have historically characterized American institutions have been under assault. As a consequence minorities and women have become part of American institutional life, and although there are still many areas where we are not to be found, the missing persons phenomenon is not as pervasive as it once was. However, the presence of the *other*, particularly minorities, in institutions and in institutional life is, as we say in Spanish, *a flor de tierra*: spare plants whose roots do not go deep, a surface phenomenon vulnerable to inclemencies of an economic, or political or social nature.

Some of us entered institutional life through the front door; others through the back door; and still others through side doors. Many, if not most of us, came in through windows, and continue to come in through windows. Of those who entered through the front door, some never made it past the lobby; others were ushered into corners and niches. Those who entered through back and side doors inevitably have remained in back and side rooms. And those who entered through windows found enclosures built around them. For despite the lip service given to the goal of the integration of minorities into institutional life, what has frequently occurred instead is ghettoization, marginalization, isolation.

Not only have the entry points been limited, but in addition the dynamics have been singularly conflictive. Rather than entering institutions more or less passively, minorities have of necessity entered them actively, even aggressively. Rather than taking, they have demanded. Institutional relations have thus been adversarial, infused with specific and generalized tensions.

The nature of the entrance and the nature of the space occupied have greatly influenced the view and attitudes of the majority population within those institutions. All of us are put into the same box; that is, no matter what the individual reality, the assessment of the individual is inevitably conditioned by a perception that is held of the class. Whatever our history, whatever our record, whatever our validations, whatever our accomplishments, by and large we are perceived unidimensionally and dealt with accordingly.

Over the past four decades America's demography has undergone significant changes. Since 1965 the principal demographic growth we have experienced in the United States has been of peoples whose national origins are non-European. This population growth has occurred both through births and through immigration. Conversely, as a consequence of careful tracking by government agencies, we now know that the birth rate of the majority population has decreased.

There are some additional demographic changes which should give us something to think about. Black Americans are now to be found in significant numbers in every major urban center in the nation. Hispanic Americans now number over 15,000,000 persons, and American Indians, heretofore a small and rural population, are increasingly more numerous and urban. The Asian American population, which has historically consisted of small and concentrated communities of Chinese, Filipino, and Japanese Americans, has doubled over the past decade, its complexion changed by the addition of Cambodians, Koreans, Hmongs, Vietnamese, et al.

Thus for the next few decades we will continue to see a growth in the percentage of non-European origin Americans as compared to EuroAmericans. To sum up, we now live in the most demographically diverse nation in the world and one that is growing increasingly more so.

One of my purposes here today is to address the question of whether a goal (quality) and a reality (demographic diversity) present a dilemma to one of the most important of American institutions: higher education.

Quality, according to the Oxford English Dictionary, has multiple meanings. One set defines quality as being an essential character, a distinctive and inherent feature. A second describes it as a degree of excellence, of conformity to standards, as superiority in kind. A third makes reference to social status, particularly to persons of high social status. A fourth talks about quality as being a special or distinguishing attribute, as being a desirable trait. Quality is highly desirable in both principle and practice. We all aspire to it in our own person, in our experiences, and of course we all want to be associated with people and operations of quality.

But let us move away from the various dictionary meanings of the word and to our own sense of what it represents and of how we feel about it. First of all we consider quality to be finite; that is, it is limited with respect to quantity; it has very few manifestations; it is not widely distributed. I have it and you have it, but they don't. We associate quality with homogeneity, with uniformity, with standardization, with order, regularity, neatness. Certainly it's always expensive. We tend to identify it with those who lead, with the rich and the famous. And, when you come right down to it, it's inherent. Either you've got it or you ain't.

Diversity, from the Latin *divertere*, meaning to turn aside, to differ, is the condition of being differ-

ent or having differences, is an instance of being different. Its companion word, *diverse*, means differing, unlike, distinct; having or capable of having various forms; composed of unlike or distinct elements.

Diversity is lack of standardization, of orderliness, homogeneity. Diversity introduces complications, is difficult to organize, is troublesome to manage, is problematical. The way we use the word gives us away. Something is *too* diverse, is *extremely* diverse. We want a *little* diversity.

When we talk about diversity we are talking about the *other*, whatever that *other* might be: someone of a different gender, race, class, national origin; somebody at a greater or lesser distance from the norm; someone outside the set; someone who doesn't fit into the mental configurations that give our lives order and meaning.

In short, diversity is desirable only in principle, not in practice. Long live diversity, . . . as long as it conforms to my standards, to my mind set, to my view of life, to my sense of order.

The United States, by its very nature, by its very development, is the essence of diversity. It is diverse in its geography, population, institutions, technology, its social, cultural, and intellectual modes. It is a society that at its best does not consider quality to be monolithic in form, finite in quantity, or to reside inherently in class. Quality in our society proceeds in large measure out of the stimulus of diverse modes of thinking and acting; out of the creativity made possible by the different ways in which we approach things.

One of the principal strengths of our society is its ability to address on a continuing and substantive basis the real economic, political, and social problems that have faced and continue to face us. What makes the United States so attractive to immigrants are the protections and opportunities it offers; what keeps our society together is tolerance for cultural, religious, social, political, and even linguistic difference; what makes us a unique, dynamic, and extraordinary nation are the power and creativity of our diversity.

The true history of the U.S. is the one of struggle against intolerance, against oppression, against xenophobia, against those forces that have prohibited persons from participating in the larger life of the society on the basis of their race, their gender, their religion, their national origin, their linguistic, and cultural background. These phenomena are not only consigned to the past. They remain with us and frequently take on virulent dimensions.

If you believe, as I do, that the well-being of a society is directly related to the degree and extent to which all of its citizens participate in its institutions, then you will have to agree that we have a challenge before us. In view of the extraordinary changes that are taking place in our society we need to take up the struggle again, unpleasant as it is. As educated and educator members of this society we have a special responsibility for assuring that all American institutions, not just our elementary and secondary schools, our juvenile halls, or our jails, reflect the diversity of our society. Not to do so is to risk greater alienation on the part of a growing segment of our society; is to risk increased social tension in an already conflictive world; and, ultimately, is to risk the survival of a range of institutions that for all their defects and deficiencies, provide us the opportunity and the freedom to improve our individual and collective lot.

Let me urge you, as you return to your professional responsibilities and to your personal spaces, to reflect on these two words — quality and diversity — and on the mental sets and behaviors that flow out of them. And let me urge you further to struggle against the notion that quality is finite in quantity, limited in its manifestations, or is restricted by considerations of class, gender, race, or national origin; or that quality manifests itself only in leaders and not in followers, in managers and not in workers; or that it has to be associated with verbal agility or elegance of personal style; or that it cannot be seeded, or nurtured, or developed.

Who's Got the Room at the Top? Issues of Dominance and Nondominance in Intracultural Communication

EDITH A. FOLB

"If a phenomenon is important, it is perceived, and, being perceived, it is labeled." So notes Nathan Kantrowitz, sociologist and student of language behavior. Nowhere is Kantrowitz's observation more apparent than in that realm of communication studies concerned with the correlates and connections between culture and communication—what the editors of this text have termed "intercultural communication." Our contemporary technology has brought us into both literal and voyeuristic contact with diverse cultures and customs, from the Stone Age Tasaday to the computer age Japanese. Our domestic liberation movements, moreover, have forced upon our consciousness the existence and needs of a multiplicity of groups within our own nation. So, the phenomenon of culture-linked communication is pervasively before us. And, as scholars concerned with culture and communication, we have tried to identify and characterize what we see. This attempt to "label the goods," as it were, has generated a profusion of semantic labels and categories—international communication, cross-cultural communication, intercultural communication, in-

This original essay appeared in print for the first time in the third edition. All rights reserved. Permission to reprint must be obtained from the publisher and the author. Professor Folb teaches at San Francisco State University.

tracultural communication, trans-racial communication, interracial communication, interethnic communication. What we perceive to be important, we label.

Some may chide us for our penchant for classifications—an example of Aristotelian excessiveness, they may say. However, I see it as a genuine attempt to understand what we do individually and collectively, what we focus on within the field of communication studies. I believe this effort to characterize what we do serves a useful function: It continually prods us to examine and expand our vision of what culture-linked communication is, and, at the same time, it helps us bring into sharper focus the dimensions and differences within this area of study. As Samovar and Porter (1982) remind us, "There is still a great need to specify the nature of intercultural communication and to recognize various viewpoints that see the phenomenon somewhat differently" (p. 2). It is my intention in this essay to attempt what the editors of this text suggest, to look at the correlates and connections between culture and communication from a different point of view, one that examines the properties and issues of dominance and nondominance in communicative exchange. The essay is speculative and sometimes polemical. And the focus of my interest and discussion is the realm of intracultural communication.

THE CONCEPT OF INTRACULTURAL COMMUNICATION

The label "intracultural communication" is not unknown within the field of communication studies, although it is one that has not been widely used. Sitaram and Cogdell (1976) have identified intracultural communication as "the type of communication that takes place between members of the same dominant culture, but with slightly differing values" (p. 28). They go on to explain that there are groups ("subcultures") within the dominant culture who hold a minimal number of values that differ from the mainstream, as well as from other subgroups. These differences are not sufficient to identify them as separate cultures, but diverse enough to set them

apart from each other and the culture at large. "Communication between members of such subcultures is *intracultural communication*" (Sitaram and Cogdell, 1976, p. 28).

In another vein, Sarbaugh (1979) sees intracultural communication as an indicator of the degree of cultural experience shared (or not shared) by two people—the more culturally homogeneous the participants, the greater the level of "intraculturalness" surrounding the communicative act. For Sitaram and Cogdell, then, intracultural communication is a phenomenon that operates within a given culture among its members; for Sarbaugh, it is a measure of homogeneity that well may transcend country or culture.

Like Sitaram and Cogdell, I see intracultural communication as a phenomenon that functions within a single, designated culture. However, like Sarbaugh, I am concerned with the particular variables within that context that importantly influence the degree and kind of cultural homogeneity or heterogeneity that can and do exist among members of the culture. Furthermore, the variables of particular interest to me are those that illuminate and underscore the interrelationship of power, dominance, and nondominance in a particular culture.[1] Finally, I believe that the concept of hierarchy, as it functions within a culture, has a deep impact on matters of power, dominance, and nondominance and, therefore, on both the form and content of intracultural communication.

As a backdrop for the discussion of dominance and nondominance in an intracultural context, I would like to formulate a frame of reference within which to view the discussion.

A FRAME OF REFERENCE FOR INTRACULTURAL COMMUNICATION

Society and Culture

Thomas Hobbes, the seventeenth-century political philosopher, left us an intriguing legacy in his work, *Leviathan*. He posited a hypothetical starting point for humankind's march to political and social organization. He called it "the state of nature." In this presocietal state, the biggest club ruled. Kill or be killed was the prevailing modus operandi. Somewhere along the evolutionary road, our ancestors began to recognize a need to change their ways—if any of them were to survive for very long. The principle of enlightened self-interest became the name of the game. Our forebears, however grudgingly, began to curb their inclination to kill, maim, steal, or otherwise aggress upon others and joined together for mutual survival and benefit. The move was one of expediency, not altruism. "Do unto others as you would have them do unto you," whatever its religious import, is a reiteration of the principle of enlightened self-interest.

So, this aggregate of beings came together in order to survive, and, in coming together, gave up certain base instincts, drives, and predilections. "Society" was formed. Those who may scoff at this postulated state of nature need only remember back to the United States' final pullout from Vietnam. The media showed us, in all too brutal detail, the rapidity with which a society disintegrates and we return to the force of the club.

But let us continue with the telling of humankind's tale. It was not sufficient merely to form society; it must be maintained. Controls must be established to ensure its stability. Thus, the social contract was enacted. It was, indeed, the social contract that ensured mutual support, protection, welfare, and survival for the society's members.

However, social maintenance and control did not ensure the perpetuation of the society as an intact entity, carrying along its cumulative and collective experiences, knowledge, beliefs, attitudes, the emergent relationship of self to other, to the group, to the universe, to matters of time and space. That is, it did not ensure the perpetuation of society's accoutrements—its culture. Institutions and structures were needed to house, as it were, the trappings of culture. So, culture was not only embodied in the precepts passed on from one generation to another, but also in the artifacts created by society to safeguard its culture. Looked at in a different light, culture is both a blueprint for continued societal

survival as well as the pervasive cement that holds the social mosaic together. Culture daily tells us and shows us how to be in the universe, and it informs future generations how to be.[2]

From the moment we begin life in this world, we are instructed in the cultural ways that govern and hold together our society, ways that ensure its perpetuation. Indeed, the social contract that binds us to our society and our culture from the moment of birth is neither of our own choice nor of our own design. For example, we are labeled by others almost immediately—John, Sandra, Pearl, David. Our genders are determined at once and we are, accordingly, swaddled in appropriate colors and treated in appropriate ways.[3]

As we grow from infancy to childhood, the socialization process is stepped up and we rapidly internalize the rules of appropriate and inappropriate societal behavior. Religion, education, recreation, health care, and many other cultural institutions reinforce our learning, shape and regulate our behavior and thought so they are orderly and comprehensible to other members of our society. Through the socialization process the human animal is transformed into the social animal. Thus, society is maintained through instruction and indoctrination in the ways of the culture.

But the question that pricks and puzzles the mind is: Whose culture is passed on? Whose social order is maintained? Whose beliefs and values are deemed appropriate? Whose norms, mores, and folkways are invoked?

Hierarchy, Power, and Dominance

In most societies, as we know them, there is a hierarchy of status and power. By its very nature, hierarchy implies an ordering process, a sense of the evaluative marketing of those being ordered. Our own vernacular vocabulary abounds with references to hierarchy and concomitant status and power: "top dog," "top banana," "king pin," "king of the mountain."

High status and attendant power may be accorded to those among us who are seen or believed to be great warriors or hunters, those invested with magical, divine, or special powers, those who are deemed wise, or those who are in possession of important, valued and/or vital societal resources and goods. Of course, power and high status are not necessarily—or even usually—accorded to these specially designated members of the society in some automatic fashion. Power, control, and subsequent high status are often forcibly wrested from others and forcibly maintained. Not everyone abides by the social contract, and strong-arm rule often prevails, as conquered, colonized, and enslaved people know too well.

Whatever the basis for determining the hierarchy, the fact of its existence in a society assures the evolution and continued presence of a power elite—those at the top of the social hierarchy who accrue and possess what the society deems valuable or vital. And, in turn, the presence of a power elite ensures an asymmetrical relationship among the members of the society. In fact, power is often defined as the ability to get others to do what you want and the resources to force them to do your bidding if they resist—the asymmetrical relationship in its extreme form.

But the perpetuation of the power elite through force is not the most effective or efficient way of ensuring one's position at the top of the hierarchy. It is considerably more effective to institute, encourage, and/or perpetuate those aspects of culture—knowledge, experiences, beliefs, values, patterns of social organization, artifacts—that subtly and manifestly reinforce and ensure the continuation of the power elite and its asymmetrical relationship within the society. Though we may dismiss Nazism as a malignant ideology, we should attend to the fact that Hitler well understood the maintenance of the power elite through the manipulation and control of culture—culture as propaganda.

Though I would not imply that all power elites maintain themselves in such an overtly manipulative way, I would at least suggest that the powerful in many societies—our own included—go to great lengths to maintain their positions of power and what those positions bring them. And to that end, they support, reinforce, and, indeed, create those particular cultural precepts and artifacts that are likely to guarantee their continued power. To the extent that the culture reflects implicitly or expressly the needs and desires of the power elite to sustain itself, it becomes a vehicle for propaganda. Thus, cultural precepts and artifacts that govern such matters as social organization and behavior, values, beliefs, and the like can often be seen as rules and institutions that sustain the few at the expense of the many.

So, we come back to the question of whose rules, whose culture? I would suggest that when we in communication studies refer to the "dominant culture" we are, in fact, not talking about numbers. That is why the label "minorities" is misleading when we refer to cultural groups within the larger society. Blacks in South Africa and women in the United States are not numerical minorities—but they are not members of the power elite either. In fact, when we talk about the concept of dominant culture, we are really talking about power—those who *dominate* culture, those who historically or traditionally have had the most persistent and far-reaching impact on culture, on what we think and say, on what we believe and do in our society. We are talking about the culture of the minority and, by extension, the structures and institutions (social, political, economic, legal, religious, and so on) that maintain the power of this minority. Finally, we are talking about rules of appropriate and inappropriate behavior, thought, speech, and action for the many that preserve power for the few. Dominant culture, therefore, significantly reflects the precepts and artifacts of those who dominate culture and is not necessarily, or even usually, a reference to numbers, but to power.

So, coming full circle, I would suggest that our socialization process, our social introduction to this aggregate of people who form society, is an introduction to a rule-governed milieu of asymmetrical societal organization and relationship, and the communicative behaviors and practices found there are likewise asymmetrical in nature. As the witticism goes, "All men (perhaps even women) are created equal—some are just more equal than others."

Given this frame of reference, I would now like to explore some definitions and concepts that, I believe, emerge from this perspective. It is my hope that the discussion will provide the reader with another way to look at intracultural communication.

A NOMENCLATURE FOR INTRACULTURAL COMMUNICATION

The Concept of Nondominance

As already indicated, I view intracultural communication as a phenomenon that operates within a given cultural context. However, my particular focus, as suggested, is not a focus on numbers but an attention to dominance, nondominance, and power in the cultural setting. That is, how do nondominant groups intersect and interact with the dominant culture membership (with those who enact the precepts and support the institutions and systems of the power elite)? For purposes of discussion and analysis, I will take most of my examples from the geopolitical configuration called the United States.

By "nondominant groups" I mean those constellations of people who have not historically or traditionally had continued access to or influence upon or within the dominant culture's (that is, those who dominate culture) social, political, legal, economic, and/or religious structures and institutions. Nondominant groups include people of color, women, gays, the physically challenged,[4] and the aged, to name some of the most prominent. I use the expression "nondominant" to characterize these people because, as suggested, I am referring to power and dominance, not numbers and dominance. Within the United States, those most likely to hold and control positions of real—not token—power and those who have the greatest potential ease of access to power and high status are still generally white, male, able-bodied, heterosexual, and youthful in appearance if not in age.[5]

Nondominant people are also those who, in varying degrees and various ways, have been "invisible" within the society of which they are a part and at the same time bear a visible caste mark. Furthermore, it is this mark of caste identity that is often consciously or habitually assigned low or negative status by members of the dominant culture.

The dimensions of invisibility and marked visibility are keen indicators of the status hierarchy in a given society. In his book, *The Invisible Man*, Ralph Ellison instructs us in the lesson that nondominant people—in this instance, black people—are figuratively "invisible." They are seen by the dominant culture as no one, nobody and therefore go unacknowledged and importantly unperceived.[6] Furthermore, nondominant peoples are often relegated to object status rather than human status. They are viewed as persons of "no consequence," literally and metaphorically. Expressions such as, "If you've seen one, you've seen them all"; "They all look alike to me"; "If you put a bag over their heads, it doesn't matter who you screw" attest to this level of invisibility and dehumanization of nondominant peoples, such as people of color or women. Indeed, one need only look at the dominant culture's slang repertory for a single nondominant group, women, to see the extent of this object status: "tail," "piece of ass," "side of beef," "hole," "gash," "slit," and so on.

At the same time that nondominant peoples are socially invisible, they are often visibly caste marked. Though we tend to think of caste in terms, say, of East Indian culture, we can clearly apply the concept to our own culture. One of the important dimensions of a caste system is that it is hereditary—you are born into a given caste and are usually marked for life as a member. In fact, we are all born into a caste, we are all caste marked. Indeed, some of us are doubly or multiply caste marked. In the United States, the most visible marks of caste relate to gender, race, age, and the degree to which one is able-bodied.

As East Indians do, we too assign low to high status and privilege to our people. The fact that this assignment of status and privilege may be active or passive, conscious or unconscious, malicious or unthinking does not detract from the reality of the act. And one of the major determinants of status, position, and caste marking relates back to who has historically or traditionally had access to or influence upon or within the power elite and its concomitant structures and institutions. So, historically blacks, native Americans, Chicanos, women, the old, the physically challenged have at best been neutrally caste marked and more often negatively identified when it comes to issues of power, dominance, and social control.[7]

Low status has been assigned to those people whom society views as somehow "stigmatized." Indeed, we have labels to identify such stigmatization: "deviant," "handicapped," "abnormal," "substandard," "different"—that is, different from those who dominate. As already suggested, it is the white, male, heterosexual, able-bodied, youthful person who both sets the standards for caste marking and is the human yardstick by which people within the United States are importantly measured and accordingly treated. As Porter and Samovar (1976) remind us, "We [in the United States] have generally viewed racial minorities as less than equal; they have been viewed as second class members of society—not quite as good as the white majority—and treated as such. . . . Blacks, Mexican Americans, Indians, and Orientals are still subject to prejudice and discrimination and treated in many respects as colonized subjects" (p. 11). I would add to this list of colonized, low-status subjects women, the physically challenged, and the aged. Again, our language is a telling repository for illuminating status as it relates to subordination in the social hierarchy: "Stay in your place," "Don't get out of line," "Know your place," "A woman's place is chained to the bed and the stove," "Know your station in life" are just a few sample phrases.

It is inevitable that nondominant peoples will experience, indeed be subjected to and suffer from, varying degrees of fear, denial, and self-hatred of their caste marking. Frantz Fanon's (1963) characterization of the "colonized native"—the oppressed native who has so internalized the power elite's perception of the norm that he or she not only serves and speaks for the colonial elite but is often more critical and oppressive of her or his caste than is the colonial—reveals this depth of self-hatred and denial.

In a parallel vein, the concept of "passing" which relates to a person of color attempting to "pass for" white, is a statement of self-denial. Implicit in the art of passing is the acceptance, if not the belief, that "white is right" in this society, and the closer one can come to the likeness of the privileged caste, the more desirable and comfortable one's station in life will be. So, people of color have passed for white—just as Jews have passed for Gentile or gay males and females have passed for straight, always with the fear of being discovered "for what they are." Physical impairment, too, has been a mark of shame in this country for those so challenged. Even so powerful a figure as F.D.R. refused to be photographed in any way that would picture him to be a "cripple."

If the act of passing is a denial of one's caste, the process of "coming out of the closet" is a conscious acceptance of one's caste. It is an important political and personal statement of power, a vivid metaphor that literally marks a rite of passage. Perhaps the most striking acknowledgement of one's caste marking in our society relates to sexual preference. For a gay male or lesbian to admit their respective sexual preferences is for them to consciously take on an identity that our society has deemed abnormal and deviant—when measured against the society's standard of what is appropriate. They become, quite literally, marked people. In an important way, most of our domestic liberation movements are devoted to having their membership come out of the closet. That is, these movements seek not only to have their people heard and empowered by the power elite, but to have them reclaim and assert their identity and honor their caste. Liberation movement slogans tell the story of positive identification with one's caste: "Black is beautiful," "brown power," "Sisterhood is powerful," "gay pride," "I am an Indian and proud of it."

The nature and disposition of the social hierarchy in a given society, such as the United States, is reflected not only in the caste structure, but also in the class structure and the role prescriptions and expectations surrounding caste and class. Although the power structure in the United States is a complex and multileveled phenomenon, its predominant, generating force is economic. That is, the power elite is an elite that controls the material resources and goods in this country as well as the means and manner of production and distribution. Though one of our national fictions is that the United States is a classless society, we have, in fact, a well-established class structure based largely on economic power and control. When we talk of lower, middle, and upper classes in this country, we are not usually talking about birth or origins, but about power and control over material resources, and the attendant wealth, privilege, and high status.

There is even a kind of status distinction made within the upper-class society in this country that again relates to wealth and power, but in a temporal rather than a quantitative way—how long one has had wealth, power, and high-class status. So, distinctions are made between the old rich (the Harrimans, the Gores, the Pews) and the new rich (the Hunt family, Norton Simon, and their like).

Class, then, is intimately bound up with matters of caste. Not all, or even most, members of our society have the opportunity—let alone the caste credentials—to get a "piece of the action." It is no accident of nature that many of the nondominant peoples in this country are also poor peoples. Nor is it surprising that nondominant groups have been historically the unpaid, low-paid, and/or enslaved work force for the economic power elite.

Finally, role prescriptions are linked to both matters of status and expectations in terms of one's perceived status, class, and caste. A role can be defined simply as a set of behaviors. The set of behaviors we ascribe to a given role is culture-bound and indicative of what has been designated as appropriate within the culture vis-à-vis that role. They are prescriptive, not descriptive, behaviors. We hold certain behavioral expectations for certain roles. It is a mark of just how culture-bound and prescriptive these roles are when someone is perceived to behave inappropriately—for example, the mother who gives up custody of her children in order to pursue her career; she has "stepped out of line."

Furthermore, we see certain roles as appropriate or inappropriate to a given caste. Though another of our national myths—the Horatio Alger myth—tells us that there is room at the top for the industrious, bright go-getter, the truth of the matter is that there is room at the top if you are appropriately caste

marked (that is, are white, male, able-bodied, and so on). The resistance, even outright hostility, nondominant peoples have encountered when they aspire to or claim certain occupational roles, for example, is a mark of the power elite's reluctance to relinquish those positions that have been traditionally associated with privileged status and high caste and class ranking. Though, in recent years, there has been much talk about a woman vice-president of the United States, it has remained just talk. For that matter, there has not been a black vice-president or a Hispanic or a Jew. The thought of the presidency being held by most nondominant peoples is still "unspeakable."

The cultural prescription to keep nondominant peoples "in their place" is reinforced by and reinforces what I refer to as the "subterranean self"—the culture-bound collection of prejudices, stereotypes, values, and beliefs that each of us embraces and employs to justify our world view and the place of people in that world. It is, after all, our subterranean selves that provide fuel to fire the normative in our lives—what roles people ought and ought not to perform, what and why certain individuals are ill- or well-equipped to carry out certain roles, and our righteously stated rationalizations for keeping people in their places as we see them. Again, it should be remembered that those who dominate the culture reinforce and tacitly or openly encourage the perpetuation of those cultural prejudices, stereotypes, values, and beliefs that maintain the status quo, that is, the asymmetrical nature of the social hierarchy. Those who doubt the fervent desire of the power elite to maintain things as they are need only ponder the intense and prolonged resistance to the Equal Rights Amendment. If women are already "equal," why not make their equality a matter of record?

The foregoing discussion has been an attempt to illuminate the meaning of nondominance and the position of the nondominant person within our society. By relating status in the social hierarchy to matters of caste, class, and role, it has been my intention to highlight what it means to be a nondominant person within a culture that is dominated by the cultural precepts and artifacts of a power elite. It has also been my intention to suggest that the concept of "dominant culture" is something of a fiction, as we in communication studies traditionally use it. Given my perspective, it is more accurate to talk about those who dominate a culture rather than a dominant culture per se. Finally, I have attempted to point out that cultural dominance is not necessarily, or even usually, a matter of the numbers of people in a given society, but of those who have real power in a society.

Geopolitics

The viewpoint being developed in this essay highlights still another facet of dominance and nondominance as it relates to society and the culture it generates and sustains—namely, the geopolitical facet. The United States is not merely a territory with certain designated boundaries—a geographical entity—it is a geopolitical configuration. It is a country whose history reflects the clear-cut interrelationship of geography, politics, economics, and the domination and control of people. For example, the westward movement and the subsequent takeover of the Indian nations and chunks of Mexico were justified by our doctrine of Manifest Destiny, not unlike the way Hitler's expansionism was justified by the Nazi doctrine of "geopolitik." It is no accident that the doctrine of Manifest Destiny coincides with the rapid growth and development of U.S. industrialization. The U.S. power elite wanted more land in which to expand and grow economically, so it created a rationalization to secure it.

Perhaps nowhere is a dominant culture's (those who dominate culture) ethnocentrism more apparent than in the missionary-like work carried on by its members—whether it be to "civilize" the natives (that is, to impose the conquerors' cultural baggage on them), to "educate them in the ways of the white man," or to "Americanize" them. Indeed, the very term *America* is a geopolitical label as we use it. It presumes that those who inhabit the United States are the center of the Western hemisphere, indeed its only residents.[8] Identifying ourselves as "Americans" and our geopolitical entity as "America," in light of the peoples who live to the north and south of our borders speaks to both our economic dominance in this hemisphere and our ethnocentrism.

Identifying the United States in geopolitical terms is to identify it as a conqueror and controller of other peoples, and suggests both the probability of nondominant groups of people within that territory and a polarized, even hostile relationship between these groups and those who dominate culture. What Rich and Ogawa (1982) have pointed out in their model of interracial communication is applicable to most nondominant peoples: "As long as a power relationship exists between cultures where one has subdued and dominated the other . . . hostility, tension and strain are introduced into the communicative situation" (p. 46). Not only were the Indian nations[9] and parts of Mexico conquered and brought under the colonial rule of the United States, but in its industrial expansionism, the United States physically enslaved black Africans to work on the farms and plantations of the South. It also economically enslaved large numbers of East European immigrants, Chinese, Irish, Hispanics (and more recently, Southeast Asians) in its factories, on its railroads, in its mines and fields through low wages and long work hours. It coopted the cottage industries of the home and brought women and children into the factories under abysmal conditions and the lowest of wages.

Indeed, many of the nondominant peoples in this country today are the very same ones whom the powerful have historically colonized, enslaved, disenfranchised, dispossessed, discounted, and relegated to poverty and low caste and class status. So, the asymmetrical relationship between the conquerer and the conquered continues uninterrupted. Although the form of oppression may change through time, the fact of oppression—and coexistent nondominance—remains.

It has been my desire throughout this essay to speculate about the complex ways in which society, culture, position, and place in the societal hierarchy affect and are affected by the matters of dominance, power, and social control. To this end, I have chosen to identify and characterize configurations of people within a society not only along a cultural axis but along a socioeconomic and a geopolitical axis as well. I have tried to reexamine some of the concepts and definitions employed in discussions of culture-linked communication in a different light. And I have chosen the issues and conditions surrounding dominance and nondominance as points of departure and return. As I said at the beginning of this essay, the content is speculative, exploratory, and, hopefully, provocative. Above all, it is intended to encourage dialogue and exchange about the conditions and constraints surrounding intracultural communication.

NOTES

1. See Folb (1980) for another perspective on the intersection of power, dominance, and nondominance as they operate within a discrete microcultural group, the world of the black ghetto teenager.

2. For a fascinating account of how and what kind of culture is transmitted from person to person, see Margaret Mead's *Culture and Commitment* (1970).

3. Mary Ritchie Key's book, *Male/Female Language* (1975), provides an informative discussion of the ways in which females and males are catalogued, characterized, and compartmentalized by our language. She illuminates its effects on how we perceive ourselves, as well as discussing how others perceive us through the prism of language.

4. The semantic marker "physically challenged" is used in lieu of other, more traditional labels such as "handicapped," "physically disabled," or "physically impaired," because it is a designation perferred by many so challenged. It is seen as a positive, rather than a negative, mark of identification.

5. In a country as youth conscious as our own, advanced age is seen as a liability, not as a mark of honor and wisdom as it is in other cultures. Whatever other reservations people had about Ronald Reagan's political aspirations in 1980, the one most discussed was his age. His political handlers went to great lengths—as did Reagan himself—to "prove" he was young in spirit and energy if not in years. It was important that he align himself as closely as possible with the positive mark of youth we champion and admire in this country.

6. It is no mere coincidence that a common thread binds together the domestic liberation movements in this country. It is the demand to be seen, heard, and empowered.

7. See Nancy Henley's *Body Politics* (1977) for a provocative look at the interplay of the variables power, dominance, and sex as they affect nonverbal communication.

8. The current bumper sticker, "Get the United States Out of North America," is a pointed reference to our hemispheric self-centeredness.

9. Neither the label "Indian" nor the label "native American" adequately identifies those people who inhabited the North American continent before the European conquest of this territory. Both reflect the point of view of the labeler, not those so labeled. That is why many who fought for the label "native American" now discount it as not significantly different from "Indian."

REFERENCES

Fanon, Frantz. (1963). *Wretched of the Earth*. New York: Grove Press.

Folb, Edith A. (1980). *Runnin' Down Some Lines: The Language and Culture of Black Teenagers*. Cambridge, Mass.: Harvard University Press.

Porter, Richard E., and Larry A. Samovar. (1976). "Communicating Interculturally." In Larry A. Samovar and Richard E. Porter (Eds.), *Intercultural Communication: A Reader* (2nd ed.) Belmont, Calif.: Wadsworth.

Rich, Andrea L., and Dennis M. Ogawa. (1982). "Intercultural and Interracial Communication: An Analytical Approach." In Larry A. Samovar and Richard E. Porter (Eds.), *Intercultural Communication: A Reader* (3rd ed.) Belmont, Calif.: Wadsworth.

Samovar, Larry A., and Richard E. Porter (Eds.). (1982). *Intercultural Communication: A Reader* (3rd ed.) Belmont, Calif.: Wadsworth.

Sarbaugh, L. E. (1979). *Intercultural Communication*. Rochelle Park, N.J.: Hayden Book Co.

Sitaram, K. S., and Roy T. Cogdell. (1976). *Foundations of Intercultural Communication*. Columbus, Ohio: Merrill.

An African-American Communication Perspective

SIDNEY A. RIBEAU
JOHN R. BALDWIN
MICHAEL L. HECHT

African American communication is as complex as the culture from which it emerges. Taken from the shores of Africa, the enslaved captives were forced to create a means of expression consistent with an African cultural tradition, yet responsive to life in the new world. The fusion of past traditions with slavery, and post-slavery experiences in the rural South and North, created a unique ethnic culture for the group known as African Americans.

The communicative style of African American ethnic culture is captured in a number of studies that investigate linguistic characteristics, social relationships, and verbal and nonverbal messages. This early research, which is primarily descriptive, provides an introduction to a rich and promising line of inquiry. Our work expands the discussion of African American discourse to include empirical investigations of the interpersonal dimensions that characterize this unique ethnic communication system. We are particularly interested in (1) the identification of satisfying and dissatisfying conversational themes, (2) conversational improvement strategies, and (3) communication effectiveness. A few important assumptions support our work and provide a context for this research.

This original article appears here in print for the first time. All rights reserved. Permission to reprint must be obtained from the authors and the publisher. Sidney Ribeau is Vice President for Academic Affairs at California State Polytechnic University, Pomona, John R. Baldwin is a Graduate Associate at Arizona State University, and Michael L. Hecht teaches in the Department of Communication at Arizona State University.

UNDERLYING ASSUMPTIONS

We consider communication to be problematic — an interactive event during which persons assign meanings to messages and jointly create identities and social reality. This process is multi-dimensional and extremely complex. Attribution of meaning to symbols requires the interpretation of messages and negotiation of social worlds. The process is replete with the potential for failure which is magnified when ethno-cultural factors are introduced. Ethnic cultures consist of cognitive (for example, values, beliefs, norms) and material (for example, food, dress, symbols) characteristics that distinguish them from mainstream American culture. For successful communication to occur, these potential problems must be anticipated and managed.

Here we use an interpretive approach that utilizes the perceptions of cultural actors to explain their communicative behavior. The descriptions and narrative accounts provided by interactions enable one to glimpse a world normally reserved for members of the shared community. It is this world that we seek to unfold.

Culture and ethnicity are the concepts that govern our exploration of African American communication. **Culture** consists of the shared cognitive and material items that forge a group's identity and ensure its survival. Culture is created, shared, and transmitted through communication. **Ethnicity** pertains to the traditions, heritage, and ancestry that define a people. It is particularly apparent in a group's expressive forms. (We take as axiomatic the existence of ethnic cultures in America, and recognize African American culture as a fundamental element of life in America.)

Our early work is governed by the conceptual assumptions listed, and a practical concern: *research on African American communication should assist the practitioner in improving relationships between African Americans and European Americans*. It is our belief that the communication discipline has much to offer the area of human relations. This line of research is intended to make a contribution to that effort. To that end we began with studies of (1) intragroup communication issues, (2) interethnic communication issues, and (3) conversational improvement strategies. The remainder of this paper will report our findings and discuss their implications. First, however, we frame these studies within an understanding of communication effectiveness.

COMMUNICATION EFFECTIVENESS

Many scholars have provided valuable information about what behaviors and communication people believe to be effective (Martin, 1989, 1993; Martin & Hammer, 1989; Pavitt & Haight, 1985; Ruben, 1977, 1989). "Competent" or "effective" communication has been defined in many ways (Spitzberg & Cupach, 1984; Spitzberg & Hecht, 1984; Wiemann & Bradac, 1989). One way to define **effective** behavior is that which is productive and satisfying for both partners. Communication is appropriate if it follows the rules and expectations the partners have; these expectations vary depending on the context the speakers are in or the relationship between them. The positive feelings the communicators have when their expectations are met make up the "satisfying" part of our definition (Hecht, 1978, 1984). The expectations may be met because a relationship is satisfying (McLaughlin & Cody, 1982), or because the communicators were able to function effectively in a new situation (Vause & Wiemann, 1981).

In view of effective communication, we see *communication issues* as "the agenda for effective communication held in common by members of the group" (Hecht, Collier, & Ribeau, in press, p. 127). That is, they are aspects of communication, which, if missing, pose problems for the communication; they are expectations about communication. Since different ethnic groups have different shared histories and ways of seeing the world, we believe that the unspoken, often subconscious, rules that one co-culture has for effective or satisfying communication may differ from those imposed by another. Further, given the impact of historical race and power relationships in the United States, it seems likely that African Americans (and other American cultures)

would apply differing rules for measuring effective communications with in-group and out-group members.

INTRAGROUP COMMUNICATION ISSUES

We started by trying to understand how African Americans communicate among themselves. We asked African Americans, Mexican Americans, and European Americans to describe satisfying or dissatisfying conversations they had experienced with a member of their own ethnic group (Hecht & Ribeau, 1984). We found that the expectations of the groups were in some ways different, in others similar. Mexican Americans differed the most, with African Americans and European Americans responding more similarly.

Mexican Americans, for example, tended to seek closely bonded relationships, seeing the relationship itself as rewarding. Within this ethnic group, satisfying communication involved nonverbal communication and acceptance of self. In comparison, African Americans, and to a greater extent, European Americans, were self-oriented—that is, they saw the reward in something the other partner might provide for them, instead of in the existence of the relationship.

In keeping with this idea of potential reward, European Americans tended to look more to the future of the relationship. This echoes a previous study in which European Americans found communication with friends more satisfying when there were signs of intimacy that confirmed the future of the relationship (Hecht, 1984). At the same time, European Americans demonstrated less concern and interest for the partner in the conversation (other orientation) than did African Americans.

African Americans, on the other hand, found greater satisfaction in conversations where both partners were more involved in the topic. Intimacy was therapeutic and foundational to the relationship, and trust was highly important. While conversation was goal-oriented, at the same time it was important that ideas and feelings be exchanged. Where the Mexican Americans found bonding a priority for relationships, the African Americans surveyed found bonding conditional — to be established only if that exchange of ideas took place. In light of this, genuineness ("being real") and expressiveness were important, and were communicated through expressive style, passion, and deep involvement with the topic. Helping one another was an integral part of satisfying interaction, supporting goal-oriented relationships. Because both parties may be trying to meet the same goals, it is necessary that those goals be clearly understood; thus, understanding is also important. African Americans found satisfaction when they knew where the conversation was going.

INTERGROUP COMMUNICATION ISSUES

We next sought to understand the agenda for effective interethnic communication — specifically, communication between blacks and whites (Hecht, Collier, & Ribeau, in press; Hecht, Larkey, & Johnson, 1992; Hecht & Ribeau, 1987; Hecht, Ribeau, & Alberts, 1989; Hecht, Ribeau, & Sedano, 1990). In this research, we identified seven primary issues important to those African Americans studied: (1) negative stereotyping, (2) acceptance, (3) personal expressiveness, (4) authenticity, (5) understanding, (6) goal attainment, and (7) power dynamics. In describing these issues, we provide quotes from African American responses to interviews and surveys to illuminate the findings.

Negative Stereotyping

Negative stereotyping is "the use of rigid racial categories that distort an African American's individuality. This violates the concept of uniqueness, something research has shown to be very important to African Americans" (Hecht, Collier, & Ribeau, in press). Negative stereotyping occurred in two ways. The first, and more obvious, was when European Americans in the study racially categorized African Americans — that is, when they treated them as a member of a group, or ascribed to them characteris-

tics of the group, instead of treating them like individuals.

Indirect stereotyping occurred when European Americans talked to African Americans about what were seen to be "African American topics," such as sports or music. Some African Americans reported that this type of behavior made them want to withdraw, or caused them to see their conversational partner with disdain. One male African American, while seeing the introduction of such topics as an attempt to find common interests, saw those who brought them up as "patronizing or unaware," and felt that other African Americans felt the same way. Another type of indirect stereotyping is when European Americans ask or expect African Americans to speak on behalf of all African Americans. One participant *did feel satisfied* about her conversation because she "didn't feel put on the spot to speak for the whole of the black race." Another female was satisfied when the other person spoke to her "as another person and didn't let my color interfere with the conversation."

Acceptance

The second issue is *acceptance*, "the feeling that another accepts, confirms, and respects one's opinions" (Hecht, Collier, & Ribeau, in press, p. 131). Frequently, African Americans did not feel accepted by European Americans. For example, some persons interviewed said African Americans sometimes try to make up for "cultural deprivation" and "talk rather than listen in order to cover up." They act "cool," flippant, or talkative, sometimes using stylized speech. Some of the participants saw these behaviors as responses to stereotypes, either in the sense that the African Americans were trying to control the conversation to preempt the stereotypes, or that they were trying to avoid recognizing them. One person strongly volunteered that African Americans are no longer concerned about what European Americans feel or accept. At the same time, many of those interviewed felt that acceptance was a characteristic of satisfying conversations. This acceptance might be shown by positive nonverbal behaviors, similar dress, feeling comfortable with the conversation, "mutual respect for each other's beliefs," and even, at times, acting "cool" or removed.

Personal Expressiveness

Personal expressiveness refers to the verbal and nonverbal expression of thoughts, ideas, or feelings. While many African Americans mentioned some aspect of expressiveness, how that expressiveness is played out varies from person to person. Some saw honesty, integrity, and the open sharing of ideas as valuable; others felt it important to keep their feelings hidden in intercultural communications. For example, one African American woman expressed dissatisfaction with a conversation because "I maintained control and did not curse her out." Opinions are important, but the emphasis is on expressing feelings — "talking from the heart, not the head." In contrast, non-expressive European Americans might be seen as racist or standoffish. Interestingly, many participants — more females than males — expressed the need to portray a tough exterior. African Americans need to "be cool," and not let European Americans know what they are thinking or feeling. History had an impact here with some of the women participants, pointing out that African American women have had to be strong both in response to prejudice and often as the head of the household. A possible explanation for the contrasting answers is that some African Americans value toughness and "coolness" until barriers of fear and mistrust are broken down; then, it becomes important to express who one really is.

Authenticity

Authenticity is tied directly to the concept of being oneself, of being genuine. Both African and European Americans perceived authenticity on the part of their conversational partner when the other was seen as revealing personal information — being honest, "being real," "being themselves," or expressing personal feelings freely. One African American male complained about "so many phony conversa-tions — white people trying to impress African Americans with their liberalness." Straightforwardness, or "telling it like it is," is one aspect of authenticity; the opposite of this is avoidance of the truth through double talking or fancy language.

At the same time, many African American males engage in self-presentation; they try to create an acceptable image of themselves through "high talk" and "stylin.'" "You dress as if you had money even if you don't." Creating an acceptable self-image becomes critical when a demeaning image has been externally imposed by European American society. In this light, stylized behavior to African Americans emerges as a sign of strength, not a lack of authenticity.

Understanding

Understanding is the feeling that messages are successfully conveyed. This theme was expressed when people felt that information was adequately exchanged or learning took place. One person noted that "there was a genuine exchange of thinking, feeling, and caring." Unfortunately, understanding can be hampered by cultural differences or differences in upbringing. One female commented that "if people don't share the same life experiences, they can't be expected to truly understand each other. If whites haven't been exposed to blacks, there will be a 'fear of the unknown.'"

Goal Attainment

Goal attainment, or achieving desired ends from a conversation, was mentioned more in satisfying than in dissatisfying conversations. It is closely linked to understanding in that without some mutual understanding no goals will be met. Goals might include finding the solution to some problem, exchanging information, or finishing some project. But cultural misunderstandings can get in the way of goals. As one male responded: "Blacks and whites may come away with different meanings from a conversation because concepts aren't defined in the same way. The members of the ethnic groups tend to think in a different manner." Because of this, African Americans often find conversations with European Americans unrewarding, but those rewarding conversations are "like gates opening."

Power Dynamics

Power dynamics, the last category, contains two main themes: powerlessness and assertiveness. *Powerlessness*, a feeling of being controlled, manipulated, or trapped, resulted from behaviors that rob African American conversational partners of the right to express their ideas freely. One participant objected to the term "powerlessness" as "putting things in white terms"; the label is not as important to us as the behaviors it describes. European Americans were seen as manipulating when they tried to control the topic, tried to persuade through subtlety, or would not let the African Americans finish their thoughts. One European-American communicator "tried to carry on the conversation all by himself . . . he would keep talking and interrupted me whenever I tried to say something."

Extreme assertiveness and confrontation used by African Americans, called "Mau Mauing," by one participant is the other half of power dynamics. African Americans, it was commented, often talk with one another in a way that "whites would consider antagonistic or brutal." For this reason, many African Americans *code switch*, or change their communication style and language, when they interact with European Americans. Assertive speaking among some African Americans is exemplified by "the dozens," a put-down game in which one person puts down or makes fun of another person. It should be emphasized, however, that this type of assertiveness is by no means universal to all African Americans.

COMMUNICATION IMPROVEMENT STRATEGIES

While interethnic communication issues are characteristics or behaviors that can help or hurt these communications, the African American participants believed *improvement strategies* can enhance con-versation. These are things communicators can do to help make the interaction more satisfying. While our initial research found six strategies (Hecht & Ribeau, 1987; Hecht, Ribeau, & Alberts, 1989; Martin, Larkey, & Hecht, 1991), later research has expanded the list to twelve: (1) asserting one's point of view, (2) positive self-presentation, (3) be open and friendly, (4) avoidance, (5) interaction management, (6) other-orientation, (7) inform/educate, (8) express genuineness, (9) confront, (10) internal management, (11) treat others as individuals, and (12) language management. We describe these again with quotes from African Americans to expound.

Asserting One's Point of View

Assertiveness, in both style and substance, includes using such expressions as "stress," "assert," or "emphasize my point." This strategy grew out of dissatisfying conversations and was recommended for aiding African Americans' persuasion or argumentation efforts. The purpose is not simply to inform, but to gain agreement. Examples of this point of view are expressed in these comments: "Just simply be more vocal in the conversation. This in itself will give you a sense of control or power." "I continue to put across what I believe."

Positive Self-Presentation

Two methods of positive self-presentation attempt to reverse the other person's impressions. One method of self-presentation is to deliberately contradict stereotypes: "I just make sure my actions and conversation don't fit the negative stereotype." The other method is to point out positive attributes or accomplishments: "I try to make others see what I know, that is, when I'm being talked down to I try to show my intelligence."

Be Open And Friendly

This strategy, used most often to improve dissatisfying conversations, is similar to positive self-presentation, but without the deliberate desire to impress. Again, the participants varied in their views on openness, or open-mindedness. Some respondents felt European Americans should "be more patient, not assume anything, find out first." However, some African Americans rejected openness as a European American, middle-class female attribute, preferring to present themselves as strong, more closed. Friendliness includes being considerate of the other, polite, and courteous.

Avoidance

In a dissatisfying conversation, one might avoid either the conversation itself (by leaving), or the topics that are sensitive or demeaning. The first strategy is indicated by those who "terminate the conversation," or "remove myself from the conversation." The second is used when an African American perceives that some topics just cannot be discussed with certain individuals. Possible methods of avoidance include "not bringing up the subject," or changing the subject. ("I don't think it's beneficial to try to change the other person.")

Interaction Management

Either the African or the European American can attempt to manage the flow of the interaction. This might be done to reduce problems or just to improve a conversation. Possible strategies within this category include managing immediate interaction ("take turns," "work toward a compromise"), postponing the problem ("request a time to talk it over"), or finding different means of communication ("write a note"). Sometimes the conversation can be better managed by "just talking a little more" or spending "more time" together.

Other-Orientation

A concern for or interest in the other person was a sign of satisfying relationships, and might be created in different ways. Involving the other person in the conversation or finding common ground was one method suggested: "Think or talk about something that both can identify with." Others emphasized listening to the other person's thoughts and opinions: "learn by listening," "placing them in our shoes," and "try to look at it from both sides." Either party can improve the conversation with this strategy.

Inform/Educate

Information was often shared to educate or inform the conversational partner, in contrast to "asserting one's point of view." One should "tactfully educate by giving more information," and "if the conversation is that important, try and explain whatever you feel is being misunderstood." More facts should be given, sometimes specifically citing African American history to help others understand. At the same time, African Americans sometimes mentioned the need to ask European Americans more questions. This strategy attempts to resolve the issues raised by stereotyping and lack of understanding.

Express Genuineness

This strategy, genuineness, addresses the issue of authenticity, of "being yourself." Comments in this category valued honesty and expressing feelings. Some participants opened up in hopes that their conversation partner would follow. Others saw it in terms of a need to "share your feelings of a lack of accomplishment," in attempting to have a satisfying conversation or to "ask the person to be for real." While these suggestions seem confrontational, they are geared toward moving the other into more honest expression.

Confront

Confrontation implies "either a direct confrontation of the issue or using questions to place the burden back on the other person" (Hecht, Collier, & Ribeau, in press). Strategies in this category include "Correct misconceptions in a shrewd, effective manner," or opposing "I believe you must always confront stereotyping by saying, 'It sounds as if you are making generalizations that may not be applicable to me.' " Examples of direct questions are "Just say, 'but how do *you* feel about it?' If they don't answer, it's obvious that it at least makes them feel uncomfortable," or "Ask why and how they got that stereotype."

Internal Management

Rather than focusing on specific behaviors to improve interaction, these comments described ways for African Americans to think about or deal with the situation. Some of these suggestions included acceptance, objectivity, and nondefensiveness: "I do my best to control my thoughts," "Think first of who you are, how you feel about yourself," and "Put the situation in proper perspective, that is, lose a battle to win the war."

Treat Others As Individuals and Equals

Leave race, color, or stereotypical beliefs entirely out of the conversation some suggested: "Talk to each other without having the sense of color in the conversation." Treat people based on who they are, and nothing else: "Decisions should be made based on each individual" or "Get to know me then judge me." This strategy, voiced most often to fight the stereotyping issue, primarily advocates desired behavior by the European American conversation partner.

Language Management

A few strategies that did not fit in the other categories are grouped here including: avoid slang or jargon and use clear articulation. "Refrain from using unfamiliar jargon" and "talk the same language" are examples of comments in this area. This strategy was used to resolve problems of a lack of understanding.

Note that the African American participants recommended some of these strategies primarily as things they should do (for example, assertiveness, positive self-presentation, avoidance, internal management, inform/educate, confront, language management); some as things European Americans

should do (treat others as individuals); and some as things both should do (be more open and friendly, interaction management, express genuineness, other-orientation). Second, it should be noted that within each category (for example, be more open and friendly) there is a diversity of thought among African Americans as to how or if that strategy should be used.

The African Americans we interviewed felt that these strategies might be successful for improving a conversation, but not always. When stereotyping or lack of acceptance takes place, for example, no strategies are seen as effective — it is like "bouncing off a brick wall." If African Americans "see signs of racism, patronizing behavior, or other put downs, they turn off quickly." The first few minutes of a conversation can make or break the conversation — and the relationship.

CONCLUSION

It is often tempting to state communication effectiveness theories (or others) as if they applied to the way all people behave. However, the studies described here demonstrate that rules for effective or satisfying communication behavior vary, depending on the ethnicity of the group, as well as the situation. Further, the research shows a diversity and complexity among African Americans (Hecht & Ribeau, 1991). Finally, African Americans' own descriptions reveal clear suggestions, both for African Americans and European Americans, for how to make interethnic communication more rewarding for all concerned.

REFERENCES

Hecht, M. L. (1978). "Toward a Conceptualization of Interpersonal Communication Satisfaction." *Quarterly Journal of Speech, 64,* 47–62.

Hecht, M. L. (1984). "Satisfying Communication and Relationship Labels: Intimacy and Length of Relationship as Perceptual Frames of Naturalistic Conversation." *Western Journal of Speech Communications, 48,* 201–216.

Hecht, M. L., Collier, M. J., and Ribeau, S. (in press). *African American Communication: Identity and Cultural Interpretations*. Newbury Park, CA: Sage.

Hecht, M. L., Larkey, L. K., and Johnson, J. N. (1992). "African American and European American Perceptions of Problematic Issues in Interethnic Communication Effectiveness." *Human Communication Research, 19*, 209–236.

Hecht, M. L., and Ribeau, S. "Ethnic Communication: A Comparative Analysis of Satisfying Communication." *International Journal of Intercultural Relations, 8*, 135–151.

Hecht, M. L., and Ribeau, S. (1987). "Afro-American Identity Labels and Communicative Effectiveness." *Journal of Language and Social Psychology, 6*, 319–326.

Hecht, M. L., and Ribeau, S. (1991). "Sociocultural Roots of Ethnic Identity: A Look at Black America." *Journal of Black Studies, 21*, 501–513.

Hecht, M. L., Ribeau, S., and Alberts, J. K. (1989). "An Afro-American Perspective on Interethnic Communication." *Communication Monographs, 56*, 385–410.

Hecht, M. L., Ribeau, S., and Sedano, M. V. (1990). "A Mexican American Perspective on Interethnic Communication." *International Journal of Intercultural Relations, 14*, 31–55.

Martin, J. N. (1989). "Behavioral Categories of Intercultural Communication Competence: Everyday Communicators' Perceptions." *International Journal of Intercultural Relations, 13*, 303–332.

Martin, J. N. (1993). "Intercultural Communication Competence." In R. Wiseman and J. Koester (Eds.), *International and Intercultural Communication Annual*, 17.

Martin, J. N., Larkey, L. K., and Hecht, M. L. (February, 1991). *"An African American Perspective on Conversational Improvement Strategies for Interethnic Communication."* Paper presented to the Intercultural and International Communication Conference, Miami, Florida.

Martin, J. N., and Hammer, M. R. (1989). "Behavioral Categories of Intercultural Communication Competence: Everyday Communicators' Percep-

tions." *International Journal of Intercultural Relations, 13*, 303–332.

McLaughlin, M., and Cody, M. J. (1982). "Awkward Silences: Behavioral Antecedents and Consequences of the Conversational Lapse." *Human Communication Research, 8*, 229–316.

Pavitt, C., and Haight, L. (1985). "The 'Competent Communicator' as a Cognitive Prototype." *Human Communication Research, 12*, 225–242.

Ruben, B. D. (1977). "Guidelines for Cross-cultural Communication Effectiveness." *Group and Organizational Studies, 12*, 225–242.

Ruben, B. D. (1989). "The Study of Cross-cultural Competence: Traditions and Contemporary Issues." *International Journal of Intercultural Relations, 13*, 229–239.

Spitzberg, B. H. (1989). "Issues in the Development of a Theory of Interpersonal Competence in the Intercultural Context." *International Journal of Intercultural Relations, 13*, 241–268.

Spitzberg, B. H., and Cupach, W. R. (1984). *Interpersonal Communication Competence*. Beverly Hills, CA: Sage.

Spitzberg, B. H., and Hecht, M. L. (1984). "A Component Model of Relational Competence." *Human Communication Research, 10*, 575–600.

Vause, C. J., and Wiemann, J. M. (1981). "Communication Strategies for Role Invention." *Western Journal of Speech Communication, 45*, 241–251.

Wiemann, J. M., and Bradac, J. J. (1989). "Metatheoretical Issues in the Study of Communication Competence: Structural and Functional Approaches." In B. Dervin and M. J. Voight (Eds.), *Progress in Communication Sciences*, Vol. 9, 261–284. Norwood, NJ: Ablex.

Viewing Persons with Disabilities as a Culture

DAWN O. BRAITHWAITE

Jonathan is an articulate, intelligent, 35-year-old man who has used a wheelchair since becoming a paraplegic when he was 20.[1] He recalls taking an ablebodied woman out to dinner at a nice restaurant. When the waitress came to take their order, she patronizingly asked his date, "And what would *he* like to eat for dinner?" At the end of the meal the waitress presented Jonathan's date with the check and thanked her for her patronage. Although it may be hard to believe the insensitivity of the waitress, this incident is not an isolated experience for persons with disabilities.

Jeff, an ablebodied student, was working with a group that included Helen, who uses a wheelchair. He recalls an incident that really embarrassed him. "I wasn't thinking and I said to the group, 'Let's run over to the student union and get some coffee.' I was mortified when I looked over at Helen and remembered that she can't walk. I felt like a real jerk." Helen later described the incident with Jeff, recalling,

At yesterday's meeting, Jeff said, "Let's run over to the union" and then he looked over at me and I thought he would die. It didn't bother me and I don't know why Jeff was so embarrassed. I didn't quite know what to say. Later in the group meeting I made it a point to say, "I've got to be running along now." I hope that Jeff noticed and felt OK about what he said.

Like Jonathan's experience, this situation between Helen and Jeff is also a common experience.

There has been a growing interest in the important area of health communication among communication scholars, with a core of researchers studying communication between ablebodied persons and those with disabilities. Persons with disabilities are becoming an increasingly large and active minority in U.S. culture, with the numbers growing yearly. In some states, disabled persons constitute the largest minority group, composing as much as seven percent of the population (Wheratt, 1988). There are two reasons for the increase in the number of persons with disabilities. First, as the population ages and lives longer, more people will develop disabilities. Second, advances in medical technologies now allow persons with disabilities to survive life-threatening illnesses and injuries.

In the past, persons with disabilities were kept out of public view, but today they are mainstreaming into all facets of society. Significant legislation, like the Americans with Disabilities Act, seek to guarantee equal rights to persons with disabilities. All of us have or will have contact with persons with disabilities of some kind and many of us will find family, friends, coworkers, or even ourselves part of the disabled culture. Marie, a college student who became quadriplegic after diving into a swimming pool, says "I knew there were disabled people around, but I never thought this would happen to me. I never even knew a disabled person before I became one. If before this happened I saw a person in a wheelchair, I would have been uncomfortable and not known what to say." As persons with disabilities continue to move into the mainstream, the need for both ablebodied and disabled persons to know how to communicate with members of the other culture will continue to grow.

The purpose of this article is to discuss communication between ablebodied persons and persons with disabilities as *cultural communication* (Carbaugh, 1990). Several researchers have described the communication of disabled and ablebodied persons as cultural communication (Braithwaite, 1990; Emry & Wiseman, 1987; Padden & Humphries, 1988). That is, we must recognize that persons with disabilities develop certain unique communication characteristics that are not shared by the majority of ablebodied individuals in U.S. society. In fact, individuals who were disabled after birth must assimilate from being a member of the ablebodied majority to being a member of a minority culture (Braithwaite, 1990).

This essay presents research findings from a series of interviews with persons who have visible physical disabilities. First, we introduce the communication problems that can arise between persons in the ablebodied culture and those in the disabled culture. Second, we discuss some problems with the way research into communication between ablebodied and disabled persons has been conducted. Third, we present results from the interviews. These results show persons with disabilities engaged in a process whereby they critique the prevailing stereotypes of the disabled held by the ablebodied and engage in a process that we call *redefinition*. Finally, we discuss the importance of these findings for both scholars and students of intercultural communication.

COMMUNICATION BETWEEN ABLEBODIED AND DISABLED PERSONS

Persons with disabilities seek to overcome the barriers associated with physical disability because disability affects all areas of an individual's life: behavioral, economic, and social. When we attempt to understand the effects of disability, we must differentiate between disability and handicap. Many aspects of disability put limitations on an individual because one or more of the key life functions, such as self-care, mobility, communication, socialization, and employment, is interrupted. Disabilities are often compensated for or overcome through assisting devices, such as wheelchairs or canes, or through training. Disabilities become handicaps when the disability interacts with the physical or social environment to impede a person in some aspect of his or her life (Crewe & Athelstan, 1985). For example, a disabled individual who is paraplegic can function in the environment with wheelchairs and curb cuts,

but he or she is handicapped when buildings and/or public transportation are not accessible to wheelchairs. When the society is willing and/or able to help, disabled persons have the ability to achieve increasingly independent lives (Cogswell, 1977; DeLoach & Greer, 1981).

Many physical barriers associated with disabilities can be detected and corrected, but the social barriers resulting from disabilities are much more insidious. Nowhere are the barriers more apparent than in the communication between ablebodied persons and persons with disabilities. When ablebodied and disabled persons interact, the general, stereotypical communication problem that is present in all new relationships is heightened, and both persons behave in even more constrained and less spontaneous ways, acting overly self-conscious, self-controlled, and rigid because they feel uncomfortable and uncertain (Belgrave & Mills, 1981; Weinberg, 1978). While the ablebodied person may communicate verbal acceptance to the person with the disability, his or her nonverbal behavior may communicate rejection and avoidance (Thompson, 1982). For example, the ablebodied person may speak with the disabled person but stand at a greater distance than usual, avoid eye contact, and cut the conversation short. Disability becomes a handicap, then, for persons with disabilities when they interact with ablebodied persons and experience discomfort when communicating; this feeling blocks the normal development of a relationship between them.

Most ablebodied persons readily recognize that what we have just described is representative of their own communication experiences with disabled persons. Ablebodied persons often find themselves in the situation of not knowing what is expected of them or how to act; they have been taught both to "help the handicapped" and to "treat all persons equally." For example, should we help a person with a disability open a door or should we help them up if they fall? Many ablebodied persons have offered help only to be rebuffed by the person with the disability. Ablebodied persons greatly fear saying the wrong thing, such as "See you later!" to a blind person or "Why don't you run by the store on your way home?" to a paraplegic. It is easier to avoid situations where we might have to talk with a disabled person rather than face discomfort and uncertainty.

Persons with disabilities find these situations equally uncomfortable and are well aware of the discomfort of the ablebodied person. They are able to describe both the verbal and nonverbal signals of discomfort and avoidance that ablebodied persons portray (Braithwaite, 1985, 1992). Persons with disabilities report that when they meet ablebodied persons, they want to get the discomfort "out of the way," and they want the ablebodied person to see them as a "person like anyone else," rather than focus solely on the disability (Braithwaite, 1985, 1991).

PROBLEMS WITH THE PRESENT RESEARCH

When we review the research in the area of communication between ablebodied and disabled persons, three problems come to the forefront. First, very little is known about the communication behavior of disabled persons. A few researchers have studied disabled persons' communication, but most of them study ablebodied persons' reactions to disabled persons (most of these researchers are themselves ablebodied). Second, most researchers talk *about* persons with disabilities, not *with* them. Disabled persons are rarely represented in the studies; when they are, the disabled person is most often "played," for example, by an ablebodied person in a wheelchair. Third, and most significantly, the research is usually conducted from the perspective of the ablebodied person; that is, what can persons with disabilities *do* to make ablebodied persons feel more comfortable. It does not take into consideration the effects on the person with the disability. Therefore, we have what may be called an *ethnocentric bias* in the research, which focuses on ablebodied/disabled communication from the perspective of the ablebodied majority, ignoring the perspective of the disabled minority.

We shall discuss the results of an ongoing study that obtains the perspectives of disabled persons concerning their communication with ablebodied persons. To date, fifty-seven in-depth interviews have been conducted with physically disabled adults about their communication with ablebodied persons in the early stages of relationships. Here we are concerned with understanding human behavior from the disabled person's own frame of reference. This concern is particularly important in the area of communication between ablebodied and disabled persons and, as we have said, previous research has been conducted from the perspective of ablebodied persons; disabled persons have not participated in these studies. Doing research by talking directly to the person with the disability helps to bring out information important to the individual, rather than simply getting the disabled person's reaction to what is on the researcher's mind. This research represents a unique departure from what other researchers have been doing because the focus is on the perspective of the disabled minority.

PROCESS OF REDEFINITION

When discussing their communication with ablebodied persons, disabled persons' responses often deal with what we call *redefinition*. That is, in their communication with ablebodied persons and among themselves, disabled persons engage in a process whereby they critique the prevailing stereotypes held by the ablebodied and create new definitions: (1) of the disabled as members of a "new" culture; (2) of self by the disabled; (3) of disability for the disabled; and (4) of disability for the dominant culture.

Redefinition of the Disabled as Members of a "New" Culture

Persons with disabilities report seeing themselves as a minority or a culture. For some of the subjects, this definition crosses disability lines; that is, their definition of *disabled* includes all persons who have disabilities. For others, the definition is not as broad and includes only other persons with the same type of disability. Most persons with disabilities, however, do define themselves as part of a culture. Says one person:

It's (being disabled) like West Side Story. *Tony and Maria; white and Puerto Rican. They were afraid of each other; ignorant of each others' cultures. People are people.*

According to another man:

First of all, I belong to a subculture because of the way I have to deal with things being in the medical system, welfare. There is the subculture . . . I keep one foot in the ablebodied culture and one foot in my own culture. One of the reasons I do that is so that I don't go nuts.

Membership in the disabled culture has several similarities to membership in other cultures. Many of the persons interviewed likened their own experiences to those of other cultures, particularly to African Americans and women. When comparing the disabled to both African Americans and women, we find several similarities. The oppression is biologically based, at least for those who have been disabled since birth; one is a member of the culture by being born with cerebral palsy or spina bifida, for example. As such, the condition is unalterable; the disability will be part of them throughout their lifetime.

For those persons who are not born with a disability, membership in the culture can be a process that emerges over time. For some, the process is a slow one, as in the case of a person with a degenerative disease that may develop over many years and gradually become more and more severe. If a person has a sudden-onset disability, such as breaking one's neck in an accident and waking up a quadraplegic, the movement from a member of the dominant culture—"normal person"—to the minority culture—disabled person—may happen in a matter of seconds. This sudden transition to membership in the disabled culture presents many challenges of readjustment in all facets of an individual's life, especially in communication relationships with others.

Redefinition of Self by the Disabled

How one redefines oneself, then, from normal or ablebodied to disabled, is a process of redefinition of self. While African Americans struggle for identity in a white society and women struggle for identity in a male-dominated society, the disabled struggle for identity in an ablebodied world. One recurring theme from the participants in this study is "I am a person like anyone else" (if disabled since birth) or "I'm basically the same person I always was" (if a sudden-onset disability). The person who is born with a disability learns the process of becoming identified as "fully human" while still living as a person with a disability. The individual who is disabled later in life, Goffman (1963) contends, goes through a process of redefinition of self. For example, the subjects born with disabilities make such statements as "I am not different from anyone else as far as I am concerned" or "Disability does not mean an incomplete character." Persons whose disabilities happened later say "You're the same person you were. You just don't do the same things you did before." One man put it this way:

If anyone refers to me as an amputee, that is guaranteed to get me madder than hell! I don't deny the leg amputation, but I am me. I am a whole person. One.

During the redefinition process, individuals come to terms with both positive and negative ramifications of disability. Some subjects report that "disability is like slavery to me." In contrast, one woman reports:

I find myself telling people that this has been the worst thing that has happened to me. It has also been one of the best things. It forced me to examine what I felt about myself . . . confidence is grounded in me, not in other people. As a woman, not as dependent on clothes, measurements, but what's inside me.

One man expresses his newfound relationship to other people when he says, "I'm more interdependent than I was. I'm much more aware of that now."

This process of redefinition is evident in what those interviewed have to say.

Redefinition of Disability for the Disabled

A third category of redefinition occurs as persons with disabilities redefine both disability and its associated characteristics. For example, in redefining disability itself, one man said, "People will say, 'Thank God I'm not handicapped.' And I'll say, 'Let's see, how tall are you? Tell me how you get something off that shelf up there!'" This perspective is centered on the view of the disability as a characteristic of the person rather than the person himself; it recognizes disability as situational rather than inherent or grounded in the person. In this view, everyone is disabled to some extent: by race, gender, height, or physical abilities, for example.

Redefinition of disability can be seen in the use of language. Says one subject who objected to the label *handicapped person*: "Persons with a handicapping condition. You emphasize that person's identity and then you do something about the condition." This statement ties into viewing one's self as a person first. Research reveals movement from the term *handicapped* to *disability* or *disabled*, although a wide variety of terms are used by these subjects to talk about the self. Another change in language has been the avoidance of phrases such as "polio victim" or "arthritis sufferer." Again the emphasis is on the person, not the disability. "I am a person whose arms and legs do not function very well," says one subject who had polio as a child.

There have also been changes in the terms that refer to ablebodied persons. Says one man:

You talk about the ablebodied. I will talk about the nonhandicapped . . . It's a different kind of mode. In Michigan they've got it in the law: "temporarily ablebodied."

It is common for the persons interviewed to refer to the majority in terms of the minority: "nondisabled" or "nonhandicapped," rather than "ablebodied" or "normal." More than the change in terminology, the phrase "temporarily ablebodied" or TABS serves to remind ablebodied persons that no one is immune from disability. The persons interviewed also used TABS as a humorous reference term for the ablebodied as well. "Everyone is a TAB." This view jokingly intimates, "I just got mine earlier than you . . . just you wait!"

In addition to redefining disability, the disabled also redefine "assisting devices":

Now, there were two girls about eight playing and I was in my shorts. And I'll play games with them and say, "which is my good leg?" And that gets them to thinking. Well, this one (pats artificial leg) is not nearly as old as the other one!

Says another subject:

Do you know what a cane is? It's a portable railing! The essence of a wheelchair is a seat and wheels. Now, I don't know that a tricycle is not doing the exact same thing.

Again, in these examples, the problem is not the disability or the assisting device, such as a cane, but how one views the disability or the assisting device. These assisting devices take on a different meaning for the persons using them. Subjects expressed frustration with persons who played with their wheelchairs: "This chair is not a toy, it is part of me. When you touch my chair, you are touching me." One woman, a business executive, expanded on this by saying, "I don't know why people who push my chair feel compelled to make car sounds as they do it."

Redefinition of Disability for the Dominant Culture

Along with the redefinitions that concern culture, self, and disability comes an effort to try to change society's view of the disabled and disability (Braithwaite, 1990). Persons with disabilities are attempting to change the view of themselves as helpless, as victims, or merely sick. One man says:

People do not consider you, they consider the chair first. I was in a store with my purchases on my lap and money on my lap. The clerk looked at my companion and said, "Cash or charge?"

This incident with the clerk is a story that has been voiced by every person interviewed in some form or another, just as it happened to Jonathan at the restaurant with his date. One woman who has multiple sclerosis and uses a wheelchair told of her husband accompanying her while she was shopping for lingerie. When they were in front of the lingerie counter, she asked for what she wanted, and the clerk repeatedly talked only to her husband saying, "And what size does she want?" The woman told her the size and the clerk looked at the husband and said, "and what color?" Persons with disabilities recognize that ablebodied persons often see them as disabled first and persons second (if at all), and they express a need to change this view. Says a man who has muscular dystrophy:

I do not believe in those goddamned telethons . . . they're horrible, absolutely horrible. They get into the self-pity, you know, and disabled folk do not need that. Hit people in terms of their attitudes and then try to deal with and process their feelings. And the telethons just go for the heart and leave it there.

Most of the subjects indicate they see themselves as educators or ambassadors for all persons with disabilities. All indicate they will answer questions put to them about their disabilities, as long as they determine the other "really wants to know, to learn." One man suggests a solution:

What I am concerned with is anything that can do away with the "us" versus "them" distinction. Well, you and I are anatomically different, but we're two human beings! And at the point we can sit down and communicate eyeball to eyeball . . . the quicker you do that, the better!

Individually and collectively, persons with disabilities do identify themselves as part of a culture. They are involved in a process of redefinition of disability, both for themselves and for the ablebodied.

CONCLUSIONS

This research justifies the usefulness of viewing disability from an intercultural perspective. Persons with disabilities do see themselves as members of a culture, and viewing communication between ablebodied and disabled persons from this perspective sheds new light on the communication problems that exist. Emry and Wiseman (1987) argue that intercultural training should be the focus in our perceptions of self and others: They call for unfreezing old attitudes about disability and refreezing new ones. Clearly, from these findings, that is exactly what persons with disabilities are doing, both for themselves and for others.

Of the fifty-seven persons with disabilities interviewed, only a small percentage had any sort of education or training concerning communication, during or after rehabilitation, that would prepare them for changes in their communication relationships due to their disabilities. Such education seems especially critical for those who experience sudden-onset disabilities because their self-concepts and all of their relationships undergo sudden, radical changes. Intercultural communication scholars have the relevant background and experience for this kind of research and training, and they can help make this transition from majority to minority an easier one (Emry & Wiseman, 1987; Smith, 1989).

As for ablebodied persons who communicate with disabled persons, this intercultural perspective leads to the following suggestions:

Don't assume that persons with disabilities cannot speak for themselves or do things for themselves. *Do assume* they can do something unless they communicate otherwise.

Don't force your help on persons with disabilities. *Do let* them tell you if they want something, what they want, and when they want it. If a person with a disability refuses your help, don't go ahead and help anyway.

Don't avoid communication with persons who have disabilities simply because you are uncomfortable or unsure.

Do remember that they have experienced others' discomfort before and understand how you might be feeling.

Do treat persons with disabilities as *persons first*, recognizing that you are not dealing with a disabled person but with a *person* who has a disability.

NOTE

1. The names of all the participants in these studies have been changed to protect their privacy.

REFERENCES

Belgrave, F. Z., and Mills, J. (1981). "Effect upon Desire for Social Interaction with a Physically Disabled Person of Mentioning the Disability in Different Contexts." *Journal of Applied Social Psychology*, 11(1), 44–57.

Braithwaite, D. O. (February, 1985). "Impression Management and Redefinition of Self by Persons with Disabilities." Paper presented at the annual meeting of the Speech Communication Association, Denver, Colorado.

Braithwaite, D. O. (1990). "From Majority to Minority: An Analysis of Cultural Change from Ablebodied to Disabled." *International Journal of Intercultural Relations*, 14, 465–483.

Braithwaite, D. O. (1991). "Just How Much Did that Wheelchair Cost?: Management of Privacy Boundaries by Persons with Disabilities." *Western Journal of Speech Communication*, 55, 254–274.

Braithwaite, D. O. (1992). "Isn't It Great that People Like You Get Out: Communication Between Disabled and Ablebodied Persons." In E. B. Ray (Ed.), *Case Studies in Health Communication*. Lawrence Erlbaum Associates, Publishers.

Carbaugh, D. (Ed.). 1990. *Cultural Communication and Intercultural Contact*. Hillsdale, NJ: Lawrence Erlbaum Associates, Publishers.

Cogswell, Betty E. (1977). "Self Socialization: Readjustments of Paraplegics in the Community." In R. P. Marinelli and A. E. Dell Orto (Eds.), *The Psychological and Social Impact of Physical Disability*, pp. 151–159. New York: Springer Publishing Company.

Crewe, N., and Athelstan, G. (1985). *Social and Psychological Aspects of Physical Disability*. Minneapolis: University of Minnesota, Department of Independent Study and University Resources.

DeLoach, C., and Greer, B. G. (1981). *Adjustment to Severe Disability*. New York: McGraw-Hill Book Company.

Emry, R., and Wiseman, R. L. (1987). "An Intercultural Understanding of Ablebodied and Disabled Persons' Communication." *International Journal of Intercultural Relations*, 11, 7–27.

Goffman, E. (1963). *Stigma: Notes on the Management of Spoiled Identity*. New York: Simon & Schuster.

Padden, C., and Humphries, T. (1988). *Deaf in America: Voices from a Culture*. Cambridge, MA: Harvard University Press.

Smith, D. H. (1989). "Studying Health Communication: An Agenda for the Future." *Health Communication*, 1(1), 17–27.

Thompson, T. L. (1982). "Disclosure as a Disability-Management Strategy: A Review and Conclusions." *Communication Quarterly*, 30, 196–202.

Weinberg, N. (1978). "Modifying Social Stereotypes of the Physically Disabled." *Rehabilitation Counselling Bulletin*, 22(2), 114–124.

Wheratt, R. (August 1, 1988). "Minnesota Disabled to Be Heard." *Star Tribune*, 1, 6.

Gender, Communication, and Culture

JULIA T. WOOD

"MEN AND WOMEN: CAN WE GET ALONG?
SHOULD WE EVEN TRY?"

Blazing across the cover of a January 1993 popular magazine, this headline announces the drama of gender, communication, and culture. Asking whether we should *even try* to get along, the magazine suggests the effort to build relationships between women and men may require more effort than it's worth. Useful as this media hype might be in selling the magazine, it's misleading in several respects. One problem is that the headline focuses on sex as the source of differences when actually, as we will see in this article, sex has very little to do with how people get along. Gender, however, has a great deal of impact on human interaction. The magazine's cover also exaggerates the difficulty of creating and sustaining satisfying relationships between the genders. If you understand why feminine and masculine cultures differ and how each communicates, it's likely you won't have a great deal of trouble getting along with people of both genders. It's also likely you'll decide it is worth the effort of trying to get along!

This article will help you understand how differences between gender cultures infuse communication. We follow the drama of culture, communication, and gender in two ways. In Act I of this drama, we consider how communication produces and re-produces cultural definitions of masculinity and femininity. Act II explores masculine and feminine cultures to discover why the genders differ in when, how, and why they use communication. To conclude, Act III offers suggestions for ways we might bridge communication gaps that sometimes interfere with effective interaction in cross-cultural gender communication.

What makes something a culture instead of just a quality common to a number of individuals? For instance, although all people with blue eyes share a common characteristic, we don't consider them a culture. Why then would we regard masculinity and femininity as different cultures? What are feminine and masculine gender cultures, and how are they created? How do differences in gender cultures affect communication? How do we learn to translate each other's communication and to develop a second language ourselves? These are the questions we pursue in this reading.

THE SOCIAL-SYMBOLIC CONSTRUCTION OF GENDER

Perhaps you have noticed that I use the terms *feminine* and *masculine* rather than women and men. The former refer to gender and the latter to sex, which are distinct phenomena. *Women, men, male,* and *female* are words that specify sexual identities, which biology determines. In contrast, feminine and masculine designate genders, which are socially constructed meanings for sex. Before we can understand why gender is a culture, we need to clarify what gender is and how it differs from sex.

Sex

Sex is determined by genetic codes that program biological features. Of the forty-nine pairs of human chromosomes, one pair controls sex. Usually this unit has two chromosomes, one of which is always an X chromosome. If the second chromosome is a Y, the fetus is male; if it is an X, the fetus is female. (Other combinations have occurred: XYY, XXY, XO, and XXX.) During gestation, genetic codes direct the production of hormones so that fetuses receive hormones that develop genitalia and secondary sex characteristics consistent with their genetic makeup. (Again there are exceptions, usually caused by medical interventions. See Wood, 1933a for a more thorough discussion.)

Aided and abetted by hormones, genetics determine biological features that we use to classify male and female sex: external genitalia (the clitoris and vagina for a female, the penis and testes for a male) and internal sex organs (the uterus and ovaries in females, the prostate in males). Hormones also control secondary sex characteristics such as percentage of body fat (females have more fat to protect the womb when a fetus is present), how much muscle exists, and amount of body hair. There are also differences in male and female brains. Females generally have greater specialization in the right hemisphere which controls integrative and creative thinking, while males typically have more developed left lobes, which govern analytic and abstract thought. Generally, females also have better developed corpus callosa, which are the bundles of nerves connecting the two brain lobes. This suggests women may be more able to cross to the left hemisphere than men are to cross to the right. All of these are sex differences directed by genetics and biology.

Gender

Gender is considerably more complex than sex. For starters you might think of gender as the cultural meaning of sex. A culture constructs gender by arbitrarily assigning certain qualities, activities, and identities to each sex and by then inscribing these assignments into the fabric of social life. Cultural constructions of gender are communicated to individuals through a range of structures and practices that make up our everyday world. From birth on, individuals are besieged with communication that presents cultural prescriptions for gender as natural and right. Beginning with the pink and blue blankets still used in many hospitals, gender socialization continues in interactions with parents, teachers, peers, and media. Throughout our interaction with others, we receive constant messages that reinforce females' conformity to femininity and males' to masculinity. This reveals gender is a social creation, not an individual characteristic.

The process of gender socialization is constant and thorough, so it generally succeeds in persuading individuals to adopt the gender society endorses for them. This means that individuals are not born with a gender, but we *become* gendered as we internalize and then embody our society's views of femininity and masculinity. Although some people resist gender socialization, the intensity and pervasiveness of social prescriptions for gender ensure most females will become feminine and most males will become masculine. This article should give you insight into your own gender so that you may decide whether you are masculine, feminine, or a combination of genders.

Gender refers to social beliefs and values that specify what sex *means* and what it allows and precludes in a particular society at a specific time. Because cultures vary and each one changes over time, the meaning of gender is neither universal nor stable. Instead, femininity and masculinity reflect the beliefs and values of particular cultures at certain points. The pervasive presence of socially constructed meanings of gender in our lives makes them seem natural, normal, right. Since cultures systematically normalize arbitrary definitions of gender, we seldom reflect on how *unnatural* it is that half of humans are assumed to be more passive, emotional, and interested in caring for others than the other half. If we do reflect on social definitions of masculinity and femininity, they don't make a great deal of sense (Janeway, 1971; Miller, 1986)!

In summary, gender and sex are not synonymous. Sex is biological, while gender is socially constructed. Sex is established by genetics and biology, while gender is produced and reproduced by society. Barring surgery, sex is permanent, while gender varies over time and across cultures. Sex is an individual property, while gender is a social and relational quality which gains meaning from prevailing social interests and contrast with the other gender. What we've covered so far explains the first relationship among gender, communication, and culture: We see that societies create meanings of gender that are communicated through an array of cultural structures and practices; in turn, individuals become gendered as they embody social prescriptions in their personal identities. We turn now to the second relationship, which concerns how social-symbolic constructions of gender establish codes of conduct, thought, and communication that create distinct gender cultures.

FEMININE AND MASCULINE COMMUNICATION CULTURES

Beginning in the 1970s scholars noticed that some groups of people share communication practices not common to outsiders. This led to the realization that there are distinctive speech communities, or communication cultures. William Labov (1972, p. 121) defined a communication culture as existing when a set of norms regarding how to communicate is shared by a group of people. Within a communication culture, members embrace similar understandings of how to use talk and what purposes it serves.

Once scholars realized distinctive communication cultures exist, they identified many, some of which are discussed in this book: African Americans, older people, Indian Native Americans, gay men, lesbians, and people with disabilities. Members in each of these groups share perspectives that outsiders don't have, and their distinctive values, viewpoints, and experiences influence how each culture uses language. This holds true for gender cultures since women and men in general have different perspectives on why, when, and how to communicate.

Feminine and masculine communication cultures have been mapped out by a number of scholars (Aries, 1987; Beck, 1988; Coates & Cameron, 1989; Johnson, 1989; Kramarae, 1981; Spender, 1984; Tannen, 1990a, b; Treichler & Kramarae, 1983; Wood, 1993a, b, c, e; Wood & Inman, 1993). Their research reveals that most girls and women operate from assumptions about communication and use rules for communicating that differ significantly from those endorsed by most boys and men. I use the qualifying word, "most," to remind us we are discussing general differences, not absolute ones based on sex. Some women are not socialized into feminine culture or they reject it; likewise, some men do not identify with masculine culture. For the most part, however, females are socialized into feminine culture and males into masculine culture. How that transpires is our next consideration.

COMMUNICATION CONSTRUCTS GENDER CULTURES

How are different gender cultures created and sustained? At the heart of the process is human communication. It is through interaction with others that we learn what masculine and feminine mean in our society and which we are supposed to be. Communication is also the primary means by which we embody gender personally so that our ways of talking conform to and, thereby, reproduce social views of masculinity and femininity. We'll now look more closely at how boys and girls are socialized into masculine and feminine gender identities.

Clinicians and researchers have identified two primary influences on gender socialization: family communication, particularly between mothers and children, and recreational interaction among children. In each of these areas, communication reflects and reproduces gender cultures.

Psychodynamic Influences on Gender Identity

Gender is not merely a role; it is a core aspect of identity which is central to how we perceive ourselves and how we act in the world (Rakow, 1986; Zimmerman & West, 1975). In her classic book, *The Reproduction of Mothering*, psychiatrist Nancy Chodorow (1978) claims that gender identity is profoundly shaped by psychological dynamics in families and most particularly by mother-child relationships in the early years. According to Chodorow, it is significant that the primary caregiver for most children is a female, usually the mother. Mothers form different relationships with sons and daughters, and these differences cultivate masculine and feminine gender identities.

Between a mother and daughter, argue Chodorow and other clinicians (Eichenbaum & Orbach, 1983; Miller, 1986; Surrey, 1983), there is a basic identification as members of the same sex. Because daughters identify with mothers, they can develop their identities inside of that primary relationship. A son, however, cannot identify fully with the mother because she is female. Thus, to develop a gender identity, sons must differentiate from mother — must pull away from the first relationship to establish selfhood. We see, then, a basic difference in the foundation of the sexes' identities: Girls tend to define self in relation to others, while boys typically define self independent of others.

Whether we think of ourselves as fundamentally connected to others (within relationship) or separate from them (independent of relationship) influences how we perceive ourselves and how interact with others (Gilligan, 1982; Riessman, 1990; Surrey, 1983). In general, males (children and adults) maintain a greater degree of distance between themselves and others than do females. This makes sense since closeness with mothers facilitates daughters but interferes with sons in their efforts to define a self. Given these different bases of identity, it's hardly surprising that girls and women are generally comfortable building close relationships and disclosing to others, while most boys and men are reserved about involvements and disclosures (Aries, 1987; Wood, 1993a). Important as the mother-child relationship is, however, it isn't the only factor that cultivates gender identities.

The Games Children Play

Augmenting psychodynamic influences on gender identity is communication that occurs in childhood games. Insight into this area was pioneered by Daniel Maltz and Ruth Borker (1982), who studied children at play. The researchers noticed recreation was usually sex-segregated, and boys and girls tended to favor discrete kinds of games. While girls were more likely to play house, school, or jump rope, boys tended to play competitive team sports like football and baseball. Because different goals, strategies and relationships characterize girls' and boys'

games, the children learned divergent rules for interaction. Engaging in play, Maltz and Borker concluded, contributes to socializing children into masculine and feminine communication cultures.

Girls Games. Most girls' games require just two or three people so they promote personal relationships. Further, these games don't have preset or fixed rules, roles, and objectives. While touchdowns and home runs are goals in boys' games and roles such as pitcher, lineman, and blocker are clearly specified, how to play house is open to negotiation. To make their games work, girls talk with each other and agree on rules, roles, and goals: "You be the mommy and I'll be the daddy, and we'll clean house." From unstructured, cooperative play, girls learn three basic rules for how to communicate:

1. Be cooperative, collaborative, inclusive. It's important that everyone feel involved and have a chance to play.

2. Don't criticize or outdo others. Cultivate egalitarian relationships so the group is cohesive and gratifying to all.

3. Pay attention to others' feelings and needs and be sensitive in interpreting and responding to them.

In sum, girls' games occur within a gender culture that emphasizes relationships more than outcomes, sensitivity to others, and cooperative, inclusive interpersonal orientations.

Boys' Games. Unlike girls' games, those that boys tend to play involve fairly large groups (baseball requires nine players plus extras to fill in) and proceed by rules and goals that are externally established and constant. Also, boys' games allow for individual stars — MVP, for instance — and, in fact, a boy's status depends on his rank relative to others. The more structured, large, and individualized character of boys' games teaches them three rules of interaction:

1. Assert yourself. Use talk and action to highlight your ideas and to establish your status and leadership.

2. Focus on outcomes. Use your talk and actions to make things happen, to solve problems, and achieve goals.

3. Be competitive. Vie for the talk stage. Keep attention focused on you, outdo others, and make yourself stand out.

Boys' games, then, emphasize achievement—both for the team and the individual members. The goals are to win for the team and to be the top player on it. Interaction is more an arena for negotiating power and status than for building relationships with others, and competitiveness eclipses cooperativeness as the accepted style in masculine communication cultures.

The characteristics of boys' and girls' games lead to distinctive understandings of what talk does and how we should use it. Differences Maltz and Borker identified in children's play are ones that we carry forward into adulthood so they punctuate communication between adult women and men. So divergent are some of women's and men's understandings of communication that linguist Deborah Tannen (1990b, p. 42) claims "communication between men and women can be like cross culture communication, prey to a clash of conversational styles."

In combination, psychodynamic theories and social science research offer a coherent picture of how gender cultures are produced and what they entail. Feminine socialization emphasizes relationships and sensitivity to people and the process of interaction, while masculine socialization stresses independence, power, and attention to outcomes. Table 1 summarizes how these differences in gender cultures affect communication.

MEN AND WOMEN IN CONVERSATION: CROSS-CULTURAL COMMUNICATION

As males and females learn the rules of distinctive gender cultures, they embody them in their personal identities, and this reproduces prevailing social meanings of the genders. One implication of being socialized into gendered identities is that there are generalizable differences in feminine and masculine styles of communication. These differences frequently lead to misunderstandings in cross-gender interaction.

Gender Gaps in Communication

To illustrate the practical consequences of differences we've identified, let's consider some concrete cases of cross-cultural gender communication. Following are five examples of common problems in communication between women and men. As you read them, you'll probably find that several are familiar to you.

What counts as support? Rita is really bummed out when she meets Mike for dinner. She explains that she's worried about a friend who has begun drinking heavily. When Mike advises her to get her friend into counseling, Rita repeats how worried she feels. Next, Mike tells Rita to make sure her friend doesn't drive after drinking. Rita explodes that she doesn't need advice. Irritated at her lack of appreciation for his help, Mike asks, "Then why did you ask for it?" In exasperation Rita responds, "Oh, never mind, I'll talk to Betsy. At least she cares how I feel."

Tricky feedback. Roseann and Drew are colleagues in a marketing firm. One morning he drops into her office to run an advertising play by her. As Drew discusses his ideas, Roseann nods and says "Um," "Un huh" and "Yes." When he finishes and asks what she thinks, Roseann says "I really don't think that plan will sell the product." Feeling misled, Drew demands, "Then why were you agreeing the whole time I presented my idea?" Completely confused, Roseann responds, "What makes you think I was agreeing with you?"

Expressing care. Dedrick and Melita have been dating for two years and are very serious. To celebrate their anniversary Melita wants to spend a quiet evening in her apartment where they can talk about the relationship and be with just each other. When Dedrick arrives, he's planned a dinner and concert. Melita feels hurt that he doesn't want to talk and be close.

Table 1 Differences Between Feminine and Masculine Communication Culture

Feminine Talk	*Masculine Talk*
1. Use talk to build and sustain rapport with others.	1. Use talk to assert yourself and your ideas.
2. Share yourself and learn about others through disclosing.	2. Personal disclosures can make you vulnerable.
3. Use talk to create symmetry or equality between people.	3. Use talk to establish your status and power.
4. Matching experiences with others shows understanding and empathy ("I know how you feel.")	4. Matching experiences is a competitive strategy to command attention. ("I can top that.")
5. To support others, express understanding of their feelings.	5. To support others, do something helpful — give advice or solve a problem for them.
6. Include others in conversation by asking their opinions and encouraging them to elaborate. Wait your turn to speak so others can participate.	6. Don't share the talk stage with others; wrest it from them with communication. Interrupt others to make your own points.
7. Keep the conversation going by asking questions and showing interest in others' ideas.	7. Each person is on her or his own; it's not your job to help others join in.
8. Be responsive. Let others know you hear and care about what they say.	8. Use responses to make your own points and to outshine others.
9. Be tentative so that others feel free to add their ideas.	9. Be assertive so others perceive you as confident and in command.
10. Talking is a human relationship in which details and interesting side comments enhance depth of connection.	10. Talking is a linear sequence that should convey information and accomplish goals. Extraneous details get in the way and achieve nothing.

I'd rather do it myself. Jay is having difficulty writing a paper for his communication class, because he's not sure what the professor wants. When he mentions this to his friend Ellen, she suggests he ask the professor or a classmate to clarify directions. Jay resists, saying "I can figure it out on my own."

Can we talk about us? Anna asks her fiancé, Ben, "Can we talk about us?" Immediately Ben feels tense — another problem on the horizon. He guards himself for an unpleasant conversation and reluctantly nods assent. Anna then thanks Ben for being so supportive during the last few months when she was under enormous pressure at her job. She tells him she feels closer than ever. Then she invites him to tell her what makes him feel loved and close to

her. Although Ben feels relieved to learn there isn't any crisis, he's also baffled: "If there isn't a problem, why do they need to talk about the relationship? If it's working, let it be."

You've probably been involved in conversations like these. And you've probably been confused, frustrated, hurt, or even angry when a member of the other sex didn't give you what you wanted or didn't value your efforts to be supportive. If you're a woman, you may think Mike should be more sensitive to Rita's feelings and Dedrick should cherish time alone with Melita. If you're a man, it's likely that you empathize with Mike's frustration and feel Rita is giving him a hard time when he's trying to help. Likewise, you may think Melita is lucky to have a guy willing to shell out some bucks so they can do something fun together.

Who's right in these cases? Is Rita unreasonable? Is Melita ungrateful? Are Dedrick and Mike insensitive? Is Jay stubborn? Did Roseann mislead Drew? When we focus on questions like these we fall prey to a central problem in gender communication: the tendency to judge. Because Western culture is hierarchical, we're taught to perceive differences as better and worse not simply as different. Yet, the inclination to judge one person as right and the other wrong whenever there's misunderstanding usually spells trouble for close relationships.

But judging is not the only way we *could* think about these interactions, and it's not the most constructive way if our interest is building healthy relationships. Disparaging what differs from our own style only gets in the way of effective communication and satisfying relationships. All of the energy invested in fixing fault or defending our behaviors diminishes what we can devote to learning how to communicate better. What might be more productive than judging is understanding and respecting unique styles of communication. Once we recognize there are different and distinctly valid styles of interacting, we can tune into others' perspectives and interact more constructively with them.

Understanding Cross-Gender Communication

Drawing upon earlier sections of this article, we can analyze the misunderstandings in these five dialogues and see how they grow out of the different interaction styles cultivated in feminine and masculine communication cultures. Because men and women typically rely on distinct communication rules, they have different ways of showing support, interest, and caring. This implies they may perceive the same communication in dissimilar ways.

In the first scenario, Rita's purpose in talking with Mike isn't just to tell him about her concern for her friend; she also sees communication as a way to connect with Mike (Aries, 1987; Riessman, 1990; Tannen, 1990b; Wood, 1993b). She wants him to respond to her and her feelings, because that will enhance her sense of closeness to him. Schooled in masculinity, however, Mike views communication as an instrument to do things, so he tries to help by giving advice. To Rita it seems he entirely disregards her feelings, so she doesn't feel close to Mike, which was her primary purpose in talking with him. Rita might welcome some advice, but only after Mike responds to her feelings.

In the second example, the problem arises when Drew translates Roseann's feedback according to rules of communication in masculine culture. Women learn to give lots of response cues — verbal and nonverbal behaviors to indicate interest and involvement in conversation — because that's part of using communication to build relationships with others. Masculine culture, however, focuses on outcomes more than processes, so men tend to use feedback to signal specific agreement and disagreement (Beck, 1988; Fishman, 1978; Tannen, 1990b; Wood, 1993a). When Drew hears Roseann's "ums," "uh huhs," and "yeses," he assumes she is agreeing. According to her culture's rules, however, she is only showing interest and being responsive, not signaling agreement.

Dedrick and Melita also experience culture clash in their communication. Within feminine culture, talking is a way — probably the primary way — to express and expand closeness. For women there is closeness in dialogue (Aries, 1987; Riessman, 1990; Wood, 1993b). Masculine socialization, in contrast, stresses doing things and shared activities as primary ways to create and express closeness (Cancian, 1987; Swain, 1989; Wood & Inman, 1993). A man is more likely to express his caring for a woman by doing something concrete for her (washing her car, fixing an appliance) or doing something with her (skiing, a concert, tennis) than by talking explicitly about his feelings. Men generally experience "closeness in doing" (Swain, 1989). By realizing doing things is a valid way to be close, feminine individuals can avoid feeling hurt by partners who propose activities. In addition, women who want to express care in ways men value might think about what they could do for or with the men, rather than what they could say (Riessman, 1990).

Masculinity's emphasis on independence underlies Jay's unwillingness to ask others for help in understanding his assignment. As Tannen (1990b) points out rather humorously, men invariably resist asking directions when they are lost on the road while women don't hesitate to ask strangers for help. What we've discussed about gender identity helps us understand this difference. Because women initially develop identity within relationship, connections with others are generally sought and welcomed — even the casual connection made in asking for directions or help with an assignment. In contrast, men differentiated from their first relationship to develop identity, so relationships have an undertone of danger — they could jeopardize independence. So Jay's refusal to ask others for help reflects the masculine emphasis on maintaining autonomy and not appearing weak or incompetent to others. Unless Ellen realizes this difference between them, Jay will continue to baffle her.

In the final case we see a very common example of culture-clash in gender communication. Feminine culture prioritizes relationships so they are a constant source of interest, attention, and communication. In contrast, within masculine culture relationships are not as central and talk is perceived as a way to do things such as solve problems rather than a means to enhance closeness (Wood, 1993a, b, c). Given these disparate orientations, "talking about us" means radically different things to most men and women. As Tannen (1986) points out, men generally feel a relationship is going along fine if there's no need to talk about it, while women tend to feel a relationship is good as long as they are talking about it! Anna's wish to discuss the relationship because it's so good makes no sense to Ben, and his lack of interest in a conversation about the relationship hurts Anna. Again, each person errs in relying on inappropriate rules to interpret the other's communication.

Most problems in cross-cultural gender communication result from faulty translations. This happens when men interpret women according to rules of masculine culture and when women interpret men according to rules of feminine culture. Just as

we wouldn't assume Western rules apply to Asian people, so we'd be wise not to imagine one gender's rules pertain to the other. When we understand there are distinct gender cultures and when we respect the logic of each one, we empower ourselves to communicate in ways that enhance our relationships.

COMMUNICATING EFFECTIVELY BETWEEN GENDER CULTURES

Whether it's a Northern American thinking someone who eats with hands is "uncouth" or a woman assuming a man is "closed" because he doesn't disclose as much as she does, we're inclined to think what differs from our customs is wrong. Ethnocentric judgments seldom improve communication or enhance relationships. Instead of debating whether feminine or masculine styles of communication are better, we should learn to see differences as merely that — differences. The information we've covered, combined with this book's emphasis on understanding and appreciating culturally diverse communication, can be distilled into six principles for effective cross-gender communication.

1. *Suspend judgment*. This is first and foremost, because as long as we are judging differences, we aren't respecting them. When you find yourself confused in cross-gender conversations, resist the tendency to judge. Instead, explore constructively what is happening and how you and your partner might better understand each other.

2. *Recognize the validity of different communication styles*. In cross-gender communication, we need to remind ourselves there is a logic and validity to both feminine and masculine communication styles. Feminine emphases on relationships, feelings, and responsiveness don't reflect inability to adhere to masculine rules for competing any more than masculine stress on instrumental outcomes is a failure to follow feminine rules for sensitivity to others. It is inappropriate to apply a single criterion — either masculine or feminine — to both gen-

ders' communication. Instead, we need to realize different goals, priorities, and standards pertain to each.

3. *Provide translation cues.* Now that you realize men and women tend to learn different rules for interaction, it makes sense to think about helping the other gender translate your communication. For instance, in the first example Rita might have said to Mike, "I appreciate your advice, but what I need first is for you to deal with my feelings." A comment such as this helps Mike interpret Rita's motives and needs. After all, there's no reason why he should automatically understand rules that aren't a part of his gender culture.

4. *Seek translation cues.* We can also improve our interactions by seeking translation cues from others. If Rita didn't tell Mike how to translate her, he could have asked "What would be helpful to you? I don't know whether you want to talk about how you're feeling or ways to help your friend. Which would be better?" This message communicates clearly that Mike cares about Rita and he wants to support her if she'll just tell him how. Similarly, instead of blowing up when Roseann disagreed with him and assuming she had deliberately misled him, Drew might have taken a more constructive approach and said, "I thought your feedback during my spiel indicated agreement with what I was saying. What did it mean?" This kind of response would allow Drew to learn something new.

5. *Enlarge your own communication style.* Studying other cultures' communication teaches us not only about other cultures, but also about ourselves. If we're open to learning and growing, we can enlarge our own communication repertoire by incorporating skills more emphasized in other cultures. Individuals socialized into masculinity could learn a great deal from feminine culture about how to support friends. Likewise, people from feminine cultures could expand the ways they experience intimacy by appreciating "closeness in the doing" that is a masculine specialty. There's little to risk and much to gain by incorporating additional skills into our personal repertoires.

6. *Suspend judgment.* If you're thinking we already covered this principle, you're right. It's important enough, however, to merit repetition. Judgment is so thoroughly woven into Western culture that it's difficult not to evaluate others and not to defend our own positions. Yet as long as we're judging others and defending ourselves, we're probably making no headway in communicating more effectively. So, suspending judgment is the first and last principle of effective cross-gender communication.

SUMMARY

As women and men, we've been socialized into gendered identities, ones that reflect cultural constructions of femininity and masculinity. We become gendered as we interact with our families, childhood peers, and others who teach us what gender means and how we are to embody it in our attitudes, feelings, and interaction styles. This means communication produces, reflects, and reproduces gender cultures and imbues them with a taken-for-granted status that we seldom notice or question. Through an ongoing, cyclical process communication, culture, and gender constantly recreate one another.

Because we are socialized into distinct communication cultures, women and men tend to communicate for different reasons and in different ways. When we fail to recognize that genders rely on dissimilar rules for talk, we tend to misread each other's meanings and motives. To avoid the frustration, hurt, and misunderstandings that occur when we apply one gender's rules to the other gender's communication, we need to recognize and respect the distinctive validity and value of each style.

"Men and Women: Can We Get Along? Should We Even Try?"

Chances are pretty good we will keep trying to get along. Relationships between women and men are far too exciting, frustrating, and interesting not to! What we've covered in this article provides a good foundation for the ongoing process of learning not just how to get along with members of the other gender, but to appreciate and grow from valuing the different perspectives on interaction, identity and relationships that masculine and feminine cultures offer.

REFERENCES

Aries, E. (1987). "Gender and Communication." In P. Shaver (Ed.), *Sex and Gender*, pp. 149–176. Newbury Park, CA: Sage.

Beck, A. (1988). *Love Is Never Enough*. New York: Harper and Row.

Cancian, F. (1987). *Love in America*. Cambridge: Cambridge University Press.

Chodorow, N. J. (1978). *The Reproduction of Mothering: Psychoanalysis and the Sociology of Gender*. Berkeley, CA: University of California Press.

Coates, J., and Cameron, D. (1989). *Women in Their Speech Communities: New Perspectives on Language and Sex*. London: Longman.

Eichenbaum, L. and Orbach, S. (1983). *Understanding Women: A Feminist Psychoanalytic Approach*. New York: Basic.

Fishman, P. M. (1978). "Interaction: The Work Woman Do." *Social Problems, 25*, 397–406.

Gilligan, C. (1982). *In a Different Voice: Psychological Theory and Women's Development*. Cambridge: Harvard University Press.

Janeway, E. (1971). *Man's World, Woman's Place: A Study in Social Mythology*. New York: Dell.

Johnson, F. L. (1989). "Women's Culture and Communication: An Analytic Perspective." In C. M. Lont and S. A. Friedley (Eds.), *Beyond Boundaries: Sex and Gender Diversity in Communication*. Fairfax, VA: George Mason University Press.

Kramarae, C. (1981). *Women and Men Speaking: Frameworks for Analysis*. Rowley, MA: Newbury House.

Labov, W. (1972). *Sociolinguistic Patterns*. Philadelphia: University of Pennsylvania Press.

Lakoff, R. (1975). *Language and Woman's Place*. New York: Harper and Row.

Maltz, D. N. and Borker, R. (1982). "A Cultural Approach to Male-Female Miscommunication." In J. J. Gumpertz (Ed.), *Language and Social Identity*, pp. 196–216. Cambridge: Cambridge University Press.

Miller, J. B. (1986). *Toward a New Psychology of Women*. Boston: Beacon.

Rakow, L. F. (1986). "Rethinking Gender Research in Communication." In *Journal of Communication, 36*, 11–26.

Riessman, J. M. (1990). *Divorce Talk: Women and Men Make Sense of Personal Relationships*. New Brunswick, NJ: Rutgers University Press.

Spender, D. (1984). *Man Made Language*. London: Routledge and Kegan Paul.

Surrey, J. L. (1983). "The Relational Self in Women: Clinical Implications." In J. V. Jordan, J. L. Surrey, and A. G. Kaplan (Speakers), *Women and Empathy: Implications for Psychological Development and Psychotherapy*, pp. 6–11. Wellesley, MA: Stone Center for Developmental Services and Studies.

Swain, S. (1989). "Covert Intimacy: Closeness in Men's Friendships." In B. J. Risman and P. Schwartz (Eds.), *Gender and Intimate Relationships*, pp. 71–86. Belmont, CA: Wadsworth.

Tannen, D. (1986). *That's Not What I Meant!: How Conversational Style Makes or Breaks Relationships*. New York: Ballentine.

Tannen, D. (1990a). "Gender Differences in Conversational Coherence: Physical Alignment and Topical Cohesion." In B. Dorval (Ed.), *Conversational Organization and Its Development: XXXVIII*, pp. 167–206. Norwood, NJ: Ablex.

Tannen, D. (1990b). *You Just Don't Understand: Women and Men in Conversation*. New York: William Morrow & Co.

Treichler, P. A., and Kramarae, C. (1983). "Women's Talk in the Ivory Tower." *Communication Quarterly, 31*, 118–132.

Wood, J. T. (1994a). *Gendered Lives*. Belmont, CA: Wadsworth.

Wood, J. T. (1993b). "Engendered Relationships: Interaction, Caring, Power, and Responsibility in Close Relationships." In S. Duck (Ed.), *Processes in Close Relationships: Contexts of Close Relationships*, vol. 3. Beverly Hills: Sage.

Wood, J. T. (1993c). "Engendered Identities: Shaping Voice and Mind Through Gender." In D. Vocate

(Ed.), *Intrapersonal Communication: Different Voices, Different Minds*. Hillsdale, NJ: Lawrence Erlbaum & Associates.

Wood, J. T. (1993e). *Who Cares?: Women, Care, and Culture*. Carbondale, IL: Southern Illinois University Press.

Wood, J. T. and Inman, C. C. (1993). "In a Different Mode: Masculine Styles of Communicating Closeness." *Journal of Applied Communication Research*.

Zimmerman, D. H., and West, C. (1975). "Sex Roles, Interruptions, and Silences in Conversation." In B. Thorne and N. Henley (Eds.), *Language and Sex: Difference and Dominance*, pp. 105–129. Rowley, MA: Newbury House.

Discovering Gay Culture in America

RANDALL E. MAJORS

Growing up gay or lesbian in America is like growing up in a foreign country. You never really feel as though you "fit in" with what is going on around you. This feeling gets worse as people begin to place expectations on you to behave heterosexually—to show interest in the opposite sex, to date, to want to marry and have children, to get "serious" with someone of the opposite sex. But these things never happen to you when you are gay, and you begin to feel left out. Worst yet, you begin to feel as though there may be something "wrong" with you because sexual feelings do begin to emerge—for members of your own sex! If you think puberty and adolescence are hard for the average person, imagine what they are like for someone who is "different."

There is no matter of choice in this issue. No one "chooses" his or her biological sexuality. The only people who think so are those who have absolutely no idea what gay people are like. The world is full of sexual-orientation bigots who preach and orate about how gay people ought to be and ought to behave. But they have never known a gay person as a friend, never really tried to understand what it is like to be different, and are totally unwilling to consider the possibility that being gay is a perfectly natural biological variety of sexuality. Mother Nature loves variety, and this is nowhere more evident in human affairs than in the broad range of the forms of human sexuality.

When you talk to someone who is gay or lesbian, you soon discover that everyone has a story to tell about being different and the difficulties that were created for them by this difference. The struggle to overcome these difficulties creates a sense of commonality for most gay people — at least for the ones who survive adolescence with a measure of self-esteem. These similar experiences tie gay and lesbian people together into a unique social group, call it a culture, subculture, brotherhood, sisterhood, or community of like-minded people.[1] In this essay I will explain the process by which a gay person becomes aware of his or her sexuality and manages the conflict that this discovery creates. Gay people must come to terms with their sexuality, and they must learn the methods of survival in a fairly hostile cultural environment by discovering for themselves the social resources for creating a full and productive life within the larger American culture. These factors create a sense of cultural identity in gay people, and understanding this process will open the doors to understanding what it means to be gay in America.

COMING TO TERMS WITH BEING GAY

Enormous pressures from heterosexual culture to conform to the myth of "normal" sexuality make the process of maturation a particularly difficult one for gay and lesbian people. Gay people have always been a part of every culture.[2] Likewise, gay people are everywhere in American culture — some studies suggest that as many as one in ten people is gay — but they are forced to hide their identity and cultural heritage. Look at the people around you. If one in ten is gay, are you aware of who they are? Probably not, and the reason is that most gay people learn early on to hide their true feelings in order to pass as straight and avoid the hassles they would otherwise receive.

Lest you think that I am exaggerating this need for secrecy, let me propose a little experiment. I challenge you to make a little sign on a piece of paper about four inches square. If you are male, print the words "Gay Power" on the paper; if female, print

the words "Lesbian Power." Now for the kicker. I challenge you to pin this piece of paper to your shirt and wear it for a day and see what happens. If anyone asks you what it means, you can explain that it is just an experiment for your communication class. Just pretend that your message is like any other — Jesus Power, Black Power, Dolphin Power. Remember, this is just an experiment. Does it matter that your sign says "Gay Power"?

One of two things usually happens with this experiment. Some people will absolutely refuse to wear such a sign. When questioned as to their reasons, they admit quite vehemently that they do not want to be identified as "one of them" by anybody. Why not? What is so wrong with being perceived as being gay? The answers to these questions get at the phenomenon known as homophobia — the bigoted, irrational hatred of gay people. The brave ones who do wear the sign for a day have some interesting stories to tell. Invariably jeers of "faggot" or "dyke" will be hurled at some; others will tell about disdainful glances and sneers. Both of these results demonstrate the hostility of the environment in which gay people must live.

Having to hide is not a healthy way to grow up, and most gay people can bear witness to the difficulties they faced when younger. Most gay men and lesbians go through periods of confusion, self-doubt, low self-image, and fear of being discovered.[3] These feelings lead to a sense of isolation ("I'm the only one in the world") and alienation ("No one can understand me"). Cases of intense brainwashing to "straighten out" gay people are common, including enforced psychotherapy, casting out of demons, and verbal abuse. Few gay people can talk about a warm and accepting family that encouraged them to be themselves and develop as their natural instincts led them.

Despite this hostile environment, many gay people come to terms with their sexuality and decide to admit it to themselves and to others. This is called the process of "coming out." Many wonderful books recount the funny, horrible, and even heartwarming stories of gay men and lesbians coming out.[4] The thread running through all these authors' stories is the drive to be themselves and to be true to their inner natures. Coming out is not an easy process. Several good resources discuss the various issues gay people must face when they come out and the solutions they must find to build a satisfying life in the face of social disapproval.[5] To be healthy human beings, we need the support of other people. Families, friends, and communities provide these forms of emotional, physical, and psychological support, but gay people are threatened with the loss of these forms of support when they come out of the closet. It takes an extremely strong person to be able to admit to something that may cause him or her the loss of friends, ridicule, or even physical danger.

If a gay person's biological family and childhood community do not provide the necessary support for maturing naturally, he or she must find those forms of support elsewhere. Thus, gay people look to other gay people to form new kinds of families and new communities.[6] One of the major forms of assistance for gay people in coming out are the services provided by the culture of the gay community. Informal social groups provide the support and nurturing that gay people need to become their true selves.

THE ROLE OF COMMUNITY IN GAY CULTURE

Times have changed greatly since the 1967 "Stonewall Riots" in New York's Greenwich Village when a group of gay men fought back at police repression and ushered in a national movement for more understanding and protection for this minority group.[7] Only 25 years ago, gay culture was a furtive and hidden urban subculture, never discussed by and mostly unknown to the general public. Since then, gay culture has blossomed to include gay neighborhoods in most large American cities, thriving gay businesses and social services, gay publications and scholarship, and an increasing share of political clout and media coverage.

Gay Neighborhoods

Most cultural groups define themselves by marking out a home territory. Gay people are doing this in-creasingly in larger American cities by creating gay neighborhoods. How do you know when a neighborhood is gay? As with any generality, it is a relative matter. A good rule of thumb is that "enough gay people in a neighborhood and it becomes a gay neighborhood." Rarely do gay people want to paint the street lamps lavender, but the presence of gay people on the street as they take up residence in a district gives a gay character to an area. Word spreads in the community that a certain area is starting to look attractive and open to gay members. There is often a move to "gentrify" older, more affordable sections of a city and build a new neighborhood out of the leftovers from the rush to the suburbs. Gay businesses, meaning those operated by or catering to gay people, often develop once enough clientele is in the area to support commercial enterprise. The Castro area in San Francisco, Greenwich Village in New York, New Town in Chicago, the Westheimer district in Houston, and West Hollywood and Silverlake in Los Angeles are examples of the many emergent gay neighborhoods in cities across America.

Gay neighborhoods satisfy many needs. First, a gay person's sense of identity is reinforced if there is a special place that is somehow imbued with "gayness." Signs of gayness, whether overt symbols like rainbow flags or more subtle cues such as the presence of other gay people on the streets create the feeling that a certain territory is special to the group and hospitable to the group's unique values. Gay neighborhoods also create a meeting ground for gay people. Because of early experiences of isolation, the need for a safe meeting and living space is very important for gay people. Merely knowing that there is a specific place where other gay people live and work and play does much to anchor the psychological aspect of gayness in a tangible, physical reality. A person's sense of identity is reinforced by knowing that there is a home base where others of similar persuasion are nearby. Finally, gay neighborhoods create physical and psychological safety. Members of subcultural groups usually experience some degree of persecution from the larger, surrounding culture. For gay people, physical safety is a very real concern.[8] Incidences of homophobic assaults or harassment are common in most cities. By centralizing gay activities, some safeguards can be mounted. Large numbers of gay people living in proximity create a deterrence to violence, whether through informal "watching out for each other" or more formal programs such as street patrols. A sense of psychological safety and comfort follows from these physical measures.

Gay Social Groups

The need for affiliation—to make friends, to share recreation, to find life partners, or merely to pass the time—is a strong drive in any group of people. Specialized businesses and social groups fulfill the social needs of gay people. While gay people in rural areas and smaller towns often suffer because there is no developed gay culture and no way for meeting each other, in larger cities an elaborate array of clubs, social groups, churches, service agencies, entertainments, stores, restaurants, and bars add to the substance of the culture.

In the 1970s and 1980s the gay bar was often the first public gay experience for a gay person. Bars provided a place to meet potential relationship partners as well as entertainment and social activities. This central role has changed as gay issues are more integrated into American culture. Gay people now meet through computer networks, high school youth support groups, and a myriad of social institutions. In large urban areas, where gay culture is more widely developed, social groups include athletic organizations that sponsor teams and tournaments; leisure activity clubs such as dancing, music, yoga, bridge, and hiking; religious groups such as Dignity (Roman Catholic), Integrity (Episcopal), and the Metropolitan Community Church, a gay congregational denomination; volunteer agencies such as information and crisis hotlines and charitable organizations; and gay businesses and political groups. A directory of groups and activities is usually published in urban gay newspapers, another important element in the mixture of phenomena that create gay culture.

Gay businesses also emerge as the culture develops. Bookstores, often with culturally affirming names such as A Different Light, the Oscar Wilde Memorial Bookstore, or Women and Children First, satisfy intellectual needs. Other consumer needs are satisfied through a variety of restaurants, hotels, travel agencies, pet stores, and just about any other service that a thriving community desires. These businesses advertise through gay publications, often employing symbols and promotional appeals that are uniquely attuned to their target consumer populations.

Gay Publications

Gay publications and scholarship have played a vital role in creating and defining gay culture. Where gayness was once never discussed, we now see national debate over gay issues. This revolution was led by the founding of gay newspapers and magazines. An early trendsetter was *The Advocate*, a national news magazine for the gay community. Local gay newspapers are vital sources for spreading news, investigating issues important to the community, and providing information about gay social groups and services. Gay newspapers are also the forum for public debate about issues that affect the community: who to vote for in coming elections, how best to respond to threats to the community, how best to resolve the tensions between conflicting group values, (for example, should gay people in prominent public office be "outed" by disclosing their homosexuality or should their rights to privacy in this matter be respected?). These journalistic sources of information have been matched by independent scholarship published through gay presses and sold through gay bookstores. The research into gay sociological and psychological issues, the proliferation of gay and lesbian literature, and the increase of writing on gay consumer and personal issues, such as making relationships work, raising children, getting legal protection, and the like, demonstrates the vitality of the gay community across the nation.[9]

Gay Political Power

Finally, the emergence of gay culture in America can be seen in terms of the political clout it is beginning to develop. In the tradition of American grassroots democracy, gay people are winning their greatest battles at the local community level. As gay people create neighborhoods and demonstrate their value as regular citizens, they win political power. The concerns of gay people are taken more seriously by politicians and elected officials who represent an area where voters can be registered and mustered into service during elections. In many areas, openly gay politicians represent gay constituencies directly and voice their concerns in ever-widening forums. The impact of this kind of democracy-in-action is felt on other institutions as well. Police departments, social welfare agencies, schools, churches, and businesses are becoming increasingly accepting of gay participation and programs. This rise in political power is accompanied by, and some critics say caused by, an increasing coverage in national media. Certainly, more news articles about gay cultural issues, positive gay characters in television and movies, and distribution of books with gay themes by national publishers have increased steadily. Thus, gay people have become more accepted and more integrated into the life of the larger communities around them.

CONCLUSION

This essay has illustrated how a gay culture has developed within the larger American culture of the past 25 years. When an individual confronts his or her own sexual orientation, a decision must be made: continue hiding or come out. What we know as gay culture today is the result of millions of individuals making that decision to come out of hiding, one step at a time.

This process has not been without its limitations. Gay culture is still largely confined to major cities. Gay people in rural areas, suburbs, and small towns across America have very little access to the life-affirming support and services that the gay commu-

nity can provide. Thus, those isolated ones are often frustrated and intimidated in their progress toward self-actualization. Likewise, gay culture is largely an adult phenomenon. Most gay people do not come out until their mid-twenties because of intense familial and peer pressure to conform to a heterosexual norm. They internalize these norms and go through considerable anguish as they struggle to overcome these pressures to be straight. Very few services are available to young gay people to help them deal with this struggle. Thus, young gay people must wait until they are old enough to make the break from their childhood settings in order to start the process of self-affirmation. The cost of this delay, in terms of individual confusion and torment, is considerable.

Finally, as a substantive gay culture emerges, it creates its own enemies. The more successful gay culture becomes in affirming its values and creating its place in the larger culture, the more some other cultural groups become envious or increasingly hostile toward it. Thus, we have seen increasing attacks upon positive gay values in national politics and by spokesmen for powerful conservative groups. This "backlash" against gay rights advances is probably the best evidence that headway is being made. Perhaps fortunately, history teaches us that the harder you try to suppress a group, the greater the spirit of resistance grows and the louder the demand for equality will be sounded. We probably have seen only the opening chapter in the story of the emerging gay culture.

NOTES

1. The relative differences and similarities between gay men and lesbian women is a hotly debated issue in the gay/lesbian community. For the purposes of this essay, however, I have chosen to speak of them as a single cultural group. For an introduction to this issue, see Celia Kitzinger, *The Social Construction of Lesbianism* (Beverly Hills: Sage Publications, 1987).

2. Several good reviews of famous homosexuals include the following: Barbara Grier and Coletta Reid, *Lesbian Lives* (Oakland, CA: Diana Press, 1976); Noel I. Garde, *Jonathan to Gide: The Homosexual in History*

(New York: Nosbooks, 1969); and A. L. Rowse, *The Homosexual in History* (Metuchen, NY: Scarecrow Press, 1975).

3. For a discussion of these issues, see Don Clark, *(The New) Loving Someone Gay* (Berkeley: Celestial Arts, 1987), and George Weinberg, *Society and the Healthy Homosexual* (New York: Doubleday, 1973).

4. While there are many to choose from, three good coming-out stories include John Reid, *The Best Little Boy In the World* (New York: E. P. Putnam Sons, 1973); Rita Mae Brown, *Rubyfruit Jungle* (New York: Daughters Pub. Co., 1973); and Aaron Fricke, *Reflections of a Rock Lobster* (New York: Alyson, 1981).

5. See Mary V. Borhek, *Coming Out to Parents: A Two-Way Survival Guide* (New York: Pilgrim Press, 1983) and Betty Berzon, *Positively Gay* (Los Angeles: Mediamix Associates, 1979). Also useful are Wes Muchmore and William Hensen, *Coming Out Right: A Handbook for Gay Male Beginners* (Boston: Alyson Press, 1982) and Rob Eichberg, *Coming Out: An Act of Love* (New York: Dutton, 1990).

6. For a discussion of these new families, see Joseph Harry, "Gay Male and Lesbian Relationships," in Eleanor D. Macklin and Roger H. Rubin, *Contemporary Families and Alternative Lifestyles* (Beverly Hills: Sage Publications, 1983), p. 220.

7. For a discussion of the Stonewall Riots, see Laud Humphreys, *Out of the Closets: The Sociology of Gay Liberation* (Englewood Cliffs: Prentice-Hall, 1972).

8. A discussion of violence against gay people and its effects is in Dennis Altman, *The Homosexualization of America: The Americanization of Homosexuality* (New York: St. Martin's Press, 1982), pp. 100–101.

9. For examples of books on these issues see Betty Burzon, *Permanent Partners: Building Gay and Lesbian Relationships That Last* (New York: E. P. Dutton, 1988); *Gay Fathers: Some of Their Stories, Experiences and Advice* (Trumansburg, NY: Crossing Press, 1984); and Paul P. Ashley, *Oh! Promise Me, But Put It in Writing: Living Together Arrangements Without, During and After Marriage* (New York: McGraw Hill, 1978).

CONCEPTS AND QUESTIONS FOR CHAPTER 3

1. By what means can you approach interaction with members of co-cultures without making assumptions that are harmful to their sense of self-worth?

2. Arturo Madrid points out the difficulties members of co-cultures face in becoming full-fledged members of American institutions. How would you propose to solve that problem?

3. How does Madrid address the concept of cultural diversity?

4. Can you think of other co-cultures that fall into Folb's category of nondominant groups?

5. How do you suppose someone from a foreign culture would respond to one of our co-cultures? Be specific.

6. How do erroneous stereotypes affect intercultural communication?

7. How would you set about trying to make people realize that their stereotypes of other cultures and co-cultures are probably erroneous and that they need to be changed or eliminated?

8. What are the basic assumptions Ribeau, Baldwin, and Hecht make regarding African-American communication?

9. What recommendations do Ribeau, Baldwin, and Hecht make to improve intercultural communication between Euro-Americans and African Americans? How can you incorporate these recommendations into your own communicative behavior?

10. How does becoming disabled change a person's communication patterns?

11. What are some of the cultural problems inherent in communication between ablebodied and disabled persons?

12. What does Wood mean when she asserts that communication constructs gender cultures?

13. What methods does Wood suggest to help improve understanding in cross-gender communication?

14. What function does gay communicative behavior serve?

15. In what ways have gay people adopted specific nonverbal behaviors that signify the manifestation of their co-culture?

16. Do you believe that co-cultures seeking to practice their own ways of life ought to be permitted this freedom? What are the limits of this behavior?

17. In what different ways have racial and ethnic co-cultures been treated in the United States?

18. Why does the history of a co-culture offer us insight into its communication behaviors?

PART THREE

Intercultural Interaction: Taking Part in Intercultural Communication

If we seek to understand a people we have to put ourselves, as far as we can, in that particular historical and cultural background. . . . One has to recognize that countries and people differ in their approach and their ways, in their approach to life and their ways of living and thinking. In order to understand them we have to understand their way of life and approach. If we wish to convince them, we have to use their language as far as we can, not language in the narrow sense of the word, but the language of the mind.

—Jawaharlal Nehru

In this part we are concerned with taking part in intercultural communication. Our interest focuses on both verbal and nonverbal forms of symbolic interaction. As we pointed out in introducing Part Two, meanings reside within people, and symbols serve as stimuli to which these meanings are attributed. Meaning-evoking stimuli consist of both verbal and nonverbal behaviors. Although we consider these forms of symbolic interaction separately for convenience, we hasten to point out their interrelatedness. As nonverbal behavior accompanies verbal behavior, it becomes a unique part of the total symbolic interaction. Verbal messages often rely on their nonverbal accompaniment for cues that aid the receiver in decoding the verbal symbols. Nonverbal behaviors not only serve to amplify and clarify verbal messages but can also serve as forms of symbolic interaction without verbal counterparts.

When we communicate verbally, we use words with seeming ease, because there is a high consensus of agreement about the meanings our words evoke. Our experiential backgrounds are similar enough that we share essentially the same meanings for most of the word symbols we use in everyday communication. But even within our culture we disagree over the meanings of many word symbols. As words move farther from sense data reality they become more abstract, and there is far less agreement about appropriate meanings. What do highly abstract words such as *love, freedom, equality, democracy,* or *good time* mean to you? Do they mean the same things to everyone? If you are in doubt, ask some friends; take a poll. You will surely find that people have different notions of these concepts and consequently different meanings for these words. Their experiences have been different, and they hold different beliefs, attitudes, values, concepts, and expectations. Yet all, or perhaps most, are from the same culture. Their backgrounds, experiences, and concepts of the universe are really quite uniform. When cultures begin to vary, much larger differences are found.

Culture exerts no small influence over our use of language. In fact, it strongly determines just what our language is and how we use it. In the narrowest sense, language is a set of symbols (vocabulary) that evoke more or less uniform meanings among a particular population and a set of rules (grammar and syntax) for using the symbols. In the broadest sense, language is the symbolic representation of a people, and it includes their historical and cultural backgrounds as well as their approach to life and their ways of living and thinking.

What comes to be symbolized and what the symbols represent are very much functions of culture. Similarly, how we use our verbal symbols is also a function of culture. What we think about or speak with others about must be capable of symbolization, and how we speak or think about things must follow the rules we have for using our language. Because the symbols and rules are culturally determined, how and what we think or talk about are, in effect, a function of our culture. This relation between language and culture is not unidirectional, however. There is an interaction between them—what we think about and how we think about it also affect our culture.

As we can see, language and culture are inseparable. To be effective intercultural communicators requires that we be aware of the relationship between culture and language. It further requires that we learn and know about the culture of the person with whom we communicate so that we can better understand how his or her language represents that person.

Another important aspect of verbal symbols or words is that they can evoke two kinds of meanings: *denotative* and *connotative*. A denotative meaning indicates the referent or the "thing" to which the symbol refers. For example, the denotative meaning of the word *book* is the physical object to which it refers; or, in the case of the set of symbols "*Intercultural Communication: A Reader*," the referent is the book you are now reading. Not all denotations have a physical correspondence. As we move to higher levels of abstraction, we often deal with words that represent ideas or concepts, which exist only in the mind and do not necessarily have a physical basis. For example, much communication research is directed toward changes in attitude. Yet attitude is only a hypothetical construct used to explain behavior; there is no evidence of any physical correspondence between some group of brain cells and a person's attitudes.

The second type of meaning—connotative—indicates an evaluative dimension. Not only do we identify referents (denotative meaning), we place them along an evaluative dimension that can be described as positive-neutral-negative. Where we place a word on the dimension depends on our prior experiences and how we "feel" about the referent. If we like books, we might place *Intercultural Communication: A Reader* near the positive end of the dimension. When we are dealing with more abstract symbols, we do the same thing. In fact, as the level of abstraction increases, so does our tendency to place more emphasis on connotative meanings. Most will agree that a book is the object you are holding in your hand, but whether books are good or bad or whether this particular book is good or bad or in between is an individual judgment based on prior experience.

Culture affects both denotative and connotative meanings. Consequently, a knowledge of how these meanings vary culturally is essential to effective intercultural communication. To make the assumption that everyone uses the same meanings is to invite communication disaster.

There are other ways in which culture affects language and language use. We tend to believe that our way of using language is both correct and universal and that any deviation is wrong or substandard. This belief can and does elicit many negative responses and judgments when we encounter someone from another culture whose use of language deviates from our own specifications.

What all of these examples are trying to point out should be quite obvious—language and culture are inseparable. In fact, it would be difficult to determine which is the voice and which is the echo. How we learn, employ, and respond to symbols is culturally based. In addition, the sending and the receiving of these culturally grounded symbols are what enable us to interact with people from other cultures. Hence, it is the purpose of this part of the book to highlight these verbal and nonverbal symbols to help you understand some of the complexities, subtleties, and nuances of language.

It is obvious that communication involves much more than the sending and receiving of verbal and nonverbal messages. Human interaction takes place within some social and physical setting that influences how we construct and perceive messages. The sway of context is rooted in three interrelated assumptions. First, communication is *rule* governed, that is to say, each encounter has implicit and explicit rules that regulate our conduct. These rules tell us everything from what is appropriate attire to what topics can be discussed. Second, the *setting* helps us define what "regulations" are in operation. Reflect for a moment on your own communication behavior as you move to and from the following arenas: classroom, courtroom, church, hospital, and dance hall. Visualize yourself behaving differently as you proceed from place to place. Third, most of the communication rules we follow have been *learned* as part of cultural experiences. While cultures might share the same general settings, their specific notion of proper behavior for each context manifests the values and attitudes of that culture. Concepts of turn-taking, time, space, language, manners, nonverbal behavior, silence, and control of the communication flow are largely an extension of each culture.

In this part of the book we offer some readings that demonstrate the crucial link that exists between context, culture, and communication. What emerges from these essays is the realization that to understand another culture you must appreciate the rules that govern that culture's behavior in a specific setting. While we might find ourselves in a variety of contexts, in this part of the book we have selected environments related to business, education, and health care.

4

Verbal Processes: Thinking and Speaking

Some people have suggested that our most unique feature is our ability, as a species, to receive, store, manipulate, and generate symbols. All 5.5 billion of us deal with past, present, and future experiences by using language; we make sounds and marks on paper that stand for something. In short, language is that special, simple, and yet magical instrument that lets us share our internal states with others.

It is the premise of this chapter that a culture's use of language involves much more than words and phrases. Forms of reasoning, techniques of problem solving, and specialized linguistic devices such as metaphors, similes, and analogies are all part of a culture's approach to language. Hence, to understand the language of any culture demands that you look beyond the vocabulary, grammar, and syntax. This philosophy has guided us in our selection of readings. We urge you to view language from this larger perspective as you read the articles in this chapter; this eclectic outlook toward language will help you understand the interaction patterns of cultures that are different from your own.

We begin this chapter with an essay by Devorah A. Lieberman, "Ethnocognitivism, Problem Solving, and Hemisphericity," that advances the claim that thinking, problem solving, and language are not only interrelated but are grounded in culture. She maintains that an understanding of differences among cultures in cognitive processing in regard to problem solving is essential for successful intercultural communication. To facilitate that understanding Lieberman develops three major themes in her essay. First, she explores the possible reasons for and approaches to differences among cultures in problem solving and cognitive processing. Second, teaching styles that reinforce and perpetuate culture-specific problem-solving approaches are presented. Finally, by means of the case study method, five culturally different teachers and classrooms (Japanese, Hebrew, French, Spanish, and English) are examined to determine what problem-solving approaches are encouraged in each of these five learning environments.

Continuing our theme that language goes beyond words, we present a selection that declares a direct connection between perception and language, a point of view that is at the heart of the Sapir-Whorf hypothesis of "linguistic relativity." This classic and sometimes controversial hypothesis maintains that each language embodies and imposes upon its users and their culture a particular view of reality that functions not only as a device for reporting experience but also, and more significantly, as a way of defining experience. To help explain this argument and its ramifications, Harry Hoijer introduces the basic assumptions, usability, and plausibility of linguistic relativity.

As you might suspect, foreign language translation is becoming ever more commonplace as our society grows increasingly multilingual and culturally diverse. Therefore, our next essay examines this crucial topic of translation. As we noted in the introduction of this part, language involves attaching meanings to word symbols, whether they are sounds or marks on a piece of paper. If those symbols have to be translated, as in a foreign language, numerous problems arise. Without accurate translations those trying to communicate often end up simply exchanging meaningless sounds. What usually happens is that the interpretations lack a common vocabulary and familiar referents.

As a means of helping us understand some of the problems that plague the translation process, Stephen P. Banks and Anna Banks examine this important subject in "Translation as Problematic Discourse in Organizations." They begin by summarizing current theories of organizations and translation before they offer a specific case study involving a multicultural organization. By analyzing what happens in a multilingual work force they are able to isolate specific translation difficulties (inaccuracies, losses of common socio-cultural contexts, and changes in power relationships) and also offer some guidelines for overcoming these problems.

All cultures introduce new members into their group by employing a rather elaborate symbol system. We are born with the tools to learn these systems, so passing on culture by speaking and listening is universal, but what is not universal is a culture's knowledge of the skills necessary to read and write. Literacy entails more than learning how to read and write; it influences thinking patterns, perceptions, cultural values, communication styles, and social organizations as well. Because we often interact with people who have no written language, it is useful to know something of how cultures such as the Hmong of Laos share experiences. So many Asian refugees have migrated to the United States that it seems appropriate to look at this culture, as Robert Shuter does in his essay "The Hmong of Laos: Orality, Communication, and Acculturation."

The purpose of this chapter is to introduce you to the various forms of verbal communication found among and between cultures. Our use of language not only gives us the gift of sharing ideas and information with those we encounter, but language is one of the primary ways we learn our culture.

In this book we encourage you to see that there are almost as many communication styles as there are cultures. The overriding assumption is that if you know something about the way other people communicate, how they use language, you can improve the quality of your communication with them and your understanding of their behavior. This study of language is important because one's language is a model of one's culture; language functions as a reflection of a culture's unique experiences. In no instance is this point more vivid than in the black community. Here the study of language not only reveals something about that group's view of the world, but it is also an examination of how past experiences find their way to the present. In our next essay, "The Need to Be: The Socio-Cultural Significance of Black Language," Shirley N. Weber uses black language to show how the African people attempted to adjust to slavery, an adjustment that is still being acted out today. She isolates five aspects of black language that she suggests might "help others understand and appreciate black language styles and the reasons blacks speak the way they do, in hopes of building respect for cultural differences."

Ethnocognitivism, Problem Solving, and Hemisphericity

DEVORAH A. LIEBERMAN

Intercultural communication theory is grounded in the concept that participants in any interaction bring with them "a system of symbols and meanings" (Schneider, 1976) that shapes their perceptions of a shared phenomenon. Based upon this approach to intercultural communication, much of the research in the field and the teaching of intercultural communication in our own college classrooms has claimed that differences (for example, values, beliefs, attitudes, frames of reference) are the basic variables that influence these perceptions (Kohls, 1984). However, few intercultural communication scholars have addressed specific differences among cultures in their approach to solving problems. Condon and Yousef (1975) and Samovar and Porter (1988, 1991) are notable exceptions. A great deal of research has addressed the different ways cultures vary in values, beliefs, and ways of classifying, but "there is a lack of research addressing differences in problem solving by culture. This research needs to be done" (Cole & Scribner, 1974, p. 174). The "cultural differences in the problem-solving" debate among ethnocognitivists (Bogen, DeZare, TenHouten, & Marsh, 1972; Cole & Scribner, 1974) ranges from whether there are inherent cultural differences in cognitive abilities to whether cultures merely teach culture-specific cognitive processes. Thus, based upon the

assumption that cultures reason and problem solve differently, this article has a threefold purpose. First, it explores the possible reasons for and approaches to differences among cultures in problem solving and cognitive processing. Second, it examines teaching styles that reinforce and perpetuate culture-specific problem-solving approaches. Third, it identifies case study problem-solving approaches utilized and encouraged by five culturally disparate teachers.

CULTURE AND PROBLEM-SOLVING APPROACHES

Cognitive processes are universal cerebral means employed to handle a specific task or problem at hand. According to Luria (1966) everyone has the same cognitive components, but learns to use them differently throughout life. Cole and Scribner (1974) support Luria, contending that it is the cultural influence that conditions the alternative cognitive processes chosen to complete tasks or solve problems. Each culture teaches, trains, and molds those within its system to exhibit what is considered the most appropriate range of problem-solving methods. For example, "Research on cultural difference . . . indicates that members of industrialized societies and members of nonindustrial societies respond to visual illusions quite differently" (Reid, p. 87).

Anthropological research has traditionally examined culture and problem solving from a group, content-observation, field-description approach. Psychological research has examined cognition, elementary functions, process, the individual laboratory and explanation (Cole, 1985). This chapter integrates these two approaches (culture and cognition), examining problem-solving approaches in different cultures. These approaches range from concrete participative problem solving to abstract individualistic problem solving.

COGNITIVE STYLES

Cultures tend to encourage and reinforce the cognitive style individuals employ when faced with refining information during the problem-solving process. Mestenhauser (1981) explains that learning as well as problem solving involves "the way a person abstracts information from the environment, remembers it, [and] classifies it into concepts and categories . . ." (p. 161). Furthermore, "Logic [the problem-solving approach] . . . is evolved out of a culture; it is not universal" (Kaplan, 1988, p. 208). Thus, a particular problem-solving approach may be considered either the "most logical" or the "most commonsensical" within a particular culture and situation (Lieberman, Kosokoff, & Kosokoff, 1988). Witkin and Goodenough (1981) claim that there are stark differences in the global and abstract functioning of individuals in different cultures and that different modes of thinking are characteristic of different cultures. Cognitive styles considered in this article are: field-dependence/field-independence, reflectivity/impulsivity, tolerance/intolerance of ambiguity, left hemisphere/right hemisphere, and "4MAT" styles.

The individual who employs the *field-dependent* cognitive style tends to take elements or background variables from the environment into account. This individual tends to perceive the event holistically including the emotionality and the feelings associated with the entire event. Scarcella (1990) claims that field-dependent individuals enjoy working with others in solving a problem. They are sensitive to the feelings and opinions of the others in the group. He asserts that Hispanic and African-American students tend to employ more field-dependent rather than field-independent strategies in learning and problem solving. Scarcella explains these cognitive behaviors as resulting from cultures that are more group-oriented and more sensitive to the social environment.

The individual who employs the *field-independent* cognitive style tends to isolate given details of the field, placing the elements into a cause-effect, linear, or sequential frame. This style emphasizes the logic of the problem, while de-emphasizing the feelings or emotions within the field. Brown (1980) claims that the field-dependent cognitive style is encouraged and reinforced in more traditional societies that also reinforce high-context behavior and authoritarian behavior. The field-independent cog-

nitive style is more predominant in highly industrialized, low-context, competitive societies.

Reflectivity and *impulsivity* refer to the length of time individuals are encouraged to spend on "thinking about a problem." Certain cultures expect an individual to reflect on multiple variables surrounding a problem to ascertain the most correct answer. Impulsivity in these cultures is not rewarded. "To make a mistake is painful; to guess is to admit not having spent enough time in finding the correct answer. Being only partially 'right,' which may be acceptable to the impulsive learners and in other cultures, is often seen as totally 'wrong' by those whose reflective learning styles are culturally sanctioned" (Damen, 1987, p. 302).

Tolerance of ambiguity describes cultures that downplay bipolar language. The English language emphasizes bipolarity. In a problem-solving situation, bipolar language might be: "This is either right or wrong," "black or white," "good or bad," "yes or no," "correct or incorrect." Bipolar language encourages cause-effect thinking and linearity (Korzybsky, 1921). Thus, there is less tolerance for ambiguity where there is greater bipolarity in the structure and meaning of the language itself.

Contradictions are not as glaring in cultures that have a greater tolerance of ambiguity. "Tolerance of ambiguity, as a cognitive style, is ill-received in the scientifically oriented, competitive ambiance of the average classroom in the United States. On the contrary, particularly at higher levels of education, field-independence, impulsivity, and intolerance of ambiguity are generally rewarded" (Damen, p. 302).

Positive relationships exist among these three problem-solving cognitive styles. Cultures that tend to encourage and reward individuals who display field-independence also may reward impulsivity and intolerance of ambiguity. Whereas, cultures that tend to encourage field-dependence also may reward reflectivity and tolerance of ambiguity (see Figure 3 on page 183).

Please note however, as I write this particular article and make sense out of the information with which I am presented, I want to avoid my own culturally encouraged Aristotelian "intolerance of ambiguity," in which I categorize cultures and individuals as "either field independent or field dependent," "impulsive or reflective," or "high context or low context." "The English language and its related thought patterns have evolved out of the Anglo-European cultural pattern. The expected sequence of thought in English is essentially a Platonic-Aristotelian sequence, descended from the philosophers of ancient Greece and shaped subsequently by Roman, medieval European, and later Western thinkers" (Kaplan, 1988, p. 208). Thus, it is difficult for this writer to avoid linear, cause-effect reasoning when formulating the reasoning within this article.

Try to avoid reading *this* article from your own culturally imposed perspective, instead attempting to examine ranges of cognitive styles and approaches to problem solving that are encouraged and reinforced within other cultures. Categorizing individual thought and behavior as either "left hemisphere" or "right hemisphere," "reflective" or "impulsive," and so on encourages "either-or" thinking. This article instead stresses such categories as continua, suggesting that behaviors may occur anywhere along the dimension dependent upon the context and situation.

CULTURAL DIFFERENCES

Two culture-based continua that directly relate to the investigation of ethnocognitivism and problem solving are low context/high context and individualism/collectivism.

Hall (1976) classifies cultures as exhibiting high-context or low-context behaviors. In high-context communication, most of the meaning of the message is "either in the physical context or internalized in the person, while very little is in the coded, explicit, transmitted part of the message" (p. 91). Low-context communication finds most "of the information . . . vested in the explicit code" (p. 91).

Similarly, cultures that encourage low-context communication also advocate individualism while those that encourage high-context communication advocate collectivism (Gudykunst & Ting-Toomey, 1988). Individualistic cultures invite individuality of thought and personal achievement of the individual as supraordinate to the group. Collectivistic cultures promote group goals and the belief that the group is supraordinate to the individual. The goals of the group take precedence, with interdependence and reciprocal obligations highly valued (Hofstede, 1986).

PROBLEM SOLVING OF THE KPELLE, FIJI, POMO, AND TROBRIAND

Following are four examples of cultures that use problem-solving techniques acquired through group participation, field dependence and reflectivity: Kpelles of Liberia, Fijians, Native Americans, and Trobriands. Each is a relatively high-context culture (Hall, 1976), gathering information from the immediate environment, and employing concrete approaches to attend to unsolved tasks. In each, there seems little leeway for inferential problem solving.

The Kpelle rice farmers are from central Liberia. They work together clearing land and raising rice and cooperate in the forest, gathering materials for buildings, tools, and medicine. The researcher seated two of the Kpelles at a table facing each other with a small partition between them. In front of each man were ten sticks (pieces of wood of different kinds); each stick matched one stick in the other pile. The researcher chose a stick from one of the men and told him to describe the stick so that the other Kpelle farmer could choose the matching stick from his pile. The procedure continued until all ten sticks had been described and selected.

With the partition lifted, the men compared the two rows of sticks and described and discussed errors. The barrier was replaced and they repeated the entire process of choosing one stick and describing it to the other. Examples of the descriptions on the first trial were: "one of the sticks," "not a large one," "piece of bamboo," "one stick," "one of the thorny." Examples of the descriptions on the second trial were: "one of the sticks," "curved bamboo," "large bamboo," and "has a thorn."

The problem-solving technique of "hit and miss" description used to transfer information did not take into account the precise information the other person needed to know to choose the stick. These farmers, through observation of one another, always participate together in tasks and do not *need* to share the information the other person lacks. All information is observable and available to all individuals (Cole, Gay, & Glick, 1969). In this high-context culture, where information is gathered from the environment, the Kpelles thus problem solve in a concrete manner.

Griffin (1982) found that the Fijian language does not allow for abstract problem solving as there is inadequate verbal coding to identify a new problem. Thus, when a problem arises that had not been previously confronted, the Fijian is "unable to think out new rules, verbalize problems, and generate options" (p. 60). Anxiety and frustration often follow as outlets for the problem-solving barrier. The Fijians employ field dependence as their cognitive style, drawing from the immediate environment to address solutions.

Another concrete approach to reasoning is evident in the native American (Freedle, 1981). When Pomo native Americans were asked to recall a story and could not remember a piece of information their response was that they could not recount the story at all. Thus, a subject's recall was either null or perfect. Similarly, a problem could either be perceived as solvable or not, depending on information availability. All pieces of the puzzle were required for problem solving to occur. Other Native American languages (for example, Hopi and Navajo) also lend themselves to concrete rather than abstract thinking, leading to less analytic and more absolute problem solving.

The Trobriand, also concrete in language, do not problem solve from the cause-and-effect approach that is associated with linear-thinking cultures. They do not have the traditional stimulus-response system; thus, when confronted with a problem the solution approach is present oriented. As the language has no "to be" verbs, the concept of delayed gratification or a solution emerging in the future does not exist. Thus sequential logic is not part of their cognitive process. Trobriand students present an example of a negative consequence of the differences in problem solving among cultures. They have been refused entrance to colleges because the autobiographic sketches accompanying their applications were assessed as lacking purposefulness and ability to plan. They were rated as questionable in character as well as intellectually inadequate (Lee, 1950).

PROBLEM SOLVING IN MAINSTREAM CULTURES

Kaplan (1970) examined problem-solving approaches and patterns of thought in more mainstream cultures. He concluded that English-speaking persons from the United States were more linear and direct than Semitic, Asian, Romance, or Russian speakers. The Semitic individuals solved problems using a combination of tangential and semidirect approaches. Asians employed a circular approach. Romance cultures used a more consistently circuitous approach, and Russians employed a combination of direct and circuitous approaches.

Kaplan asserts that in learning another language, one must learn the logic and problem-solving approach encouraged in that culture. A basis for identifying the problem-solving approach (as noted in Figure 1) is to study the paragraph format of a particular culture. "Each language and each culture has a paragraph order unique to itself, and that part of the learning of a particular language is mastering its logical system" (1988, p. 222). Kaplan cites an activity performed in U.S. schools that exemplifies how the educational system encourages linear, sequential cognition (see Figure 2). Students are told to categorize commercial television by type and purpose (p. 219). The instructor provides the programming types for the student and supplies supporting spaces that the student is expected to fill in. However, the essential category and format is designed by the instructor; thus there is no room for nonlinear, nonsequential thought on the part of the students.

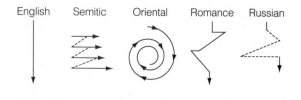

English   Semitic   Oriental   Romance   Russian

Figure 1 Sequencing Differences by Culture

Patterns of thought, first identified by Pribram (1949), vary situationally within and among cultures. Each culture teaches its members which patterns of thought and problem-solving approaches are most appropriate when confronted with particular situations (Condon & Yousef, 1975). These patterns have been identified by various authors as universalistic, nominalistic, hypothetical, intuitional, organismic, dialectical, temporal, axiomatic, affective, inductive/deductive, analytic, global, sequential, concrete sequential, and abstract random (Condon & Yousef, 1975; Felder & Silverman, 1988; Gregorc, 1979; Pribram, 1949).

Particular patterns predominate within specific cultures. For example the United States is predominantly factual-inductive (ascertain facts, find similarities, and formulate conclusions); the former Soviet Union is predominantly axiomatic-deductive (move from general principle to particulars, which can be easily deduced); and, Arab cultures are predominantly intuitive-affective (facts are secondary to emotions).

An extension of the cognitive process for problem solving is an individual's style of presentation. Confronted with a problem, an individual from the United States might respond with two or three specific alternative solutions. The U.S. culture perpetuates either thinking in three's (for example, "Tom, Dick, and Harry," "I came, I saw, I conquered"; and [when telling a joke] "and then the third man came up and said"), or in dichotomies (for example, either/or; right or wrong; good or bad). Conditioning to perceive a situation or problem from a particular style as well as from a particular perspective dictates the appropriate response (Condon & Yousef, 1975).

Though individuals have the ability to use any process, the culture stresses only two or three (Gre-

I. Programs of Serious Interest

  A. News Broadcasts:

    1. _____

    2. _____

  B. Special Features:

    1. _____

    2. _____

II. Programs Intended Primarily as Entertainment

  A. Variety Shows:

    1. _____

    2. _____

  B. Situational Comedies:

    1. _____

    2. _____

  C. Adventure Tales:

    1. _____

    2. _____

III. Advertising

  A. _____

    1. _____

    2. _____

  B. _____

    1. _____

    2. _____

Figure 2 Outlining in the U.S. Educational System

gorc, 1979). Even though these styles and patterns are idiosyncratic to the individual "they must be heavily influenced by cultural transmission" (Collins & Dedre, 1987, p. 263).

Intercultural communication research that addresses cultural patterns of thought and problem-solving approaches has only scratched the surface of cognitive functioning and differences among cultures. Springer and Deutsch (1985) contend that different languages (whether oriented toward concrete or abstract thought) are very likely responsible for differential hemispheric involvement (p. 241). They maintain that particular cognitive functions are hemisphere-specific. Thus, if a culture produces individuals who exhibit predominant problem-solving patterns and these patterns have been associated with particular hemisphericity, then it follows that **ethnocognitivism** (thought patterns dominant within a culture) and **hemisphericity** (hemisphere dominance in the brain) should be a greater consideration in the examination of intercultural interactions.

ETHNOCOGNITIVISM AND HEMISPHERICITY

The left hemisphere has traditionally been associated with the following processes: sequential, verbal, auditory, analytic, symbolic, abstract, temporal, rational, digital, logical, theoretical, cause-effect, and linear (see Figure 3). Left-hemisphere processing is systematic. "Analysis and planning are key strategies. Problems are solved by looking at the parts, and sequence is critical" (McCarthy, 1990, p. 32). The right hemisphere has traditionally been associated with the following processes: nonverbal, visual, synthetic, concrete, analogic, emotional, creative, nontemporal, nonrational, spatial, intuitive, tactile, holistic, and global (Edwards, 1979; Springer & Deutsch, 1985). "Right-mode processing seeks patterns and solves problems by looking at the whole picture. Intuition, beliefs, and opinions are key processing strategies" (McCarthy, 1990, p. 32).

The "cultural cognition" paradox asks whether a culture trains its individuals to have dominant left or right hemispheres or whether cultures are inherently left- or right-hemisphere dominant (Paredes & Hepburn, 1976). Springer and Deutsch (1985) resolve the paradox by suggesting that "every human brain is capable of more than one kind of logical process, but cultures differ with respect to the processes used with various situations." A segment of

Left Hemisphere	Right Hemisphere
Verbal, analytic, symbolic, abstract, temporal, rational, digital, logical, linear, cause-effect, sequential, theoretical, auditory	Nonverbal, synthetic, concrete analogic, nontemporal, holistic, intuitive, nonrational, spatial, tactile, creative, emotive, global
Field independent	Field dependent
Intolerance of ambiguity	Tolerance of ambiguity
Impulsivity	Reflectivity
Low context	High context
Individualistic	Collectivistic

Figure 3 Types of Cognitive Problem-solving Styles

the cultural paradox research (Tsunoda, 1978, cited in Science, 1980), suggests that the Japanese brain, as opposed to the Western brain, actually functions differently. However, Tsunoda suggests that the Japanese left hemisphere processes nonverbal human sounds, animal sounds, and Japanese instrumental music, while the right hemisphere processes Western instrumental music. Previous research claimed all nonverbal sounds (human, animal, and musical) were processed in the right hemisphere. Also, he contends that Westerners process emotion in their right hemisphere, the Japanese in the left. The language first learned develops the person's patterns of thought and influences "the way the brain's two halves process language" (Tsunoda, p. 25). Furthermore, Western children raised in the Japanese culture speaking Japanese "typically acquire Japanese brains," (p. 25) and vice versa concerning Japanese children raised in Western culture. Very little of this research has been translated from Japanese into English, and understandably "much more work is needed to determine if cultural differences in hemispheric utilization are real and, if so, to what they are attributable" (Springer & Deutsch, p. 242). Though this research has not been corroborated it raises exciting questions regarding culture as it relates to hemisphericity and problem solving.

Considering the problem-solving cognitive styles illuminated thus far within this article, a pattern emerges for style and hemisphericity. Researchers caution that cultures encourage individuals to apply particular cognitive tools (for example, reflectivity or impulsivity), though not necessarily to the exclusion of the other. For example, McCarthy (1990) addresses four styles of learning and problem solving, each with a preference, though not exclusively, for either right- or left-hemisphere skills. The four styles are (1) imaginative, (2) analytic, (3) common sense, and (4) dynamic. The imaginative approach (primarily right hemisphere) "perceives information concretely and processes it reflectively" (p. 32). The analytic approach (emphasizes left- and right-hemisphere processing) "perceives information abstractly and processes it reflectively" (p. 32). The commonsense approach (emphasizes left- and right-hemisphere processing) integrates theory and practice, by perceiving information abstractly and immediately applying it to concrete situations (p. 32). The dynamic approach (primarily right hemisphere) perceives information concretely and applies it immediately to concrete situations (p. 32).

CULTURE, HEMISPHERICITY, AND EDUCATION

Given the potential for cultural influence on hemisphere dominance and problem-solving patterns, it is essential to understand the responsibility educational systems have toward understanding their effect on developing students' patterns of thought, approaches to problem solving, and, in turn, communication styles. For example, Blakeslee (1980) contends that the U.S. educational system has not realized that it is almost singularly teaching its students to process information and formulate responses using traditionally accepted left-hemisphere skills (for example, linear thought, analytic, rational, and nonemotional). Qualities of the right hemisphere, often termed the "unconscious hemisphere," are not only deemphasized but often are associated with less important or irrelevant qualities. "Because we operate in such a sequential world [U.S.] and because the logical thought of the left hemisphere is so honored in our culture, we gradually damp out, devalue, and disregard the input of our right hemispheres. It is not that we stop using it altogether; it just becomes less and less available to us because of established patterns" (Prince, 1978, p. 57). Blakelee goes so far as to contend that "there is a decadence in the field of higher education that is the natural result of an ignorance of the unconscious side of the brain . . . The system thus feeds itself and becomes more and more scholarly and less and less intuitive" (1980, p. 76).

Consequently, as patterns of thought develop accompanying world view, the educational system is encouraging a world view and world interpretation constructed by the individual and the culture (Ong, 1973, p. 36). This world view will be influenced by the mode of thought most condoned and rewarded by the particular culture. Hale-Benson (1969) asserts that U.S. schools encourage analytic approaches to learning and problem solving. He claims that U.S. children "who have not developed these skills and those who function with a different cognitive style will not only be poor achievers early in school, but . . . also become worse as they move to higher grade levels" (p. 31).

The researchers cited in this article claim that cultures encourage problem-solving approaches viewed as "most appropriate for particular situations." Furthermore, where particular cognitive styles may be encouraged, others may be discouraged. The discouraged styles are considered "less effective," "less suitable," or "less reasonable." In some cases, particular approaches might fly in the face of what individuals from a particular culture would label "common sense reasoning" (Lieberman, Kosokoff, & Kosokoff, 1988). Claxton and Murrell (1987) go so far as to ask the question, "Are the learning styles [problem-solving styles] of minority students different from those of students of the dominant culture?" (p. 69). Numerous researchers suggest that reasoning and problem-solving approaches are encouraged in the classroom (Gregorc, 1979; Kolb, 1984; Kaplan & Kaplan, 1981). Though their explanations of the various reasoning and problem-solving approaches may differ, each asserts that classroom education reinforces the dominant thinking patterns of that particular culture.

Felder and Silverman (1988) claim that most college students, either of traditional college age or beyond, need teaching methods that stress right-hemisphere visual information. Unfortunately, the information usually is presented via predominantly auditory methods (lecturing) or visual representations of auditory information (words and mathematical symbols written in texts and handouts, on transparencies, or on a chalkboard). Silverman (1987) found that U.S. students retain 10 percent of what they read; 26 percent of what they hear; 30 percent of what they see; 50 percent of what they see and hear; 70 percent of what they say; and 90 percent of what they say as they do something.

Helgesen (1988) claims that the teacher usually teaches in the style he or she has been trained in (traditionally left hemisphere in the United States) and that the student tries to match his or her learning style to that of the teacher. This frequently leads to learning some material, missing some material, and often tuning out. Numerous educators suggest that teachers learn to "understand the duality of their students' minds" (Blakeslee, 1980, p. 59), in this way, stimulating both the verbal and nonverbal minds.

ANALYSIS OF TEACHING STYLES: FIVE CASE STUDIES

Few researchers have compared and contrasted the problem-solving approaches encouraged by teachers of various cultures. Ideally, this would be accomplished by observing teachers and classrooms in cultures around the globe. Unable to undertake this global scope, I observed culturally disparate teachers in the Pacific Northwest and identified the problem-solving approaches they encourage.

In spring of 1991, I contacted five private elementary schools in the U.S. Pacific Northwest. Each employs teachers who instruct in the language and adhere to the academic philosophy of their original country. The five private schools represented are: Japanese speaking, Hebrew speaking, French speaking, Spanish speaking, and English speaking. The Japanese-speaking instructors are from Japan. The Hebrew-speaking instructors are from Israel. The French-speaking instructors are from France and Belgium. The Spanish-speaking instructors are from Columbia and Peru. The English-speaking instructors are from the United States.

I was granted permission to videotape teachers of math and art classes in each of the five schools; the Japanese school was the exception, as they do not offer an art class. Each teacher was told that he or she was being observed and videotaped as part of a research endeavor identifying different ways of teaching throughout the Pacific Northwest private school system. The videotapes were subsequently translated into English (for analysis purposes) by speakers fluent in English and the language of the videotaped teacher. Though it is impossible to generalize any of these findings to the cultures of the respective instructors, the study takes a step toward noting differences in teaching styles of five teachers trained in different cultures and languages.

Math classes were chosen because of the basic left-hemisphere skills utilized for arithmetic understanding; art classes were chosen because of the basic right-hemisphere skills utilized for visualization and tactility. Specific math classes were chosen that addressed numbers and formulae on the day of observation and taping.

This basic analysis addresses verbal and nonverbal differences among the various teachers and schools (Figures 4 and 5). The nonverbal differences focus on room adornments, teacher-student interactive behaviors, teacher-student ratio, teacher-

	Room Adornments	Room Arrangement
Japanese Math (M)	Very little on walls	Desks in rows Individual desks Teacher in front
Art (not offered)	Pictures of scenery	Chalkboard Students called up
Israeli Math (F)	Math projects by students on walls	All on floor Common project At desks at times
Art (F)	Art projects by students on walls	All on floor Group project
French Math (M)	No numbers on walls Projects on walls	Teacher in front Student desks in rows 3 or 4 per row/desk
Art (F)	Student projects on walls	Common project on floor and at desks
U.S. Math (F)	Math as appears in other projects	One teacher in front Group project at separate desks
Art (F)	Art projects combined with other subjects	One teacher Individual projects at desks, instructed by teacher
Spanish Math (F)	Picturesque scenes	Desks pushed together
Art (F)	Student work individualized	Partly on floor, partly at desks No obvious order

Figure 4a Analysis of Nonverbal Differences Among Classrooms

student haptics (touch behaviors), and teacher-student vocalics. The verbal differences focus on differences in encouraging problem solving, levels of tolerance or intolerance of ambiguity encouraged, impulsivity or reflectivity encouraged, and individualistic or collectivistic reasoning encouraged. A summary analysis of the five classroom observations follows.

Nonverbal Elements in the Classrooms (See Figures 4a and 4b)

Even though the teachers were responsible for adorning the classroom walls in whatever style they desired, there were some practical limitations to doing so. Specifically, the Japanese classrooms were

	Teacher/Student Ratio	Teacher/Student Haptics	Teacher/Student Vocalics
Japanese	1 to approximately 20	No touching	Little noise. No speaking unless directly asked a question. No group verbal interaction
Israeli	1 to approximately 12	Hugging to reinforce answer. Touching to discipline	Dyad and triad interaction when responding to teacher questions. Group interaction while teacher addressed other students
French	1 to approximately 20	Few touches. Touching of shoulders	Very little student/student interaction in math. Much student socio-emotional interaction during art
U.S.	1 to approximately 20	Some touching: shoulders, back of hands, middle of back to direct student movements	Some student interaction during math. Primarily focused on teacher/student questions. Small group interaction during art
Spanish	1 to approximately 10	Many hugs to display affection and reinforce positive behavior	Students discussing answers before speaking out loud. Little structured interaction. Greatest noise level

Figure 4b Analysis of Nonverbal Differences Among Classrooms

shared with the public schools during the week and the U.S. classrooms were used for several different classes throughout the day so these teachers may have been limited in how and if they adorn the classroom wall.

Interestingly, the U.S., French, and Israeli teachers' math classes were each adorned with projects that included math as one of their functions. The proj-

ects were holistic, nonlinear, and collectivistic. For example, some projects were geographically oriented; these examined particular countries and the math focused on percentages of the population that were male or female, of specific age groups, and of particular occupations. The Japanese math class had very little on the walls, other than photographed landscape scenes. There were no humans in the scenes and nothing to identify what subject was studied in this classroom. The Spanish teacher's walls were adorned with students' individualized work and pictures of scenes from various countries in Central and South America.

Each of the art classes displayed individual art projects completed by the students in the class. However, the U.S. class combined the art projects with other subjects. Art theory, presented by the art teacher, was displayed on the walls.

Each of the classes had only one teacher with no teacher aides. The Japanese, U.S., and French teachers taught approximately 20 children for one hour per academic subject. The Israeli and Spanish teachers each taught between 10 and 12 students for one hour per academic subject.

The classroom observations included teacher-initiated haptics (touch behavior). On a continuum, the Japanese instructor initiated the least amount of touch and the Spanish teachers the most. The Japanese instructor did not touch any of the students throughout the math lesson. The U.S. teachers used touch *functionally* as part of their teaching, with both the math and art teachers touching the shoulders and backs of the students to guide them in a particular direction or their hands to demonstrate how to hold a particular art tool. They used no emotive haptics to reinforce or discipline. The French teachers touched infrequently — to encourage physical movement, for positive reinforcement, and to lead a few students back to their desks. The French art class teacher touched a few students on their shoulders to positively reinforce their participation and work. The Israeli and Spanish teachers used touching, hugs and hand pats, as positive reinforcement and for disciplining. Disciplining was done when children were on the floor, as in touching the foot or shoulder and asking the child to pay attention or to stop talking to fellow students. The Israeli teachers each sat with their arms loosely around students who had been told repeatedly to pay more attention.

I also analyzed the teacher-student vocalics and noise level during the class. Specific attention was paid to the teacher's nonverbal encouragement of group interaction or the amount of student-student interaction tolerated while the teacher was addressing a question to another student. The Japanese teacher's class exhibited the least unstructured interaction among the students and the least amount of noise as opposed to the Spanish classes, which exhibited the greatest unstructured interaction among the students and the loudest noise level. The Japanese students interacted only with the teacher and only answered questions when called upon. The Spanish students discussed the problems posed by the teacher among themselves and responded without definite order. For example, the art teacher asked a student what colors she thought would go nicely in the art project. Four of her fellow students all started to discuss what they thought would be appropriate for the project. Each then responded to the teacher with opinions, speaking for the group. Music played in the background during the art and music classes, adding to the overall noise levels.

Analysis of Verbal Differences Among Classrooms (See Figures 5a and 5b)

The student problem-solving styles encouraged by the teachers varied among the classes observed (see Figure 5a). The math class teaching styles varied from very theoretical with almost no application to pure application with almost no theory introduced. The Japanese and French math classes were the most theoretical. The Japanese teacher wrote equations on the board and then called on students with their hand raised to come up to the board and write the answer. Similarly, the French teacher wrote a formula on the board and then gave a signal for all the students to hold up their individual slates with the formula and the answer they had written.

The U.S. math class employed a combination of theoretical, linear, and verbal with nonverbal, visual, tactile problem solving. First, the students each wrote a formula for percentage and ratio on their individual papers. The teacher then directed each

	Types of Reasoning Encouraged	Tolerance of Ambiguity
Japanese Math	Linear Sequential Digital	High intolerance of ambiguity
Israeli Math	Holistic Tactile	Some intolerance of ambiguity
Art	Tactile Abstract	
French Math	Analytic Linear Rational	High intolerance of ambiguity
Art	Analogic Intuitive Tactile	
U.S. Math	Verbal, logical Nonverbal Abstract	Some intolerance of ambiguity
Art	Tactile, cause- effect, temporal	
Spanish Math	Spatial, holistic, digital, symbolic	High tolerance of ambiguity
Art	Nonrational, tactile, spatial	

Figure 5a Analysis of Verbal Differences Among Classrooms

student to stand and emulate a bird, flapping his or her wings a specific number of times per minute. After the activity, the student applied his or her "wing flapping" behavior to the formula written on the paper. The teacher then explained the theory behind the formula.

Both the Israeli and Spanish teachers discussed math problems with their students; neither the teachers nor the students wrote formulas. Teachers used different colors of paper to represent different sizes, ratios, or percentages. Students solved the numbers, ratios, and percentages problems as a group based upon the figures, shapes, and sizes presented to them.

Both the Japanese and French math instructors encouraged reflectivity among the students, by writ-

	Impulsivity/Reflectivity	Individualistic/Collectivistic
Japanese Math	Reflectivity encouraged Impulsivity discouraged	Individualistic
Israeli Math Art	Impulsivity encouraged Impulsivity encouraged	Collectivistic and individualistic Collectivistic
French Math Art	Reflectivity encouraged Impulsivity discouraged Reflectivity encouraged	Individualistic Collectivistic
U.S. Math Art	Impulsivity encouraged Reflectivity encouraged	Collectivistic and individualistic Individualistic
Spanish Math Art	Impulsivity encouraged Impulsivity encouraged	Collectivistic Collectivistic

Figure 5b Analysis of Verbal Differences Among Classrooms

ing the formula on the board and directing "Think about your answer as you solve it." The Japanese instructor added, "Remember all that I have taught you." Both teachers emphasized phrases such as, "Don't answer too quickly. You want to be correct." The French teacher waited for everyone to complete their responses and then announced "Hold up your answers now." In the other three classrooms, impulsivity was encouraged. Teachers verbalized the problems with students responding quickly either verbally or by raising their hands. A few even raised their hands before the teachers had finished the questions. This type of impulsivity did not occur in either the Japanese or French math classes.

Both the Japanese and the French teachers encouraged reflectivity among their students; however, neither greatly rewarded or chastised the stu-

dents for correct or incorrect answers. The students worked individually on the problems but "face" was always saved when a student offered an incorrect answer. The teacher would ask the other students, "Does anyone else have the answer?"

Collectivistic and individualistic collaboration on solving problems and separating behaviors were examined in the classroom. No teachers in this research chastised a student for incorrect answers, thereby singling (or individualizing) him or her from the rest of the group. However the Spanish math and art teachers, the U.S. math teacher, Israeli math and art teachers, and the French art teacher all encouraged collectivistic student involvement when working on a math problem or an art project. The U.S. art class was the only art class observed that had no collectivistic-collaborative approach. Each student worked on his or her own art project. The teacher circulated among the students to answer questions and offer suggestions on their particular "sponge" art projects, but students did not ask each other information. The teacher also offered bits of art theory throughout the assignment.

Tolerance of ambiguity (concerning how a problem was solved) varied in the classrooms. This research examined whether the various teachers expected students to solve a problem employing a particular method, rather than allowing students to apply various methods. In other words, was there a tolerance or intolerance for choice of solution format selected by the students? The Japanese math class, Israeli math and art classes, and French math class seemed to tolerate little ambiguity in method chosen to solve the problem presented. The teachers explained how the problem was to be solved and expected the students to employ that particular approach. The French art class and the Spanish art and math classes allowed students to choose various methods for solving the problem and each student proffered his or her method to the rest of the group.

Finally, the type of reasoning encouraged by the teachers varied. The Japanese and French math teachers encouraged linear, sequential, rational, and digital processing of math problems. They presented theory in digital formula, with little association to application, verbally giving students the format for its solution. The English math class mirrored the theory of the Japanese and French classes, but encouraged cognitive processing of theory to visual, application-oriented events (for example, number of times a bird flaps its wings). The Israeli and Spanish math classes promoted relationship of symbols to other functions, presented tactily and holistically.

Honest research must address the obvious limitations in this cursory study: these classroom tapings were of a limited number of teachers (not generalizable to a larger population), on a particular day, teaching a particular subject matter. However, patterns do emerge among this sample in regard to type of problem solving encouraged. The French and Japanese math instructors encouraged

the least collaboration among the students, the most reflectivity, and the greatest adherence to a single linear, theoretical method of problem solving. The Spanish and Israeli math teachers encouraged the greatest collaboration among students, the most impulsivity and the greatest adherence to a holistic and application-oriented approach to methods of problem solving. The U.S. math class used the strongest combination of theory and application.

Though this research cannot begin to support or question education and neurological research addressing hemisphericity, ethnocognitivism, and problem solving, it is an initial step in the direction of understanding differences in methods of problem solving encouraged within the classroom. This basic project suggests that more extensive research be completed addressing patterns of problem solving encouraged cross-culturally, dependent upon the cultures of the students and instructors and the subjects taught.

Whether the intercultural interactants are in the classroom, socializing, or in a business environment, differences in cognitive processing and problem solving are inherent within the interaction. Hofstede (1986) claims that in the multicultural classroom "the focus of the teacher's training should be on learning about his or her own culture: getting intellectually and emotionally accustomed to the fact that in other societies, people learn [problem solve] in different ways. This means taking one step back from one's values and cherished beliefs, which is far from easy" (p. 315). Consideration and understanding of differences among cultures in cognitive processing and presentation styles in problem solving is a major step toward successful intercultural communication.

REFERENCES

Blakeslee, T. R. (1980). *The Right Brain: A New Understanding of the Unconscious Mind and Its Creative Powers*. New York: Anchor Press.

Bogen, J., Dezare, W., TenHouten, W., and Marsh, J. (1972). "The Other Side of the Brain. IV: The A/P

Ration," *Bulletin of the Los Angeles Neurological Societies, 37,* 49–61.

Brislin, R. (1981). *Cross-Cultural Encounters.* New York: Pergamon Press.

Brown, H. (1980). *Principles of Language Learning and Teaching.* Englewood, Cliffs, NJ: Prentice-Hall.

Claxton, C., and Murrell, P. (1987). *Learning Styles: Implications for Improving Educational Practices.* George Washington University, Washington, D.C.: ASHE (Association for the Study of Higher Education).

Cole, M. (1985). "The Zone of Proximal Development: Where Culture and Cognition Create Each Other." In J. Wertsch (Ed.), *Culture, Communication and Cognition: Vygotskian Perspectives* (pp. 146–162). Cambridge: Cambridge University Press.

Cole, M., Gay, J., and Glick, J. (1969). "Communication Skills Among the Kpelle of Liberia." Paper presented at the Society for Research in Child Development Meeting, Santa Monica, CA.

Cole, M., and Scribner, S. (1974). *Culture and Thought: A Psychological Introduction.* New York: John Wiley & Sons.

Collins, A., and Dedre, G. (1987). "How People Construct Mental Models." In D. Holland and N. Quinn (Eds.), *Cultural Models in Language and Thought* (pp. 243–269). New York: Cambridge University Press.

Condon, J., and Yousef, F. (1975). *An Introduction to Intercultural Communication.* Indianapolis: Bobbs-Merrill Educational Publishing.

Damen, L. (1987). *Culture Learning: The Fifth Dimension in the Language Classroom.* Reading, MA: Addison-Wesley.

Edwards, B. (1979). *Drawing on the Right Side of the Brain.* Los Angeles: J. P. Tarcher.

Felder, R., and Silverman, L. (1988). "Learning and Teaching Styles in Engineering Education." *Engineering Education,* 674–681.

Freedle, R. (1981). "The Need for a Cross-Cultural Perspective." In J. Harvey (Ed.), *Cognition, Social Behavior and the Environment.* Hillsdale, NJ: Lawrence Erlbaum Associates.

Gregorc, A. F. (1979). "Learning/Teaching Styles: Potent Forces Behind Them." *Educational Leadership, 36,* 234–236.

Griffin, C. (1983). "Social Structure, Speech and Silence: Fijian Reactions to the Problems of Social Change." In W. Maxwell (Ed.), *Thinking: The Expanding Frontier* (pp. 57–69). Philadelphia: The Franklin Institute Press.

Hale-Benson, J. (1969). *Black Children: Their Roots, Culture and Learning Styles.* Baltimore, MA: Johns Hopkins University Press.

Hall, E. (1976). *Beyond Culture.* New York: Doubleday.

Helgesen, M. (1988). *Natural Style and Learning Style Preferences: Their Effect on Teaching and Learning.* University of Illinois and Urbana-Champaign: Instruction and Management Services.

Hofstede, G. (1986). "Cultural Differences in Teaching and Learning." *International Journal of International Relations, 10,* 301–320.

Kaplan, R. (1988). "Cultural Thought Patterns in Inter-Cultural Education." In J. Wurzel (Ed.), *Toward Multiculturalism: A Reader in Multicultural Education* (pp. 207–222). Yarmouth, MA: Intercultural Press, Inc.

Kaplan, R. B. (1970). "Cultural Thought Patterns in Intercultural Education." *Language Learning, 16,* Vols. 1 & 2, 1–20.

Kaplan, S., and Kaplan, R. (1981). *Cognition and Environment.* New York: Pergamon Press.

Kohls, L. (1984). *Survival Kit for Overseas Living* (rev. ed.). Yarmouth, MA: Intercultural Press, Inc.

Kolb, D. (1984). *Experiential Learning.* Englewood Cliffs, NJ: Prentice-Hall.

Korzybsky, A. (1933). *Science and Sanity: An Introduction to Non-Aristotelian Systems and General Semantics.* Lakeville, CT: The Institute of General Semantics.

Lee, D. (1950). "Codifications of Reality: Lineal and Nonlineal." *Psychosomatic Medicine, 12*(2), 89–97.

Lieberman, D., Kosokoff, S., and Kosokoff, J. (1988). "What Is Common About Common Sense?" *ORTESOL.*

Luria, A. R. (1966). *Higher Cortical Function in Man*. New York: Basic Books.

McCarthy, B. (1990). "Using the 4MAT System to Bring Learning Styles to Schools." *Educational Leadership*, 31–37.

Mestenhauser, J. (1981). "Selected Learning Concepts and Themes." In G. Althen (Ed.), *Learning Across Cultures: Intercultural Communication and International Educational Exchange*. Washington, D.C.: National Association for Foreign Student Affairs.

Ong, W. (1973). "Word as View and World as Event." In M. Prosser (Ed.), *Intercommunication Among Nations and Peoples* (pp. 27–45). New York: Harper & Row.

Paredes, J., & Hepburn, K. (1976). "The Split Brain and the Culture-and-Cognition Paradox." *Current Anthropology, 17*, 121–127.

Prince, G. (1978). "Putting the Other Half of the Brain to Work." *Training: The Magazine of Human Resources Development, 15*, 57–61.

Pribram, K. (1949). *Conflicting Patterns of Thought*. Washington: Public Affairs Press.

Reid, J. (1987). "The Learning Style Preferences of ESL Students." *TESOL Quarterly*, 87–111.

Samovar, L., and Porter, R. (Eds.). (1988). *Intercultural Communication: A Reader* (rev. ed.). Belmont, CA: Wadsworth Publishing Company.

Samovar, L., and Porter, R. (Eds.). (1991). *Intercultural Communication: A Reader* (rev. ed.). Belmont, CA: Wadsworth Publishing Company.

Scarcella, R. (1990). *Teaching Language Minority Students in the Multicultural Classroom*. Englewood Cliffs, NJ: Prentice-Hall.

Schneider, D. (1976). "Notes Toward a Theory of Culture." In K. Basso and H. Silby (Eds.), *Meanings in Anthropology*. Albuquerque, NM: University of New Mexico Press.

Silverman, L. (1987). "Global Learners: Our Forgotten Gifted Children." Paper presented at the Seventh World Conference on Gifted and Talented Children, Salt Lake City, Utah.

Springer, S., and Deutsch, G. (1985). *Left Brain, Right Brain*. New York: W. H. Freeman and Company.

Tsunoda, T. (1978). *The Japanese Brain Function*. Cited in Sibatani, A. (1980). "It May Turn Out that the Language We Learn Alters the Physical Operation of Our Brains." *Science*, 24–26.

Witkin, H., and Goodenough, D. (1981). *Cognitive Styles: Essence of Origins*. New York: International Universities Press.

The Sapir-Whorf Hypothesis

HARRY HOIJER

The Sapir-Whorf hypothesis appears to have had its initial formulation in the following two paragraphs, taken from an article of Sapir's, first published in 1929.

Language is a guide to "social reality." Though language is not ordinarily thought of as of essential interest to the students of social science, it powerfully conditions all of our thinking about social problems and processes. Human beings do not live in the objective world alone, nor alone in the world of social activity as ordinarily understood, but are very much at the mercy of the particular language which has become the medium of expression for their society. It is quite an illusion to imagine that one adjusts to reality essentially without the use of language and that language is merely an incidental means of solving specific problems of communication or reflection. The fact of the matter is that the "real world" is to a large extent unconsciously built up on the language habits of the group. No two languages are ever sufficiently similar to be considered as representing the same social reality. The worlds in which different societies live are distinct worlds, not merely the same world with different labels attached.

The understanding of a simple poem, for instance, involves not merely an understanding of the single words in their average significance, but

From *Language in Culture*, edited by Harry Hoijer, Copyright 1954 by The University of Chicago. Reprinted by permission of the publisher and the author. Professor Hoijer taught in the Department of Anthropology, University of California at Los Angeles.

a full comprehension of the whole life of the community as it is mirrored in the words, or as it is suggested by their overtones. Even comparatively simple acts of perception are very much more at the mercy of the social patterns called words than we might suppose. If one draws some dozen lines, for instance, of different shapes, one perceives them as divisible into such categories as "straight," "crooked," "curved," "zigzag" because of the classificatory suggestiveness of the linguistic terms themselves. We see and hear and otherwise experience very largely as we do because the language habits of our community predispose certain choices of interpretation. [In Mandelbaum 1949: 162]

The notion of language as a "guide to social reality" is not entirely original with Sapir. Somewhat similiar ideas, though far less adequately stated, may be found in Boas' writings, at least as early as 1911. Thus we find in Boas' introduction to the *Handbook of American Indian Languages* a number of provocative passages on this theme, to wit:

It seems, however, that a theoretical study of Indian languages is not less important than a practical knowledge of them; that the purely linguistic inquiry is part and parcel of a thorough investigation of the psychology of the peoples of the world [p. 63].

. . . language seems to be one of the most instructive fields of inquiry in an investigation of the formation of the fundamental ethnic ideas. The great advantage that linguistics offer in this respect is the fact that, on the whole, the categories which are formed always remain unconscious, and that for this reason the processes which lead to their formation can be followed without the misleading and disturbing factors of secondary explanation, which are so common in ethnology, so much so that they generally obscure the real history of the development of ideas entirely [pp. 70–71].

The Sapir-Whorf hypothesis, however, gains especial significance by virtue of the fact that both these scholars had a major interest in American Indian languages, idioms far removed from any in the Indo-European family and so ideally suited to contrastive studies. It is in the attempt to properly interpret the grammatical categories of an American Indian language, Hopi, that Whorf best illustrates his principle of linguistic relativity, the notion that "users of markedly different grammars are pointed by their grammars toward different types of observations and different evaluations of externally similar acts of observations, and hence are not equivalent as observers but must arrive at somewhat different views of the world" (1952: 11).

The purpose of this paper is twofold: (1) to review and clarify the Sapir-Whorf hypothesis, (2) to illustrate and perhaps add to it by reference to my own work on the Navajo language. . . .

The central idea of the Sapir-Whorf hypothesis is that language functions, not simply as a device for reporting experience, but also, and more significantly, as a way of defining experience for its speakers. Sapir says (1931: 578), for example:

Language is not merely a more or less systematic inventory of the various items of experience which seem relevant to the individual, as is so often naively assumed, but is also a self-contained, creative symbolic organization, which not only refers to experience largely acquired without its help but actually defines experience for us by reason of its formal completeness and because of our unconscious projection of its implicit expectations into the field of experience. In this respect language is very much like a mathematical system which, also, records experience in the truest sense of the word, only in its crudest beginnings, but, as time goes on, becomes elaborated into a self-contained conceptual system which previsages all possible experience in accordance with certain accepted formal limitations. . . . [Meanings are] not so much discovered in experience as imposed upon it, because of the tyrannical hold that linguistic form has upon our orientation in the world.

Whorf develops the same thesis when he says (1952: 5):

. . . the linguistic system (in other words, the grammar) of each language is not merely a reproducing instrument for voicing ideas but rather is itself the shaper of ideas, the program and guide for the individual's mental activity, for his analysis of impressions, for his synthesis of his mental stock in trade. . . . We dissect nature along lines laid down by our native languages. The categories and types that we isolate from the world of phenomena we do not find there because they stare every observer in the face; on the contrary, the world is presented in a kaleidoscopic flux of impressions which has to be organized by our minds—and this means largely by the linguistic systems in our minds.

It is evident from these statements, if they are valid, that language plays a large and significant role in the totality of culture. Far from being simply a technique of communication, it is itself a way of directing the perceptions of its speakers and it provides for them habitual modes of analyzing experience into significant categories. And to the extent that languages differ markedly from each other, so should we expect to find significant and formidable barriers to cross-cultural communication and understanding. These barriers take on even greater importance when it is realized that "the phenomena of a language are to its own speakers largely of a background character and so are outside the critical consciousness and control of the speaker" (Whorf 1952: 4).

It is, however, easy to exaggerate linguistic differences of this nature and the consequent barriers to intercultural understanding. No culture is wholly isolated, self-contained, and unique. There are important resemblances between all known cultures—resemblances that stem in part from diffusion (itself an evidence of successful intercultural communication) and in part from the fact that all cultures are built around biological, psychological, and social characteristics common to all mankind. The languages of human beings do not so much determine the perceptual and other faculties of their speakers vis-à-vis experience as they influence and direct these faculties into prescribed channels. Intercultural communication, however wide the difference between cultures may be, is not impossible. It is simply more or less difficult, depending on the degree of difference between the cultures concerned.

Some measure of these difficulties is encountered in the process of translating from one language into another language that is divergent and unrelated. Each language has its own peculiar and favorite devices, lexical and grammatical, which are employed in the reporting, analysis, and categorizing of experience. To translate from English into Navaho, or vice versa, frequently involves much circumlocution, since what is easy to express in one language, by virtue of its lexical and grammatical techniques, is often difficult to phrase in the other. A simple illustration is found when we try to translate the English phrases *his horse* and *his horses* into Navaho, which not only lacks a plural category for nouns (Navaho lí·? translates equally English *horse* and *horses*) but lacks as well the English distinction between *his, her, its,* and *their.* (Navaho bìlí·? may be translated, according to context, *his horse* or *horses, her horse* or *horses, its horse* or *horses,* and *their horse* or *horses.*) These Navaho forms lí·?, bìlí·? make difficulties in English also because Navajo makes a distinction between a third person (the bì- in bìlí·?) psychologically close to the speaker (e.g., *his* [that is, a Navajo's] *horse*) as opposed to a third person (the hà- of hàlí·?) psychologically remote (e.g., *his* [that is, a non-Navaho's] *horse*).

Differences of this order, which reflect a people's habitual and favorite modes of reporting, analyzing, and categorizing experience, form the essential data of the Sapir-Whorf hypothesis. According to Whorf (1952: 27), it is in these "constant ways of arranging data and its most ordinary everyday analysis of phenomena that we need to recognize the influence . . . [language] has on other activities, cultural and personal."

The Sapir-Whorf hypothesis, it is evident, includes in language both its structural and its semantic aspects. These are held to be inseparable, though it is obvious that we can and do study each more or less independently of the other. The structural aspect of language, which is that most easily analyzed and described, includes its phonology, morphology, and syntax, the numerous but limited frames into which utterances are cast. The semantic aspect consists of a self-contained system of meanings, inex-

tricably bound to the structure but much more difficult to analyze and describe. Meanings, to reiterate, are not in actual fact separable from structure, nor are they, as some have maintained (notably Voegelin 1949: 36), to be equated to the nonlinguistic culture. Our interest lies, not in questions such as "What does this form, or form class, mean?" but, instead, in the question, "In what manner does a language organize, through its structural semantic system, the world of experience in which its speakers live?" The advantage of this approach to the problem of meaning is clear. As Bloomfield long ago pointed out, it appears quite impossible, short of omniscience, to determine precisely the meaning of any single form or form class in a language. But it should be possible to determine the limits of any self-contained structural-semantic system and the ways in which it previsages the experiences of its users.

To illustrate this procedure in brief, let us turn again to Navaho and one of the ways in which it differs from English. The Navaho color vocabulary includes, among others, five terms: lìgài, dìlxìl, lìžìn, lìčí·?, and dò·ƛìž, to be taken as one way of categorizing certain color impressions. Lìgài is roughly equivalent to English *white*, dìlxìl and lìžìn to English *black*, lìčí·? to English *red* and dò·ƛìž to English *blue* or *green.* Clearly then, the Navaho five-point system is not the same as English white-black-red-blue-green, which also has five categories. English *black* is divided into two categories in Navaho (dìlxìl and lìžìn), while Navaho has but one category (dò·ƛìž) for the English *blue* and *green.* We do not, it should be noted, claim either that English speakers cannot perceive the difference between the two "blacks" of Navaho, or that Navaho speakers are unable to differentiate "blue" and "green." The difference between the two systems lies simply in the color categories recognized in ordinary speech, that is, in the ordinary everyday ways in which speakers of English and Navaho analyze color phenomena.

Every language is made up of a large number of such structural-semantic patterns, some of which pertain to lexical sets, as in the case of the Navaho and English color terms, and others of which pertain to sets of grammatical categories, such as the distinction between the singular and plural noun in English. A monolingual speaker, if his reports are to be understood by others in his speech community, is bound to use this apparatus, with all its implications for the analysis and categorization of experience, though he may of course quite often select from a number of alternative expressions in making his report. To quote Sapir again (Mandelbaum 1949: 10–11):

. . . as our scientific experience grows we must learn to fight the implications of language. "The grass waves in the wind" is shown by its linguistic form to be a member of the same relational class of experiences as "The man works in the house." As an interim solution of the problem of expressing the experience referred to in this sentence it is clear that the language has proved useful, for it has made significant use of certain symbols of conceptual relations, such as agency and location. If we feel the sentence to be poetic or metaphorical, it is largely because other more complex types of experience with their appropriate symbolisms of reference enable us to reinterpret the situation and to say, for instance, "The grass is waved by the wind" or "The wind causes the grass to wave." The point is that no matter how sophisticated our modes of interpretation become, we never really get beyond the projection and continuous transfer of relations suggested by the forms of our speech. . . . Language is at one and the same time helping and retarding us in our exploration of experience, and the details of these processes of help and hindrance are deposited in the subtler meanings of different cultures.

It does not necessarily follow that all the structural-semantic patterns of a language are equally important to its speakers in their observation, analysis, and categorizing of experience. In describing a language, we seek to uncover all its structural-semantic patterns, even though many of these exist more as potentialities of the system than in actual usage. For ethnolinguistic analysis we need to know, not only that a particular linguistic pattern exists, but also how frequently it occurs in everyday speech. We also need to know something of the degree of complexity of the pattern of expression. There are numerous patterns of speech, particularly among peoples who have well-developed arts of oratory and writing, that are little used by any except specialists in these pursuits. The patterns of speech significant to ethnolinguistic research fall clearly into the category of habitual, frequently used, and relatively simple structural-semantic devices; those, in short, which are common to the adult speech community as a whole, and are used by its members with the greatest of ease.

Not all the structural patterns of the common speech have the same degree of semantic importance. In English, for example, it is not difficult to ascertain the semantic correlates of the structural distinction between singular and plural nouns; in most cases this is simply a division into the categories of "one" versus "more than one." Similarly, the gender distinction of the English third-person singular pronouns, as between "he," "she," and "it," correlates fairly frequently with the recognition of personality and sex.

In contrast to these, there are structural patterns like that which, in many Indo-European languages, divides nouns into three great classes: masculine, feminine, and neuter. This structural pattern has no discernible semantic correlate; we do not confuse the grammatical terms "masculine," "feminine," and "neuter" with the biological distinctions among male, female, and neuter. Whatever the semantic implications of this structural pattern may have been in origin, and this remains undetermined, it is now quite apparent that the pattern survives only as a grammatical device, important in that function but lacking in semantic value. And it is perhaps significant that the pattern is an old one, going back to the earliest history of the Indo-European languages and, moreover, that it has disappeared almost completely in some of the modern languages of this family, notably, of course, in English.

In ethnolinguistic research, then, it is necessary to concentrate on those structural patterns of a language which have definable semantic correlates, and to omit those, like the Indo-European gender system, which survive only in a purely grammatical function. The assumption behind this procedure is as follows: every language includes a number of active structural-semantic categories, lexical and grammatical, which by virtue of their active status serve a function in the everyday (nonscientific) analysis and categorizing of experience. It is the study of these categories, distinctive when taken as a whole for each language, that yields, or may yield, significant information concerning the thought world of the speakers of the language.

One further point requires emphasis. Neither Sapir nor Whorf attempted to draw inferences as to the thought world of a people simply from the fact of the presence or absence of specific grammatical categories (e.g., tense, gender, number) in a given language. To quote Whorf (1952: 44) on this point: the concepts of time and matter which he reports for the Hopi

do not depend so much upon any one system (e.g., tense, or nouns) within the grammar as upon the ways of analyzing and reporting experience which have become fixed in the language as integrated "fashions of speaking" and which cut across the typical grammatical classifications, so that such a "fashion" may include lexical, morphological, syntactic, and otherwise systematically diverse means coordinated in a certain frame of consistency.

To summarize, ethnolinguistic research requires the investigator to perform, it seems to me, the following steps:

1. To determine the structural patterns of a language (that is, its grammar) as completely as possible. Such determination should include not only a statement of the modes of utterance but as well a careful indication of the frequency of occurrence of these modes, lexical and grammatical, in the common speech.

2. To determine, as accurately as possible, the semantic patterns, if any, that attach to structural patterns. This is a task neglected by most structural

linguists who, as is repeatedly mentioned in the discussions that follow, are frequently content simply to label rather than to define both lexical units and grammatical categories. In this connection it is important to emphasize that the analyst must not be taken in by his own labels; he is to discover, where possible, just how the form, or form class, or grammatical category functions in the utterances available to him.

3. To distinguish between structural categories that are active in the language, and therefore have definable semantic correlates, and those that are not. It goes without saying that such distinction requires a profound knowledge of the language, and possibly even the ability to speak and understand it well. Mark Twain's amusing translation of a German folktale into English, where he regularly translates the gender of German nouns by the English forms "he," "she," and "it," illustrates, though in caricature, the pitfalls of labeling the grammatical categories of one language (in this case, German gender) by terms belonging to an active structural-semantic pattern in another.

4. To examine and compare the active structural-semantic patterns of the language and draw from them the fashions of speaking there evidenced. As in Whorf's analysis of Hopi (1952: 25–45), while clues to a fashion of speaking may be discovered in a particular grammatical category or set of lexical items, its validity and importance cannot be determined until its range and scope within the language as a whole is also known. Whorf's conclusions as to the nature of the concept of time among speakers of English rest not alone on the tense distinctions of the English verb (mixed as these are with many other and diverse distinctions of voice, mode, and aspect) but as well on techniques of numeration, the treatment of nouns denoting physical quantity and phases of cycles, and a host of other terms and locutions relating to time. He says (1952: 33):

The three-tense system of SAE verbs color all our thinking about time. This system is amalgamated with that larger scheme of objectification of the subjective experience of duration already noted in other patterns—in the binomial formula applicable to nouns in general, in temporal nouns, in plurity and numeration.

Taken together, the fashions of speaking found in a language comprise a partial description of the thought world of its speakers. But by the term "thought world" Whorf means

more than simply language, i.e., than the linguistic patterns themselves. [He includes] . . . all the analogical and suggestive value of the patterns . . . and all the give-and-take between language and the culture as a whole, wherein is a vast amount that is not linguistic yet shows the shaping influence of language. In brief, this "thought world" is the microcosm that each man carries about within himself, by which he measures and understands what he can of the macrocosm [1952: 36].

It follows then that the thought world, as derived from ethnolinguistic studies, is found reflected as well, though perhaps not as fully, in other aspects of the culture. It is here that we may search for connections between language and the rest of culture. These connections are not direct; we see, instead, in certain patterns of nonlinguistic behavior the same meaningful fashions that are evidenced in the patterns of the language. Whorf summarizes this facet of his researches in a discussion of "Habitual Behavior Features of Hopi Culture and Some Impressions of Linguistic Habit in Western Civilization" (1952: 37–52).

It may be helpful to outline briefly some aspects of Navaho culture, including the language, as illustration of the Sapir-Whorf hypothesis. In particular, I shall describe first some of the basic postulates of Navaho religious behavior and attempt to show how these fit in a frame of consistency with certain fashions of speaking evidenced primarily in the morphological patterns of the Navajo verb.

A review of Navaho religious practices, as described by Washington Matthews, Father Berard Haile, as many others, reveals that the Navaho conceive of themselves as in a particular relationship with the environment—physical, social, and supernatural—in which they live. Navaho man lives in a universe of eternal and unchanging forces with which he attempts to maintain an equilibrium, a kind of balancing of powers. The mere fact of living is, however, likely to disturb this balance and throw it out of gear. Any such disturbance, which may result from failure to observe a set rule of behavior or ritual or from the accidental or deliberate committal of some other fault in ritual or the conduct of daily activities, will, the Navaho believe, be revealed in the illness or unexplained death of an individual, in some other personal misfortune or bad luck to an enterprise or in some community disaster such as a food shortage or an epidemic. Whereupon, a diviner must be consulted, who determines by ritual means the cause of the disturbance and prescribes, in accordance with this knowledge, the appropriate counteracting religious ceremony or ritual.

The underlying purpose of the curing ceremony is to put the maladjusted individual or the community as a whole back into harmony with the universe. Significantly, this is done, not by the shaman or priest acting upon the individual and changing him, nor by any action, by shaman or priest, designed to alter the forces of the universe. It is done by reenacting one of a complex series of religious dramas which represent, in highly abstract terms, the events, far back in Navaho history, whereby the culture heroes first established harmony between man and nature and so made the world fit for human occupation. By re-enacting these events, or some portion of them, the present disturbance, by a kind of sympathetic magic, is compensated and harmony between man and universe restored. The ill person then gets well, or the community disaster is alleviated, since these misfortunes were but symptoms of a disturbed relation to nature.

From these numerous and very important patterns of Navaho religious behavior, it seems to me we can abstract a dominant motif belonging to the Navaho thought world. The motif has been well put by Kluckhohn and Leighton, who also illustrate it in many other aspects of Navaho culture. They call it, "Nature is more powerful than man," and amplify this in part by the Navaho premise "that nature will take care of them if they behave as they should and do as she directs" (1946: 227–28). In short, to the Navaho, the way to the good life lies not in modifying nature to man's needs or in changing man's nature but rather in discovering the proper relation of nature to man and in maintaining that relationship intact.

Turning now to the Navaho language, let us look at some aspects of the verb structure, illustrated in the following two forms:

nìńtį́ *you have lain down*
nìšíńłtį́ *you have put, laid me down*

Both these verbs are in the second person of the perfective mode (Hoijer 1946); the ń- marks this inflection. Both also have a prefix nì-, not the same but subtly different in meaning. The nì- of the first means [*movement*] *terminating in a position of rest*, that of the second [*movement*] *ending at a given point*. The second form has the causative prefix t- and incorporates the first person object, expressed in this form by ši-. The stem -tį́, common to both forms, is defined *one animate being moves*.

The theme of the first verb, composed of nì- . . . tį́, means *one animate being moves to a position of rest*, that is, *one animate being lies down*. In the second verb the meaning of the theme, nì- . . . . -ł-tį́, is *cause movement of one animate being to end at a given point* and so, by extension, *put an animate being down* or *lay an animate being down*.

Note now that the first theme includes in its meaning what in English we should call both the actor and the action; these are not, in Navaho, expressed by separate morphemes. The subject pronoun prefix ń- serves then simply to identify a particular being with the class of possible beings already delimited by the theme. It functions, in short, to individuate one belonging to the class *animate being in motion to a position of rest*. The theme of the second verb, by reason of the causative l-, includes in its meaning what in English would be called action and goal. Again the pronoun ši, as a consequence, simply identifies or individuates one of a class of possible beings defined already in the

theme itself. It should be emphasized that the forms used here as illustration are in no sense unusual; this is the regular pattern of the Navaho verb, repeated over and over again in my data.

We are now ready to isolate, from this necessarily brief analysis, a possible fashion of speaking peculiar to Navaho. The Navaho speaks of "actors" and "goals" (the terms are inappropriate to Navaho), not as performers of actions or as ones upon whom actions are performed, as in English, but as entities linked to actions already defined in part as pertaining especially to classes of beings. The form which is glossed *you have lain down* is better understood you [*belong to, equal one of*] *a class of animate beings which has moved to rest*. Similarly the second form, glossed *you have put, laid me down* should read *you, as agent, have set a class of animate beings, to which I belong, in motion to a given point*.

This fashion of speaking, it seems to me, is wholly consistent with the dominant motif we saw in Navaho religious practices. Just as in his religious-curing activities the Navaho sees himself as adjusting to a universe that is given, so in his habits of speaking does he link individuals to actions and movements distinguished, not only as actions and movements, but as well in terms of entities in action or movement. This division of nature into classes of entity in action or movement is the universe that is given, the behavior of human beings or of any being individuated from the mass is customarily reported by assignment to one or other of these given divisions. . . .

REFERENCES

Boas, Franz (Ed.) (1911). "Introduction," *Handbook of American Indian Languages*, Part I. Washington, D.C., Government Printing Office.

Hoijer, Harry (1946). "The Apachean Verb, Part III: The Prefixes for Mode and Tense," *International Journal of American Linguistics*, 12:1–13— (1953); "The Relation of Language to Culture." In *Anthropology Today* (by A. L. Kroeber and others), pp. 554–73. Chicago, University of Chicago Press.

Kluckhohn, Clyde, and Dorothea Leighton (1946). *The Navaho*. Cambridge, Harvard University Press.

Mandelbaum, David G. (Ed.) (1949). *Selected Writings of Edward Sapir*. Berkeley and Los Angeles, University of California Press.

Sapir, Edward (1931). "Conceptual Categories in Primitive Languages," *Science* 74:578.

Voegelin, C. F. (1949). "Linguistics without Meaning and Culture without Words," *Word* 5:36–42.

Whorf, Benjamin L. (1952). *Collected Papers on Metalinguistics*. Washington, D.C., Department of State, Foreign Service Institute.

Translation as Problematic Discourse in Organizations

STEPHEN P. BANKS
ANNA BANKS

During a 1989 homicide trial in a New Jersey courtroom, the prosecution called a Polish-speaking witness to the stand. A court-approved translator assisted the witness. When the prosecutor asked his first question, the Polish witness responded with a long-winded reply. Then the translator rendered an English interpretation that was noticeably briefer than the original. When the prosecutor then asked the translator if the Polish testimony wasn't longer than the English rendition, the translator replied, "Yes, but everything else was not important" (Sanders, 1989).

This incident exemplifies how language translation plays a crucial role in the accomplishment of work — in this case the work of a municipal court system — and can critically influence the outcomes of institutional processes. According to a recent *Time* magazine estimate, 43,000 requests for translation in 60 languages are made annually in federal courts alone. Municipal courts in major cities issue as many as 50,000 translation requests per year each.

Translation as a workplace communication activity, however, is not confined to legal settings. With increasing frequency, simultaneous translation of politicians' and diplomats' statements can be seen

From *Journal of Applied Communication Research* (November 1991), 223–237. Copyright by the Speech Communication Association. Reprinted by permission of the publisher. Professors Stephen P. Banks and Anna Banks teach at the University of Idaho.

on the evening television news and in print news media. More widespread but less obvious to the general public is the growth of multilingualism in nearly all other sectors of employment, making this "an era of a growing need for translation" (Klein, 1982, p. 134). Fishman, Gertner, Lowy, and Milan (1986) have demonstrated that multiethnic and multilingual membership in U.S. workplaces is expanding; moreover, Glazer (1983) argues persuasively that the new influx of workers whose home language is other than English will be neither easily nor soon assimilated into the dominant, English–speaking society. So great has the impact of language differences in the workplace become that conferences and exhibitions, such as The London Language Show, are being held to provide information, training, and services for employers in all areas of language, including translation and interpreting.[1] In addition to an expanding multilingualism among workforces, translation also occurs because of increased international data flows. As Klein (1982, p. 134) points out, "when data cross borders, translation is needed."

With rare exceptions, however, communication researchers have paid scant attention to translation activities in organizational life (but see Delabastita, 1989; Diaz-Duque, 1989; Gonzalez, 1989; Nida, 1976). Lack of research concern for translation in an increasingly multilingual workplace is particularly problematic when organizations are understood as symbolic activity, as is advocated within the currently popular "interpretive turn" in organizational communication studies (Eisenberg & Riley, 1988). Viewing organizations as symbolic activity focuses research and theory on the sensemaking processes of members and situates meaning at the center of analysis (Pondy, Frost, Morgan & Dandridge, 1983; Eisenberg, 1986). In such an approach, language is widely acknowledged as the pre-eminent symbolic system, and language-in-use, or discourse, is recognized as the quintessential instance of organizational symbolism whose consequence is members' sensemaking.

Our purpose here is threefold. First we briefly describe theoretical perspectives on organizational sensemaking and on translation that allow for the identification and diagnosis of translation-based problems in organizational discourse. Second, through a discourse analysis of a case involving translation in a business meeting we develop guidelines for organizations for managing translation in institutional settings. Finally, and more globally, we hope that by developing and presenting a program of research on translation we can sensitize researchers and practitioners to the importance of translation as an aspect of organizational communication.

THEORIES OF ORGANIZING AND TRANSLATING

Organizational theorists have long recognized that a key identifying feature of organizations is the coordination of action among members (Katz & Kahn, 1978). As attention has turned, however, toward the culture metaphor and toward understanding organizations as symbolic activity, concern for the instrumental aspects of coordinated activity has given way to concern for subjective meanings (Eisenberg & Riley, 1988; Frost, 1985; Frost, Moore, Louis, Lundberg & Martin, 1985). Moreover, earlier assumptions about the necessity for and benefits of shared meanings (Putnam & Pacanowsky, 1983; Smircich, 1983) have been called into question. The challenges to sharedness come from scholars who argue that mutuality of meaning among managers and workers is difficult to achieve and largely accidental (Weick, 1976), often is intentionally eschewed as a goal (Eisenberg, 1984), and is neither a necessary nor a sufficient condition for effective organizing (Eisenberg & Riley, 1988; Gray, Bougon & Donnellon, 1985; Morgan, 1986).

What is relevant about subjective meanings, however, is their contribution as "equivalence structures" (Weick, 1976) to the ongoingness of organizational life. Sensemaking more or less overlaps, in terms of members' participation in symbolic systems; meaning's importance lies in its very capability to be more or less compatible among members as a collateral attribute of shared modes of expression (Carbaugh, 1988; Hymes, 1974) and to implicate coordinated action.

Gray, Bougon, and Donnellon (1985) argue that meaning has three aspects: fundamental cognitions whose content is socially constructed, maps of causal relationships that link fundamental concepts, and interpretations based on values and ideology. Meaning thus has conceptual, relational, and deep-structural aspects, and it acts as an equivalence structure only to the degree that concepts, relationships, and values and ideology are coincident among members. Particular meanings become coincident when the expectations and related actions of members coincide, most crucially in situations where members' self-interest and ideology are at stake.

Not all members of an organization, however, view the world from the same perspective: Power and authority hierarchies, reference group allegiances, cultural training, the polysemic nature of language, and the evanescence of meaning itself are all sources of contradictions that can break down the coincidence of meaning. Gray et al. point out that the order of organizational life is precarious and the coincidence of meanings is in constant flux. Consequently, every instance of interaction is a reformulation of coincidence and contains the possibility of degrading coincident meanings, as well as building or reaffirming them. Gray et al. identify four situations in which the degradation of those coincident meanings advocated by the powerful can occur: changes of organizational contexts, abuses of legitimate authority, increased environmental turbulence, and organizational resistance movements by members with contradictory views.

Translation as an organizational practice is relevant to the Gray et al. analysis of institutional meaning in several ways. First, translation typically is an effort to make communication easier between members of two different language groups. As such, the practice itself is a potential source of degradation of coincidence because it mediates between reference group allegiances (Tajfel, 1982) and between cultures (Delabastita, 1989). Second, the perceived need for translation as a legitimate practice

in an organization's life is itself evidence that members are facing new organizational circumstances and environmental turbulence. In addition, ethnolinguistic minorities, who are the reason translation is seen as needed in the first place, typically are not members of the powerholding sector and are likely to join organizational resistance movements if they have not been coopted (Banks, 1988).

Thus, in theory at least, translation has potential for inhibiting coincident meanings, which is an ironic possibility in view of the commonly held belief that translation is intendedly a practice for conveying meanings. Understanding how it can contribute to the loss of coincidence in organizational sensemaking is made clearer by examining an integrated theory of translation. A more detailed discussion of our approaches to the theory of translation is included in our earlier work (see Banks & Banks, 1990); here we briefly present the integration of three approaches to translation that assembles the goals, dynamics, and problematics of translation.

In the past, scholars have analyzed and explained the nature of translation by three distinctive approaches. We find all three of the approaches valuable, but each is an incomplete account for translation on its own. We find them not inconsistent with one another: Although the conceptualizations come from different epistemologies, each describes a valid, relevant aspect of translation, asks pertinent though differing questions about it, and entails its own problematic for investigating and managing translation. We call the three distinctive approaches, respectively, translation as mediation, translation as creation, and translation as domination.

Translation as mediation (see Brislin, 1986; Brower, 1959; Kelley, 1979; Rose, 1981) is concerned with the mechanisms of transferring meanings from one language system to another. Meanings are conceived as being attached in various ways to texts or "working dictionaries" (Quine, 1959), and translation ferries meanings back and forth between source and receptor languages. The mediation approach asks questions about ostensive reference (Bagwell, 1986) in messages, and its central problematic is inaccuracy of representation. Examples of the mediation approach abound in *Translation Review*, where the overwhelming majority of papers focus on the language comprehension of translators, the fidelity with which images in the source language (SL) are transferred to receptor language (RL), or the adequacy of RL to render meanings from SL.

Translation as creation recognizes that all forms of discourse are translations of previous texts into new texts (Steiner, 1975), and no text in this view is ever repeated identically (de Man, 1985). Translating is conceived as a cultural transformation of texts, and the translator is viewed as an author/speaker whose sociocultural context and features of discourse become central to meanings generated by the process. Suzanne Levine argues for the relevance of sociocultural contexts in translation, and she demonstrates in her research that translation is a creative act which answers the question, "how do cultures/languages/readers [or hearers] 'read' the texts produced by other cultures?" (Levine, 1989, p. 34). Levine's answer is that translation subverts the original text and creates a new version (see also Alexieva, 1990). Translation is concerned with meaning as the socioculturally conditioned creation and readings of texts (Shaw, 1987); its problematic is the loss of the original sociocultural context of the discourse.

Finally, *translation as domination* confronts the political and ideological implications of translating (Glassgold, 1987). Evolving from the line of inquiry called "the politics of interpretation" in literary criticism (e.g., Mitchell, 1983), the domination approach to translation recognizes that meanings are emergent in hearers'/readers' experience of texts but that sources, including translators, simultaneously constrain meanings by their communicative acts. In addition, this approach explicitly recognizes that power relations are both encoded in and partially constituted in discourse. The problematic here is "to find the ideological devices that permit elements from one discursive formation (or register) to become part of another" (Klor de Alva, 1989, p. 144).

These three approaches, taken together, can be placed within the framework of Gray, Bougon, and Donnellon's scheme of meaning in organizations—meaning is multifaceted and is constituted of concepts, contextualized interpretations of causal relationships, and interpretations of values and ideology. Each instance of translation, each line or utterance translated, poses for researcher or practitioner multiple types of problem issues. The integrated theory of translation yields three classes of problem issues that parallel Gray et al.'s three aspects of meaning: (a) issues involving inaccuracies in carrying over referential meanings from one language to another; (b) issues involving the loss of common sociocultural contexts; and (c) issues involving the change or sedimentation of power relationships. In the following section we analyze the discourse of a business meeting to illustrate these problem issues and to develop guidelines on translation practice for researchers and organization members.

A CASE ANALYSIS OF ORGANIZATIONAL TRANSLATION

A progressive and highly successful international hotel chain developed in 1987 a guest incentive program modelled on the airlines' frequent flyer programs and installed it in their nearly one hundred hotels. The marketing effort, called the "gold points program" (a pseudonym), was implemented in each Major Hotel (also a pseudonym) by local management; training materials, including a videotape about the program narrated by the corporate president, were provided by corporate headquarters.

The translation case we examined is a meeting in which the general manager of a Major Hotel on the West Coast introduced the gold points program to a gathering of approximately 75 workers, mostly housekeepers, in one of the hotel's conference rooms. The housekeeping staff were predominantly recent immigrants from Mexico, Central America, and Puerto Rico; because of this demographic fact, it was decided that the general manager's remarks would be simultaneously translated into Spanish. To accomplish this aim, the executive asked one of her personnel managers, who is Mexican-American, to translate for her. However, neither the account given for who would be speaking and the purpose of the meeting nor the videotape, which comprised nearly half the meeting, was in Spanish. Consequently, those members of the audience who were truly dependent on Spanish to understand what was happening were not fully oriented to the meeting's purpose, procedure, and content.

The data were obtained by recording the meeting from a seat in the first row of the audience, using a hand-held audio tape recorder. The general manager and personnel manager faced the audience in traditional classroom style and stood side by side, except when visual aids were shown.

The English portions of the tape recording were transcribed by the first author, using the transcription techniques advocated by Hopper and others (see Hopper, Koch, & Mandelbaum, 1986; Ochs, 1979; Orletti, 1984). Similarly, the Spanish portions were transcribed by a bilingual professor of Spanish language studies, who then back-translated (Brislin, 1986) the Spanish into English. The Spanish transcriber did not know the specific aims or background of the study.

The discourse analysis examines the audible talk exhibited during the meeting; it focuses particularly on analyzing the degree of (dis)similarity between the English and the Spanish versions.[2] Discourse analysis provides a descriptive interpretation of naturally occurring oral or written communication to achieve understanding of the social functions of specific instances of discourse (Brown & Yule, 1983; Stubbs, 1983). The interpretation of discourse proceeds by taking into consideration the sociocultural and institutional context of the participants, the influence on sensemaking contributed by interaction that proceeded and followed any utterances under analysis, and the linguistic context of material being analyzed (Brown & Yule, 1983).

Problems of Inaccuracies

Gerver (1976) cites six types of inaccuracies in translation: a) simple omission; b) escape, or cutting off the input with simultaneous talk; c) error, or incorrect processing; d) queueing, or delaying response during heavy load periods and catching up during lulls; e) filtering, or systematic omission of certain types of information; and f) approximation, or less precise renderings of information than the original contained. Simple omission, escape, and queueing are all types of causes for omitted material; regardless of the reason, the outcome is the RL version of the utterance lacks explicit information present in the SL version. Consequently, we treat as one category of inaccuracy any instance of omission. Filtering is retained as a unique problem of inaccuracy because the systematic nature of repetitive omission has severe implications for the organization.

Inaccuracies by omission occurred throughout the Major Hotel meeting translation. For example, the general manager described the implementation of the gold points program this way:

lemme tell you what th'gol = what's (.) happening = we are introducing, on April first (.) a brand new Gold Points program (.) for our guests.

The Spanish translation was:

Ya conocen el programa de puntos de oro que se llama gold points . . . este programa se va a comenzar en el mes de abril para los clients (You already know the gold points program, what's called "gold points" . . . this program is going to begin in the month of April for the clients)

Management intended to kick off the program on the first of April. Housekeepers who understood only the Spanish version will believe that the program will begin at some still unspecified time during April; thus, they will be unable to anticipate the events associated with the beginning of the program, and they will be more likely to contribute to operational problems because of their lack of information. More subtly, they miss the sense of urgency that is conveyed by specifying a particular date for the inauguration of the program, and the advent of gold points has less importance as an organizational activity for them because of that lack of preciseness. It also has diminished urgency because the manager's characterization of the program as "brand new" is omitted from the RL version; instead the translator implies in *"ya conocen el programa"* that the program is something already familiar to the workers.

Similarly, filtering is evident in two places in the meeting when the manager's direct reference to the intendedly service aspect of the program was omitted in the translation. The corporate concept for the program was to enhance the already high quality of guest service by awarding points and prizes to both guests and employees. In this, the only direct discussion of the program between top local management and workers, the vital service emphasis is lost on the non-English speaking workforce.

Error inaccuracies directly substitute different information in the translated version from that of the original. One of the most obvious errors in the transcript occurred in the description of the prizes guests can earn with their accumulated program points:

An they'll collect points = just like a lotta airlines do presently. So that after they they (.) have perhaps two thousand points in any Major Hotel they might get a free night. And after they have five thousand points they may get a weekend.

The translation was:

Asi se van aumentando puntos, y pueden ganar mas y vamos a decir, se tienen mil puntos, se dan una noche gratis en el hotel, si tienen tres mil puntos les dan un fin de semana. (So the points can accumulate, and they can earn more, let's say, if they have a thousand points, they are given a free night in the hotel, if they have three thousand points, they are given a weekend.)

The lack of agreement in the source and receptor language versions on numbers of points required for guest prizes is obvious. The hazard is that line workers, who are boundary spanners having most frequent personal contact with guests, will be uninformed about the terms of the program. Moreover, the manager portrayed the accumulation of points as something the guests do, while the translator por-

trayed it in passive terms, as if the impetus for earning points is inherent in the program itself. In fact, the marketing goal was to induce guests to spend more discretionary money on food, beverages, and services while staying in the hotel and for workers to help motivate guests to increase their in-hotel spending by providing information and higher quality service.

Approximation inaccuracies are paraphrasings in translation that contain low-level omissions and errors resulting in retention of the general sense of the original but loss of its precision and detailed effects. A clear example of approximation occurred when the general manager attempted to personalize the workers' orientation to the hotel floor that had been designated as the floor for the gold points guests:

you know that many of you see many of our guests every day. And they're gonna start saying to you: (.) especially the ladies that work on the tenth floor, the tenth floor is our official gold points floor

The RL version was:

ya saben que el piso decimo es especial para lo del puntos de oro. Asi, claro el trabajo en ese piso . . . (you already know that the tenth floor is special for the gold points business. So, of course the work on that floor . . .)

The executive's discourse tied a particular segment of the meeting's audience to the tenth floor and made that floor a special locus of the program. By describing the status of the tenth floor in less precise terms and by failing to invoke the "ladies" connection to that work site, the translator interjected an aspect of routine expectation about the program. In addition, by referring to the tenth floor as being "para lo del puntos de oro," the translator diminished the extraordinary status of the program conveyed in the manager's discourse.

Inaccurate translation creates losses of critical information from the source's discourse and inhibits coincidence of meanings. These losses imply that members will be less able to anticipate events and operational problems, will be less aware of the reasons for policies and practices they are directed to follow, and might be destined to perform their tasks incorrectly. A more systemic and deeply rooted loss — and one that is a special concern to organizational culture scholars — is the deterioration of common sociocultural contexts between managers who are speakers and other members who are receivers of translated discourse.

Problems of Sociocultural Contexts

While it is likely that most coincident meanings deteriorate over time and lead to both cyclic and random changes in organizations' social order (Gray et al., 1985), many institutional processes depend crucially on preserved coincidence of sociocultural meanings in relationships. Motivation and rewards systems, for example, succeed to the extent that members subscribe to their logics and believe their rationales within a framework of the relationship between rewarders and those who are rewarded. Likewise, changes of programs and policies call for members to "sign on" with the new vision of success being offered by powerholding members in the institutional relationship (Tichy & DeVanna, 1986). In the Major Hotel case, translation interferes in three ways with the general manager's effort to prompt members to sign on with the gold points program. First it contradicts images of social unity by displaying the ethnolinguistic differences in the relationship of managers to housekeepers. The management decision that translation was needed in the meeting is prima facie evidence that differences of ethnolinguistic identity exist to a consequential degree (Edwards, 1985; Giles & St. Clair, 1979; Tajfel, 1982). Furthermore, in the meeting, the manager's discourse segments participants in the gold points program into two parties, while the translator segments participants into three:

. . . the purpose of the program is to give our: special guests (.) the ultimate in service, and at the

sa:me ti:me let them collect points for all the dollars that they spend in our hotel (.) toward prizes.

The pronouns and nouns in this passage refer to us and them, to members of the hotel as a unity and to guests; the presence and emphasis on "our" is conspicuous in slots that otherwise could take "the" or "this/these." The Spanish rendition, however, omits the first person plural pronouns and segments the relevant parties into three groups:

Para los clientes en cada hotel y gastan dinero en los cuartos y la comida, les dan puntos para todos los dolares que gastan, para ganar premios. (They give points to the clients in each hotel for spending money on rooms and food, so they [can] earn points.)

"They" does not include the housekeepers in the audience or the speaker; it might include the general manager. The presence of "they" in this discourse context and the absence of first person plural pronouns leaves, minimally, the clients, the company, and audience members as relevant groups. In this way, the general manager's rhetoric of social unity is undercut by the linguistic choices of the translator, resulting in a different, more segmented set of organizational relationships.

The third way translation intervenes in the corporation's efforts to promote workforce solidarity around the program is by breaking down cultural bonds in a local sense. The translation diminishes the general manager's capacity for bringing members into a local culture of enthusiasm, ambition, and excitement about hotel operations:

The gold points program is a program that Major is developing (.) t' recognize the people that (.) stay with us on a regular basis 'n' are rea:l impor:tant guests (.) for us.

Here, as elsewhere throughout the meeting, the general manager's presentation is filled with vocal emphatics, such as the elongation and stressing of "real important guests." The RL version, however, flattens out the emphasis and removes the tone of advocacy from the utterance by omitting reference to guests' importance:

Este programa esta comenzida para esos clientes que vienen constantemente al hotel u hoteles Majores. (This program is [being] started for those clients who constantly come to the hotel or Major Hotels.)

Guests are depersonalized from people who "stay with us" regularly to people who "constantly come" to the hotels. In addition, this example further illustrates the problem of group segmentation mentioned above. Without coincidence of meaning about relationships like those depicted here, workers will take different actions in response to organizational changes (Gray et al., 1985). The most fundamental contradictions of meaning that emerge in translation, however, involve relationships of power and ideology.

PROBLEMS OF POWER RELATIONSHIPS

Gray, Bougon, and Donnellon point out that

prevailing systems of meaning sanctioned by powerful organizational leaders will be accepted only as long as they are perceived as legitimate, that is as long as they create meanings which are consistent with and supportive of the tacit values to which organizational members subscribe. (1985, p. 89)

Other researchers have noted the links among language, power, and domination in the workplace (e.g., Clegg, 1987; Kress & Hodge, 1979; Thomas, 1985), and most conclude that hearers' perceptions and attributions of speech contribute to the degree and direction of domination in institutional relationships. But what if the speaker is a surrogate? How does another's voice—a creator of a subver-

sive text, according to Levine (1989)—influence the power relationships, either actual or as officially sanctioned?

The possibilities are that translation can detract from, reinforce, or fail to influence power relationships. Our limited experience from analyzing the Major Hotel meeting leads us to believe that the predominant direction of influence is detraction, especially in settings where the translator is neither professionally qualified to translate nor sensitized to the ideology of the SL speaker. All translation situations have one positive aspect: Hearers will be likely to perceive power interests positively because speakers care enough about hearers' participation in the life of the organization to provide translation. That advantage is counterbalanced by hearers' simultaneous knowledge that the powerholders operate in the dominant, privileged language, thus resist erosion of discourse in the dominant language, and do not care enough to provide equal treatment for all members. Pool (1986, p. 17) argues that equal treatment of members is a "more comprehensive standard of linguistic nondiscrimination" than identical or equal treatment of languages in the workplace.

Beyond the mere fact of translation's occurrence, divergences of values and ideology can be constituted in the manner of translation. It is widely recognized that leaders influence others by using various expressive styles and devices (Pfeffer, 1981; Tompkins & Cheney, 1985). Translation can undermine the intended style of influence, either undoing managers' rhetorical aims and cultural sensitivity or mitigating the intended directness and force of dominance (Gray et al., 1985). In general, it simply is more difficult to be persuasive through a translator. The Major Hotel general manager used an indirect appeal to encourage housekeepers to be realistic and committed to the new program and take responsibility for ensuring its success:

We are having meetings every single day (.) this week to let every employee (.) learn about gold points. Because the only way the program is gonna be truly successful is if all of us really know about it, and really produce what we say we're gonna produce, and really believe it.

The speech has the repetitions and rhythmic patterns of good pulpit oratory. The Spanish rendition shows no such call to action and involvement:

Vamos a . . . juntos todo el departmento este semana para los empleados sepan de este programa es lo que nosotros tenemos que hacer para para que triunfe este programa. (We're going to . . . together with all the department[s] this week [so that] employees will all know of this program; it's what we have to do so that this program will be successful.

At other points in the meeting the general manager frames the meeting's agenda ("lemme tell you . . . what's happening"), indicates her exclusive knowledge of the discussion's significance ("does anybody know . . . about our gold points and what it means, or do you want me to start from scratch"), and uses terms of special symbolic value and, thus, ambiguity (such as "service" in "the purpose . . . is to emphasize the service part of the program") as conversational devices. These discourse devices are functionally (whether consciously or not) power strategies which work to mystify, control, or dominate audiences (Shuy, 1987). None of these power strategies was included in the RL version of the meeting; consequently, the intended rhetorical efforts to shape and reinforce the existing power relationships were subverted by the translation process.

IMPLICATIONS

The foregoing theoretical discussion and case analysis demonstrate that translation has the potential to degrade coincident meanings so that worker task accomplishment, productivity, commitment to programs and institution, and compliance all are vulnerable to erosion. The key practical issue is what can be done to mitigate the negative effects of translation. Although research is just beginning, there appear to be two classes of remedies that can help the situation—procedural actions and attitudinal changes.

For organizations the most critical action is to avoid the ready-to-hand translator who typically is a bilingual member of the staff (Sanders, 1989). Instead, firms should employ specialists trained as professional translators, whether hired as internal resource persons or as contractors from consultant agencies or translator cooperatives (Klein, 1982). Many of the inaccuracy problems can be avoided by the simple expedient of using expert translators.

In addition, expert translators must have opportunities to grasp the sociocultural context of the organizational setting, to learn the strategic importance of the discourse being translated, and to become familiar with the history of employee relations in the firm where translation is to occur. To facilitate this process, the translation activity should be included as a special communication function to be reckoned with during planning stages of any marketing, public relations, or productivity enhancement campaign. By these practices the degradation of common sociocultural contexts can be minimized.

Finally, multilingual workplaces should issue communications of strategic importance—policy interpretations, program and product changes, key job information, etc.—in writing as well as in face-to-face discussion. Written translation is more accurate and more stylistically congruous with the original than simultaneous or sequential oral translation because translators have time to more carefully create their texts. Content will be improved if firms strive to standardize technical terms and other key concepts of ongoing strategic importance; this practice requires native language literacy and broad-based training that emphasizes the use and relevance of those standard vocabularies.

Two types of attitudinal change can mitigate the hazards of multilingual settings. Klein (1982) notes that languages are constantly in flux and that translation will never be an invisible process. Consequently, the problems described here cannot be reduced to zero; minimization is the best realistic goal. Nonetheless, an attitude about communication that is fully audience-centered, one which has due regard for the linguistic, sociocultural, and institutional contexts of hearers/readers, is a sine qua non for achieving that goal. Diaz-Duque (1989) describes efforts at the University of Iowa Hospitals and Clinics that approach this ideal. There a formal interpreting and translation unit is staffed with professional translators who are trained both to be sensitive to cultural, stylistic, and linguistic needs of medical personnel and their non-English speaking clients and to understand and take account of the influence of medical practice and settings on communication.

If translation cannot be perfected so that it is an invisible process, organization members must recognize that linguistic discrimination will occur as long as multiple languages are used in the same organizational discourses (Pool, 1986). In saying this, we do not recommend acceptance of linguistic discrimination in the workplace: long-term organizational ends will be fostered by an attitude of appreciation for language diversity while recognizing the impracticability of treating all languages identically or equally. The apparent difficulty of achieving such an attitude is a measure of how much work remains to be done to address the sensitive problems of language standardization and diversity in the workplace.

NOTES

1. We use the term "translation" to include the rendering of both spoken and written discourse from source to receptor language, whether simultaneous, sequential, or delayed; we reserve the term "interpretation" to refer to the cognitive processes of making sense of communicative phenomena.

2. We recognize the hazards inherent in relying on back-translated data; however, the English back-translations are more likely to be highly valid and more reliable than the simultaneous translation being investigated because the translator is an expert and had unlimited time to work with the tape-recorded material. Transcription conventions are as follows: double slash marks contain transcriber comments; latches, [ ], indicate overlapping talk; a number or a period in parentheses indicates a pause in seconds or a noticeable pause less than one second; inaudible material is shown by ellipses; colon indicates elongated sound; and underlining indicates vocal emphasis.

REFERENCES

Alexieva, B. (1990). Creativity in simultaneous interpretation. *Babel, 36,* 1, 1–6.

Bagwell, J. (1986). *American formalism and the problem of interpretation*. Houston: Rice University Press.

Banks, A. & Banks, S. P. (1990). Unexplored barriers: The role of translation in interpersonal communication. In S. Ting-Toomey and F. Korzenney (Eds.) *International and Intercultural Communication Annual, Vol. 15.*

Banks, S. (1988). Achieving "unmarkedness" in organisational discourse: A praxis perspective on ethnolinguistic identity. In W. Gudykunst (Ed.), *Language and ethnic identity*. Clevedon: Multilingual Matters Ltd.

Brislin, R. (1986). The wording and translation of research instruments. In W. J. Lonner and J. W. Berry (Eds.) *Field methods in cross-cultural research* (pp. 137–164). Newbury Park, CA: Sage.

Brower, R. A. (Ed.) (1959). *On translation*. Cambridge, MA: Harvard University Press.

Brown, G. & Yule, G. (1983). *Discourse analysis*. Cambridge: Cambridge University Press.

Carbaugh, D. (1988). Cultural terms and tensions in the speech at a television station. *Western Journal of Speech Communication, 52,* 216–237.

Clegg, S. (1987). The language of power and the power of language. *Organization Studies, 8/1,* 61–70.

de Man, P. (1985). *The lesson of Paul de Man: Yale French studies*. New Haven, CT: Yale University Press.

Delabastita, D. (1989). Translation and mass communication: Film and T.V. translation as evidence of cultural dynamics. *Babel, 35,* 4, 193–218.

Diaz-Duque, O. (1989). Communication barriers in medical settings: Hispanics in the United States.

International Journal of the Sociology of Language, 79, 93–102.

Edwards, J. (1985). *Language, society and identity.* Oxford: Basil Blackwell.

Eisenberg, E. (1984). Ambiguity as strategy in organizational communication. *Communication Monographs, 51,* 227–242.

Eisenberg, E. (1986). Meaning and interpretation in organizations (book review). *The Quarterly Journal of Speech, 72,* 88–97.

Eisenberg, E. & Riley, P. (1988). Organizational symbols and sensemaking. In G. Goldhaber (Ed.), *Handbook of Organizational Communication.* Norwood, NJ: Ablex.

Fishman, J., Gertner, M., Lowy, E. & Milan, W. (1986). Ethnicity in action: The community resources of ethnic languages in the United States. In J. Fishman (Ed.), *The rise and fall of the ethnic revival: Perspectives on language and ethnicity* (pp. 195–282). New York: Mouton.

Frost, P. (Ed.) (1985). Organizational symbolism [Special Issue]. *Journal of Management, 11,* 2.

Frost, P., Moore, L., Louis, M., Lundberg, C. & Martin J. (Eds.) (1985). *Organizational culture.* Beverly Hills: Sage.

Gerver, D. (1976). Empirical studies of simultaneous interpretation: A review and a model. In R. W. Brislin (Ed.), *Translation: Applications and research* (pp. 165–207). New York: Gardner Press.

Giles, H. & St. Clair, R. (1979). *Language and social psychology.* Oxford: Basil Blackwell.

Glassgold, P. (1987). Translation: Culture's driving wedge. *Translation Review, 23,* 18–21.

Glazer, N. (1983). *Ethnic dilemmas 1964–1982.* Cambridge, MA: Harvard University Press.

Gonzales, C. F. (1989). "Translation." In M. Asante and W. B. Gudykunst (Eds.). *Handbook of International and Intercultural Communication,* pp. 484–501. Newbury Park, CA: Sage.

Gray, B., Bougon, M. & Donnellon, A. (1985). Organizations as constructions and destructions of meaning. In P. Frost (Ed.), Organizational symbolism [Special Issue]. *Journal of Management, 11,* 83–98.

Hopper, R., Koch, S. & Mandelbaum, J. (1986). Conversational analysis methods. In D. Ellis and W. Donohue (Eds.). *Contemporary issues in language and discourse processes* (pp. 169–186). Hillsdale, NJ: Lawrence Erlbaum.

Hymes, D. (1974). *Foundations in sociolinguistics: An ethnographic approach.* Philadelphia: University of Pennsylvania Press.

Katz, D. & Kahn, R. (1978). *The social psychology of organizations, 2nd ed.* New York: John Wiley.

Kelly, L. (1979). *The true interpreter: A history of translation theory and practice in the West.* New York: St. Martin's Press.

Kirk, R. (1986). *Translation determined.* Oxford: Claredon Press.

Klein, F. (1982). Trends in translation. *Babel,* XXVIII, No. 3, 134–139.

Klor de Alva, J. (1989). Language, politics, and translation: Colonial discourse and Classical Nahuatl in New Spain. In R. Warren (Ed.), *The art of translation: Voices from the field* (pp. 143–162). Boston: Northeastern University Press.

Kress, G. & Hodge, R. (1979). *Language as ideology.* London: Routledge & Kegan Paul.

Levine, S. (1989). From 'little painted lips' to heartbreak tango. In R. Warren (Ed.), *The art of translation: Voices from the field* (pp. 30–46). Boston: Northeastern University Press.

Malone, J. (1988). *The science of linguistics in the art of translation.* Albany, NY: SUNY Press.

Mitchell, W. (Ed.) (1983). *The politics of interpretation.* Chicago: University of Chicago Press.

Morgan, G. (1986). *Images of organization.* Beverly Hills: Sage.

Newmark, P. (1988). *A textbook of translation.* New York: Prentice-Hall.

Nida, E. (1976). Translation as communication. In G. Nichel (Ed.), *Proceedings of the 4th International Congress of Applied Linguistics* (vol. 2). Stuttgart: Hochschulverlag.

Ochs, E. (1979). Transcription as theory. In E. Ochs & B. Schieffelin (Eds.), *Developmental pragmatics* (pp. 43–72). New York: Academic Press.

Orletti, F. (1984). Some methodological problems

in data gathering for discourse analysis. *Journal of Pragmatics, 8*, 559–567.

Pfeffer, J. (1981). *Power in organizations*. Marchfield, MA: Pitman.

Pondy, L., Frost, P., Morgan, G. & Dandridge, T. (Eds.) (1983). *Organizational symbolism*. Greenwich, CT: JAI.

Pool, J. (1986). Thinking about linguistic discrimination. *Language Policy and Language Planning*, 3–21.

Putnam, L. & Pacanowsky, M. (Eds.) (1983). *Organizational communication: An interpretive approach*. Beverly Hills: Sage.

Quine, W. (1959). Meaning and translation. In R. Brower (Ed.), *On translation* (pp. 148–172). Cambridge, MA: Harvard University Press.

Rose, M. (Ed.) (1981). *Translation spectrum: Essays in theory and practice*. Albany, NY: SUNY Press.

Sanders, A. (1989). Libertad and justicia for all. *Time*, May 29, 65.

Shaw, R. (1987). The translation context: Cultural factors in translation. *Translation Review, 23*, 25–29.

Shuy, R. (1987). Conversational power in FBI covert tape recordings. In L. Kedar (Ed.), *Power through discourse* (pp. 43–56). Norwood, NJ: Ablex.

Smircich, L. (1983). Concepts of culture and organizational analysis. *Administrative Sciences Quarterly, 28*, 339–358.

Steiner, G. (1975). *After Babel: Aspects of language and translation*. London: Oxford University Press.

Stubbs, M. (1983). *Discourse Analysis*. Chicago: University of Chicago Press.

Tajfel, H. (Ed.) (1982). *Social identity and intergroup relations*. Cambridge: Cambridge University Press.

Tichy, N. & DeVanna, M. (1986). *The transformational leader*. New York: John Wiley.

Thomas, J. (1985). The language of power: Toward a dynamic pragmatics. *Journal of Pragmatics, 9*, 765–783.

Tompkins, P. & Cheney, G. (1985). Communication and unobtrusive control in contemporary organizations. In R. McPhee & P. Tompkins (Eds.) *Organizational communication: Traditional themes and new directions* (pp. 179–210). Beverly Hills: Sage.

Warren, R. (1989). Introduction. In R. Warren (Ed.), *The art of translation: Voices from the field* (pp. 3–9). Boston: Northeastern University Press.

Weick, Karl (1976). *The Social Psychology of Organizing*, 2d ed. Reading, MA: Addison-Wesley.

The Hmong of Laos: Orality, Communication, and Acculturation

ROBERT SHUTER

Although human beings have inhabited this planet between thirty thousand and fifty thousand years, the first written scripts date back to 3500 B.C. and only during the last fifteen hundred years has writing been used extensively. In fact, of three thousand reported languages currently in use, only 78 possess a written literature and hundreds may have no written component to their language.[1] Evidently orality is the foundation of all languages, with written codes emerging late in the development of most languages.

It has been argued that acquiring literacy entails more than learning how to read and write, for literacy appears to influence thinking patterns, perception, cultural values, communication style, and the social organization of societies.[2] For example, it has been reported that people from oral cultures—societies that do not have a written language—are inextricably bound to social context and are incapable of conceiving of spoken words as separate from objects or deeds.[3] Hence, unlike literates, oral people are reportedly unable to identify abstract geometric shapes or to classify objects. Instead, the shape is identified as an object familiar to them, and classification is supplanted by function (i.e., saw cuts logs). Similarly, oral and literate communication

This original essay was written for the fourth edition. All rights remain with the author. Permission to reprint must be obtained from the author. Robert Shuter teaches at Marquette University in Milwaukee, Wisconsin.

may also reflect differences in social contexting, with oral people, for example, communicating in narratives bereft of detail that describe critical incidents, while literates use more sequential speech that is often abstract and nonsituational.[4]

Despite the prevalence of cultures in the developing world that are either exclusively oral or possess a high degree of orality, few field studies have been conducted on oral societies.[5] In addition, no reported research has limited its scope to the interpersonal patterns of oral people or examined how these patterns influence acculturation into a literate society, the focus of this study. Instead, reported studies on orality have been limited to ethnographic and historical analysis of oral literature and investigation of oral traditions in ancient Greece.[6]

This paper examines the influence of orality on communication and acculturation by focusing on the Hmong of Laos, a predominantly preliterate culture that has over 90,000 people living in the United States. Since many of the most recent Southeast Asian refugees who have migrated to the United States are from oral cultures, an understanding of orality in Hmong society should provide insight into the acculturation of oral people who have settled in literate societies.[7]

The immigration of the Hmong to the U.S. occurred in the late 1970s after they were attacked by Communist Laotians and Vietnamese regimes for assisting the United States during the Vietnam war. Apparently, the Hmong were trained first by the CIA and then by the American military to serve as flight personnel on bombing missions to Laos and Vietnam. They also engaged in ground surveillance and guided U.S. pilots by radio to enemy targets deep in the jungles of Laos and Vietnam. After the United States pulled out of Vietnam, Hmong villages in Laos were frequently attacked by Laotians and Vietnamese. As a result, the Hmong fled to Thailand where they lived in refugee camps.[8]

The Hmong lived isolated in the mountains of northern Laos in a traditional society characterized by slash-and-burn cultivation, a kinship-based social and political organization, and an animistic belief system consisting of spirit curing, shamanism, and ancestor worship.[9] In addition, the Hmong are essentially an oral people who had no written language until the 1950s when a missionary developed rudimentary written Hmong, which is still unfamiliar to most Hmong.

Field research for this study began with the selection of 22 interviewees from the Hmong community in Milwaukee, Wisconsin. Most of the Hmong living in the United States reside in three states: California, Minnesota, and Wisconsin. Wisconsin is home to 16,000 Hmong. Ranging in age from 31 to 68, 15 oral and 7 literate Hmong were interviewed using in-depth interview techniques.[10] Subjects were interviewed twice for approximately three hours per session; interviews were taped and then transcribed; and selected interviews were videotaped. The principal investigator conducted all interviews over eight months and was assisted by two Hmong translators.

Interviews probed various dimensions of Hmong culture, but primarily examined five research questions, the focus of the study.

1. What is the structure and content of interpersonal messages communicated in an oral society?

2. How do communicators in an oral society transmit information? Do types of communication transmission affect the selection of cultural values regarding individualism and group centeredness?

3. How do communicators in an oral society retain information?

4. Do communicators from oral societies retain distinct oral communication patterns after they become literate?

5. How do the communication patterns of an oral society affect the acculturation of oral people into a literate society?

RESULTS

Oral Hmong are narrative communicators; that is, the structure and content of their interpersonal messages is generally in the form of a story. Structurally, a typical interpersonal disclosure consists of a plot, normally a critical incident, and a cast of characters, either living or dead. Description of the event or deed is highlighted, and details about time, date, and even place are often omitted. While the content of these stories varies, the plot generally focuses on events or deeds that occurred during the communicator's day or consists of stories about past ancestors and/or memorable events.

For the older oral Hmong, the past is communicated through stories about agriculture, war, and migration—dominant historical themes—and the activities and role responsibilities of significant ancestors. Consider the following description of grandfather provided by Wang, a 68-year-old oral Hmong who has lived in the U.S. for seven years.

"My grandfather was born in Laos. He was a leader of the village when the French came to Laos. He was looked up to by the French soldiers. He was a soldier with the French in Laos."

Wang remembered his grandfather through the roles he enacted, principally soldier and village leader, and the activity he engaged in, fighting. Wang could not provide specific information about his grandfather's age, appearance, personality, or the battles in which he fought: he only seemed to know that grandfather was a leader. Similar descriptions of parents who died in Laos are provided by Hmong interviewees: "My parents taught me to be a good person. They also taught me how to do a slash and burn." Like Wang's description of his grandfather, parental memories highlighted farming of fighting, and never included character descriptions or other person-centered information.

Hmong communication about the present is also activity oriented and, in Laos, reportedly focused on agriculture, war, migration, climate, and cultural events like funerals, weddings, and animistic rituals. Like communication about the past, interpersonal messages transmitted in Laos generally highlighted what someone *did* and sometimes included a comment about the reactions of others.

"We talked about slash and burn and what we must do tomorrow. We talked about fighting in the war. We talked about leaving the village again. We talked about who will teach our children."

Bereft of detail, these messages focused on the main event, while time, dates, character titles, and sometimes places were normally absent from the communication.

The narrative communication style of the Hmong reflects a central world view of oral people: they tend to "totalize."[11] That is, words cannot be disconnected from deeds and events, and people cannot be separated from social context. The word and the event are one, inextricably united. As a result, the Hmong's interpersonal messages tend to be narrative, situational, activity oriented, and lacking detail, characteristics similar to the oral rhetoric of ancient Greece.[12] In contrast, the communication style of literates tends to be categorical rather than narrative, conceptual not situational. This style may reflect the contextual distance literacy bestows on the speaker, a distance that emerges from being able to think of words as being separate from objects, deeds, and events. Once disconnected from social context, the communicator can think and speak conceptually, and messages need not dwell solely on events and deeds.

Tied to social context, the Hmong culture relies strictly on people and groups to transmit information and consequently places inordinate value on these sources of information. The society is arranged sociologically and politically into groups, with clan and family the preeminent groups. In Laos the Hmong farmed in small groups, socialized in small groups and, as children, were often taught about agriculture, Hmong customs, and animistic beliefs in small groups. Without books, oral people like the Hmong learned only from others and became dependent on people and groups in the community, their only sources of information. For example, consider how the Hmong in Laos learned important cultural customs and sacred beliefs.

"Normally, when the person who knows most of the things in the community, most of the cultural things, when they realize that the man is old, people will go to his house at night and ask him to teach them. As many people that can will go to the house and learn, but they know that a lot of people can go and learn but a few can remember. So

maybe 10 or 20 will go to an elderly's house and learn at night, but probably two or three remember. And there is subject matter that they should learn at night because it is sacred, like spiritual beliefs."

Apparently, small groups were also used extensively to assist individuals to remember information, an enormous problem in oral societies. As a result, the Hmong learned all essential information about cultural events and slash-and-burn agriculture in small groups, often from an elder in the community who was known to have a good memory.

"There are so many things the old man teaches and in different ways. . . . When he realizes that he is old enough and has concerns about the next generation, he will ask the village chief and they should send some of the young men to go to his house and to work with him on the farm and learn the different types of cultural events he knows. When they are 11 to 14 they go and learn. When you and I learn together, you may remember one thing and I remember one thing; we share and discuss. In case I forget something I ask you—you may remember what I forgot. I may remember what you forgot."

In oral societies like the Hmong, learning must take place in groups since individuals do not have written material to study. Hence, individual study does not exist in an oral society, which promotes group-centered values. In contrast, literacy provides individuals with the opportunity to learn alone, since reading and writing are solitary experiences. As a result, literates are less dependent on groups for information and seem to develop a keener sense of independence than oral people. In fact, becoming literate requires individuals to separate themselves from others and instead communicate with a new appendage—a pen or pencil. Separation from the group appears to be one of the costs of literacy and may restrict an oral person's acculturation into a literate society, an issue examined later in this paper.

As indicated earlier, memory plays a unique role in oral society: it is the only repository of the past. In

Hmong culture, for example, each clan may depend on only one or two persons who remember cultural customs and beliefs. These individuals have no title and do not belong to a particular family, social class, or caste: they are persons who are known to have an extraordinary memory, a highly valued trait.

"This is a simple society—they know each other. When they (Hmong community) learn who remembers better, that one will be famous for it, and they (Hmong community) know."

As a result, persons with excellent memories are respected and are the most credible members of the Hmong community. What appears to make these individuals unique is their retention of detail about significant customs and events, an unusual capacity in a society that communicates in narratives. For example, Hmong culture, like many oral societies, has many animistic beliefs that were practiced daily in Laos and that ranged from animal sacrifices when a new home was built to healing rituals like Kakong, an ancient verbal poem used to cure certain sicknesses and physical injuries. These shared beliefs still serve as the ideological cement that binds clan members together and distinguishes one Hmong clan from another. Not surprisingly, individuals who can remember these detailed rituals are vital members of the clan.

Because the Hmong rely strictly on memory, they usually retain deeds, events, and customs that are repeated and, hence, part of their daily activities. Moreover, the rituals that each male in Laos was supposed to retain were limited to selected activities: birth rituals, how to get married, how to arrange a wedding, funeral procedures, burying the dead, and agricultural practices. Hmong frequently communicated in Laos about these subjects, the basics of a "simple" society, and their messages tend to be repetitive, a characteristic of their present communication as well.

"Here in the United States there's a lot of difficulty in remembering, but back in Laos, in the simple society, we are able to remember. . . . In Hmong society, to me it's because it was so simple and we use day after day most of the same thing, that helps the people to remember the different steps that we should do. For example, in the procedure of holding a ceremony or whatever, because we use day after day and it was so simple, not so complex that we could remember, but that it was so simple that we could learn easily and we can remember what we learned. And once we got it in the mind, it cannot be forgotten total."

The preceding speaker is Hmong and, though he speaks English and is literate, his message is redundant, for he repeats his thesis, that simplicity aids memory, four times in four consecutive sentences. Similar repetition patterns occur in the messages of oral and literate Hmong interviewees and they are empirical evidence of the narrative, repetitive communication style of oral communicators, a style that seems to be a product of a culture that relies on memory.

That oral and literate Hmong interviewees have similar communication styles suggests that oral stylistic patterns may not disappear after a person becomes literate. This is called residual orality, and it appears to influence more than just communication style for literate Hmong. For example, literate Hmong appear to have difficulty following written directions that explain how to perform an activity, operate a mechanical object, or assemble something. Reared in an oral culture, Hmong traditionally learned through "doing," that is, elders taught Hmong how to perform an activity by involving them in the process: learning was always experiential. For many literate Hmong, the printed word is an inadequate mode of communication, a poor substitute for the oral, experiential learning of the traditional society.

"If Hmong students used to learn by doing and if they went to school and learned just the theory, they have problems when they practice. For example, myself—when I go to school and I learn something by reading, I could understand when I read, but if I was supposed to do it by hand, I didn't know how. So I had to get help from someone in order to be able to do it."

It is difficult to determine which oral patterns of the Hmong survive literacy; nevertheless, residual orality poses additional obstacles for acculturating oral people into a literate society.

Each oral pattern of the Hmong described in this essay significantly influences their acculturation into the United States; consider their communication style, for example. Narrative and situational in nature, the Hmong communication style collides with the communication demands of a literate society that they be categorical, detailed, and, at times, abstract and conceptual. The collision takes place daily in schools and factories, government offices and social service agencies, where the Hmong are required to know birthdates, titles, time of day, definitions; in short, details and categories that are normally omitted from their communication. Lacking temporal and categorical perspective on their past and present, the Hmong cannot provide sufficiently detailed information about age, date of birth, type and dates of employment, children's birthdates — information necessary to survive in a literate society.

In schools they encounter definitions and detailed explanations of words that are disconnected from objects and about concepts they cannot see and touch: this is an abstract, categorical world detached from situation and nature. As a result, many older Hmong become frustrated and drop out of school, particularly the men who appear to have less experience with detail and tolerate it less than Hmong women. Females in Hmong society are responsible for cooking, a sequential, categorical activity, and for sewing, a detailed procedure consisting of putting symbolic designs on cloth. These domestic activities may account for Hmong gender differences in becoming literate and, hence, acculturated.

Literacy threatens the very fabric of Hmong oral society, its group-centeredness, and it is another major obstacle to acculturation. For older Hmong, the very concept of independent study is alien to them, since learning always occurred in the present with cohesive groups of community people. Learning in groups of strangers, homework, independent study—hallmarks of literacy—run counter to the group-centered value of the Hmong and, as a result,

many adult Hmong have resisted literacy. For young Hmong, literacy often distances them from their families.

For example, when school-age Hmong begin public school, parents, elders, and the clan—traditionally the only sources of information—now must share their teaching role with groups of strangers: unfamiliar teachers and American peers. As Hmong students become more literate and engage in independent study, they rely less on traditional groups and more on themselves and alien others. This often divides the Hmong family: parents are disturbed by the loss of centrality and power, and often become dependent on literate children, which produces additional family tension. Sensing the consequences of schooling and literacy, Hmong elders want their children to become literate but they do not want it to affect their relationship with them, a difficult request that may impede literacy and acculturation.

Finally, residual orality poses unique acculturation problems for literate Hmong. As indicated earlier, literate Hmong, particularly adults, have difficulty following written instructions unless they are accompanied by oral explanation and demonstrations. This residual pattern, for example, may be an obstacle to certain types of job training, particularly training that is primarily theoretical. As a result, it may limit literate Hmong to occupations that are activity-oriented and taught experientially. Having fewer occupational choices, literate Hmong have less access to American jobs and to goods and services, which may impede their acculturation. Similarly, the narrative, repetitive communication style of many literate Hmong may further narrow job options, since it delays the acquisition of a mainstream American communication style, a prerequisite for employability. Stylistically different from many of their American peers, Hmong literates may have more difficulty acculturating than Southeast Asians from literate societies.

CONCLUSION

Evidently, the oral tradition of the Hmong is reflected in the structure, content, transmission, and

Table 1

	Exclusively Oral	High-Residual Orality	Low-Residual Orality
Structure of message	Narrative; critical incident; high repetition	Narrative; critical incident; high repetition	Categorical/sequential; detailed; low repetition
Content of message	Situational topics	Primarily situational topics	Abstract and situational topics
	Low in temporal and chronological data	Low in temporal and chronological data	High in temporal and chronological data
Transmission of message	Interpersonal interaction: small group interaction; value group relations	Interpersonal interaction; small group interaction; additional media secondary; value group relations	Multiple media: priority on mass media; value individualism
Retention of message	Memory	Primarily memory	Multiple media
Communication world view	Words, objects, and events inseparable	Words, objects, and events closely connected	Words, objects, and events separate

retention of interpersonal communication. And because these oral patterns seem to collide with the values of a literate society and the expected communication of literates, they seem to slow the acculturation of the Hmong into a literate society. This is significant, since a sizable percentage of recent Southeast Asian refugees, possibly as high as 80%, are either exclusively oral or predominantly oral, having grown up in rural oral villages with few schools outside large cities. It is likely that oral patterns and acculturation problems described for the Hmong may be shared by many of the recent Southeast Asian refugees and by others who have migrated from South and Central America, the Middle East, Asia, and Africa, where there seem to be high levels of orality and residual orality.[13]

Conceptually, orality has unique implications for furthering our understanding of communication across cultures. For example, oral cultures may possess significantly different values and communication patterns from literate societies. By being able to classify cultures along an orality continuum, consisting of exclusively oral, high-residual orality, and low-residual orality, a researcher should be able to assess potential intercultural misunderstandings and conflicts. To determine how to classify a culture, communication characteristics of a society can be compared with the list of oral interaction patterns in Table 1, generated from the preceding study.

The table indicates that communicators in each of the three categories may differ in five communication areas: structure of message, content of message, transmission of message, retention of message, and communication world view. In terms of the structure and content of the message, exclusively oral and high-residual oral speakers tend to be narrative communicators emphasizing situational topics, with little temporal and chronological data provided. In contrast, low-residual communicators tend to structure messages categorically and generally provide chronological and temporal information. Societies that are placed in each category also differ in the way information is normally transmitted: exclusively oral and high-residual oral cultures rely primarily on face-to-face interaction, while low-residual oral societies use multiple media to transmit messages, including print and electronic channels. Reliance on face-to-face transmission in exclusively oral and high-residual oral societies produces group-centered values; in contrast, low-residual oral societies tend to be more individualistic. Without print, exclusively oral cultures depend on memory to retain information. High-residual oral cultures also rely heavily on memory and may also employ other media as a repository of information, though they are of less importance. In contrast, low-residual oral cultures use multiple media to retain information and tend to stress print and electronic media. Finally, communicators from exclusively oral and high-residual oral cultures have varying degrees of difficulty separating spoken words from objects and events and, hence, are tied to social context. Speakers from low-residual oral societies can disconnect words from objects and events.

This paradigm can be used in a variety of ways. For example, in intercultural transactions, researchers may be able to identify areas of potential communication conflict and misunderstandings, once the communicators' cultures have been classified. Similarly, acculturation problems due to differences in degrees of orality can be isolated with greater ease. Potentially useful, this paradigm should be tested in future studies to determine with greater certainty both the communication patterns of the three types of oral societies and systematic methods for classifying world cultures.

NOTES

1. Munro E. Edmonson, *Lore: An Introduction to the Science of Fiction* (New York: Holt, Rinehart and Winston, 1971).

2. See, for example, John Foley, "The Traditional Oral Audience," *Balkan Studies* 18, 145–153; Jack Goody, *Literacy in Traditional Societies* (Cambridge, England: Cambridge University Press, 1968); Walter Ong, *Orality and Literacy* (London: Methuen, 1982); Sylvia Scriber and Michael Cole, "Literacy Without Schooling: Testing for Intellectual Effects," *Harvard Educational Review* 48, 1978, 448–461.

3. Aleksandr Romanovich Luria, *Cognitive Development: Its Cultural and Social Foundations*, ed. Michael Cole (Cambridge, Mass.: Harvard University Press, 1976).

4. Ibid.

5. See, for example, Roger Abrahams, "The Training of the Man of Words in Talking Sweet," *Language in Society* 1, 15–29; John Miles Foley, "The Traditional Oral Audience," *Balkan Studies* 18, 1977, 145–153; Aleksandr Romanovich Luria, *Cognitive Development: Its Cultural and Social Foundations*, ed. Michael Cole (Cambridge, Mass.: Harvard University Press, 1976).

6. See, for example, Ruth Finnegan, *Oral Literature in Africa* (Oxford: Clarendon Press, 1970); Eric Havelock, "The Ancient Art of Oral Poetry," *Philosophy and Rhetoric* 19, 187–202, 1979.

7. It is difficult to ascertain the exact percentage of Southeast Asian refugees who are either exclusively oral or predominantly oral. But since most of the recent refugees migrated from rural communities where there were no schools, it has been estimated that most of them are predominantly oral, particularly women, who generally did not receive education even when it was available.

8. Robert William Geddes, *Migrants of the Mountains: The Cultural Ecology of the Blue Miau (Hmong) of Thailand* (Oxford: Clarendon Press, 1976).

9. Timothy Dunnigan, "Segmentary Kinship in an Urban Society: The Hmong of St. Paul, Minneapolis," *Anthropological Quarterly*, 1981, 126–133.

10. Lewis Dexter, *Elite and Specialized Interviewing* (Evanston, Ill.: Northwestern University Press, 1971).

11. Walter Ong, *Orality and Literacy* (London: Methuen, 1982), p. 56.

12. Ibid, pp. 16–30.

13. Walter Ong first used the term residual orality and argues that contemporary cultures have different degrees of residual orality. See Walter Ong, *Orality and Literacy* (London: Methuen, 1982), pp. 28–29.

The Need to Be: The Socio-Cultural Significance of Black Language

SHIRLEY N. WEBER

"Hey blood, what it is? Ah, Man, ain't notin to it but to do it."
"Huney, I done told ya', God, he don't lak ugly."
"Look-a-there. I ain't seen nothin like these economic indicators."

From the street corners to the church pew to the board room, black language is used in varying degrees. It is estimated that 80 to 90 percent of all black Americans use the black dialect as least some of the time.[1] However, despite its widespread use among blacks at all social and economic levels, there continues to be concern over its validity and continued use. Many of the concerns arise from a lack of knowledge and appreciation for the history of black language and the philosophy behind its use.

Since the publication of J. L. Dillard's book *Black English* in 1972, much has been written on the subject of black language. Generally, the research focuses on the historical and linguistic validity of black English, and very little has been devoted to the communications and cultural functions black language serves in the black community. It seems obvious that given the fact that black English is not "formally" taught in schools to black children and, yet, has widespread use among blacks, it must serve some important functions in the black community

that represent the black's unique experience in America. If black language served no important function, it would become extinct like other cultural relics because all languages are functional tools that change and adapt to cultural and technological demands. If they cease to do this, they cease to exist as living languages. (The study of the English languages' evolution and expansion over the last hundred years, to accommodate changing values and technological advancements, is a good example.) This article looks at the "need to be," the significance of black language to black people.

One's language is a model of his or her culture and of that culture's adjustment to the world. All cultures have some form of linguistic communications; without language, the community would cease to exist. To deny that a people has a language to express its unique perspective of the world is to deny its humanity. Furthermore, the study of language is a study of the people who speak that language and of the way they bring order to the chaos of the world. Consequently, the study of black language is really an examination of African people and of their adjustment to the conditions of American slavery. Smitherman says that black English (dialect) is

an Africanized form of English reflecting Black America's linguistic-cultural African heritage and the conditions of servitude, oppression and life in America. . . .

(It) is a language mixture, adapted to the conditions of slavery and discrimination, a combination of language and style interwoven with and inextricable from Afro-American culture.[2]

Much has been written about the origins of black language, and even though the issue seems to be resolved for linguists, the rest of the world is still lingering under false assumptions about it. Basically, there are two opposing views: one that says there was African influence in the development of the language and the other that says there was not. Those who reject African influence believe that the African arrived in the United States and tried to speak English. And, because he lacked certain intellectual and physical attributes, he failed. This hypothesis makes no attempt to examine the phonological and grammatical structures of West African languages to see if there are any similarities. It places the African in a unique position unlike any other immigrant to America. Linguistic rationales and analyses are given for every other group that entered America pronouncing words differently and/or structuring their sentences in a unique way. Therefore, when the German said *zis* instead of *this*, America understood. But, when the African said *dis*, no one considered the fact that consonant combinations such as *th* may not exist in African languages.

Countering this dialectical hypothesis is the creole hypothesis that, as a result of contact between Africans and Europeans, a new language formed that was influenced by both languages. This language took a variety of forms, depending on whether there was French, Portuguese, or English influence. There is evidence that these languages were spoken on the west coast of Africa as early as the sixteenth century (before the slave trade). This hypothesis is further supported by studies of African languages that demonstrate the grammatical, phonological, and rhythmic similarities between them and black English. Thus, the creole hypothesis says that the African responded to the English language as do all other non-English speakers: from the phonological and grammatical constructs of the native language.

The acceptance of the creole hypothesis is the first step toward improving communications with blacks. However, to fully understand and appreciate black language and its function in the black community, it is essential to understand some general African philosophies about language and communications, and then to see how they are applied in the various styles and forms of black communications.

In Janheinz Jahn's *Muntu*, basic African philosophies are examined to give a general overview of African culture. It is important to understand that while philosophies that govern the different groups in Africa vary, some general concepts are found throughout African cultures. One of the primary principles is the belief that everything has a reason for being. Nothing simply exists without purpose or consequences. This is the basis of Jahn's explanation of the four basic elements of life, which are

Muntu, mankind; Kintu, things; Hantu, place and time; and Kuntu, modality. These four elements do not exist as static objects but as forces that have consequences and influence. For instance, in Hantu, the West is not merely a place defined by geographic location, but a force that influences the East, North, and South. Thus, the term "Western world" connotes a way of life that either complements or challenges other ways of life. The Western world is seen as a force and not a place. (This is applicable to the other three elements also.)

Muntu, or man, is distinguished from the other three elements by his possession of Nommo, the magical power of the word. Without Nommo, nothing exists. Consequently, mankind, the possessor of Nommo, becomes the master of all things.

All magic is word magic, incantations and exorcism, blessings and curse. Through Nommo, the word, man establishes his mastery over things. . . .

If there were no word all forces would be frozen, there would be no procreation, no changes, no life. . . . For the word holds the course of things in train and changes and transforms them. And since the word has this power every word is an effective word, every word is binding. And the muntu is responsible for his word.[3]

Nommo is so powerful and respected in the black community that only those who are skillful users of the word become leaders. One of the main qualifications of leaders of black people is that they must be able to articulate the needs of the people in a most eloquent manner. And because Muntu is a force who controls Nommo, which has power and consequences, the speaker must generate and create movement and power within his listeners. One of the ways this is done is through the use of imaginative and vivid language. Of the five canons of speech, it is said that Inventio or invention is the most utilized in black American. Molefi Asante called it the "coming to be of the novel," or the making of the new. So that while the message might be the same, the analogies, stories, images, and so forth must be fresh, new, and alive.

Because nothing exists without Nommo, it, too, is the force that creates a sense of community among communicators, so much so that the speaker and audience become one as senders and receivers of the message. Thus, an audience listening and responding to a message is just as important as the speaker, because without their "amens" and "right-ons" the speaker may not be successful. This interplay between speaker and listeners is called "call and response" and is a part of the African world view, which holds that all elements and forces are interrelated and indistinguishable because they work together to accomplish a common goal and to create a sense of community between the speaker and the listeners.

This difference between blacks and whites was evident, recently, in a class where I lectured on Afro-American history. During the lecture, one of my more vocal black students began to respond to the message with some encouraging remarks like "all right," "make it plain," "that all right," and "teach." She was soon joined by a few more black students who gave similar comments. I noticed that this surprised and confused some of the white students. When questioned later about this, their response was that they were not used to having more than one person talk at a time, and they really could not talk and listen at the same time. They found the comments annoying and disruptive. As the lecturer, I found the comments refreshing and inspiring. The black student who initiated the responses had no difficulty understanding what I was saying while she was reacting to it, and did not consider herself "rude."

In addition to the speaker's verbal creativity and the dynamic quality of the communication environment, black speech is very rhythmic. It flows like African languages in a consonant-vowel-consonant-vowel pattern. To achieve this rhythmic effect, some syllables are held longer and are accented stronger and differently from standard English, such as DE-troit. This rhythmic pattern is learned early by young blacks and is reinforced by the various styles it complements.

With this brief background into the historical and philosophical foundation of black language, we can examine some of the styles commonly employed and their role in African-American life.

Among the secular styles, the most common is *rappin'*. Although the term *rappin'* is currently used by whites to mean simply talking (as in *rap sessions*), it originally described the dialogue between a man and a woman where the main intention is to win the admiration of the woman. A man's success in rappin' depends on his ability to make creative and imaginative statements that generate interest on the part of the woman to hear more of the rap. And, although she already knows his intentions, the ritual is still played out; and, if the rap is weak, he will probably lose the woman.

To outsiders, rappin' might not appear to be an important style in the black community, but it is very important and affects the majority of black people because at some time in a black person's life, he or she will be involved in a situation where rappin' will take place. For, in the black community, it is the mating call, the introduction of the male to the female, and it is ritualistically expected by black women. So that while it is reasonable to assume that all black males will not rise to the level of "leader" in the black community because only a few will possess the unique oral skills necessary, it can be predicted that black men will have to learn how to "rap" to a woman.

Like other forms of black speech, the rap is rhythmic and has consequences. It is the good *rapper* who *gets over* (scores). And, as the master of Nommo, the rapper creates, motivates, and changes conditions through his language. It requires him to be imaginative and capable of responding to positive and negative stimuli immediately. For instance:

R: Hey Mama, how you doing?

L: Fine.

R: Yeah, I can see! (looking her up and down) Say, you married?

L: Yes.

R: Is your husband married? (bringing humor and doubt)

The rap requires participation by the listener. Thus, the speaker will ask for confirmation that the listener is following his line of progression. The rap is an old style that is taught to young men early. And, while each male will have his own style of rappin' that will adapt to the type of woman he is rappin' to, a poor, unimaginative rap is distasteful and often repulsive to black women.

Runnin' it down is a form of rappin' without sexual overtones. It is simply explaining something in great detail. The speaker's responsibility is to vividly recreate the event or concept for the listener so that there is complete agreement and understanding concerning the event. The speaker gives accurate descriptions of the individuals involved, describing them from head to toe. Every object and step of action is minutely described. To an outsider this might sound boring and tedious. However, it is the responsibility of the speaker to use figurative language to keep the listener's attention. In a narrative of a former slave from Tennessee, the following brief excerpt demonstrates the vivid language used in runnin' it down:

I remember Mammy told me about one master who almost starved his slaves. Mighty stingy I reckon he was.

Some of them slaves was so poorly thin they ribs would kinda rustle against each other like corn stalks a-drying in the hot winds. But they gets even one hog killing time, and it was funny, too, Mammy said.[4]

Runnin' it down is not confined to secular styles. In C. L. Franklin's sermon, "The Eagle Stirreth Her Nest"—the simple story of an eagle, mistaken for a chicken, that grows up and is eventually set free—the story becomes a drama that vividly takes the listener through each stage of the eagle's development. And even when the eagle is set free because she can no longer live in a cage, she does not simply fly away. Instead, she flies from one height to the other, surveying the surroundings, and then flies away. The details are so vivid that the listener can "see" and "feel" the events. Such is the style and the effect of runnin' it down.

Another common style of black language is *the dozens*. The dozens is a verbal battle of insults between speakers. The term dozens was used during slavery to refer to a selling technique used by slavers. If an individual had a disability, he was considered "damaged goods" and was sold with eleven other "damaged" slaves at a discount rate. The term dozens refers to negative physical characteristics. To an outsider, the dozens might appear cruel and harsh. But to members of the black community, it is the highest form of verbal warfare and impromptu speaking. The game is often played in jest.

When the dozens is played, there is usually a group of listeners that serves as judge and jury over the originality, creativity, and humor of the comments. The listeners encourage continuation of the contest by giving comments like "Ou, I wouldn't take that," "Cold," "Rough," "Stale," or any statement that assesses the quality of the comments and encourages response. The battle continues until someone wins. This is determined by the loser giving up and walking away, or losing his cool and wanting to fight. When a physical confrontation occurs, the winner is not determined by the fight, but by the verbal confrontation. The dozens is so popular that a rock 'n' roll group made a humorous recording of insults between friends. Some of the exchanges were:

Say Man, your girlfriend so ugly, she had to sneak up on a glass to get a drink of water.

Man, you so ugly, yo mamma had to put a sheet over your head so sleep could sneak up on you.

The dozens, like other forms of black language, calls on the speaker to use words to create moods. More than any other form, it pits wit against wit, and honors the skillful user of Nommo.

The final secular style to be discussed is proverbial wisdom. Sayings are used in the black community as teaching tools to impart values and truths. Their use demonstrates the African-American's respect for the oral tradition in teaching and socializing the young. Popular phrases, such as "what goes around comes around," "if you make you bed hard you gon lay in it," "God don't like ugly," and "a hard head make a soft behind," are used in everyday conversation by blacks from all social, economic, and educational strata. At some time in a black child's life, the sayings are used to teach them what life expects of them and what they can expect in return. It is also used to expose the truth in an artful and less offensive manner, such as "you don't believe fat meat is greasy." In this saying the listener is being put down for having a narrow or inaccurate view of things. And while it might appear that proverbial wisdoms are static, they are constantly changing and new ones are being created. One of the latest is said when you believe someone is lying to you or "putting you on." It is, "pee on my head and tell me it's raining." Or, if someone is talking bad about you, you might say, "don't let your mouth write a check your ass can't cash." Proverbial wisdom can be found on every socioeconomic level in the black community, and it is transmitted from generation to generation. Listening to speech that is peppered with proverbial sayings might seem strange to nonblacks. But, because proverbial sayings are generally accepted as "truths" because they are taught to children at a very early age, they effectively sum up events and predict outcome.

Like the secular, the nonsecular realm places a tremendous emphasis on the creative abilities of the speaker. The speaker (preacher) creates experiences for his listeners, who are participants in the communication event. The minister calls and his audience responds, and at some point they become one. The minister actively seeks his audience's involvement and when he does not receive it, he chides and scolds them. The audience also believes that the delivery of a good sermon is dependent upon them encouraging the minister with their "amens" and "right-ons." And if the minister preaches false doctrine, the audience also feels obliged to tell him, "Uh, oh Reb, you done gone too far now!"

The language used by the minister, who is probably very fluent in standard English, is generally seasoned with black English. Seldom will you hear the term *Lord* used, but you will hear *Lawd* because the *Lord* is the man in the big house who is an overseer, but the *Lawd* is a friend who walks, talks, and comforts you. The relationship between the *Lawd* and his people is more personal than the *Lord*'s.

Also, the speaker may overaccent a word for black emphasis. In C. L. Franklin's sermon, he said,

"*extra*-ordinary sight." He then came right back and said *extraordinary*, to demonstrate that he knew how to "correctly" enunciate the word. The nonsecular style of speech is generally the most dramatic of all forms and has the highest degree of audience participation. It encompasses all the elements of black language, and of all the styles it is the most African in form.

Black language and the numerous styles that have been developed are indications of the African-American's respect for the spoken word. The language has often been called a hieroglyphic language because of the vivid picture created by the speaker for the listener about the activities or feelings taking place. To say someone is "all jawed up," or "smacking on some barnyard pimp," or "ready to hat," is more imaginative and creative than saying they had "nothing to say," or "eating chicken," or "ready to leave." The responsibility of the speaker and the listener to participate in the communication event also emphasizes the African world view, which stresses the interrelatedness of all things to each other. And finally, the dynamics of the communication, and the responsibility of man as the user of Nommo, places communication and the spoken word in the arena of forces and not static objects. The rhythm and flow of the language approximates the style and flow and unity of African life.

Despite all of the explanation of the Africanness found in black language, many continue to ask, why use it? Why do blacks who have lived in America for hundreds of years continue to speak "black"? Why do those who possess degrees of higher learning and even write scholarly articles and books in standard English continue to talk "black"?

There are many reasons for the continued use of black language. A language expresses an experience. If the experiences of a group are culturally unique, the group will need a different vocabulary to express them. If white folks in white churches don't *get happy* because they have been socialized to be quiet listeners in church, then they don't have the vocabulary that blacks have to describe levels of spiritual possession. And if they do not have curly hair, they probably do not *press* their hair or worry about *catching up* their *kitchins*. Thus, because blacks experience the world differently from other groups in America, there is a need for a language that communicates that experience.

Secondly, black language reaches across the superficial barriers of education and social position. It is the language that binds, that creates community for blacks, so that the brother in the three-piece Brooks Brothers suit can go to the local corner where folks "hang out" and say, "hey, blood, what it is?", and be one with them. Additionally, the minister's use of black language reminds the listeners of their common experiences and struggles (for example, "I been thur the storm"). Through black language, barriers that separate blacks are lowered and they are finally "home" with each other. So, for cultural identity, the code is essential to define the common elements among them.

Finally, black language usage stands as a political statement that black people are African people who have not given up a vital part of themselves in slavery: their language. They have retained the cultural link that allows them to think and to express themselves in a non-European form. As an old adage says, The namer of names is the father of things. Thus, the ability of blacks to maintain and sustain a living language shows their control over that aspect of their lives, and their determination to preserve the culture. The use of black language is the black man's defiance of white America's total indoctrination. The use of black language by choice is a reflection not of a lack of intelligence, but of a desire to retain and preserve black life styles.

The purpose of this discussion is to help others understand and appreciate black language styles and the reasons blacks speak the way they do, in hopes of building respect for cultural difference. Now the question may be asked, what does the general society do about it? Some might ask, should whites learn black English? To that question comes a resounding *no*! Black language is, first of all, not a laboratory language and it cannot be learned in a classroom. And even if you could learn definition and grammar, you would not learn the art of creative expression that is taught when you're "knee high to a duck." Thus, you would miss the elements of rhythm and style, and you would sound like invaders or foreigners.

What one should do about the language is be open-minded and not judge the speaker by European standards of expression. If you're in a classroom and the teacher is *gettin down*, don't *wig out* because the black student says "teach." Simply realize that you must become listening participants. If some *bloods* decide to use a double negative or play *the dozens*, don't assume some social theory about how they lack a father image in the home and are therefore culturally and linguistically deprived. You just might discover that they are the authors of your college English text.

The use of black language does not represent any pathology in blacks. It simply says that, as African people transplanted to America, they are a different flower whose aroma is just as sweet as other flowers. The beginning of racial understanding is the acceptance that difference is just what it is: different, not inferior. And equality does not mean sameness.

NOTES

1. Geneva Smitherman. *Talkin' and Testifyin'.* (1972). Boston: Houghton Mifflin Company, p. 2.

2. Ibid., p. 3.

3. Janheinz Jahn. *Muntu*. (1961). New York: Grove Press, Inc., pp. 132–133.

4. Smitherman, *Talkin' and Testifyin'*, p. 156.

CONCEPTS AND QUESTIONS
FOR CHAPTER 4

1. Can you think of examples that would demonstrate the validity of linguistic relativity?

2. What is meant by the sentence, "Language is a guide to social reality"?

3. Can you conceive of some arguments that would cast doubts on the concept of linguistic relativity?

4. What intercultural difficulties could arise as a result of different speaking styles when North American and Japanese business persons are engaged in policy development?

5. In what manner does culture influence the spoken aspects of decision making in Asian countries?

6. What do Banks and Banks mean when they discuss "subjective meanings"?

7. What is meant by the phrase, "translation as creation"?

8. What are the six most common types of inaccuracies in translation?

9. What is black language and how does it function within the black community?

10. What are the "dozens" and what purpose does it play in the black community?

11. Drawing from your own experiences, can you think of any examples that demonstrate the notion that cultures often use different problem-solving techniques?

12. What might be some additional cultural differences in left- and right-brain hemisphere activity not mentioned by Lieberman?

13. What is the difference between field dependent and field independent cognitive styles?

14. What does Shuter mean when he writes, "Conceptually, orality has unique implications for furthering our understanding of communication across cultures"?

15. How do exclusively oral and low-residual orality cultures differ in their communication of world view?

5

Nonverbal Interaction:
Action, Sound,
and Silence

Successful participation in intercultural communication requires that we recognize and understand culture's influence not only on verbal interaction but on *nonverbal* interaction as well. Nonverbal behaviors, just as do verbal behaviors, constitute messages to which people attach meaning. Because nonverbal symbols are derived from such diverse behaviors as body movements, postures, facial expressions, gestures, eye movements, physical appearance, the use and organization of space, and the structuralization of time, these symbolic behaviors often vary from culture to culture. An awareness of the role of nonverbal behaviors is crucial, therefore, if we are to appreciate all aspects of intercultural interaction.

Nonverbal behavior is largely unconscious. We use nonverbal symbols spontaneously, without thinking about what posture, what gesture, or what interpersonal distance is appropriate to the situation. These factors are critically important in intercultural communication because, as with other aspects of the communication process, nonverbal behaviors are subject to cultural variation. These nonverbal behaviors can be categorized in two ways.

In the first, culture tends to determine the specific nonverbal behaviors that represent or symbolize specific thoughts, feelings, or states of the communicator. Thus, what might be a sign of greeting in one culture could very well be an obscene gesture in another. Or what might be a symbol of affirmation in one culture could be meaningless or even signify negation in another. In the second, culture determines when it is appropriate to display or communicate various thoughts, feelings, or internal states; this is particularly evident in the display of emotions. Although there seems to be little cross-cultural difference in the behaviors that represent emotional states, there are great cultural differences in which emotions may be displayed, by whom, and when or where they may be displayed.

As important as verbal language is to a communication event, nonverbal communication is just as, if not more, important. Nonverbal messages tell us how other messages are to be interpreted. They indicate whether verbal messages are true, joking, serious, threatening, and so on. Gregory Bateson has described these "second-order messages" as meta communication, which we use as frames around messages to designate how they are to be interpreted.* The importance of meta communication can be seen from communication research indicating that as much as 90 percent of the social content of a message is transmitted paralinguistically or nonverbally.†

Chapter 5 deals with nonverbal interaction. The readings examine the influence of culture on various aspects of nonverbal behavior in order to demonstrate the variety of culturally derived nonverbal behaviors and the underlying value structures that produce these behaviors.

As in the previous chapter, which dealt with verbal language, we begin this chapter with an overview. Peter Andersen's article "Explaining Intercultural Differences in Nonverbal Communication" begins with an analysis of how culture determines our nonverbal communicative behavior. Andersen goes beyond a mere cataloging of differences in nonverbal communication and offers us insights into cultural explanations for a variety of nonverbal communication differences.

In Chapter 3 we noted that the experiences of men and women often produce some significant differences in values, attitudes, and communication patterns. One of these major differences is found in the area of nonverbal communication. More specifically, researchers have found sex differences in all categories normally associated with nonverbal behavior. To demonstrate the importance of some of these behaviors Laurie P. Arliss explores the topic of touch as a form of gender

communication. She begins by noting that the dominant North American culture is basically a "noncontact culture" that tends to be fairly restrictive about who touches whom. After advancing this general thesis Arliss examines active and passive touching, ritualized, sexual, affiliative, and aggressive touch as it applies to gender. Being aware of sex differences in touching behavior should be helpful to both men and women as they attempt to exchange ideas, information, and feelings with one another.

One of the major themes of this volume is that culture touches nearly every phase of the communication process. While seldom viewed in the West as an ingredient of communication, silence also affects communication. The main focus of the next essay is the special link between culture and silence. In "Silence and Silences in Cross-Cultural Perspective: Japan and the United States," Satoshi Ishii and Tom Bruneau discuss the cultural bases of silence, define the concept of silence, and then compare how the East and West use silence as a form of communication. Their analysis of East-West differences in the use of silence goes a long way toward helping us understand the problems that can exist in American-Japanese intercultural communication when the role and function of silence is not understood by both sides.

Our next essay examines a culture's use of *space* as yet another aspect of human interaction. The assumption behind this analysis is that our use of space is a message that transmits meaning to those around us. As noted in several selections in this chapter, our perception of space and the use we make of it are directly related to our culture. This relationship is documented and illustrated by Carol Zinner Dolphin in her article "Variables in the Use of Personal Space in Intercultural Transactions." Dolphin, like the editors of this book, conceives of a culture as more than simply the country one calls home; she therefore includes the influence of age, sex, relationships, environment, and ethnicity on the communication encounter. Dolphin concludes by presenting a number of suggestions for further research. She believes that the issues raised by these questions will increase our

---

*Gregory Bateson, "A Theory of Play and Fantasy," *Psychiatric Research* 2 (1955), 39–51.

†Albert Mehrabian and Morton Wiener, "Decoding in Inconsistent Messages," *Journal of Personality and Social Psychology* 6 (1967), 109–114.

understanding of the link between culture, communication, and space.

In our final essay, Edward T. Hall looks at the conscious and unconscious ways cultures use time. Hall maintains that cultures organize and respond to time in two different ways, which he refers to as Polychronic (P-time) and Monochronic (M-time). While these systems are not meant to be perceived as either/or categories, they do offer two distinct approaches to time. Cultures such as those found in the Mediterranean, Africa, and South America are P-time cultures in that they do many things at the same time, are more concerned with people and the present moment than with schedules, and believe that they are in command of time rather than being controlled by it. M-time cultures of Northern Europe and North America, on the other hand, emphasize schedules, the segmentation of time, and promptness. It is easy to imagine the potential for misunderstanding when people from these diverse orientations come together. Hall's essay helps us avoid communication problems by introducing us to the many forms these two interaction patterns take.

Explaining Intercultural Differences in Nonverbal Communication

PETER ANDERSEN

Culture has been equated with communication by a number of scholars. Culture and communication are inseparable because culture is both learned and maintained through human interaction (Andersen, Lustig, and Andersen, 1986; Prosser, 1978; Saral, 1977). Moreover, culture is primarily a nonverbal phenomenon because most aspects of one's culture are learned through observation and imitation rather than explicit verbal instruction or expression. The primary level of culture is communicated implicitly, without awareness, by primarily nonverbal means (Hall, 1984).

Intercultural communication occurs when two or more individuals with different cultural backgrounds interact. This process is rarely smooth and problem free. In most situations, intercultural interactants do not share the same language, but languages can be learned and larger communication problems occur in the *nonverbal* realm. Nonverbal communication is a subtle, multidimensional, and usually spontaneous process (Andersen, 1986). Indeed, individuals are not aware of most of their own nonverbal behavior, which is enacted mindlessly, spontaneously, and unconsciously (Andersen, 1986; Burgoon, 1985; Samovar and Porter, 1985). Since we are not usually aware of our *own* nonverbal behavior, it is extremely difficult to identify and master the

This essay was prepared especially for the fifth edition. All rights reserved. Permission to reprint must be obtained from the publisher and the author. Peter Andersen teaches at San Diego State University.

nonverbal behavior of another culture. At times we feel uncomfortable in other cultures because we intuitively know something isn't right. "Because nonverbal behaviors are rarely conscious phenomena, it may be difficult for us to know exactly why we are feeling uncomfortable" (Gudykunst and Kim, 1984, p. 149).

This article reviews briefly the codes of nonverbal communication, locates culture as a part of interpersonal behavior, then discusses five main dimensions of cultural variation, including *immediacy*, *individualism*, *masculinity*, *power distance*, and *high* and *low context*. It is argued that each of these dimensions produces differences in a culture's communication, particularly in a culture's nonverbal communication.

NONVERBAL CODES

Most discussions of nonverbal intercultural communication take an anecdotal approach, where numerous examples of intercultural differences for each nonverbal code are discussed in detail. Recapitulation of the various nonverbal codes of intercultural communication is not a primary purpose of the present article. Thus each code will be discussed only briefly along with references that provide detailed and excellent analyses of how each nonverbal code differs interculturally.

Two of the most fundamental nonverbal differences in intercultural communication involve space and time. *Chronemics*—or the study of meanings, usage, and communication of time--is probably the most discussed and well-researched nonverbal code in the intercultural literature (Bruneau, 1979; Burgoon and Saine, 1978; Gudykunst and Kim, 1984; Hall, 1959, 1976, 1984; Malandro and Barker, 1983; Merriam, 1983). The analyses suggest that the time frames of various cultures differ so dramatically that even if only chronemic differences existed, intercultural misunderstandings would still be abundant. A second nonverbal code that has attracted considerable attention is *proxemics*, the communication of interpersonal space and distance. Research has documented that cultures differ substantially in their use of personal space, the dis-

tances they maintain, and their regard for territory, as well as the meanings they assign to proxemic behavior (Burgoon and Saine, 1978; Gudykunst and Kim, 1984; Hall, 1959, 1976; Malandro and Barker, 1983; Samovar, Porter, and Jain, 1981; Scheflen 1974).

Many intercultural differences have been reported in people's *kinesic* behavior, including their facial expressions, body movements, gestures, and conversational regulators (Burgoon and Saine, 1978; Gudykunst and Kim, 1984; Hall, 1976; Jensen, 1985; Malandro and Barker, 1983; Rich, 1974; Samovar, Porter, and Jain, 1981; Scheflen, 1974). Interpersonal patterns of tactile communication called *haptics* also reveal substantial intercultural differences (Andersen and Leibowitz, 1978; Malandro and Barker, 1983; Prosser, 1978; Samovar, Porter, and Jain, 1981).

Other important codes of nonverbal communication have attracted considerably less space in publications on nonverbal intercultural communication. *Physical appearance*, the most important nonverbal code during initial encounters, is of obvious importance because many intercultural encounters are based on stereotypes and are of short duration. Some discussion of intercultural differences in appearance is provided by Scheflen (1974) and Samovar, Porter, and Jain (1981). *Oculesics*—the study of messages sent by the eyes, including eye contact, blinks, eye movements, and pupil dilation—has received only marginal attention by intercultural communication scholars (Gudykunst and Kim, 1984; Jensen, 1985; Samovar, Porter, and Jain, 1981). Since eye contact has been called an "invitation to communicate," the way it varies cross-culturally is an important communication topic. *Vocalics* or *paralanguage*—the nonverbal elements of the voice—also has received comparatively little attention from intercultural researchers (Gudykunst and Kim, 1984; LaBarre, 1985; Rich, 1974; Scheflen, 1974; Samovar, Porter, and Jain, 1981). Music and singing—a universal form of aesthetic communication—has been almost completely overlooked in intercultural research except for one excellent study (Lomax, 1968) that identified several groups of worldwide cultures through differences and similarities in folk songs. Finally, *olfactics*—the

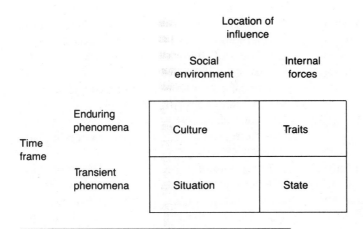

Location of
influence

	Social environment	Internal forces
Enduring phenomena	Culture	Traits
Transient phenomena	Situation	State

Time frame

Figure 1 Sources of Influence on Interpersonal Behavior

LOCATING CULTURE IN INTERPERSONAL BEHAVIOR

Culture is a critical concept to communication scholars because every communicator is a product of her or his culture. Culture, along with traits, situations, and states, is one of the four primary sources of interpersonal behavior (Andersen, 1987a, 1987b) (see Figure 1). Culture is the enduring influence of the social environment on one's behavior, including one's interpersonal communication behavior. Culture exerts a considerable force on individual behavior through what Geetz (1973) called "control mechanisms—plans, recipes, rules, instructions (what computer engineers call 'programs')— for the governing of behavior" (p. 44). Culture has similar powerful, though not identical, effects on all residents of a cultural system. "Culture can be behaviorally observed by contrasting intragroup homogeneity with intergroup heterogeneity" (Andersen, Lustig, and Andersen, 1986, p. 11).

Culture has been confused with personal traits because both are enduring phenomena (Andersen, 1987a, 1987b). Traits have multiple causes (An-

derson, 1987b), only some of which are the result of culture. Culture has also been confused with the situation because both are part of one's social environment. However, culture is an enduring phenomenon whereas the situation is a transient one with an observable beginning and end. Culture is one of the most enduring, powerful, and invisible shapers of our behavior.

DIMENSIONS OF CULTURAL VARIATION

Thousands of anecdotes regarding misunderstandings caused by nonverbal behaviors between persons from different cultures have been reported. While it may be useful to know that Arabs stand closer to one another than do Americans, that the Swiss are more time-conscious than the Italians, and that Orientals value silence more than Westerners, this anecdotal approach is not sufficient. Because the number of potential pairs of cultures is huge, and because the number of possible misunderstandings based on nonverbal behavior between each pair of cultures is similarly large, millions of potential intercultural anecdotes are possible. What is needed is some way to organize and understand this plethora of potential problems in intercultural communication. Some initial research has shown that cultures can be located along dimensions that help to explain these intercultural differences. Most cultural differences in nonverbal behavior are a result of variations along the dimensions we discuss next.

Immediacy and Expressiveness

Immediacy behaviors are actions that simultaneously communicate warmth, closeness, and availability for communication; they signal approach rather than avoidance and closeness rather than distance (Andersen, 1985). Examples of immediacy behaviors are smiling, touching, eye contact, close distances, and vocal animation. Some scholars have labeled these behaviors as "expressive" (Patterson, 1983).

Cultures that display considerable interpersonal closeness or immediacy have been labeled "contact cultures" because people in these countries stand close and touch often (Hall, 1966). People in low-contact cultures tend to stand apart and touch less. According to Patterson (1983):

These habitual patterns of relating to the world permeate all aspects of everyday life, but their effects on social behavior define the manner in which people relate to one another. In the case of contact cultures, this general tendency is manifested in closer approaches so that tactile and olfactory information may be gained easily (p. 145).

It is interesting that contact cultures are generally located in warm countries and low-contact cultures in cool climates. Considerable research has shown that contact cultures include most Arab countries; the Mediterranean region including France, Greece, and Italy; Jewish people from both Europe and the Middle East; Eastern Europeans and Russians; and Indonesians and Hispanics (Condon and Yousef, 1983; Jones and Remland, 1982; Mehrabian, 1971; Montagu and Matson, 1979; Patterson, 1983; Samovar, Porter, and Jain, 1981; Scheflen, 1972). Australians are moderate in their cultural contact level, as are North Americans, although North Americans tend toward low contact (Patter-

son, 1983). Low-contact cultures include most of Northern Europe, including Scandinavia, Germany, and England; British-Americans; white Anglo-Saxons (the primary culture of the United States); and the Japanese (Andersen, Andersen, and Lustig, 1987; Heslin and Alper, 1983; Jones and Remland, 1982; Mehrabian, 1971; Montagu and Matson, 1979; Patterson, 1983; Samovar, Porter, and Jain, 1981; Scheflen, 1972).

Explanations for these latitudinal variations have included energy level, climate, and metabolism (Andersen, Lustig, and Andersen, 1987). Evidently, cultures in cool climates tend to be task-oriented and interpersonally "cool," whereas cultures in warm climates tend to be interpersonally oriented and interpersonally "warm." Even within the United States, people in warm latitudes tend to exhibit more contact than people in cold areas. Andersen, Lustig, and Andersen (1987) found a 0.31 correlation between the latitude of universities and touch avoidance. These data suggest that students at Sunbelt universities are more touch-oriented than their counterparts in colder climates.

Individualism

One of the most fundamental dimensions along which cultures differ is the degree of *individualism* versus *collectivism*. This dimension determines how people live together (alone, in families, or tribes; see Hofstede, 1982), their values, and how they communicate. As we shall see, people in the United States are individualists for better or worse. We take individualism for granted and are blind to its impact until travel brings us in contact with less individualistic, more collectivistic cultures.

Individualism has been applauded as a blessing and has been elevated to the status of a national religion in the United States. Indeed, the best and worst features of our culture can be attributed to individualism. Proponents of individualism have argued that it is the basis of liberty, democracy, freedom, and economic incentive and that it serves as a protection against tyranny. On the other hand, individualism has been blamed for our alienation from one another, loneliness, selfishness, and narcissism. Indeed, Hall (1976) claimed that, as an extreme, "Western man has created chaos by denying that part of his self that integrates while enshrining the parts that fragment experience" (p. 9).

There can be little doubt that individualism is one of the fundamental dimensions that distinguish cultures one from the other. Likewise, there is little doubt that Western culture is individualistic, whereas Eastern culture emphasizes harmony among people and between people and nature. Tomkins (1984) demonstrated that an individual's psychological makeup is the result of this cultural dimension. He stated, "Human beings, in Western Civilization, have tended toward self-celebration, positive or negative. In oriental thought another alternative is represented, that of harmony between man and nature" (p. 182). Prosser (1978) suggested that the Western emphasis on individuality finds its culmination in contemporary U.S. cultures, where the chief cultural value is the role of the individual. This idea is verified in the landmark intercultural study of Hofstede (1982). In his study of individualism in forty noncommunist countries, the nine most individualistic (in order) were the United States, Australia, Great Britain, Canada, the Netherlands, New Zealand, Italy, Belgium, and Denmark—all Western or European countries. The nine least individualistic (starting with the least) were Venezuela, Colombia, Pakistan, Peru, Taiwan, Thailand, Singapore, Chile, and Hong Kong—all oriental or South American cultures. Similarly, Sitaram and Cogdell (1976) reported individuality to be of primary importance in Western cultures, of secondary importance in black cultures, and of lesser importance in Eastern and Muslim cultures.

While the United States is the most individualistic country on earth (Hofstede, 1982), regions of the United States vary in their degree of individualism. Elazar (1972) has shown that the Central Midwest and the mid-Atlantic states have the most individualistic political culture, whereas the Southeast has the most traditionalistic and least individualistic. But these differences are all relative and, by world standards, even Mississippi has an individualistic culture. Bellah et al. (1985) stated:

Individualism lies at the very core of American culture. . . . Anything that would violate our right to think for ourselves, judge for ourselves, make our own decisions, live our lives as we see fit, is not only morally wrong, it is sacrilegious (p. 142).

Indeed, our extreme individualism makes it difficult for Americans to interact with and understand people from other cultures. We are unique; all other cultures are less individualistic. As Condon and Yousef (1983) stated:

The fusion of individualism and equality is so valued and so basic that many Americans find it most difficult to relate to contrasting values in other cultures where interdependence greatly determines a person's sense of self (p. 65).

The degree to which a culture is individualistic or collectivistic has an impact on the nonverbal behavior of that culture in a variety of ways. First, people from individualistic cultures are comparatively remote and distant proximically. Collectivistic cultures are interdependent and, as a result, they work, play, live, and sleep in close proximity to one another. Hofstede (1982) cites research which suggests that as hunters and gatherers, people lived apart in individualistic nuclear families. As agricultural societies developed, the interdependent extended family began to live in close proximity in large family or tribal units. Urban-industrial societies returned to a norm of individualism, nuclear families, and lack of proximity to one's neighbors, friends, and coworkers.

Kinesic behavior tends to be synchronized in collectivist cultures. Where families work collectively, movements, schedules, and actions need to be highly coordinated (Argyle, 1975). In urban cultures, family members often do their "own thing," coming and going, working and playing, eating and sleeping on different schedules. People in individualistic cultures also smile more than people in normatively oriented cultures according to Tomkins (1984). This fact can probably be explained by the fact that individualists are responsible for their relationships and their own happiness, whereas normatively or collectively oriented people regard compliance with norms as a primary value and personal or interpersonal happiness as a secondary value. Similarly, people in collectivist cultures may suppress both positive and negative emotional displays that are contrary to the mood of the group because maintaining the group is a primary value. People in individualistic cultures are encouraged to express emotions because individual freedom is of paramount value.

Research suggests that people in individualistic cultures are more nonverbally affiliative than people in collectivist cultures. The reason for this is not intuitively obvious because individualism does not require affiliation. However, Hofstede (1982) explained that:

In less individualistic countries where traditional social ties, like those with extended family members, continue to exist, people have less of a need to make specific friendships. One's friends are predetermined by the social relationships into which one is born. In the more individualistic countries, however, affective relationships are not socially predetermined but must be acquired by each individual personally (p. 163).

In individualistic countries like the United States, affiliativeness, dating, flirting, small-talk, and initial acquaintance are more important than they are in collectivist countries where the social network is more fixed and less reliant on individual initiative. Bellah et al. (1985) maintain that for centuries in the individualistic and mobile United States, society people could meet very easily and their communication was open. However, their relationships were usually casual and transient.

Finally, in an impressive study of dozens of cultures, Lomax (1968) found that the song-and-dance styles of a country are related to its level of social cohesion and collectivism. Collectivist cultures rate high in stressing groupness and in the cohesion found in their singing styles. Collectivist cultures show both more cohesiveness in singing and more synchrony in their dance style than do individualistic cultures (Lomax, 1968). It is not surprising that rock dancing, which emphasizes separateness and

"doing your own thing," evolved in individualistic cultures such as those in England and the United States. These dances may serve as a metaphor for the whole U.S. culture, where individuality is more prevalent than in any other place.

Masculinity

Masculinity is a neglected dimension of culture. Masculine traits are typically attributes such as strength, assertiveness, competitiveness, and ambitiousness, whereas feminine traits are attributes such as affection, compassion, nurturance, and emotionality (Bem, 1974; Hofstede, 1982). Cross-cultural research shows that young girls are expected to be more nurturant than boys although there is considerable variation from country to country (Hall, 1984). Hofstede (1982) has measured the degree to which people of both sexes in a culture endorse masculine or feminine goals. Masculine cultures regard competition and assertiveness as important, whereas feminine cultures place more importance on nurturance and compassion. Not surprisingly, the masculinity of a culture is negatively correlated with the percentage of women in technical and professional jobs and positively correlated with segregation of the sexes in higher education (Hofstede, 1982).

The nine countries with the highest masculinity scores, according to Hofstede (1982) (most masculine first) are Japan, Austria, Venezuela, Italy, Switzerland, Mexico, Ireland, Great Britain, and Germany. With the exception of Japan, these countries all lie in Central Europe and the Caribbean. The eight countries with the lowest masculinity scores (least masculine first) are Sweden, Norway, Netherlands, Denmark, Finland, Chile, Portugal, and Thailand—all Scandinavian or South American cultures with the exception of Thailand. Why don't South American cultures manifest the Latin pattern of machismo? Hofstede (1982) suggests that machismo occurs more often in the Caribbean region than it does in South America itself.

Considerable research suggests that androgynous patterns of behavior (those that are both feminine and masculine) result in a high degree of self-esteem, social competence, success, and intellectual development for both males and females. Nonverbal styles where both men and women are free to express both masculine (e.g., dominance, anger) and feminine (e.g., warmth, emotionality) behavior are likely to be healthy and very effective. Indeed, Buck (1984) has shown that males may harm their health by internalizing emotions rather than externalizing them as women usually do. Internalized emotions that are not expressed result in a high stress level and high blood pressure. Interestingly enough, countries considered very masculine show high levels of stress (Hofstede, 1982).

Considerable research has demonstrated significant differences in vocal patterns between egalitarian and nonegalitarian countries. Countries where women are economically important and where sexual standards for women are permissive show more relaxed vocal patterns than other countries (Lomax, 1968). Moreover, egalitarian countries show less tension between the sexes, more vocal solidarity and coordination in their songs, and more synchrony in their movement than we see in less egalitarian countries (Lomax, 1968).

It is important to note that the United States tends to be a masculine country according to Hofstede (1982) although it is not among the nine most masculine. Intercultural communicators should keep in mind that other countries may be more or less sexually egalitarian than is the United States. Similarly, most countries are more feminine (i.e., nurturant, compassionate), and people of both sexes in the United States frequently seem loud, aggressive, and competitive by world standards.

Power Distance

A fourth fundamental dimension of intercultural communication is power distance. Power distance—the degree to which power, prestige, and wealth are unequally distributed in a culture—has been measured in a number of cultures using Hofstede's (1982) power distance index (PDI). Cul-tures with high PDI scores have power and influence concentrated in the hands of a few rather than distributed more or less equally throughout the population. Condon and Yousef (1983) distinguish among three cultural patterns: democratic, authority-centered, and authoritarian. The PDI is highly correlated (0.80) with authoritarianism (as measured by the F-Scale) (Hofstede, 1982).

The nine countries with the highest PDI (highest first) are the Philippines, Mexico, Venezuela, India, Singapore, Brazil, Hong Kong, France, and Colombia (Hofstede, 1982)—all of which are South Asian or Caribbean countries, with the exception of France. Gudykunst and Kim (1984) report that both African and Asian cultures generally maintain hierarchical role relationships. Asian students are expected to be modest and nonverbally deferent in the presence of their instructors. Likewise, Vietnamese consider employers to be their mentors and will not question orders. The nine countries with the lowest PDI (lowest first) are Austria, Israel, Denmark, New Zealand, Ireland, Sweden, Norway, Finland, and Switzerland (Hofstede, 1982)—all of which are European, middle-class democracies located at high latitudes. The United States is slightly lower than the median in power distance. A fundamental determiner of power distance is the latitude of a country. Hofstede (1982) claims that latitude and climate are major forces in shaping cultures. He maintains that the key intervening variable is that technology is needed for survival in colder climates. This need produces a chain of events in which children are less dependent on authority and learn from people other than authority figures. Hofstede (1982) reports a 0.65 correlation between PDI and latitude! In a study conducted at forty universities throughout the United States, Andersen, Lustig, and Andersen (1987) report a − 0.47 correlation between latitude and intolerance for ambiguity and a − 0.45 correlation between latitude and authoritarianism. These findings suggest that residents of the northern United States are less authoritarian and more tolerant of ambiguity. Northern cultures may have to be more tolerant and less autocratic to ensure cooperation and survival in harsher climates.

It is obvious that power distance affects the non-verbal behavior of a culture. High PDI countries such as India, with its rigid caste system, may severely limit interaction, as in the case of India's "untouchables." More than 20 percent of India's population are untouchables—those who are at the bottom of India's five-caste system (Chinoy, 1967). Any contact with untouchables by members of other castes is strictly forbidden and considered "polluting." Obviously, tactile communication among castes is greatly curtailed by Indian culture. High PDI countries with less rigid stratification than India may still prohibit interclass dating, marriage, and contact, which are taken for granted in low PDI countries.

Social systems with large power discrepancies also produce different kinesic behavior. According to Andersen and Bowman (1985), subordinates' body tension is more obvious in power-discrepant relationships. Similarly Andersen and Bowman (1985) report that in power-discrepant circumstances, subordinates smile often in an effort to appear polite and to appease superiors. The continual smiles of many orientals may be an effort to appease superiors or to produce smooth social relations; they may be the result of being reared in a high PDI culture.

Vocalic and paralinguistic cues are also affected by the power distance in a culture. People living in low PDI countries are generally less aware that vocal loudness may be offensive to others. The vocal tones of people in the United States are often perceived as noisy, exaggerated, and childlike (Condon and Yousef, 1983). Lomax (1968) has shown that in countries where political authority is highly centralized, singing voices are tighter and the voice box is more closed, whereas more permissive societies produce more relaxed, open, and clear sounds.

High and Low Context

A final essential dimension of intercultural communication is that of context. Hall (1976, 1984) has described high- and low-context cultures in considerable detail. "A high-context (HC) communication or message is one in which most of the information is either in the physical context or internalized in the person, while very little is in the coded, explicit, transmitted parts of the message" (Hall, 1976, p. 91). Lifelong friends often use HC or implicit messages that are nearly impossible for an outsider to understand. The situation, a smile, or a glance provides an implicit meaning that doesn't need to be articulated. In HC situations or cultures, information is integrated from the environment, the context, the situation, and from nonverbal cues that give the message a meaning that is unavailable in the explicit verbal utterance.

Low-context (LC) messages are just the opposite of HC messages; most of the information is in the explicit code (Hall, 1976). LC messages must be elaborated, clearly communicated, and highly specific. Unlike personal relationships, which are relatively HC message systems, institutions such as courts of law and formal systems such as mathematics or computer language require explicit, LC systems because nothing can be taken for granted (Hall, 1984).

Cultures vary considerably in the degree of context used in communication. The lowest-context cultures are probably the Swiss, German, North American (including the United States), and Scandinavian (Hall, 1976, 1984; Gudykunst and Kim, 1984). These cultures are preoccupied with specifics, details, and precise time schedules at the expense of context. They utilize behavior systems built around Aristotelean logic and linear thinking (Hall, 1984). Cultures that have some characteristics of both HC and LC systems include the French, English, and Italian (Gudykunst and Kim, 1984), which are somewhat less explicit than Northern European cultures.

The highest-context cultures, found in the Orient, China, Japan, and Korea, are extremely HC cultures (Elliott, Scott, Jensen, and McDonough, 1982; Hall, 1976, 1984). Languages are some of the most explicit communication systems, but the Chinese language is an implicit high-context system. To use a Chinese dictionary, one must understand thousands of characters that change meaning when combined with other characters. People from the United States frequently complain that the Japanese never get to the point; they fail to recognize that HC cultures must provide a context and setting and let the point evolve (Hall, 1984). American Indian cultures with ancestral migratory roots in East Asia are remarkably like contemporary oriental culture in several ways, especially in their need for high context (Hall, 1984). Not surprisingly, most Latin American cultures, a fusion of Iberian (Portuguese-Spanish) and Indian traditions, are also high-context cultures. Southern and eastern Mediterranean people such as Greeks, Turks, and Arabs tend to have HC cultures as well.

Communication is obviously quite different in high- and low-context cultures. First, explicit forms of communication such as verbal codes are more prevalent in low-context cultures such as the United States and Northern Europe. People from LC cultures are often perceived as excessively talkative, belaboring the obvious, and using redundancies. People from HC cultures may be perceived as nondisclosive, sneaky, and mysterious. Second, HC cultures do not value verbal communication the same way as do LC cultures. Elliot et al. (1982) found that people who were more verbal were perceived as more attractive by people in the United States, but people who were less verbal were perceived as more attractive in Korea—a high-context culture. Third, HC cultures are more reliant on and tuned in to nonverbal communication than are LC cultures. LC cultures, and particularly the men in LC cultures, fail to perceive as much nonverbal communication as do members of HC cultures. Nonverbal communication provides the context for all communication (Watzlawick, Beavin, and Jackson, 1967), but people from HC cultures are particularly affected by contextual cues. Thus facial expressions, tensions, movements, speed of interaction, location of the interaction, and other subtleties of nonverbal behavior are likely to be perceived by and have more meaning for people from high-context cultures. Finally, people from HC cultures expect more nonverbal communication than do interactants in LC cultures (Hall, 1976). People from HC cultures expect communicators to understand unarticulated feelings, subtle gestures, and environmental cues that people from LC cultures simply do not process.

What is worse, both cultural extremes fail to recognize these basic differences in behavior, communication, and context, and both are quick to misattribute the causes for the other's behavior.

CONCLUSION

Reading about these five dimensions of culture cannot ensure competence in intercultural communication. The beauty of international travel, and even travel within the United States, is that it provides a unique perspective on one's own behavior and the behavior of others. Combining cognitive knowledge from articles and courses with actual encounters with people from other cultures is the best way to gain such competence.

A full, practical understanding of the dimensions along which cultures differ, combined with the knowledge of how specific communication acts differ cross-culturally, has several practical benefits. First, such knowledge will highlight and challenge assumptions about our own behavior. The structure of our own behavior is invisible and taken for granted until it is exposed and challenged through the study of other cultures and actual intercultural encounters. Indeed, Hall (1976) stated that ethnic diversity in interethnic communication can be a source of strength and an asset from which one can discover oneself.

Second, this discussion should make it clear that our attributions about the nonverbal communication of people from other cultures are often wrong. No dictionary or code of intercultural behavior is available. We cannot read people like books, not even people from our own culture. Understanding that someone is from a masculine, collectivist, or high-context culture will, however, make their behavior less confusing and more interpretable.

Finally, understanding about intercultural differences and actually engaging in intercultural encounters is bound to reduce ethnocentrism and make strangers from other cultures seem less threatening. Fear is often based on ignorance and misunderstanding. The fact of intercultural diversity should produce joy and optimism about the number of possible ways to be human.

REFERENCES

Andersen, P. A. (1985). "Nonverbal Immediacy in Interpersonal Communication." In A. W. Siegman and S. Feldstein (Eds.). *Multichannel Integrations of Nonverbal Behavior.* Hillsdale, N.J.: Lawrence Erlbaum.

Andersen, P. A. (1986). "Consciousness, Cognition, and Communication." *Western Journal of Speech Communication,* 50, 87–101.

Andersen, P. A. (1987a). "Locating the Sources of Interpersonal Behavior." *Distinguishing Among Traits, States, Cultures and Situations.* Unpublished paper, San Diego State University, San Diego, Calif.

Andersen, P. A. (1987b). "The Trait Debate: A Critical Examination of the Individual Differences Paradigm in Intercultural Communication." In B. Dervin and M. J. Voigt (Eds.). *Progress in Communication Sciences,* Volume VIII. Norwood, N.J.: Ablex Publishing.

Andersen, J. F., Andersen, P. A., and Lustig, M. W. (February 1987). "Predicting Opposite-Sex Touch Avoidance: A National Replication and Extension." Paper presented at the annual convention of the Western Speech Communication Association, San Diego, Calif.

Andersen, P. A., and Bowman, L. (May 1985). "Positions of Power: Nonverbal Cues of Status and Dominance in Organizational Communication." Paper presented at the annual convention of the Interpersonal Communication Association, Honolulu, Hawaii.

Andersen, P. A., and Leibowitz, K. (1978). "The Development and Nature of the Construct Touch Avoidance." *Environmental Psychology and Nonverbal Behavior,* 3, 89–106.

Andersen, P. A., Lustig, M. W., and Andersen, J. F. (1986). "Communication Patterns Among Cultural Regions of the United States: A Theoretical Perspective." Paper presented at the annual convention of the International Communication Association, Chicago.

Andersen, P. A., Lustig, R., and Andersen, J. F. (1987). Changes in Latitude, Changes in Attitude: The Relationship Between Climate and Interpersonal Communication." Unpublished manuscript, San Diego State University, San Diego, Calif.

Argyle, M. (1975). *Bodily Communication.* New York: International Universities Press.

Bellah, R. N., Madsen, R., Sullivan, W. M., Swidler, A., and Tipton, S. (1985). *Habits of the Heart: Individualism and Commitment in American Life.* New York: Harper & Row.

Bem, S. L. (1974). "The Measurement of Psychological Androgyny." *Journal of Consulting and Clinical Psychology,* 42, 155–162.

Bruneau, T. (1979). "The Time Dimension in Intercultural Communication." In D. Nimmo (Ed.). *Communication Yearbook 3.* New Brunswick, N.J.: Transaction Books.

Buck, R. (1984). *The Communication of Emotion.* New York: The Guilford Press.

Burgoon, J. K. (1985). "Nonverbal Signals." In M. L. Knapp and G. R. Miller (Eds.). *Handbook of Interpersonal Communication.* Newbury Park, Calif.: Sage Publications.

Burgoon, J. K., and Saine, T. (1978). *The Unspoken Dialogue: An Introduction to Nonverbal Communication.* Boston: Houghton Mifflin.

Chinoy, E. (1967). *Society.* New York: Random House.

Condon, J. C., and Yousef, F. (1983). *An Introduction to Intercultural Communication.* Indianapolis, Ind.: Bobbs-Merrill.

Elazar, D. J. (1972). *American Federalism: A View from the States.* New York: Thomas P. Crowell Company.

Elliot, S., Scott, M. D., Jensen, A. D., and McDonough, M. (1982). "Perceptions of Reticence: A Cross-Cultural Investigation." In M. Burgoon (Ed.). *Communication Yearbook 5.* New Brunswick, N.J.: Transaction Books.

Geertz, C. (1973). *The Interpretation of Cultures.* New York: Basic Books.

Gudykunst, W. B., and Kim, Y. Y. (1984). *Communicating with Strangers: An Approach to Intercultural Communication.* New York: Random House.

Hall, E. T. (1959). *The Silent Language.* New York: Doubleday and Company.

Hall, E. T. (1966). *The Hidden Dimension.* New York: Doubleday and Company.

Hall, E. T. (1976). *Beyond Culture*. Garden City, N.Y.: Anchor Books.

Hall, E. T. (1984). *The Dance of Life: The Other Dimension of Time*. Garden City, N.Y.: Anchor Press.

Heslin, R., and Alper, T. (1983). "Touch: A Bonding Gesture." In J. M. Wiemann and R. Harrison (Eds.). *Nonverbal Interaction*. Newbury Park, Calif.: Sage Publications.

Hofstede, G. (1982). *Culture's Consequences* (abridged ed.). Newbury Park, Calif.: Sage Publications.

Jensen, J. V. (1985). "Perspective on Nonverbal Intercultural Communication." In L. A. Samovar and R. E. Porter (Eds.). *Intercultural Communication: A Reader*. Belmont, Calif.: Wadsworth.

Jones, T. S., and Remland, M. S. (May 1982). "Cross-Cultural Differences in Self-Reported Touch Avoidance." Paper presented at the annual convention of the Eastern Communication Association, Hartford, Conn.

LaBarre, W. (1985). "Paralinguistics, Kinesics, and Cultural Anthropology." In L. A. Samovar and R. E. Porter (Eds.). *Intercultural Communication: A Reader*. Belmont, Calif.: Wadsworth.

Lomax, A. (1968). *Folk Song Style and Culture*. New Brunswick, N.J.: Transaction Books.

Malandro, L. A., and Barker, L. (1983). *Nonverbal Communication*. Reading, Mass.: Addison-Wesley.

Mehrabian, A. (1971). *Silent Messages*. Belmont, Calif.: Wadsworth.

Merriam, A. H. (1983). "Comparative Chronemics and International Communication: American and Iranian Perspectives on Time." In R. N. Bostrom (Ed.). *Communication Yearbook 7*. Newbury Park, Calif.: Sage Publications.

Montagu, A., and Matson, F. (1979). *The Human Connection*. New York: McGraw-Hill.

Patterson, M. L. (1983). *Nonverbal Behavior: A Functional Perspective*. New York: Springer-Verlag.

Prosser, M. H. (1978). *The Culture Dialogue: An Introduction to Intercultural Communication*. Boston, Mass.: Houghton Mifflin.

Rich, A. L. (1974). *Interracial Communication*. New York: Harper & Row.

Samovar, L. A., and Porter, R. E. (1985). "Nonverbal Interaction." In L. A. Samovar and R. E. Porter (Eds.). *Intercultural Communication: A Reader*. Belmont, Calif.: Wadsworth.

Samovar, L. A., Porter, R. E., and Jain, N. C. (1981). *Understanding Intercultural Communication*. Belmont, Calif.: Wadsworth.

Saral, T. (1977). "Intercultural Communication Theory and Research: An Overview." In B. D. Ruben (Ed.). *Communication Yearbook I*. New Brunswick, N.J.: Transaction Books.

Scheflen, A. E. (1972). *Body Language and the Social Order*. Englewood Cliffs, N.J.: Prentice-Hall.

Scheflen, A. E. (1974). *How Behavior Means*. Garden City, N.Y.: Anchor Press.

Sitaram, K. S., and Cogdell, R. T. (1976). *Foundations of Intercultural Communication*. Columbus, Ohio: Charles E. Merrill.

Tomkins, S. S. (1984). "Affect Theory." In K. R. Scherer and P. Ekman (Eds.). *Approaches to Emotion*. Hillsdale, N.J.: Lawrence Erlbaum.

Watzlawick, P., Beavin, J. H., and Jackson, D. D. (1967). *Pragmatics of Human Communication*. New York: W. W. Norton.

The Role of Touch in Gender Communications

LAURIE P. ARLISS

The study of communication through touch is often referred to as *haptics*. Interpersonal touching is also referred to as *tactile communication*, since it is assumed that any sensory stimulation through the skin communicates meaning. Of course, the perceived meaning of a given touch is dependent not only on the nature of the touch but also on the situation and the relationship between the individuals. In fact, touching may be the most noticed type of nonverbal communication between adults, but the least studied by researchers. Unlike many kinesic behaviors, which are usually learned without explicit discussion, we are often taught prescribed cultural norms concerning whom we can and cannot touch, along with information about where, when, and how.

Our culture has been labeled a *noncontact* culture, which indicates that we tend to be fairly restrictive about who touches whom.[1] More specifically, it seems that touching in our culture is most often associated with sexual behavior, and many touches are evaluated first and foremost in relation to potential sexual ramifications. The fact that touch can communicate sexual desire is obvious in our predominantly heterosexual culture. It has provided the basis for many romance stories, both fiction and nonfiction. But with increased publicity about child molestation and growing openness about homosexuality, even adult-child touches and touches be-

tween adults of the same sex may be regarded as potentially sexual.

Perhaps because touch is so closely linked to sexuality, sex differences in haptic communication abound. But it is important for the reader to be able to suspend his or her learned preconception that all touch is sexual in order to be able to understand the variety of messages that can be communicated through touch. We have all experienced unpleasant touches and (hopefully) warm, reassuring, and pleasurable touches of many kinds. Conversely, most readers can remember offering touches expressly intended to communicate displeasure with various others, touches expressly intended to communicate affection or arousal, touches intended to communicate intermediate emotions, and even inadvertent touches for which immediate apologies were probably offered.

Gibson classifies tactile communication as active or passive, to emphasize the distinction between touching and being touched — a distinction that most of us find quite important.[2] In fact, a good deal of the research concerning sex differences in touching has focused on precisely the issue of which sex demonstrates the most touching — both active and passive — in communication with others. As you might guess, men have been observed to be considerably more active than women in this regard, across a variety of situations. According to Deaux's review, "men are more likely to touch others, and women are more likely to be touched."[3] But this simple statement requires a good deal of clarification.

To begin with, it is crucial to specify the gender composition of the dyad in which touching behavior is reported. The obvious conclusion is that the men who are doing the touching are touching women. This conclusion about male-female dyads accounts for a good deal of the research. According to Leathers, "in both intimate and professional relationships men are expected to touch women much more frequently than they are touched by women, and they do so."[4] Research based on self-reports indicates that, indeed, both sexes tend to think that adult males touch adult females more than vice

From Laurie P. Arliss, *Gender Communication*, © 1991, pp. 97–104. Reprinted by permission of Prentice-Hall, Englewood Cliffs, New Jersey. Laurie P. Arliss teaches at Ithaca College.

versa.[5] Observational research supports this expectation. In a study conducted during the 1970s, Henley observed what she classified as *intentional touching* in public settings and reported that male-to-female touches were most common, accounting for 42% of all intentional touches observed. This figure is nearly twice that of the female-to-male touches she observed.[6]

In a 1980 replication of Henley's research, Major and Williams reported that the sex differences proposed by Henley were supported, although the contrast in the touching behavior had decreased somewhat: men touched women in 36% of the observed instances, while women touched men in 27% of the incidents. Major and Williams were also concerned with the extent to which touches were reciprocated. They found that some were and some were not, but men were more likely to initiate touches that their female counterparts did not return than vice versa.[7]

Thus, in male-female dyads, there is good reason to expect that the male will communicate through active touching, while the female will participate in passive touching communication. This empirical observation is consistent with the self-reports of adult Americans, and, coincidentally, with the stereotypic assumption that males should initiate sexual contact. It may be that in cross-sex adult interactions, even when no sexual intent is involved, the norms governing sexuality are observed. Certainly, we have inherited a system of "manners," based on notions about chivalry, which call for men to touch women as they escort them through unopened doors and into empty chairs. Like children and elderly companions, women generally occupy the role of the cared for, which often involves being the passive recipient of touch.

An alternate explanation for the uneven distribution of intentional touches between the sexes has been well articulated in the work of Nancy Henley. She points out that male-female dyads are "mixed" in the sense that there is an unequal distribution of status and power between men and women in our society. Therefore, just as any superior is freer to touch any subordinate than vice versa, so are men freer to touch women than vice versa. The tendency for men to be the touchers not only demonstrates their superiority over women, according to Henley, but also reinforces it behaviorally.[8]

Research based on male-female pairs clearly contradicts the prevailing cultural mythology that women touch more than men. However, this stereotypic portrayal accurately reflects the research on same-sex touching. Self-report data indicates that both men and women believe women are freer than men to touch members of the same sex, whether friends or relatives. Women are reportedly freer than men to dance together, walk hand-in-hand, and hug one another, to name just a few examples. Observational data supports the self-reported findings that female-female touching is more prevalent than male-male touching, and also that female-female dyads are allowed a wider range of permissible behaviors.[9]

In fact, haptic communication among males seems to be highly restricted to specific kinds of touches and specific situations. This is true even in familiar communication. Father-son touches are not as common as mother-daughter touches, or, for that matter, as common as mother-son touches.[10] Young boys are often taught to substitute a handshake for a kiss as part of their socialization. Certainly, restrictions of this sort are culturally and situationally influenced, but the tendency for males to save certain touches for females is apparent nevertheless. The touches that are deemed appropriate for male-male dyads, according to Willis and his colleagues, tend to be "purposeful and directed."[11] So, when men do touch other men, their tactile gestures tend to be like their speech—short and to-the-point: a mild punch in the arm or a firm slap on the back.

In sum, the research concerning active and passive touch clearly supports the mythology that men are the touchers and women are the receivers of touch. As expected, opposite-sex touching is the most prevalent type, largely because men initiate touch with female partners. But same-sex touching, which is not nearly as common in our culture, is female-dominated, since men tend to restrict tactile contact with other men. Because they receive more opposite-sex touching and more same-sex touching, women must be perceived as more approachable in terms of passive touch.

In the next section, several meanings that can be associated with human touches are described and examined for sex differences. Several category systems have been proposed to identify the potential messages that can be communicated through touching.[12] The list that follows admittedly does not cover every function of touch in human communication. But the touching behaviors discussed are those most clearly identified with gender differences.

RITUALIZED TOUCHING

Nearly all societies share conventions about ritualized touch. The most obvious example of a ritualized touch in our society is the handshake. This mutual gesture is widely practiced and serves as a substitute for a number of verbal messages: "Hello," "Good-bye," "It's a deal," "Congratulations," etc. Sometimes, a ritualized *pat on the back* is offered in place of the handshake, but this substitution seems to be riskier and seldom occurs between strangers or during initial meetings.

Other ritualized touches are not prevalent in our culture today, but are characteristic of other times and places: *the double kiss on the cheek* or *the kiss on the hand*. Certain situations, like weddings and funerals, invoke patterns of ritualized touching that are otherwise not typical. If you stand on the receiving line of either event, you had better be prepared; weddings are rife with simultaneous *cheek kisses*, while funerals require sharing brief *shoulder hugs*.

As stated, the handshake is the most widely used ritual touch in our daily interaction. In fact, it is impressive to note that the handshake is usually accomplished with a minimum of difficulty between men, which indicates its prevalence and importance in the male arena. But many women still encounter some difficulty in accomplishing the handshake. The norms governing when and how to extend one's hand to a female, how long and how firmly to grasp the other's hand, etc., are still indefinite. As women begin to move in political and professional circles requiring more interaction with relative strangers, the female-female and male-female handshakes will undoubtedly be accomplished with greater ease. Nevertheless, at present, the ritual handshake seems more easily and widely practiced by men.[13]

A more locally situated form of ritual touching that also tends to be male dominated at present is identified by Key as *play*, and "comprises a wide range [of touching] from very informal bantering and exchanges to contact sports."[14] It is fascinating to observe the many types of touches that men exchange in the context of their games. Apparently unconscious of any possible sexual overtones, they grab, wrestle with, and pat one another in otherwise restricted areas, whether on or off the field. In the context of the game, the touches function variously as encouragement, consolation, and congratulations.

Women seldom share a carefully tuned system of ritualized touches. In fact, many observers have commented that, when women engage in sports, they borrow an array of male behaviors, including a number of ritualized pats and embraces. Apparently, participation in group athletics, like participation in public interactions with strangers, has not traditionally been part of the female experience. As women gain access to these arenas, special forms of female ritualized touching may emerge.

SEXUAL TOUCHING

It was argued earlier that sexuality appears to be a preoccupation among Americans, which renders most any tactile contact potentially sexual. According to Morris, it may well be the possibility for confusing the two which is responsible for a prohibition against touching in middle-class America.[15] Certainly, sexual pleasure is physically and instinctually tied to various types of touching, but due to culturally determined patterns otherwise-nonerotic touches have also come to be identified as sexual. For example, hand-holding has come to be associated with romance and is often identified as a precursor to intimate tactile interaction. Of course, humans join hands for other reasons: members of groups join hands to pray; patients take their nurse's hand to squeeze during painful procedures; and even a stranger can take a child's hand in order to provide assistance.

Despite the exceptions we all acknowledge, holding hands still remains a predictable event during early stages of adult heterosexuality. It is one of a sequence of touches that Morris suggests is "spontaneously reenacted" with surprising regularity. Imagine a past (or fictional) romance and check the touching sequence against that suggested by Morris: "hand to hand, arm to shoulder, arm to waist, mouth to mouth, hand to head, hand to body, mouth to breast, hand to genitals, genitals and/or mouth to genitals."[16] To be sure, the steps become increasingly tied to physically erotic stimulation, but the fascinating truth is that, in early stages of intimacy, the various touches serve as symbols of sexuality and can be very arousing. We have learned to treat these touches as sexual and to understand their place on a continuum of romantic behavior.

Traditionally, men in our society have been believed to be the sexual aggressors and women the passive receivers of touch. Bernard points out that, in terms of sexual intercourse, this tradition appears to be consistent with the physical reality that men must be aroused in order to participate, while women can participate regardless of arousal, or even consent.[17] But with regard to the "moves" that serve as precursors to sexual interaction, there appears to be no such logic prohibiting a female from taking a male's hand or putting her arm around him. Yet, stereotypically, men have also been expected to initiate these touches, while women have traditionally used more subtle and passive techniques, sometimes known as *flirting*.

Although women are certainly freer than ever to acknowledge and cultivate their own sexuality, it is difficult to assert that cultural prescriptions concerning sexual touching are dead and gone. There is substantial evidence that the active-passive myth is real. Further evidence that the myth of male dominance lives on is contained in the contemporary language used to reference sexual involvement. Baker points out that sexual metaphors continue to portray women as passive "receptacles" and men as ex-

plosive aggressors, and that this distinction is demeaning and dangerous. While the specific sexual metaphors seemingly come and go, the trend remains unchanged.[18] Indeed, the sheer number of slang words that metaphorize women as sex objects is reportedly ten times the number used to refer to men.[19]

Actual patterns in sexual touching are difficult to study, except through self-reports. According to a well-publicized survey, women are experiencing increased freedom to act on their sexual desires.[20] Certainly, media portrayals of sexually aggressive women are increasingly abundant. But each reader is encouraged to question for himself or herself whether or not sexual touching, from hand-holding to sexual intercourse, is not free from traditional prescriptions concerning male aggression and female passivity. Remember to imagine yourself as the future parent of an adolescent boy and girl!

AFFILIATIVE TOUCHING

Certain touches appear to be offered in order to help create or maintain a sense of affiliation between individuals. Sometimes, affiliative touches represent acknowledgment of the relationship between the individuals and are offered upon meeting or parting. Exchanging hugs or kisses or placing one's hand momentarily on the other's shoulder in such situations often symbolizes a positive connection between the participants. Sadly, these tactile gestures sometimes become so ritualized that it is difficult to discern a sincere touch from a feigned expression of warmth. In much the same way that we call almost anyone "Dear," we may overuse affiliative touches of this sort.

Sometimes, affiliative touching is closely tied to an emotionally charged event. We may hug or hold hands with a friend or relative to console them or share their joy. These touches seem especially meaningful, and I hope that each reader has experienced a moment in which a relationship seemed to spontaneously grow closer during such an event. Henley concurs that the amount of affiliative touching seems to be influenced by the relationship between the actors. Logically, friends engage in more affiliative touching than acquaintances, and acquaintances more than strangers. Also, the situation between the actors is influential, i.e., friends would be more likely to touch one another at a party than at work.[21]

As you might expect, though, women report more affiliative touching than men across relationships and situations, particularly with members of the same sex. In addition, women touch children more than men, according to both self-reports and observations.[22] Similarly, women touch the elderly and disabled more often than men.[23] Coincidentally, women dominate professions that seemingly call for affiliative touching, such as elementary school teaching and nursing. As these occupations become better integrated, it will be interesting to see if men adopt similar patterns of touch to communicate affiliation and support. At present, the tendency for women to use touch in this way probably functions both to create and to reinforce the myth that women are more emotionally expressive.

AGGRESSIVE TOUCHING

Many of the scholars who have studied touch as communication have stressed its positive functions in human interaction. We have all heard stories about skin hunger suffered by neglected children and been warned that we need our daily dose of hugging. While the need for physical contact is well documented, it is important not to overlook the potential negative functions of tactile communication.

Some touches are overtly aggressive and obviously harmful. To put it plainly, they hurt! In addition to inflicting pain, tactile gestures like punching, choking, and kicking communicate information about the relationship between the participants. Yet, violent acts of this type are seldom treated as tactile communication.

Rather, physical aggression has been treated as an individual trait, one that is likely to be more pronounced in a male than in a female. Some scholars have speculated that men are biologically predisposed to aggressive behavior.[24] Others have argued that male aggression is a socially learned and re-

warded tendency—one that is neither encouraged nor allowed among females.[25] Here it is important to note that, regardless of the explanation, men are clearly more likely than women to be both the inflictors and the victims of aggressive contact.[26] Ultimately, Henley argues, women are culturally excluded from physical interaction to the point where they are often incapable of defending themselves against attack.[27]

But actual physical trauma is only one of the possible negative effects of tactile interaction. Several researchers have concluded that active touch is related to status and power, whether it hurts or not. Support for this contention is embodied, first of all, in the observational studies reporting that higher-status people touch lower-status people more than vice versa, across a wide variety of relationships and situations.[28] In addition, self-reports indicate that people believe that status affects the likelihood of active and passive touching such that people are more likely to touch lower-status people than peers and less likely to touch higher-status people than peers.[29] Finally, research suggests that people perceive active touching to be an indication of status. Several experimental studies in which subjects reacted to various types of photographs that depicted touching provide evidence that, at least between members of the same sex, the toucher was seen as dominant. This trend was accentuated in depictions of same-sex unequals, such as a boss and a subordinate. At least one of the studies, however, reports an apparent contradiction in cross-sex interactions, when a female identified as higher status was shown touching a male of lower status. The touch of a female superior did not increase her perceived dominance over the male subordinate. Despite this telling inconsistency, this research indicates "a striking and consistent finding . . . that the act of touch overwhelmed the impact of any other power indicators, namely gender, age, and initial status."[30]

So, it appears to be a well-researched conclusion that touching can serve to reinforce the power dynamic of dyadic interaction. In light of the observed tendency for men to touch women more than vice versa, it seems that touching may be one behavior by which male dominance is perpetuated. But the aggression explanation does not account for the reported and observed finding that women touch women more than men touch men. To explain this tendency, it is necessary to call on the affiliation explanation. While it may be confusing to combine explanations in this way, it is apparent that the gender composition of a given dyad appears to influence the meaning of touch and therefore to affect sex differences in tactile communication.

NOTES

1. Mark Knapp, *Nonverbal Communication in Human Interaction* (New York: Holt, Rinehart and Winston, 1978), 258.

2. James J. Gibson, "Observations on Active Touch," *Psychological Review* 69 (1962): 477–91.

3. Kay Deaux, *The Behavior of Men and Women* (Monterey, Calif.: Brooks/Cole, 1976), 64.

4. Dale G. Leathers, *Successful Nonverbal Communication: Principles and Applications* (New York: Macmillan, 1986), 137.

5. Sidney M. Jourard, "An Exploratory Study of Body-Accessibility," *British Journal of Social and Clinical Psychology* 5 (1966): 221–31; Lawrence B. Rosenfeld, Sallie Kartus, and Chett Ray, "Body Accessibility Revisited," *Journal of Communication* 26 (1976): 27–30.

6. Nancy M. Henley, "Status and Sex: Some Touching Observations," *Bulletin of the Psychonomic Society* 2 (1973): 91–93.

7. Brenda Major, "Gender Patterns in Touching Behavior," in *Gender and Nonverbal Behavior*, ed. Clara Mayo and Nancy M. Henley (New York: Springer-Verlag, 1980), 3–37.

8. Nancy Henley, *Body Politics: Power, Sex and Nonverbal Communication* (New York: Touchstone Press, 1986).

9. Major, 18–20.

10. Frank N. Willis and G. E. Hofmann, "Development of Tactile Patterns in Relationship to Age, Sex and Race," *Developmental Psychology* 11 (1975): 866.

11. Frank N. Willis, D. L. Reeves and D. R. Buchanan, "Interpersonal Touch in High School Relative to Sex and Race," *Perceptual and Motor Skills* 43 (1976): 843–47.

12. Albert Mehrabian, *Nonverbal Communication* (Chicago: Aldine-Atherton, 1972); Ashley Montagu, *The Human Significance of the Skin* (New York: Columbia University Press, 1971).

13. Henley, 1986, 110.

14. Mary Ritchie Key, *Paralanguage and Kinesics* (Metuchen, N.J.: Scarecrow Press, 1975), 103.

15. Desmond Morris, *Intimate Behavior* (New York: Random House, 1971), 104–5.

16. Morris, 74.

17. Jesse Bernard, *The Sex Game* (New York: Atheneum, 1973), 60.

18. Robert Baker, "'Pricks' and 'Chicks': A Plea for 'Persons,'" in *Sexist Language: A Modern Philosophical Analysis*, ed. Mary Betterling-Braggin (Totowa, N.J.: Littlefield-Adams, 1981), 161–82.

19. Julia Stanley, "Gender Marking in American English: Usage and Reference," in *Sexism and Language*, ed. Alleen P. Nilsen et al. (Urbana, Ill.: National Council of Teachers of English, 1977), 43–74.

20. Shere Hite, *The Hite Report* (New York: Macmillan, 1976).

21. Henley, 1986, 203–4.

22. Major, 21.

23. M. N. Blondis and B. E. Jackson, *Nonverbal Communication with Patients: Back to the Human Touch* (New York: Wiley, 1977); L. M. Verbrugge and R. P. Steiner, "Physician Treatment of Men and Women: Sex Bias or Appropriate Care?" *Medical Care* 19 (1981): 609–32.

24. Deaux, 82; T. Tieger, "On the Biological Basis of Sex Differences in Aggression," *Child Development* 51 (1980): 943–63.

25. Eleanor E. Maccoby and Carol N. Jacklin, "Sex Differences in Aggression: A Rejoinder and Reprise," *Child Development* 51 (1980): 964–80.

26. Deaux, chapter 8.

27. Henley, 1986, 183.

28. Major, 1981, 23.

29. Henley, 1986, 104.

30. Major, 1981, 24.

Silence and Silences in Cross-Cultural Perspective: Japan and the United States

SATOSHI ISHII
TOM BRUNEAU

A BRIEF FOCUS

Every deed and every relationship is surrounded by an atmosphere of silence. . . . Friendship needs no words—it is solitude delivered from the anguish of loneliness. Silence pervades the world, as do a multitude of kinds of silences and an entire spectrum of silencings. A cultural, social, and political nature. It is certainly not particular to any single cultural tradition. However, different cultural groups seem to stylize their forms of silence according to their own traditional wisdom, beliefs, and attitudes.

Hammarskjold (1971, p. 8)

Most people throughout the world experience some form of silence. However, the manner in which people's attitudes become socially and culturally disposed toward silence is dramatically different in different cultural groups. Northern European and North American societies, for example, are so involved in linear progression that even flashes of silence are filled with action and doing. In these cultures, silence is viewed as dark, negative, and full of "no things"—all of which are considered socially undesirable. In such cultures, silence is ritualized and ceremonialized by authoritative leader-

ship in a wide variety of contexts. In other cultures, however, silence is *often* achieved. Here breaking silence is a necessary evil, at best; speaking is a negative act.

Silence is the mode of communication for the contemplative throughout the world—but it is more practical in some cultural and social groupings than others. For some, Lao Tsu's (1972) simple statement, "To talk little is natural" (No. 23), is obviously and experientially descriptive. Pragmatists and people in action—those mobilized in projects and active planning, in decision making, and the like—seldom experience deep silence. Pragmatists and scientific-minded people shake their heads in utter amazement that what means nothing to them can be significant to others in many different ways.

Silence belongs to the world of being—not to the world of becoming. Silence is stillness—a mental phenomenon of some duration. *Silences*, however, while connected to the deeper level of silence, belong to the world of becoming, of linear progression, of conscious and semiconscious thinking, saying, and doing. Stillness and silence-of-being appear to concern right-brained cortical processes; silence, in its social or asocial manifestations, concerns sitting still, solitude, and inaction. Silences-of-becoming appear to concern left-brained cortical processes.

Silences

Silences lie on the surface of deeper levels of silence. Silences are like interconnected rivers and lakes; silence is like the sea to which they are connected. Silences are discontinuities; they are breaks in action. Silences are often dynamic variations of processes recognized as having signification. They are stillings of process where we attempt to impose duration (Bruneau, 1985). Some cultural groups, many of them Far Eastern, are biased in favor of lengthy silences. These groups create silences more frequently than do those from some Western cultures; they interrupt processual action with long and deep silences.

When we alter continuity significantly, we create silences; when we alter expected succession, we

This essay was prepared especially for the fifth edition. All rights reserved. Permission to reprint must be obtained from the publisher and the authors. Satoshi Ishii teaches at Otsuma Women's University, Mobara, Chiba-ken, Japan. Tom Bruneau teaches at Radford University, Radford, Virginia.

create silences; when we stop to think, we create internal silences.

Silences are not only based in the very comprehensibility of each language of the world but are also the stuff out of which social acts, social actions, social presence, and social events are created and articulated. Thus we can speak of social silences, or interpersonal or group silences. Some lengthy group silences can be viewed as "social silences." These silences are also durational breaks in process, succession, and continuity. Customs, traditions, social mannerisms, social stability, normative actions, and the like can be viewed as they relate to habitual silences.

Silencing

The process of arresting process is *silencing*. At a basic level, silencing is the imposition of volition or will to give signification or symbolic meaning (Bruneau, 1985). At a political or social level, it is a process of using a figure to gain rhetorical import; it is a persuasive act, an exercise in enforcing norms and directing others and one's self; it is many such communicative matters. As far as social and political exigencies, events, situations, and circumstances are concerned, we can speak of those who silence and those who are silenced, those who act and those who observe, those who listen and those who speak.

We silence others to gain attention, to maintain control, to protect, to teach, to attempt to eliminate distractions, to induce reverence for authority or tradition, and to point to something greater than ourselves or our groups. Silencing is also a way of positing a ground of psychological and social neutrality, so that silences and silence can occur positively. Zones of silence, or places where extraneous noise is controlled, are sometimes created as a means of silencing others. These zones can concern authority, expertise, secrecy, thinking, and the like.

Silencing can be the essence of the language of superiority and inferiority, affecting such relationships as teacher-follower, male-female, and expert-client. The definition of much role behavior across many cultural groups concerns the manner of speech and refraining from speech. The process of silencing can have both positive and negative effects. In some situations, quiet is demanded by others and by those who must themselves be quiet. Being quiet—effecting a self-imposed silence is often valued and rewarded in some social environments. Being quiet is often a sign of respect for the wisdom and expertise of others. The elderly of many Eastern cultural groups expect signs of respect, one of which is the silence of the young, as well as the silence of less authoritative family members. Westerners often do not understand this process: It was common several decades ago but is practiced less and less today.

Contrary to outspoken and often ego-driven Western women (even the milder ones), many women in Eastern cultures view their silent roles as very powerful. Some women see their silent roles as natural (some are unconscious of them) and cannot *imagine* speaking out unless violated personally. There is a power of control in silence and in the outward show of reticence. This power often goes unrecognized by those who value speech-as-power and by those who value assertiveness by all, equally and democratically. It is, without a doubt, a truism that many cultures of the world expect more silences from women and children.

SILENCES IN CROSS-CULTURAL PERSPECTIVE

Today's communication scholars, who often observe the Western rhetorical tradition uncritically, have been concerned primarily with verbal expressions or speaking out. The Western tradition is relatively negative in its attitude toward silence and ambiguity, especially in social and public relations. People seldom recognize that silences do have linking, affecting revelational, judgmental, and activating communicative functions in Western cultures (Jensen, 1973). Also, silences can convey all the various kinds and degrees of messages that may be described as cold, oppressive, defiant, disapproving or condemning, calming, approving, humble, excusing, and consenting (Samovar et al., 1981, p. 184). The intercultural implications of silent behaviors are diverse because the value and use of silence as communication vary markedly from one culture to another. Consequently, communication scholars ought to pay more attention to the cultural views of silence and the interpretations given to silence in communication interactions.

Since the time of ancient Greek philosophers, Western thought has emphasized bipolar values and concepts by opposing terms such as black versus white, good versus bad, and yes versus no. Speech versus silence has been researched and taught from the same bipolarization: Speech has a positive connotation and silence has a negative one. Recently, however, both Eastern and Western scholars have come to advocate relativistic viewpoints on such concepts and values: "A major misconception is . . . the common, basic assumption that silence is completely other than speech, its foreign opposite, its antagonist" (Bruneau, 1973, p. 17). Silence is not the "empty" absence of speech sound; silence creates speech, and speech creates silence; yin and yang are, in this view, counterdependent as well as dynamically concomitant. In Gestalt terms, the two function as the "figure" and the "ground," one being possible because of the other's existence, but dynamically so. Generally, silence is regarded as the ground against which the figures of speech are perceived and valued. The two should sometimes be perceived in the reverse way; silence should be treated as the figure against which the ground of speech functions. Most people, especially in Western cultures, are unconscious of this interdependence between speech and silence.

Some Pragmatic Comparisons

In intercultural communication, while the basic *form* of silence *may be* universal, its functions and interpretations vary among cultures. For a newcomer to a foreign culture, a general knowledge of when and where to keep silent may be a basic social requirement, just as a little knowledge of verbal communication is. That is, in intercultural communication contexts a deep understanding comes from being sensitive and open-minded to cultural differences in communicative silences. According to

Wayne (1974), the U.S. interpretations of silence are: (1) sorrow, (2) critique, (3) obligation, (4) regret, and (5) embarrassment. Australian interpretations proved to be similar to the U.S. ones. Wayne goes on to conclude, "In every case the fact that the percentage of neutral or uncommitted responses was much higher for the Japanese and thus could be interpreted as a cultural difference" (pp. 127–130).

From the perspective of an ethnography of communication, the notion and significance of silent communication competence should be positively introduced and researched along with verbal communication competence. Humans become communicatively competent by acquiring not only the structure and use of language but also a set of values and patterns of silent interaction. Anthropologically, the relative quantities and values of the silence of children in communicative settings can be said to be related to socialization and child-rearing practices. According to Caudill and Weinstein (1969), for example, Japanese mothers make more efforts than do U.S. mothers to soothe their children with physical, rather than verbal, contact. This effort apparently suggests that Japanese mothers value silence and its association with self-restraint in Japanese society. In contrast to the Western significance of eloquence and self-assertion, the general attitude of Japanese people toward language and verbalization is that fewer words, supported by the *aesthetics of vagueness*, are better than more words.

Socio-cultural impact plays an important role in the characterization of communication patterns. It may be safely said that Japanese culture nurtures silence, reserve, and formality, whereas Western cultures place more value on speech, self-assertion, and informality. Ishii and Klopf (1976) ascertained from their cross-cultural survey results that the average person in the United States devotes about twice the time to conversation (6 hours, 43 minutes) that the Japanese do (3 hours, 31 minutes).

Further evidence to support the idea that the Japanese have negative attitudes toward speaking is in order. Values regarding appropriate communicative behavior are often most clearly reflected in traditional proverbs. Katayama (1982) analyzed 504 Japanese proverbs on the values of language and found: 124 (25 percent) of them had positive values; 320 (63 percent) had negative values; and 59 (12 percent) were neutral. Inagaki (1985) also investigated 3,600 Japanese people's attitudes toward speaking and obtained data indicating that 82 percent of them agreed with the saying, *"Kuchi wa wazawai no moto,"* or, in English, "Out of the mouth comes all evil" (p. 6). This finding is not surprising given the many Japanese proverbs expressing negativity toward speech. Ishikawa's (1970) survey results on businessmen and businesswomen in Tokyo revealed that (1) men should or need to be silent to be successful in life and (2) 65 percent of the businesswomen would choose silent males to marry (p. 5).

All these survey results show a contrast between Japanese and U.S. values of speech and silence. Rader and Wunsch (1980) obtained the following results from their survey on oral communication in U.S. businesses: (1) 95 percent responded that the ability to communicate orally and in writing was considered to be important in their jobs and (2) graduates in business were spending the greatest portion of time in speaking, followed by listening, writing, and reading. Woodstock (1979), who analyzed oral and written communication problems of managerial trainees, secretaries, and immediate supervisors, concluded that oral communication is an area that should be given more emphasis in the business communication classroom.

Not only in business but in everyday social life, people in the United States like to ask questions and force others to talk to fill interpersonal silences. Because silence is not valued and therefore not tolerated socially in U.S. society (and in many European societies), one function of speech is to avoid silence, generally, as well as to fill silences during the transference of messages. Contrary to the U.S. practice, in Japanese society silence and silences are generally considered to be positively meaningful; they are socio-culturally accepted to a much higher degree.

The point here is that the quantity of silences versus the quantity of speech is interpreted and valued differently across cultures. Different norms of appropriate communicative behavior exist, and a variety of intercultural misunderstanding can occur if one does not know when, where, and how to remain silent. To promote natural and effective interaction, especially with Japanese, people in the United States need to learn to feel more comfortable in situations where silence and vagueness prevail. Learning the general rules for silence plays a more important part than generally thought for all people attempting to communicate successfully across cultures.

Japanese Enryo-Sasshi Versus U.S. Exaggeration-Reduction

Anthropologists, psychologists, sociologists, and communication scholars have often pointed out that Japanese people are oriented to nonconfrontational and nondialectical interpersonal relations. This orientation of the Japanese is unquestionably based on their nonverbal, intuitive communication practices, whereas Americans want to emphasize individualism and self-assertion supported by verbal communication. Barnlund (1975), who compared Japan-U.S. verbal and nonverbal self-disclosure, concluded: "The communicative consequences of cultural emphasis upon 'talkativeness' and 'self assertion' among Americans may cultivate a highly self-oriented person, one who prizes and expresses every inner response no manner how trivial or fleeting." As to Japanese self-disclosure, he goes on to say, "The communicative consequences of cultural encouragement of 'reserve' and 'caution' among Japanese may produce an other-oriented person, who is highly sensitive and receptive to meanings in others" (p. 160). Barnlund's observations are evidentially supported by Ishii, Klopf, and Cambra's (1979, 1984) PVB[1] findings on Japanese and U.S. students' verbal predispositions: The Japanese students were significantly different from the U.S. students, being less dominant, less inclined to initiate and maintain conversations, less apt to speak frequently and long, less inclined to talk, and less fluent than U.S. students (1984). How, then, can these

Japan-U.S. communication style differences be explained psychologically in terms of encoding and decoding messages?

In the high-context Japanese culture, most information tends to be in the physical context and internalized into the person. People, therefore, need not participate actively in verbal interaction. Ishii's (1984) study of *enryo-sasshi* communication in such a high-context culture was among the first attempts to analyze and clarify the general process of Japanese interpersonal empathic communication. The speaker, unconsciously depending on the other person and the communicative situation, simplifies and economizes messages rather than elaborating on them. His or her psychological "exit," through which the encoded messages are sent out under the impact of *enryo* (reserve or restraint), is considered to be much smaller than his or her own message-receiving "entrance," called *sasshi*. The sense of *enryo-sasshi* is of utmost importance in high-context Japanese interpersonal relations.

Intrapersonally, the person of good *enryo* considers the active, exaggerated expression of ideas and feelings to be degrading and foreign. Ideas and feelings that might hurt the other person or damage the general atmosphere when expressed are carefully sent back for re-examination in an internal self-feedback process. Only those ideas judged safe and vague are allowed to be sent out through the small exit that functions as a screening filter. This message-screening process in consideration of the other person and the context is *"enryo"*; it makes the Japanese appear silent, vague, and awkward in communicating with superiors, strangers, and people from different cultures. This observation apparently serves to explain the psychological backdrop of Japanese people's communication apprehension: Thirty-five percent of the Japanese considered themselves to be highly apprehensive in communication situations as compared to 20 percent of the Americans.

To make communicative interaction possible in the high-context situation, the Japanese listener is expected to possess good sensitivity and to receive the message through his or her wide entrance. In this message-receiving stage, the restricted and vague information is appropriately "developed" according to the listener's guess competence called *"sasshi."* In Japanese interpersonal relations, a person of good *sasshi*, who is good at mind-reading or perceiving intuitively people's ideas and feelings, is highly appreciated. This process of interaction is *enryo-sasshi* communication, one of the keys to understanding Japanese interpersonal relations.

In the U.S. multi-ethnic low-context culture, a communication process that is in contrast to the Japanese process seems to function. In low-context communication people depend on the active exchange of overt, verbal messages. The speaker is socialized and expected to send out his or her messages through the large exit, in an exaggerated way, rather than simplifying and economizing them. The psychological mechanism of American message-screening and internal self-feedback can be said to be rougher than that of Japanese *enryo-sasshi*. This fact is evidently based upon a *counter-Japanese value* of interpersonal communication that the more speaking, the better—at home, at school, and in business.

The U.S. listener, in receiving and decoding the exaggerated message, subconsciously attempts to reduce the information. The message-receiving entrance seems to be smaller than that of the Japanese; that is, the listener is not expected to guess and develop the message. Clarity and exactitude in decoding are not the norm. This whole process of sending and receiving messages can be called U.S. *exaggeration-reduction communication*.

CONCLUSION

Whereas verbal communication plays a very important role in promoting intercultural as well as interpersonal understanding, we should recognize that the ultimate goal-stage of communication—interpersonally or interculturally—may be communication through silence. Silence lends substance to speech and gives it tensive direction—being supports becoming. Baker (1955), who constructed a communication model of silence on the basis of "reciprocal identification," claims that silence *is the aim of human communication*. We do not dispute this claim, and although we have been forced here to use words to point to the muted world, we are hopeful that we have shared some of our interior silence and silences with those of the reader.

NOTE

1. PVB (Predispositions toward Verbal Behavior) is an instrument to measure a person's general feelings of his or her verbal behavior (see Mortensen et al., 1977). For details of the Japan-U.S. cross-cultural surveys, see Ishii et al., 1984.

REFERENCES

Baker, S. J. (1955). "The Theory of Silence." *Journal of General Psychology, 53,* 145–167.

Barnlund, D. C. (1975). *Public and Private Self in Japan and the United States.* Tokyo: Simul Press.

Bruneau, T. J. (1973). "Communicative Silences: Forms and Functions." *Journal of Communication, 23,* 1, 17–46.

Bruneau, T. J. (1982). "Communicative Silences in Cross-Cultural Perspective." *Media Development* (London), *29* (4), 6–8.

Bruneau, T. J. (1985). "Silencing and Stilling Process: The Creative and Temporal Bases of Signs." *Semiotica, 56* (3/4), 279–290.

Caudill, W., and Weinstein, H. (1969). "Maternal Care and Infant Behavior in Japan and America." *Psychiatry, 32,* 12–43.

Hammarskjold, D. (1971). *Markings* (Transl. L. Sjoberg and W. H. Auden). New York: Alfred A. Knopf.

Inagaki, Y. (1985). *Jiko Hyogen No Gijutsu* ("Skills in Self-Expression"). Tokyo: PHP Institute.

Ishii, S. (1984). *"Enryo-sasshi* Communication: A Key to Understanding Japanese Interpersonal Relations." *Cross Currents, 11* (1), 49–58.

Ishii, S., and Klopf, D. W. (1976). "A Comparison of Communication Activities of Japanese and American Adults." *Eigo Tembo (ELEC Bulletin), 53,* 22–26.

Ishii, S., Klopf, D. W., and Cambra, R. E. (1979). "Oral Communication Apprehension Among Students in Japan, Korea and the United States." *Jijieigogaku Kenkyu (Current English Studies), 18,* 12–26.

Ishii, S., Klopf, D. W., and Cambra, R. E. (1984). "The Typical Japanese Student as an Oral Communicator: A Preliminary Profile." *Otsuma Review, 17,* 39–63.

Ishikawa, H. (1970). "Chinmoku-gata Wa Shusse Suru" ("The Silent Type Succeeds"). *Mainichi Shimbun.*

Jensen, V. J. (1973). "Communicative Functions of Silence." *ETC: A Review of General Semantics, 30,* 259–263.

Katayama, H. (1982). "Kotowaza Ni Hanei Sareta Nipponjin No Gengokan" ("Japanese Views of Language as Reflected in Proverbs"). *Kyoiku Kiyo 8-go (Eighth General Education Annual).* Matsudo, Chiba-ken: Matsudo Dental School, Nihon University, 1–11.

Mortensen, C. D., et al. (1977). "Measurement of Verbal Predispositions: Scale Development and Application." *Human Communication Research, 3,* 146–158.

Rader, M., and Wunsch, A. (1980). "A Survey of Communication Practices of Business School Graduates by Job Category and Undergraduate Major." *Journal of Business Communication, 17,* 33–41.

Samovar, L. A., Porter, R. E., and Jain, N. C. (1981). *Understanding Intercultural Communication.* Belmont, Calif.: Wadsworth.

Tsu, Lao (1972). *Tao Te Ching* (Transl. Gia-Fu-Feng and J. English). New York: Alfred A. Knopf.

Wayne, M. S. (1974). "The Meaning of Silence in Conversations in Three Cultures." In *Patterns of Communication In and Out of Japan* (International Christian University Communication Student Group, ed.). Tokyo: ICU Communication Department, 127–130.

Woodstock, B. (1979). "Characteristic Oral and Written Business Communication Problems of Selected Managerial Trainees." *Journal of Business Communication, 16,* 43–48.

Variables in the Use of Personal Space in Intercultural Transactions

CAROL ZINNER DOLPHIN

I. BACKGROUND

The concept of personal space has been the subject of numerous analogies. David Katz compared it to the shell of a snail. Stern developed the concept of a personal world. Von Uexkull used the graphic analogy of people "surrounded by soap bubble worlds" (Sommer, 1959). Hayduk (1983), on the other hand, suggests that the bubble is not a good analogy since it does not characterize the gradual acceptance of space intrusion under varying circumstances and prefers Sundstrom's (1976) alternate analogy, which compares personal space to an electrical field which is three dimensional, possesses force which decreases with distance, and has positive/negative signs to account for attraction and repulsion of certain bodies.

Forston (1968) defined *proxemics* as "the study of how man communicates through structuring microspace—the distance that man consciously maintains between himself and another person while relating physically to others with whom he is interacting" (p. 109). *Personal space* may be viewed as "the way in which individuals expect the immediate space around them to be used," translating the "more general interpersonal goals into spatial and behavioral terms . . ." (Liebman, 1970, p. 211). Personal space differs from *territory*, "an area con-

trolled by an individual, family or other face-to-face collectivity," principally by virtue of its mobility (Sommer, 1966, p. 59). Whereas territory tends to remain stable with somewhat definable boundaries, personal space is carried with the individual. "Personal space has the body as its center; territory does not" (Sommer, 1959, p. 247). Hall (1966) adds another dimension to the concept of proxemics by terming it "the interrelated observations and theories of man's use of space as a specialized elaboration of culture" (p. 1).

Edward Hall (1966) maintains that "it is in the nature of animals including man to exhibit behavior which we call territoriality. In doing so, they use the senses to distinguish between one space or distance and another" (p. 128). The anthropologist's formal observations of interpersonal transactions led him to propose a system of classifying the use of personal space. Subjects in Hall's United States sample (middle class adults, mainly natives of the northeastern seaboard) exhibited four distance zones, marked particularly by shifts in vocal volume. The intimate zone (contact to eighteen inches) usually is reserved for spouses, lovers and close friends, people engaged in lovemaking, comforting, nursing and conversations of a private nature. The personal zone (eighteen inches to four feet) includes activities such as chatting, gossiping, playing cards and casual interactions and is the territory of friends and acquaintances. Those whom one does not know well are often kept in the social zone (four to twelve feet), the domain of interviews, business transactions and professional exchanges. The public zone (beyond twelve feet) makes interpersonal communication nearly impossible and often denotes a status difference between the speaker and listener. "Spatial changes," writes Hall (1959, p. 204), "give a tone to a communication, accent it, and at times can even override the spoken word. The flow and shift of distance between people as they interact with each other is part and parcel of the communication process."

Emphasizing the impact of culture on communication behaviors, Hall specifies that the above distances are relevant only for those who fit into his sample category and notes that, in the United States

From *The Howard Journal of Communications*, Volume 1 (Spring 1988), 23–38. Reprinted by permission of the publisher. Professor Dolphin teaches at the University of Wisconsin Center, Waukesha County.

and Northern Europe, individuals are guided in their use of space according to their concept of a partner as a stranger or as a familiar. Other cultures demonstrate other patterns such as the family/non-family distinction in Portugal and Spain or the caste/outcaste system of India (Hall, 1966, p. 128).

It is in this vein that Hall (1963), based upon Heidiger's division of animals into contact and non-contact species, expands his theories in the use of personal space to identify differences between contact and noncontact cultures. It is hypothesized that people from contact cultures, i.e. Arabs, Southern Europeans and Latin Americans, will use closer distances, maintain more direct axes and eye contact, touch each other more frequently, and speak more loudly than those from noncontact cultures, i.e. Northern Europeans, Asians, Americans and Indians.

According to Hall, then, culture inevitably plays *the* definitive role in determining how different individuals use personal space. People from different cultures are seen as not only speaking different languages, but inhabiting different sensory worlds. "Selective screening of sensory data admits some things while filtering out others, so that experience as it is perceived through one set of culturally patterned sensory screens is quite different from experience perceived through another" (Hall, 1966, p. 2). Moreover, cultural conditioning is seen as difficult if not impossible to overcome. "Cultural irrationality," writes Hall in *Beyond Culture* (1976, p. 192), "is deeply entrenched in the lives of us, and because of culturally imposed blinders, our view of the world does not normally transcend the limits imposed by culture. We are, in effect, stuck with the program culture imposes." Giving support to Hall's earlier theories were experiments by Baltus (1974) which led him to characterize proxemic behavior as "culturally conditioned and entirely arbitrary . . . binding on all concerned" (p. 7).

Early support for Hall's hypotheses was provided in experiments conducted by Watson and Graves in 1966 and by Watson in 1970. The 1966 study, which observed proxemic distances in dyads of male Arab students (from a contact culture) and male American students (from a noncontact culture), concluded that Arab subjects sat closer to one another, faced each other more directly, maintained higher degrees of eye contact, touched each other more frequently, and were generally more involved with one another during interaction than the American students. Watson expanded his work in his 1970 study which included a greater number of students from a wider range of locations. Added to the original sample of only sixteen individuals were an additional one hundred and ten male students, all of whom were involved in pairs speaking their own native languages and were observed through a one-way glass. Contact cultures were represented primarily by subjects from Saudi Arabia, Latin America and Southern Europe, while those from Northern Europe, East Asia and India/Pakistan represented natives of noncontact cultures. Again, Hall's hypotheses were generally supported with there being no overlap in mean scores between contact and non-contact groups in the areas of directness of axis, frequency of touch, and maintenance of direct eye contact. A slight variance was noted in the use of proxemic distances where Indians/Pakistanis maintained a closer mean distance than all other groups except Arabs.

Other researchers, however, have not been as supportive of Hall's theories. Forston (1968) observed eight dyads of male Latin American students and eight dyads of male North American (United States) students, all of whom had been asked to work together to solve a problem. Contrary to Forston's expectations, the North Americans (noncontact culture) sat closer to one another than the Latin Americans (contact culture); no touch interaction occurred whatsoever except that of a single handshake between two North Americans. Similarly, studies conducted by Shuter (1977), Mazur (1977), and Sanders (1985), all cited later in this paper, produced results which raise serious questions about Hall's contact/noncontact theory and his view of culture as the primary factor in behavior, "the backdrop against which all other events are judged" (Hall, 1966, p. x).

In 1972, Madeline Schmitt proposed a theoretical network which identified culture as but one of five variables to predict social distance: (1) Social Identity (the identity of a particular individual and/or his/

her social role), (2) Status, (3) Cultural Distance (difference in values influenced by cultural variations), (4) Physical Distance (actual proximity and/or ecological position), and (5) Personal Distance (emotional differences and/or interpersonal closeness). Bochner (1982) believes that the determination of the "correct" distance in a relationship depends upon two things: the type of activity and the relationship of the individuals involved (p. 14). He proposes nine variables in the use of personal space, specifically considering cross-cultural contacts: (1) On whose territory the interaction occurs, (2) Time span of the contact, (3) Purpose of the meeting, (4) Type of involvement, (5) Frequency of contact, (6) Degree of intimacy, (7) Relative status and power, (8) Numerical balance, and (9) Visible distinguishing characteristics (such as race and sex). Significantly, Bochner suggests that a major difference may exist if the exchange is between two individuals from the same culture or if the individuals come from different cultures.

Finally, Canter (1975) cautions that the amount of space necessary in order for an individual to perform a certain task must be distinguished from the use of space by individuals in their daily transactions. It is the failure to separate these two concepts, he maintains, which have led some (notably Hall) to conclude that generalizations can be made about humans' spacial requirements across a sweeping cross-section of cultures (p. 132).

Hall, an anthropologist, has gone to some pains to point out the differences in the use of space between cultures. He rather confuses the argument by detailed categorizations of the spatial zones whilst still insisting that there are large cultural and, presumably, sub-cultural variations. Large individual differences combined with large sub-cultural variations could easily find two people using similar spatial distances in quite different ways. This makes the notion of tying distances to zones of space (or "proxemic behavior," as Hall calls it) quite inappropriate (p. 142).

The purpose of the remainder of this paper is not to disprove or to devalue the theories of Edward Hall, but rather to substantiate the claim that variables other than the broad scale categorization of a country into contact- or noncontact-oriented may play equally important roles in determining inhabitants' use of space. Furthermore, evidence will be offered which suggests that some of these variables do not rely to any extent whatsoever upon cultural conditioning but might be proposed as culture-general principles.

II. AGE AND SEX

Certainly the most obvious of these additional variables are those of the age and sex of the individuals involved in an interact. Of the two areas, age appears to be the more culture-general characteristic. Studies by both Baxter (1970) and Aiello and Jones (1971) indicate that the need for personal space increases with age. Both experiments were conducted by unobtrusively observing subjects in natural settings, and both found that children interacted the most proximally, adolescents at an intermediary distance, and adults at the greatest distance. Furthermore, Dean (1976) found that adults tend to respond more favorably to their space being invaded by smaller children, with a reduction of tolerance as the age of the uninvited visitor increases.

Pegán and Aiello (1982) observed 284 Puerto Rican children (138 males and 146 females) in grades one, six, and eleven in both New York City and Puerto Rico. In each location, a confederate who appeared to be a young teacher invited dyads of children to discuss their favorite television shows; each twenty seconds, she recorded the pair's distance and axis (shoulder orientation to one another). In both samples, older pairs used more space, with first graders using a mean distance of seven inches, sixth graders twelve inches, and eleventh graders twenty-four inches, thus moving out of Hall's "intimate" range into the close range of "personal" distance. It is important that both groups, whether in the United States or Puerto Rico, showed similar results; however, it is impossible to ascertain whether this was due primarily to the children's ages or familiar cultural environment.

Of more cultural significance, then, are the results of two studies done by Richard Lerner (1975 and 1976), who asked similar groups of kindergarten through third grade children in the United States and in Japan to illustrate comfortable interaction distances by the placement of figures on a flannel board. Despite cultural differences, the two groups yielded identical findings with mean distances between subjects increasing as the ages of the children increased. Additionally, Lerner determined that, beginning in the first grade, both male and female children used greater distances between opposite sex dyads than same sex dyads, illustrating the early influences of sex upon proxemic conditioning. Finally, children with endomorphic body types were given more surrounding space than either ectomorphs or mesomorphs, with males giving more space to endomorphs than females.

The observations of Heshka and Nelson (1972) focused on the behavior of adult dyads in an outdoor environment in London, England. Following each observation, which was also unobtrusively photographed, each individual was asked to fill out a brief questionnaire revealing his/her age and relationship to the other person. While Heshka and Nelson confirmed the hypothesis that distances are closer with young people and tend to increase, they have proposed that distance may vary in a curvilinear pattern, with spatial needs beginning to decrease at about age forty and continuing to decrease into old age.

Although the use of space by persons of certain ages appears to have some culture-general applications, the same can surely not be said about the sex variable. Use of personal space as influenced by the sex(es) of interacting individuals tends to differ dramatically from one culture to another. Whereas one culture may expect physical contact between males, in another it may be a taboo. While one country may expect females to maintain distances, the same behavior may be interpreted as coldness or disinterest in another. The examples which follow confirm two hypotheses: (1) Behavioral expectations for male/male, female/female, and male/female dyads differ according to the sex of the participants, and (2) These expectations are culture-specific but do not necessarily correspond to the contact or noncontact categorization of a culture.

For example, Jeffrey Sanders (1985) and his colleagues examined personal space zones by measuring distances maintained between 32 male and 32 female Arab students (a contact culture) and 32 male and 32 female American students (a noncontact culture). In the dyads, he varied the degree of relationship between the two participants as well as using both same sex and opposite sex pairs. Although Hall's theories would lead one to expect closer interactions between the Arabs than the Americans, the experimenters found very little difference between Arab males and Americans in general (male or female). Arab females, on the other hand, showed dramatic differences from the other three groups. Male friends were kept at a much farther distance than were female friends. For these females, the primary variable appeared to be sex, as male friends were kept nearly as far away as male strangers.

Studies conducted by Julian and Nancy Edney (1974) in the United States and by H. Smith (1981) in France and Germany examined crowding patterns on the beaches in these countries. Although the personal space needs were less for the French (a contact culture) than for the Germans and Americans (noncontact cultures) and thus confirmed Hall's hypothesis, similar variations were noted in all three cultures according to sex. Larger groups, mixed sex groups, and females tended to claim less space per person than small groups and males. In general, lone females used less space than lone males; similarly they used less space within their groups, placing themselves closer to other female groups than to male groups. These results are consistent with Smith's suggestion that "cross national commonalities in territorial patterns are more important than within cultural variations" (Smith, p. 132).

Curt and Nine (1983) noted that in Puerto Rico (a contact culture), people of the same sex and age touch a great deal and stand quite close together; whereas, people of the opposite sex and age do not touch at all and tend to stand farther apart than Americans do. Upon closer observation, Curt and Nine realized that, in closer male/female relationships, women may touch the males; however the men do not reciprocate. On the other hand, females

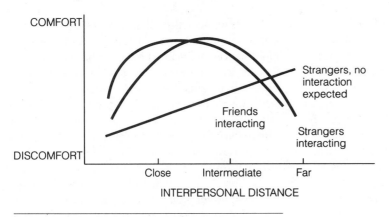

Figure 1 Sundstrom and Altman (1976, p. 61)

tend to avoid direct eye contact with males, with many Puerto Rican wives never looking directly at their husbands.

Latin Americans from three contact nations—Costa Rica, Panama and Colombia—were observed by Robert Shuter (1976) to note their proxemic angles toward one another, their proxemic distances, and their frequency of physical contact (touch). Shuter found that the mean axis score and the mean distance for Costa Ricans were significantly smaller than for those of Panamanians and Colombians; similarly, a greater number of Costa Ricans touched each other than did the two other cultures. Shuter's results indicate that the directness of interactions diminishes as one travels from Central to South America, despite the classification of all three as contact cultures. Across all three cultures, however, females tend to relate most directly, followed by male/female dyads, and, finally, by males. Accordingly, the mean distance score for females was considerably smaller than for male/female or male/male dyads—regardless of culture. Finally, in each of the three countries, female/female dyads were the most likely to make physical contact, followed by male/male and male/female in Costa Rica and Colombia (where 0% of the male/female pairs exhibited touch) and male/female, male/male in Panama.

Shuter (1977) conducted a similar study by observing interactions in Venice Mastre, Italy, Heidelberg, Germany, and Milwaukee, Wisconsin, to determine if sex and/or culture have an impact on distance, axis orientation and/or contact. Contrary to Hall's theories, Shuter's data suggest that a single culture may be both contact and noncontact oriented. For example, Italians, normally viewed as contact oriented, exhibited the greatest amount of tactility in male/male dyads; however, in male/female and female/female groupings, they did not differ significantly from the Germans (a noncontact culture). Furthermore, although male/male pairs exhibited a more active contact pattern, Italian males did not converse more closely nor more directly than the non-touching German male. Additionally, American females were as tactile as Italian women, while both were surpassed by the German female.

Based on this research, Shuter (1977) seriously questioned the validity of Hall's hypothesis:

Contrary to Hall's position, it appears that each of the cultures examined is so diverse that it cannot be classified as strictly contact or noncontact oriented. In fact, sex pairs within Germany, Italy and the United States displayed such a wide range of distance, axis, and tactile behaviors that gender-

free culture statements could not be advanced on any tested variable. Unsurprisingly, when sex pair behavior is compared across the three cultures, the limitation of Hall's categories is dramatically revealed (p. 304).

Upon an examination of even a limited number of contact and noncontact cultures, it is apparent that male/male, female/female, and male/female dyads most often respond differently within a single culture and that these patterns often vary from culture to culture. A recent experiment by Lombardo (1986) introduced yet another confounding factor, namely the influence of sex role (orientation toward androgyny) upon American males and females in their use of space. His results led Lombardo to propose that sex roles, as well as sex itself, may have an impact over how an individual uses space and his or her perception of space needs and space invasion. Clearly, it is impossible to make culture-general statements about "typical" behaviors when referring to the variable of sex.

III. RELATIONSHIPS AND ENVIRONMENT

Other than culture, age and sex, the interaction distance between two individuals can be affected by a host of other variables: relationship between the two, the environment of the transaction, attitudinal differences, occupation and/or status, the language used, etc. Of these, the first two, relationship and environment, will be considered in more detail.

In the presentation of his theory of the four distance zones, Hall (1966) notes that "how people are feeling toward each other at the time (of a meeting) is a decisive factor in the distance used" (p. 114). Yet, Hall effectively eliminates this consideration of relationships in his intercultural work. A theoretical model of personal space and interpersonal relationships, developed by Sundstrom and Altman (1976), follows three assumptions: that people seek an optimal distance for each interaction, that discomfort results from interaction outside of the optimal range (too close or too far) and that the optimal zone, as well as reactions to violations, will depend

upon the interpersonal situation. Their model (Figure 1) diagrams levels of comfort/discomfort in distances, based upon interactions with friends, strangers, and strangers where no interaction is anticipated, indicating that the highest degree of comfort at close distances occurs with friends interacting. The studies cited below support this model and suggest the basis for a culture-general hypothesis concerning the variable of relationship.

In 1968, Little studied social interaction distances by asking individuals from five countries (United States, Sweden, Scotland—noncontact cultures—and Greece and Southern Italy—contact cultures) to place figures of their own sex on a flannel board to represent various communication situations. Although Hall's contact/noncontact culture theory was supported, there was a general tendency across cultures for subjects to indicate closer proxemic distances as the indicated relationship became closer and the subjects more pleasant, leading Little to conclude that "the major single factor determining distances in dyadic schemata appears to be the relationship between the members, with the specific content or affective tone of the transaction as next important" (Little, p. 1). Identical results were noted by Watson (1970, also cited in Part I) who observed male college students from the noncontact cultures of North America, East Asia, India, Pakistan, and Northern Europe and the contact cultures of the Middle East, Latin America and Southern Europe. In Watson's expansive study, the rankings of cultural groups on interpersonal distance (far to near) was nearly identical to their rankings on average intensity of friendships within the pairs. That is, the more friendly the pairs representing a given culture, the closer their average interpersonal distance, regardless of culture. In a study cited earlier, Heshka and Nelson (1972) found that, in London, strangers, particularly females, stood farther apart than friends.

Lomranz (1976) tested three groups of sixteen to seventeen year old male sojourners (Argentineans, Iraqis, and Russians) who had lived in Israel for approximately one year. He found that proxemic distance in all three cultures varied along a continuum toward progressive greater distances as the level of friendship declined. Significantly, in dealing with a close friend, only a small variance was noted across these three very distinct cultures, a fact which did not hold true for meetings with strangers. A later study by Carolyn and E. Gregory Keating (1980) in yet another culture documented the behavioral pattern of dyads on park benches in Nairobi, Kenya. In this African culture also, the Keatings observed that those who appeared to be acquainted (spoke to each other, approached or left together) sat closer together than strangers.

Acceptable spatial distances may also vary according to the environment of a given interaction, as well as to people's (probably) cultural perception of crowding and privacy. Moreover, their use of space and tolerance for crowding may not be at all related to the concept of contact and noncontact cultures. Studies done by Robert Sommer as early as 1962 illustrate that the proxemic distances chosen by individuals may vary according to the placement of furniture, the specific setting (such as a living room or an office), and the size of the space. In the latter situation, Sommer (1962) determined that people feel more comfortable sitting at closer distances in a large room than in an intimate setting. Nasar and his colleagues (1984) further hypothesized that feelings of crowding may be affected by the amount of light available in a room. An experiment conducted by Mazur (1977), in which he observed the spacing of male strangers on park benches in the United States, Spain, and Morocco, led him to offer an alternate hypothesis to Hall's: "Under a given set of physical constraints (e.g. bench length, room dimensions, number of people per square yard, etc.), the spacing pattern of noninteracting strangers is similar across cultures" (p. 58).

On the other hand, culturally influenced privacy needs may complicate the establishment of such culture-general rules. "In the strictest sense," writes Canter (1975, p. 139), "privacy may be seen as the establishing of a physical and/or psychological barrier against the world." In Western societies, the need for privacy may take the form of territoriality and/or the setting up of physical barricades against others, thus creating the sense of aloneness. In East-

ern societies, however, the feeling of privacy may be reached even in a crowded room, as the individual simply retreats into him or herself. Neither the Arabs (a contact culture) nor the Japanese (a noncontact culture) have a word for "privacy" as we understand it in their languages. In public situations, both groups demonstrate a tolerance for crowding, pushing, and close proximity which is uncomfortable to the American. The homes of both peoples tend to be open and flexible, emphasizing a need to be with one another. (Arab homes are usually constructed without specific room dividers; whereas Japanese walls are flexible, and activity in the center of the space is emphasized.) In the use of personal interaction distance, on the other hand, the two cultures differ significantly with the Arab approaching close enough to smell the partner's breath, while maintaining direct eye contact, and the Japanese adopting a much more distant position with averted eyes.

Condon and Yousef (1975) offer a warning about careless attempts to categorize and predict nonverbal behaviors based on overly simplistic categorizations:

. . . one wonders, however, if it might be possible to anticipate relations between proxemic behavior and other cultural patterns of communication before completing detailed proxemic descriptions of many different societies. For example, are there likely to be some common value orientations among cultures which are characterized by frequent physical contact . . . ? Do relatively noncontact cultures reveal different value orientations? Or is there no more connection between values and the sound system of the language spoken in any given culture? . . . Perhaps the best we can do at this point is to warn of pushing analogies too far and point out that many codes of nonverbal interaction cannot be treated adequately by analogies to other forms of behavior (p. 141).

IV. ETHNICITY

The characteristics of age, sex, relationships, and environment can be seen as universal variables, possibly influenced by, but not dependent upon, a particular culture. The final aspect of this paper, on the other hand, focuses on an aspect of culture, namely ethnicity, which may supercede the categorization of a country or geographical area as a contact or noncontact culture. For example, will a group of Japanese Italian citizens living in a predominantly Japanese extended family group in Italy be more influenced by their ethnic background (the noncontact Japanese) than by the geographical area (the contact Italian) in which they live? This concept has particularly sweeping implications for countries such as the United States which, despite its "melting pot" composition, has been described as a noncontact culture by Hall.

In his description of the four spatial distances (public, social, personal, and intimate), Hall (1966) carefully explains the limitations of his sample:

It should be emphasized that these generalizations are not representative of human behavior in general—or even of American behavior in general—but only of the group included in the sample. Negroes and Spanish Americans as well as persons who come from southern European cultures have very different proxemic patterns (Hall, 1966, p. 116).

Interestingly, the anthropologist has had considerable experience in working with the Native Americans of United States Southwest, whom he often identifies as unique in their conceptualizations and use of time (1976, 1983). It is particularly ironic, then, that, in his writings about contact and noncontact cultures, Hall appears to adopt but two molds into which countries of the world must fit, apparently overlooking the multitude of co-cultures and subcultures which exist in most geographical areas.

Even more importantly, most researchers have been painstakingly cautious in separating contact culture and noncontact culture subjects. Studies and anecdotes abound which portray the classic behavioral patterns when two Arabs meet or when two Japanese converse. It is apparently assumed that, by studying such isolated examples, the individual from another culture can internalize and adapt to the use of personal space in countries other than his/her own. What is sorely lacking in intercultural research are experiments and observations which survey the results of interactions between individuals from two different cultures or from two co-cultures within the same country. If age, sex, and a host of other variables can affect an interaction, it stands to reason that the presence of two cultures or co-cultures interacting side-by-side may carry an even greater impact. Studies of different ethnic groups within a single country, most notably blacks and whites in the United States, imply support of this hypothesis.

As early as 1970, Baxter noted differences for personal space needs in Hispanic-American, White-American, and Black-American children, with mixed race dyads exhibiting greater distances than any single-race pairs. In studies of black and white children, Severy (1979) determined that, by age seven, black children require less personal space than white children, with mixed sex dyads needing more space than same sex dyads. Somewhat paradoxically, through observations of fifth grade boys at play, Zimmerman (1975) noted that black boys talked to each other significantly less, faced each other less directly and interacted at greater distances than white boys. Racially mixed dyads appeared to attempt to adjust to each other's needs and interacted at an intermediate distance.

Based on Hall's contact/noncontact culture theory, Aiello and Jones (1971) observed 210 same sex (male/male, female/female) first and second grade dyads from three diverse New York City subcultures: blacks, whites, and Puerto Ricans; they hypothesized that blacks and Puerto Ricans would interact at closer distances than the white children. In this study, in contrast to that of Zimmerman, the hypothesis was confirmed with whites maintaining distances nearly twice that of blacks and Puerto Ricans. An additional correlation was found, however, between distance and sex of the dyad. Both Puerto Rican and white female/female dyads stood closer than male/male dyads, with the opposite being true of blacks. Additionally, the axis orientation of white children was more direct than that of blacks or Puerto Ricans, with the latter being the least direct.

Across cultures, males tended to face their partners more directly than females. In a similar vein, Jones (1971) found that Chinese in New York City interacted at greater distances than either Puerto Ricans or Italians.

Perhaps related to their comfortability with closer proximities, there is also some indication that blacks will more readily invade the personal space of another black than will whites intrude upon the personal space of another individual of either race. When Bauer (1973) instructed blacks and whites to approach a same sex/same race confederate "as close as comfortable," white males chose the farthest distance, followed by white females, black males, and black females. An experiment by William Dick (1976) netted similar results. Four male confederates (two blacks, aged 20 and 30 years, and two whites, aged 20 and 30 years) were positioned individually on a university campus in front of a bubble gum machine so that subjects would need to invade their space in order to turn the knob to receive free gum. Significantly more black subjects invaded the space of the black confederates. Females tended to be more cautious than males, indicating that both race and sex influenced the subject's decision to "invade space."

Although conducted in the unlaboratory-like setting of the New York subway, the work of David Maines (1977) makes a unique contribution in his observation of mixed sex/mixed race dyads. In observing the elbow placement of individuals, either to the side or out to the front, Maines discovered that there was a general tendency for individuals to locate their elbows to their sides in noncrowded conditions and to the front in more crowded contexts. Movement to the front was particularly significant in mixed race and mixed sex dyads where individuals are apparently more reluctant to actually touch another person. A similar pattern was noticed in observing the physical contact patterns of the hands of passengers sharing a "balance strap." In these situations, there was an especially noticeable pattern of avoidance in the case of mixed race/same sex groupings. While Maines' observations did not include verbal interactions, his results are impor-

tant in suggesting further implications for mixed ethnic pairings. Unfortunately, studies of mixed race or mixed subculture groups in other cultures are difficult to locate.

A final significant contribution is that of Sussman and Rosenfeld (1982) who looked at the influence of culture and language on conversational distance. The researchers hypothesized that theories for contact/noncontact societies hold true primarily in same-culture interactions in which individuals speak in their native tongues and that, correspondingly, adopting the use of another language serves to create a distance which is evidenced through proxemics. Observations of Japanese, Venezuelan, and American student dyads substantiated their hypothesis, with all three groups maintaining further distances when speaking a foreign tongue than when using their native language. Although this study used dyads of individuals from the same culture, hypotheses might be suggested about the potential implications for interactions in mixed-culture pairs with differing native tongues.

V. CONCLUSIONS

The research in this paper holds suggestions for further study in the use of space in several different areas:

Can culture-general hypotheses for the following be substantiated?

• A curvilinear pattern of proxemic distances according to age

• A continuum of progressively smaller distances as relationships move from that of stranger to that of close friend

Can culture-specific theories for the following be generated?

• Interaction differences between male/male, female/female, and male/female dyads in different cultures

• The impact of environment and the perceptions of crowding and privacy in different cultures

Can (and should) Hall's theory of contact/non-contact cultures be redefined and refined?

More significantly, however, this research indicates a serious gap in the study of "intercultural" proxemics; indeed, there appears to be very little work with a truly intercultural focus being done. While anecdotal accounts are sometimes cited to explain the "East Meets West" phenomenon, I was unable to locate a single example of a study which used a scientific approach to examine interaction behaviors between individuals from different cultures. Only one (the Maines subway study) even touched upon United States patterns in racially mixed pairs. The experiments and hypotheses to date, then, have been based nearly totally on intracultural or, at best, cross-cultural studies. Some of the areas which might be probed are the following:

• Can any hypotheses be substantiated for intercultural interactions based upon contact/noncontact, noncontact/noncontact, contact/contact dyads?

• Can any hypotheses be substantiated in terms of the distance control factor for the host or the sojourner?

• Can any hypotheses be substantiated about the distance behaviors of two sojourners from different cultures interacting in a third culture?

• Can any hypotheses be substantiated about the impact of language choice in a transaction? Is there a correlation between use of the native tongue and the distance control factor?

• In any of the above cases, how might the sex, sex roles, age, relationship, status and ethnicity of the individuals influence the interaction patterns?

"Proxemics research" admits Edward Hall (1976, p. 86), "requires an inordinate amount of time." Because of the many variables present, he says, few studies have been done which examine its impact. In his first book, *The Silent Language* (1959), Hall offers this simplistic advice to the sojourner: "Watch where people stand and don't back up." In this world of multinational companies and jet travel, however, we cannot afford to be so easily placated.

REFERENCES

Aiello, J. R. and S. E. Jones (1971). Field study of proxemic behavior of young school children in three subcultural groups. *Journal of Personality and Social Psychology*, **19**: 351–356.

Baltus, D. (1974). Proxemics. Conference paper.

Bauer, E. A. (1973). Personal space: A study of blacks and whites. *Sociometry*, **36**(3): 402–408.

Baxter, J. (1970). Interpersonal spacing in natural settings. *Sociometry*, **33**(4): 444–456.

Birdwhistell, R. (1970). *Kinesics and Context: Essays on Body Motion Communication*. Philadelphia: University of Pennsylvania Press.

Bochner, S. (1982). The social psychology of cross-cultural relations. In S. Bochner (Ed.) *Cultures in Contact*. New York: Pergamon Press: 5–44.

Canter, D., *et al.* (1975). *Environmental Interactions: Psychological Approaches to Our Physical Surroundings*. London: Surrey Press.

Condon, J. C. and F. Yousef (1975). *An Introduction to Intercultural Communication*. Indianapolis: Bobbs-Merrill.

Curt, C. and J. Nine (1983). Hispanic-Anglo conflicts in nonverbal communication. In Isidora Albino (Ed.) *Perspectives Pedagogicas*. San Juan, Puerto Rico: Universidad de Puerto Rico.

Dean, L. M., F. N. Willis, and J. N. la Rocco (1976). Invasion of personal space as a function of age, sex and race. *Psychological Reports*, **38**(3)(pt.1): 959–965.

Dick, W. E. (1976). Invasion of personal space as function of age and race. *Psychological Reports*, **39**(1): 281–282.

Edney, J. and N. Jordon-Edney (1974). Territorial spacing on a bench. *Sociometry*, **37**(1): 92–104.

Edwards, D. J. (1980). Perception of crowding and tolerance of interpersonal proxemics and separation in South Africa. *Journal of Social Psychology*, **110**(1): 19–28.

Engebretson, D. and D. Fullmer (1970). Cross-cultural differences in territoriality. *Journal of Cross-Cultural Psychology*, **1**: 261–269.

Evans, G. W. (1978). Human spatial behavior: The arousal model. In Andrew Baum and Yakov M. Epstein (Eds.) *Human Response to Crowding*. N.J.: Erlbaum Associates.

Felipe, N. J. and R. Sommer (1966). Invasions of personal space. *Social Problems*, **14**: 206–214.

Forston, R. and C. Larson (1968). The dynamics of space. An experimental study in proxemic behavior among Latin Americans and North Americans. *Journal of Communication*, **18**: 109–116.

Goffman, E. (1971). *Relations in Public*. New York: Basic Books.

Hall, E. T. (1959). *The Silent Language*. New York: Doubleday.

Hall, E. T. (1960). The silent language in overseas business. *Harvard Business Review*, **38**(3): 87–96.

Hall, E. T. (1963). A system for the notation of proxemic behavior. *American Anthropologist*, **65**: 1003–1026.

Hall, E. T. (1964). Silent assumptions in social communication. *Disorders of Communication*, **42**: 41–55.

Hall, E. T. (1966). *The Hidden Dimension*. New York: Doubleday.

Hall, E. T. (1976). *Beyond Culture*. New York: Anchor Press.

Hall, E. T. (1983). *Dance of Life*. New York: Doubleday.

Hayduk, L. A. (1983). Personal space: Where we now stand. *Psychological Bulletin*, **94**: 293–335.

Heaton, J. (1978). Teaching culture as a second language. Private culture and kinesics. University of California, Los Angeles: Research Report.

Heshka, S. and Y. Nelson (1972). Interpersonal speaking distances as a function of age, sex, and relationship. *Sociometry*, **35**(4): 491–498.

Jensen, J. V. (1972). Perspectives on nonverbal intercultural communication. In Larry A. Samovar and Richard E. Porter (Eds.) *Intercultural Communication: A Reader*. Belmont, Calif.: Wadsworth.

Jones, S. E. (1971). A comparative proxemics analysis of dyadic interaction in selected subcultures of New York City. *Journal of Social Psychology*, **84**: 35–44.

Keating, C. E. and E. G. Keating (1980). Distance between pairs of acquaintances and strangers on public beaches in Nairobi, Kenya. *Journal on Social Psychology*, **110**(2): 285–286.

Kinloch, G. C. (1973). Race, socio-economic status and social distance in Hawaii. *Sociology and Social Research*, **57**(2): 156–167.

Lerner, R. M., *et al.* (1975). Effects of age and sex on the development of personal space schemata toward body build. *Journal of Genetic Psychology*, **127**: 91–101.

Lerner, R. M., *et al.* (1976). Development of personal space schemata among Japanese children. *Developmental Psychology*, **15**(5): 466–467.

Liebman, M. (1970). The effects of sex and race norms on personal space. *Environmental Behavior*, **2**: 208–246.

Little, K. B. (1968). Cultural variations in social schemata. *Journal of Personality and Social Psychology*, **10**(1): 1–7.

Lombardo, J. P. (1986). Interaction of sex and sex role in response to violations of preferred seating arrangements. *Sex Roles*, **15**: 173–183.

Lomranz, J. (1976). Cultural variations in personal space. *Journal of Social Psychology*, **99**(1): 21–27.

Maines, D. R. (1977). Tactile relationships in the subway as affected by racial, sexual and crowded seated situations. *Environmental Psychology and Nonverbal Behavior*, **2**(2): 100–108.

Mazur, A. (1977). Interpersonal spacing on public benches in contact vs. noncontact cultures. *Journal of Social Psychology*, **101**: 53–58.

Nasar, J. L., *et al.* (1984). Modifiers of perceived spaciousness and crowding among different cultural groups. Research report, November.

Noesjirwan, J. (1978). A laboratory study of proxemic patterns in Indonesians and Australians. *Journal of Social and Chemical Psychology*, **17**(4):333–334.

Pegán, G. and J. R. Aiello (1982). Development of personal space among Puerto Ricans. *Journal of Nonverbal Behavior*, **7**(2): 59–68.

Sanders, J., *et al.* (1985). Personal space amongst Arabs and Americans. *International Journal of Psychology*, **20**(1): 13–17.

Schmitt, M. H. (1972): Near and Far: A re-formulation of the social distance concept. *Sociology and Social Research*, **57**(1): 85--97.

Severy, L. J., *et al.* (1979). A multimethod assessment of personal space development in female and male, black and white children. *Journal of Nonverbal Behavior*, **4**(2): 68–86.

Shuter, R. (1976). Nonverbal communication: Proxemics and tactility in Latin America. *Journal of Communication*, **26**(3): 46–52.

Shuter, R. (1977). A field study of nonverbal communication in Germany, Italy and the United States. *Communication Monographs*, **44**(4): 298–305.

Singer, M. R. (1987). *Intercultural Communication: A Perceptual Approach.* N.J.: Prentice-Hall.

Six, B., *et al.* (1983). A cultural comparison of perceived crowding and discomfort: The United States and West Germany. *Journal of Psychology*, **114**(1): 63–67.

Smith, A. G. (Ed.) (1966). *Communication and Culture: Readings in the Codes of Human Interaction.* New York: Holt, Rinehart and Winston.

Smith, H. (1981). Territorial spacing on a beach revisited: A crossnational exploration. *Social Psychology Quarterly*, **44**: 132–137.

Sommer, R. (1959). Studies in personal space. *Sociometry*, **22**: 247–260.

Sommer, R. (1962). The distance for comfortable conversation: A further study. *Sociometry*, **25**: 111–125.

Sommer, R. (1966). Man's proximate environment. *Journal of Social Issues*, **22**(4): 59–70.

Sommer, R. (1969). *Personal Space.* N.J.: Prentice-Hall.

Sommer, R. and F. D. Becker, Territorial defense and the good neighbor. *Journal of Personality and Social Psychology*, **11**: 85–92.

Speelman, D. and C. D. Hoffman (1980). Personal space assessment of the development of racial attitudes in integrated and segregated schools. *Journal of Genetic Psychology*, **136**(2): 307–308.

Sundstrom, E. and I. Altman (1976). Interpersonal relationships and personal space: Research review and theoretical model. *Human Ecology*, **4**: 46–67.

Sussman, N. and H. M. Rosenfeld (1982). Influence of culture, language and sex on conversational distance. *Journal of Personality and Social Psychology*, **42**(1): 66–74.

Thayer, S. and L. Alban. A field experiment on the effect of political and cultural factors in the use of personal space. *Journal of Social Psychology*, **88**(2): 267–272.

Watson, O. M. (1970). *Proxemic Behavior: A Cross-Cultural Study.* The Hague: Mouton.

Watson, O. M. and T. D. Graves (1966). Quantitative research in proxemic behavior. *American Anthropologist*, **68**: 971–985.

Wysocki, B., Jr. (1986). Closed society: Despite global role, many Japanese try to avoid foreigners. *Wall Street Journal*, **68**(23): 1, 18.

Yousef, F. S. (1974). Cross-cultural communication aspects of contrastive social values between North Americans and Middle Easterners. *Human Organization*, **33**(4): 383–387.

Zimmerman, B. and G. H. Brody (1975). Race and modeling influence in the interpersonal play pattern for boys. *Journal of Educational Psychology*, **67**(5): 591–598.

Monochronic and Polychronic Time

EDWARD T. HALL

Lorenzo Hubbell, trader to the Navajo and the Hopi, was three quarters Spanish and one quarter New Englander, but culturally he was Spanish to the core. Seeing him for the first time on government business transactions relating to my work in the 1930s, I felt embarrassed and a little shy because he didn't have a regular office where people could talk in private. Instead, there was a large corner room—part of his house adjoining the trading post—in which business took place. Business covered everything from visits with officials and friends, conferences with Indians who had come to see him, who also most often needed to borrow money or make sheep deals, as well as a hundred or more routine transactions with store clerks and Indians who had not come to see Lorenzo specifically but only to trade. There were long-distance telephone calls to his warehouse in Winslow, Arizona, with cattle buyers, and his brother, Roman, at Ganado, Arizona—all this and more (some of it quite personal), carried on in public, in front of our small world for all to see and hear. If you wanted to learn about the life of an Indian trader or the ins and outs of running a small trading empire (Lorenzo had a dozen posts scattered throughout northern Arizona), all you had to do was to sit in Lorenzo's office for a month or so and take note of what was going on. Eventually all the different parts of the pattern would unfold before your eyes, as eventually they did before mine, as I lived and worked on that reservation over a five-year period.

I was prepared for the fact that the Indians do things differently from AE cultures because I had spent part of my childhood on the Upper Rio Grande River with the Pueblo Indians as friends. Such differences were taken for granted. But this public, everything-at-once, mélange way of conducting business made an impression on me. There was no escaping it, here was another world, but in this instance, although both Spanish and Anglos had their roots firmly planted in European soil, each handled time in radically different ways.

It didn't take long for me to accustom myself to Lorenzo's business ambiance. There was so much going on that I could hardly tear myself away. My own work schedule won out, of course, but I did find that the Hubbell store had a pull like a strong magnet, and I never missed an opportunity to visit with Lorenzo. After driving through Oraibi, I would pull up next to his store, park my pickup, and go through the side door to the office. These visits were absolutely necessary because without news of what was going on life could become precarious. Lorenzo's desert "salon" was better than a newspaper, which, incidentally, we lacked.

Having been initiated to Lorenzo's way of doing business, I later began to notice similar mutual involvement in events among the New Mexico Spanish. I also observed the same patterns in Latin America, as well as in the Arab world. Watching my countrymen's reactions to this "many things at a time" system I noted how deeply it affected the channeling and flow of information, the shape and form of the networks connecting people, and a host of other important social and cultural features of the society. I realized that there was more to this culture pattern than one might at first suppose.

Years of exposure to other cultures demonstrated that complex societies organize time in at least two different ways: events scheduled as separate items—one thing at a time—as in North Europe, or following the Mediterranean model of

From Edward T. Hall, *The Dance of Life: The Other Dimension of Time* (New York: Doubleday and Company, 1983), pp. 41–54. Copyright © 1983 by Edward T. Hall. Used by permission of Doubleday, a division of Bantam, Doubleday, Dell Publishing Group, Inc.

involvement in several things at once. The two systems are logically and empirically quite distinct. Like oil and water, they don't mix. Each has its strengths as well as its weaknesses. I have termed doing many things at once: Polychronic, P-time. The North European system—doing one thing at a time—is Monochronic, M-time. P-time stresses involvement of people and completion of transactions rather than adherence to preset schedules. Appointments are not taken as seriously and, as a consequence, are frequently broken. P-time is treated as less tangible than M-time. For polychronic people, time is seldom experienced as "wasted," and is apt to be considered a point rather than a ribbon or a road, but that point is often sacred. An Arab will say, "I will see you before one hour," or "I will see you after two days." What he means in the first instance is that it will not be longer than an hour before he sees you, and at least two days in the second instance. These commitments are taken quite seriously as long as one remains in the P-time pattern.

Once, in the early '60s, when I was in Patras, Greece, which is in the middle of the P-time belt, my own time system was thrown in my face under rather ridiculous but still amusing circumstances. An impatient Greek hotel clerk, anxious to get me and my ménage settled in some quarters which were far from first-class, was pushing me to make a commitment so he could continue with his siesta. I couldn't decide whether to accept this rather forlorn "bird in the hand" or take a chance on another hotel that looked, if possible, even less inviting. Out of the blue, the clerk blurted, "Make up your mind. After all, time is money!" How would you reply to that at a time of day when literally nothing was happening? I couldn't help but laugh at the incongruity of it all. If there ever was a case of time not being money, it was in Patras during siesta in the summer.

Though M-time cultures tend to make a fetish out of management, there are points at which M-time doesn't make as much sense as it might. Life in general is at times unpredictable; and who can tell exactly how long a particular client, patient, or set of transactions will take. These are imponderables in the chemistry of human transactions. What can be

accomplished one day in ten minutes, may take twenty minutes on the next. Some days people will be rushed and can't finish; on others, there is time to spare, so they "waste" the remaining time.

In Latin America and the Middle East, North Americans can frequently be psychologically stressed. Immersed in a polychronic environment in the markets, stores, and souks of Mediterranean and Arab countries, one is surrounded by other customers all vying for the attention of a single clerk who is trying to wait on everyone at once. There is no recognized order as to who is to be served next, no queue or numbers to indicate who has been waiting the longest. To the North European or American, it appears that confusion and clamor abound. In a different context, the same patterns can be seen operating in the governmental bureaucracies of Mediterranean countries: a typical office layout for important officials frequently includes a large reception area (an ornate version of Lorenzo Hubbell's office), outside the private suite, where small groups of people can wait and be visited by the minister or his aides. These functionaries do most of their business outside in this semipublic setting, moving from group to group conferring with each in turn. The semiprivate transactions take less time, give others the feeling that they are in the presence of the minister as well as other important people with whom they may also want to confer. Once one is used to this pattern, it is clear that there are advantages which frequently outweigh the disadvantages of a series of private meetings in the inner office.

Particularly distressing to Americans is the way in which appointments are handled by polychronic people. Being on time simply doesn't mean the same thing as it does in the United States. Matters in a polychronic culture seem in a constant state of flux. Nothing is solid or firm, particularly plans for the future; even important plans may be changed right up to the minute of execution.

In contrast, people in the Western world find little in life exempt from the iron hand of M-time. Time is so thoroughly woven into the fabric of existence that we are hardly aware of the degree to which it determines and coordinates everything we do, including the molding of relations with others in many subtle ways. In fact, social and business life, even one's sex life, is commonly schedule-dominated. By scheduling, we compartmentalize; this makes it possible to concentrate on one thing at a time, but it also reduces the context. Since scheduling by its very nature selects what will and will not be perceived and attended, and permits only a limited number of events within a given period, what gets scheduled constitutes a system for setting priorities for both people and functions. Important things are taken up first and allotted the most time; unimportant things are left to last or omitted if time runs out.

M-time is also tangible; we speak of it as being saved, spent, wasted, lost, made up, crawling, killed, and running out. These metaphors must be taken seriously. M-time scheduling is used as a classification system that orders life. The rules apply to everything except birth and death. It should be mentioned, that without schedules or something similar to the M-time system, it is doubtful that our industrial civilization could have developed as it has. There are other consequences. Monochronic time seals off one or two people from the group and intensifies relationships with one other person or, at most, two or three people. M-time in this sense is like a room with a closed door ensuring privacy. The only problem is that you must vacate the "room" at the end of the allotted fifteen minutes or an hour, a day, or a week, depending on the schedule, and make way for the next person in line. Failure to make way by intruding on the time of the next person is not only a sign of extreme egocentrism and narcissism, but just plain bad manners.

Monochronic time is arbitrary and imposed, that is, learned. Because it is so thoroughly learned and so thoroughly integrated into our culture, it is treated as though it were the only natural and logical way of organizing life. Yet, it is *not* inherent in man's biological rhythms or his creative drives, nor is it existential in nature.

Schedules can and frequently do cut things short just when they are beginning to go well. For example, research funds run out just as the results are beginning to be achieved. How often has the reader had the experience of realizing that he is pleasurably immersed in some creative activity, totally unaware of time, solely conscious of the job at hand, only to be brought back to "reality" with the rude shock of realizing that other, frequently inconsequential previous commitments are bearing down on him?

Some Americans associate schedules with reality, but M-time can alienate us from ourselves and from others by reducing context. It subtly influences how we think and perceive the world in segmented compartments. This is convenient in linear operations but disastrous in its effect on nonlinear creative tasks. Latino peoples are an example of the opposite. In Latin America, the intelligentsia and the academicians frequently participate in several fields at once—fields which the average North American academician, business, or professional person thinks of as antithetical. Business, philosophy, medicine, and poetry, for example, are common, well-respected combinations.

Polychronic people, such as the Arabs and Turks, who are almost never alone, even in the home, make very different uses of "screening" than Europeans do. They interact with several people at once and are continually involved with each other. Tight scheduling is therefore difficult, if not impossible.

Theoretically, when considering social organization, P-time systems should demand a much greater centralization of control and be characterized by a rather shallow or simple structure. This is because the leader deals continually with many people, most of whom stay informed as to what is happening. The Arab fellah can always see his sheik. There are no intermediaries between man and sheik or between man and God. The flow of information as well as people's need to stay informed complement each other. Polychronic people are so deeply immersed in each other's business that they feel a compulsion to keep in touch. Any stray scrap of a story is gathered in and stored away. Their knowledge of each other is truly extraordinary. Their involvement in people is the very core of their existence. This has bureaucratic implications. For example, delegation of authority and a buildup in bureaucratic levels are not required to handle high volumes of business. The principal shortcoming of P-type bureaucracies is that as functions increase, there is a proliferation of small bureaucracies that really are not set up to handle the problems of outsiders. In fact, outsiders traveling or residing in Latin American or Mediterranean countries find the bureaucracies unusually cumbersome and unresponsive. In polychronic countries, one has to be an insider or have a "friend" who can make things happen. All bureaucracies are oriented inward, but P-type bureaucracies are especially so.

There are also interesting points to be made concerning the act of administration as it is conceived in these two settings. Administration and control of polychronic peoples in the Middle East and Latin America is a matter of job analysis. Administration consists of taking each subordinate's job and identifying the activities that go to make up the job. These are then labeled and frequently indicated on the elaborate charts with checks to make it possible for the administrator to be sure that each function has been performed. In this way, it is felt that absolute control is maintained over the individual. Yet, scheduling how and when each activity is actually performed is left up to the employee. For an employer to schedule a subordinate's work for him would be considered a tyrannical violation of his individuality—an invasion of the self.

In contrast, M-time people schedule the activity and leave the analysis of the activities of the job to the individual. A P-type analysis, even though technical by its very nature, keeps reminding the subordinate that his job is not only a system but also part of a larger system. M-type people, on the other hand, by virtue of compartmentalization, are less likely to see their activities in context as part of the larger whole. This does not mean that they are unaware of the "organization"—far from it—only that the job itself or even the goals of the organization are seldom seen as a whole.

Giving the organization a higher priority than the functions it performs is common in our culture. This is epitomized in television, where we allow the TV commercials, the "special message," to break the continuity of even the most important communica-tion. There is a message all right, and the message is that art gives way to commerce—polychronic advertising agencies impose their values on a monochronic population. In monochronic North European countries, where patterns are more homogeneous, commercial interruptions of this sort are not tolerated. There is a strict limit as to the number as well as the times when commercials can be shown. The average American TV program has been allotted one or two hours, for which people have set aside time, and is conceived, written, directed, acted, and played as a unity. Interjecting commercials throughout the body of the program breaks that continuity and flies in the face of one of the core systems of the culture. The polychronic Spanish treat the main feature as a close friend or relative who should not be disturbed and let the commercials mill around in the antechamber outside. My point is not that one system is superior to another, it's just that the two don't mix. The effect is disruptive, and reminiscent of what the English are going through today, now that the old monochronic queuing patterns have broken down as a consequence of a large infusion of polychronic peoples from the colonies.

Both M-time and P-time systems have strengths as well as weaknesses. There is a limit to the speed with which jobs can be analyzed, although once analyzed, proper reporting can enable a P-time administrator to handle a surprising number of subordinates. Nevertheless, organizations run on the polychronic model are limited in size, they depend on having gifted people at the top, and are slow and cumbersome when dealing with anything that is new or different. Without gifted people, a P-type bureaucracy can be a disaster. M-type organizations go in the opposite direction. They can and do grow much larger than the P-type. However, they combine bureaucracies instead of proliferating them, e.g., with consolidated schools, the business conglomerate, and the new superdepartments we are developing in government.

The blindness of the monochronic organization is to the humanity of its members. The weakness of the polychronic type lies in its extreme dependence on the leader to handle contingencies and stay on top of things. M-type bureaucracies, as they grow larger, turn inward; oblivious to their own structure, they grow rigid and are apt to lose sight of their original purpose. Prime examples are the Army Corps of Engineers and the Bureau of Reclamation, which wreak havoc on our environment in their dedicated efforts to stay in business by building dams or aiding the flow of rivers to the sea.

At the beginning of this chapter, I stated that "American time is monochronic." On the surface, this is true, but in a deeper sense, American (AE) time is both polychronic and monochronic. M-time dominates the official worlds of business, government, the professions, entertainment, and sports. However, in the home—particularly the more traditional home in which women are the core around which everything revolves—one finds that P-time takes over. How else can one raise several children at once, run a household, hold a job, be a wife, mother, nurse, tutor, chauffeur, and general fixer-upper? Nevertheless, most of us automatically equate P-time with informal activities and with the multiple tasks and responsibilities and ties of women to networks of people. At the preconscious level, M-time is male time and P-time is female time, and the ramifications of this difference are considerable.

In the conclusion of an important book, *Unfinished Business*, Maggie Scarf vividly illustrates this point. Scarf addresses herself to the question of why it is that depression (the hidden illness of our age) is three to six times more prevalent in women than it is in men. How does time equate with depression in women? It so happens that the time system of the dominant culture adds another source of trauma and alienation to the already overburdened psyches of many American women. According to Scarf, depression comes about in part as a consequence of breaking significant ties that make up most women's worlds. In our culture, men as a group tend to be more task-oriented, while women's lives center on networks of people and their relations with people. Traditionally, a woman's world is a world of human emotions, of love, attachment, envy, anxiety, and hate. This is a little difficult for late-twentieth-century people to accept because it implies basic differences between men and women that are not fashionable at the moment. Nevertheless, for most cultures around the world, the feminine mystique is intimately identified with the development of the human relations side of the personality rather than the technical, cortical left-brain occupational side. In the United States, AE women live in a world of peoples and relationships and their egos become spread out among those who are closest to them by a process we call identification. When the relationships are threatened or broken or something happens to those to whom one is close, there are worries and anxieties, and depression is a natural result.

Polychronic cultures are by their very nature oriented to people. Any human being who is naturally drawn to other human beings and who lives in a world dominated by human relationships will be either pushed or pulled toward the polychronic end of the time spectrum. If you value people, you must hear them out and cannot cut them off simply because of a schedule.

M-time, on the other hand, is oriented to tasks, schedules, and procedures. As anyone who has had experience with our bureaucracies knows, schedules and procedures take on a life all their own without reference to either logic or human needs. And it is this set of written and unwritten rules—and the consequences of these rules—that is at least partially responsible for the reputation of American business being cut off from human beings and unwilling to recognize the importance of employee morale. Morale may well be the deciding factor in whether a given company makes a profit or not. Admittedly, American management is slowly, very slowly, getting the message. The problem is that modern management has accentuated the monochronic side at the expense of the less manageable, and less predictable, polychronic side. Virtually everything in our culture works for and rewards a monochronic view of the world. But the antihuman aspect of M-time is alienating, especially to women. Unfortunately, too many women have "bought" the M-time world, not realizing that unconscious sexism is part of it. The pattern of an entire system of time is too large, too diffuse, and too ubiquitous for most to identify its patterns. Women sense there is something alien about the way in which modern organizations handle time, beginning with how the workday, the week, and the year are set up. Such changes as flextime do not alter the fact that as soon as one enters the door of the office, one becomes immediately locked into a monochronic, monolithic structure that is virtually impossible to change.

There are other sources of tension between people who have internalized these two systems. Keep in mind that polychronic individuals are oriented toward people, human relationships, and the family, which is the core of their existence. Family takes precedence over everything else. Close friends come next. In the absence of schedules, when there is a crisis the family always comes first. If a monochronic woman has a polychronic hairdresser, there will inevitably be problems, even if she has a regular appointment and is scheduled at the same time each week. In circumstances like these, the hairdresser (following his or her own pattern) will inevitably feel compelled to "squeeze people in." As a consequence, the regular customer, who has scheduled her time very carefully (which is why she has a standing appointment in the first place), is kept waiting and feels put down, angry, and frustrated. The hairdresser is also in a bind because if he does not accommodate his relative or friend regardless of the schedule, the result is endless repercussions within his family circle. Not only must he give preferential treatment to relatives, but the degree of accommodation and who is pushed aside or what is pushed aside is itself a communication!

The more important the customer or business that is disrupted, the more reassured the hairdresser's polychronic Aunt Nell will feel. The way to ensure the message that one is accepted or loved is to call up at the last minute and expect everyone to rearrange everything. If they don't, it can be taken as a clear signal that they don't care enough. The M-time individual caught in this P-time pattern has the feeling either that he is being pressured or that he simply doesn't count. There are many instances where culture patterns are on a collision course and there can be no resolution until the point of conflict is identified. One side or the other literally gives up. In the instance cited above, it is the hairdresser who

usually loses a good customer. Patterns of this variety are what maintain ethnicity. Neither pattern is right, only different, and it is important to remember that they do not mix.

Not all M-times and P-times are the same. There are tight and loose versions of each. The Japanese, for example, in the official business side of their lives where people do not meet on a highly personalized basis, provide us an excellent example of tight M-time. When an American professor, business person, technical expert, or consultant visits Japan, he may find that his time is like a carefully packed trunk—so tightly packed, in fact, that it is impossible to squeeze one more thing into the container. On a recent trip to Japan, I was contacted by a well-known colleague who had translated one of my earlier books. He wanted to see me and asked if he could pick me up at my hotel at twelve-fifteen so we could have lunch together. I had situated myself in the lobby a few minutes early, as the Japanese are almost always prompt. At twelve-seventeen, I could see his tense figure darting through the crowd of arriving business people and politicians who had collected near the door. Following greetings, he ushered me outside to the ubiquitous black limousine with chauffeur, with white doilies covering the arms and headrests. The door of the car had hardly closed when he started outlining our schedule for the lunch period by saying that he had an appointment at three o'clock to do a TV broadcast. That set the time limit and established the basic parameters in which everyone knew where he would be at any given part of the agenda. He stated these limits—a little over two hours—taking travel time into account.

My colleague next explained that not only were we to have lunch, but he wanted to tape an interview for a magazine. That meant lunch and an interview which would last thirty to forty minutes. What else? Ah, yes. He hoped I wouldn't mind spending time with Mr. X, who had published one of my earlier books in Japanese, because Mr. X was very anxious to pin down a commitment on my part to allow him to publish my next book. He was particularly eager to see me because he missed out on publishing the last two books, even though he had written me in the United States. Yes, I did remember that he had written, but his letter arrived after the decision on the Japanese publisher had been made by my agent. That, incidentally, was the very reason why he wanted to see me personally. Three down and how many more to go? Oh, yes, there would be some photographers there and he hoped I wouldn't mind if pictures were taken? The pictures were to be both formal group shots, which were posed, and informal, candid shots during the interview, as well as pictures taken with Mr. X. As it turned out, there were at least two sets of photographers as well as a sound man, and while it wasn't "60 Minutes," there was quite a lot of confusion (the two sets of photographers each required precious seconds to straighten things out). I had to hand it to everyone—they were not only extraordinarily skilled and well organized, but also polite and considerate. Then, he hoped I wouldn't mind but there was a young man who was studying communication who had scored over 600 on an examination, which I was told put him 200 points above the average. This young man would be joining us for lunch. I didn't see how we were going to eat anything, much less discuss issues of mutual interest. In situations such as these, one soon learns to sit back, relax, and let the individual in charge orchestrate everything. The lunch was excellent, as I knew it would be—hardly leisurely, but still very good.

All the interviews and the conversation with the student went off as scheduled. The difficulties came when I had to explain to the Japanese publisher that I had no control over my own book—that once I had written a book and handed it in to my publisher, the book was marketed by either my publisher or my agent. Simply being first in line did not guarantee anything. I had to try to make it clear that I was tied into an already existing set of relationships with attached obligations and that there were other people who made these decisions. This required some explaining, and I then spent considerable time trying to work out a method for the publisher to get a hearing with my agent. This is sometimes virtually impossible because each publisher and each agent in the United States has its own representative in Japan. Thus an author is in their hands, too.

We did finish on time—pretty much to everyone's satisfaction, I believe. My friend departed on schedule as the cameramen were putting away their equipment and the sound man was rolling up his wires and disconnecting his microphones. The student drove me back to my hotel on schedule, a little after 3 P.M.

The pattern is not too different from schedules for authors in the United States. The difference is that in Japan the tightly scheduled monochronic pattern is applied to foreigners who are not well enough integrated into the Japanese system to be able to do things in a more leisurely manner, and where emphasis is on developing a good working relationship.

All cultures with high technologies seem to incorporate both polychronic as well as monochronic functions. The point is that each does it in its own way. The Japanese are polychronic when looking and working inward, toward themselves. When dealing with the outside world, they have adopted the dominant time system which characterizes that world. That is, they shift to the monochronic mode and, characteristically, since these are technical matters, they outshine us. . . .

CONCEPTS AND QUESTIONS
FOR CHAPTER 5

1. From your personal experiences can you think of additional ways that people in various cultures greet, kiss, show contempt, or beckon?

2. Are cultural differences that are based on linguistic problems harder or easier to overcome than the problems related to nonverbal actions?

3. In what ways do nonverbal behaviors reflect the values, history, and social organization of a culture?

4. What are some of the dangers of overgeneralizing from nonverbal communication?

5. Have you ever experienced situations where the nonverbal behavior of someone did not meet your expectations? How did you react? Could this have been a cultural problem?

6. How can we develop a theory of nonverbal behavior if we go beyond the anecdotal narration of bizarre behaviors?

7. Can you think of any cultural examples that would tend to support the notion that a culture's history influences its use of nonverbal communication?

8. What are the relationships between verbal and nonverbal forms of communication?

9. How might cultural differences in time conceptualization lead to intercultural communication problems?

10. What examples can you think of that illustrate differences between the sexes in touching behavior?

11. How would you prevent the occurrence of intercultural communication problems that are brought about by the unconscious and unintentional performance of nonverbal behavior that deeply offends members of another culture?

12. Why is it important to look at both intentional and unintentional forms of nonverbal communication? Can you give an example of each?

13. Is it easier to overcome problems related to nonverbal actions or verbal languages? Why?

14. Which one of the various types of nonverbal behaviors discussed in this chapter do you think is most important to the student of intercultural communication? Why?

15. What does Andersen mean when he writes, "Culture is an enduring phenomenon whereas the situation is a transient one with an observable beginning and end?"

16. Can you think of instances where your personal space was "invaded" by someone from another culture?

17. Dolphin notes that "Other than culture, age and sex, the interaction distance between two individuals can be affected by a host of other variables: relationship between the two, the environment of the transaction, attitudinal differences, occupation and/or status, the language used, etc." Can you think of any other variables not mentioned by Dolphin?

18. How have you seen Hall's concept of monochronic time reflected in your culture?

6

Cultural Contexts: The Influence of the Setting

All intercultural communication takes place within a social setting or environment that impacts on the communication event. We call this the social context because the setting is never neutral; it influences how the participants behave. We have all learned culturally appropriate patterns of communicative behavior for the various social contexts in which we normally find ourselves. But, as in other aspects of intercultural communication, the patterns of behavior appropriate to various social contexts are culturally diverse. When we find ourselves in an unfamiliar context without an internalized set of rules to govern our behavior, or when we are interacting with someone who has internalized a different set of rules, communication problems often arise.

The growth of international business during the last 30 years has been startling. Overseas transactions that generated millions of dollars annually are now multibillion dollar operations. Furthermore, the international business community has become multinational with culturally diverse organizational units. In fact, the study of the multinational organization has become a subtopic within the fields of intercultural and organizational communication. Successful businesspeople functioning in international business and world markets must learn about approaches to business practices that are different from their own or those they studied in school.

Because of this economic growth and the internationalization of business, businesspeople no longer have the luxury of dealing exclusively with those who possess the same cultural background and experiences. One's associates, clients, subordinates, and even supervisors are frequently from different countries and cultures. Such aspects as gift giving, methods of negotiation, decision making, policy formulation, marketing techniques, management structure, human resource management, and patterns of communication are now subject to culturally diverse influences.

While the globalization of business was taking place, changes also were happening within the United States; the country was becoming a more pluralistic, multicultural society. As a result, the cultural diversity of the U.S. population increased and we now often find ourselves engaged in intercultural communication in a variety of communication contexts. The workplace, schools, social service agencies, and health services, among others, are contexts that have become especially intercultural. Consequently, intercultural interaction within the U.S. continues to increase.

In this chapter we will look at a series of articles that deal with cultural diversity in communication contexts. We focus on a combination of international and domestic settings in which knowledge and appreciation of cultural diversity are important if successful intercultural communication is to occur.

All business activities involve many forms of communication, but there are two forms that are crucial to successful businesses: discussion and negotiation. These are difficult enough in intracultural communications, but intercultural communication adds further problems because culture impacts communication styles. The first two articles will examine cultural diversity in both of these forms of interaction. First, in his article, "Contrasts in Discussion Behaviors of German and American Managers," Robert A. Friday examines the effect of culture on this form of communication. Friday traces cultural expectations of both German and American managers across a number of dimensions, pointing out the differences, and how they can lead to misunderstandings and ineffective communication.

Susan A. Hellweg, Larry A. Samovar, and Lisa Skow lead us through an investigation of cultural diversity in negotiating behavior. In "Cultural Variations in Negotiation Styles," they highlight negotiation styles used by such cultures as the French, Japanese, Chinese, Brazilians, and Arabic cultures of the Middle East. They present a detailed description of various communication styles and cultural variations in decision making. They show how sen-

sitivity to cultural diversity is essential to successful intercultural business negotiations.

The next article, "The Group: A Japanese Context" focuses on the Far East. Dolores and Robert Cathcart explore how a culture's view of a specific concept can influence behavior. In this case, the concept is the Japanese view of groups. The Cathcarts examine the Japanese concept of "group" by describing the special and unique way in which the Japanese define groups. If one's experience with groups changes from culture to culture, then it follows that each culture might well bring a different way of acting to a group situation. The Cathcarts describe relevant Japanese history and analyze its influence in shaping modern Japanese culture as a basis to examine the role of groups as the significant context for communication in Japan.

A culturally diverse communication context that may occur in a variety of locations such as the workplace, schools, health care services, and social services is counseling in the multicultural setting. In their article, "Counseling and Culture," Anne and Paul Pedersen develop what they call "intrapersonal" and "interpersonal cultural grids" as a theoretical framework that combines personal and cultural perspectives of social system variables. By combining the individual and the group perspectives, the cultural grid can be used to describe a distinctive cultural orientation in each communication situation and to suggest how specific behaviors, expectations, and values are related to social system variables.

A multicultural society impacts strongly on the health care setting because cultural beliefs about health and disease are very diverse. Such a simple question as "How do you catch a cold?" can elicit a variety of answers ranging from having stood in a draft to being the victim of a supernatural spell, depending upon one's cultural background. In her article, "Negotiating Cultural Understanding in Health Care Communication," Patricia Geist examines the complex and dynamic features of communication in a health care context. She begins by developing the link between culture, health, and communication and the expansion of cultural sensitivity in the health care context. She then describes cultural differences in perceptions, treatment practices, and relationships. As she notes, "All cultures have beliefs about health and illness that have been passed down from generation to generation. The difference between the belief system of the Western biomedical model and that of other cultures can result in inappropriate assessment or complications in treatment and communication in the provider-patient relationship. Geist concludes her article with suggestions for culturally sensitive health care

While many people naively believe that all classrooms are pretty much alike, Robert G. Powell and Janis F. Andersen take the position that learning environments are culturally diverse, and that they alter the communication patterns of people within those environments. In their article, "Culture and Classroom Communication," they support this assertion by highlighting intercultural differences in educational systems, teachers, learning styles, classroom rituals, intelligence assessment, education value, time values, and nonverbal behaviors. They follow this introduction of cultural diversity in education by describing how students from diverse cultural and ethnic backgrounds interact in the classroom and how they feel about certain types of communication behaviors. In this discussion they outline norms for loquacity, discourse structure, participant relations, the construction and functions of questions, teacher behavior, and academic advising. They complete their discussion by providing a taxonomy of rules for Anglo advisors who must counsel culturally diverse students.

Contrasts in Discussion Behaviors of German and American Managers

ROBERT A. FRIDAY

AMERICAN MANAGERS' EXPECTATION

Business Is Impersonal

In any business environment, discussion between colleagues must accomplish the vital function of exchanging information that is needed for the solution of problems. In American business, such discussions are usually impersonal.[1] Traditionally the facts have spoken for themselves in America. "When facts are disputed, the argument must be suspended until the facts are settled. Not until then may it be resumed, for all true argument is about the meaning of established or admitted facts" (Weaver, 1953) in the rationalistic view. Much of post-WWII American business decision making has been based on the quantitative MBA approach which focuses on factual data and its relationship to the ultimate fact of profit or loss, writing strategy plans, and top-down direction. After all of the facts are in, the CEO is often responsible for making the intuitive leap and providing leadership. The power and authority of the CEO has prevailed in the past 40 years, with no predicted change in view (Bleicher & Paul, 1986, p. 10–11). Through competition and contact with West Germany and Japan, the more personal approach is beginning to enter some lower level decision-

From *International Journal of Intercultural Relations*, Vol. 13, 1989, pp. 429–445. Reprinted by permission of Pergamon Press, Inc. and the author.

making practices (Peters & Waterman, 1982, pp. 35–118).

Another reason for the impersonal nature of American business is that many American managers do not identify themselves with their corporations. When the goals and interests of the corporation match up with those of the American manager, he or she will stay and prosper. However, when the personal agenda of the American manager is not compatible with that of the corporation, he or she is likely to move on to attain his or her objective in a more conducive environment. Most American managers can disassociate themselves from their business identity, at least to the extent that their personal investment in a decision has more to do with their share of the profit rather than their sense of personal worth.

In contrast, "the German salesman's personal credibility is on the line when he sells his product. He spends years cultivating his clients, building long-term relationships based on reliability" (Hall, 1983, p. 67). This tendency on the part of Germans is much like American business in the early part of this century.

The cohesiveness of the employees of most German businesses is evidenced in the narrow salary spread. Whereas in the United States the ratio of lowest paid to highest paid is approximately 1 to 80, in Germany this ratio is 1 to 25 (Hall, 1983, p.74).

GERMAN MANAGERS' EXPECTATION

Business Is Not as Impersonal

The corporation for most Germans is closely related to his or her own identity. German managers at Mobay are likely to refer to "Papa Bayer" because they perceive themselves as members of a corporate family which meets most of their needs. In turn, most German managers there, as elsewhere, have made a lifelong commitment to the larger group in both a social and economic sense (Friday & Biro, 1986–87). In contrast to the American post-WWII

trend is "the German postwar tradition of seeking consensus among a closely knit group of colleagues who have worked together for decades [which] provides a collegial harmony among top managers that is rare in U.S. corporations" (Bleicher & Paul, 1986, p. 12). Our interviews suggested that many German managers may enter a three-year-plus training program with the idea of moving on later to another corporation. This move rarely occurs.

While a three-year training program appears to be excessively long by American standards, one must understand that the longer training program works on several levels that are logical within the German culture. The three or more years of entry level training is a predictable correlation to the German and USA relative values on the Uncertainty Avoidance Index[2] (Hofstede, 1984, p. 122). The longer training period is required to induct the German manager into the more formal decision-making rules, plans, operating procedures, and industry tradition (Cyert & March, 1963, p. 119), all of which focus on the short-run known entities (engineering/reliability of product) rather than the long-run unknown problems (future market demand).

On another level the "strong sense of self as a striving, controlling entity is offset by an equally strong sense of obligation to a *code* of decency" (McClelland, Sturr, Knapp, & Wendt, 1958, p. 252). Induction into a German company with an idealistic system of obligation requires a longer training period than induction into an American company in which the corporate strategy for productivity is acquired in small group and interpersonal interaction.[3] The German manager who moves from one corporation to another for the purpose of advancement is regarded with suspicion partly because of his lack of participation in the corporate tradition, which could prove to be an unstabilizing factor.

Our preliminary interview results suggested uncertainty avoidance (Hofstede, 1984, p. 130) in everyday business relationships, especially the German concern for security. For example, most of the transfer preparation from the German home office to the USA consists of highly detailed explanations of an extensive benefits package. Since the German manager sees a direct relationship between his or her personal security and the prosperity of his or her company, business becomes more personal for him or her. Similarly, Americans who work in employee-owned companies are also seeing a clear relationship between personal security and the prosperity of their company.

AMERICAN MANAGERS' EXPECTATION

Need to Be Liked

The American's need to be liked is a primary aspect of his or her motivation to cooperate or not to cooperate with colleagues. The arousal of this motivation occurs naturally in discussion situations when direct feedback gives the American the desired response which indicates a sense of belongingness or acceptance. The American "envisions the desired responses and is likely to gear his actions accordingly. The characteristic of seeing others as responses is reflected in the emphasis on communication in interaction and in the great value placed on being liked. . . . American's esteem of others is based on their liking him. This requirement makes it difficult for Americans to implement projects which require an 'unpopular' phase" (Stewart, 1972, p. 58).

For Americans, the almost immediate and informal use of a colleague's first name is a recognition that each likes the other. While such informality is common among American business personnel, this custom should probably be avoided with Germans. "It takes a long time to get on a first-name basis with a German; if you rush the process, you may be perceived as overly familiar and rude. . . . Germans are very conscious of their status and insist on proper forms of address. Germans are bewildered by the American custom of addressing a new acquaintance by his first name and are even more startled by our custom of addressing a superior by first name" (Hall, 1983, p. 57–58). When such matters of decorum are overlooked during critical discussions, an "unpopular phase" may develop.

The need to be liked is culturally induced at an early age and continued throughout life through regular participation in group activities.

They [Americans] are not brought up on sentiments of obligation to others as the Germans are, but from kindergarten on they regularly participate in many more extracurricular functions of a group nature. In fact, by far the most impressive result . . . is the low number of group activities listed by the Germans (about 1, on the average) as compared with the Americans (about 5, on the average). In these activities the American student must learn a good deal more about getting along with other people and doing things cooperatively, if these clubs are to function at all (McClelland et al., 1958, p. 250).

This cultural orientation in relation to group participation will be revisited later in the closing discussion on "learning styles, training, instruction, and problem solving."

GERMAN MANAGERS' EXPECTATION

Need to Be Credible

The German counterpart to the American need to be liked is the need to establish one's credibility and position in the hierarchy. The contrast between American informality and mobility and German formality and class structure is a reflection of the difference between these two needs. In the absence of a long historical tradition, Americans have developed a society in which friendships and residence change often, family histories (reputations) are unknown, and, therefore, acceptance of what one is doing in the present and plans to do in the future is a great part of one's identity. In order to maintain this mobility of place and relationships, Americans rely on reducing barriers to acceptance through informality.

Germans, with their strong sense of history, tradition, family, and life-long friendships, tend to move much less often, make friendships slowly, and keep them longer than Americans. Because one's family may be known for generations in Germany, the family reputation becomes part of one's own identity, which in turn places the individual in a stable social position.[4]

The stability of the social class structure and, thus, the credibility of the upper class in Germany is largely maintained through the elitist system of higher education.

Educational achievement has been a major factor in determining occupational attainment and socioeconomic status in the post-World War II era. University education has been virtually essential in gaining access to the most prestigious and remunerative positions. Some of the most enduring social divisions have focused on level of education (Nyrop, 1982, p. 113).

A German's education most often places him or her at a certain level which, in turn, determines what they can and can't do. In Germany, one must present credentials as evidence of one's qualification to perform *any* task (K. Hagemann, personal communication, May–September, 1987). Thus, the German societal arrangement guarantees stability and order by adherence to known barriers (credentials) that confirm one's credibility. In Germany, loss of credibility would be known in the manager's corporate and social group and would probably result in truncated advancement (not dismissal since security is a high value).

The rigid social barriers established by education and credentials stand in direct contrast to the concepts of social mobility in American society. "Our social orientation is toward the importance of the individual and the equality of all individuals. Friendly, informal, outgoing, and extroverted, the American scorns rank and authority, even when he/she is the one with the rank. American bosses are the only bosses in the world who insist on being called by their first names by their subordinates" (Kohls, 1987, p. 8). When Germans and Americans come together in discussion, the German's drive is to establish hierarchy, the American's is to dissolve it.

AMERICAN MANAGERS' EXPECTATIONS

Assertiveness, Direct Confrontation, and Fair Play

In comparing Americans with Japanese, Edward Stewart relates the American idea of confrontation as "putting the cards on the table and getting the information 'straight from the horses mouth.' It is also desirable to face people directly, to confront them intentionally" (Stewart, 1972, p. 52). This is done so that the decision makers can have all of the facts. Stewart contrasts this intentional confrontation of Americans to the indirection of the Japanese, which often requires the inclusion of an intermediary or emissary in order to avoid face to face confrontation and thus, the loss of face. However, this view may leave the American manager unprepared for what he or she is likely to find in his or her initial discussion with a German manager.

The American manager is likely to approach his or her first discussion with German managers in an assertive fashion from the assumption that competition in business occurs within the context of cooperation (Stewart, 1972, p.56). This balance is attained by invoking the unspoken rule of fair play.

Our games traditions, although altered and transformed, are Anglo-Saxon in form; and fair play does mean for us, as for the English, a standard of behavior between weak and the strong—a standard which is curiously incomprehensible to the Germans. During the last war, articles used to appear in German papers exploring this curious Anglo-Saxon notion called "fair play," reproduced without translation—for there was no translation.

Now the element which is so difficult to translate in the idea of "fair play" is not the fact that there are rules. Rules are an integral part of German life, rules for behavior of inferior to superior, for persons of every status, for every formal situation. . . . The point that was incomprehensible was the inclusion of the other person's weakness inside the rules so that "fair play" included in it a state-

*ment of relative strength of the opponents and it
ceased to be fair to beat a weak opponent.*

*. . . Our notion of fair play, like theirs [British],
includes the opponent, but it includes him far
more personally . . . (Mead, 1975, p. 143–145).*

I am not implying that the American is in need of
a handicap when negotiating with Germans. It is important to note however, that the styles of assertiveness under the assumption of American equality
(fair play) and assertiveness under the assumption
of German hierarchy may be very different. The
general approach of the German toward the weaker
opponent may tend to inspire a negative reaction
in the American, thus reducing cooperation and
motivation.

GERMAN MANAGERS' EXPECTATIONS

Assertiveness, Sophistication, and Direct Confrontation

The current wisdom either leaves the impression or
forthrightly states that Americans and Germans
share certain verbal behaviors which would cause
one to predict that discussion is approached in a
mutually understood fashion.

*If North Americans discover that someone spoke
dubiously or evasively with respect to important
matters, they are inclined to regard the person
thereafter as unreliable, if not dishonest. Most of
the European low-context cultures such as the
French, the Germans, and the English show a similar cultural tradition. These cultures give a high
degree of social approval to individuals whose verbal behaviors in expressing ideas and feelings are
precise, explicit, straightforward, and direct
(Gudykunst & Kim, 1984, p. 144).*

Such generalizations do not take into account
the difference between *Gespräch* (just talking
about—casually) and *Besprechung* (discussion in
the more formal sense of having a discussion about
an issue). *Besprechung* in German culture is a common form of social intercourse in which one has

high level discussions about books, political issues,
and other weighty topics. This reflects the traditional German values which revere education.
Americans would best translate *Besprechung* as a
high level, well evidenced, philosophically and logically rigorous debate in which one's credibility is
clearly at stake—an activity less familiar to most
Americans.

The typical language of most Americans is not
the language many Germans use in a high level debate on philosophical and political issues.

*In areas where English immigrants brought with
them the speech of 16th and 17th century England,
we find a language more archaic in syntax and
usage than [sic] present-day English. Cut off from
the main stream, these pockets of English have survived. But the American language, as written in
the newspapers, as spoken over the radio (and television), . . . is instead the language of those who
learned it late in life and learned it publicly, in
large schools, in the factory, in the ditches, at the
polling booth. . . . It is a language of public, external relationships. While the American-born generation was learning this public language, the
private talk which expressed the overtones of personal relationships was still cast in a foreign
tongue. When they in turn taught their children to
speak only American, they taught them a one-
dimensional public language, a language oriented to the description of external aspects of behavior, weak in overtones. To recognize this
difference one has only to compare the vocabulary with which Hemingway's heroes and heroines
attempt to discuss their deepest emotions with the
analogous vocabulary of an English novel. All the
shades of passion, laughter close to tears, joy trem-
ulous on the edge of revelation, have to be
summed up in such phrases as: 'They had a fine
time.' Richness in American writing comes from the
invocation of objects which themselves have overtones rather than from the use of words which
carry with them a linguistic aura. This tendency to
a flat dimension of speech has not been reduced
by the maintenance of a classical tradition (Mead,
1975, pp. 81–82).*

Figure 1 Development of Discussion Behavior at a Glance

American	Focus	German
Impersonal—act as own agent—will move on when business does not serve his/her needs or when better opportunity arises	**Relationship to Business**	Not as impersonal—corporation is more cohesive unit—identity more closely associated with position, and security needs met by corporation
Need to be liked—expressed through informal address and gestures	**Personal Need**	Need for order and establishment of place in hierarchy—expressed through formal address and gestures
Short-term—largely informal—many procedures picked up in progress	**Orientation to Corporation**	Long-term training—formal—specific rules of procedure learned
Based on accomplishment and image—underlying drive toward equality	**Status**	Based on education and credentials—underlying drive toward hierarchy
Assertive, tempered with fair play—give benefit of doubt or handicap	**Confrontation**	Assertive—put other in his/her place
Discussion about sports, weather, occupation: what you do, what you feel about someone. Logical, historical analysis rarely ventured. Native language sophistication usually low.	**Common Social Intercourse**	Besprechung—rigorous logical examination of the history and elements of an issue. Politics favorite topic. Forceful debate expected. Native language sophistication high.

Since many Americans tend not to discuss subjects such as world politics, philosophical and ethical issues with a large degree of academic sophistication, a cultural barrier may be present even if the Germans speak American style English. In a study of a German student exchange program, Hagemann observed that "it was crucial for the Germans, that they could discuss world-politics with their American counterparts, found them interested in environmental protection and disarmament issues and that they could talk with them about private matters of personal importance.... If they met Americans who did not meet these demands the relationships remained on the surface" (Hagemann, 1986, p. 8).

This tendency not to enter into sophisticated discussions and develop deeper relationships may be a disadvantage for many Americans who are working with Germans (see Figure 1). In addition, in a society in which one's intellectual credibility[5] establishes one's position in the group and thus determines what one can and can't do, *Besprechung* can become quite heated—as is the case in Germany.

FOCUS: WHEN *BESPRECHUNG* AND DISCUSSION MEET

The management style of German and American managers within the same multinational corporation is more likely to be influenced by their nationality than by the corporate culture. In a study of carefully matched national groups of managers working in the affiliated companies of a large U.S. multinational firm, "cultural differences in management assumptions were not reduced as a result of working for the same multinational firm. If anything, there was slightly more divergence between the national groups within this multinational company than originally found in the INSEAD multinational study" (Laurent, 1986, p. 95).

On the surface we can see two culturally distinct agendas coming together when German and American managers "discuss" matters of importance. The American character with its need to remain impersonal and to be liked avoids argumentum ad hominem. Any attack on the person will indicate disrespect and promote a feeling of dislike for the other, thus promoting the "unpopular phase," which, as Stewart indicates, may destroy cooperation for Americans.

In contrast, the German manager, with his personal investment in his position and a need to be credible to maintain his or her position, may strike with vigor and enthusiasm at the other's error. The American manager with his lack of practice in German-style debate and often less formal language, education, and training, may quickly be outmaneuvered, cornered, embarrassed, and frustrated. In short, he or she may feel attacked. This possible reaction may be ultimately important because it can be a guiding force for an American.

Beyond the question of character is the more fundamental question of the guidance system of the individual within his or her culture and what effect changing cultural milieu has on the individual guidance system. I define guidance system as that which guides the individual's actions. In discussing some of the expectations of German and American managers, I alluded several times to what could be construed as peer pressure within small groups. How this pressure works to guide the individual's actions, I will argue in the next section, has great implications for developing programs for American success in Germany.

Viewed as systems of argumentation, discussion and *Besprechung* both begin a social phase even though Americans may at first view the forcefulness of the Germans as anti-social (Copeland & Griggs, 1985, p. 105). However, a dissimilarity lends an insight into the difference in the guidance systems and how Germans and Americans perceive each other.

American discussion, with the focus on arriving at consensus, is based on the acceptance of value relativism (which supports the American value of equality and striving for consensus). The guidance system for Americans is partly in the peer group pressure which the individual reacts to but may not be able to predict or define in advance of a situation. Therefore, some Americans have difficulty articulating, consciously conceiving, or debating concepts in their guidance system but rather prefer to con-

sider feedback and adjust their position to accommodate the building of consensus without compromising their personal integrity.

German *Besprechung*, with the focus on arriving at truth or purer concepts, rejects value relativism in support of German values of fixed hierarchy and social order. The German *Besprechung* is argumentation based on the assumption that there is some logically and philosophically attainable truth. The guidance system for Germans is composed of concepts which are consciously taken on by the individual over years of formal learning (a la Hall) and debate. While a German makes the concepts his/her own through *Besprechung*, his/her position is not likely to shift far from a larger group pressure to conform to one hierarchical code.

The peer pressure of the immediate group can often become a driving force for Americans. The irony is that many Germans initially perceive Americans as conformists and themselves as individualists, stating that Americans can't act alone while Germans with their clearly articulated concepts do act alone. Americans, on the other hand, often initially perceive Germans as conformists and themselves as individualists stating that Germans conform to one larger set of rules while Americans do their own thing.

LEARNING STYLES, TRAINING, INSTRUCTION, AND PROBLEM SOLVING

Education and Training

The ultimate function of group process in American corporations is problem solving and individual motivation (being liked). For Germans motivation is more of a long term consideration such as an annual bonus or career advancement. Problem solving for Germans is more compartmentalized and individualized.

The contrasting elements discussed earlier and outlined in both "At a Glance" summaries (Figures 1 and 2) indicate that considerable cultural distance

Figure 2 Manager Background At a Glance

American	Focus	German
Peer pressure of immediate group—reluctant to go beyond the bounds of fair play in social interaction—backdrop is social relativism	**Guidance System**	Peer pressure from generalized or larger social group—forceful drive to conform to the standard—backdrop is consistent and clearly known
Generally weaker higher education—weak historical perspective and integrated thought—focus is on the future results—get educational requirements out of the way to get to major to get to career success	**Education**	Higher education standards generally superior, speak several languages, strong in history, philosophy, politics, literature, music, geography, and art
More group oriented—social phase develops into team spirit—individual strengths are pulled together to act as one	**Problem Solving**	More individualized and compartmentalized—rely on credentialed and trained professional
Informal awareness—get the hang of variations—often unconscious until pointed out	**Learning**	Formal awareness—specific instruction given to direct behavior—one known way to act—highly conscious

may have to be traveled by Germans and Americans before they can be assured that cooperation and motivation are the by-products of their combined efforts. The contrasting elements are, of course, a result of the organization and education—the acculturation—of the minds of Germans and Americans. In this section I will examine the different cultural tendencies from the perspective of Hall's definitions of formal and informal culture and discuss some implications for intercultural training and education.

The first level of concern is general preparation for the managerial position. As an educator I must take a hard look at the graduates of our colleges and universities as they compare to their German counterparts. I am not attempting to imply that Germans are better than Americans. All cultural groups excel in some area more than other cultural groups.

Germans are better trained and better educated than Americans. A German university degree means more than its U.S. equivalent because German educational standards are higher and a smaller percentage of the population wins college

entrance. Their undergraduate degree is said to be on par with our master's degree. It is taken for granted that men and women who work in business offices are well educated, able to speak a foreign language, and capable of producing coherent, intelligible, thoughtful communications. German business managers are well versed in history, literature, geography, music and art (Hall, 1983, p. 58).

Americans tend to focus on the present as the beginning of the future, whereas Germans tend to "begin every talk, every book, or article with background information giving historical perspective" (Hall, 1983, p. 20). While Hall makes a strong generalization, a contrary incident is rare. American college graduates are not known for having a firm or detailed idea of what happened before they were born. While some pockets of integrated, sophisticated thinking exist, it is by no means the standard. Indeed, many American college students are unable to place significant (newsworthy) events within an over-all political/philosophical framework two months after the occurrence.

In contrast, college educated Germans tend to express a need to know *why* they should do something—a reasoning grounded in a logical understanding of the past. Compared to the rigorous German theoretical and concrete analysis of past events, Americans often appear to be arguing from unverifiable aspirations of a future imagined. While such vision is often a valuable driving force and the basis for American innovation and inventiveness, it may not answer the German need to explicitly know why and, thus, may fall short (from a German perspective) in group problem solving when these two cultures are represented. From the educational perspective, one must conclude that more than a few days of awareness training is needed before successful discussions can result between German and American managers, primarily because of what is not required by the American education system. The contrary may also be true in the preparation of Germans to work with Americans. Tolerance for intuitive thinking may well be a proper focus in part of the German manager's training prior to working with American managers.

Formal and Informal Culture

The unannounced and largely unconscious agenda of small group process among Americans is usually more subtle than the German formal awareness but equally as important. American individuals come together in the initial and critical social phase, "size up" each other, and formally or informally recognize a leader. In a gathering of hierarchical equals the first to speak often emerges as the leader. At this point the embers of team spirit warm once again. As the group moves through purpose and task definition, members define and redefine their roles according to the requirements of the evolving team strategy. Fired with team spirit, inculcated through years of group activity and school sports, the group produces more than the sum of their individual promises.

"In the United States a high spontaneous interest in achievement is counterbalanced by much experience in group activities in which the individual learns to channel achievement needs according to

the opinions of others. . . . Interestingly enough, the American 'value formula' appears to be largely unconscious or informally understood, as compared to the German one, at any rate" (McClelland et al., 1958, p. 252). Though this observation is 30 years old, it still appears to be quite accurate. The use of modeling (imitation) as a way of acquiring social and political problem-solving strategies is also a way of adjusting to regionalisms. In taking on different roles, Americans become adept at unconsciously adjusting their character to meet the requirements of different situations. In short, says Hall, "Compared to many other societies, ours does not invest tradition with an enormous weight. Even our most powerful traditions do not generate the binding force which is common in some other cultures. . . . We Americans have emphasized the informal at the expense of the formal" (Hall, 1973, p. 72).

The German learning style is often characterized by formal learning as defined by Hall (Hall, 1973, p. 68). The characteristics of German frankness and directness are echoed in Hall's example of formal learning: "He will correct the child saying, 'Boys don't do that,' or 'You can't do that,' using a tone of voice indicating that what you are doing is unthinkable. There is no question in the mind of the speaker about where he stands and where every other adult stands" (Hall, 1973, p. 68). German formal awareness is the conscious apprehension of the detailed reality of history which forms an idealistic code of conduct that guides the individual to act in the national interest as if there was no other way.[6]

American informal awareness and learning is an outgrowth of the blending of many cultural traditions, in an environment in which people were compelled to come together to perform group tasks such as clearing land, building shelter, farming, and so on. The reduction of language to the basic nouns and functions was a requirement of communication for the multilingual population under primitive conditions. Cultural variations will always be a part of the vast American society. Americans have had to "get the hang of it" precisely because whatever *it* is, *it* is done with several variations in America.

In a sense, the informal rules such as "fair play" are just as prescriptive of American behavior as the system of German etiquette is prescriptive of much of German social interaction, including forms of address (familiar *Du* and the formal *Sie*). Even the rules for paying local taxes, entering children in schools, or locating a reputable repair person vary by local custom in America and can only be known by asking.[7] The clear difference is that the rules are not overtly shared in America.

The American expectations or informal rules for group discussion are general enough to include the etiquette of American managers from different ethnic backgrounds. As long as notions of equality, being liked, respect, fair play, and so on guide behaviors things run smoothly. "Anxiety, however, follows quickly when this tacit etiquette is breached. . . . What happens next depends upon the alternatives provided by the culture for handling anxiety. Ours include withdrawal and anger" (Hall, 1973, p. 76). In the intercultural situation, the American who participates informally in group behavior may feel that something is wrong but may not be able to consciously determine the problem. Without the ability of bringing the informal into conscious awareness, which is a function of awareness and education, many Americans may flounder in a state of confusion, withdrawal and anger.

CONCLUSION

What should become apparent to intercultural trainers working with companies that are bringing German and American personnel together is that they are working with two populations with distinct learning and problem-solving styles. The American is more likely to learn from an interactive simulation. Within the situation the American can "get the hang of" working with someone who has a German style. Trainers and educators of American managers know that the debriefing of the role play, which brings the operative informal rules into conscious awareness, is the focus of the learning activity. The short-term immersion training so often used today can only supply some basic knowledge and limited role-play experience.

What must never be forgotten in the zeal to train American managers is that their basic guidance sys-

tem in America is a motivation to accommodate the relative values of the immediate group. While the general cultural awareness exercises that begin most intercultural training may make Americans conscious of their internal workings, much more attention must be given to inculcate an understanding of German social order and the interaction permitted within it.

Knowledge of the language and an in-depth orientation to the culture for the overseas manager and spouse should be mandatory for American success in Germany and German success in the United States. "The high rate of marital difficulties, alcoholism and divorce among American families abroad is well known and reflects a lack of understanding and intelligent planning on the part of American business" (Hall, 1983, p. 88). In our pilot program we became quite aware of the fact that German spouses require much more preparation for a sojourn to America. American short-term planning is in conflict with the long-term preparation needed for most Americans who are going to work with Germans. In Germany the role of the spouse (usually the female) in business includes much less involvement than in the United States. We suspect this has much to do with the lack of attention to spouse preparation that we have observed thus far.

RECOMMENDATION

Long-term programs should be established that provide cultural orientation for overseas families at least three or four years before they start their sojourn with beginning and increasing knowledge of the language as a prerequisite for entry. Such programs should

• attend to the general instructional deficiencies of Americans in the areas of history, philosophy, and politics as studied by Germans,

• prepare Germans to expect and participate in an informal culture guided by value relativism in a spirit of equality,

• incorporate cultural sharing of German and American managers and their families in social settings so the sojourners can come together before, during, and after their individual experiences to establish a formal support network.

Segments of such programs could be carried on outside the corporate setting to allow for a more open exchange of ideas. In America, colleges and universities could easily establish such programs. Many American colleges and universities which have served as research and development sites for business and industry are also developing alternative evening programs to meet the educational needs in the community. Also, corporate colleges are an ideal setting for extended in-house preparation. In such learning environments, professors can come together with adjunct faculty (private consultants and trainers) to produce a series of seminars which combine lecture instruction, small group intercultural interaction, networking, media presentations, contact with multiple experts over time, and even a well planned group vacation tour to the sojourner's future assignment site.

Part of the programs should be offered in the evening to avoid extensive interference with the employee's regular assignments and to take advantage of the availability of other family members who should be included in intercultural transfer preparation. Cost to the corporation would be greatly reduced in that start-up funds could be partly supplied through federal grants, travel costs would be lessened, and program costs would be covered under regular tuition and materials fees. As a final note, I strongly recommend that such programs for American managers be viewed as graduate level education since they will be entering a society in which education is a mark of status.

NOTES

1. Future references to America and Americans should be understood as referring to the North Eastern United States and the citizens thereof, while references to Germany and Germans should be understood as West Germany and the citizens thereof.

2. Actual German values were 65, with a value of 53 when controlled for age of sample, while the actual USA values were 46, with a value of 36 when controlled for age of sample.

3. For a quick overview of how small group and interpersonal communication is related to corporate success in America see Peters and Austin, 1985, pp. 233–248.

4. These comparative descriptions correspond to the German social orientation and the American personal orientation discussed by Beatrice Reynolds (1984, p. 276) in her study of German and American values.

5. "In Germany, power can be financial, political, entrepreneurial, managerial or intellectual; of the five, intellectual power seems to rank highest. Many of the heads of German firms have doctoral degrees and are always addressed as 'Herr Doktor.'" (Copeland & Griggs, 1985, p. 120). While there may be exceptions to this rule, exceptions are few and hard to find.

6. "Yet this rigidity has its advantages. People who live and die in formal cultures tend to take a more relaxed view of life than the rest of us because the boundaries of behavior are so clearly marked, even to the permissible deviations. There is never any doubt in anybody's mind that, as long as he does what is expected, he knows what to expect from others" (Hall, 1973, p. 75). "In Germany everything is forbidden unless it is permitted" (Dubos, 1972, p. 100).

7. The perplexing problem for German executives who are new in the United States is that in Germany everything is known thus, *you should not have to ask* to find your way around. But in the USA where change is the watch word, *one has to ask to survive.*

REFERENCES

Bleicher, K., & Paul, H. (1986). Corporate governance systems in a multinational environment: Who knows what's best? *Management International Review*, **26**, (3) 4–15.

Copeland, L., & Griggs, L. (1985). *Going international: How to make friends and deal effectively in the global marketplace.* New York: Random House.

Cyert, R. M., & March, J. G. (1963). *A behavioral theory of the firm.* Englewood Cliffs, N.J.: Prentice-Hall.

Dubos, R. (1972). *A god within*. New York: Charles Scribner's Sons.

Friday, R. A., & Biro, R. (1986–87). [Pilot interviews with German and American personnel at Mobay Corporation (subsidiary of Bayer), Pittsburgh, PA]. Unpublished raw data.

Gudykunst, W. B., & Kim, Y. (1984). *Communicating with strangers: An approach to intercultural communication*. Reading, Mass.: Addison-Wesley.

Hagemann, K. (1986). *Social relationships of foreign students and their psychological significance in different stages of the sojourn*. Summary of unpublished diploma thesis, University of Regensburg, Regensburg, Federal Republic of Germany.

Hall, E. T. (1973). *The silent language*. New York: Doubleday.

Hall, E. T. (1983). *Hidden differences: Studies in international communication—How to communicate with the Germans*. Hamburg, West Germany: Stern Magazine Gruner + Jahr AG & Co.

Hofstede, G. (1984). *Culture's consequences: International differences in work-related values*. Beverly Hills: Sage Publications.

Kohls, L. R. (1987). *Models for comparing and contrasting cultures*, a juried paper, invited for submission to National Association of Foreign Student Advisors, June, 1987.

Laurent, A. (1986). The cross-cultural puzzle of international human resource management. *Human Resource Management*, **25**, 91–103.

McClelland, D. C., Sturr, J. F., Knapp, R. N., & Wendt, H. W. (1958). Obligations of self and society in the United States and Germany. *Journal of Abnormal and Social Psychology*, **56**, 245–255.

Mead, M. (1975). *And keep your powder dry*. New York: William Morrow.

Nyrop, R. F. (Ed.) (1982). *Federal republic of Germany, a country study*. Washington, D.C.: U.S. Government Printing Office.

Peters, T., & Austin, N. (1985). *A passion for excellence*. New York: Warner Communication.

Peters, T., & Waterman, R. (1982). *In search of excellence*. New York: Warner Communication.

Reynolds, B. (1984). A cross-cultural study of values of Germans and Americans. *International Journal of Intercultural Relations*, **8**, 269–278.

Stewart, E. C. (1972). *American cultural patterns: A cross-cultural perspective*. Chicago: Intercultural Press.

Weaver, R. M. (1953). *The ethics of rhetoric*. South Bend, IN.: Rengery/Gateway.

Cultural Variations in Negotiation Styles

SUSAN A. HELLWEG
LARRY A. SAMOVAR
LISA SKOW

As we continue through the 1990s, it seems hardly necessary to document the truth of Marshall McLuhan's prophecy about the global village. Nowhere is this international interdependence more evident than in the business arena. From a Toyota plant in Kentucky to a continuing massive U.S. trade deficit measured in hundreds of billions of dollars, the foreign influence on "doing business" is all around us. Newspapers and magazines abound with stories detailing how, if the United States is to survive, it must learn to adapt to an economic challenge that does well beyond its own boundaries. Earlier calls to engage in a financial battle with Japan have now been replaced with concerns that are far more universal. For example, the twelve-nation European Economic Community (EEC) may completely restructure Europe, making it a world-class power. Additionally, the six countries of the Association of Southeast Asian Nations (ASEAN) will soon become a major source of influence in the global marketplace.

Adapting to this new marketplace has been difficult for the United States. While talk concerning the Pacific Rim, the "twenty-four-hour stock market," and the need for joint ventures can be heard in nearly every corporate office, the facts seem to tell a story of a country that was not prepared to share the rewards of economic power.

When World War II ended, most of the world was decimated. Not only were financial institutions in disarray, but most countries had to fight the war at their front door; hence buildings, including banks, were destroyed. Such was not the case with the United States. We emerged from the war as the only superpower. Economically, we were in control. We set the tempo everywhere. Back in the early 1950s, America monopolized high tech and the majority of the world's automobiles and television sets. Then only a small portion of America's industries faced foreign competition. Even in the 1960s we were the world's largest exporter of manufactured goods. We represented only 5 percent of the world's population, yet we ruled over a vast economic empire.

What has transpired throughout the world in the last twenty years has dramatically changed this picture. For whether we like it or not, it is now a fact of life that the United States must share economic dominance with Japan, West Germany, Great Britain, the Netherlands, Korea, Canada, and a long list of other countries that also compete for a portion of the world's economic bounty. Like all cultures, our deep sense of ethnocentrism has kept us, until recently, from admitting to the economic revolution that was unfolding before us.

The purpose of this chapter is to highlight negotiation styles used by members of other cultures, ones that American business people must be aware of in their future dealings around the globe. With this knowledge, they can adapt to the styles reflected in other cultures; knowledge of only American negotiation techniques is no longer enough to compete successfully in the global marketplace. We have selected three of the most common problems that plague Americans when they attempt to negotiate with other countries. These problems can best be summarized as cultural variations concerning (1) rules for conducting business, (2) the selection of negotiators, and (3) methods of decision making.

This original article first appeared in print in the sixth edition. All rights reserved. Permission to reprint must be obtained from the publisher and the authors. Susan Hellweg and Larry Samovar teach at San Diego State University. Lisa Skow is a doctoral student at the University of Washington.

CULTURAL VARIATIONS IN CONDUCTING BUSINESS

All cultures explicitly and implicity instruct their members as to the procedural rules that should be followed in both their public and private affairs. From greetings to appropriate dress, members of a culture know the rules for that culture. Most rules for behavior are learned at a low awareness level and hence are acted out with a regularity that hides them even from the user. There are not only general rules that are unique to a culture, but there are also a series of specific cultural codes that help define a particular context. It is our contention that not knowing the rules that apply to the business environment can hinder the international negotiation process. We will now look at some cross-cultural rules for doing business that are often misunderstood by Americans.

Negotiation Atmosphere

American negotiators assume an attitude of "economic gain" in the negotiation process. They expect others to display what they conceive of as "American professionalism," including an aggressive approach toward that which is to be negotiated (Scott, 1981). As they tend to be uninterested in establishing long-term relationships in this context, they view socializing as unimportant. Rather, the American norm is to conduct business in an efficient manner; while compromises may be part of the outcome, in the eyes of the American negotiators, prestige is achieved by their ability to maneuver a debate. In keeping with the notion of American professionalism, they are more likely to presume trust of their counterparts at the onset of negotiations (Graham, 1987).

The French, in contrast to Americans, are likely to distrust their counterparts at first. Their negotiations are conducted through formal hospitality. As the French are represented by a heavily bureaucratic government with a history of involvement in international negotiations, they see themselves as more experienced negotiators (Fisher, 1980).

The Japanese believe that socializing is integral to the negotiation process. They are concerned with establishing long-term business/personal relationships through such transactions—the Japanese view a contract as the beginning of an adaptive process rather than as the end of one. Negotiators from this culture rely on the trust established between the parties involved and on an implicit understanding (Fisher, 1980).

Like the Japanese, Chinese negotiators feel that mutual interests and friendships are important in the negotiation process, so socialization during the contract agreement process is an expectation. Favorable terms are anticipated from friends; the nature of the relationship between the parties involved is critical to the Chinese. Trust is acquired between negotiators through favorable direct experience. Contracts are not considered as binding by the Chinese as the trust between those involved (Weiss and Stripp, 1985).

In the Middle East, personal relationships are also an important part of negotiations. Hospitality is a first priority in their business transactions (Weiss & Stripp, 1985), and negotiations are initiated with prenegotiation social graces. Trust and respect must be secured for successful negotiations (Scott, 1981).

The general business approach utilized by Brazilians and Mexicans is similar to the approach taken by Middle Eastern negotiators. Since Brazilians cannot rely on a legal system "to iron things out," they focus on establishing and maintaining personal relationships in business transactions (Graham and Herberger, 1983). For Mexicans, the public forum is not considered the appropriate place to consummate negotiations. Likewise, formal negotiations are not viewed by Mexicans as a time for objective analysis and pragmatic matters (Fisher, 1980).

Detail: Depth Versus Breadth

American negotiators assume that many small agreements will be consummated before the final agreement. Members of American negotiating teams want "the facts" pertaining to the negotiation only. Like the French, Americans put considerable emphasis on written agreements or contracts, believing that American integrity is at stake (Fisher, 1980). They are more concerned with quantity versus quality and with issues that deal with the amount of time involved, rather than with details that might be important to their counterparts (Moran and Harris, 1982).

Believing that much detail is comprehended implicitly in negotiation processes, the Japanese identify fewer specific issues and are less detail oriented than their American counterparts. "The Japanese tend to avoid any appearance of a petty focus on details in negotiations, striving to reach a broad agreement where details are not clearly spelled out" (March, 1985, p. 57). The Japanese rely primarily on general, brief written agreements. They believe that agreed-upon "principles" between negotiators are important, not the specifics of an agreement, principles that are designed to "guide" the agreement relationship (Weiss and Stripp, 1985).

Like the Japanese, the Chinese also prefer written agreements that would probably appear general to American and French negotiators; they leave room for "trust and common sense" (Weiss and Stripp, 1985). The Chinese tend to bargain away details at the negotiation table, preferring to use generalities (Fisher, 1980). Middle Eastern and Mexican negotiators prefer agreements that are bound by an oral understanding; they believe the written agreement is secondary and only represents the strong bond of the oral obligation (Weiss and Stripp, 1985). Thus, like Japanese and Chinese negotiators, a detailed, written agreement is not central to the negotiation process in the Middle East and Mexico.

Communication Style

According to Scott (1981), Americans tend to convey warmth, sincerity, confidence, and positiveness in their communication. March (1985) suggests that Americans are always ready to engage in bargaining. Americans often engage in compromise activity in the negotiation context. Negotiators from the United States tend to automatically assume that English will be spoken in the sessions. The use of translators may put the American participants at a disadvantage since the other side is likely to know a fair amount of English and will have more time to contemplate what is taking place during the translation period. American negotiators tend to be more interested in logical arguments than in the people they are dealing with. They may employ threats, warnings, and continual pushiness, even if their counterparts are signaling "no" (Graham and Herberger, 1983). Americans tend to express their ideas bluntly, silence being perceived as uncomfortable and indicative of trouble.

According to Graham, Campbell, and Meissner (1988), Americans employ a negotiating style similar to that of the British, but less silence is utilized and they are more egalitarian. The British interrupt less in their negotiations than their American counterparts and they have a polite yet indistinct style of negotiating. Scott (1981) describes British negotiators as kind, friendly, sociable, agreeable, flexible, and responsive.

The Japanese appear to be easily persuadable because of their seemingly accepting, passive mien, and they show little reaction to their counterparts during negotiations save for nodding. Japanese negotiators take long pauses, appear not to be rushed, and expect patience from other participants and no interruptions. The Japanese keep their emotions in check (Zimmerman, 1985), but seek simple symbolic expression (Morrison, 1972). According to Yotsukura (1977), the Japanese process 10 percent of a message through its verbal or overt expression and the other 90 percent through personal meaning. The Japanese encourage covert, fragmented expression. The fact that their language leads to a variety of interpretations through its ambiguity leads to frequent communication failures. Furthermore, Japanese verbal expression is encased in layers of indirectness through such phrases as "I think," "perhaps," "probably," and "maybe" (Ishii, 1985; Okabe, 1973; Yotsukura, 1977).

Silence is also part of the Japanese negotiation process. They are more evasive with their feelings and ideas than their Western counterparts. Harmony is crucial to their negotiations; they desire to achieve smoothness in all their transactions, both business and personal, and they may therefore appear standoffish or inscrutable to the other side (Fisher, 1980). The Japanese are most polite as negotiators and because of their behaviors in this context, they are among the least aggressive among cultures. Their communication is more frequently positive than expressive of "no's" and commands (Graham, Campbell, and Meissner, 1988).

The Chinese tend to be suspicious of Western negotiators. They do not wish to openly confront conflict and therefore shun any proposal-counterproposal style of negotiating. The Chinese must not be forced to withdraw from a stand, due to a possible loss of face (Scott, 1981). Chinese negotiators make concessions slowly and refrain from small talk. They do not accept hypothetical examples (Weiss and Stripp, 1985).

Unlike the Japanese, the French employ frequent "no" communication and often insist on using their own language in the negotiation settings (Scott, 1981). Said to be the most "difficult" of Europeans, French negotiators may be long-winded and rationalize a great deal without bargaining or compromising. They tend to put forth all their information and establish principles of reasoning first; new information is not easily accepted by them. They may thus be perceived as inflexible by opposing negotiation teams (Fisher, 1980). According to Weiss and Stripp (1985), the French relish debate and welcome and respect dissent. They are confrontational and competitive—to the French, negotiation involves a search for well-reasoned arguments.

For Germans, strength lies in the bidding stage of negotiation. They do not tend to compromise. German negotiators are generally clear, firm, and assertive in their expression—once a bid is put forth, it becomes sacrosanct and they are less likely to accept other possibilities (Scott, 1981). The Germans may not ask many questions in the negotiation process but will disclose a great deal and may frequently interrupt (Graham, Campbell, and Meissner, 1988).

In sharp contrast to American negotiators, "rhetoric and the grand idea are pursued" by Mexican negotiators (Fisher, 1980, p. 20). These negotiators do not see any advantage in frank talk. They may play the weaker side because of the perception that Americans have sympathy for the disadvantaged, the side that needs special consideration, but at the same time they are still extremely wary of patronizing assistance or concessions. Compromise to them threatens dignity in the negotiation process. Mexican negotiators prefer the deductive approach; they start with a general proposal, define the issues, and then make conclusions with the little detail or evidence used. More emphasis is placed upon contemplation and intuition. Mexicans stand closer than Americans and Japanese; they use more physical contact to show confidence (Fisher, 1980).

Brazilian negotiators are very aggressive by American standards, use a lot of commands, and employ a high frequency of "no's" and "you's." They do not engage in silence tactics, frequent touching, or facial gazing (Graham, Campbell, and Meissner, 1988). Brazilians may compete with each other for the floor and often appear to Americans to be rude and poor listeners (Graham and Herberger, 1983).

CULTURAL VARIATIONS IN SELECTING NEGOTIATORS

Our research and experience has led us to conclude that Americans also fail to understand the type of person they will be facing at the negotiating table. Like language, person perception is culturally based. While in the United States and Mexico one might consider a dynamic speaker to be a highly credible source, in Japan such a person is not to be trusted. Because of cultural variations in person perception, status, rank, and so on, not all cultures select the same type of individual to attend negotiating sessions. A few cultural differences in personnel selection will help illustrate this second variation in negotiation styles.

Younger negotiators (in the thirties or even twenties) are more common among American teams than in other cultures. Women may be included although few hold top-level positions (Greenwald, 1983). Technical expertise is a critical concern in the selection of American negotiation representatives. The social background, education, and age of candidates have little to do with their selection as negotiating team members or leaders.

Americans believe that relying on social status for such selection is unreasonable. In the international arena, team members from the United States make the assumption that they are world leaders and advisors, solicited or unsolicited (Fisher, 1980). Using a "John Wayne" type of strategy, American negotiators often believe they can do it alone and handle any negotiation situation. This strategy saves money on personnel and Americans pride themselves on having full authority to make decisions (Graham and Herberger, 1983).

French negotiation team members are usually selected on the basis of their social and professional status (Fisher, 1980). In addition, Weiss and Stripp (1985) report that French team members are selected based on social, professional, academic, and family ties. Similarity in personality and background among French negotiators is important and appears to be influential in the negotiation process. Among German negotiators similarity does not seem to be an important factor. And while the status and role of negotiators is crucial among British negotiators, similarity among them has been found to have little effect (Campbell, Graham, Jolibert, and Meissner, 1988).

The average age of Japanese business negotiators is the late thirties, with the leader being at least in his forties. Women are not usually participants on a Japanese negotiation team (Greenwald, 1983). Selection of negotiators is based largely on status and knowledge (Weiss and Stripp, 1985), with age seniority being the single most important criterion used in the selection of team leaders (Fisher, 1980). Chinese negotiators expect to deal with someone of authority and high status, and they feel slighted if they do not negotiate with such individuals (Scott, 1981).

Middle Eastern negotiators select negotiation team members similarly to the Japanese: The oldest member is usually the leader and younger members may even be ignored on Iranian teams (Soderberg, 1985). Negotiators from Saudi Arabia are generally selected on the basis of status and loyalty. Americans have commented that Saudis like to work alone when negotiating and take credit for accomplishments while passing blame on to others. The

first person to enter the room often has the highest rank in Saudi negotiations and titles are frequently used (Weiss and Stripp, 1985).

Personal qualities and connections are often the criteria for selection on Mexican negotiating teams. Group dynamics depend upon the social relationships among team members. Who holds authority on these teams is not always apparent; a subordinate present with a team member (for example, personal secretary) may indicate authority. Even personal secretaries to high authorities may be given more respect than an official who does not have *palanca* (leverage). Authority tends to be inherent in the individual on the team, not in the individual's position (Fisher, 1980).

CULTURAL VARIATIONS IN DECISION MAKING

There are vast cultural differences in how people think, apply forms of reasoning, and make decisions. Unless individuals have had experiences with people from other cultures who follow different patterns of thought, most will assume everyone thinks in much the same manner. In the Western view, we believe that we can discover truth if we just apply the correct steps of the scientific method. We believe that if we follow the Aristotelian modes of reasoning all problems will be solved. The Eastern version, best illustrated by Taoist thought, holds that truth, not the individual, is the active agent, and ways of knowing take a variety of forms. Even the simple Western notion of introduction, body, and conclusion is not found in most of the world. In short, cultural variations in decision making represent yet another problem facing American negotiators.

Problem-Solving Process

American negotiators view negotiation sessions as problem-solving sessions, even if no real problem exists. They tend to compartmentalize issues, focusing on one issue at a time, instead of negotiating many issues together. They are preoccupied with who makes the decisions on the opposing side, to whom they should be directing their proposals. Americans see themselves in the negotiating setting as universal problem solvers, working in everyone's best interests (Fisher, 1980). They rely on rational thinking and concrete data in their negotiations (Weiss and Stripp, 1985) and utilize a factual inductive style of persuasion (Glenn, Witmeyer, and Stevenson, 1977).

The French have no problem with open disagreement—they debate more than they bargain and are less apt than Americans to be flexible for the sake of agreement. Decisions are made with self-assurance. They start with a long-range view of their purposes, as opposed to Americans, who work with more short-range objectives (Fisher, 1980). The French are generally conservative, safe decision makers. Decisions are centrally made and by top authorities (Weiss and Stripp, 1985).

The Western concept of decision making is not applicable to the Japanese, who depend heavily on middle-level expertise; subordinates brief superiors who in turn use their influence to negotiate and make decisions. The Japanese use a consensus-building, direction-taking process where everyone affected by the decision is included in the process. For the Chinese, on the other hand, decision making is more authoritative than consensual; decisions are made by higher authorities without the inclusion of subordinates (Weiss and Stripp, 1985). The Japanese allow little room for flexibility in their negotiations, and they are slow in producing conclusions but fast in implementation. They stick to a decision once it is made (Fisher, 1980). The Japanese will not often ask for more than they need, although they may offer less than they can eventually offer. Proposal-counterproposal negotiating with the Japanese is not effective because their teams take so long to make decisions. Japanese negotiators make decisions on the basis of detailed information rather than persuasive arguments. Informal agreements and then written agreements are reached among all concerned.

Middle-Easterners can be described as having an intuitive-affective approach to persuasion. Broad issues that do not appear to be directly related to the issue at hand are brought up; issues are linked together on the basis of whether or not the speaker likes the issues. Personal bias is often exercised (Glenn, Witmeyer, and Stevenson, 1977). Negotiation teams from Saudi Arabia do not make decisions on the basis of empirical reasoning; while subordinates are consulted informally, the leader always makes the final decision, and Saudis expect the top man to negotiate with them (Weiss and Stripp, 1985).

The Mexicans use a centralized decision-making process. They view authority as being inherent within the individual, not his position; delegating of authority by an individual would be seen as a surrendering of assets. Making trade-offs is common for Mexican negotiators, including additional issues that are not part of the business at hand (Fisher, 1980).

Organizational Structure

For Americans the task-related stage is the most important for successful negotiations, where the most information is given (Adler, Graham, and Gehrke, 1987). But Americans tend to move toward the persuasion (bargaining) stage too quickly, not spending enough time gathering information. Americans usually approach negotiations sequentially, taking one thing at a time. For Americans, concessions on individual issues lead to the final agreement (Graham and Herberger, 1983). Negotiation outcomes to Americans depend upon events at the negotiation table, not the role of the negotiator or prenegotiation socializing (Campbell, Graham, Jolibert, and Meissner, 1988).

The French engage in a lateral style of negotiation; the whole deal is covered each step of the way. First comes the outline agreement, then the principal agreement, and then the headings agreement (Scott, 1981).

The Japanese do not discuss bargaining tactics. Prenegotiations move slowly and cautiously. The Japanese do not openly disagree during formal negotiations; they would consider this distasteful and embarrassing. They often use mediators during negotiations, and they basically take one position throughout the process; adjustments or modifications can be made once the final agreement is decided upon. American negotiators might see this as devious (Fisher, 1980). A seller may often express regret and apologies before offering a request. The Chinese state their proposition in the beginning and do not enhance it if the opposing side raises doubts (Weiss and Stripp, 1985). Concessions may come only at the end with negotiators from the Far East (Graham and Herberger, 1983).

Prenegotiation is crucial for successful Middle Eastern negotiations; it is only after respect and trust have been acquired that the hard negotiations will take place. Establishing a comfortable climate and spending time on the exploratory phase of negotiations are therefore crucial (Scott, 1981).

For Mexicans also the beginning stage of negotiations is used for social discourse and gaining trust among participants. This phase is crucial to them for successful and harmonious negotiations (Weiss and Stripp, 1985). In negotiations with Brazilians, the first stage of the process, nontask sounding (where pleasantries and nonbusiness information are exchanged) may be lengthened if the Brazilians feel that the other side is impatient. Such impatience may lead them to be apprehensive about beginning information seeking that starts the actual business negotiations. Brazilians offer high prices and eventually make concessions (Graham and Herberger, 1983).

CONCLUSION

Most of the reasons why Americans overlook cultural differences are traceable to strong feelings of ethnocentrism that influence how they send and receive messages. What makes ethnocentrism such a powerful and insidious force in communication is that it often exists invisibly (for example, we only study Western philosophers) and is usually invisible in its manifestations (for example, we approach problems with a Western orientation). The fact that many other cultures also demonstrate these feelings of conscious and unconscious superiority makes ethnocentrism especially difficult to control in the negotiating context.

It is our contention that sensitivity to cultural differences must begin before negotiation teams confront their counterparts from other countries. Most critics seem to agree that currently our universities are contributing to ethnocentric behavior instead of reducing it, by training people to do things "the American way" (Graham and Herberger, 1983, p. 161), a way, as we have argued, that may hinder international negotiations.

REFERENCES

Adler, N. J., Graham, J. L., and Gehrke, T. S. (1987). "Business Negotiations in Canada, Mexico, and the United States." *Journal of Business Research*, *15*, 411–429.

Campbell, N. C. G., Graham, J. L., Jolibert, A., and Meissner, H. G. (1988). "Marketing Negotiations in France, Germany, the United Kingdom, and the United States." *Journal of Marketing*, *52*, 49–62.

Fisher, G. (1980). *International Negotiation: A Cross-Cultural Perspective*. Chicago, Ill.: Intercultural Press, Inc.

Glenn, E. S., Witmeyer, D., and Stevenson, K. A. (1977). "Cultural Styles of Persuasion." *International Journal of Intercultural Relations*, *1* (3), 52–66.

Graham, J. L. (1987). "Deference Given the Buyer: Variations Across Twelve Cultures." In F. Lorange and F. Contractor (Eds.), *Cooperative Strategies in International Business*. Lexington, Mass.: Lexington Books.

Graham, J. L., Campbell, N., and Meissner, H. G. (1988). *Culture, Negotiations, and International Cooperative Ventures*. Unpublished manuscript.

Graham, J. L., and Herberger, R. A., Jr. (1983). "Negotiators Abroad—Don't Shoot from the Hip." *Harvard Business Review*, *61*, 160–168.

Greenwald, J. (1983, August 1). "The Negotiation Waltz." *Time*, pp. 41–42.

Hall, E. T. (1977). *Beyond Culture*. New York: Anchor Books.

Ishii, S. (1985). "Thought Patterns as Modes of Rhetoric: The United States and Japan." In L. A. Samovar and R. E. Porter (Eds.), *Intercultural Communication: A Reader* (4th ed.) Belmont, Calif.: Wadsworth.

March, R. (1985, April). "East Meets West at the Negotiating Table." *Winds*, pp. 47–55.

Moran, R. T., and Harris, P. R. (1982). *Managing Cultural Synergy*. Houston: Gulf.

Morrison, J. L. (1972). "The Absence of a Rhetorical Tradition in Japanese Culture." *Western Speech*, *36*, 89–102.

Okabe, R. (1973). "Yukichi Fukuzawa: A Promulgator of Western Rhetoric in Japan." *Quarterly Journal of Speech*, *59*, 186–195.

Scott, B. (1981). *The Skills of Negotiating*. New York: Wiley.

Soderberg, D. C. (1985). *A Study of the Influence of Culture on Iranian and American Negotiations*. Unpublished master's thesis, San Diego State University, San Diego, Calif.

Weiss, S. E., and Stripp, W. (1985). *Negotiating with Foreign Businesspersons: An Introduction for Americans with Propositions on Six Cultures*. Working paper no. 1, New York University, Graduate School of Business Administration.

Yotsukura, S. (1977). "Ethnolinguistic Introduction to Japanese Literature." In W. C. McCormack and S. A. Wurm (Eds.), *Language and Thought: Anthropological Issues*. Hague, The Netherlands: Mouton.

Zimmerman, M. (1985). *How to Do Business with the Japanese*. New York: Random House.

The Group: A Japanese Context

DOLORES CATHCART
ROBERT CATHCART

Examining the cultural context of Japanese communication and other social behavior is a process fraught with complexity. Everyone seriously interested in Japan knows that nation as a group culture where individualism is submerged and expression is found in "hidden" ways. Personal honor, reward, prestige, and wealth all depend on one's group affiliation and its position in a larger hierarchy. But, not so easily discerned, is how the Japanese came to be this way. There is no one factor such as hard work or group consensus that can readily account for Japan's highly organized, extremely productive society. Most studies of the Japanese use comparisons with the West, frequently citing examples that present opposing paradigms as if somehow we can understand Japan by thinking of it as a nation completely opposite from our own (see Cleaver, 1976). Perhaps a better way would be to look at Japanese historical development, tracing how the group tradition arose, how it survived major crisis, and how it continues to provide a secure foundation for the inclusion of the modern, the exotic, and even the previously unimagined.

Social context in Japan is circumscribed by numerous historical, social, political, and economic factors. First and foremost, Japan is a tiny nation — a collective of relatively small islands separated from

This original essay appears here in print for the first time. All rights reserved. Permission to reprint must be obtained from the authors and the publisher. Dolores Cathcart is a freelance writer. Robert Cathcart is Professor Emeritus at Queens College of the City of New York.

the Asian mainland by the Sea of Japan. This archipelago covers about 377,000 square kilometers (147,000 square miles), an area slightly larger than the size of California and Oregon combined. About 70 percent of the area is mountainous, leaving only 30 percent of the land for farming and urbanization. Japan has less than half the U.S. population but its approximately 124 million people live crowded together in this small area.

Despite Japan's recent prominence as a major world power its home territory is only a small spot on the world globe and its population is far smaller than other world powers. Its isolation, its almost total lack of natural resources, the constant and continual threat of earthquakes and typhoons, along with its small, dense, and homogenous population have fostered attitudes of dependency within the social unit and a sense of separateness from the outside. Japan's geography and its history form an ongoing context apart from which one cannot appreciate or understand the significance of Japanese group culture. We will describe some of this history and analyze its influence in shaping modern Japanese culture. From this basis we will examine the role of the group as the significant context for communication in Japan.

HISTORICAL DEVELOPMENTS

The Japanese Way, *Nihonjin-ron*

Japan's early civilization was based on rice agriculture, a process that demanded cooperation and communal sharing. Rice cultivation is labor intensive, leaving little time for other activities. So demanding was this farming that in the early villages families became extremely interdependent, living so closely together their rooftops often touched. Group values became dominant and the village came to be thought of as an extended family (*ie*). Loyalty to the village group, hard work, and harmony were enshrined as cardinal virtues. With no central source of national power and influence, villages remained insular and established their own

codes and rules (Worden, 1992). Any offense could result in ostracism (*mura hichibu*) and for the individual this was the worst of fates since other groups would be unlikely to accept an outsider. The values of the village group were internalized and formalized over time creating what is known as "the Japanese way" (*Nihonjin-ron*; see Taylor, 1983). Through the centuries there has been practically no influx of foreigners into Japan to alter Nihonjin-ron. Imported foreign influences such as Confucianism, Buddhism, and the introduction of Chinese character writing have been blended with the already established Japanese way without changing the group character of society. The Japanese still assimilate foreign ideas, fashions, and designs in this manner. Each is filtered through traditional Japanese concepts of group harmony and loyalty (Irokawa, 1973).

During the "middle ages" of Japanese history strong *shogunates* (ruling families) created a social structure similar in some ways to the feudal societies of Europe but different in function. In Japan, there were no religious or ethnic factions to deal with. There was little wealth to covet beyond the rice stored in granaries. Still, battles to acquire territory and political power were fought. Powerful families secured their large land holdings by building castles, creating samurai armies, and engaging in court intrigues in a constant jostling for power.

The concept of family or ie already included an extended group of villagers, and as strong shoguns gained power they set up daimyos in the large villages and demanded that all their serfs pay allegiance to them as head of family. In their own realms the daimyo represented unchallenged authority and held the power of life and death over all subjects. A strict hierarchy was established and elaborate rules requiring conformity, subservience, and the show of humility governed everyone's behavior. A court was established in Edo (now Tokyo) and all daimyos were required to spend part of each year there to keep them from becoming too independent of central authority and to control their powers. Foreigners and foreign influences were kept out except when it served the ruling shogunate's purposes. Foreign trade was severely limited, and travel abroad prohibited (Taylor, 1983, p. 35).

In Edo, power was concentrated and reinforced by establishing a strict hierarchy that demanded a show of deference and humility to those at the top. At court, every nuance of speech, movement, and dress acquired meaning. Every act of communication became highly dependent on context. The Japanese language itself came to reflect this stratification of society; for example, grammar requires recognition of male superiority, there is an ingroup language and an outgroup one, and there are generational variations. Different disciplines or schools use different language to describe identical things. Important differences also extend beyond the grammatical: "There are differences (in speech) in communicational settings (where and when speech occurs), in topics, in channels (e.g., handwriting etc.)" (Hayashi, 1974). Highly refined ways of nonverbal communication were also given great importance. In negotiation, the nobler the aspiration, the more exquisite and subtle was the expression required, and the greater was the demand on others to interpret. These courtly customs left an indelible mark on the Japanese in as much as Japan's feudalism lasted almost sixteen hundred years (A.D. 300–1868). Its residue continues to influence Japanese social interaction and to shape modern politics (Worden, 1992).

After the demise of the shogunates and the establishment of a central government (the Meiji Restoration period, 1868–1919) there was a drastic reorganization of population and productivity. Japan brought in machinery, created industrial cities, and opened its doors (under pressure from the United States and other powers) to world trade. Despite this upheaval, concepts of extended family, group affiliation, and loyalty not only survived but were reinforced by a national civil code that strengthened Confucian ideas of filial piety and the hierarchical status that had been assimilated in the Diamyo period (Long, 1992, p. 104). The Confucian notion of ranking in the family—men and women, father and child—was applied to the new industries and used to create groups of workers dependent on those at the top. In the move from countryside to city there was almost no change toward individual autonomy although some Western ideas of equality were adopted by small numbers of people in the liberalizing atmosphere of the 1920s. Foreign ideas seeped in and in the rapidly developing industrial cities new opportunities arose for small enterprises that were least affected by the traditional codes and rituals. The rise of militarism, however, quickly altered the course of Japan and the old customs were appropriated in the service of a military empire. Powerful generals restored the samurai code and, with fanatic zeal mobilized the nation for war by evoking the traditional loyalty of every group to the larger group, which now was the nation or empire.

Post-World War II Japan

Japan's defeat in World War II signaled another drastic change in social control. The nation was in complete disarray; people were starving and American atomic and fire bombs had devastated cities and countryside alike. The American occupation (al forces) faced the enormous task of organizing a unified work force for rebuilding. American occupational officials looked to heads of important families from prewar Japan, who still commanded much respect. These modern day daimyos were able to use their rank to establish the new hierarchies that became the corporate entities of a newly rebuilt Japan. Again, the traditional social structure was reaffirmed and in the most unlikely circumstances.

The American occupation (1945–1952) brought many changes but it did not radically reform the social order. The constitution guaranteed individual freedoms. The political structure was completely reformed. Yet, half a century later the Japanese continue to live lives centered on group responsibility rather than individual liberty. Nihonjin-ron (the Japanese way) continues alongside constitutional guarantees of individual rights and the people live, somewhat uncomfortably, with the resultant dichotomies. Economically, however, the results have been tremendously successful for the Japanese. Set on a new course with economic development as a priority, the Japanese have used traditional concepts of group effort and hard work to not only rebuild but to catch up with and surpass the West.

Out of this history has evolved a modern nation of diligent workers rewarded by being a part of a greatly successful whole. Japan's most prominent and lasting achievement has been to produce a society that revolves totally around the concept of "group." Long (1992) sees this history as the dominant context for all Japanese social interaction today:

Creating harmonious relations with others through reciprocity and the fulfillment of social obligations is more significant for most Japanese than an individual's relationship to a transcendent God. Harmony, order, and self-development are three of the most important values that underlie social interaction. . . . Religious practice, too, emphasizes the maintenance of harmonious relations with others (both spiritual beings and other humans) and the fulfillment of social obligations as a member of a family and a community (p. 93).

Women in Japanese Society

We note here that this essay does not address the role of women in Japanese society. The civil code enacted during the Meiji Restoration legally defined women as inferior to men. As Japan became industrialized women were used as workers but were denied access to any advancement in the hierarchy since they were always hired as "temporary" employees. Most women in modern Japan are still denied lifetime employment offered to men despite the fact that the democratic constitution enacted after World War II granted women equal rights. Some observers claim that women's roles are changing (see Iwao, 1976), but within the context of group and the male-dominated hierarchy, women have little direct influence except through the traditional role of "young daughter" (office lady) within the company, and later, wife and mother in the family. Many women accept this as "the way things are." Some Japanese women we know say they would welcome change but most see little possibility of real change, and instead, say they would like to have been born male.

THE GROUP AS CONTEXT

Taylor (1983) offers this apt description of modern day Japanese:

One of Japan's most prominent national characteristics is the individual's sense of the group. At every level of society the Japanese have a very strong sense of who is on the inside [uchi] and who is on the outside [soto]. The group draws firm boundaries between "us" and "them" and, hierarchy, is an essential guidepost to proper behavior. Group ties can be so close that members feel collective responsibility for each other's actions. Loyalty to the group and willingness to submit to its demands are thus key virtues in Japanese society. It is the values of the group rather than abstract principles, that serve as morality for many Japanese (p. 67).

This special way of defining "group" exists in contrast to our Western view which holds that each individual has a unique identity, a "self" separate from, though influenced by, other members of the group. There is no counterpart in Japan to the American debate over "what is a group?" or whether committees make better decisions than individuals, and so on. In Japan there is no need to define groups, they simply "are," the "natural" or normal milieu in which human interaction takes place.

Every Japanese person belongs to a primary group. Even hippies, for instance, or people who from our [Japanese] standards are ruffians, have primary groups of which they are members. There has never in Japan been a stratum of drifters who have been caste out of society and forced to make their own way on their own. The elite have built their own clearly differentiated "islands" as well, and other "islands" can be found everywhere down to the very bottom of society. Everybody has a group he or she is part of (Nakane 1977, p. 8).

The individual does not believe it is possible to "go it alone" for each Japanese, at birth, is drawn into this system. A Japanese legal scholar, Takeoyoshi (1967), describes the Japanese way of viewing the individual in the group:

There is no place for the concepts of the individual as an independent entity equal to other individuals. In (Japanese) culture, the social order consists of social obligations, which are defined not in specific determinate terms, but in diffuse, indeterminate terms. . . . The indeterminateness of social obligations — hence the lack of concepts of equality and independent individual — does not allow the existence of [individual] "right" as the counterpart of social obligations (p. 274).

Each person is thought of as part of a group and each small group as part of a larger one. Within each group individuals are ranked hierarchically according to sex, seniority, and age. In a Japanese group an individual has no problem fitting in or finding a role. A person's place in the group is determined at the time of entrance into the group and remains that ever after. In the family each member is ranked. The youngest daughter in the family remains in that inferior role no matter what occupational or marital status she attains. In the business world the newly hired worker is junior to all those who were there before and senior to all those who follow. This will not change. No bright young member of a group ever leap frogs over those more senior or is assigned a task not commensurate with his or her place in the hierarchy.

An experience we had in Japan exemplifies this. We had spent a long arduous day establishing research procedures for a study of stereotypes with our Japanese and French counterparts. We noticed the Japanese seemed ill at ease, particularly at lunchtime and during our coffee or tea breaks. At dinnertime we were escorted to our places in a restaurant dining room. Our Japanese hosts now appeared very pleased and relaxed. We interpreted this as their pride and pleasure in bringing us to such a fine Tokyo restaurant. This interpretation was proven inaccurate when one of the Japanese researchers whispered that *now* they were happy because, for the first time in the entire day, we were seated in the correct order. The oldest person and most senior researcher, who happened to be an American, was placed at the head of the group; next in age and

status was a Japanese team member, now seated to the left; and so on down the line, everyone arranged, this time, according to age and status. The change in the attitude of the Japanese was amazing. You could hear and feel the difference. They were at ease, comfortable, able to fully participate because the correct order (hierarchy) had been established.

As Taylor (1983) points out, hierarchy is the context for all relationships in Japan:

All societies establish hierarchies. In few societies, however, are they so widespread or important as in Japan. For the Japanese, rank is so finely determined that equality is rare — everyone and everything are at least slightly above or below the nearest apparent equal. Family members, work mates, schools, companies, even nations and races all have their places. Hierarchy is inseparable from orderliness; a group is not properly organized unless its members are ranked (p. 42).

Group Concepts

This dependency and the interdependency of all members of a group is reinforced by the concept of *on*. A Japanese is expected to feel an indebtedness to those others in the group who provide security, care, and support. This indebtedness creates obligation and when combined with dependency is called *on*. On functions as a means of linking all persons in the group in an unending chain because obligation is never satisfied, but continues throughout life. *On* is fostered by a system known as the *oyabun-kobun* relationship (Hall & Beardsley, 1965). Traditionally the *oyabun* is a father, boss, or patron who protects and provides for a son, employee, or student in return for his or her service and loyalty. This is not a one-way dependency. Each boss or group leader recognizes his own dependency on those below. Without their undivided loyalty he or she could not function. Oyabun are also acutely aware of this double dimension because of having had to serve a long period of *kobun* on the way up the hierarchy to the position at the top. All had oyabun who protected and assisted them, much like a father, and now each must do the same for their kobun. Oyabun have one or more kobun whom they look after much as if they were children. The more loyal and devoted the "children" the more successful the "father."

This relationship is useful in modern life where large companies assume the role of superfamily and become involved in every aspect of their workers' lives. Bosses are oyabun and employees are kobun. The company is not viewed as just a place of employment apart from one's life at home. The company or corporation becomes the center of the individual's social and economic life. Off-work hours are spent with one's fellow employees; vacations are taken at the company-owned retreat; health services, insurance, and transportation are provided. In even the most personal situations the company is involved. It isn't unusual for the company to help arrange marriages. In exchange the worker gives the company priority in his or her life. Thus, *on* based on the oyabun-kobun relationship works to promote both company and individual needs and creates a tight bond.

On and oyabun-kobun stress dependency and loyalty of superior and inferior in a vertical hierarchy. Without some balance, however, these concepts would produce a highly factional system where each group would have no regard for the interests of the whole. A mutual regard or loyalty to something larger than one's faction or oyabun-kobun link is therefore necessary. It is the concept of *giri* which serves in checking factionalism. Giri controls the horizontal relationships in this vertically organized society.

Giri, a term difficult for Westerners to interpret, is widely used in Japan. Hall and Beardsley (1965) offer the following explanation:

To some Japanese today, giri *is the blanket term for obligation between persons in concrete, actual situations as contrasted with a universalistic ethic of duty. . . . Giri [is the form of] obligations . . . [without] superiority on one side and inferiority on the other [as in the* on *relationship]. . . . Giri connotes obligation and as such sets up the tone of relationship toward specified other persons (p. 94).*

Giri is well-suited to a society that induces life-long group relationships. These life-long relationships extend obligation horizontally to all the other groups that Japanese are members of or that contain associates from former groups. Japanese spend most of their days in close proximity with the members of their group, and without giri such an intense interaction over such an extended period of time would be impossible to bear. The highly ritualized modes of interpersonal interaction developed to accommodate giri and obligate persons to other group members prevent situations that produce hostility.

Japanese Decision Making

This uniquely Japanese way of viewing relationships creates a distinctive style of decision making known as *consensus decision*. The Japanese devotion to consensus building seems difficult for most Westerners to grasp but loses some of its mystery when looked at as a solution to representing every member of the group. In a system that operates on oyabun-kobun relationships nothing is decided without concern for how the outcome will affect all. Ideas and plans are circulated up and down the company hierarchy until everyone has had a chance to react. This reactive process is not to exert pressure but to make certain that all matters affecting the particular groups and the company are taken into consideration. Much time is spent assessing the mood of everyone involved and only after all the ramifications of how the decision will affect each group can there be a quiet assent. A group within the company may approve a decision that is not directly in its interest (or even causes it difficulties) because its members know they are not ignored, their feelings have been expressed and they can be assured that what is good for the company will ultimately be good for them. For this reason consensus decisions cannot be hurried along without chancing a slight or oversight that will cause future problems.

The process of consensus building in order to make decisions is a time-consuming one, not only because everyone must be considered, but also because the Japanese avoid verbalizing objections or doubts in order to preserve group harmony. The advice, often found in American group literature, that group communication should be characterized by open and candid statements expressing individual personal feelings, wishes, and dislikes, is the antithesis of the Japanese consensus process. No opposing speeches are made to argue alternate ideas; no conferences are held to debate issues. Instead, the process of assessing the feelings and mood of each work group proceeds slowly until there exists a climate of agreement. This process is possible because of the tight relationships that allow bosses and workers to know each other intimately and to know the group so well that needs and desires are easy to assess. As Kyozaburo (1979) states

The members of a small, closed society know almost everything about each other, so they do not need too many words to convey meaning. They are accustomed to understanding the other person's feelings through his or her facial expression and attitude. It was considered foolish, even impolite, to explain everything from beginning to end in words (p. 5).

The Japanese place a high value on the display of feelings and sensitivity rather than on verbal skill. The first virtue is group harmony; therefore, the free voicing of personal opinions is avoided. Some of our Japanese friends have said they can communicate with persons in their *nakama* (life-long group) by a kind of telepathy, claiming they do not need words to express their thoughts but depend on an exchange of feelings. A Japanese explains: "It might be said that the culture is primarily visual, not verbal, in orientation, and social decorum provides that silence, not eloquence, is rewarded" (Miyoshi, 1974).

French philosopher Roland Barthes (1982) found the Japanese quite unique:

[In Japan] it is not the voice (with which we identify the "rights" of the person) which communicates (communicates what? our—necessarily beautiful—soul? our sincerity? our prestige?), but the whole body (eyes, smile, hair, gestures, clothing)

which sustains with you a sort of babble that the perfect domination of the codes strips of all regressive, infantile character. To make a date (by gestures, drawings on paper, proper names) may take an hour, but during that hour, for a message which would be abolished in an instant if it were to be spoken (simultaneously quite essential and quite insignificant), it is the other's entire body which has been known, savored, received, and which has displayed (to no real purpose) its own narrative, its own text (p. 10).

Consensus building is utterly dependent on this sort of communication and dovetails with other values and ideas regarding the individual in society.

One of the consequences of making decisions through consensus is it makes the group and not the individual morally responsible for the decisions. Golden (1982) notes

Once an opinion is acceptable, it becomes the group's opinion and is no longer associated with its originator. This convention helps keep group unity intact by not singling out any one individual on the basis of performance or initiative (p. 137).

When a person commits a transgression it is the group that is embarrassed and, in the final analysis, responsible for the misdeed. It is commonly accepted in Japanese law and practice that the group should make amends and restitution resulting from individual misconduct (Kawashima, 1967). Usually, the person at the head of the particular group offers the necessary apology or makes the restitution expected. Individual Japanese, thus, feel a great deal of pressure and anxiety to always behave appropriately so that the group will not be embarrassed or looked upon with disfavor.

In dealing with such issues as corruption, bribe taking, pollution and price fixing the Japanese government is faced with a new problem because the international news media look to assign blame. It can be very difficult in Japan to investigate groups and assess blame because group members will not talk to outsiders about what happens in their group and they do not express dissatisfaction publicly.

THE MODERN CONTEXT

The Japanese replicate this ancient model of family hierarchy and process throughout their society. The nuclear family is the first circle in the many circles of groups that dominate life in Japan. Dependency on others is central to this system. It is, therefore, commonly accepted that the Japanese family must teach a child to become a member of society, learning to behave according to the assigned role he or she is born to. "Japanese children learn from their earliest days that human fulfillment comes from close association with others" (Long, 1992). All the intricate rituals and modes of honorific speech are learned within the family in preparation for life in a hierarchical group society. Most importantly, each child learns that personal desire (*ninjo*) must be fulfilled *within the group*. Ninjo is submerged in the opinion and action of the group. This lesson could be hard without the rewards that accrue. Japanese children, at a young age, are extremely indulged and given tender care, learning that comfort and intimacy are to be found by controlling ninjo and accepting the group as a means of personal fulfillment (Kizaemon, 1954). Japanese psychologist Takeo Doi (1962) describes the dependency that results from such care as *amae* or "the sweet dependency" first experienced through mother love within the family. He contends that throughout life a Japanese participates in close groups in an everlasting quest to duplicate this sweet dependency.

In modern Japan government service or employment with a large important corporation provides the path to success. Children are early groomed to compete for acceptance into that hierarchy. Once that path is entered it is extremely difficult to deviate from; it is rare for a person to withdraw from a group because group affiliation confers identity and security. All through school Japanese children prepare for university entrance exams because their whole future is dependent on scores made during the week of "Exam Hell." The top two universities admit those with the highest scores. The best companies and the government civil service hire graduates from those two universities. All other universities are arranged hierarchically and their graduates are placed in the appropriate business, government, and education hierarchies.

High school students cram for exams and mothers devote themselves to making sure study comes before all else. The goal of gaining admission to a university dominates life; anxiety and work mark these years for both student and mother. Once accepted at a university it is rare for anyone to drop out or leave even temporarily to travel or work. Universities rarely grant readmittance after an absence and credits cannot be transferred. Therefore, everyone who enters the university stays and becomes part of the group hierarchy. Peer groups are formed around those who entered at the same time and are the same age. This has special importance because the connections made while in the university will continue throughout each person's life.

It is commonly reported that Japanese university students do not study hard once they have been admitted to a school. After the grueling competition for admission, students view university life as a time to throw off restraints, to drink, to make love, to protest, or act out against the older established order. Evidence of this seems to abound in the news stories and pictures of youth in Tokyo. These portrayals fail to explain the overnight transformation that occurs when upon graduation day the former student emerges a company man — cutting his hair; dressing in a suit, white shirt, and tie; and adopting a reserved attitude and impeccable manners. This is yet another case of a Japanese trait that seems mysterious until seen in its context. The rigid system that requires constant observance of hierarchy has its safety valves and the period at the university is one of those times when the strict code that controls behavior is relaxed. This time of nonconformity doesn't threaten the whole because it is virtually impossible to deviate from the chosen path that leads to company life. Then too, even though students appear to only be having a good time, they are actually serving the established order by making necessary and important contacts with others that will serve the company later on.

Students at the university form their own nakamas (small groups), usually around special interest clubs such as poetry, photography, hiking, or golf. They drink together, confide in one another, and learn to know each other intimately. This is not only practice for joining a company group, it forms links with others who go on to other groups and who will be valuable contacts that help connect company groups. A Japanese company man never actually leaves his university nakama but maintains and nourishes the close contacts with the group by continuing the sport or special interest the group shares as an extension of his business obligations. This interaction provides the necessary connection between groups that maintains the close connections among business, government, and educational institutions. In Japan, groups not only spiral out concentrically from nuclear family to school, to university, to company, to nation but also intersect horizontally on a less hierarchical plane — that is, company to company or agency to agency.

The Company Man

In this overlapping and connecting of groups, it is always understood that one's loyalty belongs unquestionably to one's company. This is acknowledged in the ritual and ceremony that surround any transition from one hierarchy to another. Transitions, such as leaving the university to join a company are circumscribed by ceremony and marked as symbolic rights of passage. For example, when a new recruit is welcomed into the company the new worker's parents participate, symbolizing the approval and acknowledgment of the transfer of loyalty from the natural family to the company family. The family metaphor is so pervasive the worker is thought of as being adopted by the company. Still, since one never really leaves a group, the child, the member of a student nakama, and the worker are all roles with continuing obligations. For sociologist Matsumoto (1960), it is this context that circumscribes the role of the individual:

The individual does not interact as an individual but as a son in a parent-child relationship, as an apprentice in a master-apprentice relationship, or as a worker in an employer-employee relationship. Furthermore, the playing of a role of son, appren-tice, student, or worker persists twenty-four hours a day. There is no clear-cut demarcation between work and home life (p. 60).

Nonconformist

While it is nearly impossible for persons enmeshed in corporate hierarchy to make personal decisions to change there is room in modern Japan for non-conformity outside the monolithic government-business enterprises. Not all Japanese, of course, conform to the image of the "company man." Some exceptions to corporate life are the many small entrepreneurs who own bars, beauty shops, noodle stands, imo (hot potato) carts, and so on and the many Japanese who participate in the entertainment world of film, radio, television, photography, and fashion where foreign ideas and techniques are explored safely without threat (presumably) of changing the central group structure.

Throughout Japanese history there have been individuals alienated from traditional groups for one reason or another, producing some interesting and provocative results. Some outsiders have joined the gangster group known as the *yakuzi*. The yakuzi run the gambling, prostitution, bar enterprises, and other rackets in Japan and are tolerated by the establishment until they overstep boundaries somehow understood but never stated. The yakuzi are not only tolerated but it is said that some corporations are known to hire yakuzi to control stockholder meetings and perform other fringe services. Interestingly, the yakuzi have an internal group structure that rivals any other in the nation in its requirements for loyalty and ritual.

MODERN DAY CONTEXTS

Outside Influences

There are, of course, pressures toward change in present day Japan. Japan's goal to catch up with and bypass the West has presented challenges in dealing with other nations. It has become increasingly difficult to protect society from outside influences when businesses must send their employees to foreign countries and when television brings foreign nations to Japan everyday. As the Japanese become aware of how the rest of the world perceives them, their sense of themselves as unique is being challenged and they are seeing outsiders in a different light (see A Report on Television Stereotypes of Three Nations: France, U.S., and Japan, 1968). *Uchi* and *soto* are now harder to define. The necessity to communicate with foreign governments and to do business with foreign companies presents the Japanese with formidable problems. In face-to-face negotiations the Japanese have tried to adapt to the exigencies of dealing with styles of negotiation and decision making totally different from their own.

Uchi and *Soto*

The Japanese view that they are a unique people in a unique nation is, to the outsider, the most frustrating characteristic of the Japanese. It seems to deny what most Americans believe, that there are fundamental beliefs and feelings that unite all people in the modern world. Americans feel strongly that if they just try hard enough they can find that common ground on which to resolve differences with other peoples. Yet, the Japanese we know feel equally strongly that Americans can never really understand "ware, ware, Nihonjin" or "we Japanese" as they so often refer to themselves; the "we" meaning unique or different from anyone else, anywhere. Gould (1972) concurs with his statement that the Japanese have

an unshakable conviction that no non-Japanese can ever understand the nuances and intuitive perceptions of the Japanese. In many travels over many years in all parts of Japan, I have never met a Japanese who truly believes that the foreign mentality can share the Japanese experience or aspirations. . . . It seems (to be) the Japanese perspective that experiences of Japan are by that fact alone totally different from the rest of the world (p. 71).

Most intercultural studies assume there are basic human qualities that are found in every race and people and that by understanding other cultures we can create common goals for humanity. The Japanese do participate in intercultural endeavors but they do not see themselves as "the same" in any way as the soto, or other. Further, their uniqueness is unquestionable to them, though not because of any physiological or psychological difference in nature but because of the extremely intimate and complex group orientation that has been the center of their culture for all its centuries. It is also true that no foreigner in Japan can ever be completely accepted no matter how well the language is spoken or the cultural nuances understood. A foreigner cannot be uchi (inside), and therefore one can never behave or speak in the Japanese way. The Japanese way (ninhonji-ron) has been carefully protected from outside influences and even in these times when the Japanese must deal with outsiders that way is protected. The Japanese are extremely interested in and ready to import foreign ideas, fashions, and trends but only when they are filtered through the traditional system. Japan imports and views more American movies than any other nation. All the French fashion houses have posh showrooms in Tokyo. Coca-Cola and Big Macs thrive on the scene. T-shirts with foreign language logos abound. But, when getting down to business the Japanese insist on maintaining the old ways.

In the international business and political worlds there are tremendous pressures on Japan to change but so far the Japanese have been able to adapt their methods to the exigencies of modern international life. To do business with the outside world, companies and corporations have not only had to admit foreigners to Japan and find ways to negotiate but they have also had to send many of their own employees to other countries. This requires the Japanese to be away from the nakama for months, sometimes years, posing a real threat to maintaining groups in the traditional way. If the Japanese employee in America or Europe adapts too well to his foreign assignment it will be very difficult to return to his nakama or family. The Japanese believe that a person who leaves Japan, even temporarily, chances losing the true Japanese spirit. Persons in foreign positions for any length of time are scrutinized on their return to assess if they have lost their Japaneseness. *Nakama doshi*, or being in one's group, requires diligent and constant participation. When a Japanese has been away from the group it is a hard task to become nakama doshi once again.

To conduct business or diplomatic relations with the Japanese it is often necessary to make the concessions to Japanese style. This is not a stubborn refusal on the part of the Japanese to meet half way, rather it is the real danger to the group that Japanese feel when dealing with soto (outsiders) whose seemingly direct and brash ways disrupt harmony and undermine obligation.

Various styles have evolved but it is very difficult for the Japanese to proceed in any encounter until the relative importance of persons (hierarchical status) they are dealing with is ascertained. Among themselves the Japanese use business cards to accomplish this and they have convinced many foreigners to use business card exchange as a way to begin communication. If the exchange is taking place in Japan the next move is to learn as much as possible about the others they must deal with. This too is done in a traditional Japanese fashion. Foreign businesspeople are entertained in restaurants and bars in an attempt to discover the style and direction the proceedings will take. The Westerner often thinks of this as becoming friends but friendship is not the purpose. The Japanese are getting a feel for things, assessing the aspirations of the others, and deciding when they feel they know enough to start business. Once negotiations are finally begun matters proceed slowly because everyone in the company must be kept involved (even those not present). If the Japanese decide to stop negotiations or to withdraw it can be very difficult to know this. Nothing happens and only vague and noncommittal responses are offered. There is not a definite "no." There is just a reluctance that must be interpreted. This lack of directness often frustrates foreigners. These behaviors, though, are simply adapted from the normal Japanese way of conducting business. Terasawa (1974) gives this advice:

When you do business in Japan you must be prepared to take your time, to be alert to indirection. The Japanese businessman is intent on harmony, *even if the deal falls through, and he will spend whatever time is necessary to determine his "you to you" approach and he will communicate his own views indirectly and with great sensitivity. . . . This places time in a different perspective. In Japan the Western deadline approach is secondary to a thorough job. Japanese are thorough in their meetings as well as in their production. Thus Americans are often exasperated by the seemingly endless sequences of meetings of many Japanese businessmen (p. A41).*

CONCLUSION

Clearly, the Japanese are now facing demands on them as a prominent power in the world that requires accommodation and new ways of behaving internationally, yet the context for all Japanese behavior remains the group. Group orientation has produced the highly successful blend of big business and government at the top of a hierarchy supported by loyal, hardworking employees and this isn't likely to change in the immediate future.

According to American cultural critic Louis Menand (1992), "Culture isn't something that comes with one's race or sex. It comes only through experience; there isn't any other way to acquire it. And in the end everyone's culture is different because everyone's experience is different." While Menand's statement stands as a justification for American individuality, curiously, the Japanese would find it acceptable as a justification of their view that cultural and racial differences are intractable. They believe that the gulf that separates one people from the next is always, at base, unbridgeable.

REFERENCES

"A Report on Television Stereotypes of Three Nations: France, U.S., and Japan." (1968). International Television Flow Project—Japan. Tokyo: NHK Broadcasting Co.

Barthes, R. (1982). *Empire of Signs.* (Translated by Richard Howard). NY: Hill & Wang.

Cleaver, C. (1976). *Japanese and Americans: Cultural Parallels and Paradoxes*. Minneapolis: University of Minnesota Press.

Doi, L. T. (1962). "Amae: A Key Concept for Understanding Japanese Culture." In R. J. Smith and R. K. Beardsley (Eds.), *Japanese Culture: Its Developments and Characteristics*. (pp. 130–144). NY: Aldine.

Golden, A. S. (1982). "Group Think in Japan, Inc." *The New York Times Magazine* (December, 5) pp. 133–140.

Gould, R. (1972). "Japan Alone." *Japan Quarterly*. 19 (1).

Hall, J., and Beardsley, R. (1965). *Twelve Doors to Japan*. NY: McGraw-Hill.

Hayashi, T. (1974). "Modernization of the Japanese System of Communication." *Language in Society*. April.

Irokawa, D. (1973). "Japan's Grass-Roots Tradition: Current Issues in the Mirror of History." *Japan Quarterly*. 20 (1).

Iwao, S. (1976). "A Full Life for Modern Japanese Women." In *Text of Seminar on "Changing Values in Modern Japan."* (pp. 95–133). Tokyo: Nihonjin Kenkyukai.

Kawashima, T., and Takeoyoshi, K. (1967). "The Status of the Individual in the Notion of Law, Right, and Social Order in Japan." In C. Moore (Ed.), *The Japanese Mind*. Honolulu: University Press of Hawaii.

Kizaemon, A. (1954). "The Family in Japan." *Marriage and Family Living*. 16 (4). p. 362.

Kyozaburo, D. (1979). "Japanese Culture." *About Japan 11*. Tokyo: Kinji Kawamura.

Long, S. O. (1992). "The Society and Its Environment." In R. E. Dolan and R. L. Worden (Eds.), *Japan: A Country Study*. (pp. 69–128). Washington, D.C.: Library of Congress.

Matsumoto, Y. (1960). "Contemporary Japan: The Individual and the Group." *Transactions of the American Philosophical Society*, 50 (1), p. 60.

Menand, L. (1992). "The Hammer and the Nail." *The New Yorker*, July 20, 84.

Miyoshi, M. (1974). *Accomplices of Silence*. Berkeley: University of California Press. p. xv.

Nakane, C. (1977). "Speaking of the Japanese." *About Japan*. Tokyo: Kinji Kawamura.

Taylor, J. (1983). *Shadows of the Rising Sun*. NY: Harcourt Brace Jovanovich.

Terasawa, Y. (1974). "Japanese Style in Decision-Making." *The New York Times*. Sunday, May 12.

Worden, R. L. (1992). "Historical Setting." In R. E. Dolan and R. L. Worden (Eds.), *Japan: A Country Study*. (pp. 1–68). Washington, D.C.: Library of Congress.

Counseling and Culture

ANNE PEDERSEN
PAUL PEDERSEN

During the last 20 years the social-psychological concept *culture* has become recognized as a powerful framework for use in analyzing ourselves — *who we are* and *who others are*. These others are those with whom we live, work, and serve.

I. DEFINING CULTURE

What is culture? Some anthropologists find culture in artifacts — for example, tools, rock etchings, temples of the Mayan and Incan peoples, and other architecture; but these are products of culture. Social anthropology, a subdiscipline of anthropology, is primarily concerned with the study of **culture** as complex social structures that make up communities, societies, and nations. Both physical and social anthropology address wider concerns than individuals. But to complete our understanding we must look at the originators of culture, *people*. We are the essence of the culture process. How do we create our culture? From the moment of birth we don't just see we *look for*, we don't just hear, we *listen for*. We are actively creating our culture through our sense of the social and physical environment. Baby smiles and mother rewards baby with a smile and a hug. A smiling face, thus, becomes a pleasurable event in this parent-child culture.

This original article appears in print here for the first time. All rights reserved. Permission to reprint must be obtained from the authors and the publisher. Anne and Paul Pedersen teach at Syracuse University.

The mind-body interaction begins the process of cultural orientation, forming patterns of behavior, expectations, and values. *Behavior* justifies our existence, *expectations* motivate us, and *values* order our priorities as well as contribute to the "rightness" or "wrongness" of our activities.

Culture exists in people. It is not static. Our concepts grow more complex and agile to accommodate to life around us. As our life space expands, our perceptions widen. We change, we become more aware, more knowledgeable, more skillful in adapting to our surroundings. The individual process of differentiation suggests change, mental diversification, and development.

Understanding this process we can say that we are all *multicultural*. We need not be in contact with exotic or unique people, different ethnic groups, or international visitors to experience multiculturalism. The multicultural set is *in* us. Hence, the counselor and the client are moving with one another, attempting to match perceptions that can be only partly isomorphic. To be most effective the counselor must recognize both the ways that a client is culturally similar and the ways that a client is culturally different from him or her.

A complex model is needed to capture, describe, and assess the dynamic factors that influence a person's behaviors and expectations. Such a model will allow the more fluid analysis of counseling judgments, yet encourage the creation of orderly categories to help the counselor interpret relationships.

That model should see culture as intrinsic, located in the person. This way it can be understood as a key to unlocking individual behavior, expectations, and values. A skilled counselor will then be more likely to accurately identify the salient social system variables that influence a client's expectations and the values that explain that individual's attendant behavior (Hines & Pedersen, 1981a, 1981b; Pedersen, A. & Pedersen, P., 1989, 1991; Pedersen, P. & Pedersen, A., 1989; Pedersen, P., 1988). This article will describe a Cultural Grid that seeks to meet these two criteria and help the counselor organize the complicated variables of a multicultural counseling interview.

II. THE INTRAPERSONAL CULTURAL GRID

The Cultural Grid provides direction for counselors to accomplish three functions:

1. represent a unique personal orientation

2. identify and describe the cultural aspect of the situation

3. form hypotheses about cultural versus personal differences.

Not all differences, misunderstandings, or conflicts are derived from contrasting cultural orientations. Some conflicts result from deliberate and intentional personal behavior. There is an important difference between cultural and personal behavior.

The Cultural Grid provides an open-ended analytical tool for understanding selected social system variables such as age, gender, educational level, and aspects of comembership as they interact within the kaleidoscope of personally generated experience.

If you think of your culture as an accumulation of everything that everyone has ever taught you or that you have learned on your own then you have an idea of how complex interpersonal culture is. This almost unlimited list of social system variables may include any one or more of those "teachers." This definition of culture has heuristic value for counselors who seek to understand a client's intrapsychic reality from the viewpoint the client is presenting at a point in time. The value of a broad reservoir of social system variables is that no matter how idiosyncratic, different, and even unacceptable a client's behavior might be that behavior is almost certainly learned — linked to a salient social system variable shared by others.

We present and discuss two versions of the Cultural Grid. The first emphasizes *intra*personal dynamics of the individual, the internal variables that control behaviors. This version of the Cultural Grid is like a photographic snapshot of the social system characteristics that taught you the *values* that shaped the *expectations* that dictated the *behaviors* you are presenting right now — like reading this chapter. Think of the Intrapersonal Cultural Grid as a framework for understanding how your social system's variables control your each and every behavior (see Figure 1).

This Intrapersonal Cultural Grid serves many different purposes:

1. combines both the personal and group identity in a specific cultural context

2. helps each individual gain insight into his or her own personal-cultural orientation

3. identifies ways in which each individual is both different and similar in comparison with others

4. accounts for and predicts changing priorities and behaviors as different social system variables become salient

5. provides a meaningful network of cues to counselors seeking to understand culturally different clients

The Intrapersonal Cultural Grid might help understand the effect an individual's personal cultural orientation has on making a particular decision in a certain way at a certain time. Knowing how culture controls behavior will help a client and a counselor make better decisions.

You may benefit from filling out the grid to chart a particular behavior or decision in your life. For example, what are the expectations, the values, and the salient social system variables behind your decision to read this book? By systematically identifying the ways that these social system variables have shaped your behavior you will gain information about your own intrapersonal cultural orientation — meaning the ways you are both similar and different from those around you. You may display the particular behavior of reading this book because you *expect* to learn something. That expectation is important to you because you *value* learning. Who taught you that learning was important? your family? your peers? your socio-economic group? others from your nationality? from your ethnic back-

Cognitive Perspective

Social system variable	Role behavior	Expectation	Value-Meaning

Demographic
  race
  gender
  age
  other			

Ethnographic
  nationality
  ethnicity
  language			

Status level
  economic
  social
  educational			

Affiliation
  formal
  non-formal
  informal			

Figure 1 The Intrapersonal Cultural Grid

ground? Which social system variables are salient here? Take a minute now to fill in your personal cultural orientation.

Why did you decide to take the course for which you are reading this chapter? Perhaps your family has always valued education. You are 20 years old and a junior in college. You have a brother with a learning disability. While you patiently try to help your brother, you realize that you don't have the necessary skill. You enroll in this course and read this book because you expect your behavior to better equip you to help your brother and others.

Different people commit the same behavior with very different expectations or for different reasons. On the other hand, people who display very different behaviors might have very similar expectations and values. "Culture" is the name we have given to understanding and making sense out of how people can be both similar and different at the same time. Compare your explanation of your behavior in taking this course and reading this book with another person in your class and pay attention to the similarities and differences. Try to understand the ways you are both similar and different.

In analyzing a particular behavior we begin by identifying the expectation behind the behavior. What was it that the person expected to happen as a result of enacting that particular behavior? Then we move from the expectation to the values behind the expectation. Why is this expectation important? Finally, we identify the source of those values. Where did the individual learn that some things are more important than others? This process is important for all communication but it is essential for multicultural counseling where very different behaviors might easily be otherwise misunderstood.

III. THE INTERPERSONAL CULTURAL GRID

The second model we examine is the Interpersonal Cultural Grid, which looks at the similarities and differences between two or more people (see Figure 2). This model has two dimensions; one looks at similarities and differences in behaviors, the other at comparative expectations.

In analyzing conflict between two individuals we begin by identifying shared expectations that the two people have for competence, friendliness, trust, safety, and so on. Note that people can behave differently even though they have the same expectations. Once you have identified those areas of shared expectations the reasons for different behaviors may become clearer. The two people may agree to disagree or they may voluntarily modify their behavior toward the other.

Think for a moment of your best friend. Is that person exactly like you? Probably not. Would you accept behaviors and statements from that person you would not accept from others? Probably yes. Why? Because you share the same expectation of friendship. Multicultural counseling is the process of seeking out those shared expectations among strangers of differing cultural backgrounds.

Likewise, the same behavior may mean something quite different for two different individuals or even for the same individual at a different time or place. When someone bumps into you almost daily in front of the door to the classroom, you may interpret that behavior as hostile, uncivilized at best. However, the bumper may just be exhibiting daily anxiety about getting to class, sitting in the front, and setting up his work desk — or he may have a hearing deficit.

Also different behaviors may have the same meaning; one student looks down because she is taking notes of her professor's lecture, another looks at the professor as she gathers the words in her mind. They display dissimilar behavior, yet have the same expectation — organizing the knowledge of the lecture.

Now that we have considered the implications of misinterpreting behaviors and expectations it is use-

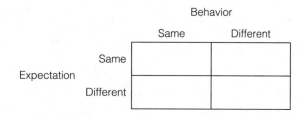

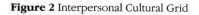

Figure 2 Interpersonal Cultural Grid

ful to consider the implications of similarity and difference in behavior and expectation between two people. Similarity of behavior and expectation are not always possible, or perhaps even desirable. It is necessary to consider the importance of accurate interpretation and mutual agreement of expectations in the analysis of personal interaction. Both people may quite rightly agree to disagree if each accurately understands the other's intention.

One student is constantly being urged to study with a group of students in her class. She prefers working alone and the self-management that goes with studying alone. The other students interpret this as "stuck up behavior" that implies that they are not good enough for her; they believe she doesn't want to help them for selfish reasons. Yet, it is possible that all these students expect to benefit from hard study but choose different situations to accomplish their learning. Different behaviors may or may not indicate similar expectations.

Personal misunderstandings are common within all organized life, including the family, friends, and so on. Personal conflict is more likely to result from disagreement in expectations. For example, you expect to get the family car and drive to a party this evening but your parents expect you to stay home and study — conflicting expectations!

Cultural misunderstanding and conflict occur when two people with differing cultural orientation assume that they share the same expectations for a situation but choose different behaviors to convey their intentions. Each inaccurately interprets the other's behavior from the viewpoint of his or her own personal cultural expectations.

Through matching behaviors and expectations from the grid, the counselor can identify criteria to interpret and understand the type of misunderstanding and propose the appropriate intervention. Accurately identifying someone else's expectation is never easy and the best you can hope for is a "best guess" based on the information at hand. Rather than jump to a negative conclusion it might be useful to include among your working hypotheses potentially positive or shared expectations when trying to interpret negative or very different behaviors.

Think of a conflict you have had recently and map it on the summary Cultural Grid (see Figure 3). Try to fill in data for all four cells of the grid demonstrating similarities and differences of behavior expectations. Chart how that conflict has changed over time moving, perhaps, from cells emphasizing shared or positive expectations toward those cells emphasizing different or negative expectations. Is this a personal or cultural misunderstanding? Knowing what you know now, what could you have done to resolve that conflict earlier? What could you still do to retrieve that relationship from increased conflict?

The Interpersonal Cultural Grid separates personal (same behavior but different expectation) from cultural (same expectation but different behavior) conflict. It

1. combines both the personal (behavior) and the cultural (expectation) aspects of a conflict situation

2. helps people script and rewrite their own behavior based on their cultural orientation

3. compares each person's behavior with the behavior of others in the context of culturally learned expectations

4. accounts for and predicts changing priorities in relation to the salience of a situation

5. provides a network of cues for the counselor to guide a complex interview

The two examples of the grid framework, intrapersonal and interpersonal, might be useful for under-

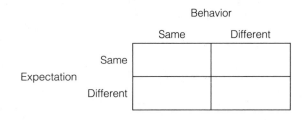

Figure 3 Interpersonal Cultural Grid: Summary

standing an individual's "personal cultural framework" to make a particular decision in a particular way at a particular time.

Identify a particular behavior you have acted out but do not entirely understand; see if the grid framework is helpful to you (see Figure 4). First, identify one specific behavior. Second, cite three possible expectations that enacted that behavior. Then, specify three possible values that led to each expectation. Last, determine the salient social system variables that may have taught you the values, that led to the expectations, that led to the behavior.

Now, try to map the following case on an Interpersonal Cultural Grid. Mrs. Smith is 82 years old; German-American; and a widow, former beauty queen, and grandmother. She is fighting a chronic lung disease in a private care facility. Mrs. Smith chooses to stay apart from other patients in the group and rarely interacts with them. Her favorite pastimes are working crossword puzzles and playing solitaire. The counselor now thinks that she may have a loss of hearing and would like her to see an audiologist, but Mrs. Smith will not leave her part of the facility and may reject any assessment. Is this a personal or a cultural misunderstanding?

1. Identify the possible positive expectations that Mrs. Smith and the counselor share.

2. Identify the possible different or negative expectations that Mrs. Smith and the counselor may have.

3. What are the behaviors that the counselor wants Mrs. Smith to enact?

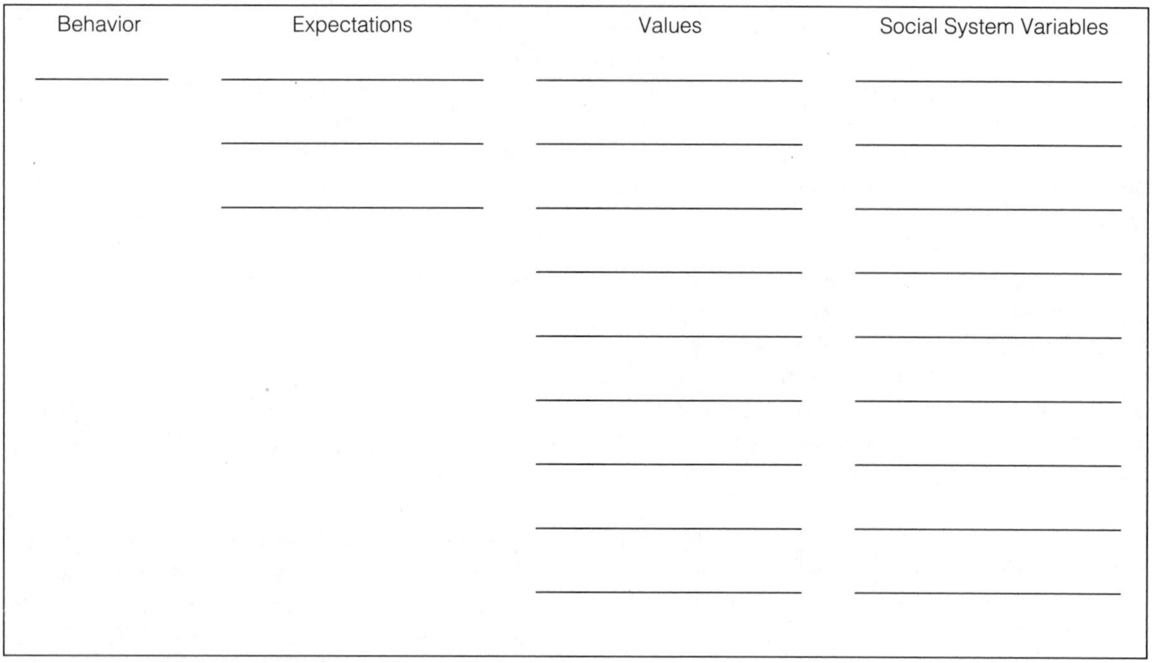

Behavior	Expectations	Values	Social System Variables
_____	_____	_____	_____
	_____	_____	_____
	_____	_____	_____
		_____	_____
		_____	_____
		_____	_____
		_____	_____
		_____	_____
		_____	_____

Figure 4 Using the grid framework to understand behavior.

4. What are the behaviors that the counselor wants Mrs. Smith to stop?

5. What has to happen to make this counseling interaction successful?

6. What are the conditions that would probably cause the counseling interaction to fail?

7. Change the race, ethnicity, gender, and age of Mrs. Smith. Does this make a difference?

CONCLUSION

We have examined two models for accurately understanding cultural similarities and differences in a counseling relationship. The first, the Intrapersonal Cultural Grid, looks inside the person to identify his or her own expectations and values that likely led to a particular behavior. These values were learned from a network of social system variables we refer to as a "cultural context." By linking behavior to expectation to values to social system variables, it is possible to understand the behavior in its own cultural context. This model may be used to understand your own behaviors or it may be useful to generate working rival hypotheses about someone else's behavior to better understand the ways that culture controls behavior.

The second, the Interpersonal Cultural Grid, looks at the relationship between two or more people to identify the ways that those persons are similar and the ways they are different. To the extent that a counselor can identify shared positive expectations between two persons in conflict the counselor has identified common ground between the two persons that may lead to reconciliation. This is more likely to succeed when the counselor is not distracted by negative or disruptive behaviors.

Culture controls behavior. This has been an attempt to help counselors understand the ways that culture controls behavior so that multicultural counseling can accurately and appropriately include the client's cultural context in understanding the client's behaviors.

REFERENCES

Hines, A., and Pedersen, P. (1981a). "The Cultural Grid: Management Guidelines to Personal Cultural Orientation." *Culture Learning Institute Report*. Honolulu, HI: East-West Center.

Hines, A., and Pedersen, P. (1981b). "The Cultural Grid: Matching Social System Variables and Cultural Perspectives." *Asian Pacific Training Development Journal, 1*, 6–8.

Pedersen, A., and Pedersen, P. (1989). "The Place of Age in Culture: An Application of the Cultural Grid." In L. Adler (Ed.), *Cross-Cultural Research in Human Development: Focus on Lifespan* (pp. 234–246). Westport, CT: Praeger/Greenwood Press.

Pedersen, A., and Pedersen, P. (1991). "The Cultural Grid: A Framework for Multicultural Counseling." In L. A. Samovar and R. E. Porter (Eds.), *Intercultural Communication: A Reader*. Belmont, CA: Wadsworth Publishing.

Pedersen, P., and Pedersen, A. (1989). "The Cultural Grid: A Complicated and Dynamic Approach to Multicultural Counseling." *Counseling Psychology Quarterly, 2*(2), 133–141.

Pedersen, P. (1988). *A Handbook for Developing Multicultural Awareness*. Alexandria, VA: American Association for Counseling and Development.

Negotiating Cultural Understanding in Health Care Communication

PATRICIA GEIST

While knowledge and appreciation of cultural diversity is growing in all types of contexts, providers in the health care setting have more to learn about the effects of culture on individuals' perception and expression of their symptoms. The white coat and high technology image of modern medicine dominating American medicine coincides with what many people see as an excessive medical emphasis on disease and a biological understanding of illness (Littlewood, 1991). The reality of our contemporary society is that it is a culturally diverse community of individuals with many different national, regional, ethnic, racial, socioeconomic, and occupational orientations that influence interactions in health care settings (Kreps, 1992).

This article examines the complex and dynamic features of communication in a health care context challenged by the culturally diverse expectations and behaviors of individuals seeking health care. In the last decade, with increasing numbers of immigrants admitted to the United States, greater attention has been paid to cross-cultural caring, cultural sensitivity, and transcultural care. The article begins with a discussion of the long-standing interest in considering sociocultural backgrounds of patients in health care delivery. What we discover is that the movement to communicate in culturally sensitive ways is constrained by the Western emphasis on the biomedical model and its inherent progressive ideology. The article continues by presenting specific case examples where providers and patients face difficulties when the culturally specific beliefs and practices of patients are not discussed or considered in diagnosing and determining appropriate treatment. Finally, the article concludes with avenues for overcoming the obstacles revealed in the case examples and for expanding our notions of culture and culturally sensitive health care.

LINKING CULTURE, HEALTH, AND COMMUNICATION

In 1989 the United States admitted over one million immigrants from all over the world (See Table 1). In fact, California is expected to be the first mainland state with a nonwhite majority in the coming decades (Howe-Murphy, Ross, Tseng, & Hartwig, 1989). With the diversity of individuals entering the United States comes increasing diversity in health care beliefs and practices of persons seeking health care. However, medical education, generally, has failed to integrate intercultural communication training into its curriculum.

Sectors of health care education have long been concerned with cultural influences upon health care delivery. Three decades ago, the field of transcultural nursing was established, and with it an emphasis on culture-specific care, culturally congruent care, and culturally sensitive care (Leininger, 1991). Transcultural nursing, a humanistic and scientific area of formal study and practice, focuses upon differences and similarities among cultures with respect to human care, health (or well-being), and illness based upon the people's cultural values, beliefs, and practices (Leininger, 1991). Operating from this philosophy, nurses work to avoid imposing their cultural beliefs on their patients, and provide them with cultural-specific or culturally congruent care.

Transcultural nursing has been criticized for its limited notion of culture. One criticism is that it views culture as a unified whole with a direct cause and effect relationship upon behavior. Instead, in viewing culture as dynamic, and the experiences of individuals from similar cultures as varied, we begin to focus on the unique requirements of individuals—their feelings, opinions, and experiences (Mason, 1990). Second, critics believe that transcultural nursing must include more of a global perspective (Lindquist, 1990), one that goes beyond traditional cultural beliefs and practices to the history and political situation in the country from which individuals have immigrated. Finally, culturally sensitive care needs to address the stressful and traumatic experiences of immigrants in adapting to their new home in the United States (Boyle, 1991).

Today, the significant influence of culture on perceptions, treatment, and interaction is being recognized and written about in a wide array of texts, including *Patients and Healers in the Context of Culture* (1980), *Medicine and Culture* (1988), *Culture, Health and Illness* (1990), *Caring for Patients from Different Cultures: Case Studies from American Hospitals* (1991), and *Cross-Cultural Caring* (1991), to name a few. What is clear in just about every examination of health and culture is that "miscommunication, noncompliance, different concepts of the nature of illness and what to do about it, and above all different values and preferences of patients and their physicians limit the potential benefits of both technology and caring" (Payer, 1989, p. 10). Cross-cultural caring considers health care a social process in which professionals and patients bring a set of beliefs, expectations, and practices to the medical encounter (Waxler-Morrison, Anderson, & Richardson, 1991). The task of negotiating an understanding of the problem, diagnosis, or treatment often is complicated by these cultural differences.

In the United States, the emphasis on technological progress and the biomedical model complicates the task of communicating to negotiate understanding even further. A progressive ideology has produced a society of experts who possess the technical knowledge, not social knowledge, and whose communication to the public places priority on the "body," not the "person" (Hyde, 1990). This progres-

Table 1 Immigrants to the United States in 1989

Country or Region	Number of Immigrants	Percent of Immigrants
Mexico	405,660	37%
Asia	296,420	27%
Central America	101,273	9%
Europe	94,338	9%
Caribbean	87,597	8%
South America	59,812	5%
Africa	22,486	2%
Canada	18,294	2%
Oceania*	4,956	<1%

*Includes Australia, Fiji, New Zealand, Tonga, and Western Samoa

sive ideology places great emphasis on the functioning and malfunctioning of the human machine. One physician points out that this emphasis permeates medical education.

Disease, we were told [in medical school] was caused by a malfunction of the machine, the body. . . . The emphasis began and ended with the body. . . . For this reason the modern medical model is called the molecular theory of disease causation. . . . (Dossey, 1982, pp. 6–8)

But, as a growing number of providers are discovering, this model does not account for the part of the human psyche that is most centrally involved in the cure of illness, namely varying perceptions of what constitutes health, illness, treatment, and the appropriate interaction between provider and patient (Lowenberg, 1989; Needleman, 1985). In fact, many would argue as Lowenberg (1989) does, that the single, most overriding conflict in the health care system is the polarization between humanistic and technological advances in health care. Fisher (1986) suggests that crosscutting all interactions between providers and patients is an ideology that supports the authority of the medical perspective over the patient's perspective. Consequently, the asymmetry of the medical relationship creates difficulties for patients in raising topics of interest to them and/or providing information they see as relevant (Fisher, 1986; Mishler, 1984).

Negotiating cultural understanding in the health care context necessitates willingness on the part of providers and patients to communicate honestly; to build a supportive, trusting relationship — "a relationship based not on unrealistic certainty, but on honesty in facing the uncertainty in clinical practice" (Inlander, Levin, & Weiner, 1988, p. 206). We need to understand illness and care as embedded in the social and cultural world (Kleinman, 1980). For Kleinman, "medicine is a cultural system, a system of symbolic meanings anchored in particular arrangements of social institutions and patterns of interpersonal interactions" (p. 24). He uses the term *clinical reality* to describe health-related aspects of social reality — especially attitudes and norms concerning sickness and health, clinical relationships, and treatment or healing activities (p. 37).

Increasing immigration of individuals from diverse cultures brings with it an amalgam of modern and traditional beliefs, values, and institutions that often conflict and contradict (Kleinman, 1980). The call to expand our understanding and appreciation of clinical realities implies that we need to acknowledge our ethnocentrism in dictating the proper way to provide care (Leininger, 1991); internationalize our professional education system (Linquist, 1990); consider the sociocultural background of patients (Boyle, 1991; Giger & Davidhizar, 1991); develop our cultural sensitivity (Waxler-Morrison et al., 1991); understand traditional (folk-healing) health care beliefs and incorporate them into care (Krajewski-Jaime, 1991); and generally communicate interculturally, recognizing the problems, competencies, prejudices, and opportunities for adaptation (Barna, 1991; Brislin, 1991; Kim, 1991; Spitzberg, 1991).

EXPANDING CULTURAL SENSITIVITY IN THE HEALTH CARE CONTEXT

A growing crisis in the U.S. health care system is the culture gap between the medical system and the huge number of ethnic minorities it employs and serves (Galanti, 1991). Assessment is a clinical art that combines sensitivity, clinical judgment, and scientific knowledge (Anderson, Waxler-Morrison, Richard, Herbert, & Murphy, 1991). Rather than using phrases like "taking the history," "physical examination," or "case management," health care providers negotiate a plan that will be acceptable to both themselves and their patients. The following cases reveal the difficulties that providers and patients face negotiating appropriate care. Differences in beliefs about health and illness, perceptions of appropriate treatment, and expectations about interaction in the medical setting complicate the communication process in health care delivery.

CULTURAL DIFFERENCES IN PERCEPTIONS, TREATMENT PRACTICES, AND RELATIONSHIPS

All cultures have beliefs about health and illness that have been passed down from generation to generation (Galanti, 1991; Krajewski-Jaime, 1991). The difference between the belief system of the Western

biomedical model and that of other cultures can result in inappropriate assessment or complications in treatment and communication in the provider-patient relationship. The research investigating the intersection of health and culture abounds with vivid examples of these challenges and the successes and failures in negotiating understandings acceptable to both providers and patients.

One source of misunderstanding in health care delivery stems from the practice of folk-healing medicine. Some practices can result in misdiagnosis; others simply contradict scientific medicine; and still others can result in improper medical treatment (Galanti, 1991). Curanderismo, a Hispanic folk-healing belief system originating in Europe, is the treatment of a variety of ailments with a combination of psychosocial interventions, mild herbs, and religion (Chesney, Thompson, Guevara, Vela, & Schottstaedt, 1980; Comas-Diaz, 1989; Krajewski-Jaime, 1991; Maduro, 1983). The three most common beliefs about the causes of disease are (a) natural and supernatural forces; (b) imbalances of hot and cold; and (c) emotions (Krajewski-Jaime, 1991, p. 161). Three practices central to this belief system are: (a) the role of the social network, particularly kin, in diagnosing and treating illness; (b) the relationship between religion and illness, which includes the use of religious ritual in many healing processes; and (c) consistency (but not uniformity) of beliefs among Hispanic communities about symptoms and regimens of healing (Krajewski-Jaime, 1991, p. 160).

Knowledge of folk-healing beliefs and practices enables providers to communicate with empathy, sensitivity, and open-mindedness. Social workers, physicians, and nurses who receive special training in interviewing and communication may build trust and mutual sharing of cultural information in their relationships with their patients (Krajewski-Jaime, 1991). When this training has not been part of medical education, differences in health beliefs between predominant-culture providers and minority patients may result in inappropriate assessment. Providers may interpret folk-healing beliefs and practices as ignorance, superstition, abuse, or neglect because patients do not follow prescribed treatments. In the following case, described by Krajewski-Jaime in her research on folk-healing beliefs and practices among Mexican-American families, she reveals how a non-Hispanic caseworker's recommendations could have resulted in the unnecessary removal of a Mexican-American child from his caring and nurturing family.

The assessment indicated that the child in question was ill and in need of medical care, but the mother had obvious emotional problems and appeared to be irrational: the mother had kept on saying, in broken English, that she could not allow any evil spirits to come near her child and had locked the child in his room; hung from the ceiling a pair of sharp scissors just above his head, and would not allow anyone, including the caseworker and the doctor, to enter the child's room. The caseworker's supervisor, who had some knowledge of the folk-healing practices among some of the agency's Mexican-American clients, asked a Mexican-American child protective service worker to reinvestigate the case. The worker visited the mother, who, while upset about the child's illness, welcomed someone who spoke Spanish. The mother explained that she had used several home remedies to help her child's fever go away, but evil spirits had already taken possession of her child and the usual remedies no longer helped. The only thing left to do was to prevent new spirits from entering the child's body. The scissors would immediately cut any spirits that would try to enter the child's body. Since evil spirits could attach to anyone who entered the room, she could not allow anyone to enter the room, thus preventing any further harm to her child. The Mexican-American worker, although familiar with folk-healing practices had not seen this particular cure before. She understood the validity of this belief within the client's cultural context, but to successfully obtain the mother's permission to see the child, to remove the dangerous scissors, and to see that the child received medical attention, she had to validate the mother's beliefs and gain her trust. She told the mother that although she had not seen anyone use this cure before, she had heard her grandmother

talk about it. To protect the patient and his or her entire surroundings, however, the grandmother usually nailed the scissors on the room's entrance door. The worker explained that, should the spirits attach themselves to anyone who wished to enter the room, the scissors on the entrance door would immediately prevent them from doing so and thus provided stronger protection to the patient. The Mexican-American worker went on to ask the mother if this made sense to her. She asked the mother if she thought this would be more beneficial since it would allow her child to be seen by the caseworker and the doctor. The mother agreed and emphasized that she wanted only what was best for her child. She changed the location of the scissors and welcomed the caseworker and the doctor to examine the child (pp. 158–159).

As Krajewski-Jaime points out, although this is an extreme example because of the dangerousness of the practice, most folk-healing practices are harmless. This case demonstrates how folk-healing, if understood, can become a resource on which to capitalize in building rapport in relationships with patients or families and negotiating appropriate diagnosis and treatment.

Similar to curanderismo, Chinese folk medicine bases many of its beliefs on maintaining a harmonious balance between the two opposing forces of "hot" and "cold," often substituted for yang and yin (Lai & Yue, 1990). Illness may be seen as an imbalance in hot or cold foods and thus people may seek cures from food substances they associate with their own deficiency.

For instance, a traditional Chinese may eat animals' brains in order to grow wiser. A diabetic may eat an animal's pancreas in hope of cure. People thought to be anaemic often eat red foods. These examples illustrate why traditional Chinese may have difficulty in regarding plastic capsules as a cure (Lai & Yue, p. 80).

These beliefs and practices provide evidence of the Chinese people's great concern about questions of health and healthcare, more so than Americans (Kleinman, 1980). However, along with this emphasis comes a belief in self-medication that may cause serious health problems.

Three specific examples of health practices reveal the problems that may develop with a patient's self-medication. First, Chinese, embracing the maxim of "all things in moderation," may believe that taking medicine over an extended period of time may weaken their bodies (Li, 1987). As a result, they often feel that:

Western medicine is too potent for them or their small bodies and they may reduce dosages to a quantity they believe suitable. For example, an elderly Chinese with diabetes may reduce his insulin because it is "foreign" and jeopardizes his health (Lai & Yue, 1990, pp. 83–84).

In fact, Chinese may refuse blood tests, believing that loss of blood will weaken their bodies or that the tests are too invasive (Lai & Yue). Second, dual use of Western medicine and folk medicine is common in the Korean, Bahamian, Haitian, Puerto Rican, Cuban, and Southern U.S. black cultures (Scott, 1974). However, Western prescriptions may contain the same chemical ingredients as herbal prescriptions patients are presently consuming; consequently patients may experience overdose or adverse reactions (Park & Peterson, 1991). Finally, in this third example, we see how the beliefs of a Guatemalan patient's husband led to double dosages of birth control pills:

One couple that came together for family planning counseling returned in only two weeks asking for more pills. The husband responded to all the questions for his wife regarding how she felt, if she was experiencing any irregular bleeding or pain, without consulting her even though she did understand enough Spanish to know what was being asked. She sat next to him silently as he explained that apparently the woman had taken two pills a day, thinking that they work better if the dosage is doubled. During the initial counseling, the husband also responded to all the questions by the female nurse and translator and stated he understood the procedures required for use of the Pill.

However, the subsequent visit indicated that he did not fully understand why he had to take extra precaution during the first few weeks, and thus he had encouraged his wife to double the dosage (Miralles, 1989, pp. 102–103).

In these three examples, the significance of communication in the provider-patient relationship is pronounced. And it is clear that providers who lack knowledge of health care beliefs and practices must negotiate and construct understanding during their interactions with patients.

The advice to health care providers in communicating with individuals from diverse cultures is to ask specifically about their beliefs and practices concerning herbal medicines or folk-healing practices (Park & Peterson, 1991). Asking these questions directly, rather than waiting for patients to volunteer the information or to ask about such issues, is especially important considering that Chinese and other immigrant groups generally have been taught to respect doctors and not to ask questions (Lai & Yue, 1990). In fact, for many Chinese, agreement and use of the word "yes" help to avoid the embarrassment of saying "no," as the following case illustrates:

Linh Lee, a sixty-four-year-old Chinese woman [was] hospitalized for an acute evolving heart attack. At discharge, her physician suggested that she come back in two weeks for a follow-up examination. She agreed to do so, but never returned. It is likely that she never intended to do so but agreed because he was an authority figure. Chinese are taught to value accommodation. Rather than refuse to the physician's face and cause him dishonor, Mrs. Lee agreed. She simply did not follow through, sparing everyone embarrassment. When Nancy, her Chinese-American nurse, saw her in Chinatown several weeks later, Mrs. Lee was very cordial and said she was feeling fine (Galanti, 1991, p. 21).

In a case such as this we find that negotiating an agreed upon "yes" cannot be taken at face value. Providers who understand how cultural values can lead patients to communicate in prescribed ways will be sensitive to different communication styles in order to avoid the difficulties created by situations such as the one described above.

One additional factor complicating efforts to construct understanding in the provider-patient relationship is the common problem of patients not possessing English language competence. And although the use of translators can help to mitigate this problem, for a variety of reasons, translators, patients, or family members can complicate and obstruct efforts to negotiate understanding (Fitzgerald, 1988; Galanti, 1991; Hartog & Hartog, 1983; Miralles, 1989).

Miscommunication is a frequent problem with the use of translators (Fitzgerald, 1988; Galanti, 1991; Miralles, 1989). Even with expert translation, problems such as linguistic differences between the terms in English and other languages can present difficulties, especially languages such as Vietnamese which includes diverse dialects.

[Vietnamese] words that translate "feeling hot" don't mean "fever." What they mean is "I don't feel well" and generalized malaise. And if you should ask your Vietnamese patients, "Have you ever had hepatitis?" the translator [may] translate that into "liver disease," and liver disease in Vietnam means itching. . . . Similarly, the kidney is the center of sexual potency to Indochinese and Vietnamese, and therefore "kidney trouble" may really mean decreased libido or other sexual difficulty (Fitzgerald, 1988, p. 67).

In addition, translators sometimes choose not to translate exactly what the patient says for any number of reasons — embarrassment, desire to portray the culture in a certain light, or lack of understanding:

[Translators] are sometimes reluctant to translate what they think is ignorance or superstition on the part of the patient. So they are sophisticated and tell you what they think rather than what the patient said. [Or the provider may ask] "How do you feel?" The translator then spends five to ten minutes in discussion with the patient and comes back and says, "Fine" (Fitzgerald, 1988, p. 65).

Linguistic variations, slang, and culturally specific terminology existing within any culture can create communication difficulties even for an excellent translator. In addition, translators often selectively choose what to communicate from the patient's or provider's narratives, giving a synopsis of what the patient says or grossly altering the meaning of the communication (Anderson et al., 1991).

A translator's use of medical jargon and technical vocabulary also may contribute to communication difficulties. In the following case, the provider and patient *appeared* to have negotiated understanding, but unfortunately this was not the case:

Jackie, an anglo nurse, was explaining the harmful side effects of the medication [that] Adela Samillan, a Filipino patient, was to take at home after her discharge. Although Mrs. Samillan spoke some English, her husband, who was more fluent, served as interpreter. Throughout Jackie's explanation, the Samillans nodded in agreement and understanding and laughed nervously. When Jackie verbally tested them on the information, however, it was apparent that they understood very little. What had happened? Dignity and self-esteem are extremely important for most Asians. Had the Samillans indicated they did not understand Jackie's instructions, they would have lost their self-esteem for not understanding or they would have caused Jackie to lose hers for not explaining the material well enough. By pretending to understand, Mr. and Mrs. Samillan felt they were preserving everyone's dignity. Jackie's first clue should have been their nervous laughter. Asians usually manifest discomfort and embarrassment by giggling. Once Jackie realized they had not understood the material, she went over it until they were able to explain it back to her (Galanti, 1991, p. 20).

This case, as well as other previous cases, demonstrates how important it is not to take smiles and nods of agreement as understanding when communicating with Asian patients. The nurse in this case communicated with the patients in order to assess their understanding and it was only through her continued time, patience, and effort that they were able to negotiate understanding.

And still another complicating factor is the fact that often professional translators are not available in the medical setting and the patient's friends or family members are asked to serve as translators. For a wide variety of reasons, these circumstances can contribute to miscommunication. In the following case, we begin to understand how awkward, embarrassing, or difficult it might be for family members to communicate what they are being asked to translate.

A Hispanic woman, Graciela Garcia, had to sign an informed consent for a hysterectomy. Her bilingual son served as the interpreter. When he described the procedure to his mother, he appeared to be translating accurately and indicating the appropriate body parts. His mother signed willingly. The next day, however, when she learned that her uterus had been removed and that she could no longer bear children, she became very angry and threatened to sue the hospital. What went wrong? Because it is inappropriate for a Hispanic male to discuss private parts with his mother, the embarrassed son explained that a tumor would be removed from her abdomen and pointed to that general area. When Mrs. Garcia learned that her uterus had been removed, she was quite angry and upset because a Hispanic woman's status is derived in large part from the number of children she produces (Galanti, 1991, p. 15).

There are a whole set of issues complicating communications in the health care setting when children serve as translators. In the case above, cultural rules dictate who can discuss what with whom (Galanti, 1991). In other cases, asking a patient's child to interpret can undermine the patient's competence in the eyes of the child, creating tensions in their relationship (Anderson et al., 1991). Once again we find that selection and use of translators is a complex issue that can interfere with providers' and patients' efforts to negotiate cultural understanding. In the final section of this article we discuss avenues for overcoming the obstacles faced in negotiating cultural understanding and for expanding our notions of culturally sensitive health care.

CULTURALLY SENSITIVE HEALTH CARE

The past ten years have seen a growing body of literature offering advice for increasing cultural sensitivity in health care delivery. Although, many of these suggestions focus on what actions providers should take, it is possible to see the implications these ideas have for anyone's efforts to increase their sensitivity to and understanding of other culture's health care beliefs and practices.

One useful starting point for health professionals is training that assists individuals in examining their own cultural beliefs and values as a basis for understanding and appreciating other cultural beliefs and values (Gorrie, 1989). At the University of Southern California, a course in cross cultural communication sensitizes physician assistants to their personal biases and prejudices through videotaped mock interviews. Believing that self-awareness of personal discomfort can become a tool for promoting sensitive cross-cultural communication, the curriculum is based on the model, "Differences + Discomforts = Discoveries." Critiquing the interviews, students are encouraged to investigate their own feelings of prejudice and bias and to use their sensitivity to discomfort as "a cue that they are perceiving a difference and to inquire further rather than seek safety in the harbor of fear and prejudice" (Stumpf & Bass, 1992, p. 115).

In a system-wide approach, Howe-Murphy et al. (1989) describe the Multicultural Health Promotion Project, a multidisciplinary, multicultural, and participative model designed to address the need for changes in allied health service delivery to minority populations. Their training efforts are focused on faculty from three allied health departments (Health Science, Nutrition and Food Science, and Occupational Therapy), students preparing for careers in these three professions, and community health care practitioners—all of whom face issues of health promotion in the multicultural environment.

Viewing cultures as dynamic, and not static unified wholes, means that variations exist among individuals of any one culture. Accordingly, health care providers need to assess each patient individually before deciding on a plan of care (Park & Peterson, 1991). Taking a more holistic approach, concentrating on "individual's own experience and understanding of illness" may assist in this assessment (Littlewood, 1991). Providers should acquire a knowledge of the specific language of distress utilized by patients and providers' diagnosis and treatment must make sense to patients, acknowledging patients' experience and interpretation of their own condition (Helman, 1990). Individuals from similar cultural groups often share metaphors (sayings or idioms) that express their perspective on situations, problems, and dilemmas. Providers may use these metaphors in the form of anecdotes, stories, or analogies to build rapport in relationships with patients and to magnify the patient's need to make the changes recommended in treatment plans (Zuniga, 1992).

Listening to the patient's stories (Kreps & Thornton, 1992), soliciting their illness narratives (Kleinman, 1988), and building partnerships (Geist & Dreyer, 1993) will facilitate negotiation of cultural understanding in provider-patient relationships. Since relationships among patients and providers inevitably are shaped by the health care context (Geist & Hardesty, 1992), the complexities and uncertainties of cultural diversity in medical work must continually be negotiated as patients and providers communicate in ways to meet their needs.

REFERENCES

Adams, R., Briones, E. H., and Rentfro, A. R. (1992). "Cultural Considerations: Developing a Nursing Care Delivery System for a Hispanic Community." *Nursing Clinics of North America, 27*, 107–117.

Alexander, F. (1965). *Psychosomatic Medicine*. New York: Norton.

Anderson, J. M., Waxler-Morrison, N., Richardson, E., Herbert, C., and Murphy, M. (1991). "Conclusion: Delivering Culturally Sensitive Health Care." In N. Waxler-Morrison, J. M. Anderson, and E. Richardson (Eds.), *Cross-Cultural Caring: A Handbook for Health Professionals in Western Canada*. Vancouver: University of British Columbia.

Balch, J. F., and Balch, P. A. (1990). *Prescription for Nutritional Healing*. Garden City Park, NY: Avery.

Barna, L. M. (1993). "Stumbling Blocks in Intercultural Communication." In L. A. Samovar and R. E. Porter (Eds.), *Intercultural Communication: A Reader*, 7th ed. Belmont, CA: Wadsworth, pp. 345–353.

Boyle, J. S. (1991). "Transcultural Nursing Care of Central American Refugees." *Imprint, 38*, 73–79.

Brislin, R. W. (1991). "Prejudice in Intercultural Communication." In L. A. Samovar and R. E. Porter (Eds.), *Intercultural Communication: A Reader,* 6th ed. Belmont, CA: Wadsworth, pp. 366–370.

Bulger, R. J. (1989). "The Modern Context for a Healing Profession." In R. J. Bulger (Ed.), *In Search of the Modern Hippocrates* (pp. 3–8). Iowa City: University of Iowa Press.

Chesney, A. P., Thompson, B. L., Guevara, A., Vela, A., and Schottstaedt, M. F. (1980). "Mexican-American Folk Medicine: Implications for the Family Physician." *The Journal of Family Practice, 11*, 567–574.

Comas-Diaz, L. (1989). "Culturally Relevant Issues and Treatment Implications for Hispanics." In D. R. Kowlow and E. P. Salett (Eds.), *Crossing Cultures in Mental Health* (pp. 31–48). Washington, D.C.: Sietar.

Corea, G. (1985). *The Hidden Malpractice: How American Medicine Mistreats Women*. New York: Harper & Row.

Coward, R. (1989). *The Whole Truth: The Myth of Alternative Health*. Boston: Faber & Faber.

Dossey, L. (1982). *Space, Time, and Medicine*. Boston: New Science.

Fisher, S. (1986). *In the Patient's Best Interest: Women and the Politics of Medical Decisions*. New Brunswick, NJ: Rutgers University Press.

Fitzgerald, F. T. (1988). "How They View You, Themselves, and Disease." *Consultant, 28*, 65–77.

Galanti, G. (1991). *Caring for Patients from Different Cultures: Case Studies from American Hospitals*. Philadelphia: University of Pennsylvania Press.

Geist, P., and Dreyer, J. (1993). "Juxtapositioning Accounts: Different Versions of Different Stories in the Health Care Context." In S. Herndon and G. Kreps (Eds.), *Qualitative Research: Applications in Organizational Communication* (pp. 79–105). Cresskill, NJ: SCA Applied Communication Series/Hampton Press.

Geist, P., and Hardesty, M. (1992). *Negotiating the Crisis: DRGs and the Transformation of Hospitals*. Hillsdale, NJ: Lawrence Erlbaum.

Giger, J. N., and Davidhizar, R. E. (1991). *Transcultural Nursing: Assessment and Intervention*. St. Louis: Mosby-Year Book.

Gorrie, M. (1989). "Reaching Clients Through Cross Cultural Education." *Journal of Gerontological Nursing, 15* (10), 29–31.

Gould, R. (July 7, 1989). "Dissident Doctoring." *The Times Literary Supplement*, D 748.

Hartog, J., and Hartog, E. A. (1983). "Cultural Aspects of Health and Illness Behavior in Hospitals." *The Western Journal of Medicine, 139*, 106–112.

Helman, C. G. (1990). *Culture, Health, and Illness: An Introduction for Health Professionals*. Boston: Wright.

Howe-Murphy, R., Ross, H., Tseng, R., and Hartwig, R. (1989). "Effecting Change in Multicultural Health Promotion: A Systems Approach." *Journal of Allied Health, 18*, 291–305.

Howze, E. H., Broyden, R. R., and Impara, J. C. (1992). "Using Informal Caregivers to Communicate with Women about Mammography." *Health Communication, 4*, 171–181.

Hyde, M. J. (1990). "Experts, Rhetoric, and the Dilemmas of Medical Technology: Investigating a Problem of Progressive Ideology." In M. J. Medhurst, A. Gonzalez, and T. R. Peterson (Eds.), *Communication and the Culture of Technology* (pp. 115–136). Pullman, WA: Washington State University.

Inlander, C. B., Levin, L. S., and Weiner, E. (1988). *Medicine on Trial: The Appalling Story of Medical Ineptitude and the Arrogance that Overlooks It*. New York: Pantheon.

Jones, J. A., and Phillips, G. M. (1988). *Communicating with Your Doctor*. Carbondale, IL: Southern Illinois University Press.

Kim, Y. Y. (1991). "Communication and Cross-Cultural Adaptation." In L. A. Samovar and R. E. Porter (Eds.), *Intercultural Communication: A Reader,* 6th ed. Belmont, CA: Wadsworth, pp. 401–411.

Kleinman, A. (1980). *Patients and Healers in the Context of Culture: An Exploration of the Borderland Between Anthropology, Medicine, and Psychiatry*. Berkeley: University of California Press.

Kleinman, A. (1988). *The Illness Narratives: Suffering, Healing, and the Human Condition*. New York: Basic Books.

Kleinman, A. (1992). "Local Worlds of Suffering: An Interpersonal Focus for Enthographies of Illness Experience." *Qualitative Health Research, 2*, 127–134.

Krajewski-Jaime, E. R. (1991). "Folk-Healing Among Mexican-American Families as a Consideration in the Delivery of Child Welfare and Child Health Care Services." *Child Welfare, 70*, 157–167.

Kreps, G. L., and Thornton, B. C. (1992). *Health Communication: Theory and Practice* (2nd ed). New York: Longman.

Lai, M. C., and Yue, K. K. (1990). "The Chinese." In N. Waxler-Morrison, J. A. Anderson, and E. Richardson (Eds.), *Cross-Cultural Caring: A Handbook for Health Professionals in Western Canada* (pp. 68–90). Vancouver: University of British Columbia Press.

Leininger, M. (1991). "Transcultural Nursing: The Study and Practice Field." *Imprint, 38* (2), 55–66.

Li, K. C. (February 1987). "*The Chinese Perspective Towards Mental Illness and Its Implications in Treatment*." Paper presented at Haughnessy Hospital, Vancouver.

Lindquist, G. J. (1990). "Integration of International and Transcultural Content in Nursing Curricula: A Process for Change." *Journal of Professional Nursing, 6*, 272–279.

Littlewood, R. (1991). "From Disease to Illness and Back Again." *The Lancet, 337*, 1013–1015.

Lowenberg, J. S. (1989). "*Caring and Responsibility: The Crossroads Between Holistic Practice and*

Traditional Medicine." Philadelphia: University of Pennsylvania Press.

Maduro, R. (1983). "Curanderismo and Latino View of Disease and Curing." *The Western Journal of Medicine, 139*, 868–874.

Mason, C. (1990). "Women as Mothers in Northern Ireland and Jamaica: A Critique of the Transcultural Nursing Movement." *International Journal of Nursing Studies, 27*, 367–374.

Miralles, M. A. (1989). "*A Matter of Life and Death: Health-Seeking Behavior of Guatemalan Refugees in South Florida*." New York: AMS Press.

Mishler, E. G. (1984). *The Discourse of Medicine: Dialectics of Medical Interviews*. Norwood, NJ: ABLEX.

Needleman, J. (1985). "*The Way of the Physician*." San Francisco: Harper & Row.

Northouse, P. G., and Northouse, L. L. (1985). *Health Communication: A Handbook for Health Professionals*. Englewood Cliffs, NJ: Prentice-Hall.

O'Brien, M. E. (1981). "Transcultural Nursing Research: Alien in an Alien Land." *Image, 13*, 37–39.

Park, K. Y., and Peterson, L. M. (1991). "Beliefs, Practices, and Experiences of Korean Women in Relation to Childbirth." *Health Care for Women International, 12*, 261–267.

Payer, L. (1989). *Medicine and Culture: Notions of Health and Sickness in Britain, the U.S., France, and West Germany*. London: Victor Gallancz LTD.

Scott, C. (1974). "Health and Healing Practices Among Five Ethnic Groups in Miami, Florida." *Public Health Report, 89*, 524–532.

Siegel, B. S. (1986). *Love, Medicine, and Miracles: Lessons Learned About Self-Healing from a Surgeon's Experience with Exceptional Patients*. New York: Harper & Row.

Simon, S. (June 25 1992). "A Dose of Their Own Medicine." *Los Angeles Times*, A1, 9.

Sirott, L., and Waitzkin, H. (1984). "Holism and Self-Care: Can the Individual Succeed Where Society Fails?" In V. W. Sidel and R. Sidel (Eds.), *Reforming Medicine: Lessons from the Last Quarter Century* (pp. 245–264). New York: Pantheon.

Spitzberg, B. H. (1991). "Intercultural Communication Competence." In L. A. Samovar and R. E. Porter (Eds.), *Intercultural Communication: A Reader*, 6th ed. Belmont, CA: Wadsworth, pp. 353–365.

Stumpf, S. H., and Bass, K. (1992). "Cross Cultural Communication to Help Physician Assistants Provide Unbiased Health Care." *Public Health Records, 107*, 113–115.

U.S. Bureau of the Census. (1991). *Statistical Abstract of the U.S.: 1991* (11th ed.). Washington, D.C.

Wallis, C. (November 4, 1991). "Why New Age Medicine Is Catching On." *Time*, 68–76.

Waxler-Morrison, N., Anderson, J., and Richardson, E. (1991). *Cross-Cultural Caring: A Handbook for Health Professionals in Western Canada*. Vancouver: University of British Columbia.

Zuniga, M. E. (1992). Using Metaphors in Therapy: Dichos and Latino Clients. *Social Work, 37*, 55–60.

Culture and Classroom Communication

ROBERT G. POWELL
JANIS ANDERSEN

One of the most striking features of today's classroom is the cultural diversity of the student body. Students from Asian, Hispanic, African, European, and Native American cultural backgrounds are participating in all levels of our educational systems. Further, these students have culturally based canons and expectations about education and classroom communication behavior. As classrooms shift and change, educators must come to understand how culture might influence the classroom communication. While it is relatively easy to identify cultural artifacts in the classroom (names, dress, faces), it is far more difficult to unpack the more subtle ways in which culture influences classroom activities, communication, and learning. The purpose of this article is to reveal some of the ways in which culture shapes and structures classroom communication. The first part addresses the issue comparatively by illustrating how educational practices vary around the world. The second explores the way in which student cultural diversity influences instructional communication in the United States.

This original essay appears in print here for the first time. All rights reserved. Permission to reprint must be obtained from the publisher and the authors. Robert Powell teaches at California State University, Fresno and Janis Andersen teaches at San Diego State University.

CULTURAL ASSUMPTIONS ABOUT CLASSROOMS

People tend to believe that all classrooms look and function in much the same way. If you were asked to imagine a classroom in central Illinois, southern California, upstate New York, or even France, Mexico, or China, you would probably envision a classroom like that with which you are most familiar. Even though you might picture different kinds of people in the different locations—nattily dressed students in an Ivy league school or suntanned students in shorts and T-shirts in southern California—your notion of what the classroom looks like and what people do in it is tied to your personal experiences. If you are from the United States, you probably visualize a classroom with rows of desks for students to sit and take notes, a large desk, and perhaps a lectern where the teacher imparts information and directs classroom activities.

People tend to believe that the learning environments with which they are most familiar are representative of learning environments in general. Even if these culturally based assumptions do not generalize as we suggest, they are often held up as models for what a learning environment ought to be.

Culture provides us with a heritage and a set of expectations about educational settings. If you were asked to create a classroom context and to structure the interaction to provide the best possible learning situation, chances are you would create something very similar to the classroom you go to everyday. You may not find the current situations ideal, but your images of a proper learning environment are inextricably linked to your familiarity with and experience in learning environments. Teachers tend to teach the way they were taught; parents tend to treat their children the way they were treated. The entire educational system, together with the rules and procedures for effective classroom interaction, reflects a cultural dictate rather than a universal mandate. With this in mind, it should not be surprising that parents and teachers have resisted the movement toward year-round school systems. Yet, many of the criticisms about a year-round schedule have little to do with education and learning and much more to do with the way schools are supposed to be structured. In this country, we expect to begin school in September and get out in June. Family vacations are organized around a nine-month school year and a three-month summer vacation. Any deviation from this expected norm is perceived by many as disruptive.

CULTURAL DIVERSITY IN INSTRUCTION

This section highlights some cultural differences in educational practices. An in-depth, systematic study of an individual culture, its institutions, and its people is necessary for us to know enough about another culture's educational system to improve our instructional encounters with individuals from that culture. The differences highlighted here are useful not so much for understanding other cultures but for facilitating heightened awareness of our own culture. The discussion that follows, therefore, offers insights into our own educational system. Hall, a pioneer in intercultural communication, believes that we can never really understand another's culture but being aware of its diversity is a tremendous aid in understanding our own culture better.[1] Further, by studying culture's role in education, we can put our own educational assumptions into perspective.

Educational Systems

If asked to describe a generic educational system, most of us would probably begin by talking about a classroom, a teacher, and some students. These seemingly basic components, however, reflect cultural assumptions. Classrooms, for example, are a relatively recent innovation. Socrates, Plato, Aristotle, and Confucius taught without the benefit of a blackboard, and the comfort — or discomfort — of a classroom building. And, the students of these teachers did quite well even though they did not take notes and their teachers did not provide hand-outs or behavioral objectives. A modern version of a school without classrooms comes from Chicago in the early 1970s where the Metro School was a complete high school without walls.[2] The classes met in museums, libraries, bookstores, and other significant places. A sociology class was taught by having students walk the length of Halsted Street through numerous ethnic neighborhoods. Students ate in restaurants, visited families, and carefully observed street activity.

Teachers

What constitutes a teacher also reflects a cultural bias. In the United States, it was not until around the Civil War period (1860s) that women replaced men as teachers.[3] Presently, women make up almost 70 percent of the teaching force in the United States.[4] In preliterate societies, kin were and are responsible for educating the young. Deciding which category of kin will assume which teaching responsibility is highly systematized and is related in many ways to having a teaching credential in a content area. Instead of learning art from Mrs. Ruiz, home economics from Mrs. Sullivan, and woodworking from Mr. Yang, children learn to make pottery from their uncle, cooking from their mother, and toolmaking from their grandfather.

Many of us think of teachers as being older than their students, but cultural anthropologist Margaret Mead states that this perception reflects a culturally determined, postfigurative learning paradigm.[5] Only in postfigurative societies, do older people tend to disseminate their knowledge to younger, less experienced, and less knowledgeable individuals; cofigurative cultures adopt primarily peer learning patterns, and prefigurative societies learn from their younger members who are more up to date. The one-room schoolhouses of the early 1900s relied mainly on cofigurative or peer instruction. Due to teacher shortages and developments in cooperative learning, the utilization of cofigurative learning strategies emerged again in the United States in the 1980s.[6] Prefigurative learning patterns are used in complex industrial societies where rapid technological and scientific advances quickly outdate previously acquired knowledge. Thus, we may find 50-year-old executives attending special seminars on computer technology that are taught by people 20 or 30 years younger.

Learning

Student orientations to learning are also affected by culture. Many theorists contend that culture helps shape and structure the "learning style" of the student.[7] In Eastern cultures, for example, knowledge and insight are believed to come from reflection and meditation.[8] The student is expected to receive information, and then reflect upon it. Students in Eastern cultures seldom disagree with a teacher or ask questions because such behavior would threaten the "face" of the teacher who is a revered and respected individual. Native American students, on the other hand, utilize a visual learning style that is dependent on observation and imitation rather than explicit verbalization.[9]

In the United States, a teacher may consider knowledge more relative and negotiable. Lively class discussions play an important role in these types of learning contexts. Questions such as "Do you agree with the author on this point?" are intended to evoke classroom interaction and not compliance.

A good deal of research has examined the relationship between learning style and culture. Even though no clear-cut causal links have been identified, there are some perspectives worth examining. Gay, indicates that there are two cultural orientations to learning—an *analytic style* and a *relational style*.[10] The analytic style involves breaking things down into their component parts. A relational style, on the other hand, is more holistic; meanings and knowledge are situated in global constructs. Research indicates that Anglo and Asian children are more likely to embrace an analytic communication style while Native-American, Hispanic, and African-American students are more likely to embrace a relational style. In terms of communication structures in the classroom, then, Hispanics, Native Americans and African Americans will respond positively to teaching strategies utilizing holistic thinking and cooperative learning.

Classroom Rituals

Rituals and patterns of classroom interaction vary from culture to culture. We probably picture students speaking their native languages in classroom interactions throughout the world, and we might picture all students raising their hands to ask or answer a question. In fact, mathematics is taught in English in the Philippines, since Tagalog (the primary language of the Philippines) does not have sufficient technical terms for mathematics instruction. In Jamaica, primary students flap or snap their fingers to signal that they know the answer. In Trinidad, students put their index fingers to their forehead with the inside facing out to ask permission to be excused.[11] Some cultures do not have a way for students to signal a desire to talk to a teacher; in these cultures, students speak only after the teacher has spoken to them. There is virtually no classroom interaction in Vietnamese classrooms and in Mexico most classroom interaction is tightly controlled by the teacher.

The classroom in an Israeli kibbutz is very noisy and interaction is spontaneous.[12] In sharp contrast, Chinese classrooms are so quiet that North Americans teaching there often find the silence unnerving.[13] Chinese culture tends to reflect a Buddhist tradition which holds that knowledge, truth, and wisdom come to those whose quiet silence allows the spirit to enter. Classrooms in the United States tend to reflect a Socratic ideal where student-teacher interaction plays a central role in the pursuit of knowledge.

Intelligence Assessment

The way intelligence and learning are measured are certainly related to culture. In the United States a single score may be used to index a student's intelligence. Consider, for example, the importance that standardized test scores have in this country—students' academic future are dramatically affected by their verbal and math SAT scores. But, in Iran, a child might be considered intelligent if he has memorized the Koran and mastered the Arabic language.[14] Gardner rightly reminds us that different cultures cultivate an assortment of intelligences.[15]

Formal Education Value

The value placed on formal education also has a cultural dimension. In Japan, for example, education is a high national priority. The Japanese believe that the best way to ensure their future is to develop their most valued national resource — their people. In 1980, more students graduated from the twelfth grade in Japan than in any country in the world, and this trend will continue into the next decade.[16]

Competition to get into Japanese colleges and universities is especially keen. Almost four applications are submitted for each college opening. The entrance examinations for universities are as important to the Japanese as are the World Series or the Super Bowl in the United States. With such a commitment to education, it is not surprising that the Japanese have become world leaders in technology.

Time Value

Our use of time and our view of time also reflect a cultural bias that alters our educational process.[17] Punctuality is valued in the United States. Students who turn their work in late are considered lazy or less intelligent than those who work more slowly. A Western "monochronic" view of time also influences the manner in which curriculum is developed. Classes and activities are structured according to a preestablished time schedule. The time schedule is seldom developed in terms of how much time a learning task may require. One time-related problem that is often overlooked involves testing: Students are often graded on how many questions they can answer correctly in a designated period of time. This grading philosophy is a disadvantage for students raised in Hispanic cultures because they have not been conditioned to use every moment in a task-oriented manner. The following idioms show the contrast between Western and Hispanic views of time. For Westerners the "clock races" and "time is money," while for Hispanics the "clock walks" (*el reljo anda*).

In contrast to the Western monochronic view of time, American Indians have a "polychronic" view of time. These individuals engage in activities when they believe that the time is right, not according to some preestablished calendar. In many cultures, classes end when the subject matter has been thoroughly discussed rather than when the clock designates the end of a period. In the United States, we measure education itself in time — years spent in school — and it is only recently that our system has allowed credit to be given for knowledge when one has not spent the requisite time in the classroom. The entire notion of education as a time process, however, is a product of nineteenth-century Western thought.

Nonverbal Behavioral Differences

Many nonverbal behaviors are culturally learned, and the literature on nonverbal behavior is brimming with examples of cross-cultural differences in interpreting these behaviors.[18] These differences are also manifest in classroom environments. In the United States, we show respect to teachers by looking at them when they talk to us, but in Jamaica looking at teachers is a sign of disrespect, while not looking at them is a sign of respect. African Americans and many West African cultures also reflect the Jamaican pattern.[19]

In Italian classrooms, teachers and students touch each other frequently, and children greet a teacher with a kiss on both cheeks while putting their arms around the teacher. On the other hand, Chinese and Japanese children show complete emotional restraint in classrooms.[20] In Western cultures it is common to show affection by patting children on the head. For Hmong children, a pat on the head is considered a significant transgression.[21]

CULTURE AND INSTRUCTIONAL PRACTICES IN THE UNITED STATES

Now that we have discussed some of the more obvious cultural differences characterizing the'educational process, we would like to shift our attention and focus to some of the ways that culture impacts communication and instruction in the United States. Specifically, we will examine how students from diverse cultural and ethnic backgrounds interact in the classroom and how they feel about certain types of communication behaviors.

Interaction in the classroom is oriented toward and guided by mainstream forms of discourse.[22] Rubin states that problems occur in the classroom when the interaction expectations of the classroom teacher do not match the communication expectations of students from nonmainstream ethnic cultures. These mismatches fall into six general areas: (1) norms for loquacity, (2) norms for the structure of interaction, (3) norms for participant relations, (4) norms for construing questions, (5) judgments of teacher behavior, and (6) academic advisement.

Norms for Loquacity

As we have indicated, students differ in their orientations to classroom interaction. When the first author asked his class to comment on the role of culture in the classroom, three Anglo women and one Anglo man quickly raised their hands and began offering their opinion. When the instructor pointed out that the students most willing to offer their opinions were Anglo, not the African American, Hispanic, or Asian, they looked at him curiously but continued to offer their opinions. This episode reflects the differences that these students hold about classroom discourse. Anglos and inner-city African Americans tend to embrace the verbosity norm of the classroom. These students have been taught that access to learning is shaped and structured through talk. Native American and Asian students, however,

do not tend to embrace this norm and tend to be more verbally passive.

Norms for the Structure of Interaction

The second cultural difference identified by Rubin involves norms for discourse structure and sequence. Cazden has conducted extensive research in this area and has noted some important distinctions that relate to the structure of classroom discourse.[23] She noted cultural differences in the way Anglo and African Americans structure *sharing time* narratives. Sharing time consists of those events when children reveal aspects of their private worlds. Anglo children were more inclined to develop topic-centered narratives that focused on a single topic or event. African-American children, on the other hand, were more inclined to develop episodic narratives. Episodic stories are longer and include shifting scenes and changing characters. Cazden's research indicated that white listeners considered episodic stories difficult to comprehend and that the students generating episodic stories were perceived as less competent. The opposite impression of these forms were obtained from African-American listeners.

Another way in which culture influences the structures of interaction concerns the way in which students gain access to interaction. Beyers and Beyers found differences in the way students captured the attention of the teacher.[24] A young white girl, for example, looked at the teacher 14 times and managed to establish eye contact 8 times. An African-American girl, on the other hand, looked at the teacher 35 times but established eye contact with the teacher only 4 times. Analysis of videotapes indicated that the white child timed her glances so that she was looking at the teacher during those moments the teacher was scanning the room. The African-American child timed her glances to correspond to the times when the teachers's attention was drawn away from her. According to Beyers and Beyers, this finding suggests that the white child and white teacher shared an implicit rule for interaction that resulted in more access to classroom communication.

Norms for Participant Relations

A third way that culture influences classroom interaction concerns norms for participant relations. Some children can be highly participative outside of class but very quiet and reserved once the classroom activities begin. Rubin theorizes that culture influences the manner in which individuals contextualize classroom events. For some, the classroom is a place open for interaction just as is the playground. For others, the classroom is not a place for talk but one for reflection. Cherokee Indian children, for example, do not have a construct for one-to-one teacher-student interaction.

Norms for Construing Questions

Culture influences the way that questions are construed. Teacher questions are ubiquitous, and they serve numerous functions. Teachers may ask genuine questions to solicit unknown information, pseudoquestions designed to check student knowledge, or directives masked as questions ("Do you have the salt?"). Students must understand the type of question posed before responding and the problems that occur when the function of the question is misread.

The use of pseudoquestions, for example, is a predominantly middle-class Anglo characteristic.[25] The use of this pattern of communication is not as evident in Asian, African-American, or Hispanic homes. It is not surprising that Anglo children are most likely to raise their hands to any number of questions posed in the class. The difficulty, of course, is confusing a cultural rule with an attribution of what the student knows. Students who do not raise their hands to pseudoquestions may "know"

just as much as the students who do; culture, however, has shaped a different construct on how that knowledge is appropriately shared.

Judgments of Teacher Behavior

Judgments about teacher classroom communication are also affected by culture. Several investigations have examined the effects of teacher *immediacy* on a variety of instructional outcomes. Immediacy concerns those behaviors that signal approach and acceptance.[26] Powell and Harville examined the relationship between teacher immediacy and teacher clarity for students from diverse ethnic backgrounds. The results of their investigation indicated that the relationship between verbal immediacy and teacher clarity was statistically higher for students from Latino and Asian ethnic groups.[27] This finding suggests that immediacy played an especially important role in the way that meaning is shaped for Latino and Asian students.

In a related study, Sanders and Wiseman assessed the effects of verbal and nonverbal immediacy on cognitive, affective, and behavioral learning. They found that immediacy played an especially important role in affective learning for Hispanic students and was more highly related to affective learning than cognitive learning for white, Asian, and Hispanic students.[28]

Collier and Powell studied the relationship between teacher immediacy and teacher effectiveness over time and found differences across the groups they examined. Immediacy early in the course was most important for the Latino group. In contrast, African Americans indicated that immediacy was more important later in the course. Immediacy had a fairly stable effect for Anglos and Asians.[29]

The results of these studies suggest that the behaviors we assume are effective communication strategies for teachers have cultural implications. Gudykunst and Ting-Toomey state that "culture is the normative frame in which expectations concerning appropriate or competent nonverbal behaviors are defined consensually."[30] Thus, teacher behavior may have different implications and consequences for students from diverse cultural orientations.

Academic Advisement

The expectations that students have about academic advisement also have a cultural dimension. Collier assessed communication in the advisement relationships between Anglo advisors and Asian-American, African-American, and Latino students.[31] She asked students to describe a conversation with an Anglo advisor in which the advisor behaved inappropriately and ineffectively. Culturally based expectations about appropriate communication from the Anglo advisor were thus obtained. A significant number of Asian-American and Latino students felt that references to their accents were inappropriate. Asian Americans felt that embarrassing criticism and openness were inappropriate. African Americans described distance and hostility as inappropriate. Latinos cited distance and lack of individual concern as inappropriate behaviors. Collier also found some similarity across the groups. Asian Americans, African Americans, and Latinos mentioned behaviors such as mismanagement of time (being late, rushing the student) interrupting the student, and not attending nonverbally to the student as inappropriate.

Collier concludes her research by providing a taxonomy of rules for Anglo advisors. Following are the rules she provides for (1) politeness, (2) cultural appropriateness, (3) relational appropriateness, and (4) approaching tasks in advisement contexts.

1. *Politeness rules*: With Asian Americans, manage time appropriately, attend nonverbally, allow mutual talk time, greet warmly, pronounce names correctly, and do not use foul language. With African Americans, allow time for mutual talk, manage time appropriately, show recognition and respect for the student as an individual, attend appropriately, and greet warmly. With Latinos, attend appropriately and pronounce names correctly.[32]

2. *Culturally appropriate rules*: Avoid over-generalizing and stereotyping or criticizing stu-

dents' ability or preparation for school; avoid negative comments about accents, and allow adequate time for students.[33]

3. *Relationally appropriate rules*: With Asian Americans, show respect; do not use or ask for too much openness, and avoid confronting or embarrassing the advisee. With African Americans, be friendly and direct, show respect for the individual student, and allow trust to build slowly. With Latinos, take time to show concern and friendliness, and show support and empathy verbally and nonverbally.[34]

4. *Rules for approaching the task*: With Asian Americans, provide adequate advice throughout the meeting, allow a mutual role in decision making, and be direct. With African Americans, provide adequate advice throughout the meeting, allow a mutual role in decision making, be direct, and verify information to avoid mistakes. With Latinos, establish the relationship first through a warm greeting and small talk and then provide adequate advice, allow a mutual role in decision making, and verify information to avoid mistakes.[35]

SUMMARY

In an informative and interesting book on intercultural behavior, Geert Hofstede explores the differences in thinking and action among people from 40 different nations.[36] He argues that people have mental problems based on their cultural experiences that are both developed and reinforced by schools and other social institutions. Many of these patterns are so subtle that people fail to realize that things can be another way. By highlighting intercultural differences in educational environments, we begin to realize that nothing about the educational process is absolute. Every component reflects a cultural choice, conscious or unconscious, about whom to educate, how, when, in what subjects, for what purposes, and in which manner. Perhaps this realization will not only increase our awareness of, but sensitivity to, the culturally diverse classroom in the United States.

NOTES

1. Edward T. Hall, *The Hidden Dimension* (Garden City, NY: Doubleday and Company, 1966).

2. Chicago *Sun Times*, December 6, 1972.

3. Jules Henry, "Cross Cultural Outline of Education," in Joan I. Roberts and Sherrie C. Adinsanya (eds.), *Educational Patterns and Cultural Configurations* (New York: David McKay, 1970).

4. Los Angeles *Times*, March 13, 1988.

5. Margaret Mead, *Culture and Commitment: A Study of Learning and Development* (Garden City, NY: Natural History Press, Doubleday and Company, 1970).

6. D. A. Kolb, *Experiential Learning: Experience as a Source of Learning and Development* (Englewood Cliffs, NJ: Prentice-Hall, 1984).

7. Charles Claxton, "Learning Styles, Minority Students, and Effective Education, *Journal of Developmental Education, 1* (1990), 6–9.

8. D. Lawrence Kincaid, *Communication Theory: Eastern and Western Perspectives* (San Diego, CA: Academic Press, 1987).

9. Geneva Gay, "Interactions in Culturally Pluralistic Classrooms, in J. A. Bales (ed.), *Education in the 80's: Multiethnic Education* (Washington, DC: National Educational Association, 1981).

10. Geneva Gay, "Viewing the Pluralistic Classroom as a Cultural Microcosm," *Educational Research Quarterly, 2* (1978), 45–59.

11. Aaron Wolfgang, "The Teacher and Nonverbal Behavior in the Multicultural Classroom," in Aaron Wolfgang (ed.), *Nonverbal Behavior, Application and Cultural Implications* (New York: Academic Press, 1979).

12. M. Spiro, *Children of the Kibbutz* (Cambridge, MA: Harvard University Press, 1975).

13. Wolfgang, p. 167.

14. Howard Gardner, *Frames of Mind* (New York: Basic Books, 1983).

15. Gardner.

16. Thomas P. Rohlen, *Japan's High Schools* (Los Angeles: University of California Press, 1983).

17. William R. Todd-Mancillas, "Classroom Environments and Nonverbal Behavior," in Larry Barker (ed.), *Communication in the Classroom* (Englewood Cliffs, NJ: Prentice-Hall, 1982).

18. See for example, Edward T. Hall, *The Silent Language* (Greenwich, CN: Fawcett Publications, 1959); Loretta Malandro and Larry Barker, *Nonverbal Communication* (Reading, MA: Addison-Wesley, 1983); Marianne LaFrance and Clara Mavo, *Moving Bodies: Nonverbal Communication in Social Relationships* (Monterey, CA: Brooks/Cole, 1978).

19. Wolfgang, p. 167.

20. Wolfgang, p. 169.

21. Gail Sorensen, "Teaching Teachers from East to West: A Look at Common Myths," *Communication Education, 38* (1989), 331–332.

22. Donald Rubin, "'Nobody Play by the Rule He Know': Ethnic Interference in Classroom Questioning Events," in Young Yun Kim (ed.), *Interethnic Communication: Current Research* (Beverly Hills, CA: Sage Publications, 1986).

23. Courtney Cazden, *Classroom Discourse: The Language of Teaching and Learning* (Portsmouth, NH: Heinemann, 1988).

24. P. Beyers and H. Beyers, "Non-Verbal Communication in the Education of Children," in Courtney Cazden, V. Sohn, and Dell Hymes (eds.), *Functions of Language in the Classroom* (New York: Teachers College Press, 1972).

25. Rubin.

26. Albert Mehrabian, *Silent Messages: Implicit Communication of Emotions and Attitudes* (Belmont, CA: Wadsworth, 1981).

27. Robert Powell and Barbara Harville, "The Effects of Teacher Immediacy and Clarity on Instructional Outcomes: An Intercultural Assessment," *Communication Education, 39* (1990), 369–379.

28. Judith Sanders and Richard Wiseman, "The Effects of Verbal and Nonverbal Teacher Immediacy on Perceived Cognitive, Affective, and Behavioral Learning in the Multicultural Classroom," *Communication Education, 39* (1990), 341–354.

29. Mary Jane Collier and Robert Powell, "Ethnicity, Instructional Communication and Classroom Systems," *Communication Quarterly, 38* (1990), 334–349.

30. William Gudykunst and Stella Ting-Toomey, *Culture and Interpersonal Communication* (Newbury Park, CA: Sage Publications, 1988), p. 117.

31. Mary Jane Collier, "Competent Communication in Intercultural Unequal Status Advisement Contexts," *Journal of Communication, 1* (1988), 3–22.

32. Collier, p. 16.

33. Collier, p. 16.

34. Collier, p. 17.

35. Collier, pp. 17–18.

36. Geert Hofstede, *Culture's Consequences: International Differences in Work-Related Values* (Newbury Park, CA: Sage Publications, 1980).

CONCEPTS AND QUESTIONS FOR CHAPTER 6

1. What differences must a manager be concerned about when managing human resources in a multinational organization?

2. How do peer group relations in multinational/multicultural business organizations differ from those in U.S. business organizations?

3. As an employee of a U.S. company, you have just been assigned to the international division and will soon take a position as a department manager at a facility in Germany. What differences in the cultural context of the workplace might you expect to encounter? How would you prepare yourself for the new assignment?

4. How would you approach a business discussion with a German managerial counterpart knowing the German impersonal approach to business?

5. How would you reconcile the American need to be liked with the German need to be credible if you were undertaking a discussion of management techniques with a German business counterpart?

6. What is the German of *Besprechung*, and how does it apply to business discussions?

7. What are the three major problems associated with international negotiations?

8. How does the American perspective of the negotiation atmosphere differ from the perspective held by other cultures?

9. In what ways does the American communication style differ from that of the Japanese, the French, and the Mexican?

10. How does the Japanese concept of group differ from that perceived in the United States?

11. In what manner did the Japanese *shogunates* (ruling families) contribute to the development of the Japanese concept of group?

12. How do the Cathcarts view the Japanese concept of group as a communication context?

13. What are the differences between the intrapersonal cultural grid and the interpersonal cultural grid?

14. How can you personally use the personal grids to improve your ability to be an intercultural communicator?

15. What cultural functions are served by medical systems?

16. What communication problems might a health care provider working within the Western biomedical health care system orientation encounter when dealing with patients coming from a different medical orientation? What should he or she do to minimize these problems?

17. What considerations should a health care provider give when she or he is working with a care receiver who does not possess English language competence?

18. What influence does culture have on the context of the classroom?

19. How does the culturally defined role of teacher affect the classroom context?

20. How has your culture shaped the expectations for your classroom behavior?

21. What suggestions do Powell and Andersen offer to help teachers in the United States cope with culturally diverse classrooms?

PART FOUR

Intercultural Communication: Seeking Improvement

Happy are they that hear their detractions and can put them to mending.

—*Shakespeare*

Understanding is the beginning of approving.
— *André Gide*

In a sense, this entire volume has been concerned with the practice of intercultural communication. We have looked at a variety of cultures and a host of communication variables that operate when people from different cultures attempt to interact. However, our analysis thus far has been somewhat theoretical. Previous selections have concentrated primarily on the issue of understanding intercultural communication. We have not, at least up to this point, treated the act of practicing intercultural communication.

We have already pointed out many of the problems that cultural differences can introduce into the communication process. And we have shown how an awareness of not only other cultures but also of one's own culture can help mediate some of the problems. But intercultural communication is not exclusively a single party activity. Like other forms of interpersonal communication, it requires for its highest and most successful practice the complementary participation of all parties to the communication event.

When elevated to its highest level of human activity, intercultural communication becomes what David Berlo described as "Interaction: The Goal of Human Communication": the communicative act in which "two individuals make inferences about their own roles and the role of the other at the same time."* Berlo calls this reciprocal role taking: In order for people to achieve the highest level of communication there must be a mutual reciprocity in achieving an understanding of each other. In

---

*David K. Berlo, *The Process of Communication*. New York: Holt, Rinehart & Winston, 1960, p. 130.

333

intercultural communication, this means that you must not only know about your culture and the culture of the one with whom you are communicating, but that that person must also know about his or her own culture and about your culture as well. Unless there is mutual acknowledgment of each other's cultures and a willingness to accept those cultures as a reality governing communicative interactions, intercultural communication cannot rise to its highest possible level of human interaction.

In this final section we have slightly modified our orientation so that we can include a discussion based on the activity of communication. For although the readings in this portion of the book will increase your understanding, their main purpose is to improve your behavior *during* intercultural communication.

The motivation for this particular section grows out of an important precept found in the study of human communication. It suggests that human interaction is a behavioral act in which people engage for the purpose of changing their environment. Inherent in this notion is the idea that communication is something people *do*—it involves action. Regardless of how much you understand intercultural communication, when you are communicating with someone from another culture you are part of a behavioral situation. You, and your communication counterpart, are doing things to each other. This final part of the book deals with that "doing." In addition, it is intended to help your communication become as effective as possible.

As you might well imagine, personal contact and experience are the most desirable methods for improvement. Knowledge and practice seem to work in tandem. The problem, however, is that we cannot write or select readings that substitute for this personal experience. Therefore, our contribution by necessity must focus on the observations of those who have practiced intercultural communication with some degree of success.

7

Communicating Interculturally: Becoming Competent

The primary purpose of this book is to help you become more effective intercultural communicators. To this end, the articles in this chapter offer advice and counsel aimed at improving the way you communicate when you find yourself in intercultural encounters. To help you achieve this goal, most of the essays discuss problems as well as solutions. Being alert to potential problems is the first step toward understanding. Once problems have been identified it is easier to seek means of improvement.

The first essay looks at both problems and solutions. In "Stumbling Blocks in Intercultural Communication," LaRay M. Barna deals with some specific reasons why intercultural communication often fails to bring about mutual understanding. She has selected six important causes for communication breakdown across cultural boundaries: assuming similarity instead of difference, language problems, nonverbal misunderstanding, the presence of preconceptions and stereotypes, the tendency to evaluate, and the high anxiety that often exists in intercultural encounters.

Our second essay moves us from potential problems to possible solutions. In his article "Intercultural Communication Competence" Brian H. Spitzberg offers a profile of the effective intercultural communicator. More specifically, he suggests a course of action that is likely to enhance our competence when we are in an intercultural situation. These suggestions take the form of propositions that can be used to guide our actions. We are told that intercultural competence is increased if we (1) are motivated, (2) are knowledgeable, (3) possess interpersonal skills, (4) are credible, (5) meet the expectations of our communication partner, (6) can strike a balance between autonomy needs and intimacy needs, (7) reflect similarities, (8) manifest trust, (9) offer social support, and (10) have access to multiple relationships.

Our next essay, "Managing Intercultural Conflicts Effectively," Stella Ting-Toomey moves us from a general analysis of communication competency to a specific topic associated with intercultural communication: intercultural conflict. The rationale behind this selection is clearly stated in the opening line of the essay: "Conflict is inevitable in all social and personal relationships." To preempt the problems created by interpersonal disharmony, particularly in the intercultural setting, Ting-Toomey maintains that conflict must be defined and managed. To help us improve our capacity to clarify and regulate conflict the author explains three significant features of intercultural conflict. First, a framework using low-context versus high-context and monochronic and polychronic time is advanced to demonstrate why and how cultures are different and similar. Second, some basic assumptions and factors that contribute to conflict are discussed. Finally, Ting-Toomey offers a series of skills that can help manage conflict when it develops in the intercultural encounter.

Humor, as we all know from personal experience, is an integral part of human interaction. In fact, humor is so commonplace that we often take it for granted. However, Wen-Shu Lee attempts to alert us to some of the problems in the use of humor when our communication partner is from a culture different from our own. Lee maintains that humor breakdowns are more than linguistic problems. For her, the use of humor often "takes us into the heart of cultural understanding." To increase intercultural understanding Lee offers numerous examples that will assist us in using humor in an effective manner. Specifically, she sees humor sharing as a two-stage process. First, the successful use of humor demands a new set of conversational rules between native and non-native speakers so that humor becomes socially acceptable. The second stage would have us employing Aristotle's enthymematic-reasoning pattern as a guide to explaining and appreciating cross-cultural humor.

Our next essay is based on a premise that has been at the core of this entire book. Simply stated, we have become a multicultural, multiracial, and multilingual society. This profound change on North American culture has touched economic, social, legal, political, and educational systems. For these institutions to survive they need to meet the inevitable challenge of cultural diversity. To facilitate that challenge in "A Model for Cultural Diversity Training" Derald Wing Sue offers a model that seeks to incorporate cultural diversity in organizations. The model is based on a $3 \times 3 \times 3$ matrix, which analyzes an organization's functional focus (recruitment, retention, and promotion), barriers to effective intercultural communication (differences, discrimination, and systemic factors), and cross-cultural competencies (beliefs/attitudes, knowledge, and skills).

The final article deals with cross-cultural adaptation, a unique and often overlooked aspect of intercultural communication. Young Yun Kim examines this subject in her essay "Adapting to a New Culture." Because over a million immigrants are coming to the United States each year, the issues of adaptation is indeed an important one. For as Kim notes, "cross-cultural adaptation is achieved mainly through communication." This means that these new arrivals to the United States must learn new ways to think, feel, and behave so as to coordinate their activities with those of the dominant culture. The process of learning these new modes of communication is called "acculturation." As you would suspect, attempting to learn a new culture, while trying to maintain some behaviors of the original culture, can be very stressful. Understanding the roots of some of these tensions and frustrations, and how to overcome them, is the central goal of this essay. Our role in the acculturation process is rather clear. Kim tells us that successful adaptation is a joint activity between the "strangers" and members of the dominant culture. By taking a positive role in that activity we can help immigrants with the difficult transition they face in their efforts to preserve their original ethnicity while adapting to a new and often confusing environment.

Stumbling Blocks in Intercultural Communication

LARAY M. BARNA

Why is it that contact with persons from other cultures so often is frustrating and fraught with misunderstanding? Good intentions, the use of what one considers to be a friendly approach, and even the possibility of mutual benefits don't seem to be sufficient — to many people's surprise. A worse scenario is when rejection occurs just because the group to which a person belongs is "different." It's appropriate at this time of major changes in the international scene to take a hard look at some of the reasons for this. New proximity and new types of relationships are presenting communication challenges that few people are ready to meet.

THE SIX STUMBLING BLOCKS

I. Assumption of Similarities

One answer to the question of why misunderstanding and/or rejection occurs is that many people naively assume there are sufficient similarities among peoples of the world to make communication easy. They expect that simply being human, having common requirements of food, shelter, security, and so on, makes everyone alike. Unfortunately they overlook the fact that the forms of adaptation to these

common biological and social needs and the values, beliefs, and attitudes surrounding them are vastly different from culture to culture. The biological commonalities are not much help when it comes to communication, where we need to exchange ideas and information, find ways to live and work together, or just make the kind of impression we want to make.

Another reason many people are lured into thinking that "people are people" is that it reduces the discomfort of dealing with difference. If someone acts or looks "strange," (different from them) it's then possible to evaluate this as "wrong" and treat everyone ethnocentrically.

The assumption of similarity does not often extend to the expectation of a common verbal language but it does interfere with caution in decoding nonverbal symbols, signs, and signals. No cross-cultural studies have proven the existence of a common nonverbal language except those in support of Darwin's theory that facial expressions are universal.[1] Ekman (1976) found that "the particular visible pattern on the face, the combination of muscles contracted for anger, fear, surprise, sadness, disgust, happiness (and probably also for interest) is the same for all members of our species" (pp. 19–20).

This seems helpful until it is realized that a person's cultural upbringing determines whether or not the emotion will be displayed or suppressed, as well as on which occasions and to what degree (Ekman & Friesen, 1969, p. 1). The situations that bring about the emotional feeling also differ from culture to culture; for example the death of a loved one may be a cause for joy, sorrow, or some other emotion, depending upon the accepted cultural belief.

Since there seem to be no universals or "human nature" that can be used as a basis for automatic understanding, we must treat each encounter as an individual case, searching for whatever perceptions and communication means are held in common and proceed from there. This is summarized by Vinh The Do: "If we realize that we are all culture bound and culturally modified, we will accept the fact that, being unlike, we do not really know what someone else 'is.' This is another way to view the 'people are people' idea. We now have to find a way to sort out the cultural modifiers in each separate encounter to find similarity."[2]

Persons from the United States seem to hold this assumption of similarity more strongly than some other cultures. The Japanese, for example, have the reverse belief that they are distinctively different from the rest of the world. This notion brings intercultural communication problems of its own. Expecting no similarities they work hard to figure out the foreign stranger but do not expect foreigners to be able to understand them. This results in exclusionary attitudes and only passive efforts toward mutual understanding (Tai, 1986, pp. 45–47).

As Western trappings permeate more and more of the world the illusion of similarity increases. A look-alike facade deceives representatives from contrasting cultures when each wears Western dress, speaks English, and uses similar greeting rituals. It is like assuming that New York, Tokyo, and Tehran are all alike because each has the appearance of a modern city. But without being alert to possible underlying differences and the need to learn new rules for functioning, persons going from one city to the other will be in immediate trouble, even when taking on such simple roles as pedestrian or driver. Also, unless a foreigner expects subtle differences it will take a long time of noninsulated living in a new culture (not in an enclave of his or her own kind) before he or she can be jarred into a new perceptual and nonevaluative thinking.

The confidence that comes with the myth of similarity is much stronger than with the assumption of differences, the latter requiring tentative assumptions and behaviors and a willingness to accept the anxiety of "not knowing." Only with the assumption of differences, however, can reactions and interpretations be adjusted to fit "what's happening." Without it someone is likely to misread signs and symbols and judge the scene ethnocentrically.

The stumbling block of assumed similarity is a *troublem*, as one English learner expressed it, not only for the foreigner but for the people in the host country (United States or any other) with whom the international visitor comes into contact. The native inhabitants are likely to be lulled into the expectation that, since the foreign person is dressed appropriately and speaks some of the language, he or she will also have similar nonverbal codes, thoughts, and feelings. In the United States nodding, smiling, and affirmative comments from a foreigner will probably be confidently interpreted by straightforward, friendly Americans as meaning that they have informed, helped, and pleased the newcomer. It is likely, however, that the foreigner actually understood very little of the verbal and nonverbal content and was merely indicating polite interest or trying not to embarrass himself or herself or the host with verbalized questions. The conversation may even have confirmed a stereotype that Americans are insensitive and ethnocentric.

In instances like this, parties seldom compare impressions and correct misinterpretations. One place where opportunities for achieving insights does occur is in an intercultural communication classroom. Here, for example, U.S. students often complain that international student members of a discussion or project group seem uncooperative or uninterested. One person who had been thus judged offered the following explanation:[3]

I was surrounded by Americans with whom I couldn't follow their tempo of discussion half of the time. I have difficulty to listen and speak, but also with the way they handle the group. I felt uncomfortable because sometimes they believe their opinion strongly. I had been very serious about the whole subject but I was afraid I would say something wrong. I had the idea but not the words.

The classroom is also a good place to test whether one common nonverbal behavior, the smile, is actually the universal sign people assume it to be. The following enlightening comments came from international students newly arrived in the United States.[4]

Japanese student: On my way to and from school I have received a smile by non-acquaintance American girls several times. I have finally learned they have no interest for me; it means only a kind of greeting to a foreigner. If someone smiles at a stranger in Japan, especially a girl, she can assume he is either a sexual maniac or an impolite person.

Korean student: An American visited me in my country for one week. His inference was that people in Korea are not very friendly because they didn't smile or want to talk with foreign people. Most Korean people take time to get to be friendly with people. We never talk or smile at strangers.

Arabic student: When I walked around the campus my first day many people smiled at me. I was very embarrassed and rushed to the men's room to see if I had made a mistake with my clothes. But I could find nothing for them to smile at. Now I am used to all the smiles.

Vietnamese student: The reason why certain foreigners may think that Americans are superficial — and they are, some Americans even recognize this — is that they talk and smile too much. For people who come from placid cultures where nonverbal language is more used, and where a silence, a smile, a glance have their own meaning, it is true that Americans speak a lot. The superficiality of Americans can also be detected in their relations with others. Their friendships are, most of the time, so ephemeral compared to the friendships we have at home. Americans make friends very easily and leave their friends almost as quickly, while in my country it takes a long time to find out a possible friend and then she becomes your friend — with a very strong sense of the term.

Statements from two U.S. students follow.[5] The first comes from someone who has learned to look for differing perceptions and the second, unfortunately, reflects the stumbling block of assumed similarity.

U.S. student: I was waiting for my husband on a downtown corner when a man with a baby and two young children approached. Judging by small quirks of fashion he had not been in the U.S. long. I have a baby about the same age and in appreciation of his family and obvious involvement as a father I smiled at him. Immediately I realized I did the wrong thing as he stopped, looked me over from head to toe and said, "Are you waiting for me? You meet me later?" Apparently I had acted as a prostitute would in his country.

U.S. student: In general it seems to me that foreign people are not necessarily snobs but are very unfriendly. Some class members have told me that you shouldn't smile at others while passing them by on the street in their country. To me I can't stop smiling. It's just natural to be smiling and friendly. I can see now why so many foreign people stick together. They are impossible to get to know. It's like the Americans are big bad wolves. How do Americans break this barrier? I want friends from all over the world but how do you start to be friends without offending them or scaring them off — like sheep?"

The discussion thus far threatens the popular expectation that increased contact with representatives of diverse cultures through travel, student exchange programs, joint business ventures, and so on will automatically result in better understanding and friendship. Indeed, tests of that assumption have been disappointing.[6] For example, research found that Vietnamese immigrants who speak English well and have the best jobs are suffering the most from psychosomatic complaints and mental problems and are less optimistic about the future than their counterparts who remain in ethnic enclaves without attempting to adjust to their new homeland. One explanation given is that these persons, unlike the less acculturated immigrants, "spend considerable time in the mainstream of society, regularly facing the challenges and stresses of dealing with American attitudes" (Horn, 1980, pp. 103–104).

After 24 years of listening to conversations between international and U.S. students and professors and seeing the frustrations of both groups as they try to understand each other, this author, for one, is inclined to agree with Charles Frankel (1965) who says, "Tensions exist within nations and between nations that never would have existed were these nations not in such intensive cultural communication with one another" (p. 1). Recent world events have proven this to be true.

From a communicative perspective it doesn't have to be that way. Just as more opportunities now exist for cross-cultural contact so does more information about how to meet this challenge. There are more orientation and training programs around the country, more courses in intercultural communication in educational institutions, and more published material.[7] Until persons can squarely face the likelihood of meeting up with difference and misunderstanding, however, they will not be motivated to take advantage of these resources.

Many potential travelers who do try to prepare for out-of-country travel (for business conferences, government negotiations, study tours, or whatever) might gather information about the customs of the other country and a smattering of the language. Behaviors and attitudes of its people are sometimes researched, but necessarily from a secondhand source, such as a friend who has "been there." Experts realize that information gained in this fashion is general, seldom sufficient, and may or may not be applicable to the specific situation and area that the traveler visits. Also, knowing "what to expect" often blinds the observer to all but what confirms his or her image. Any contradictory evidence that does filter through the screens of preconception is likely to be treated as an exception and thus discounted.

A better approach is to begin by studying the history, political structure, art, literature, and language of the country if time permits. This provides a framework for on-site observations. Even more important is to develop an investigation, nonjudgmental attitude, and a high tolerance for ambiguity—all of which require lowered defenses. Margaret Mead (1960) suggests sensitizing persons to the kinds of things that need to be taken into account instead of developing behavior and attitude stereotypes. She reasons that there are individual differences in each encounter and that changes occur regularly in cultural patterns, making research information obsolete.

Stewart and Bennett (1991) also warn against providing lists of "do's and don'ts" for travelers for several reasons, mainly that behavior is ambiguous; the same action can have different meanings in different situations and no one can be armed with prescriptions for every contingency. Instead they encourage persons to understand the assumptions and values on which their own behavior rests. This can then be compared with what is found in the other culture, and a "third culture" can be adopted based on expanded cross-cultural understanding (pp. 15–16).

II. Language Differences

The remainder of this article will examine some of the variables of the intercultural communication process itself and point out danger zones therein. The first stumbling block has already been discussed at length, the hazard of *assuming similarity instead of difference*. A second danger will surprise no one: *language difference*. Vocabulary, syntax, idioms, slang, dialects, and so on, all cause difficulty, but the person struggling with a different language is at least aware of being in trouble.

A worse language problem is the tenacity with which someone will cling to just one meaning of a word or phrase in the new language, regardless of connotation or context. The infinite variations possible, especially if inflection and tonal qualities are present, are so difficult to cope with that they are often waved aside. This complacency will stop a search for understanding. The nationwide misinterpretation of Krushchev's statement "We'll bury you" is a classic example. Even "yes" and "no" cause trouble. When a non-native speaker first hears the English phrase, "Won't you have some tea?" he or she listens to the literal meaning of the sentence and answers, "No," meaning that he or she wants some. The U.S. hostess, on the other hand, ignores the double negative because of common usage, and the guest gets no tea. Also, in some cultures, it is polite to refuse the first or second offer of refreshment. Many foreign guests have gone hungry because they never got a third offer. This is another case of where "no" means "yes."

III. Nonverbal Misinterpretations

Learning the language, which most visitors to foreign countries consider their only barrier to understanding, is actually only the beginning. As Frankel (1965) says, "To enter into a culture is to be able to hear, in Lionel Trilling's phrase, its special 'hum and buzz of implication'" (p. 103). This suggests the third stumbling block, *nonverbal misinterpretations*. People from different cultures inhabit different sensory realities. They see, hear, feel, and smell only that which has some meaning or importance for them. They abstract whatever fits into their personal world of recognition and then interpret it through the frame of reference of their own culture. An example follows:

An Oregon girl in an intercultural communication class asked a young man from Saudi Arabia how he would nonverbally signal that he liked her. His response was to smooth back his hair, which to her was just a common nervous gesture signifying nothing. She repeated her question three times. He smoothed his hair three times. Then, realizing that she was not recognizing this movement as his reply to her question, automatically ducked his head and stuck out his tongue slightly in embarrassment. This behavior *was* noticed by the girl and she expressed astonishment that he would show liking for someone by sticking out his tongue.

The lack of comprehension of nonverbal signs and symbols that are easy to observe — such as gestures, postures, and other body movements — is a definite communication barrier. But it is possible to learn the meanings of these messages, usually in informal rather than formal ways. It is more difficult to note correctly the unspoken codes of the other culture that are less obvious such as the handling of time and spatial relationships and subtle signs of respect or formality.

IV. Preconceptions and Stereotypes

The fourth stumbling block is the presence of *preconceptions and stereotypes*. If the label "inscrutable" has preceded the Japanese guest, his behaviors (including the constant and seemingly inappropriate smile) will probably be seen as such. The stereotype that Arabs are "inflammable" may cause U.S. students to keep their distance or even alert authorities when an animated and noisy group from the

Middle East gathers. A professor who expects everyone from Indonesia, Mexico, and many other countries to "bargain" may unfairly interpret a hesitation or request from an international student as a move to manipulate preferential treatment.

Stereotypes help do what Ernest Becker (1962) asserts the anxiety-prone human race must do — reduce the threat of the unknown by making the world predictable (pp. 84–89). Indeed, this is one of the basic functions of culture: to lay out a predictable world in which the individual is firmly oriented. Stereotypes are overgeneralized, secondhand beliefs that provide conceptual bases from which we "make sense" out of what goes on around us, whether or not they are accurate or fit the circumstance. In a foreign land their use increases our feeling of security and is psychologically necessary to the degree that we cannot tolerate ambiguity or the sense of helplessness resulting from inability to understand and deal with people and situations beyond our comprehension.

Stereotypes are stumbling blocks for communicators because they interfere with objective viewing of stimuli — the sensitive search for cues to guide the imagination toward the other person's reality. They are not easy to overcome in ourselves or to correct in others, even with the presentation of evidence. Stereotypes persist because they are firmly established as myths or truisms by one's own national culture and because they sometimes rationalize prejudices. They are also sustained and fed by the tendency to perceive selectively only those pieces of new information that correspond to the image held. For example, the Asian or African visitor who is accustomed to privation and the values of self-denial and self-help cannot fail to experience American culture as materialistic and wasteful. The stereotype for the visitor becomes a reality.

V. Tendency to Evaluate

Another deterrent to understanding between persons of differing cultures or ethnic groups is the *tendency to evaluate,* to approve or disapprove, the statements and actions of the other person or group rather than to try to comprehend completely the thoughts and feelings expressed from the world view of the other. Each person's culture or way of life always seems right, proper, and natural. This bias prevents the open-minded attention needed to look at the attitudes and behavior patterns from the other's point of view. A mid-day siesta changes from a "lazy habit" to a "pretty good idea" when someone listens long enough to realize the mid-day temperature in that country is over 115°F.

The author, fresh from a conference in Tokyo where Japanese professors had emphasized the preference of the people of Japan for simple natural settings of rocks, moss, and water and of muted greens and misty ethereal landscapes, visited the Katsura Imperial Gardens in Kyoto. At the appointed time of the tour a young Japanese guide approached the group of 20 waiting U.S. Americans and remarked how fortunate it was that the day was cloudy. This brought hesitant smiles to the group who were less than pleased at the prospect of a shower. The guide's next statement was that the timing of the summer visit was particularly appropriate in that the azalea and rhododendron blossoms were gone and the trees had not yet turned to their brilliant fall colors. The group laughed loudly, now convinced that the young man had a fine sense of humor. I winced at his bewildered expression, realizing that had I come before attending the conference I would have shared the group's inference that he could not be serious.

The communication cutoff caused by immediate evaluation is heightened when feelings and emotions are deeply involved; yet this is just the time when listening with understanding is most needed. As stated by Sherif, Sherif, and Nebergall (1965), "A person's commitment to his religion, politics, values of his family, and his stand on the virtue of his way of life are ingredients in his self-picture — intimately felt and cherished" (p. vi). It takes both the awareness of the tendency to close our minds and the courage to risk changing our own perceptions and values to dare to comprehend why someone thinks and acts differently from us. Religious wars and negotiation deadlocks everywhere are examples of this.

On an interpersonal level there are innumerable illustrations of the tendency to evaluate, resulting in a breach in intercultural relationships. Two follow:[8]

U.S. student: A Persian friend got offended because when we got in an argument with a third party, I didn't take his side. He says back home you are supposed to take a friend's or family's side even when they are wrong. When you get home then you can attack the "wrongdoer" but you are never supposed to go against a relative or a friend to a stranger. This I found strange because even if it is my mother and I think she is wrong, I say so.

Korean student: When I call on my American friend he said through window, "I am sorry. I have no time because of my study." Then he shut the window. I couldn't understand through my cultural background. House owner should have welcome visitor whether he likes or not and whether he is busy or not. Also the owner never speaks without opening his door.

The admonition to resist the tendency to immediately evaluate does not intend to suggest that one should not develop one's own sense of right and wrong. The goal is to look and listen empathically rather than through a thick screen of value judgments that would cause one to fail to achieve a fair and total understanding. Once comprehension is complete it can be determined whether or not there is a clash in values or ideology. If so, some form of adjustment or conflict resolution can be put into place.

VI. High Anxiety

High anxiety or tension, also known as *stress,* is common in cross-cultural experiences due to the number of uncertainties present. The two words, "anxiety" and "tension," are linked because one cannot be mentally anxious without also being physically tense. Moderate tension and positive attitudes prepare one to meet challenges with energy. Too much anxiety or tension requires some form of relief which too often comes in the form of defenses, such as the skewing of perceptions, withdrawal, or hostility. That's why it is considered a serious stumbling block. As stated by Kim (1991):

Stress, indeed, is considered to be inherent in intercultural encounters, disturbing the internal equilibrium of the individual system. Accordingly, to be interculturally competent means to be able to manage such stress, regain internal balance, and carry out the communication process in such a way that contributes to successful interaction outcomes (p. 267).

High anxiety or tension, unlike the other five stumbling blocks (assumption of similarity, language, nonverbal misinterpretations, preconceptions and stereotypes, and the practice of immediate evaluation), is not only distinct but often underlies and compounds the other stumbling blocks. The use of stereotypes and evaluations are defense mechanisms in themselves to alleviate the stress of the unknown or the intercultural encounter, as previously explained. If the person was tense or anxious to begin with these would be used even more. Falling prey to the aura of similarity is also a protection from the stress of recognizing and accommodating to differences. Different language and nonverbal patterns are difficult to use or interpret under the best of conditions. The distraction of trying to reduce the feeling of anxiety (sometimes called "internal noise") makes mistakes even more likely. Jack Gibb (1961) remarks,

Defense arousal prevents the listener from concentrating upon the message. Not only do defensive communicators send off multiple value, motive, and affect cues, but also defensive recipients distort what they receive. As a person becomes more and more defensive, he becomes less and less able to perceive accurately the motives, the values, and the emotions of the sender (pp. 141–148).

Anxious feelings usually permeate both parties in an intercultural dialogue. The host national is uncomfortable when talking with a foreigner because he or she cannot maintain the normal flow of verbal and nonverbal interaction. There are language and perception barriers; silences are too long or too short; proxemic and other norms may be violated. He or she is also threatened by the other's unknown knowledge, experience, and evaluation—the visitor's potential for scrutiny and rejection of the person and/or the country. The inevitable question "How do you like it here?" which the foreigner abhors, is a quest for reassurance, or at least a "feeler" that reduces the unknown. The reply is usually more polite than honest but this is seldom realized.

The foreign members of dyads are even more threatened. They feel strange and vulnerable, helpless to cope with messages that swamp them. Their own "normal" reactions are inappropriate. Their self-esteem is often intolerably undermined unless they employ such defenses as withdrawal into their own reference group or into themselves, screen out or misperceive stimuli, use rationalization or overcompensation, or become aggressive or hostile. None of these defenses leads to effective communication.

Culture Shock. If a person remains in a foreign culture over time the stress of constantly being "on guard" to protect oneself against making "stupid mistakes" takes its toll and he or she will probably be affected by "culture fatigue," usually called *culture shock.* According to Barna (1983):

. . . the innate physiological makeup of the human animal is such that discomfort of varying degrees occurs in the presence of alien stimuli. Without the normal props of one's own culture there is unpredictability, helplessness, a threat to self-esteem, and a general feeling of "walking on ice"—all of which are stress producing (pp. 42–43).

The result of several months of this sustained anxiety or tension (or excitation if the high activation is perceived positively) is that reserve energy supplies become depleted, the person's physical capacity is weakened, and a feeling of exhaustion, desperation, or depression may take over (Selye, 1969). He or she, consciously or unconsciously, would then use psychological defenses such as those described previously. If this temptation is resisted, the sojourner suffering from the strain of constant adjustment may find his or her body absorbing the stress in the form of stomach or back aches, insomnia, inability to concentrate, or other stress-related illnesses (Barna, 1983, pp. 29–30).

The following account by a sojourner to the United States illustrates the trauma of culture shock:

Soon after arriving in the U.S. from Peru, I cried almost every day. I was so tense I heard without hearing, and this made me feel foolish. I also escaped into sleeping more than twelve hours at a time and dreamed of my life, family, and friends in Lima. After three months of isolating myself in the house and speaking to no-one, I ventured out. I then began to have severe headaches. Finally I consulted a doctor, but she only gave me a lot of drugs to relieve the pain. Neither my doctor nor my teachers ever mentioned the two magic words that could have changed my life: culture shock! When I learned about this I began to see things from a new point of view and was better able to accept myself and my feelings.

I now realize most of the Americans I met in Lima before I came to the U.S. were also in one of the stages of culture shock. They demonstrated a somewhat hostile attitude toward Peru, which the Peruvians sensed and usually moved from an initially friendly attitude to a defensive, aggressive attitude or to avoidance. The Americans mostly stayed within the safe cultural familiarity of the embassy compound. Many seemed to feel that the difficulties they were experiencing in Peru were specially created by Peruvians to create discomfort for "gringos." In other words, they displaced their problem of adjustment and blamed everything on Peru.[9]

Culture shock is a state of dis-ease, and, like a disease, it has different effects, different degrees of severity, and different time spans for different people. It is the least troublesome to those who learn to accept cultural diversity with interest instead of anxiety and manage normal stress reactions by practicing positive coping mechanisms, such as conscious physical relaxation (Barna 1983, pp. 33–39).

Physiological Reactions. Understanding the physiological component of the stumbling block of anxiety/tension helps in the search for ways to lessen its debilitating effects (Selye, 1974, 1976). It is hard to circumvent because, as human animals, our biological system is set so that anything that is perceived as being "not normal" automatically signals an alert (Toffler, 1970, pp. 334–342; Ursin, 1978). Depending on how serious the potential threat seems to be, extra adrenalin and noradrenalin pour into the system; muscles tighten; the heart rate, blood pressure, and breathing rate increase, the digestive process turns off, and other changes occur (Oken, 1974).

This "fight or flight" response was useful, actually a biological gift for survival or effective functioning, when the need was for vigorous action. However, if the "danger" is to one's social self, which is more often the case in today's world, too much anxiety or tension just gets in the way. This is particularly true in an intercultural setting where the need is for understanding, calm deliberation, and empathy in order to untangle misperceptions and enter into smooth relationships.

All is not "doom and gloom" however. As stated by Ursin (1978), "The bodily response to changes in the environment and to threatening stimuli is simply activation" (p. 219). Researchers believe that individuals control their emotional response to that activation by their own cognitions (Brown, 1980; Keating, 1979; Schachter and Singer, (1962)). If a person expects something to be exciting rather than frightening, he is more likely to interpret the somatic changes that he feels in his body as excitement. Selye (1978) would label that "the good stress" that does much less harm unless it continues for some time without relief. Feeling "challenged" facilitates functioning as opposed to a person who feels "threatened" (Lazarus, 1979).

People also differ in their stress tolerance. Whatever the reasons, everyone knows people who "fall apart at the least thing" and others who seem unflappable in any crisis. If you are one of the former there are positive ways to handle the stress of intercultural situations, whether these be one-time encounters; frequent dialogues in multicultural settings like a school or workplace, vacation trips; or wherever. For starters, you can find opportunities to become familiar with many types of people so that differences become normal and interesting instead of threatening. And you can practice body awareness so that changes that signify a stress reaction can be identified and counteracted.

CONCLUSION

Being aware of the six stumbling blocks is certainly the first stop in avoiding them, but it isn't easy. For most people it takes insight, training, and sometimes an alteration of long-standing habits or thinking patterns before progress can be made. The increasing need for global understanding, however, gives all of us the responsibility for giving it our best effort.

We can study other languages and learn to expect differences in nonverbal forms and other cultural aspects. We can train ourselves to meet intercultural encounters with more attention to situational details. We can use an investigative approach rather than stereotypes and preconceptions. We can gradually expose ourselves to differences so that they become less threatening. We can even learn to lower our tension level when needed to avoid triggering defensive reactions.

The overall goal should be to achieve *intercultural communication competence,* which is defined by Kim (1991) as "the overall internal capability of an individual to manage key challenging features of intercultural communication: namely, cultural differences and unfamiliarity, intergroup posture, and the accompanying experience of stress" (p. 259).

Roger Harrison (1966) adds a final thought:

. . . the communicator cannot stop at knowing that the people he is working with have different customs, goals, and thought patterns from his own. He must be able to feel his way into intimate contact with these alien values, attitudes, and feelings. He must be able to work with them and within them, neither losing his own values in the confrontation nor protecting himself behind a wall of intellectual detachment (p. 4).

NOTES

1. See Charles Darwin, *The Expression of Emotions in Man and Animals* (New York: Appleton, 1872); Irenaus, Eibl-Eibesfeldt, *Ethology: The Biology of Behavior* (New York: Holt, Rinehart & Winston, 1970); Paul Ekman and Wallace V. Friesan, "Constants Across Cultures in the Face and Emotion," *Journal of Personality and Social Psychology, 17* (1971), pp. 124–129.

2. Personal correspondence. Mr. Do is Multicultural Specialist, Portland Public Schools, Portland, Oregon.

3. Taken from student papers in a course on intercultural communication taught by the author.

4. Ibid.

5. Ibid.

6. See for example: Bryant Wedge, *Visitors to the United States and How They See Us* (Princeton, NJ: D. Van Nostrand Company, 1965); and Milton Miller et al., "The Cross-Cultural Student: Lessons in Human Nature," *Bulletin of Menninger Clinic* (March 1971).

7. One good source is the Intercultural Press, Inc., P.O. Box 768, Yarmouth, Maine 04096 U.S.A.

8. Taken from student papers in a course on intercultural communication taught by the author.

9. Personal correspondence.

REFERENCES

Barna, L. M. (1983). "The Stress Factor in Intercultural Relations." In D. Landis and R. W. Brislin (Eds.), *Handbook of Intercultural Training,* Vol. II. New York: Pergamon Press.

Becker, E. (1962). *The Birth and Death of Meaning.* New York: Free Press.

Brown, B. B. (1980). "Perspectives on Social Stress." In H. Selye (Ed.), *Selye's Guide to Stress Research,* Vol. 1. New York: Van Nostrand Reinhold.

Ekman, P. (Summer 1976). "Movements with Precise Meanings." *Journal of Communication, 26.*

Ekman, P., and Friesen, W. (1969). "The Repertoire of Nonverbal Behavior — Categories, Origins, Usage and Coding." *Semiotica 1.*

Frankel, C. (1965). *The Neglected Aspect of Foreign Affairs.* Washington, D.C.: Brookings Institution.

Gibb, J. R. (September 1961). "Defensive Communication." *Journal of Communication 2.*

Harrison, R. (1966). "The Design of Cross-Cultural Training: An Alternative to the University Model." In *Explorations in Human Relations Training and Research.* Bethesda, MD: National Training Laboratories. NEA No. 2.

Horn, J. (June 1980). "Vietnamese Immigrants: Doing Poorly by Doing Well." *Psychology Today.*

Keating, J. P. (1979). "Environmental Stressors: Misplaced Emphasis Crowding as Stressor." In I. G. Sarason and C. D. Spielberger (Eds.), *Stress and Anxiety,* Vol. 6. Washington, D.C.: Hemisphere Publishing.

Kim. Y. Y. (1991). "Intercultural Communication Competence: A Systems-Theoretic View." In S. Ting-Toomey, and F. Korzenny (Eds.), *Cross-Cultural Interpersonal Communication* (International and Intercultural Communication Annual, Vol. XV). Newbury Park, CA: Sage Publications, Inc.

Lazarus, R. S. (November, 1979). "Positive Denial: The Case for Not Facing Reality." *Psychology Today.*

Mead, M. (1960). "The Cultural Perspective." In *Communication or Conflict.* Mary Capes (Ed.), Associated Press.

Oken, D. (1974). "Stress — Our Friend, Our Foe." In *Blue Print for Health.* Chicago: Blue Cross Association.

Schachter, S., and Singer, J. E. (1962). "Cognitive, Social and Physiological Determinants of Emotional State." *Psychological Review 69.*

Selye, H. (September 1969). "Stress: It's a G.A.S." *Psychology Today.*

Selye, H. (1974). *Stress Without Distress.* New York: J. B. Lippincott.

Selye, H. (1976). *The Stress of Life.* New York: McGraw-Hill.

Selye, H. (March 1978). "On the Real Benefits of Eustress." *Psychology Today.*

Sherif, C. W., Sherif, W., and Nebergall, R. (1965). *Attitude and Attitude Change.* Philadelphia: W. B. Saunders Co.

Stewart, E. C., and Bennett, M. J. (1991). *American Cultural Patterns.* Yarmouth, Maine: Intercultural Press, Inc.

Tai, E. (1986). "Modification of the Western Approach to Intercultural Communication for the Japanese Context." Unpublished master's thesis, Portland State University, Portland, Oregon.

Toffler, A. (1970). *Future Shock.* New York: Bantam Books.

Ursin, H. (1978). "Activation, Coping and Psychosomatics." In E. Baade, S. Levine, and H. Ursin (Eds.), *Psychobiology of Stress: A Study of Coping Men.* New York: Academic Press.

A Model of Intercultural Communication Competence

BRIAN H. SPITZBERG

The world we live in is shrinking. Travel that once took months now takes hours. Business dealings that were once confined primarily to local economies have given way to an extensively integrated world economy. Information that once traveled through error-prone and time-consuming methods now appears in the blink of an eye across a wide range of media. People in virtually all locations of the globe are more mobile than ever, and more likely to traverse into cultures different from their own. Literally and figuratively, the walls that separate us are tumbling down. Though we may not have fully become a "global village," there is no denying that the various cultures of the world are far more accessible than ever before, and that the peoples of these cultures are coming into contact at an ever increasing rate. These contacts ultimately comprise interpersonal encounters. Whether it is the negotiation of an arms treaty, or the settlement of a business contract, or merely a sojourner getting directions from a native, cultures do not interact, people do.

The purpose of this essay is to examine the concept of interactional competence in intercultural contexts. For the purposes of this essay, *intercultural communication competence* is considered very broadly as an impression that behavior is appropriate and effective in a given context. Normally, *competence* is considered an ability or a set of skilled behaviors. However, any given behavior or ability may be judged competent in one context, and incompetent in another. Consequently, competence cannot inhere in the behavior or ability itself. It must instead be viewed as a social evaluation of behavior. This social evaluation is composed of the two primary criteria of appropriateness and effectiveness.

Appropriateness means that the valued rules, norms, and expectancies of the relationship are not violated significantly. *Effectiveness* is the accomplishment of valued goals or rewards relative to costs and alternatives. With these dual standards, therefore, communication will be competent in an intercultural context when it accomplishes the objectives of an actor in a manner that is appropriate to the context and relationship.

These two standards obviously bear on the concept of interactional quality. Communication that is *in*appropriate and *in*effective (that is, minimizing) is clearly of low quality. Communication that is appropriate but *in*effective (that is, sufficing) suggests a social chameleon who does nothing objectionable, but also accomplishes no personal objectives through interaction. Finally, communication that is *in*appropriate but effective (that is, maximizing) would include such behaviors as lying, cheating, stealing, bludgeoning, and so forth, messages that are ethically problematic. While there may be instances in which such actions could be considered competent, they are rarely the ideal behaviors to employ in any given circumstance. Only the interactant who is both simultaneously appropriate and effective seems to meet the requirements of the optimal interpersonal communicator. The remainder of this essay examines issues surrounding appropriateness and effectiveness in intercultural interaction.

A MODEL OF INTERCULTURAL COMPETENCE

Most existing models of intercultural competence have been fairly fragmented. Typically, the literature

Table 1 Empirically Derived Factors of Intercultural Competence

Ability to adjust to different cultures	Frankness
Ability to deal with different societal systems	General competence as teacher (task)
Ability to deal with psychological stress	Incompetence
Ability to establish interpersonal relationships	Intellectualizing future orientation
Ability to facilitate communication	Interaction involvement
Ability to understand others	Interpersonal flexibility
Adaptiveness	Interpersonal harmony
Agency (internal locus and efficacy/optimism)	Interpersonal interest
Awareness of self and culture	Interpersonally sensitive maturity
Awareness of implications of cultural differences	Managerial ability
Cautiousness	Nonethnocentrism
Charisma	Nonverbal behaviors
Communication apprehension	Personal/Family adjustment
Communication competence (ability to communicate)	Opinion leadership
Communication efficacy	Rigidity (task persistence)
Communicative functions	Task accomplishment
Controlling responsibility	Transfer of "software"
Conversational management behaviors	Self-actualizing search for identity
Cooperation	Self-confidence/Initiative
Cultural empathy	Self-consciousness
Cultural interaction	Self-disclosure
Demand (long-term goal orientation)	Self-reliant conventionality
Dependent anxiety	Social adjustment
Differentiation	Spouse/Family communication
Empathy/Efficacy	Strength of personality
Familiarity in interpersonal relations	Verbal behaviors

is reviewed and a list of skills, abilities, and attitudes is formulated to summarize the literature (Spitzberg & Cupach, 1989). Such lists appear on the surface to reflect useful guidelines for competent interaction and adaptation. For example, Spitzberg's (1989) review of studies, along with other more recent studies, produces the partial list in Table 1. While each study portrays a reasonable list of abilities or attitudes, there is no sense of integration or coherence across lists. It is impossible to tell which skills are most important in which situations, or even how such skills relate to each other.

A more productive approach would be to develop an integrative model of intercultural competence that is both consistent with the theoretical and empirical literatures, and also provides specific pre-

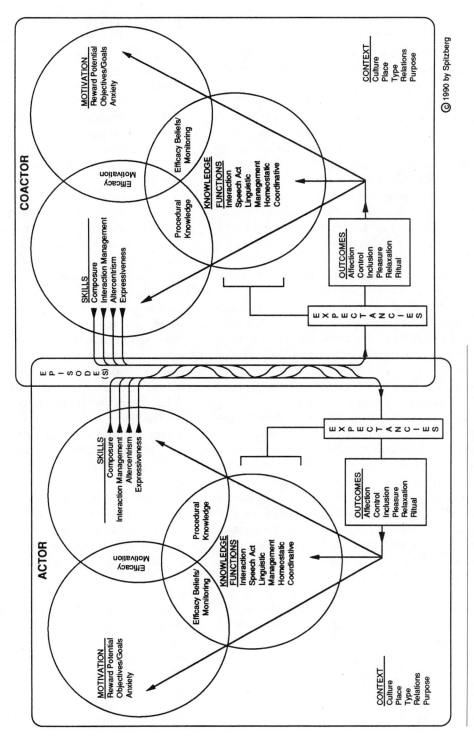

Figure 1 A Diagrammatic Representation of Relational Competence

dictions of competent behavior. This approach is reflected in basic form in Figure 1, and is elaborated on by means of the series of propositions that follow. The propositions are broken down into three levels of analysis: (1) the individual system, (2) the episodic system, and (3) the relational system. The *individual system* includes those characteristics an individual may possess that facilitate competent interaction in a normative social sense. The *episodic system* includes those features of a particular Actor that facilitate competence impressions on the part of a specific Coactor in a specific episode of interaction. The *relational system* includes those components that assist a person's competence across the entire span of relationships rather than in just a given episode of interaction. Each successive system level subsumes the logic and predictions of the former. The propositions serve both to provide an outline of a theory of interpersonal competence in intercultural contexts as well as offer practical advice. To the extent that interactants can analyze intercultural situations sufficiently to understand initial conditions, then each proposition suggests a course of action that is likely to enhance their competence in the situation encountered.

The model portrays the process of dyadic interaction as a function of two individuals' *motivation* to communicate, *knowledge* of communication in that context, and *skills* in implementing their motivation and knowledge. Over the course of the interaction both within and across episodes, behavior is matched to expectancies that each interactant has of the other and the interaction process. If expectancies are fulfilled in a rewarding manner, then interactants are likely to perceive both self and other as communicatively competent, and feel relatively satisfied that objectives were accomplished. Interactants may be seen as incompetent because they lack motivation to perform competently, knowledge of the competent lines of action in the context concerned, or the communication skills to carry off a deft interaction. Also, interactants may be viewed as incompetent because their partner has unrealistic expectancies for the person or episode. These and other implications are discussed next.

Individual System

1. *As communicator motivation increases, communicative competence increases.* Very simply, the more a person wants to make a good impression and communicate effectively, the more likely it is that this person will view self, and be viewed by others, as competent. The question then, becomes what constitutes or leads to high levels of motivation. The following propositions address this question.

1a. *As communicator confidence increases, communicator motivation increases.* Confidence results from several individual experiences. For example, a person who is nervous meeting strangers is likely to be less confident when encountering a new person from a different culture. Further, the more unfamiliar a person is with a given type of situation, the less confident that person is regarding what to do and how to do it. Finally, some situations carry more significant implications and are more difficult to manage than others. For example, getting directions to a major urban landmark is likely to permit greater confidence than negotiating a multimillion dollar contract for your company. Thus, social anxiety, familiarity with the situation, and the importance or consequences of the encounter all influence an interactant's confidence in a social context.

1b. *As reward-relevant efficacy beliefs increase, communicator motivation increases.* Efficacy beliefs are self-perceptions of ability to perform a given set of behaviors (Bandura, 1982). Basically, the more actors believe that they are able to engage in a set of valued or positive actions, the more prone they are to do so. A professional arbitrator is likely to have much higher efficacy beliefs in negotiating disputes or contracts than the average person. However, this arbitrator might not have any greater confidence than the average person in developing friendships with others in a different culture. Efficacy beliefs are therefore usually task specific, and correlated to familiarity with the task(s) and context(s).

1c. *As communicator approach dispositions increase, communicator motivation increases.* Approach dispositions refer to personality characteristics that prompt someone to value communicative activity. People who are higher in self-esteem, who consistently seek relatively high levels of sensory stimulation, who believe they have high levels of control over their environment, who are low in social anxiety, and who are generally well-adjusted psychologically, are likely to seek out communication encounters and find them positively reinforcing.

1d. As the relative cost/benefit ratio of a situation increases, communicator motivation increases. Very simply, every situation can be viewed as having certain potential costs and benefits. Even in no-win situations (for example, "true" conflicts), the behavior that leads to the least costly or painful outcomes is considered the most preferable or beneficial. Likewise, in a win-win situation the least desirable outcomes are also the most costly. Thus, as the perception of potential benefits increases relative to the potential costs of a course of action, the more motivated a person is to pursue that particular course of action. Obviously, the weighing of costs and benefits must always be done relative to alternatives. Asking directions from someone who does not speak your language may be considered too much effort, but only relative to the alternatives of consulting a map, trial-and-error exploration, seeking someone who speaks your language who might be familiar with the locale, or getting hopelessly lost.

2. Communicative knowledge increases, communicative competence increases. A stage actor needs to be motivated to give a good performance to be viewed as a competent actor. However, merely wanting to perform well, and being unhampered by stage fright, are probably insufficient to produce a competent performance. For an actor to give a good performance, it is also important that the actor know the script, the layout of the stage, the type of audience to expect, and so on. So it is with social interaction as well. The more an interactant knows about how to communicate well, the more competent that person is likely to be.

Knowledge of interaction occurs at several microscopic levels (Greene, 1984). As identified in Figure 1, an actor needs to know the interaction func-

tion, the basic goals the interaction is to pursue. These interaction behaviors combine to form speech acts, which express content functions such as asking questions, asserting opinions, and so on. To perform speech acts in turn requires knowledge of linguistics — semantics, syntax, and the constituents of a meaningful sentence. Actual performance of these actions requires adaptation of this behavior to the other person. Thus, behaviors need to be adapted to achieve the following functions: management — coherence and continuity of topic, and relatively smooth flow of speaking turns; homeostatic — a relative balance of physiological activity level; and coordinative — individual matching of verbal and nonverbal components. Several predictions help specify the relevance of knowledge to competent interaction.

2a. As task-relevant procedural knowledge increases, communicator knowledge increases. Procedural knowledge concerns the "how" of social interaction rather than the "what." For example, knowing the actual content of a joke would be considered the substantive knowledge of the joke. Knowing how to tell it, with all the inflections, the timing, and the actual mannerisms, are all matters of the procedural knowledge of the joke. This knowledge is typically more "mindless" than other forms of knowledge. For example, many skill routines are overlearned to the point that the procedures are virtually forgotten, as in driving a familiar route home and not remembering anything about the drive upon arrival. You "know" how to drive, but you can use such knowledge with virtually no conscious attention to the process. Thus, the more a person actually knows how to perform the mannerisms and behavioral routines of a cultural milieu, the more knowledgeable this person is likely to be in communicating generally with others in this culture. In general, as a person's exposure to a culture increases, his or her stores of relevant subject matters, topics, language forms, and so on, as well as procedural competencies, are likely to increase.

2b. As mastery of knowledge-acquisition strategies increases, communicator knowledge increases. A person who does not already know how to behave is not necessarily consigned to incompetence. People have evolved a multitude of means for finding out what to do, and how to do it, in unfamiliar contexts. The metaphor of international espionage illustrates some of the strategies by which people acquire information about others, such as interrogating (asking questions), surveilling (observing others), exchanging information (disclosing information to elicit disclosure from other), posturing (violating some local custom and observing reactions to assess the value of various actions), bluffing (acting as if we know what we are doing and allowing the unfolding action to inform us and define our role), or engaging double agents (using the services of a native or mutual friend as an informant). The more of these types of strategies actors understand, the more capable they are in obtaining the knowledge needed to interact competently in the culture.

2c. As identity and role diversity increases, communicator knowledge increases. In general, the more diverse a person's exposure to distinct types of people, roles, and self-images, the more this person is able to comprehend various roles and role behaviors characteristic of a given cultural encounter. Some people live all their lives in a culture within very narrow ranges of contexts and roles. Others experience a wide variety of societal activities (jobs, tasks), roles (parent, worshiper, confidant), and groups (political party, religious affiliation, volunteer organization, cultures and co-cultures). A person who has a highly complex self-image reflecting these social identities (Hoelter, 1985), and who has interacted with a diversity of different types of persons and roles (Havighurst, 1957) is better able to understand the types of actions encountered in another culture.

2d. As knowledge dispositions increase, communicator knowledge increases. Many personality characteristics are related to optimal information processing. Specifically, persons high in intelligence, cognitive complexity, self-monitoring, listening skills, empathy, role-taking ability, nonverbal sensitivity, perceptual accuracy, problem-solving ability, and so on, are more likely to know how to behave in any given encounter. In short, while mere possession of information may help, a person also needs to know how to analyze and process that information.

3. As communicator skills increase, communicator competence increases. Skills are any repeatable, goal-oriented actions or action sequences. An actor who is motivated to perform well, and knows the script well, still may not possess the acting skills required to give a good performance. All of us have probably encountered instances in which we knew what we wanted to say, but just could not seem to say it correctly. Such issues concern the skills of performing our motivation and knowledge. Research indicates that there are four specific types or clusters of interpersonal skills, and one more general type of skill.

Before specifying the skills that facilitate intercultural communication competence, an important qualifier needs to be considered. There are probably no specific behaviors that are universally competent. Even if peoples from all cultures smile, the smile is not always a competent behavior. However, there may be skill modes or clusters that are consistently competent according to standards of appropriate usage within each culture. For example, probably all cultures value the smooth flow of conversation, even though they may differ in the specific behaviors and cues used to accomplish such interaction management. Any skill or ability is constrained by its own culturally and relationally appropriate rules of expression. It is in this sense that the following propositions are developed regarding communication skills.

3a. As conversational altercentrism increases, communicator skill increases. Altercentrism ("alter" means other, "centrism" means to focus upon) involves those behaviors that reveal concern for, interest in, and attention to, another person. Behaviors such as eye contact, asking questions, maintenance of others' topics, appropriate body lean and posture, and active listening all indicate a responsiveness to the other person.

3b. As conversational coordination increases, communicator skill increases. Conversational coordination involves all those behaviors that assist in the smooth flow of an encounter. Minimizing response latencies, providing for smooth initiation and conclusion of conversational episodes, avoiding disruptive interruptions, providing transitions between themes or activities, and providing informative feedback cues all assist in managing the interaction and maintaining appropriate pacing and punctuation of a conversation.

3c. As conversational composure increases, communicator skill increases. To be composed in a conversation is to reflect calmness and confidence in demeanor. Thus, composure consists of avoiding anxiety cues (nervous twitches, adaptors, lack of eye contact, breaking vocal pitch) and displaying such behaviors as a steady volume and pitch, relaxed posture, and well-formulated verbal statements. A composed communicator comes across as assertive, self-assured, and in control.

3d. As conversational expressiveness increases, communicator skill increases. Expressiveness concerns those skills that provide vivacity, animation, intensity, and variability in communicative behavior. Specifically, expressiveness is revealed by such behaviors as vocal variety, facial affect, opinion expression, extensive vocabulary usage, and gestures. Expressive communication is closely associated with the ability to display culturally and contextually appropriate effect and energy level through speech and gesture.

3e. As conversational adaptation increases, communicator skill increases. Adaptation is a commonly noted attribute of the competent intercultural communicator. It typically suggests several characteristics. First, rather than radical chameleonlike change, adaptation implies subtle variation of self's behavior to the behavioral style of others. Second, it implies certain homeostatic, or consistency-maintaining, regulatory processes. That is, verbal actions are kept relatively consistent with nonverbal actions. Similarly, amount of personal altercentrism, coordination, composure, and expressiveness, are kept relatively consistent with personal style tendencies. Third, adaptation suggests accommodation of both the actions of the other person as well as one's own goal(s) in the encounter Rather than implying completely altercentric or egocentric orientations, adaptation implies altering and balancing self's goals and intentions to those of the other person. Thus, the skill of adaptation implies such behaviors as shifts of vocal style, posture, animation, and topic development as the behaviors of the other person vary and as changes in self's goals change over the course of a conversation.

The propositions in this section have examined three basic components of interculturally competent communication. In general, the more motivated, knowledgeable, and skilled a person is, the more competent this person is likely to be. It is possible that a person can be viewed as highly competent if high in only one or two of these components. For example, a person who is very motivated may compensate for lack of knowledge and skill through perseverance and effort alone. Likewise, someone who is extremely familiar with a given type of encounter may be able to "drift" through ("I've written so many contracts in my life I can negotiate one in my sleep") with minimal motivation and little conscious awareness of the exact procedures involved. Nevertheless, across most encounters, the more of each of these components a person possesses or demonstrates, the more competent this person's interaction is likely to be.

Episodic System

The first three primary propositions entailed factors that increase the likelihood that an actor will produce behaviors that are normatively competent. As such, the actor producing them, and others generally, will tend to believe that the interactant has behaved competently. However, given that competence is an impression, there is no guarantee that a person who has performed behaviors that normally would be viewed as competent, will be viewed as competent by a particular conversational partner in a particular relational encounter. The propositions in this section address this latter issue. These propositions are episodic in the sense that characteristics of an Actor influence the impressions of the Coactor in a specific episode of interaction. The statements concern those characteristics of an Actor that predict a Coactor's impression of the Actor's competence.

4. As actor's communicative status increases, coactor's impression of actor's competence increases. Communicative status is meant here to represent all those factors that enhance this person's positive evaluation. Competence is, after all, an evaluation. Generally, as a person's status goes, so goes his or her competence. There are obvious exceptions, but it is instructive to consider those status characteristics particularly relevant to communicative competence.

4a. As Actor's motivation, knowledge, and skills increase, Coactor's impression of Actor's competence increases. The logic of the individual system also applies to the episodic system; the factors that lead a person to behave competently in a normative sense will usually lead to a competent relational performance as well (Imahori & Lanigan, 1989; Spitzberg & Cupach, 1984). This is true in two slightly different senses. In one sense, norms comprise the majority of people's views and behaviors, so a person who is normatively competent will usually be viewed as competent in any given encounter. In another sense an Actor who is motivated to interact competently with a particular Coactor, knowledgeable about this particular Coactor, and skilled in interacting with this particular Coactor, is also more likely to communicate better and be viewed as competent by this Coactor in a given encounter.

Factors that facilitate motivation, knowledge, and skill in a particular episodic system are likely to be logical extensions of the individual system components. For example, motivation is likely to increase as attraction to the Coactor increases and as positive reinforcement history with the Coactor increases. Knowledge of the Coactor is likely to increase with the duration of the relationship and the depth and breadth of self-disclosure between Actor and Coactor increase. Skill in interacting with the Coactor is likely to increase as adaptation and refinement increase over the lifetime of the relationship.

4b. As contextual obstruction of Actor's performance increases, Coactor's impression of Actor's competence increases. When forming an impression of an Actor, a Coactor is left to determine the extent to which the Actor's outcomes are due to the Actor's own abilities and effort, rather than the context or other factors. For example, a physically unattractive Actor who consistently makes friends and has dates is likely to be viewed as more communicatively competent than a person who is physically attractive. The reasoning is that the social context is weighted against the unattractive Actor and in favor of the attractive Actor. Thus, the attractive Actor would achieve the same outcomes due to attractiveness rather than his or her competence, whereas the unattractive actor must overcome the contextual barriers through competent action. In essence, all other things being equal, an Actor's competence is "discounted" if there are obvious alternative explanations for the Actor's good fortune. Similarly, an Actor's competence is "forgiven" if there are many apparent alternative reasons for his or her failure.

4c. As Actor's receipt of valued outcomes increases, Coactor's impression of Actor's competence increases. While the discounting effect just discussed influences impressions of competence, it is not likely to outweigh other factors entirely. If an Actor is perceived as consistently achieving positive outcomes, a Coactor is likely to assume that the Actor has something to do with this success (Kaplowitz, 1978). The negotiator who consistently presides over significant agreements is likely to be viewed as more communicatively competent as a simple result of the tangible outcomes, almost regardless of extenuating circumstances.

4d. As Actor's extant-attributed communicative status increases, Coactor's impression of Actor status increases. An actor who comes into an encounter with an established high level of status is more likely to be viewed as competent in subsequent interactions. Additionally, an Actor who has established a satisfying relationship with a particular Coactor has, in effect, established a reserve of competence in the Coactor's views. Thus, Desmond TuTu, Boris Yeltsin, or even Lee Iaccoca enter any communicative situation with considerable communicative status in tow. In essence then, the impression we initially have of an Actor is likely to be the basis for our later impressions until such time that significant events alter these impressions. Furthermore, certain cultures develop higher regard for other cultures generally. The mutual regard that Americans and Japanese-Americans may share is probably quite different than that which South African blacks and whites may share.

5. *Coactor's impression of actor's competence is a function of actor's fulfillment of coactor's expectancies.* Over time, interactants develop expectations regarding how interpersonal interaction is likely to, and should, occur in particular contexts. Not surprisingly, therefore, a person's competence in a given relationship is due partly to expectancy fulfillment and violation. Research indicates that expectancies generally develop along three fundamental dimensions: *evaluation, potency,* and *activity* (commonly referred to as the E-P-A dimensions respectively; see Osgood, May, & Miron, 1975; Spitzberg, 1989). Most contexts are viewed in terms of their valence (good versus bad), power (dominant versus passive), and animation (noisy versus quiet) characteristics. A typical, noncharismatic church service is expected to be good, the audience passive and relatively quiet. A typical party, in contrast, is expected to be good, strong, fast and noisy. Upon being fired, an exit interview is expected to be unpleasurable, and the interviewee as weak and relatively passive. The point is that experience with interpersonal encounters produces expectancies and evaluations regarding both anticipated and appropriate behavior. The propositions that follow elaborate on the influence of these cognitions on impressions of competence.

5a. *As Actor's fulfillment of positive Coactor expectancies increases, Coactor's impression of Actor's competence increases.* To the extent that a Coactor expects an encounter with an Actor to be positive, the Actor is likely to be viewed as competent to the extent that he or she fulfills these expectancies. Since the expectancies typically form a consistent system in a Coactor's mind, an Actor needs to fulfill each of the E-P-A dimensions. If an interviewer expects interviews to be good (E), his or her own role to be relatively powerful and the role of the inter-

viewee to be relatively powerless (P), and for the encounter to be generally quiet but quick (A), then the Actor is well-advised to behave according to these expectancies. Since the interviewer has developed these expectancies along all three dimensions, they tend to be "set" in relationship to each other. Thus, part of what makes the interview "good" in the interviewer's opinion is that the interviewer's role is typically powerful, and the interviews tend to go quietly and quickly.

5b. *As Actor's normative violation of Coactor's negative expectancies increases, Coactor's impression of Actor's competence increases.* The logic of the former proposition reverses itself when a Coactor expects an encounter to be negative. Consider the previous interview example from the interviewee's perspective. An interviewee may find interviews highly anxiety-producing, threatening, and difficult. As such, the interview context is expected to be unpleasurable, the interviewee's role as submissive, and the encounter as generally slow and inactive. If the interviewer wants to make a good impression, therefore, he or she needs to violate the interviewee's expectations in an appropriate manner. Such an interviewer might change the setting to a less-formal lunchroom context, dress more casually, tell some stories and initially discuss topics unrelated to the position, and generally spend some time putting the interviewee in a good mood. Such an encounter violates the interviewee's expectancies, but does so in a way that is normatively acceptable and positive.

5c. *As Actor's fulfillment of Coactor's competence prototype expectancies increases, Coactor's impression of Actor's competence increases.* A prototype in this usage is basically a cognitive outline of concepts, analogous to a mental map of the competence territory. The prototype of a competent person is likely to consist of several levels of concepts varying in their abstraction. A simplified and hypothetical example of a prototype for a competent communicator is displayed in Figure 2.

At the highest level is the category label that determines what types of inferences are relevant to a given set of observed behavior. For example, ob-

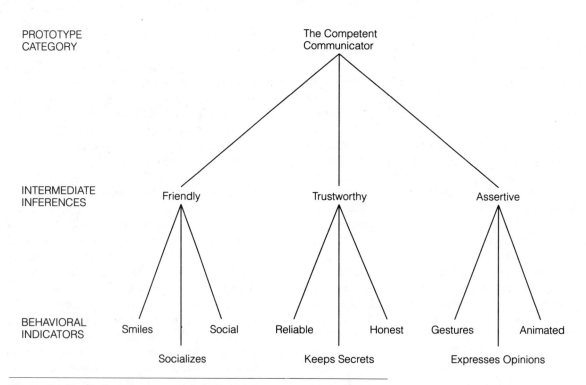

PROTOTYPE CATEGORY

The Competent Communicator

INTERMEDIATE INFERENCES

Friendly   Trustworthy   Assertive

BEHAVIORAL INDICATORS

Smiles   Social   Reliable   Honest   Gestures   Animated

Socializes   Keeps Secrets   Expresses Opinions

Figure 2 A Simple Cognitive Prototype of a Competent Communicator (Adapted from Pavitt and Haight (1985))

serving someone changing the oil in a car is not relevant to the category of "competent communicator." At the next level are types of inferences or impressions that collectively make up the label of competent communicator. In this hypothetical example, a competent communicator is someone who is believed to be friendly, trustworthy, and assertive. Each of these inferences, in turn, is based upon certain types of behavior. To the extent that these behaviors are observed, the inferences follow. Observed behaviors are matched or compared to those that over time have come to occupy the position of category indicators. If there is a good match, then the inferences and evaluations that define the label of competent communicator (in this case, friendly, trustworthy, assertive) are attributed to the interactant observed. If only some of the behaviors match, then the inference of competence is diminished proportionately. Certain behaviors in any given encounter may also be weighted in their importance to the im-

pression. When judging whether or not someone is being deceptive, for example, many people would rely most heavily on that person's eye contact, relative to other behaviors, in assessing this person's competence.

5c. As Actor's normative reciprocity of positive effect and compensation of negative effect increases, Coactor's impression of Actor's competence increases. Reciprocity implies a matching or similarity of response, whereas compensation suggests an opposite or homeostatic response. Research indicates that across most types of relationships and encounters, interactants are generally considered more competent when they reciprocate positive effect and feel more competent when they compensate for negative effect (Andersen, 1989; Spitzberg, 1989). To the extent that the Coactor expresses positive effect, the Actor's response in kind is likely to produce more positive impressions. When the Coactor expresses negative effect, the Actor is likely to be more competent responding with more neutral or positive effect.

5d. As Actor's normative compensation of power relations increases, the more Coactor's impression of Actor's competence increases. Across most types of interpersonal relationships, complementary power relationships tend to produce higher impressions of competence. This is a sweeping statement, and obviously is an overstatement in many ways. For example, optimal negotiation outcomes tend to result when parties begin in fairly competitive, and end up in cooperative, orientations. Still, this principle is useful in most types of relations.

Specifically, dominance is more competently met with passivity, and passivity with dominance. The validity of this proposition is best illustrated by consideration of its alternative. Imagine, for example, what work relationships would be like if every time superiors gave a subordinate orders, the superior was met with orders or refusal. Imagine married couples in which neither person ever actually offered to make a decision. In other words, relationships and encounters tend to work more smoothly and comfortably when dominant moves are responded to with complementary passive moves, and passive moves are met with more directive moves. This does not imply that people should adopt a role of passivity or dominance, but that on a statement-by-statement basis, most interaction will be viewed as competent to the extent that its power balance is complementary rather than reciprocal.

This section has examined the episodic system of intercultural competence. Specifically, the propositions in this section have involved those characteristics of an Actor that increase the likelihood that the Coactor views the Actor as competent in a given episode of interaction. The following section concerns an abbreviated excursion into the relational system, in which characteristics that facilitate competence across the lifespan of a relationship are considered.

Relational System

Relationships are not simply sums of episodes over time. Certainly there is likely to be a strong correlation, such that the more competent the average episode of interaction is, the more relationally stable and satisfying the relationship tends to be. Thus, the logic of the individual system and episodic system are also likely to extend to the relational system. However, there are other factors at work, and this section examines some of these features. In this discussion, the phrase "relational competence" refers to the level of communicative quality in an established relationship. It is an index of the mutual adaptation and satisfaction achieved by a relationship.

6. As mutual fulfillment of autonomy and intimacy needs increases, relational competence increases. Autonomy and intimacy are two fundamental human needs (McAdams, 1988). Typically, they exist in a form of dialectical tension, in that both "struggle" for dominance over the other at any given time, but both are ever-present to some degree. The need for intimacy involves the desire for human contact, connection, belonging, inclusion, camaraderie, communal activity, and nurturance. The need for autonomy, in contrast, is a need for self-control, independence, power, privacy, and solitude. Individuals seem to fluctuate between these two needs over time. And, as with virtually all needs, as each need is fulfilled, it ceases to dominate the individual's behavior. A lonely person continuously thinks about companionship. Once companionship is found, other needs begin to influence this person's thoughts and actions. It follows that if a relationship is competent over the course of its lifespan, the members' need to fulfill the needs of the other as these dialectical needs fluctuates (Spitzberg, 1993).

7. As mutual attraction increases, relational competence increases. This highly intuitive proposition simply indicates that as partners grow more and more attracted to each other, the more this is both likely to reflect, and result in, mutually competent interaction over time (Eagly, Ashmore, Makhijani, & Longo, 1991). This proposition gains support from the consistent finding that attraction is closely associated, at least initially, with interpersonal similarity (Feingold, 1988). Highly similar persons provide a world view of similar values and orientations. These in turn are reflected in a reinforcing and self-confirming manner of symbolic expression. In general, we enjoy interacting with those who are similar because they seem to "speak our language." One implication is that initial interactions with culturally dissimilar others should focus upon areas of similarity that can support sufficient motivation and reinforcement for continued interaction. This is not to imply that differences are always negatively reinforcing. However, differences tend to make the *process* of communication more effortful and difficult, and thereby, generally less rewarding.

8. *As mutual trust increases, relational competence increases.* Similar to the above proposition, the more partners trust one another, the more competent interaction is likely to be, and the more competent the relationship is likely to be (Canary & Spitzberg, 1989). Trust provides a context in which interaction can be more honest, spontaneous, direct, and open. Over time, such a trusting climate is likely to be mutually reinforcing, and lead to a productive and satisfying communicative relationship.

9. *As access to social support increases, relational competence increases.* Social support is anything offered by another that assists a person in coping with problematic or stressful situations. Types of support range from tangible (lending money) to informational (offering advice) to emotional (comforting words) forms. Since stresses stimulate personal and often relational crises, anything that diminishes the effects of these stresses is likely to enhance the person's ability to manage the relationship itself. One of the common problems of sojourner couples or families is that the stresses of being in a new culture often cannot be resolved by the social support of a friendship network, since the friendship network has yet to be established in the new culture.

10. *As relational network integration increases, relational competence increases.* When discussing relationships, it is ironically easy to forget that individuals are always simultaneously members of multiple relationships. When two people come together and form a relationship, part of what determines the competence of this relationship is the extent to which each member's personal network integrates with the other person's network of social relationships. Increasingly, as businesses become multinational and move entire management teams to work with labor in other countries, the problems of social network integration will become substantial. The development of common activities and goals that require cooperation or interaction across social networks, and the development of easier access to the network, are likely to facilitate this aspect of intercultural competence.

CONCLUSIONS

Before examining the implications of this essay, an important qualification needs to be considered. Specifically, most of the propositions presented here have what can be considered upper limits. Basically, too much of a good thing can be bad. For example, someone can be *too* motivated, use *too* much expressiveness, or be *too* composed. Virtually any piece of advice, when carried to extremes, tends to lose its functional value. This can be viewed as a curvilinearity principle. In essence, as motivation, knowledge, and skill increase, so do impressions of competence, to a point, after which the relationship reverses, and competence impressions decrease.

Sir Karl Popper, an eminent philosopher of science, has warned that theories are only useful if they are in danger of failing. Theories that tell us what we already know must be true, tell us nothing. The point is that theories are only valuable to the extent they make risky predictions that may be proved false. It is in this sense that this essay must be viewed with caution.

The predictions offered in this essay represent statements that in the daily interplay of lives are often in danger of being false. None of the predictions should be considered absolutely true, or as an infallible view of the complex canvas of intercultural relations. Nevertheless, progress in the development of knowledge results from such risky propositions, and this essay has attempted to chart a path to progress. In doing so, I have attempted to paint with very broad brush strokes the outline of a theory of intercultural competence. The lines of this theory are strained by their abstraction to the point of no longer resembling the vibrant landscape they are meant to represent. Thus, like any theory or work of abstract art, the key is that the benefactor will find some significant personal meaning in it, and be ever mindful that the symbol is not the thing to which it refers.

REFERENCES

Andersen, P. A. (May 1989). *"A Cognitive Valence Theory of Intimate Communication."* Paper presented at the Iowa Network on Personal Relationships Conference, Iowa City, IA.

Bandura, A. (1982). "Self-Efficacy Mechanism in Human Agency." *American Psychologist, 37,* 122–147.

Canary, D. J. and Spitzberg, B. H. (1989). "A Model of the Perceived Competence of Conflict Strategies." *Human Communication Research, 15,* 630–649.

Eagly, A. H., Ashmore, R. D., Makhijani, M. G., and Longo, L. C. (1991). "What Is Beautiful Is Good, But . . . : A Meta-Analytic Review of Research on the Physical Attractiveness Stereotype." *Psychological Bulletin, 110,* 109–128.

Feingold, A. (1988). "Matching for Attractiveness in Romantic Partners and Same-Sex Friends: A Meta-Analysis and Theoretical Critique." *Psychological Bulletin, 104,* 226–235.

Greene, J. O. (1984). "A Cognitive Approach to Human Communication: An Action Assembly Theory." *Communication Monographs, 51,* 289–300.

Havighurst, R. J. (1957). "The Social Competence of Middle-Aged People." *Genetic Psychology Monographs, 56,* 297–375.

Hoelter, J. W. (1985). "A Structural Theory of Personal Consistency." *Social Psychology Quarterly, 48,* 118–129.

Kaplowitz, S. A. (1978). "Towards a Systematic Theory of Power Attribution." *Social Psychology, 41,* 131–148.

Imahori, T. T., and Lanigan, M. L. (1989). "Relational Model of Intercultural Communication Competence." *International Journal of Intercultural Relations, 13,* 269–286.

McAdams, D. P. (1988). "Personal Needs and Personal Relationships." In S. Duck (Ed.), *Handbook of Personal Relationships: Theory, Research and Interventions* (pp. 7–22). New York: John Wiley & Sons.

Osgood, C. E., May, W. H., and Miron, S. (1975). *Cross-Cultural Universals of Affective Meaning.* Urbana, IL: University of Illinois Press.

Pavitt, C. and Haight, L. (1985). "The 'Competent Communicator' as a Cognitive Prototype." *Human Communication Research, 12,* 225–241.

Spitzberg, B. H. (1989). "Issues in the Development of a Theory of Interpersonal Competence in the Intercultural Context." *International Journal of Intercultural Relations, 13,* 241–268.

Spitzberg, B. H. (1993). "The Dialectics of (In)competence." *Journal of Social and Personal Relationships, 10,* 137–158.

Spitzberg, B. H., and Cupach, W. R. (1984). *Interpersonal Communication Competence.* Beverly Hills, CA: Sage.

Spitzberg, B. H., and Cupach, W. R. (1984). *Handbook of Interpersonal Competence Research.* New York: Springer-Verlag.

Spitzberg, B. H., and Hecht, M. L. (1989). "A Component Model of Relational Competence." *Human Communication Research, 10,* 575–599.

Managing Intercultural Conflicts Effectively[1]

STELLA TING-TOOMEY

Conflict is inevitable in all social and personal relationships. The Latin root words for conflict, "com" and "fligere," means "together" and "to strike" or more simply, "to strike together." Conflict connotes a state of dissonance or collision between two forces or systems. This state of dissonance can be expressed either overtly or subtly. In the context of intercultural encounters, *conflict* is defined in this chapter as the perceived and/or actual incompatibility of values, expectations, processes, or outcomes between two or more parties from different cultures over substantive and/or relational issues. Such differences oftentimes, are expressed through different cultural conflict styles. Intercultural conflict typically starts off with miscommunication. Intercultural miscommunication often leads to misinterpretations and pseudoconflict. If the miscommunication goes unmanaged or unclarified, however, it can become actual interpersonal conflict.

This article is developed in three sections: (1) A cultural variability perspective which emphasizes identity construal variations, low-context versus high-context, and monochronic and polychronic time patterns is presented; (2) assumptions and factors leading to conflict induced by violations of expectations are explained; and (3) effective conflict-management skills in managing intercultural conflicts are discussed.

A CULTURAL VARIABILITY PERSPECTIVE

To understand differences and similarities in communication across cultures, it is necessary to have a framework to explain why and how cultures are different or similar. A cultural variability perspective refers to how cultures vary on a continuum of variations in accordance with some basic dimensions or core value characteristics. While there are many dimensions in which cultures differ, one that has received consistent attention from both cross-cultural communication researchers and psychologists around the world is individualism-collectivism. Countless cross-cultural studies (Chinese Culture Connection, 1987; Gudykunst & Ting-Toomey, 1988; Hofstede, 1980, 1991; Hui & Triandis, 1986; Schwartz & Bilsky, 1990; Triandis, Brislin, & Hui, 1988; Wheeler, Reis, & Bond, 1989) have provided theoretical and empirical evidence that the value orientations of individualism and collectivism are pervasive in a wide range of cultures. Ting-Toomey and associates (Ting-Toomey, 1988, 1991; Ting-Toomey, Gao, Trubisky, Yang, Kim, Lin, & Nishida, 1991; Trubisky, Ting-Toomey, & Lin, 1991), related individualism-collectivism to conflict styles, providing clear research evidence that the role of cultural variability is critical in influencing cross-cultural conflict negotiation process.

The cultural socialization process influences individuals' basic assumptions and expectations, as well as their process and outcome orientations in different types of conflict situations. The dimension of individualism-collectivism, as existing on a continuum of value tendency differences, can be used as a beginning point to understand some of the basic differences and similarities in individualistic-based or group-based cultures. *Culture* is defined as a system of knowledge, meanings, and symbolic actions that is shared by the majority of the people in a society.

Individualism-Collectivism Value Tendencies

Basically, *individualism* refers to the broad value tendencies of a culture to emphasize the importance of individual identity over group identity, individual rights over group rights, and individual needs over group needs. In contrast, *collectivism* refers to the broad value tendencies of a culture to emphasize the importance of the "we" identity over the "I" identity, group obligations over individual rights, and ingroup-oriented needs over individual wants and desires. An *ingroup* is a group whose values, norms, and rules are deemed as salient to the effective functioning of the group in the society and these norms serve as the guiding criteria for everyday behaviors. On the other hand, an "outgroup" is a group whose values, norms, and rules are viewed as inconsistent with those of the ingroup and these norms are assigned a low priority from the ingroup standard. Macro-level factors such as ecology, affluence, social and geographic mobility, migration, cultural background of parents, socialization, rural or urban environment, mass media exposure, education, and social change have been identified by Triandis (1988, 1990) as some of the underlying factors that contribute to the development of individualistic and collectivistic values. High individualistic values have been found in the United States, Australia, Great Britain, Canada, the Netherlands, and New Zealand. High collectivistic values have been uncovered in Indonesia, Colombia, Venezuela, Panama, Equador, and Guatemala (Hofstede, 1991). In intercultural communication research (Gudykunst & Ting-Toomey, 1988), Australia, Canada, and the United States have been identified consistently as cultures high in individualistic value tendencies, while strong empirical evidence has supported that China, Taiwan, Korea, Japan, and Mexico can be identified clearly as collectivistic, group-based cultures. Within each culture, different ethnic communities can also display distinctive individualistic and collectivistic value tendencies. For example, members of first-generation, Asian immigrant cultures in the United States may retain some basic group-oriented value characteristics.

The core building block of individualism-collectivism is its relative emphasis on the importance of the "autonomous self" or the "connected self" orientation. In using the terms "independent construal of self" and "interdependent construal of self" to represent individualistic versus group-oriented identity, Markus and Kitayama (1991) argue that the placement of our sense of self-concept in our culture has a profound influence on our communication with others. They argue that the sense of individuality that accompanies this "independent construal of self" includes a sense of

oneself as an agent, as a producer of one's actions. One is conscious of being in control over the surrounding situation, and of the need to express one's own thoughts, feelings, and actions of others. Such acts of standing out are often intrinsically rewarding because they elicit pleasant, ego-focused emotions (e.g., pride) and also reduce unpleasant ones (e.g., frustration). Furthermore, the acts of standing out, themselves, form an important basis of self-esteem (p. 246).

Conversely, the self-concept that accompanies an "interdepedent construal of self" includes an

attentiveness and responsiveness to others that one either explicitly or implicitly assumes will be reciprocated by these others, as well as the willful management of one's other-focused feelings and desires so as to maintain and further the reciprocal interpersonal relationship. One is conscious of where one belongs with respect to others and assumes a receptive stance toward these others, continually adjusting and accommodating to these others in many aspects of behavior. Such acts of fitting in and accommodating are often intrinsically rewarding, because they give rise to pleasant, other-focused emotions (e.g., feeling of connection) while diminishing unpleasant ones (e.g., shame) and, furthermore, because the self-restraint required in doing so forms an important basis of self-esteem (p. 246).

Thus, the cultural variability of independent versus interdependent construal of self frames our existential experience and serves as an anchoring point in terms of how we view ourselves and our communicative actions. For example, if we follow an independent construal of self-orientation, our communicative action will tend to be more self-focused, more ego-based, and more self-expressive.

Concurrently, the value we place on particular self-conception also influences the criteria we use to perceive and evaluate others' communicative actions. To illustrate, if we follow an interdependent construal of self-orientation, we will tend to use group norms, group interests, and group responsibilities to interpret and evaluate others' conflict behaviors. Overall, the cultural variability dimension of individualism-collectivism and the independent and interdependent construal of self help us to "make sense" or explain why people in some cultures prefer certain approaches or modes of conflict negotiation than people in other cultures.

Low Context and High Context

In addition to individualism-collectivism, Edward T. Hall's (1976, 1983) low-context and high-context communication framework helps to enrich our understanding of the role of communication in individualistic and collectivistic cultures. According to Hall (1976), human transaction can be basically divided into low-context and high-context communication systems:

HC [High Context] transactions featured pre-programmed information that is in the receiver and in the setting, with only minimal information in the transmitted message. LC [Low Context] transactions are the reverse. Most of the information must be in the transmitted message in order to make up what is missing in the context (p. 101).

Although no one culture exists exclusively at one extreme of the communication context continuum, in general, low-context communication refers to communication patterns of linear logic interaction approach, direct verbal interaction style, overt intention expressions, and sender-oriented value (Ting-Toomey, 1985). High-context communication refers to communication patterns of spiral logic interaction approach, indirect verbal negotiation mode, subtle nonverbal nuances, responsive intention inference, and interpreter-sensitive value

(Ting-Toomey, 1985). Low-context (LC) communication patterns have been typically found in individualistic cultures and high-context (HC) communication patterns have been typically uncovered in collectivistic cultures.

For individualistic, LC communicators, the bargaining resources in conflict typically revolve around individual pride and self-esteem, individual ego-based emotions, and individual sense of autonomy and power. For collectivistic, HC interactants, the negotiation resources in conflict typically revolve around relational "face" maintenance and group harmony, group-oriented status and self-esteem, face-related emotions, and reciprocal sense of favors and obligations. For individualistic, LC negotiators, conflict typically arises because of incompatible personalities, beliefs, or goal orientations. For collectivistic, HC negotiators, conflict typically arises because of incompatible facework or relational management.

The concept of *face* is tied closely to the need people have to a claimed sense of self-respect in any social interactive situations (Ting-Toomey, 1985, 1988, in press a; Ting-Toomey & Cole, 1990). As human beings, we all like to be respected and feel approved in our everyday communicative behaviors. However, how we manage face and how we negotiate "face loss" and "face gain" in a conflict episode differs from one culture to the next. As Cohen (1991) observes:

Given the importance of face, the members of collectivistic cultures are highly sensitive to the effect of what they say on others. Language is a social instrument — a device for preserving and promoting social interests as much as a means for transmitting information. [Collectivistic], high-context speakers must weigh their words carefully. They know that whatever they say will be scrutinized and taken to heart. Face-to-face conversations contain many emollient expressions of respect and courtesy alongside a substantive element rich in meaning and low in redundancy. Directness and especially contradiction are much disliked. It is hard for speakers in this kind of culture to deliver a blunt "no" (p. 26).

M-Time and P-Time

Finally, the concept of time in the conflict-negotiation process also varies in accordance with the individualism-collectivism dimension. Time is reflective of the psychological and the emotional environment in which communication occurs. Time flies when two friends are enjoying themselves and having a good time. Time crawls when two enemies stare at each other and have nothing more to say to one another. Time influences the tempos and pacings of the developmental sequences of a conflict-negotiation session. It also influences the substantive ideas that are being presented in a conflict-bargaining episode.

Hall (1983) distinguished two patterns of time that govern the individualistic and collectivistic cultures: Monochronic Time Schedule (M-time) and Polychronic Time Schedule (P-time). According to Hall (1983):

P-time stresses involvement of people and completion of transactions rather than adherence to preset schedules. Appointments are not taken as seriously and, as a consequence, are frequently broken. P-time is treated as less tangible than M-time. For polychronic people, time is seldom experienced as "wasted," and is apt to be considered a point rather than a ribbon or a road, but that point is often sacred (p. 46).

For Hall (1983), Latin American, Middle Eastern, African, Asian, French, and Greek cultures are representatives of P-time patterns, while Northern European, North American, and German cultures are representatives of M-time patterns. M-time patterns appear to predominate in individualistic, low-context cultures, and P-time patterns appear to predominate in group-based, high-context cultures. People that follow individualistic, M-time patterns usually compartmentalize time schedules to serve individualistic-based needs, and they tend to separate task-oriented time from socioemotional time. In addition, they are more future-conscious of time than centered in the present or the past. People who follow collectivistic, P-time patterns tend to hold more fluid attitudes toward time schedules, and they tend

to integrate task-oriented activity with socioemotional activity. In addition, they are more past and present-conscious than future-oriented.

Members of individualistic, M-time cultures tend to view time as something that can be possessed, drained, and wasted, while members of collectivistic, P-time cultures tend to view time as more contextually based and relationally oriented. For individualistic, M-time people, conflict should be contained, controlled, and managed effectively within certain frames or within certain preset schedules. For collectivistic, P-time people, the clock time in resolving conflict is not as important as in taking the time to really know the conflict parties who are involved in the dispute. For P-time individuals, the time spent in synchronizing the implicit interactional rhythms between people is much more important than any preset, objective timetable.

In sum, in individualistic cultures, people typically practice "I" identity-based values, low-context direct interaction, and M-time negotiation schedules. In collectivistic cultures, people typically treasure "we" identity-based values, high-context indirect interaction, and P-time negotiation rhythms.

VIOLATIONS OF CONFLICT EXPECTATIONS[2]

Drawing from the key ideas of the cultural variability perspective, we can now apply these concepts to understanding the specific conflict assumptions, conflict issues and process factors, and the conflict interaction styles that contribute to intercultural miscommunication or intercultural conflict. When individuals from two contrastive cultures meet one another especially for the first time, they typically communicate out of their culturally based assumptions and beliefs, stereotypic images of each other, and habitual communication patterns. These assumptions create expectations for others' conflict behavior.

It is inevitable that we hold anticipations or expectations of how others should or should not behave in any communicative situation. These expectations, however, are grounded in the social norms of the culture and also depend on the symbolic meanings individuals assign to behaviors (Burgoon, 1991). Intercultural miscommunication or intercultural conflict often occurs because of violations of normative expectations in a communication episode. Expectation violations occur frequently, especially if one party comes from an individualistic-based culture and the other party comes from a collectivistic-based culture.

Cultural Conflict Assumptions

Different cultural value assumptions exist as the metaconflict issues in framing any intercultural conflict episode. Based on the individualism-collectivism dimension, we can delineate several cultural assumptions concerning LC and HC communicators' basic attitudes toward conflict. For individualistic, LC communicators, conflict typically follows a "problem-solving" model: (1) Conflict is viewed as an expressed struggle to air out major differences and problems; (2) conflict can be both dysfunctional and functional; (3) conflict can be dysfunctional when it is repressed and not directly confronted; (4) conflict can be functional when it provides an open opportunity for solving problematic issues; (5) substantive and relational issues in conflict should be handled separately; (6) conflict should be dealt with openly and directly; and (7) effective management of conflict can be viewed as a win-win problem-solving game.

For the collectivistic, HC interactants, their underlying assumptions of conflict follow a "face maintenance" model: (1) Conflict is viewed as damaging to social face and relational harmony and should be avoided as much as possible; (2) conflict is, for the most part, dysfunctional; (3) conflict signals a lack of self-discipline and self-censorship of emotional outbursts, and hence, a sign of emotional immaturity; (4) conflict provides a testing ground for a skillful facework negotiation process; (5) substantive conflict and relational face issues are always intertwined; (6) conflict should be dealt with discreetly and subtly; and (7) effective management of conflict can be viewed as a win-win face negotiation game.

From the conflict as a "problem-solving" model, conflict is viewed as potentially functional, personally liberating, and an open forum for "struggling against" or "struggling with" one another in wrestling with the conflict issues as hand. From the conflict as a "face maintenance" model, conflict is viewed as primarily dysfunctional, interpersonally embarrassing and distressing, and a forum for potential group-related face loss and face humiliation. These fundamental cultural conflict assumptions influence the mindsets and the attitudinal level of the conflict parties in terms of how they should approach an interpersonal conflict episode. Appropriate and inappropriate conflict behaviors, in short, are grounded in the basic value assumptions of the cultural conflict socialization process.

Conflict Issues and Process Violations

Every conflict entails both substantive and relational issues. Individualistic conflict negotiators typically attend to the objective, substantive issues more than the relational, socioemotional issues. Collectivistic conflict negotiators, in contrast, typically attune to the relational, affective dimension as the key issue in resolving task-related or procedural-related conflict. When collectivistic communicators are in sync with one another and their nonverbal rhythms harmonize with one another, peaceful resolutions can potentially follow. When individualistic communicators are able to rationalize the separation of the people from the problems, and emphasize compartmentalizing affective issues and substantive issues, conflict can be functional.

In reviewing diplomatic negotiation case studies between individualistic, low-context (United States) and collectivistic, high-context (China, Egypt, India, Japan, and Mexico) cultures, Cohen (1991) concludes:

Individualistic, low-context negotiators can be described as primarily problem oriented and have the definition of the problem and the clarification of alternative solutions uppermost in their thoughts, [collectivistic] high-context negotiators

are seen to be predominantly relationship ori-
ented. For them, negotiation is less about solving
problems (although, obviously, this aspect cannot
be dismissed) than about attending a relationship.
For interdependent cultures it is not a conflict that
is resolved but a relationship that is mended. . . . In
international relations the consequence is con-
cern both with the international relationship and
with the personal ties between the interlocutors
(p. 51).

In individualistic, LC cultures such as Australia and the United States, control of one's autonomy, freedom, territory, and individual boundary is of paramount importance to one's sense of self-respect and ego. In collectivistic, HC cultures such as Japan and Korea, being accepted by one's ingroup members and being approved by one's superiors, peers, and/or family members is critical to the development of one's sense of self-respect. Thus, conflict issues in individualistic cultures typically arise through the violation of autonomous space, privacy, individual power, and sense of individual fairness and equity. In collectivistic cultures, conflict issues typically revolve around the violation of ingroup or outgroup boundaries, norms of group loyalty and commitment, and reciprocal obligations and trust.

In terms of different goal orientations in inter-cultural conflict, individualists' conflict-management techniques typically emphasize a win-win goal orientation and the importance of a tangible out-come action plan. For collectivists, typically time and energy are invested in negotiating face loss, face gain, and face protection issues throughout the various developmental phases of conflict. While indi-vidualists tend to be highly goal or result-oriented in conflict management, collectivists tend to empha-size heavily the relational or facework process of conflict resolution. This collectivistic conflict face-work negotiation process can also take place be-yond the immediate conflict situation.

Several writers (Cohen, 1991; Leung, 1987, 1988; Ting-Toomey, 1985) indicate that collectivists tend to display a stronger preference for informal third-party conflict mediation procedure than individual-ists. For example, for the Chinese culture, conflict typically is diffused through the use of third-party intermediaries. However, there exists a key differ-ence in the use of third-party mediation between the individualistic, Western cultures and the collec-tivistic, Asian cultures. In the Western cultures, con-flict parties tend to seek help with an impartial third-party mediator (such as a professional mediator or family therapist). In many Asian cultures, conflict parties typically seek the help of an older (and hence assumed to be wiser) person who is related to both parties. It is presumed that the informal me-diator has a richer data base to arbitrate the conflict outcome. Expectations may be violated when an in-dividualistic culture sends an impartial third-party to arbitrate an international conflict with no prior relationship-building sessions. Conflict-process vio-lations also arise if an individualistic culture sends an intermediary that is perceived to be of lower ranking or lower status than the representative ne-gotiators of the collectivistic culture. Conversely, a collectivistic culture tends to violate the individu-alistic fairness norm when it sends an "insider" or ingroup person to monitor or arbitrate the conflict outcome situation.

The concept of power in a conflict-negotiation situation also varies from an individualistic culture to a collectivistic culture. Power, in the context of individualistic culture, often means tangible re-sources of rewards and punishments that one con-flict party has over another. Power, in the context of collectivistic culture, often refers to intangible re-sources such as face loss and face gain, losing pres-tige or gaining reputation, and petty-mindedness versus benevolent generosity as displayed in the conflict anxiety-provoking situation.

Finally, the interpretation of conflict-resolution rhythm also varies along the individualism-collectiv-ism dimension. For individualistic, M-time people, conflict-resolution processes should follow a clear agenda of opening, expressing conflicting interests, negotiating, and closing sequences. For collectivis-tic, P-time people, conflict facework processes have no clear beginning and no clear end. For M-time individuals, conflict-resolution time should be filled with decision-making activities. For P-time individ-uals, time is a "being" construct that is governed by the implicit rhythms in the interaction between people. While M-time negotiators tend to emphasize agenda setting, objective criteria, and immediate, future-oriented goals in the conflict-negotiation process, P-time negotiators typically like to take time to engage in small talk, to delve into family or personal affairs, and also to bring in the historical past to shed light on the present conflict situation. As Cohen (1991) observes:

[North] Americans, then, are mostly concerned with addressing immediate issues and moving on to new challenges, and they display little interest in (and sometimes little knowledge of) history. The idea that something that occurred hundreds of years ago might be relevant to a pressing problem is almost incomprehensible. . . . In marked contrast, the representatives of non-Western societies possess a pervasive sense of the past. . . . This preoccupation with history, deeply rooted in the consciousness of traditional societies, cannot fail to influence diplomacy. Past humiliations for these societies (which are highly sensitive to any slight on their reputations) are not consigned to the archives but continue to nourish present concerns (p. 29).

The arbitrary division of clock time or calendar time holds little meaning for collectivistic, P-time people. For them, a deadline, in one sense, is only an arbitrary human construct. For P-time individuals, a deadline is always subject to revision and renegotiation. Graceful handling of time pressure is viewed as much more important than a sense of forceful urgency. In sum, people move with different conflict rhythms in conflict-negotiation sessions. For M-time individuals, a sense of timeline and closure-orientation predominate their mode of conflict resolution. For P-time individuals, a sense of the relational commitment and synchronized relational rhythm signal the beginning stage of a long-term, conflict-bargaining process.

Expectation violations often occur when a person from an individualistic culture engages a person from a collectivistic culture in an interpersonal conflict situation. Different cultural conflict assumptions lead to different attitudes toward how to approach a basic conflict episode. Miscommunication often gives rise to escalatory conflict spirals or prolonged misunderstandings. While common feelings of anxiety, frustration, ambivalence, and a sense of emotional vulnerability typically exist in individuals in any conflict situation, how we go about handling this sense of emotional vulnerability varies from one culture to the next. Individualists and collectivists typically collide over their substantive orientation versus relational face maintenance orientation; goal orientation versus process orientation; formal versus informal third-party consultation process; tangible versus intangible power resources; and different time rhythms that undergird the conflict episode. In addition, the verbal and nonverbal messages they engage in, and the distinctive conflict styles they carry with them can severely influence the overall outcome of the conflict dissonance process.

Cross-Cultural Conflict Interaction Styles

In a conflict situation, individualists typically rely heavily on direct requests, direct verbal justifications, and upfront clarifications to defend one's action or decision. In contrast, collectivists typically use qualifiers ("Perhaps we should meet this deadline together"), tag questions ("Don't you think we might not have enough time"), disclaimers ("I'm probably wrong but . . ."), tangential response ("Let's not worry about that now"), and indirect requests ("If it won't be too much trouble, let's try to finish this report together") to make a point in the subtle, conflict face-threatening situation. From the collectivistic orientation, it is up to the interpreter of the message to pick up the hidden meaning or intention of the message and to respond either indirectly or equivocally. In addition, in an intense conflict situation, many collectivists believe that verbal messages can oftentimes compound the problem. However, by not using verbal means to explain or clarify a decision, collectivists are often viewed as "inscrutable."

Silence is viewed as demanding immense self-discipline in a collectivistic conflict situation. On the other hand, silence can be viewed as an admission of guilt or incompetence in an individualistic culture. In addition, while open emotional expression during a stressful conflict situation oftentimes is viewed as a signal of caring in an individualistic culture, proper emotional composure and emotional self-restraint are viewed as signals of a mature, self-disciplined person in most collectivistic, Asian cultures. In comparing verbal and nonverbal exchange processes in Japan and the United States, Okabe (1983) summarizes:

The digital is more characteristic of the [North] American mode of communication. . . . The Japanese language is more inclined toward the analogical; its use of ideographic characters . . . and its emphasis on the nonverbal aspect. The excessive dependence of the Japanese on the nonverbal aspect of communication means that Japanese culture tends to view the verbal as only a means of communication, and that the nonverbal and the extra-verbal at times assume greater importance than the verbal dimension of communication. This is in sharp contrast to the view of Western rhetoric and communication that the verbal, especially speech, is the dominant means of expression (p. 38).

In short, in the individualistic cultures, the conflict-management process relies heavily on verbal offense and defense to justify one's position, to clarify one's opinion, to build up one's credibility, to articulate one's emotions, and to raise objections if one disagrees with someone else's proposal. In collectivistic conflict situations, ambiguous, indirect verbal messages often are used with the intention of saving mutual face, saving group face, or protecting someone else's face. In addition, subtle nonverbal gestures or nonverbal silence is often used to signal a sense of cautionary restraint toward the conflict situation. The use of deep-level silence can also reflect a sense of resignation and acceptance of the fatalistic aspect of the conflict situation. The higher the person is in positional power in a collectivistic culture, the more likely she or he will use silence as a deliberate, cautionary conflict strategy.

In terms of the relationship between the norm of fairness and cross-cultural conflict interaction style,

results from past research (Leung & Bond, 1984; Leung & Iwawaki, 1988) indicate that individualists typically prefer to use the equity norm (self-deservingness norm) in dealing with reward allocation in group conflict interaction. In comparison, collectivists oftentimes prefer to use the equality norm (the equal distribution norm) to deal with ingroup members and thus avoid group disharmony. However, like their individualistic cohorts, collectivists prefer the application of the equity norm (the self-deservingness norm) when competing with members of outgroups, especially when the conflict involves competition for scarce resources in the system.

Findings in many past conflict studies also indicate that individuals do exhibit quite consistent cross-situational styles of conflict negotiation in different cultures. While dispositional, relationship, or conflict salient factors also play a critical part in conflict-management patterns, culture assumes the primary role of conflict-style socialization process. Based on the theoretical assumptions of the "I" identity and the "we" identity, and the concern of self-face maintenance versus mutual-face maintenance in the two contrastive cultural systems, findings across cultures (China, Japan, Korea, Taiwan, Mexico, and the United States) clearly indicate that individualists tend to use competitive control conflict styles in managing conflict, while collectivists tend to use integrative or compromising conflict styles in dealing with conflict. In addition, collectivists also tend to use more obliging and avoiding conflict styles in task-oriented conflict situations (Chua & Gudykunst, 1987; Leung, 1988; Ting-Toomey et al., 1991; Trubisky, Ting-Toomey, & Lin, 1991).

Different results have also been uncovered concerning ingroup and outgroup conflict in the collectivistic cultures. For example, Cole's (1989) study reveals that Japanese students in the United States tend to use obliging strategies more with members of ingroups than with members of outgroups. They also tend to actually use more competitive strategies with outgroup members than ingroup members. In addition, the status of the ingroup person plays a critical role in the collectivistic conflict process.

Previous research (Ting-Toomey et al., 1991) suggests that status affects the conflict-management styles people use with members of their ingroup. For example, in a collectivistic culture, while a high-status person can challenge the position or opinion of a low-status person, it is a norm violation for a low-status person to directly rebut or question the position or the opinion of the high-status person, especially in the public arena. Again, the issue of face maintenance becomes critical in high–low-status conflict interaction. The low-status person should always learn to "give face" or protect the face of the high-status person in times of stressful situations or crises. In return, the high-status person will enact a reciprocal face-protection system that automatically takes care of the low-status person in different circumstances.

Overall, the preferences for a direct conflict style, for the use of the equity norm, and for the direct settlement of disputes reflect the salience of the "I" identity in individualistic, HC cultures; while preferences for an indirect conflict style, for the use of the equality norm, and for the use of informal mediation procedures reflect the salience of the "we" identity in the collectivistic, HC cultures. In individualistic, LC cultures, a certain degree of conflict in a system is viewed as potentially functional and productive. In collectivistic, HC cultures in which group harmony and consultative decision-making are prized, overt expressions of interpersonal conflict are highly avoided and suppressed. Instead, nonverbal responsiveness, indirect verbal strategies, the use of informal intermediaries, and the use of cautionary silence are some of the typical collectivistic ways of dealing with interpersonal conflict.

EFFECTIVE CONFLICT MANAGEMENT

Effective conflict management requires us to communicate effectively, appropriately, and creatively in different conflict interactive situations. Effective conflict management requires us to be knowledgeable and respectful of different worldviews and ways of dealing with a conflict situation. It requires us to be sensitive to the differences and similarities between low-context and high-context communication patterns and to attune to the implicit negotiation rhythms of monochronic-based and polychronic-based individuals.

Effective conflict management also requires the awareness of the importance of both goal-oriented and process-oriented conflict negotiation pathways, and requires that we pay attention to the close relationship between cultural variability and different conflict communication styles. For both individualists and collectivists, the concept of "mindfulness" can serve as the first effective step in raising our awareness of the differences and similarities in cross-cultural conflict-negotiation processes. Langer's (1989) concept of mindfulness helps individuals to tune-in conscientiously to their habituated mental scripts and expectations. According to Langer, if mindlessness is the "rigid reliance on old categories, mindfulness means the continual creation of new ones. Categorization and recategorization, labeling and relabeling as one masters the world are processes natural to children" (p. 63). To engage in a mindfulness state, an individual needs to learn to (a) create new categories, (b) be open to new information, and (c) be aware that multiple perspectives typically exist in viewing a basic event (Langer, 1989, p. 62).

Creating new categories means that one should not be boxed in by one's rigid stereotypic label concerning cultural strangers. One has to learn to draw out commonalities between self and cultural strangers and also learn to appreciate the multifaceted aspects of the individuals to whom the stereotypic label is applied. In order to create new categories, one has to be open to new information. New information relies strongly on responsible sharing and responsive listening behavior.

Some specific suggestions can be made based on differences in individualistic and collectivistic styles of conflict management. These suggestions, however, are not listed in order of importance. *To deal with conflict effectively in the collectivistic culture, individualists need to:*

1. Be mindful of the face-maintenance assumptions of conflict situations that take place in this culture. Conflict competence resides in the strategic skills of managing the delicate interaction balance of humiliation and pride, and shame and honor. The face moves of one-up and one-down in a conflict episode, the use of same status negotiators, and the proprieties and decorum of gracious "face fighting" have to be strategically staged with the larger group audience in mind.

2. Be proactive in dealing with low-grade conflict situations (such as by using informal consultation or the "go between" method) before they escalate into runaway, irrevocable mutual face-loss episodes. Individualists should try to realize that by helping their opponent to save face, they may also enhance their own face. Face is, intrinsically, a bilateral concept in the group-based, collectivistic culture.

3. "Give face" and try not to push their opponent's back against the wall with no room for maneuvering face loss or face recovery. Learn to let their opponent find a gracious way out of the conflict situation if at all possible, without violating the basic spirit of fundamental human rights. They should also learn self-restraint and try not to humiliate their opponent in the public arena or slight her or his public reputation. For collectivists, the concept of "giving face" typically operates on a long-range, reciprocal interaction system. Bilateral face-giving and face-saving ensures a continuous, interdependent networking process of favor-giving and favor concessions — especially along a long-term, historical time sense.

4. Be sensitive to the importance of quiet, mindful observation. Individualists need to be mindful of the historical past that bears relevance to the present conflict situation. Restrain from asking too many "why" questions. Since collectivistic, LC cultures typically focus on the nonverbal "how" process, individualists need to learn to experience and manage the conflict process on the implicit, nonverbal pacing level. Use deep-level silence, deliberate pauses, and patient conversational turn-taking in conflict interaction processes with collectivists.

5. Practice attentive listening skills and feel the copresence of the other person. In Chinese characters, hearing or *wun* (聞) means "opening the door to the ears," while the word *listening* or *ting* (聽) means attending to the other person with your "ears, eyes, and heart." Listening means, in the Chinese character, attending to the sounds, movements, and feelings of the other person. Patient and deliberate listening indicates that one person is attending to the other person's needs even if it is an antagonistic conflict situation.

6. Discard the Western-based model of effective communication skills in dealing with conflict situations in the collectivistic, HC cultures. Individualists should learn to use qualifiers, disclaimers, tag questions, and tentative statements to convey their point of view. In refusing a request, learn not to use a blunt "no" as a response because the word "no" is typically perceived as carrying high face-threat value in the collectivistic culture. Use situational or self-effacing accounts ("Perhaps someone else is more qualified than I am in working on this project"), counterquestions ("Don't you feel someone else is more competent to work on this project . . ."), or conditional statements ("Yes, but . . .") to convey the implicit sense of refusal.

7. Let go of a conflict situation if the conflict party does not want to deal with it directly. A cooling period sometimes may help to mend a broken relationship and the substantive issue may be diluted over a period of time. Individualists should remember that avoidance is part of the integral, conflict style that is commonly used in the collectivistic, LC cultures. Avoidance does not necessarily mean that collectivists do not care to resolve the conflict. In all likelihood, the use of avoidance is strategically used to avoid face-threatening interaction and is meant to maintain face harmony and mutual face dignity.

In sum, individualists need to learn to respect the HC, collectivistic ways of approaching and handling conflicts. They need to continuously monitor their ethnocentric biases on the cognitive, affective, and behavioral reactive levels, and learn to listen attentively, and observe mindfully and reflectively.

Some specific suggestions also can be made for collectivists in handling conflict with individualists. *When encountering a conflict situation in an individualistic, LC culture, collectivists need to:*

1. Be mindful of the problem-solving assumptions. The ability to separate the relationship from the conflict problem is critical to effective conflict negotiation in an individualistic, LC culture. Collectivists need to learn to compartmentalize the task dimension and the socioemotional dimension of conflict.

2. Focus on resolving the substantive issues of the conflict, and learn to openly express opinions or points of view. Collectivists should try not to take the conflict issues to the personal level, and learn to maintain distance between the person and the conflict problem. In addition, try not to be offended by the upfront, individualistic style of managing conflict. Learn to emphasize tangible outcomes and develop concrete actions plans in implementing the conflict-decision proposal.

3. Engage in an assertive, leveling style of conflict behavior. Assertive style emphasizes the rights of both individuals to speak up in a conflict situation and to respect each other's right to defend her or his position. Collectivists need to learn to open a conflict dialogue with an upfront thesis statement, and then develop the key point systematically, with examples, evidence, figures, or a well-planned proposal. In addition, collectivists need to be ready to accept criticisms, counterproposals, and suggestions for modification as part of the ongoing, group dialogue.

4. Own individual responsibility for the conflict decision-making process. Owning responsibility and using "I" statements to describe feelings in an ongoing conflict situation constitute part of effective conflict-management skills in an individualistic, LC culture. Collectivists need to learn to verbally explain a situation more fully and learn not to expect others to infer their points of view. Assume a sender-based approach to resolving conflict; ask more "why" questions and probe for explanations and details.

5. Provide verbal feedback and engage in active listening skills. Active listening skills, in the individualistic, LC culture, means collectivists have to engage in active verbal perception checking and to ensure that the other person is interpreting their points accurately. Collectivists need to use verbal paraphrases, summary statements, and interpretive messages to acknowledge and verify the storyline of the conflict situation. Learn to occasionally self-disclose feelings and emotions; they cannot rely solely on nonverbal, intuitive understanding to "intuit" and evaluate a situation.

6. Use direct, integrative verbal messages that clearly convey their concern over both the relational and substantive issues of a conflict situation. Collectivists should also not wait patiently for clear turn-taking pauses in the conflict interaction, as individualistic conversation typically allows overlap talks, simultaneous messages, and floor-grabbing behavior. Collectivists also may not want to engage in too many deliberate silent moments as individualists will infer that as incompetence or inefficient use of time.

7. Commit to working out the conflict situation with the conflict party. Collectivists should learn to use task-oriented integrative strategies and try to work out a collaborative, mutual goal dialogue with the conflict party. Work on managing individual defensiveness and learn to build up trust on the one-to-one level of interaction. Finally, confirm the conflict person through explicit relationship reminders and metacommunication talks, while simultaneously working on resolving the conflict substantive issues, responsibly and constructively.

In sum, collectivists need to work on their ethnocentric biases as much as the individualists need to work out their sense of egocentric superiority. Collectivists need to untangle their historical sense of cultural superiority—especially in thinking that their way is the only "civilized" way to appropriately deal with conflict. Both individualists and collectivists need to be mindful of their cognitive, affective, and behavioral blinders that they bring into a conflict-mediation situation. They need to continuously learn new and novel ideas in dealing with the past, present, and the future for the purpose of building a peaceful community that is inclusive in all ethnic and cultural groups.

In being mindful of the potential differences between individualistic, LC and collectivistic, HC conflict styles, the intercultural peacemaking process can begin by affirming and valuing such differences as diverse human options in resolving some fundamental, human communication phenomenon. While it is not necessary that one should completely switch one's basic conflict style in order to adapt to the other person's behavior, mutual attuning and responsive behavior in signalling the willingness to learn about each other's cultural norms and rules may be a first major step toward a peaceful resolution process. In addition, conflicting parties from diverse ethnic or cultural backgrounds can learn to work on collaborative task projects and strive toward reaching a larger-than-self, community goal.

To be a peacemaker in the intercultural arena, one has to be first at peace with one's self and one's style. Thus, the artificial switching of one's style may only bring artificial results. Creative peacemakers must learn first to affirm and respect the diverse values that exist as part of the rich spectrum of the basic human experience. They may then choose to modify their behavior to adapt to the situation at hand. Finally, they may integrate diverse sets of values and behaviors, and be able to move in and out of different relational and cultural conflict boundaries. Creative peacemakers can be at ease and at home with the marginal stranger in their search toward common human peace. *Peace* means, on a universal level, a condition or a state of tranquility—with an absence of oppressed thoughts, feelings, and actions, from one heart to another, and from one nation state to another nation state.

NOTES

1. I want to thank Bill Gudykunst for his thoughtful suggestions on an earlier version of the manuscript.

2. Many of the ideas in this section are drawn from Ting-Toomey (in press b).

REFERENCES

Burgoon, J. (1991). "Applying a Comparative Approach to Expectancy Violations Theory." In J. Blumer, J. McCleod, and K. Rosengren (Eds.), *Communication and Culture Across Space and Time*. Newbury Park, CA: Sage.

Chinese Culture Connection. (1987). "Chinese Values and Search for Culture-Free Dimensions of Culture." *Journal of Cross-Cultural Psychology, 18,* 143–164.

Chua, E., and Gudykunst, W. (1987). Conflict Resolution Style in Low- and High-Context Cultures. *Communication Research Reports, 4,* 32–37.

Cohen, R. (1991). *Negotiating Across Cultures: Communication Obstacles in International Diplomacy*. Washington, D.C.: U.S. Institute of Peace.

Cole, M. (May 1989). "Relational Distance and Personality Influence on Conflict Communication Styles." Unpublished master thesis. Arizona State University, Tempe, AZ.

Gudykunst, W., and Ting-Toomey, S. (1988). *Culture and Interpersonal Communication*. Newbury Park, CA: Sage.

Hall, E. T. (1976). *Beyond Culture*. New York: Doubleday.

Hall, E. T. (1983). *The Dance of Life*. New York: Doubleday.

Hofstede, G. (1980). *Culture's Consequences: International Differences in Work-Related Values*. Beverly Hills, CA: Sage.

Hofstede, G. (1991). *Cultures and Organizations: Software of the Mind*. London: McGraw-Hill.

Hui, C., and Triandis, H. (1986). "Individualism-Collectivism: A Study of Cross-Cultural Researchers." *Journal of Cross-Cultural Psychology, 17,* 225–248.

Langer, E. (1989). *Mindfulness*. Reading, MA: Addison-Wesley.

Leung, K. (1987). "Some Determinants of Reactions to Procedural Models for Conflict Resolution: A Cross-National Study." *Journal of Personality and Social Psychology, 53,* 898–908.

Leung, K. (1987). "Some Determinants of Conflict Avoidance." *Journal of Cross-Cultural Psychology, 19,* 125–136.

Leung, K., and Bond, M. (1984). "The Impact of Cultural Collectivism on Reward Allocation." *Journal of Personality and Social Psychology, 47,* 793–804.

Leung, K., and Iwawaki, S. (1988). "Cultural Collectivism and Distributive Behavior." *Journal of Cross-Cultural Psychology, 19,* 35–49.

Markus, H., and Kitayama, S. (1991). "Culture and the Self: Implications for Cognition, Emotion, and Motivation." *Psychological Review, 2,* 224–253.

Okabe, R. (1983). "Cultural Assumptions of East-West: Japan and the United States." In W. Gudykunst (Ed.), *Intercultural Communication Theory.* Beverly Hills, CA: Sage.

Schwartz, S., and Bilsky, W. (1990). "Toward a Theory of the Universal Content and Structure of Values." *Journal of Personality and Social Psychology, 58,* 878–891.

Ting-Toomey, S. (1985). "Toward a Theory of Conflict and Culture." In W. Gudykunst, L. Stewart, and S. Ting-Toomey (Eds.), *Communication Culture, and Organizational Processes* (pp. 71–86). Beverly Hills, CA: Sage.

Ting-Toomey, S. (1986). "Conflict Styles in Black and White Subjective Cultures." In Y. Kim (Ed.), *Current Research in Interethnic Communication.* Beverly Hills, CA: Sage.

Ting-Toomey, S. (1988). "Intercultural Conflict Styles: A Face-Negotiation Theory." In Y. Kim and W. Gudykunst (Eds.), *Theories in Intercultural Communication.* Newbury Park, CA: Sage.

Ting-Toomey, S. (1991). "Intimacy Expressions in Three Cultures: France, Japan, and the United States." *International Journal of Intercultural Relations, 15,* 29–46.

Ting-Toomey, S. (Ed.) (in press a). *The Challenge of Facework: Cross-Cultural and Interpersonal Issues.* Albany, NY: State University of New York Press.

Ting-Toomey, S. (in press b). *Intercultural Communication Process: Crossing Boundaries.* New York: Guildford.

Ting-Toomey, S., and Cole, M. (1990). "Intergroup Diplomatic Communication: A Face-Negotiation Perspective." In F. Korzenny and S. Ting-Toomey (Eds.), *Communicating for Peace: Diplomacy and Negotiation.* Newbury Park, CA: Sage.

Ting-Toomey, S., Gao, G., Trubisky, P., Yang, Z., Kim, H. S., Lin, S. L., and Nishida, T. (1991). "Culture, Face Maintenance, and Styles of Handling Interpersonal Conflict: A Study in Five Cultures." *The International Journal of Conflict Management, 2,* 275–296.

Triandis, H. (1988). "Collectivism vs. Individualism: A Reconceptualization of a Basic Concept in Cross-Cultural Psychology." In G. Verma and C. Bagley (Eds.), *Cross-Cultural Studies of Personality, Attitudes and Cognition.* London: Macmillan.

Triandis, H. (1990). "Cross-Cultural Studies of Individualism and Collectivism." In J. Berman (Ed.), *Nebraska Symposium on Motivation.* Lincoln: University of Nebraska Press.

Triandis, H., Brislin, R., and Hui, C. H. (1988). "Cross-Cultural Training Across the Individualism-Collectivism Divide." *International Journal of Intercultural Relations, 12,* 269–289.

Trubisky, P., Ting-Toomey, S., and Lin, S. L. (1991). "The Influence of Individualism-Collectivism and Self-Monitoring on Conflict Styles." *International Journal of Intercultural Relations, 15,* 65–84.

Wheeler, L., Reis, H., and Bond, M. (1989). "Collectivism-Individualism in Everyday Social Life: The Middle Kingdom and the Melting Pot." *Journal of Personality and Social Psychology, 57,* 79–86.

Communication About Humor as Procedural Competence in Intercultural Encounters

WEN-SHU LEE

At one time or another in our lives we all fail to understand humor. A high school freshman surrounded by seniors in a locker room may easily miss their ingroup jokes and feel embarrassed or socially inept. On your first day at a new job, your coworkers' giggles about the boss may suddenly leave you in the dark. However, if English is your native language, as familiarity increases gradually you begin to pick up the jokes. But, for people from a different culture, and especially when English is the second language, failure to understand humor is an everyday thing. Native speakers asked to explain their humor become confused; they are not used to explaining humor to people who share minimal cultural and linguistic experiences with them. Humor, thus, presents a peculiar type of intercultural communication problem that deserves our attention.

HUMOR AS A PATHWAY TO INTERCULTURAL COMMUNICATION COMPETENCE

It is tempting to treat humor breakdown as a language problem — "They [non-native speakers] just

do not speak our language well." Yet, even when non-native speakers get all of the definitions of words right they still may not "get the joke." At times, we may throw up our hands thinking: "If they don't get it, they don't. You simply can't explain humor. If you explain it, you kill it!"

This essay offers a different approach; we do not treat humor as a linguistic problem. In fact, humor goes beyond language; it takes us into the heart of cultural understanding. We may not explain successfully all jokes and cartoons, but learning how to *explain* humor and how to *ask questions* about humor provides an opportunity, in a happy and unexpected way, to understand different cultures and become competent intercultural communicators.

The goal of this essay is to provide a method for achieving *procedural competence;* it spells out how to initiate and engage in the process of humor explanation effectively. We deal with the most difficult humor problem in intercultural communication — that between native and non-native English speakers by laying out a two-stage process for sharing humor. The first stage requires making *new conversational rules* between native and non-native speakers. This stage makes communication about humor problems socially acceptable. It also sets up a free and encouraging context for both native and non-native speakers to begin the next stage — actually learning to explain humor. The second stage, *explaining humor,* employs Aristotle's *enthymematic reasoning* to present ways in which humor is not only understood but can truly be appreciated by non-native speakers. Let's turn to the first stage.

STAGE 1: MAKING NEW CONVERSATIONAL RULES

There are many reasons why it is hard to explain humor; ordinary conversational rules regulating the encounter between two adults often prohibit them from bringing up humor openly as an object for discussion. This section lays out new conversational rules for native and non-native speakers, respectively. Through the process of making these new conversational rules, native and non-native speakers can together cultivate a new intercultural context in which both parties are freer to learn and practice the process of asking questions and explaining humor.

Rule for Non-Native Speakers

As a rule, it is embarrassing for most of us to admit that we did not get a joke. It gives the impression of incompetence or inadequacy—"When they all laugh so hard, I don't want to ask stupid questions to spoil the fun!" However, if we do not signal to others that explanations are necessary, we may never get to the point of talking about humor and the intercultural problems related to it. Non-native speakers have to abandon the old rule that "admitting to incomprehension and asking questions about humor is stupid" and make a new conversational rule for themselves "asking questions about humor is acceptable and it is a sign of courage rather than incompetence" (see Table 1). As Confucius said, "It's better to be stupid for three minutes than for the entire life time."

What follows from this new rule is that non-native speakers are freer to communicate their confusion to native speakers. Yet new ways of voicing problems with humor have to be learned. The general principle is that non-native speakers need to communicate incomprehension in ways that are easy for them, so that they are more willing and motivated to continue the new practice and, at the same time, cultivate a context in which native speakers are more relaxed and willing to work with them. What then are ways that are easy for non-native speakers and relaxing and friendly for both native and non-native speakers? The answer lies in cultural and personal idiomatic verbal and nonverbal expressions.

Idiomatic verbal expressions

It's way over my head!

I didn't get it.

It left me out in the cold.

It left me in the dark.

Whoa! That was too quick for me.

Table 1 Stage 1: Making New Conversational Rules

Purpose of Stage 1

For native and non-native partners to learn to foster a friendly and encouraging learning context by making a lot of "inadequate (either stupid or rude) behaviors" not only acceptable but also welcomed!

Non-Native Speakers' Step

Abandon the old conversational rule:

"Admitting to incomprehension and asking questions about humor is stupid"

Make a new conversational rule:

"Asking questions about humor is acceptable and it is a sign of courage rather than incompetence."

Behaviors necessary to implement the new conversational rule:

Asking questions and regulating conversations in terms of idiomatic verbal and nonverbal expressions

Native Speakers' Step

Abandon the old conversational rule:

"Checking whether the partner understands humor is treating him or her as an ignorant child, which is rude and inappropriate."

Make a new conversational rule:

"Actively checking incomprehension and encouraging questions is to pave the way for intercultural understanding, which is a sign of maturity and honesty rather than impropriety."

Behaviors necessary to implement the new conversational rule and uphold non-native speakers' rules:

(a) double check non-native partner's comprehension
(b) indicate the fact that even native speakers sometimes fail to understand humor
(c) affirm and encourage the necessity of asking questions

Idiomatic nonverbal expressions

A "T" gesture [time out]

Passing the flat of the hand beginning on a plain at the middle of the forehead rising up over the head accompanied by a jet light sound [it's way over my head]

The expressions above are important because non-native speakers usually learn English in a formal classroom setting. They speak "academic" English. As a consequence, they often appear polite but uncomfortably formal. Saying "I don't understand it" over and over won't do. Non-native speakers must learn to communicate incomprehension in ways that are used not in dictionaries but are used among friends. They need to learn and use idiomatic and folk expressions, so that native speakers will be more willing and relaxed in working with them. Non-native speakers also need to know how to use the non-verbal gestures friends employ in regulating the conversation and signaling confusion.

Rule for Native Speakers

It takes two parties to converse; it also takes two to change conversational rules. We turn to a discussion about ways in which native speakers can learn to establish new conversational rules. (See native speakers' step in Table 1.)

As a rule, it is inappropriate, rude, or imposing to ask a communication partner if she or he understands the meaning of a humor. We do not want to insult our partner by treating him or her as an ignorant child. However, because the non-native partner may not be aware of missing the humor and, even when aware, may be reluctant to bring up the confusion, humor problems may be ignored jointly. Therefore, native speakers need to make a step to replace the old rule (checking whether the partner understands humor is treating him or her as an ignorant child, which is rude and inappropriate) with a new set of rules holding that *actively checking incomprehension and encouraging questions paves the way for intercultural understanding. Checking is a sign of maturity and honesty rather than impropriety.*

Some behavioral changes follow from making these new conversational rules. First, native speakers are free to ask about the responses which non-native speakers politely give when listening to an explanation. For example, non-native speakers may nod frequently, but often times nodding means

"I am listening to you" rather than "I understood your explanations." Native speakers need to double check the comprehension by asking further questions without assuming that the partner understands the explanations.

Second, these new rules encourage native speakers to make non-native speakers' newly established conversational rules their rules. Hopefully this will enable native speakers to admit that native speakers sometimes fail to understand humor: "My friends and myself only understand a third of the Far Side cartoons." When non-native speakers hear this, instead of feeling inadequate or stupid, they are more likely to feel that it is alright to ask questions. Third these new rules encourage native speakers to remind their partners that whenever they do not understand that they need to stop the explanation by using a gesture or by asking a question.

The point of establishing new conversational rules is to foster a friendly and encouraging learning context to make a lot of "inadequate (either stupid or rude) behaviors" not only acceptable but also welcomed! We may conclude from the above discussions that (a) non-native speakers need to overcome fear and hesitation and learn to ask questions, like a friend engaging in an informal conversation, and (b) native speakers need to admit that humor incomprehension also occurs among native speakers and remind non-native speakers to be brave and forward about explanations given. After giving an explanation, native speakers need to double check non-native speakers' comprehension before moving on to another subject. With these new conversational rules spelled out, we turn to the next stage — explaining humor.

STAGE 2: EXPLAINING HUMOR

Humor usually plays off the contradictions or ironies commonly experienced in a culture in an unexpected way. We need to know what is ordinarily done in a culture in order to understand and laugh at messages poked at the "out of the ordinary." The problem here is that culture is usually imparted in a

Table 2 Comparison of Syllogism and Enthymeme

Syllogism	Enthymeme
Major Premise(s)	- - - - - - - - - -
Minor Premise(s)	Minor Premise(s)
Conclusion	- - - - - - - - - -

Table 4 Native Speaker's Ability to Understand Humor

Can provide the missing premise
Can understand the humor text
Can reach a funny conclusion and laugh

tacit way, meaning we are often unaware of the fact that we know what we know. The fish is not quite aware of water because the water is everywhere. We rarely talk about our culture; so explaining our culture to a partner is really difficult. Culture is all around us. Inside us. We may not even know where to begin!

Let's begin with Aristotle. Aristotle introduced two concepts that help us understand how we reason: enthymeme and syllogism (see Table 2). A syllogism involves a three-step formal reasoning process associated with formal logic. It consists of a major premise, broad cultural assumptions about ways of doing, perceiving, or defining things; a minor premise, which provides a specific case or event; and a conclusion which follows logically from the premises. The following is an example of a syllogism:

Scientists are usually nerdy and ugly [the major premise].
Samuel is a scientist [the minor premise].
Samuel is quite nerdy and ugly [the conclusion].

When humor is presented (in the form of a cartoon or joke), pieces of the syllogism are usually missing; they are assumed understood. At this point, humor is better understood as a form of what Aristotle calls *enthymeme*. This is where a speaker relies on his or her audience to provide the missing premises to reach the conclusion which, in the case of humor, is laughter (a funny conclusion). A speaker adopts a more abbreviated form of persuasion; using enthymematic reasoning (see Table 3) she or he can more effectively persuade the audience. The speaker only has to provide the minor premise and rely on the audience to supply the missing major premise. The conclusion, provided by the speaker or the audience, will be better received because the audience participates in the reasoning process with the speaker. If we use our earlier syllogism example, its enthymeme might look like this:

[the major premise is missing]
Samuel is a scientist [the minor premise]
[the conclusion is missing]

If we apply enthymematic-syllogistic principles to humor, a humor text (joke) offers an explicit minor premise — a specific case or event (Samuel is a scientist). A common or shared body of cultural knowledge is the implicit or missing major premise (Scientists are usually nerdy and ugly); it is not discussed or represented in the humor text. In order to reach a conclusion — the laughter — the audience or the hearer has to fill in the missing premise (Samuel is nerdy and ugly; see Table 3). Stated differently, humor is an *enthymematic form of persuasion*. To appreciate the humor the audience must

Table 3 Humor as an Enthymeme

Major Premise(s) Missing
Minor Premise(s) Provided [humor text]
Conclusion Missing

Table 5 Non-Native Speaker's Ability to Understand Humor

Can rarely provide the missing premise
May not understand the given humor text
Cannot reach a funny conclusion

THE FAR SIDE   By GARY LARSON

Scientific meat markets.

provide two of the three syllogistic steps: (a) the cultural knowledge, and (b) the laughter.

When we treat humor as a type of enthymeme, it is understandable why it's relatively easy for native speakers (see Table 4) but hard for non-native speakers to get the joke. They may not understand the verbal and nonverbal messages in a humor text, and they are rarely able to provide the appropriate cultural knowledge to reach a humorous conclusion (see Table 5).

Converting Enthymemes Into Syllogisms

The process of humor explanation requires native speakers to explain explicit premises (a humor text) and reconstruct the missing premises (cultural knowledge) for the non-native speakers. The goal briefly stated, is to convert enthymemes back into syllogisms. This job is more easily said than done. We will use a "Far Side" cartoon to illustrate this process.

It's a scientific meat market! From a native speaker's perspective, all you have is a cartoon, your laughter, and your partner's confusion. Where should you begin? You may begin with the cartoon, the explicit minor premises (see Table 6, step 1). Non-native speakers usually understand English in a literal way; when they see the word "meat market" they think about beef and pork. You need to explain to your non-native partner that a meat market is also a "meet market," a bar or night club where people can "meet" for social and romantic purposes. Different people may provide different explanations

Table 6 Converting an Enthymeme into a Syllogism

Step 1: Explaining the Minor Premise(s)

Explain the explicit messages seen in the cartoon.

Step 2: Constructing the missing Major Premises
Missing premise (a): The ordinary meatmarket behaviors
Missing premise (b): The stereotype of scientists

Step 3: Funny Conclusion can be reached if an analogous cultural context can be located

Funny conclusion cannot be reached in the partner's culture because:
(a) their bar is different from the bars in America and
(b) the stereotype of scientists is positive

Search for analogous humor context in the partner's culture by asking:
(a) Where do people flirt and have romantic encounters? (students' dancing party)
(b) Who is the least desired in romantic encounters? (military intelligence officers)

Reconstruct the cartoon by using the partner's cultural context — place the military officers at a dancing party (rather than scientists in the meat market).

Metastep: Steps 1 through 3 are usually difficult. Therefore, a different measure has to be taken to overcome the problem, a metastep. This step is about how to make other steps easier; it encourages discussions among people from the same culture to discuss given and missing premises and how to locate translatable contexts.

about the cartoon. For our purposes, we assume that you have explained the explicit premise — a couple of scientists in a bar trying to "meet" people.

But it is still not funny. You need to move away from the cartoon and explain two necessary missing premises (see Table 6, step 2): (a) how people usually behave in a meat market, and (b) the stereotype of a scientist in the American culture.

People in a meat market try to strike up conversations with strangers who appear to be attractive and available at the same time. Strategies commonly used include:

Haven't we met before?
What's your sign?
Don't you know so and so?
You are very attractive.
That's a really cute outfit you have on.

Once a conversation begins people may try to prolong the encounter by saying:

Can I buy you a drink?
May I sit down?
What are you drinking? [martini] Bartender, two martinis!

The person initiating the encounter then tries to impress the partner:

I am trying to get rid of my Mercedes and buy a Porsche.
I could have sworn that I saw you this summer on the Riviera.
I just sold my property in Beverly Hills, and I'm having the hardest time deciding whether I should invest in Monterey or Palo Alto.

Because of differences in ethnicity, region, social class, gender, political, or sexual orientations, you may spell out different behaviors commonly observed in the meat market. But the purpose of this exercise is to provide the cultural knowledge (the premises that are missing in a humor text) that native speakers possess, and which non-native speakers may need to understand the cartoon.

Another missing premise concerns the stereotype of scientists in American culture. Scientists are often portrayed as "nerdy," meaning awkward, unfashionable, boring, and socially inept. They are unable to produce the melodious voice associated with flirting. All these "nerdlike" characteristics are at odds with what works in the meat market.

With the two missing premises reconstructed (meat-market behavior and the stereotype of scientists), non-native speakers may finally understand the cartoon: A "scientific meat market" is a bar where nerdy people try to flirt and strike up a conversation by showing off impressive scholarly or academic credentials rather than physical attractiveness, social status, and wealth. When you finish a detailed explanation of the explicit and implicit premises, your partner may "understand" the cartoon, but not get the joke! Instead of hearty laughter, you may only get polite and kind but emotionless smiles. Take heart! Rather than feeling frustrated, take a third step, beyond converting enthymemes into syllogisms, to help your partner appreciate the humor (see Table 6, step 3). It is to this difficult yet necessary and creative step we now turn.

Locating Analogous Cultural Contexts

Culturally shared premises may vary by culture. It is important for native speakers to ask questions about similar contexts or stereotypes in the partner's culture, for example, "What do people in your country usually do in a bar?" If the partner is from Taiwan, she or he will tell you that a bar is a place where male customers go to buy bar girls' time, to drink or dance together. They may also take the bar girls out to spend the night, but they will have to pay extra. People in Taiwan do not flirt to cultivate romantic relationships in a bar. In brief, it is a place where decent women do not go, and single or married men go to 打野食 (hunt for wild food). A bar is also a place where men take business partners to

cultivate business relationships. Because there is a lot of drinking and pleasure, it is easier to feel like pals and cut friendly deals. Businessmen's wives and girlfriends do not go with them. Businesswomen of course do not go there, either! It is an exclusive pleasure and business domain for men. Knowing this cultural difference, it is easier to understand why it is hard for your partner to appreciate the humor.

Along the same vein, stereotypes about scientists differ. People in Taiwan respect scientists. They are thought to be logical and intelligent. The word "scientist" usually connotes positive meanings, in sharp contrast to the negative associations scientists have in American culture.

If we take the premises about bars or meat markets and scientists and place them in the Taiwanese culture, we have intelligent and logical male scientists going to the bar "hunting for wild food" or doing business with each other. What we have is NOT FUNNY! American humor, in this instance, does not translate well into Taiwanese cultural experience.

This joke died. End of conversation. Not necessarily! To get across the humor, you need to ask questions to (a) locate in your partner's culture where and how people flirt and try to arrange romantic encounters (without assuming a bar is the place), and to (b) identify the people who are least likely to do well in romantic encounters (without assuming that will be or should be "scientists").

In Taiwan, engineering and medical schools have predominantly male students, while the school of liberal arts has mostly female students. Students arrange social gatherings to encourage the possibility of meeting romantic partners. Engineering or medical male students often set up dancing parties in private homes (when parents are gone), inviting a whole class of female students from the school of liberal arts. There may be a lot of looking and searching and some flirting at the party, but the "partiers" usually talk about school or extracurricular activities.

Who are least likely to be associated with such romantic gatherings? Not scientists, but military intelligence officers who instruct high school students in military drills and discipline them over their physical appearance and moral conduct. This requires explanation!

Female high school students are expected to wear their hair straight (they are not allowed to perm their hair) along the neckline. If a student violates this rule, her female military intelligence officer has the right to discipline her. Usually, the officer cuts one side of the student's hair above the ear, forcing the female student to cut all of her hair that short. Male students are to wear their hair no longer than ½ inch. If a student violates this rule, the male military intelligence officer can discipline him by shaving the center of his head — like an airport runway. The student is said to have an 飛機頭 (airplane head). He has to shave his head bald and remain "ugly" for one or two months. High school students in Taiwan are normal teenagers; they want to impress the opposite gender. Hair length and style, therefore, are an area of bitter and intense struggle at school between students and officers. Those who are least likely to be a romantic partner in Taiwan, given their stereotype (rigid, boring, unfashionable, unintelligent, and altogether obnoxious), are the military intelligent officers.

Armed with this knowledge, you may help your partner appreciate the meat market cartoon by asking him or her to imagine a cartoon where a male and female military intelligence officer meet at a dancing party. The male officer wearing a proud face may say, "I made SIX airplane heads last week." The female officer wearing a warm smile with lots of hearts flying around responds, "I cut THIRTY-FIVE girls' hair today!" The title of the cartoon: "Military Intelligence Officers at the Dancing Party." At this moment, you get a good laugh out of your partner — she or he may even "split a gut."

Up to this point, we have explored three steps in explaining humor. Still, you may wonder if you can ever figure out how to reconstruct the missing premises and locate analogous contexts in someone else's culture. In other words, you may have difficulties with steps 2 and 3. The next section will offer a metastep, a step *about* the other suggested steps, to help you overcome explanation problems (see Figure 6, the Metastep).

The Metastep

In the meat market cartoon, some people in my intercultural class could not narrow the massive cultural knowledge to two areas (major premises) — the meat market context and the stereotype of scientists in American culture. Similar difficulties were experienced by non-native speakers trying to locate the analogous humor context in their cultures for native speakers. In the case of the meat market cartoon, people from Taiwan may or may not offer the college dancing party context as analogous to the bar or meat market in America, or the military intelligence officer as analogous to the stereotype of scientists in American culture. You may find help at this juncture by talking with people from your own culture about the missing premises. This is instrumental for both native and non-native speakers to go through steps 1 through 3 successfully. Stated differently, you may not immediately figure out explanations for a specific humor text and its accompanying cultural assumptions. This does not mean that you are ignorant or incompetent. Rather, it tells you that you should talk with people from your own culture. By collectively articulating each other's version of cultural knowledge through dialogue, you may piece together a cultural quilt. This puts you in a better position to share with people from different cultures.

This last step makes our "taken-for-granted" world (the world we live in but do not talk about) the topic of discussion. While swimming, the fish ponders the nature of water. When you [native and non-native speakers] engage your fellows in a discussion of your cultural world, you become more knowledgeable about your own culture and are more able to articulate it in intercultural humor explanation processes.

One final note about humor explanations, and this is crucial: the process of establishing conversational rules to facilitate communication about humor (stage 1); explaining the humor text (stage 2, step 1); reconstructing missing cultural knowledge (stage 2, step 2); locating analogous humor context in the partner's culture (stage 2, step 3); and becom-

Table 7 The Complete Procedure of Humor Sharing

Stage 1: Making New Conversational Rules

  Non-native and native partners learn to make inadequate (either stupid or rude) behaviors not only acceptable but also welcomed!

Stage 2: Explaining Humor

  Step 1: Explain the humor text [given minor premise(s)]

  Step 2: Reconstruct tacit cultural knowledge [missing premise(s)]

  Step 3: Locate analogous humor context in partner's culture [reach a funny conclusion]

  Metastep: Talk with same-culture partners about steps 1, 2, 3 to figure out the content of each step.

---

ing more knowledgeable about one's own culture by talking with fellow speakers about premises (the Metastep) remains more or less constant (see Table 7). The *process* remains constant, but the *content* of each step may vary because native and non-native partners may have different views from those provided in the meat market case about the knowledge necessary to comprehend and appreciate the cartoon. Carry out the two stages of humor sharing, but strive to be creative in reconstructing the content of various premises.

SUMMARY

When we communicate with members from a group different in gender, social class, educational background, ethnicity, or nationality, humor (in the form of joking, story telling, and cartoons) creates a potential for communication breakdown. This chapter takes on the most difficult case — humor breakdown between native and non-native English speakers — offering a procedural solution.

What is accomplished in learning to communicate about humor is quite fruitful! First of all, communication about humor requires *procedural com-*

petence. Both native and non-native partners come from specific subcultures of their native cultures. This means that the *content* of their conversational rules and humor explanations may differ substantially. But the *process* of making new conversational rules, explaining given premises, reconstructing missing premises, locating analogous cultural contexts, and engaging in discussions with people from the same cultural backgrounds about all of these steps rises above content! Process provides a tool for taking in, transforming, and creating content. Becoming procedurally competent, you are able to search and understand different cultures on your own. Procedural competence means that you are equipped to begin exciting and thoughtful cultural experiences, to search for means of improvement and be alert to potential problems. Your competence is not limited to encounters with a specific culture. Rather, you can go through this process with people from all kinds of cultures.

Second, we do not naturally "know about" our own culture. To explain humor to people from different cultures, we are forced to talk with people from our own culture (remember the metastep) about the world we take for granted. We learn to articulate what we are used to but usually do not need to talk about. As a result, we cease to know our own culture passively, and begin to actively identify and articulate tacit cultural assumptions. In this process, we may discover that people from different subcultures in our own "culture" may explain the premises in quite different ways.

Third, when discussing humor, the conversation can lead effortlessly to the discovery of what we do not know about each other's culture; for example, we discovered that scientists are nerdy in one culture, but not in another culture. We become more humble and cautious in insuing intercultural encounters. We learn to ask questions in order to know what we do not know, not just to learn things we want to know.

This chapter takes up the question of humor and lays out ways to "do" intercultural communication competently. It's now time for you to look for cartoons you enjoy and share with a partner. You may struggle trying out different ways to solve the problems. You may fail to explain some cartoons and jokes, but ultimately, you can and will achieve some intercultural understanding, and in the process, share fun and humor with intercultural friends.

A Model for Cultural Diversity Training

Derald Wing Sue

Recently, renewed interest in the role that counselors and psychologists may play in the world of work (business and industry) has surfaced in several major publications. *The Counseling Psychologist* (Vol. 10, No. 3, 1982) devoted an entire special issue ("Counseling Psychology in Business & Industry") to the topic discussing how counselors may apply their unique skills to this target population. In addition to discussing the roles and relationships that counselors may develop in organizations, Osipow (1982) and Toomer (1982) analyzed barriers that have impeded the counselor's involvement in business and industry. Likewise, two issues of the *American Psychologist* (February, 1990 — "Organizational Psychology," and October, 1990 — "Stress in the Workplace") made a strong case for psychologists to become involved in occupational health and aid organizations to cope with the enormous changes occurring in the nature of work and the work force (Keita & Jones, 1990; Millar, 1990).

Perhaps no area is experiencing more rapid changes than in the area involving characteristics of our workers. Our work sites are fast reflecting the fact that we are becoming a multicultural, multiracial, and multilingual society (Johnston & Packer, 1987; Offermann & Gowing, 1990; Sue & Sue, 1990). Already, 75% of those entering the United States

Reprinted from *Journal of Counseling and Development,* Vol. 70 September/October 1991, pp. 99–105. © ACA. Reprinted with permission. Derald Wing Sue is a professor of counseling psychology in the Department of Educational Psychology at California State University, Hayward. No further reproduction authorized without written permission of American Counseling Association.

(U.S.) work force are minorities and women. By the time the so-called "baby boomers" retire (those born between 1946 and 1961), racial-ethnic minorities will be the major contributors to social security and pension plans. With the declining birthrates of White Americans and the relatively higher rates for racial minorities, we are not only becoming an older population, but one in which the complexion of the country is truly changing (Johnston & Packer, 1987). Couple this fact with the number of immigrants from Pacific Rim and Latin American countries, and it becomes clear that White Americans will become the numerical minority within the next 20 or so years.

These demographic changes will have major impact upon our economic, social, legal, political, educational, and cultural systems. As counselors involved in organizational change, we will need to face and convince others about the inevitable challenge of cultural diversity. Although the tasks for counselors in educational and mental health settings are slightly different from those for their business and industry counterparts, there are enough similarities and overlap for each to learn from one another.

For example, the diversification trend means that professional counselors and other mental health service providers need to (a) increase their cultural sensitivity, (b) obtain greater knowledge and understanding of various racial-ethnic groups, and (c) develop culturally relevant counseling strategies (Sue, 1990). To accomplish these goals, several things need to happen. First, counselor education programs need to do a better job of recruiting, admitting, and supporting minority counselor trainees (Atkinson, Morten, & Sue, 1989). Yet, surveys of graduate programs continue to reveal that ethnic minorities are underrepresented (Atkinson, 1983; Parham & Morland, 1981; Russo, Olmedo, Stapp, & Fulcher, 1981). Second, it has become quite clear that nonminority mental health providers also need to be trained to work with culturally diverse clients. Both the American Psychological Association (APA) and the Association for Counseling and Development (AACD) have developed training standards that incorporate cultural diversity. Yet, these standards are only slowly being implemented in programs. Last, traditional counseling practice that uses the one-to-one therapy role has been seriously criticized by minority individuals as being culture and class bound. It assumes that the problem resides in the individual (Sue & Sue, 1990). Counselors need to get out of the office to meet clients in their own home environment (outreach) and to learn that many problems encountered by the culturally different individual reside in institutions. Thus, counselors must learn to intervene in the system (institutions) and act as change agents.

The task of this article is to present a model for diversity assessment and training. It looks at the levels of organizational intervention, the barriers to multicultural change, and the ways of incorporating multicultural competencies in organizations. Although developed primarily in application to business and industry, it seems to have equal validity for organizational change in other settings as well.

THE CHALLENGE OF CULTURAL DIVERSITY

Industry exists for different reasons (products or services) but always for profit. . . . Counseling psychologists have tended to shy away from profit statements. Yet, in order to be accepted and have a function in the industry, such a perspective must be at least acceptable and, to some extent, promoted. We must be willing to accept the view that profits, humanely obtained, are an integral part of our society. (Osipow, 1982, p. 19)

No statement better summarizes the issues facing the counselor or psychologists working in business and industry. Although the values and ethics of industry may not be shared by those of the counselor, profits drive a business; and profits may provide the fuel for change in the workplace (Beer & Walton, 1990; Foster, Jackson, Cross, Jackson, & Hardiman, 1988). Businesses and industries need to be convinced that their survival depends on how they manage cultural diversity. Likewise, schools, mental health institutions, and our professional societies cannot continue to ignore the diversification trend. Will we compete with only a dwindling portion of our traditional human resources, or will we face the challenge and learn to deal with a diverse population? To be successful and competitive, organizations need to address the following issues.

1. The labor pool in the USA (United States of America) is shrinking. To attract and retain new workers, businesses will have to reach out to employ people of different cultures and color. As a result, old definitions of "fit" in the workplace will have to be drastically altered (Goldstein & Gilliam, 1990).

2. At this time, the USA minority marketplace equals the GNP (gross national product) of Canada. The minority market now purchases more goods and consumes more services than does any USA trading partner (Adler, 1986; Foster et al., 1988). By the year 2000, it will represent 25% of the market. To tap into such a vast market means a culturally sensitive approach on the part of companies. A company that values diversity and employs a diverse work force retains a competitive edge.

3. The majority of large corporations is no longer bound by national boundaries. Many corporations derive increasing profits from outside their home country in the international marketplace (Adler, 1986; Beer & Walton, 1990). Yet, American businesses seem ill-equipped to deal with the diversity and complexity of a global economic world. Organizational behavior differs from country to country, and such lack of understanding can lead to major blunders and losses. The manager or worker in a multicultural world and society will need special skills and sensitivities to conduct appropriate transactions.

4. Companies will need to value diversity. This goes beyond hiring minority employees at the lower levels of employment. A "glass ceiling" often exists for women and minorities preventing advancement and promotion to higher levels (Morrison & Von Glinow, 1990; Sue, Sue, Zane, & Wong, 1985). Unfortunately, we have the greatest diversity at the lower levels, and need it most at the higher ones. A successful organization will need to review its policies, practices, and organizational structure to remove potential barriers. It will need to create new policies, practices, and internal structures that will support and advance cultural diversity. This means that organizations must be willing to include minorities in decision-making positions and share power with them (Jackson & Holvino, 1988).

5. Valuing diversity is a long-term, ongoing commitment on the part of organizations. United States companies, our schools, and mental health services are often seeking either quick profits or easy solutions. There are no "quick fixes," "magic wands," or simple solutions. Success is directly proportional to the investment of time, energy, and financial resources devoted to the development of a truly multicultural organization. It begins at the top levels of government, business, and industry. Without such support and commitment, organizations may be doomed to failure.

6. It seems that education will be significantly affected. More and more minority students are entering the public school systems. In California, for example, the number of White students dropped below 50% in 1988, and in 1990, statistics reveal that one in four of the students lives in a home in which English is not spoken. Furthermore, one in every six students was born outside the United States. Some of the greatest challenges to our educational system will be how to (a) make the curriculum more relevant to the needs of minority students, (b) deal with differences in learning styles/teaching styles that may affect minority student performance, and (c) clarify communication style differences that may be misunderstood by teachers and counselors.

7. We can no longer rely on ethnocentric orientation in the delivery of mental health services. This bias has been highly destructive to the natural help-giving networks of minority communities. We need to expand our perception of what constitutes appropriate counseling/therapy practice by becoming acquainted with equally legitimate methods of treatment delivered by minority groups like nonformal or natural support systems (Brammer, 1985; Pearson, 1985) (family, friends, community self-help

programs, and occupation networks), folk-healing methods (Padilla & DeSnyder, 1985), and indigenous formal systems of therapy (Draguns, 1981).

INCORPORATING DIVERSITY IN ORGANIZATIONS: FUNCTIONS

Training programs on cultural diversity need to be tailored to institutional and individual needs. Organizations possess their own corporate, work, or extracurricular cultures (Schein, 1990). They are also at various stages in their receptivity and implementation of cultural diversity goals (Jackson & Holvino, 1988). Some institutions are primarily exclusionary and monocultural in their focus. Others vary in the degree to which they have moved to multiculturalism. No one universal training package can meet the complexity of multiculturalism in the workplace. Extensive work in this area points to three functions and three barriers in an organization where diversity training, intervention, or both would most likely be helpful.

Recruitment (Labor Pool)

Organizations must reach out to attract minority applicants and expand the pool of workers from which they recruit. How often have we heard the statement, "We can't find enough qualified minorities?" Oftentimes, such a statement reflects bias on the part of the selection process. The implication is that most minorities are not qualified or must fit a White definition fostered by the organization to be considered qualified (Sue & Sue, 1990). Such attitudes and beliefs on the part of those in positions of power automatically restrict the labor pool and may eliminate many potentially excellent minority workers.

Likewise, repeated criticisms have been launched at mental health institutions for being disproportionately composed of White counselors. The underrepresentation is often used to suggest why minority clients terminate counseling at such a high rate or fail to use traditional services (Atkinson, Morten, & Sue, 1989; Sue & Sue, 1990). Graduate

programs have been unsuccessful in recruiting significant numbers of minority applicants because the pool they drew from may have few minority individuals. Counselor education programs with successful affirmative action recruitment efforts need to identify and solicit applications not only from those minority individuals who already have plans to enter but also from potential students who may have ruled out graduate education for less than valid reasons (Atkinson, 1983). We must begin to reach out to those who may settle for a less appealing vocation because of their experiences with an oppressive environment that restricts their outlook on life. Recruitment must be active and well intentioned.

Factors that impede recruitment of minority candidates (e.g., image of the company or school, low representation in the work force or graduate programs, biased recruitment admission and selection criteria) need to be analyzed, and steps need to be taken to eradicate obstacles. This may also mean that companies and universities need to become more involved in the community to change their image and to help develop the pool of workers or students.

Retention (Corporate Culture)

To keep qualified minority workers and students means that a company or university needs to accommodate cultural diversity and make minority individuals feel comfortable at their work sites or educational environment. Minorities must perceive themselves as part of a team whose contributions are valued. Racism, sexism, stereotyping, and discrimination must be minimized. Managers, workers, school administrators, counselors, and teachers need to understand the "minority experience" and feel comfortable in dealing with unpleasant racial-cultural issues arising from a culturally diverse population. To simply recruit more minority individuals without consequent changes in the internal operation of the company or university and its "culture" would result in only misunderstandings, frustrations, and loss of valuable minority employees and students. Ultimately, the competitive edge of the company will be lost resulting in economic failure.

Counselor education programs seem to suffer from their inability to retain minority students once admitted into graduate school. Retention is not only a function of major curricular changes (relevance to the minority experience) but extracurricular as well. Oftentimes, minorities who are the victims of discrimination and oppression may need economic, social, and emotional support not needed by nonminorities. Graduate institutions need to carefully and systematically provide culturally relevant support services.

Promotion (Career Path)

One of the greatest impediments to valuing diversity is the perception by racial-ethnic minorities that for them promotion and advancement in an organization are limited. Equal access and opportunity must be open to everyone regardless of race, culture, ethnicity, sex, sexual orientation, and religion. We can no longer equate equality with sameness. For companies and universities to be successful, they must challenge the "myth of color blindness" and the belief that equal treatment is desirable. Oftentimes, equal treatment can be discriminatory, whereas differential treatment that recognizes differences is not necessarily preferential. Organizations often have great difficulty comprehending this statement. Indeed, the blind application of a single standard to all populations may be unfair. For example, because Asian Americans may be less vocal in unit meetings, they are often denied promotion to management positions (Sue et al., 1985). In U.S. businesses, leadership is often equated with how vocal and articulate a person is in an interpersonal encounter. A verbal individual is perceived as assertive and a leader. To evaluate an Asian American worker's management or executive potential on this criteria may be totally invalid. Promotion of minority workers, then, may dictate a differential approach or standard that is truly nondiscriminatory! Equal access and opportunities may mean treatment that recognizes differential experiences, values, and behaviors of minority populations.

In education, this may translate into a recognition that different styles of learning may dictate different styles of teaching. Although the term "promotion" is used by the business sector, the equivalent term "graduation" is used in education. Admitting increased numbers of minorities may not be productive unless subsequent changes occur in the educational process, which also increases the rates of retention and graduation.

INCORPORATING DIVERSITY IN ORGANIZATIONS: BARRIERS

In addition to the three levels of organizational intervention (recruitment, retention, and promotion), three major barriers to incorporating diversity may be identified: (a) differences in communication styles, characteristics, or both; (b) interpersonal-attitudinal discrimination and prejudice; and (c) systemic barriers.

1. *Differences in communication styles and differences in characteristics of racial-ethnic minorities* are often postulated for their lack of success in the business and educational sectors (Sue, 1990). For example, it is often believed that Asians lack the assertive leadership skills needed to become effective leaders or managers in an organization (Sue et al., 1985); or, that women and minorities have certain traits, attitudes, behaviors, and values that clash with those that achieve success in business and education (Morrison & Von Glinow, 1990). Although studies offer some limited support for this belief, care must be exercised not to "blame the victims." In most cases, it is institutional policies and practices that are at the heart of the problem. Nevertheless, there are times when it seems that minority workers or managers may profit from becoming aware of their social impact on others and/or developing multicultural communication skills. In addition, minority students may benefit from study-skills training, job-

interviewing training, and the like. Effectiveness training for minorities (developing communication and leadership skills, helping immigrant workers adapt to the U.S. workplace, understanding merit review, learning stress management, and understanding organization values) may be of immense value in retention and promotion. Workshops for racial-ethnic minority and female employees or students may include lectures, role-playing, small-group exercises, videotaped interactions, and team building.

2. *Interpersonal discrimination and prejudice* also serve to seriously impair cultural diversity goals. In this respect, White workers and management may believe that minorities and women are less suitable for management roles or positions in the company than are nonminorities and men. Stereotypes that Blacks make "good athletes but poor scholars" are a convenient way to justify not promoting Blacks to decision-making positions (Sue & Sue, 1990). Likewise, teachers and counselors may have preconceived notions (stereotypes) that place minority students or clients in an unenviable position. Discrimination may occur from a conscious or unconscious basis. The latter is especially challenging because the person discriminating may believe he or she is acting in a rational and good-faith manner. Such is the case when a White worker, teacher, or fellow student may tell an ethnic joke in "good humor" and not realize its impact on his or her minority counterpart. Or, during a merit review, a White manager may rate a Hispanic worker as low in leadership qualities because he or she speaks with an accent. Training at this level focuses on interpersonal interaction and attitude and behavior change of White teachers, support staff, counselors, and workers and management. Workshops aimed at consciousness raising, increased knowledge, increased sensitivity, and development of cross-cultural communication and management skills are indicated. Such training needs to be implemented at all levels of the organization from the top to the bottom.

3. *Systemic barriers* may also exist in an organization that mirrors the nature of race relations in the United States. For example, high-status positions are

usually White dominated, whereas low-status positions are occupied by minority groups (Foster et al., 1988; Morrison & Von Glinow, 1990). The dominance of White men in management and academic positions poses a structural problem for underrepresented groups because evaluation of minority members is likely to be distorted. The corporate or academic culture may create culture conflicts for the minority person (leading to alienation). Formal institutional policies and practices may maintain exclusion of minorities, and powerful informal liaisons ("old boy's network") may be equally discriminatory. To truly value diversity means altering the power relations in an organization to minimize structural discrimination (Foster et al., 1988). The strategy involves changing structural relations in an organization and constructing programs and practices with the same economic and maintenance priorities as other valued aspects of the company. Multicultural policy statements supporting cultural diversity; formation of pluralism councils to oversee progress in a company; accountability programs that reward diversity; use of role models, mentors, and networks for minority employees; and elimination of racist or sexist language and jokes are only a few of the approaches that companies have begun to explore. Many of these strategies may prove useful for counselor education programs as well. Strong affirmative action statements in "recruiting" literature, hiring minority tenure track faculty, funding educational support services, changing biased admission criteria, and using selection procedures that use cross-cultural experiences as one criteria may prove fruitful.

Figure 1 attempts to illustrate a 3 × 3 design (Functional Levels × Barriers) to ascertain the types of training or intervention that may be most appropriate for the organization. For example, if our goal is to aid minorities in *promotion* and our analysis is that *leadership skills* are needed, then effectiveness training may be called for. If *interpersonal discrimination* in the work force is preventing *promotion*, then consciousness raising or cross-cultural management training for White workers may be dictated. If *retention* of minorities is difficult because of

FUNCTIONAL LEVELS	BARRIERS		
	Differences	Interpersonal Discrimination	Systemic Barriers
Promotion/ Advancement (Career Path)	Effectiveness training for minorities and majority individuals	Consciousness raising Sensitivity training Increased knowledge Cross-cultural counseling, teaching, and management skills	Organizational development Systems intervention Creating new programs and practices
Retention (Corporate Culture)	Effectiveness training for minorities and majority individuals	Consciousness raising Sensitivity training Increased knowledge Cross-cultural counseling, teaching, and management skills	Organizational development Systems intervention Creating new programs and practices
Recruitment (Labor Pool)	Effectiveness training for minorities and majority individuals	Consciousness raising Sensitivity training Increased knowledge Cross-cultural counseling, teaching, and management skills	Organizational development Systems intervention Creating new programs and practices

Figure 1 Cultural Diversity Training: A Systemic Approach

systemic barriers, working on the corporate culture (e.g., organizational development, systems intervention) seems indicated.

INCORPORATING DIVERSITY IN ORGANIZATIONS: COMPETENCIES

In addition to the 3 × 3 design used to get a clearer picture of organizational needs, numerous cross-cultural specialists have stressed the importance of training from a competency-based approach (Carney & Kahn, 1984; Corvin & Wiggins, 1989; Sue et al., 1982). Although originally developed for counselors undergoing cross-cultural training, a competency-based approach seems to have equal validity in application to managers, workers, employers, or employees. These multicultural competencies have been adequately described elsewhere (Carney & Kahn, 1984; Sabnani, Ponterotto, & Borodovsky, 1991; Sue et al., 1982) so only a very brief presentation is given here. The competencies are organized along three dimensions: beliefs and attitudes, knowledge, and skills.

1. *Beliefs and attitudes* that workers or counselors have about racial or ethnic minorities may be totally inaccurate and may lead to stereotyping or negativism toward certain minority groups. For example, beliefs that Blacks and Hispanics are intellectually inferior and will not do well in school, or that Asians make good technical workers but poor managers, are good examples of widespread stereotyping that

may hinder recruitment, retention, and promotion. Likewise, there is widespread belief among White workers that recent immigrants have taken jobs away from Whites and that they are draining economic resources (welfare programs) from our society. Contrary to this belief are studies indicating that recent immigrants actually create more jobs and contribute more financial resources into our economy than they take away (Johnston & Parker, 1987). It is also important for White employers, workers, teachers, and counselors to realize that they have directly or indirectly benefitted from individual, institutional, and cultural racism. Although no one was ever born wanting to be a racist, Whites have been socialized in a racist society and need to accept responsibility for their own racism and to deal with it in a nondefensive, guilt-free manner.

If a training program is directed toward this domain, then an expansion of awareness regarding one's own culture and the cultures of other ethnic groups is needed. Movement toward valuing and respecting differences, becoming aware of one's own values and biases, becoming comfortable with differences that exist in terms of race and culture, among other characteristics, are built into the training.

2. *Knowledge* encompasses the acquisition of information regarding one's own and the other cultures' values, worldviews, and social norms. Being knowledgeable about the history, experiences, cultural values, and life-styles of various racial-ethnic groups is very important. How do these factors affect Asian American, African American, American Indian, and Hispanic education, achievement, career, vocational choice, and work? The greater the depth of knowledge an employer or counselor has about various minority groups, the more likely the company or program will be successful in incorporating diversity. Furthermore, it is important that workers and counselors understand the concepts of prejudice and racism, and the organizational barriers that impede cultural diversity in the workplace.

3. *Skills* involve building the foundation for effective multicultural counseling management and commu-

nication. The effective multicultural counselor-manager and worker is able to send and receive both verbal and nonverbal messages accurately and appropriately. What we are dealing with here is communication styles (Sue, 1990). The key words "send," "receive," "nonverbal," "verbal," "accurately," and "appropriately" are important. These words recognize several things about the effective cross-cultural counselor or manager.

First, communication is a two-way process. The skilled counselor and manager must not only be able to communicate (send) his or her thoughts to the client or employee, but he or she must also be able to read (receive) messages from the client or employee.

Second, cross-cultural effectiveness may be highly correlated with the counselor's and manager's ability to recognize and respond not only to verbal but also to nonverbal messages.

Third, sending and receiving a message accurately means the ability to consider cultural cues operative in the setting.

Fourth, accuracy of communication must be tempered by its appropriateness. In many cultures, subtlety and indirectness of communication is a highly prized art (Sue, 1990; Sue & Sue, 1990).

Perhaps equally important is the multicultural counselor's and manager's ability to exercise institutional intervention skills and strategies on behalf of cultural diversity goals. Although being able to intervene at the individual classroom, small-group, or unit level is important, such activity may be more remedial than preventive. The entire organization needs to develop a human resource management strategy that ultimately affects its culture and organizational structure (Foster et al., 1988). A strong multicultural policy statement, when genuinely implemented, can help in this regard. One that seems beneficial and effective is the following definition distilled from those given by Jackson and Holvino (1988) and Strong (1986).

A multicultural organization is genuinely committed (action as well as words) to diverse representation throughout its organization and at all

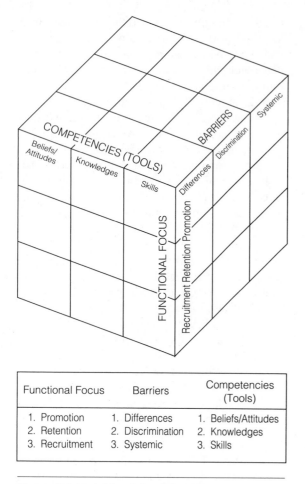

Functional Focus	Barriers	Competencies (Tools)
1. Promotion	1. Differences	1. Beliefs/Attitudes
2. Retention	2. Discrimination	2. Knowledges
3. Recruitment	3. Systemic	3. Skills

Figure 2 A Model for Cultural Diversity Training: Functional Focus, Barriers, and Competencies (Developed by Derald Wing Sue, PhD. A Psychological Corporation. Not to be reproduced without written consent.)

levels. It is sensitive to maintaining an open, supportive, and responsive environment. It is working toward and purposefully including elements of diverse cultures in its ongoing operations (organization policies and practices are carefully monitored to the goals of multiculturalism). It is authentic in responding to issues confronting it (commitment to changing policies and practices that block cultural diversity).

Depending on the specific goal or goals chosen, a training package may use different strategies. If the focus is attitudes and beliefs, then exercises aimed at revealing stereotypes or racial-cultural images are addressed. If the focus is on knowledge, then guided self-study, lectures, audiovisual presentations, and interviews with experts or consultants may be indicated. If the focus is on skills, role-playing, communication training, watching cross-cultural interactions, behavioral rehearsal, and analyzing organizational development and goals may be more appropriate. Again, it is important to note that no one method or approach is likely to be effective unless it is systematically geared to the needs of the organization and workers.

The cultural diversity training model shown in Figure 2 is based on a careful assessment of the corporate culture, organizational structure, and employees using the $3 \times 3 \times 3$ matrix outlined earlier: Functional Focus—promotion, retention, and recruitment; Barriers—differences, discrimination, and systemic; Competencies—beliefs/attitudes, knowledge, and skills. A total of 27 cells can be identified for training intervention. Each cell allows us to develop the appropriate training programs and strategies that will lead to movement toward a multicultural organization.

CONCLUSION

Cultural diversity training, when applied to organizations, is a complex and long-term process. The model being proposed here, though originally developed for business and industry, seems equally applicable to institutions of higher education, mental health organizations, and professional organizations (AACD and APA) as well. There are, however, some major cautions and limitations that need to be considered in using this model for change. First, the cube model presented should be used as a conceptual framework for assessment and suggestions of possible intervention strategies. It should be used in a "wholistic" fashion that integrates the overall goals of multiculturalism. To focus on only a few cells (i.e., Discrimination × Attitudes × Retention) without seeing the global picture may ultimately defeat multicultural objectives. Individual consciousness raising without consequent economic-structural-behavioral change may have limited success in the workplace and may actually thwart multiculturalism (Jackson & Holvino, 1988; Sue & Sue, 1990). Second, recent work on White identity development (Hardiman, 1982; Helms, 1990; Sabnani, Ponterotto, & Borodovsky, 1991; Sue & Sue, 1990) suggests the importance of incorporating the degree of White racial awareness of the worker, student, or counselor. The trainer is likely to encounter different challenges or resistances depending upon the developmental level of the target population. Last, it is important to realize that any multicultural training program must ultimately contain a strong antiracism component (Corvin & Wiggins, 1989). Moving toward multiculturalism is more than the acquisition of knowledge and skills. If that were not the case, we would have eradicated racism years ago. Our biases, prejudices, and stereotypes run deep and die hard! If we are to truly become a multicultural society, we cannot continue to avoid this battleground.

REFERENCES

Adler, N. J. (1986). *International dimensions of organizational behavior*. Belmont, CA: Wadsworth.

Atkinson, D. R. (1983). Ethnic minority representation in counselor education. *Counselor Education and Supervision, 23*, 7–19.

Atkinson, D. R., Morten, G., & Sue, D. W. (1989). *Counseling American minorities: A cross-cultural perspective* (3rd ed.). Dubuque, IA: William C. Brown.

Beer, M., & Walton, E. (1990). Developing the competitive organization: Interventions and strategies. *American Psychologist, 45*(2), 154–161.

Brammer, L. (1985). Nonformal support in cross-cultural counseling and psychotherapy. In P. B. Pedersen (Ed.), *Handbook of cross-cultural counseling and therapy* (pp. 85–92). Westport, CT: Greenwood Press.

Carney, C. G., & Kahn, K. B. (1984). Building competencies for effective cross-cultural counseling: A developmental view. *The Counseling Psychologist, 12*(1), 111–119.

Corvin, S. A., & Wiggins, F. (1989). An antiracism training model for White professionals. *Journal of Multicultural Counseling and Development, 17*, 105–114.

Draguns, J. G. (1981). Cross-cultural counseling and psychotherapy. In A. J. Marsella & P. B. Pedersen (Eds.), *Cross-cultural counseling and psychotherapy* (pp. 3–27). New York: Pergamon.

Foster, B. G., Jackson, G., Cross, W. E., Jackson, B., & Hardiman, R. (1988). Workforce diversity and business. *Training & Development Journal, April*, 15–19.

Goldstein, I. L., & Gilliam, P. (1990). Training system issues in the year 2000. *American Psychologist, 45*(2), 143.

Hardiman, R. (1982). White identity development: A process oriented model for describing the racial consciousness of White Americans. *Dissertation Abstracts International, 43*, 104A. (University Microfilms No. 82-10330).

Helms, J. E. (1990). *Black and White racial identity: Theory, research and practice*. New York: Greenwood Press.

Jackson, B. W., & Holvino, E. (1988). Developing multicultural organizations. *Journal of Religion and the Applied Behavioral Sciences, 9*(2), 14–19.

Johnston, W. B., & Packer, A. H. (1987). *Workforce 2000: Work and workers for the twenty-first century*. Indianapolis, IN: Hudson Institute.

Keita, G. P., & Jones, J. N. (1990). Reducing adverse reaction to stress in the workplace. Psychology's expanding role. *American Psychologist, 45*, 1137–1141.

Millar, J. D. (1990). Mental health and the workplace: An interchangeable partnership. *American Psychologist, 45*, 1165–1168.

Morrison, A. M., & Von Glinow, M. A. (1990). Women and minorities in management. *American Psychologist, 45*, 200–207.

Offermann, L., & Gowing, M. K. (1990). Organizations of the future: Changes and challenges. *American Psychologist, 45*, 95–108.

Osipow, S. H. (1982). Counseling psychology: Applications in the world of work. *The Counseling Psychologist, 10*(3), 19–25.

Padilla, A. N., & DeSnyder, N. S. (1985). Counseling Hispanics: Strategies for effective intervention. In P. B. Pedersen (Ed.), *Handbook of cross-cultural counseling and therapy* (pp. 157–164). Westport, CT: Greenwood Press.

Parham, W., & Morland, J. R. (1981). Non-White students in counseling psychology: A closer look. *Professional Psychology, 12,* 499–507.

Pearson, R. E. (1985). The recognition and use of natural support systems in cross-cultural counseling. In P. B. Pedersen (Ed.), *Handbook of cross-cultural counseling and therapy* (pp. 299–306). Westport, CT: Greenwood Press.

Russo, N. F., Olmedo, E. L., Stapp, J., & Fulcher, R. (1981). Women and minorities in psychology. *American Psychologist, 36,* 1315–1363.

Sabnani, H. B., Ponterotto, J. G., & Borodovsky, L. G. (1991). White racial identity development and cross-cultural counselor training. *The Counseling Psychologist, 19*(1), 76–102.

Schein, E. H. (1990). Organizational culture. *American Psychologist, 45,* 109–119.

Strong, L. J. (1986). *Race relations for personal and organizational effectiveness.* Unpublished manuscript.

Sue, D. W. (1990). Culture specific techniques in counseling: A conceptual framework. *Professional Psychology, 21*(6), 424–433.

Sue, D. W., Bernier, J. E., Durran, A., Feinberg, L., Pedersen, P. B., Smith, E., & Vasquez-Nuttall, E. (1982). Position paper: Cross-cultural counseling competencies. *The Counseling Psychologist, 10*(2), 45–52.

Sue, D. W., & Sue, D. (1990). *Counseling the culturally different: Theory & practice.* New York: Wiley.

Sue, S., Sue, D. W., Zane, N., & Wong, H. Z. (1985). Where are the Asian American leaders and top executives? *P/AAMHRC Review, 4,* 13–15.

Toomer, J. E. (1982). Counseling psychologists in business and industry. *The Counseling Psychologist, 10*(3), 9–18.

Adapting to a New Culture

YOUNG YUN KIM

One of the dramatic changes we witness today is the enormous interface of cultures in human affairs—from political and economic to art and leisure activities. At the forefront of this global reality are the countless people who are on the move crossing cultural boundaries. Each year, millions of immigrants and refugees change homes. Finding themselves driven by natural disaster and economic need, or looking for better hopes of freedom, security, or social and economic betterment, people uproot themselves from their familiar homes and embark on the journey of building a new life into an alien, and sometimes hostile, milieu. Along with immigrants and refugees are numerous temporary sojourners: diplomats, military personnel, and other governmental and intergovernmental agency employees on overseas assignments. Peace Corps volunteers have worked in nearly 100 nations since President John F. Kennedy initiated the program in 1960. Researchers, professors, and students visit and study at foreign academic institutions, along with missionaries carrying out their religious endeavors. Many business employees today are given overseas assignments, while an increasing number of accountants, teachers, construction workers, athletes, artists, musicians, and writers find employment in foreign countries.

These and many others like them are, indeed, the contemporary pioneers. They face, firsthand, some

This original essay was written especially for this seventh edition. All rights reserved. Permission to reprint must be obtained from the publisher and the author. Professor Young Yun Kim teaches at the University of Oklahoma, Norman, Oklahoma.

of the most drastic and all-encompassing challenges of having to construct a new life in an unfamiliar milieu. Confronted with the process of cross-cultural adaptation, they will discover this process is achieved mainly through communication.

STRESS, ADAPTATION, AND GROWTH

Individuals move to another country for varied reasons and circumstances and with differing levels of commitment to the host society. For more immigrants, the move is permanent, or is at least regarded as such initially, in the sense that it is now the primary setting for the conduct of their lives. For many short-term sojourners, reasons for a sojourn are often very pragmatic and specific and contacts with new cultures are mostly peripheral, requiring less overall commitment. Foreign students, for example, can reduce their adaptation to the bare minimum required to fulfill their role as a student and may confine their social contact to fellow students from their home country. A similar observation can be made about military personnel and their families in foreign countries, and about migrant workers as well (Brislin, 1981; Dyal & Dyal, 1981; Furnham & Bochner, 1982; Taft, 1977).

What is common to both immigrants and sojourners, however, is that they begin their life in the host society as *strangers* (Gudykunst & Kim, 1992; Simmel, 1908/1950). Many of their previously held beliefs, taken-for-granted assumptions, and routinized behaviors are no longer relevant or appropriate. Faced with things that do not follow their unconscious "script," they must cope with a high level of uncertainty and anxiety (Gudykunst, 1988). They must also learn new ways to think, feel, and behave so as to coordinate their activities with local people—a process commonly called *acculturation* (Berry, 1990; Broom & Kitsuse, 1955; Shibutani & Kwan, 1965; Spicer, 1968). In varying degrees, they go through the further process of *deculturation* (Bar-Yosef, 1968; Eisenstadt, 1954), or unlearning some of their childhood cultural patterns. New responses are adopted in situations that previously would have evoked old ones.

The experiences of acculturation and deculturation, in turn, inevitably produce *stress* (Barna, 1983; Dyal & Dyal, 1981; Kim, 1988, in press; Moos, 1976), or forms of temporary psychic disturbance and even "breakdown" in some extreme cases. As parts of their internal organization undergo changes, the strangers are temporarily in a state of disequilibrium manifested in emotional "lows" of confusion and anxiety. This state of internal flux is met by the strangers' tendency to use various "defense" mechanisms such as selective attention, denial, hostility, cynicism, avoidance, and withdrawal (Lazarus, 1966, p. 262). All of these hinder the activities of acculturation and deculturation necessary for adapting to the host milieu. Such cross-cultural stress experiences are particularly acute during the initial phase of sojourn or immigration, as indicated by the difficulties and disruptions that have been documented amply in "culture shock" and related studies (cf. Adler, 1972/1987, 1975; Furnham, 1984, 1988; Furnham & Bochner, 1986; Oberg, 1960; Torbiorn, 1982).

Yet, the stress they experience works as a necessary impetus for new learning. In time, most strangers manage to achieve an increasing level of *adaptation* to their changed circumstances. Prompted by the cross-cultural challenges they face in the host environment, they work out new ways of handling their daily activities. In the ongoing relationship with the environment, strangers gradually modify their cognitive, affective, and behavioral habits, and acquire increasing proficiency in expressing themselves, understanding the host cultural practices, and coordinating their thoughts and actions with those of the local people. The interplay of stress and adaptation further leads to an internal *growth*—a transformation in the direction of increased functional fitness and psychological health vis-à-vis the host environment (Kim, 1988, in press; Kim & Ruben, 1988).

Stress, then, is part-and-parcel of strangers' adaptation and growth experiences over time. Together, the three elements—stress, adaptation, and growth—help define the nature of strangers' psychological movement forward and upward in the direction of increased chances of success in meeting the demands of the host environment. The *stress-*

adaptation-growth dynamic plays out not in a smooth, arrowlike linear progression, but in a cyclic and continual "draw-back-to-leap" pattern similar to the movement of a wheel: Each stressful experience is responded to by strangers with a "draw back" (or temporary disintegration and disengagement), which then activates their adaptive energy to help them reorganize themselves and "leap forward" (temporary integration or engagement). The process is simultaneously disturbing and promising, as it involves continual new cultural learning (acculturation) and unlearning of the old culture (deculturation). As strangers work through the setbacks, they come out "victorious" with an increased capacity to see others, themselves, and situations in a new light and to face new challenges yet to come.

THE ROLE OF COMMUNICATION

Given the developmental process of cross-cultural adaptation, we now turn to the phenomenon of differential adaptation rates, or speeds at which different strangers adapt. Even though most strangers in alien cultures have demonstrated an impressive capacity to manage cross-cultural challenges successfully without damaging their overall integrity, some do suffer more from an extreme inability to find ways to overcome the challenges they face in the host environment. Some may strongly resist the idea of having to change their original cultural habits, thereby raising psychological barriers to work against their own adaptive change. Others may be ill-equipped to deal with states of panic, causing a prolonged damage to their internal system, often leading to a more extreme withdrawal and alienation from the host society or a decision to return to their home country prematurely.

The fact that individual strangers differ in their adaptation rate leads to the question, "Why do some strangers adapt faster than others?" or "Given the same length of time, why do some strangers attain a higher-level of adaptation?" To explain differential adaptative changes, we need to focus on the fact that *communication* — the process of encoding and de-coding verbal and nonverbal information — lies at the heart of cross-cultural adaptation. After all, adaptation occurs through the communication interface between the stranger and the host milieu — just as the natives acquire their capacity to function in their society through communicative interactions throughout their lives. It is only through communication that strangers can come to learn the significant symbols of the host culture, and thereby to organize their own and others' activities successfully.

Strangers' communication activities can be conceptualized into two basic, inseparable dimensions — personal communication and social communication. According to Ruben (1975), *personal communication* is the "private symbolization" activities — all the internal mental activities that occur that dispose and prepare people to act and react in certain ways in actual social situations. Personal communication is linked to *social communication* when two or more individuals interact with one another, knowingly or not. Ruben (1975) defines social communication as the process underlying "inter-subjectivization," a phenomenon that occurs as a consequence of "public symbolization." As Geyer (1980) suggests, the personal communication process can be compared to the "off-line functions" of computer systems, which interfaces with the environment through the "on-line functions" of input-out transactions of messages (p. 32).

Personal Communication

Personal (or intrapersonal) communication refers to the mental processes by which we organize ourselves in and with our sociocultural milieu, developing ways of seeing, hearing, understanding, and responding to the environment. As Ruben (1975) states, "Personal communication can be thought of as sensing, making-sense-of, and acting toward the objects and people in one's milieu. It is the process by which the individual informationally fits himself into . . . his environment" (pp. 168–169). In the context of cross-cultural adaptation, personal communication can be examined in terms of *host communication competence,* that is, the overall internal capacity of a stranger to decode and encode information in accordance with host cultural practices of communication. For the natives, such communication competence has been acquired from so early in life and has been so internalized into their personal communication system that, by and large, it operates automatically and unconsciously. For strangers, however, such competence has to be acquired and cultivated through trial and error. Until they have acquired a sufficient level of host communication competence, they are handicapped in their ability to relate to the host environment.

The many elements of host communication competence—from the knowledge about the host language and social norms to the ability to manage interpersonal relationships to solve impending problems at work—can be grouped into three categories that have been commonly employed in the study of communication competence: cognitive, affective, and operational or behavioral (Kim, 1991; Spitzberg & Cupach, 1984). *Cognitive competence* includes such internal capacities as the knowledge of the host language and culture including the history, social institutions, worldviews, beliefs, laws and regulations, social norms, and rules of interpersonal conduct. Knowledge of the host language goes beyond linguistics—phonetics, syntax, and vocabulary—to include the pragmatic uses of the language in everyday life. This also entails command of the many subtle nuances in the way the language is used and interpreted by the natives in various formal and informal contexts of social engagement. Linguistic and cultural knowledge is accompanied by a development of cognitive complexity (Kelly, 1955; Schroder, Driver, & Streufert, 1967), that is, the structural differentiation and integration in an individual's information-processing capacity. During the initial phase of adaptation, a stranger's perception of the host culture is relatively simple; gross stereotypes are salient in the perception of the unfamiliar environment. As the stranger learns more about the host culture, however, his or her perception becomes more refined and complex, enabling him or her to participate in the host social processes meaningfully.

Along with cognitive competence, *affective competence* facilitates cross-cultural adaptation by providing an emotional and motivational capacity to deal with the various challenges of living in the host environment. Included in this competence is strangers' willingness and determination to learn the host language and culture. Also included is their ability to understand and empathize with the emotional and aesthetic sensibilities of the natives, and to participate in the local experiences of joy, excitement, humor, and triumph as well as sadness, anger, and despair. Relatedly, strangers' affective competence also include their attitude toward the host society and toward themselves. Strangers who feel positive and respectful toward the host society are likely to maintain less psychological distance from and prejudice against its members, compared with other strangers who may resent or look down on the natives, or who have little genuine interest in understanding them. In addition, strangers lack affective competence when they feel insecure or confused about themselves and their own cultural identity, and thus feel "marginal" (Stonequist, 1935).

Closely linked with cognitive and affective competence is *operational competence* or the "enactment tendencies" (Buck, 1984, p. vii). The operational competence of strangers refers to their capacity to enact, or express, their cognitive and affective experiences outwardly when communicating with others. Strangers' operational competence, as such, is based on their cognitive and affective competence. As they try to come up with a mental plan for action, they must base the decision on their current knowledge about the host culture and language, the degree of sophistication in their information-processing capacity, as well as their ability and motivation to appreciate, empathize, and participate in, the emotions and aesthetic experiences of the natives. As such, strangers' operational competence enables them to choose a "right" combination of verbal and nonverbal activities to meet the demands of daily activities—from managing face-to-face encounters, initiating and maintaining relationships, seeking appropriate information sources to solve various problems they may encounter, to finding ways to succeed in accomplishing their goals.

Social Communication

Strangers' host communication competence is directly and reciprocally connected to their participation in the social communication activities of the host society (Kim, 1986, 1987). On the one hand, their social communication activities are constrained by their capacity to communicate effectively and appropriately in the host cultural context. On the other hand, every social communication event offers them an opportunity to cultivate their communication competence — cognitively, affectively, and behaviorally. In particular, *interpersonal communication,* or direct face-to-face interactions, helps strangers to secure vital information and insight into the mindsets and behaviors of the local people. In interacting with natives face to face, strangers also learn about themselves — how they think, express themselves, and respond to others. As such, strangers' interpersonal communication activities can not only enable them to carry out their daily tasks but also provide them with needed emotional support and points of reference for checking and validating their own thoughts and actions.

In addition to interpersonal communication, strangers' adaptation is facilitated by attending to the *mass communication* activities of the host society. Mass communication refers to social communication that occurs through various forms of media such as radio, television, newspaper, magazine, movie, art, music, and drama. By engaging in such communication activities, strangers interact with their host milieu without direct involvement in relationships with specific individuals, and thereby expand the scope of their adaptive learning beyond the immediate social context with which they come into contact. In transmitting messages that reflect the aspirations, myths, work and play, and specific issues and events of the host society, the media explicitly or implicitly convey the worldviews, beliefs, values, mores, and norms of the culture. Of strangers' various mass communication experiences, exposure to information-oriented mass media messages such as newspapers, magazines, television news, and other informational programs have been found to be particularly associated with greater adaptation, when compared to more entertainment-oriented media contents (Kim, 1976).

The adaptation function of mass communication should be particularly significant during the initial phase of resettlement. During this phase, strangers have not yet developed a level of host communication competence sufficient to develop interpersonal relationships with local people. The communication experiences in direct face-to-face contact with the natives can be intensely frustrating or intimidating to many strangers. They may feel awkward and out of place in relating to others, and the direct negative feedback from another person can be too overwhelming for the strangers to have pleasurable interpersonal encounters with the natives. Under such circumstances, strangers naturally tend to withdraw from such direct contact and, instead, prefer mass media as an alternative, pressure-free channel through which elements of the host culture can be experienced (Kim, 1979b; Ryu, 1978).

ENVIRONMENT

The adaptation function of strangers' personal and social (interpersonal, mass) communication cannot be fully understood in isolation from the conditions of the new sociocultural milieu. Societies and communities present different environments for strangers, who, in turn, may be more successful in adapting to a particular environment than to others. Many of the environmental characteristics can be grouped into two: (1) host receptivity and conformity pressure and (2) ethnic group strength. These factors are discussed here as crucial to defining the relative degrees of "push and pull" that a receiving society offers to strangers, thereby influencing their cross-cultural adaptation.

Host Receptivity and Conformity Pressure

The *receptivity* of the host environment refers to the degree to which the environment is open to, welcomes, and accepts strangers into its social communication networks and offers them various forms of informational, technical, material, and emotional support. Receptivity incorporates the meaning of other similar terms such as *interaction potential* (Kim, 1979a) or *acquaintance potential* (Cook, 1962) that have been employed to refer to the access that strangers have to the host social communication processes. A given environment can be more receptive toward certain groups of strangers while unwelcoming toward certain others. For example, Canadian visitors arriving in a small town in the United States are likely to find a large receptive environment. On the other hand, the same town may show less receptivity toward visitors from a lesser known and vastly different culture such as Turkey or Iran. Such differences in host receptivity extended to strangers can be attributed to a number of plausible reasons including: (1) the nature of the relationships, friendly or hostile, between the host country and the stranger's home country; (2) the degree of cultural and ideological difference and incompatibility between the two cultures; (3) the perceived or actual status or power of the stranger's home country and culture; (4) the perceived or actual economic, social, and political standing (or merit) of the stranger's ethnic group within the host society; (5) the perceived or actual economic, social, and political threat to the host society brought about by the stranger's ethnic group; and (6) the racial or ethnic prejudice predominantly held by the society against strangers in general or that particular group. These and related factors, individually and interactively, help shape the degree of receptivity a particular host environment offers a particular stranger.

Along with receptivity, *conformity pressure* (Zajonc, 1952) on the part of the host society influences the social communication activities of strangers. Here, conformity pressure refers to the extent to which the society challenges strangers to adopt the normative patterns of the host culture. Different host environments show different levels of acceptance of strangers and their ethnic characteristics. Heterogeneous and "open" host environments such as the United States generally tend to hold a more pluralistic political ideology concerning ethnic differences and thereby exert less pressure on strangers to change their habitual ways. Even within a country, ethnically more heterogeneous metropolitan areas tend to demand that strangers conform less than do small, ethnically homogeneous rural towns. Even within a city, certain neighborhoods may be more homogeneous and thus expect more conformity from strangers.

Ethnic Group Strength

Another important aspect of an environment that influences strangers' cross-cultural adaptation is the strength of their ethnic group relative to the host society at large. Ethnic groups differ in their relative status or power within the host society. An insight into ethnic group strength has been provided by sociologists Clarke and Obler (1976), who proposed a three-stage theory of ethnic group development. The first is economic adjustment, which is ongoing from the arrival of the group until they become an integral part of the permanent economy. Second, community building, or the development of community leadership and institutional resources used to assert the ethnic group's identity and interests, corresponds to the concept of "institutional completeness" (Breton, 1964). Third, is the period of political growth and aggressive self-assertion needed to strengthen the collective ethnic identity and common interests of the group as a whole.

In social psychology, the phenomenon of ethnic group strength has been discussed in terms of *ethnolinquistic vitality*. In research on the influences of the social milieu and the collective consequences of fluency in a second language, Giles, Bourhis, and Taylor (1977) have suggested that the influence of ethnolinguistic vitality on individual behavior can be defined in terms of three structural variables: (1) the status of a language in a community, (2) the absolute and relative number of its locuters, and (3) the institutional support (governmental services, schools, mass media) for the ethnic language. Ethnolinguistic vitality as an objective environmental condition has been linked to what Giles et al. (1977) propose as the "subjective ethnolinguistic vitality" or perceived legitimacy of the position of one's ethnic group. For example, speakers who perceive a subordinate position of their group as legitimate are likely to adjust their communication behaviors and "converge" to those of the dominant outgroup.

These views offer implications for the role of ethnic group strength in a stranger's adaptation to the host society. Integrating these views, we can describe the strength of an ethnic group in terms of one or more of the following elements: (1) ethnolinguistic vitality; (2) economic status, (3) institutional completeness, and (4) ethnic political activism. Frequently, these community characteristics are closely associated with the size of the ethnic population and the historical "maturity" of the community in the host society. From this view, Cuban Americans in Miami, Florida, for example, have an ethnic community that is stronger than a smaller Russian community in Chicago. Exceptions are seen, for example, in the small group of Americans who recently began working and living in Czechoslovakia. In spite of the fact that this group is small and unorganized, their political and economic status or prestige as Americans renders it a strength as an ethnic group.

Because a stronger ethnic group provides its members with a stronger subculture and offers many of the vital services to its members, it is likely to facilitate the cross-cultural adaptation of strangers during the initial phase. In the long run, however, a strong ethnic community is likely to discourage their adaptation to the host society, as it encourages ethnolinguistic maintenance. A strong ethnic community is further likely to exert a subtle or explicit pressure to conform to the ethnic community norms and thereby discourage an active participation in the host social communication activities. Empirical evidence supporting this observation is provided by Rosenthal and Hrynevich (1985), who found that, in Australia, the Greek immigrant community is more cohesive and organized than is the Italian, and that Greek-Australian adolescents were reported to place more emphasis than did Italian-Australian adolescents on their ethnic identity and maintaining their heritage. In addition, according to

the investigators, the Greek-Australian adolescents placed less emphasis on adapting to the dominant Australian culture at large. Similar results were reported by Driedger (1976), who found in Canada that an ethnic group's status within the society interacted with its institutional completeness, so that groups high on both status and institutional completeness (French and Jews) had the strongest sense of ethnic identity.

PREDISPOSITION

The adaptation of strangers is influenced not only by the environmental condition, but also by the condition of the strangers. Each stranger begins the cross-cultural adaptation process with a different set of preexisting characteristics. Some may begin with enthusiasm, while others may find themselves "forced" into it by unavoidable circumstances. Some may be young, while others may feel they are too old to make changes in their lifetime habits. The internal conditions with which they begin their life in the host society help set the parameters for their own subsequent adaptive changes. The various ways in which strangers differ in their internal conditions can be organized into three categories: (1) preparedness, (2) ethnicity, and (3) personality. Together, these characteristics help define the degree of a stranger's "adaptive potential" (Kim, 1979a) or "permeability" (De Vos, 1990) into the host environment.

Preparedness

Strangers come to their new environment with differing levels of readiness for dealing with that environment. Specifically, *preparedness* refers to the level of host communication competence prior to moving to the host culture, or the cognitive, affective, and operational abilities to participate in the social communication activities of the host society. This ranges from the knowledge of the host culture and language and the attitude toward the host society to the ability to empathize with the local people's emotional and aesthetic experiences and to perform and engage in various social situations appropriately and effectively. Influencing strangers' readiness are a wide range of formal and informal learning activities they may have had prior to moving to the host society. Included in such activities are the schooling and training in, and the media exposure to, the host language and culture, as well as their prior contacts with members of the host society. In addition, the strangers' preparedness is often influenced by whether their move to the host society is voluntary or involuntary and for how long. Voluntary, long-term immigrants, for example, are likely to enter the host society with a greater readiness and willingness for making necessary changes in themselves compared to the temporary visitors who unwillingly relocate for reasons other than their own volition.

Ethnicity

Strangers arrive in a host society with different cultural, racial, and linguistic backgrounds (McGuire et al., 1978). The term *ethnicity,* is used here as inclusive of the various characteristics of strangers that make them distinctive as a people. Japanese sojourners and immigrants, for example, bring to a given host society common physical, linguistic, and cultural features that are different from, say, Mexicans or French. Such ethnic characteristics play a crucial role in the cross-cultural adaptation process. It does so by affecting the ease or difficulty with which the stranger is able to develop the communication competence in a given host society, and to participate in its social communication activities. For instance, many of the Japanese business executives in the United States are likely to face a greater amount of challenge in overcoming their language barrier than are their British counterparts. In particular, strangers' physical features (such as height, skin color, and facial features) play an important role in their cross-cultural adaptation by influencing the degree to which the natives are psychologically prepared to welcome them into their interpersonal networks. Compared to Colombian visitors, for instance, Caucasian visitors from Ireland would be more readily accepted in the United States.

The ethnicity of a given stranger influences strangers' adaptation process in two interrelated manners. First, each presents its particular level of linguistic and cultural barriers for the stranger to overcome in order to develop the host communication competence and participate in the host social communication activities. Second, each creates a certain level of psychological barrier (or affinity) in the minds of the natives, which, in turn, affects the natives' receptivity toward the stranger. As such, strangers embark on their cross-cultural adaptation process with certain levels of "advantage" (or "handicap") simply due to their ethnic characteristics (Phinney & Rosenthal, 1992, p. 145).

Personality

Along with ethnic backgrounds, strangers enter a host environment with a *personality,* a set of enduring traits of sensibilities. They begin the challenges of the new environment within the context of their existing personality, which serves as the basis upon which they pursue and internalize new experiences with varying degrees of success. Of particular interest to the present theory are those personality resources that would help facilitate strangers' adaptation by enabling them to endure stressful challenges and to maximize new learning—both of which are essential to their adaptive transformation.

Openness is such a personality trait. In the systems theoretical perspective, openness is defined as an internal posture that is receptive to new information (Gendlin, 1962, 1978). Openness, like a child's innocence, enables strangers to minimize their resistance and to maximize their willingness to attend to the new and changed circumstances. Openness further enables strangers to perceive and interpret various events and situations in the new environment as they occur with less rigid, ethnocentric judgments. As a theoretical concept, openness is accepted as varying in degree among strangers. It is a broad term that incorporates other similar but more specific concepts such as "flexibility," "open-mindedness," and "tolerance for ambiguity." Also, openness embraces the level of optimism and affirmative orientation in strangers' basic outlook on life in general, as well as their fundamental "self-trust" in the face of adverse circumstances. As such, it is a dimension of personality that enables strangers to continually seek to acquire new cultural knowledge, to cultivate greater emotional and aesthetic sensitivity, and to expand the range of their behavioral repertoire. All of these are vital to actively participating in and accommodating to the demands of the host milieu.

Strength is an additional personality trait closely related to openness. Along with openness, the present theory recognizes personality strength as vital to cross-cultural adaptation. Like openness, the concept of personality strength is a broad concept that represents a range of interrelated personality attributes such as resilience, risk-taking, hardiness, persistence, patience, elasticity, and resourcefulness. As such, personality strength means the inner quality that absorbs "shocks" from the environment and bounces back without being seriously damaged by them. Low levels of personality strength are reflected in tendencies to be shy, fearful, and easily distressed by uncertain or stressful situations. On the other hand, individuals with high levels of personality strength tend to be stimulated by new challenges and remain effervescent and confident.

Strength, together with openness, helps define the personality predisposition that serves as the inner resource that helps strangers "push" themselves in their adaptation process. Strong and open strangers are less likely to give up easily and are more likely to take risks willingly under challenging situations in the host society. They are better equipped to work toward developing host communication competence because they would continually seek new learning and new ways to handle their life activities. In doing so, they are better able to make necessary adjustments in themselves to facilitate their own intercultural transformation and growth. Serious lack of these qualities, on the other hand, weakens their adaptive capacity, and thereby

works as self-imposed psychological barriers against their own cross-cultural adaptation process (Hettema, 1979).

AN INTEGRATION

In essence, cross-cultural adaptation is about change in individuals. As sojourners and immigrants undergo continual communication activities in the host society, they will become more functionally fit and psychologically healthier vis-à-vis the environment. The internal change process is possible because of the stress-adaptation-growth dynamic strangers experience as they try to cope with and manage the challenges of the unfamiliar milieu. In doing so, strangers acculturate (learn) new cultural patterns, as well as deculturate (unlearn) at least some of the old cultural patterns. All of the learning and unlearning takes place via communication interfaces between the stranger and the host environment. As such, the quantity and quality of communication strangers have with the host environment critically contribute to the different rates of adaptive change they achieve in a given period of time.

Realistically, no stranger's adaptation can ever be complete no matter how long he or she interacts with the host environment. Most of them, nonetheless, do make a workable adaptation given a sufficient amount of time, as they continue to interact with the host environment. Gradually the strangers are transformed so that they become increasingly capable of managing their daily activities. At the heart of interactive adaptation lies the communication process linking the individual strangers to the host sociocultural milieu. The importance of communication to adaptation cannot be overemphasized. Acquisition of communication competence by the stranger is not only instrumental to all other aspects of his or her life activities, but also vital for the host society if it is to effectively accommodate diverse elements and, at the same time, maintain the necessary societal unity and strength. As long as common channels of communication remain, consensus and patterns of concerted action will persist in the society. As Mendelsohn (1964) describes it, communication makes it possible to merge minority groups into one democratic social organization of commonly shared ideas and values.

The dimension of personal communication—the cognitive, affective, and operational components of strangers' host communication competence—serves as the very "engine" that "moves" them along the adaptive journey. Inseparably linked with the host communication competence is the dimension of social communication, through which strangers participate in the ongoing social milieu of the host society. As strangers participate in various forms of interpersonal and mass communication activities, they are both encouraged and pressured by the host environment as well as by their ethnic community environment. The three environmental conditions—host receptivity, conformity pressure, and ethnic group strength—help define the relative degree of "push and pull" that a receiving society offers to strangers. An environment offering an optimal influence on strangers' adaptation is viewed as one in which the native population welcomes and supports the strangers while expecting them to conform to the local norms. At the same time, an optimal environment includes an ethnic community that provides informational, material, and emotional support during the initial transition period, without exerting social pressure on the strangers against their adaptation to the host society at large. In facing such environmental forces, the strangers' own readiness, ethnicity, and personality strength and openness set the initial parameters for the subsequent unfolding of their own cross-cultural experiences.

Should strangers choose to become successfully adapted, they must, above all, be prepared and willing to face the stressful experiences of coping with the uncertainties and anxieties in an unfamiliar milieu. They must concentrate on acquiring new cultural communication practices and putting aside some of the old ones. They must recognize the importance of host communication competence as the fundamental mechanism by which they adapt successfully. Through openness and strength of personality, strangers can better overcome temporary setbacks and embrace cultural differences. They must also maximally participate in the interpersonal and mass communication processes of the host society. Through active participation, the strangers can in turn develop a more realistic understanding of, and appreciation for, the native culture and ways of life.

Strangers, however, cannot accomplish their adaptive goals alone. The process of adaptation is an interactive process of "push and pull" between them and the new environment. Indeed, members of the host society can facilitate strangers' adaptation by maximizing its receptivity toward them—by accepting their original ethnicity and providing them with a supportive interpersonal communication milieu. The host society can more actively encourage strangers to adapt through communication training programs. Such training programs should facilitate the strangers' acquisition of the host communication competence. In addition, the ethnic community can play a significant adaptive function for the strangers in their early stages of resettlement. Ethnic communities can provide support systems to assist new arrivals in coping with the stresses and initial uncertainties and can guide them toward effective adaptation. At the same time, however, strangers must realize that exclusive and prolonged reliance on their ethnic community alone would delay and eventually limit the opportunities for them to adapt to the host milieu in the long run.

Few strangers can escape cross-cultural adaptation completely. Adaptation is a phenomenon that occurs naturally and that is desired by most, if not all, strangers as long as they are engaged in direct and continual communication interactions with the host environment. Through interactions, strangers acquire at least some degree of new cultural learning (acculturation) and, at the same time, lose some of the original cultural patterns (deculturation)—regardless of the ideological viewpoint they themselves may have concerning their future in the host society. As such, the ongoing debate between "assimilationists" (who adhere to the "melting-pot" view) and "cultural pluralists" (proponents of conversation of ethnicity) loses its relevance. It is too simplistic to view adaptation and ethnicity maintenance as mutually incompatible or exclusive phenomena and argue that strangers choose one or the other. They are two sides of the same coin; they are interrelated and inseparable. What is important is that both the assimilationist and the pluralist perspectives must acknowledge that at least some adaptive changes do occur in individuals over time and that such changes do accompany a certain degree of loss of ethnicity.

All in all, the cross-cultural adaptation process is a joint, interactive venture between the conditions of strangers themselves and those of the new environment. Out of the dynamic interface arises a fluctuating psychic movement of stress, adaptation, and growth. In time, most strangers advance in the direction of an increasingly intercultural realm of personhood, where they are better able to see both the host culture and the home culture with clarity, depth, and appreciation. Cross-cultural adaptation is fundamentally a special manifestation of the ever-present human capacity—the capacity to face challenges, learn from them, and evolve into a greater self-integration. We are never a "finished product."

REFERENCES

Adler, P. (1972/1987). "Culture Shock and the Cross-Cultural Learning Experience." In L. Luce and E. Smith (Eds.), *Toward Internationalism* (pp. 24–35). Cambridge, MA: Newbury.

Adler, P. (1975). "The Transition Experience: An Alternative View of Culture Shock." *Journal of Humanistic Psychology, 15*(4), 13–23.

Bar-Yosef, R. (1968). "Desocialization and Resocialization: The Adjustment Process of Immigrants." *International Migration Review, 2,* 27–42.

Barna, L. (1983). "The Stress Factor in Intercultural Relations." In D. Landis and R. Brislin (Eds.), *Handbook for Intercultural Training: Vol. II. Issues in Training Methodology* (pp. 19–49). New York: Pergamon Press.

Berry, J. (1990). "Psychological Acculturation: Understanding Individuals Moving Between Cultures." In R. Brislin (Ed.), *Applied Cross-Cultural Psychology* (pp. 232–253). Newbury Park, CA: Sage.

Breton, R. (1964). "Institutional Completeness of Ethnic Communities and the Personal Relations of Immigrants." *American Journal of Sociology, 70,* 193–205.

Brislin, R. (1981). *Cross-Cultural Encounters.* Elmsford, NY: Pergamon.

Broom, L., and Kitsuse, J. (1955). "The Validation of Acculturation: A Condition to Ethnic Assimilation." *American Anthropologist, 62,* 44–48.

Buck, R. (1984). *The Communication of Emotion.* New York: Guilford.

Clarke, S., and Obler, J. (1976). "Ethnic Conflict, Community-Building, and the Emergence of Ethnic Political Traditions in the United States." In S. Clarke and J. Obler (Eds.), *Urban Ethnic Conflict: A Comparative Perspective* (pp. 1–34). Chapel Hill, NC: University of North Carolina.

Cook, S. (1962). "The Systematic Analysis of Socially Significant Events." *Journal of Social Issues, 18*(2), 66–84.

De Vos (1990). "Self in Society: A Multilevel, Psychocultural Analysis." In G. De Vos and M. Suarez-Orozco (Eds.), *Status Inequality: The Self in Culture* (pp. 17–74). Newbury Park, CA: Sage.

Driedger, L. (1976). "Ethnic Self-Identity: A Comparison of Ingroup Evaluations." *Sociometry, 39,* 131–141.

Dyal, J., and Dyal, R. (1981). "Acculturation, Stress and Coping." *International Journal of Intercultural Relations, 5*(4), 301–328.

Eisenstadt, S. (1954). *The Absorption of Immigrants.* London: Routledge & Kegan Paul.

Furnham, A. (1984). "Tourism and Culture Shock." *Annals of Tourism Research, 11*(1), 41–57.

Furnham, A. (1988). "The Adjustment of Sojourners." In Y. Kim and W. Gudykunst (Eds.), *Cross-Cultural Adaptation* (pp. 42–61). Newbury Park, CA: Sage.

Furnham, A., and Bochner, S. (1982). "Social Difficulty in a Foreign Culture: An Empirical Analysis of Culture Shock." In A. Furnham and S. Bochner (Eds.), *Cultures in Contact* (pp. 161–198). Elmsford, NY: Pergamon.

Furnham, A., and Bochner, S. (1986). *Culture Shock: Psychological Reactions to Unfamiliar Environments*. London: Mathuen.

Gendlin, E. (1962). *Experiencing and the Creation of Meaning*. New York: The Free Press.

Gendlin, E. (1978). *Focusing*. New York: Everest House.

Geyer, R. (1980). Alienation Theories: A General Systems Approach. New York: Pergamon.

Giles, H., Bourhis, R., and Taylor, D. (1977). "Towards a Theory of Language in Ethnic Group Relations." In H. Giles (Ed.), *Language, Ethnicity, and Intergroup Relations* (pp. 307–348). London: Academic.

Gudykunst, W. (1988). "Uncertainty and Anxiety." In Y. Kim and W. Gudykunst (Eds.), *Theories in Intercultural Communication* (pp. 123–156). Newbury Park, CA: Sage.

Gudykunst, W., and Kim, Y. (1992). *Communicating with Strangers: An Approach to Intercultural Communication* (2nd ed). New York: McGraw-Hill.

Hettema, P. (1979). *Personality and Adaptation*. New York: North-Holland.

Kelly, G. (1955). *The Psychology of Personal Constructs: Vol. 1. A Theory of Personality*. New York: Norton.

Kim, Y. (1979a). "Toward an Interactive Theory of Communication-Acculturation." In B. Ruben (Ed.), *Communication Yearbook III* (pp. 435–453). New Brunswick, NJ: Transaction Books.

Kim, Y. (May 1979b). "Mass Media and Acculturation." Paper presented at the annual conference of the Eastern Communication Association, Philadelphia, PA.

Kim, Y. (1986). "Understanding the Social Context of Intergroup Communication: A Personal Network Approach." In W. Gudykunst (Ed.), *Intergroup Communication* (pp. 86–95). London: Edward Arnold.

Kim, Y. (1987). "Facilitating Immigrant Adaptation: The Role of Communication and Interpersonal Ties." In T. Albrecht and M. Adelman (Eds.), *Communicating Social Support* (pp. 192–211). Newbury Park, CA: Sage.

Kim, Y. (1988). *Communication and Cross-Cultural Adaptation: An Integrative Theory*. Clevedon, England: Multilingual Matters.

Kim, Y. (1991). "Intercultural Communication Competence: A Systems-Theoretic View." In S. Ting-Toomey and F. Korzenny (Eds.), *Cross-Cultural Interpersonal Communication* (pp. 259–275). Newbury Park, CA: Sage.

Kim, Y. (in press). *Becoming Intercultural: An Integrative Theory of Cross-Cultural Adaptation*. Newbury Park, CA: Sage.

Kim, Y., and Ruben, B. (1988). "Intercultural Transformation." In Y. Kim and W. Gudykunst (Eds.), *Theories in Intercultural Communication* (pp. 299–321). Newbury Park, CA: Sage.

Lazarus, R. (1966). *Psychological Stress and the Coping Process*. St. Louis, MO: McGraw-Hill.

McGuire, W., McGuire, C., Child, P., and Fujioka, T. (1978). "Salience of Ethnicity in the Spontaneous Self-Concepts as a Function of One's Ethnic Distinctiveness in the Social Environment." *Journal of Personality and Social Psychology, 36,* 511–520.

Mendelsohn, H. (1964). "Sociological Perspective on the Study of Mass Communication." In L. Dexter and D. White (Eds.), *People, Society, and Mass Communication* (pp. 29–36). New York: The Free Press.

Moos, R. (1976). *Human Adaptation: Coping with Life Crisis*. Lexington, MA: Heath.

Oberg, K. (1960). "Culture Shock: Adjustment to New Cultural Environments." *Practical Anthropology, 7,* 170–179.

Phinney, J., and Rosenthal, M. (1992). "Ethnic Identity in Adolescence." In G. Adams, T. Gullota, and R. Montemayor (Eds.), *Adolescent Identity Formation* (pp. 145–172). Newbury Park, CA: Sage.

Rosenthal, D., and Hrynevich, C. (1985). "Ethnicity and Ethnic Identity: A Comparative Study of Greek-, Italian-, and Anglo-Australian Working-Class Adolescents." *Journal of Youth and Adolescence, 12,* 117–135.

Ruben, B. (1975). "Intrapersonal, Interpersonal, and Mass Communication Process in Individual and Multi-Person Systems." In B. Ruben and J. Kim

(Eds.), *General Systems Theory and Human Communication* (pp. 164–190). Rochelle Park, NJ: Hayden.

Ryu, J. (May 1978). "Mass Media's Role in the Assimilation Process: A Study of Korean Immigrants in the Los Angeles Area." Paper presented to the annual meeting of the International Communication Association, Chicago.

Schroder, H., Driver, M., and Streufert, S. (1967). *Human Information Processing: Individuals and Groups Functioning in Complex Social Situations.* New York: Holt, Rinehart & Winston.

Shibutani, T., and Kwan, K. (1965). *Ethnic Stratification: A Comparative Approach.* New York: Macmillan.

Simmel, G. (1908/1950). "The Stranger." In K. Wolff (Ed. and Trans.), *The Sociology of Georg Simmel.* New York: Free Press.

Spicer, E. (1968). "Acculturation." In D. Sills (Ed.), *International Encyclopedia of the Social Sciences* (pp. 21–27). Macmillan & Free Press.

Spitzberg, B., and Cupach, W. (1984). *Interpersonal Communication Competence.* Beverly Hills, CA: Sage.

Stonequist, E. (1935). "The Problem of the Marginal Man." *American Journal of Sociology, 41,* 1–12.

Taft, R. (1977). "Coping with Unfamiliar Cultures." In N. Warren (Ed.), *Studies in Cross-Cultural Psychology: Vol. 1* (pp. 121–153). London: Academic Press.

Torbiorn, I. (1982). *Living Abroad: Personal Adjustment and Personnel Policy in the Overseas Setting.* New York: John Wiley & Sons.

Zajonc, R. (1952). "Aggressive Attitude of the 'Stranger' as a Function of Conformity Pressures." *Human Relations, 5,* 205–216.

CONCEPTS AND QUESTIONS FOR CHAPTER 7

1. If you were going to travel abroad, what preparation would you make to ensure the best possible opportunity for effective intercultural communication?

2. What specific suggestions can you make that could improve your ability to interact with other ethnic or racial groups in your community? How would you go about gaining the necessary knowledge and experience?

3. What are the six stumbling blocks in intercultural communication discussed by LaRay Barna? How can you learn to avoid them?

4. Can you think of any mannerisms, behaviors, or styles that the North American businessperson might reflect that could stifle successful intercultural communication?

5. Why is it important to locate similarities between cultures as well as differences?

6. What are some basic differences between cultures that value individualism and those that value collectivism?

7. What does Ting-Toomey mean when she talks about "face loss" and "face gain"?

8. Can you think of examples of conflict situations that entailed both substantive and relational issues?

9. What are some differences between direct and indirect conflict styles?

10. What does Lee mean when she speaks of "new conversational rules"?

11. What is an enthymeme? How do enthymemes relate to intercultural humor?

12. According to Sue, what are three major barriers that often prevent organizations from incorporating diversity into their training programs?

13. What are three important "competency tools" that can facilitate diversity training?

14. Can you think of intercultural examples of what Spitzberg refers to as "individual, episodic, and relational" systems?

15. Can you think of specific examples of what Spitzberg calls "appropriate and effective" message behavior? How might appropriateness and effectiveness differ from culture to culture?

16. What is acculturation? Why is acculturation often a difficult task for immigrants?

17. What does Kim mean by the phrase "ethnic group strength"?

18. What does Kim mean when she writes, "Strangers cannot accomplish their adaptive goals alone"?

8

Ethical Considerations: Prospects for the Future

"Everything that looks to the future elevates human nature."

— Gillett

The goal of this book is to help you understand intercultural communication and to assist you in appreciating the issues and problems inherent in interactions involving people from foreign and alien cultures. To this end we have examined a series of diverse essays that presented a variety of variables operable during intercultural encounters. But what we have looked at up to now is what is already known about intercultural communication. We now shift our emphasis and focus on two issues that are much harder to pin down. These are the ethical considerations that must be inherent in intercultural interactions and the future prospects of this developing field of study. In short, this chapter examines some of the following questions: What do we need to accomplish, what may we expect to accomplish, what philosophical issues must we deal with, and what kinds of personalities must we develop if we are to improve the art and science of intercultural communication during the remainder of this century?

To set the tone for this final chapter, we begin with an essay that deals with the ethical questions centering around how we go about judging the actions of people from different cultures. As you would suspect, this issue is indeed a difficult and complex one. In "The Evaluation of Culture," Elvin Hatch tackles this question with a rather optimistic premise. He maintains that "it is possible to arrive at a general principle for evaluating institutions without assuming that ours is a superior way of life." Admittedly, such an idealistic stance is not easy to put into operation. Yet Hatch does offer a framework that can be used to evaluate cultures. His philosophy is predicated on three generalizations: first, that humanistic values seem to be widespread among most human beings; second, that humanistic values are better than ethnocentrism— even though it too is universal; and third, that much of what we evaluate with regard to other cultures falls out of the scope of humanistic philosophy, and therefore we need a way to judge and evaluate such things as sexual mores, kinship relations, styles of leadership, and the like. Hatch offers some guidelines to help us make these ethical decisions.

Our next essay, by Young Yun Kim, is based on one of the basic themes of this book—that today's interconnected and fast-changing world demands that we all change our assumptions about culture and our individual places within that culture. Recognizing these changes, Kim advances a philosophical orientation that she calls *intercultural personhood*. For Kim, intercultural personhood combines the key attributes of Eastern and Western cultural traditions, and she presents a model using these attributes. This model takes into account basic modes of consciousness, cognitive patterns, personal and social values, and communication behavior. The notion of intercultural personhood also leads us into the concept of the multicultural person as set forth in the next article.

The next selection in this chapter is by Rosita D. Albert and Harry C. Triandis. It calls our attention to a topic that is bound to generate a great deal of discussion in the next few years. It is the issue of multicultural education. The concept behind multicultural education is rather simple to state but very complex and controversial to implement. Advocates of multicultural education maintain that pupils who are culturally different from the majority need multicultural education so that they can learn to function effectively in their own culture as well as in the majority culture. Some educators believe that students of the dominant culture can also benefit from education that asks them to learn about the patterns of perception, values, and behaviors of culturally different classmates. Because this philosophy is not without its critics, Albert and Triandis discuss some of the objections to multicultural education. They also point out three different approaches to teaching multicultural education and some advantages and disadvantages of each. Regardless of your personal feeling about multicultural education, it is a topic that is going to be debated by all people who are interested in the large influx of new minorities seeking an education in the United States educational system.

Our final selection, while touching on some of the same issues discussed by Hatch in the first essay of this chapter, extends the importance of ethical judgments beyond those suggested by him. David W. Kale not only grants the significance of developing an ethical orientation toward other cultures, but he offers a number of specific challenges for the future. It is the future that is made real by Kale as he presents us with current examples, ranging from our role in the rain forests of Brazil to events taking place in the Soviet Union.

Kale begins by acknowledging that most people feel uncomfortable addressing cultural beliefs about what is right and wrong. He reminds us that most of these beliefs are at the very foundation of our lives and our culture. Yet even with this uneasiness, increased contact with diverse cultures, combined with the problems that can occur when cultures clash, demand that we must examine the issues associated with questions of right and wrong. To assist us in that examination, Kale asks that we begin by looking at five interrelated issues directly associated with any evaluation of intercultural ethics: (1) a definition of communication ethics, (2) cultural relativity versus universal ethics, (3) the concept of spirit as a basis for intercultural ethics, (4) peace as the fundamental value in intercultural ethics, and (5) a universal code of ethics in intercultural communication. Kale amplifies the fifth issue by advancing a specific code, which he urges us to follow, predicated on four principles that should guide the actions of *ethical communicators*: (a) Address people of other cultures with the same respect that they would like to receive themselves, (b) seek to describe the world as they perceive it as accurately as possible, (c) encourage people of other cultures to express themselves in their uniqueness, and (d) strive for identification with people of other cultures.

It might be well to view Kale's exploration, and all the other selections in this chapter, as only a sampling of the many issues that confront those involved in intercultural communication. The field is relatively new and the challenges are so varied that it is impossible to accurately predict future directions. Our intent in this chapter, therefore, is simply to introduce you to a few of the concepts that await further discussion in the 1990s.

One final note: Much of what we offer in this chapter is subjective, and, to some, might even appear naive. Neither we nor the authors of the articles apologize for maintaining that in intercultural contacts each person should aim for the ideal. What we introduce here are some suggestions for developing new ways of perceiving oneself and others. In so doing we can all help make this complex and shrinking planet a more habitable and peaceful place for its nearly five and one-half billion residents.

The Evaluation of Culture

ELVIN HATCH

If relativism is in such difficulty as a moral philosophy, is there any role at all left for it to play in our thinking? I believe so, and one of my purposes . . . is to indicate what that is. There is another purpose: Given that much of ethical relativism has been nudged aside by recent events, I want to advance a set of principles that will cover much of the ground that relativism has relinquished. These principals constitute a framework that we can use in evaluating cultures, including our own.

The first principle is that there is merit to the criticism that relativism has been accompanied by a conservative bias. What is at issue here is the relativist claim that all cultures or institutions are equally valid or fitting: Anthropologists tended to assume that the mere presence of a cultural trait warrants our valuing it. Elizabeth Colson has put the case quite simply; she wrote, "Ethnographers have usually presented each social group they study as a success story. We have no reason to believe that this is true" (1976, p. 264). A people may get by with inadequate solutions to their problems even judging by their own standards. For example, if the people are genuinely interested in ensuring the productivity of their gardens, they will find innovations like crop rotation and fertilization more effective than human sacrifice—although they will not have the statistical evidence to realize this (cf. Bagish 1981, pp. 12–20).

Second, a general principle is at hand for judging the adequacy of institutions. It may be called the hu-

From Elvin Hatch, *Culture and Morality: The Relativity of Values in Anthropology* (New York: Columbia University Press, 1983), 133–144. Copyright © 1983 Columbia University Press. Reprinted by permission of the publisher and author.

manistic principle or standard, by which I mean that the well-being of people ought to be respected. The notion of well-being is a critical aspect of the humanistic principle, and three points can be made with respect to it. For one, I assume that human well-being is not a culture-bound idea. Starvation and violence, for example, are hardly products of Western thought or a function of Western thinking, although they may be conceived in a peculiarly Western idiom. Starvation and violence are phenomena that are recognized as such in the most diverse cultural traditions. Another is that the notion of human well-being is inherently value-laden, and concepts of harm and beneficence are inseparable from it: it seems impossible to imagine the idea of human well-being divorced from moral judgments of approval and disapproval. Whereas such notions as sky or earth may conceivably be held in purely neutral terms in a given culture, such ideas as hunger and torture cannot be. It is even reasonable to argue that the *point* of morality, as a philosophical if not a sociological issue, is to promote the well-being of others (Warnock 1971, esp. pp. 12–26). Finally, the notion of human well-being, when used as the central point of morality, serves to root moral questions in the physical, emotional, and intellectual constitution of people. It may be that any rigorous attempt to work out the content of morality will have to include an analysis of such notions as human wants, needs, interests, and happiness.

The humanistic principle can be divided into two parts. First is Redfield's point about humaneness, that it is good to treat people well, or that we should not do one another harm. We can judge that human sacrifice, torture, and political repression are wrong, whether they occur in our society or some other. Similarly, it is wrong for a person, whatever society he or she may belong to, to be indifferent toward the suffering of others. The matter of coercion, discussed earlier, fits here, in that we may judge it to be wrong when some members of a society deliberately and forcefully interfere in the affairs of other people. Coercion works against the well-being of those toward whom it is directed. Second is the notion that people ought to enjoy a reasonable level of material existence: we may judge that poverty, mal-

nutrition, material discomfort, human suffering, and the like are bad. These two ideas may be brought together to form one standard since both concern the physical well-being of the members of society, and the difference between them is that the former refers to the quality of interpersonal relations, and the latter to the material conditions under which people live.

The humanistic principle may be impossible to define very tightly; it may even be that the best we can do to give it shape is to illustrate it with examples as I have done here. And surely it is difficult to apply in actual situations. Yet these are not good reasons to avoid making judgments about the relative merit of institutions or about the desirability of change. Although we may do harm by expressing judgments across cultural boundaries, we may do as much or more harm by failing to do so.

The orthodox relativist would perhaps argue that there is no humanistic moral principle that we can use for this purpose, in that notions like harm and discomfort are quite variable from one culture to the next. Pain and personal injury may even be highly valued by some people. For example, the Plains Indian willingly engaged in a form of self-torture that a middle-class American could hardly tolerate. The Indians chopped off finger joints and had arrows skewered through their flesh; tied to the arrows were cords, by which the sufferer dragged buffalo skulls around the village. Some American Indians were also reported to have placed a very high value on bravery, and the captive who withstood torture without showing pain was highly regarded by the enemies who tormented him.

Yet cases like these do not make the point that notions of pain and suffering are widely variable. Following this same logic one could say that middle-class Americans value pain since they willingly consent to surgery, and the man or woman who bears up well is complimented for his or her strength of character. The Indian who was tortured to death would surely have preferred a long and respectable life among his people to the honorable death that came to him. The Plains Indian who engaged in self-torture was trying to induce a vision (in our idiom, a hallucination) for the power and advantages it was believed such an experience would bring. The pain was a means to an end, and surely was not seen as a pleasurable indulgence to look forward to. The difference between middle-class Americans and Plains Indians on this point could be a difference in judgments of reality and not a difference in values—the American would not believe that the vision has the significance attributed to it by the Indian, so he or she would not submit to the pain. Similarly, the plains warrior might not believe in the efficacy of surgery and might refuse to suffer the scalpel.

The widespread trend among non-Western peoples to want such material benefits as steel knives and other labor-saving devices is a clear indication that all is not relative when it comes to hard work, hunger, discomfort, and the like. Cultural values may be widely different in many ways, but in this sphere at least, human beings do seem to have certain preferences in common.

The Yanomamö are an instructive case, for here is a people who do not seem to share the humanistic value I am suggesting. The level of violence and treachery in this society suggests that their regard for pain and suffering is demonstrably different from what I am arguing is the norm among human beings. Yet this is not clearly the case either: Individuals in Yanomamö society are more willing than middle-class Americans to inflict injury on others, yet they want to avoid injury to themselves. Why else would the wife flee in terror when her husband comes at her with a machete, and why else would a village seek refuge from enemies when it is outnumbered and weak? The Yanomamö seem rather to be a case in which we are warranted in making a value judgment across cultural boundaries: They do not exhibit as much regard for the well-being of other persons as they have for themselves, and this can be judged a moral error.

Does this point about the generality of the humanistic principle among human beings not make the same mistake that Herskovits, Benedict, and other relativists were accused of making, which is to derive an "ought" from an "is"? My argument is not quite that simple, for it has two parts. First is the

generalization that the humanistic value seems to be widespread among human beings. Second, I am making the moral judgment (quite separately from the empirical generalization) that this is an estimable value to hold, or that it warrants acceptance—in contrast, say, to another widespread value, ethnocentrism, which is not meritorious even if it is universal.

A third principle in the scheme that I propose is that a considerable portion of the cultural inventory of a people falls outside the scope of the humanistic standard mentioned above. In other words, once we have considered those cultural features that we can reasonably judge by this standard, a large portion remains, and it consists of those items which have little if anything to do with the strictly practical affairs of life and which then cannot be appraised by practical considerations. Included are sexual mores, marriage patterns, kinship relations, styles of leadership, forms of etiquette, attitudes toward work and personal advancement, dietary preferences, clothing styles, conceptions of deity, and others. Some of these nonappraisable features are closely linked to others that are, in that there are always nonessential cultural accouterments or trappings associated with institutions that are important on practical grounds. Western medicine provides a surfeit of examples. Health care clearly falls within the orbit of the humanistic principle, yet much of the medical system in the United States is hardly necessary for health's sake, including the rigid social hierarchy among doctors and nurses and the traditional division of labor between them. Successful health care systems can assume different forms from the one exhibited in this country. It is essential (but difficult) to keep in mind this division between what is essential and what is not in such matters as medicine, for otherwise civilization will tend to pack a good deal of unnecessary cultural baggage along with the genuinely useful features when it sets out to share its advantages with others.

Relativism prevails in relation to the institutions that fall outside the orbit of the humanistic principle, for here a genuine diversity of values is found and there are no suitable cross-cultural standards for evaluating them. The finest reasoning that we or anyone else can achieve will not point decisively to the superiority of Western marriage patterns, eating habits, legal institutions, and the like. We ought to show tolerance with respect to these institutions in other societies on the grounds that people ought to be free to live as they choose.

This leads to the fourth principle: Is it possible to identify any areas of culture in which we may speak of improvement? Are there any criteria that will produce a hierarchical ordering of societies that we may say represents a pattern of advance? Or is the distinction between primitive and civilized societies but an expression of our cultural bias?

The first criterion that comes to mind is Redfield's and Kroeber's, according to which civilization has brought a more humane existence, a higher level of morality to mankind, inasmuch as people treat one another better in complex societies. This judgment is very difficult to accept today, however. Recent events have left most of us with considerable ambivalence about Western democracy, to cite one instance. Politicians seem too often to be both incompetent and dishonest, and to be willing to allow private economic interests to influence programs and policies at all levels. Similarly, there is a very strong distrust of the power and intentions of big business, which seems to set its policies chiefly by looking at its margin of profit. The risk of producing a dangerous product is calculated by assessing how much the company is liable to lose in lawsuits relative to its profits, and not by considering the real dangers to human life. Much of the difficulty of assessing moral advance is that this is a highly impressionistic matter. The ledger sheets on which we tote up the pluses and minuses for each culture are so complex that summary calculations of overall moral standing are nearly meaningless. Perhaps the most one can say about whether or not there has been moral advance is that it is impossible to tell—but that it is not very likely.

It is important to distinguish between this conclusion and Herskovits'. According to him, we cannot speak of progress in this sphere because any humanistic principle we might use will necessarily be culture-bound; we have no yardstick to measure with. My point is that we do have a suitable yardstick, but that there are so many measures to take in each culture that the sum total is too complicated to assess.

Another criterion for gauging improvement is the material well-being of people: disregarding whether or not the members of society behave well or ill toward one another, can we say that the material conditions of life have gotten better with civilization? In pursuing this question I need to digress somewhat. The issue of material improvement places the focus on economics and technology, and also on such technical knowledge as that which is provided by medical and agricultural research. So we need first to ask if it is possible to arrive at an objective and meaningful hierarchy of societies based on these features. Herskovits questioned that we can. To him, an ordering of societies according to our criteria of economic production and technological complexity will merely reflect our cultural perspective and not some fundamental principle of general significance to all peoples.

Herskovits' argument is off the mark. On one hand, the criteria of economic complexity and technological sophistication are objective in the sense that they are definable by reference to empirical features that are independent of our culture. For example, the intensity and scale of economic transactions have a physical aspect which is identifiable from other cultural perspectives than ours, and the same is true of such measures as the amount of food produced per farm worker.[1] What is more, the social hierarchy that results from the use of these criteria has historical significance: One would be astonished, say, to discover evidence of complex forms of agricultural production in the Paleolithic. But on the other hand, and even more important, this is a meaningful hierarchy, in that the point of this ordering of societies would not be lost on people from other cultures; it would be meaningful to them because they see the value of increasing agricultural productivity, the use of bicycles (and automobiles), the availability of running water, and the like. It is surely the case that non-Western peoples all over the world are more interested in the products of Western industrial production than they are in the intricacies of Australian kinship, and are more likely to incorporate such Western innovations as fertilizers and matches into their cultures than they are the particulars of the Australian system of marriage and descent. This is an important message we get from the post-World War II drive for economic development among the newly independent nations.

There is a danger in using people's perceptions of the relative superiority of economic and technological systems as a test for the meaningfulness of this social hierarchy, because not all of the world's populations agree about what it is that is good about development and modernization. For example, Burma and Iran are highly selective in the changes they will accept, and at least some very simple societies (like the Andaman Islanders) want little if any change.

There is another way to establish the hierarchy without relying completely and directly on people's opinions. However another society may feel about what they do or do not want with regard to development, the economic and technological relationship between them and Western societies is asymmetrical. It is true that the fully developed nations rely on the less developed ones for natural resources like oil, but processed goods, and both economic and technological innovations, flow chiefly to and not away from the societies that are lower on the scale. To take an extreme case, there is little in the sphere of technology and economics that the Australian aborigines or Andaman Islanders can offer to the developed nations, whereas the reverse is not true. For example, some of the most isolated Andaman Islanders occasionally find empty gasoline drums washed upon their shore. They cut these in half and use them as enormous cooking pots (Cipriani 1966, p. 52). It is unthinkable that this relationship could be reversed—that we would find some technological item from their cultural inventory to be especially useful in our everyday lives. It is true that we may value their pottery or other artifacts as examples of primitive art, but the use we have for such items is esthetic, not practical, and consequently such items are of a different order from the gasoline drums that the Andamanese find so useful.

In noting this asymmetry I do not mean that cultures which are lower in the hierarchy do not have a very sophisticated technical knowledge of their own (they must in order to survive), and in this sense "they have something to teach us," as Brokensha and Riley remark concerning the Mbeere of Kenya. "In fact," these writers continue, "Mbeere and other folk-belief systems contain much that is based on extremely accurate, detailed and thoughtful observations, made over many generations" (1980, p. 115). It is easy to depreciate or ignore the cultural practices and ideas of another society, say, when assisting them in the process of development. In particular, it is tempting to want to replace their traditional practices with "modern" ones in wholesale fashion, instead of building on or incorporating the indigenous knowledge in helping to bring about change. Nevertheless, the presence of such useful knowledge in indigenous systems of thought does not negate the fundamental asymmetry that exists among societies or the hierarchy which the asymmetry suggests.

The pluralistic notion of development . . . has bearing on the way we should conceive this hierarchy. The idea that Third World countries should become more and more like Western industrial societies is subject to criticism, and it may be preferable to define development differently for each society according to the interests of the people concerned and the nature of their economic and ecological conditions. A people may have achieved as much development as they need and want without embarking on a trajectory of industrial "growth" in the Western sense. In other words, the hierarchy I am suggesting does not represent a set of stages through which all societies will necessarily want to pass. It is simply a ranking of cultural systems according to degrees of economic complexity, technological sophistication, and the like.

Yet this begs a crucial question. Is it not true that to suggest this hierarchy is to imply that the societies higher on the scale are preferable? Does the existence of the hierarchy not mean that the societies that fall below would be better off if only they could manage to come up to a higher level of economic complexity and technological sophistication?

The discussion now comes back to the issue that prompted this digression. Can we say that the social hierarchy we have arrived at represents improvement or advance? The response unfortunately is as indecisive as the one concerning moral progress, and for the same reason. On one hand, civilization has brought a lower infant mortality rate due to better diet, hygiene, and medical care; less vulnerability to infectious disease for the same reasons; greater economic security due to increased economic diversification; less danger from local famine due to improved systems of transportation and economic organization; greater material comfort due to improved housing, and the like. But on the other hand, we have pollution, the horrors of modern warfare, and the boredom and alienation of factory work, to name a few. On one hand we have labor-saving devices like automatic dishwashers, but on the other hand we have to spend our lives on a treadmill to pay for them. The tally sheet is simply too complicated to make an overall judgment. It is not at all clear that other people should want to become like Western civilization.

What we can say about the hierarchy is that the nations that fall toward the upper end of the scale have greater resources than the others. They have better technical knowledge from which the entire world may benefit—knowledge about hygiene, diet, crop rotation, soils, and the like. They also have the physical capacity to undertake programs of assistance when other societies are interested. Yet the higher civilizations also have the capacity to do far greater harm. The industrial system has exploited the powerless, ravaged the environment, meddled in the affairs of other countries, and conducted war in ways that the simpler societies never dreamed of. Even when we set out altruistically to help others we often mismanage the effort or misunderstand what it is we should do. Just as it is not at all clear that industrial civilization provides a happier or more fulfilling life for its members, so it is not clear whether its overall influence on those below it in

the hierarchy has been to their detriment or benefit. This is a pessimistic age, and at this point it is difficult to suppress a strong sense of despair on this score.

The place of Western civilization in the hierarchy of human societies is very different from what it was thought to be by Victorian anthropologists, who saw the differences among societies at bottom as a matter of intelligence: Civilization is more thoughtful and shows greater sense than the lower societies, and it provides a happier and more benign mode of living; savages would embrace our way of life if they had the intelligence to understand it, for their institutions are but imperfect specimens of our own. Clearly this is inadequate. Many areas of life cannot be judged by standards that apply across cultural boundaries, for in many respects cultures are oriented in widely different directions. Still, all people desire material comfort and security, and in this sense Western civilization is distinguished from other cultures. The relationship among societies in this respect is one of asymmetry. Just as we may do far more harm to others than they can do to us, so we may do them more good, and we have the obligation to share the material advantages our civilization has to offer. Yet this asymmetry should not be confused with superiority. As a total way of life ours may not be preferable to others, and we need not try to turn them into copies of Western civilization.

An important implication follows from these conclusions: It is possible to arrive at a general principle for evaluating institutions without assuming that ours is a superior way of life. Herskovits for one seems to have believed that this could not be done, and that any general moral principle we might advance would express our own cultural bias and would tacitly make us appear to occupy a position superior to the rest. But this is not so. The matter of arriving at general moral principles and of how we measure up to these principles are two very separate issues.

The idea of ethical relativism in anthropology has had a complicated history. Through the 1930s the discipline expressed an overwhelming confidence in the notion, a confidence that was fortified by the empirical findings about the variability of moral values from culture to culture. And relativism was thought to be an idea of signal importance, for it could be used in world affairs and would contribute to peace and human understanding. But suddenly and with firm conviction, relativism was swept aside. It had all been a mistake.

Was relativism completely mistaken? After we have excised what is unacceptable, is there something left, a residuum of some kind, that still warrants approval? Certainly the relativists' call for tolerance contained an element that is hard to fault. This is the value of freedom: People ought to be free to live as they choose, to be free from the coercion of others more powerful than they. Equally fundamental, perhaps, is the message that relativism contained about the place of Western civilization among human societies. Rejected was the smug belief in Western superiority that dominated anthropological thinking during the 1800s. Just as the universe has not looked the same since the Copernican revolution, so the world and our place in it has not looked the same since ethical relativism appeared at about the turn of the century.

NOTE

1. The World Bank and other organizations commonly use a number of objective measures in assessing such matters as poverty, physical quality of life, and economic and social development. For example, see Lizer 1977, and World Bank 1979, pp. 117–188.

REFERENCES

Bagish, H. (1981). *Confessions of a Former Cultural Relativist.* (Second Annual Faculty Lecture, Santa Barbara City College) Santa Barbara: Santa Barbara City College Publications.

Benedict, R. (1934). *Patterns of Culture.* Boston: Houghton Mifflin.

Benedict, R. (1934). "Anthropology and the Abnormal." *Journal of General Psychology, 10,* 59–82.

Brokensha, D. and Riley, D. (1980). "Mbeere Knowledge of Their Vegetation, and Its Relevance for Development (Kenya)" in D. Brokensha, D. Warren, and O. Werner, eds., *Indigenous Knowledge Systems and Development.* Lanham, Md.: University Press of America.

Cipriani, L. (1966). *The Andaman Islanders,* edited and translated by D. Cox. New York: Praeger.

Colson, E. (1976). "Culture and Progress," *American Anthropologist, 78,* 261–271.

Herskovits, M. (1947). *Man and His Works.* New York: Knopf.

Herskovits, M. (1973). *Cultural Relativism: Perspectives in Cultural Pluralism.* New York: Vintage Books.

Kroeber, A. (1917). "The Superorganic," *American Anthropologist, 19,* 163–213.

Kroeber, A. (1948). *Anthropology,* rev. ed. New York: Harcourt Brace.

Kroeber, A. (1952). *The Nature of Culture.* Chicago: University of Chicago Press.

Redfield, R. (1953). *The Primitive World and Its Transformations.* Ithaca: Cornell University Press, 1957 ed.

Redfield, R. (1957). "The Universally Human and Cultural Variable," *Journal of General Education, 10,* 150–160.

Intercultural Personhood: An Integration of Eastern and Western Perspectives

YOUNG YUN KIM

Today we live in a world of global community. Rigid adherence to the culture of our youth is neither feasible nor desirable. The tightly knit communication web has brought cultures of the world together closer than ever before. Strong cultural identity is more a nostalgic conception than a realistic assessment of our attributes. Indeed, we live in an exciting time in which we are challenged to examine ourselves critically. As Toffler (1980) states in *The Third Wave*, "Humanity faces a quantum leap forward. It faces the deepest social upheaval and creative restructuring of all time. Without clearly recognizing it, we are engaged in building a remarkable new civilization from the ground up" (p. 10).

Reflecting the interactive realities of our time, a number of attempts have been made to explore ideologies that are larger than national and cultural interests and that embrace all humanity. As early as 1946, Northrop, in *The Meeting of the East and the West*, proposed an "international cultural ideal" to provide intellectual and emotional foundations for what he envisioned as "partial world sovereignty." Among contemporary critics of culture, Thompson (1973) explored the concept of "planetary culture" in which Eastern mysticism was integrated with Western science and rationalism. Similarly, Elgin (1981) proposed "voluntary simplicity" as an emerging global "common sense" and a practical life style to reconcile the willful, rational approach to life of the West and the holistic, spiritual orientation of the East.

In this frame of ideas, the present writer has presented the concept "intercultural person" as an image of future human development (Kim, 1988; Kim & Ruben, 1988). The intercultural person represents a type of person whose cognitive, affective, and behavioral characteristics are not limited but are open to growth beyond the psychological parameters of his or her own culture. Other similar terms such as "international" (Lutzker, 1960), "universal" (Walsh, 1973), and "multicultural" (Adler, 1982) person have also been used to project an essentially similar image of personhood with varying degrees of descriptive and explanatory utility.

To envision how we may renew ourselves and grow beyond our own cultural conditioning in this intercultural world, we need to comprehend and to seek meaning and order in the complexity of the fundamental human condition. Our task is to look at both Eastern and Western cultures in their "original form" rather than in their contemporary cultural patterns. The linking back to the origin not only enables us to see the respective foundation of the two cultures clearly, but also creates the possibility of recognizing and bringing into play new lines of development. In this essay, we will examine the basic cultural *a priori* or world view of East and West, concepts deeply rooted in the religious and philosophical traditions of the two cultural groups. Once we rediscover the cultural roots of Eastern and Western worlds, we will then be able to develop a broad perspective on the ground-level human conditions without being restricted by our own cultural "blind spots." Such a pan-human understanding will enable us to construct an image of intercultural personhood—a way of life that is called for by the increasingly intercultural realities of our world.

EASTERN AND WESTERN WORLD VIEWS

Traditional cultures throughout Asian countries including India, Tibet, Japan, China, Korea, and Southeast Asia have been profoundly influenced by such religious and philosophical systems as Buddhism, Hinduism, Taoism, and Zen. On the other hand, the Western European nations have historically followed the Greek and the Judaeo-Christian traditions. Of course, any attempt to present the cultural *a priori* of these two broadly categorized civilizations inevitably sacrifices specific details and the uniqueness of variations within each group. No two individuals or groups are identical in their beliefs and behaviors, and whatever we characterize about one culture or cultural group must be thought of as variable rather than as rigidly structured. Nevertheless, there are several key factors in the two perspectives that distinguish each group clearly from the other. To examine these factors is to indicate the equally evident interconnectedness that ties different nations together to constitute the Eastern or Western cultural group.

The characterization of Eastern and Western world views in this section and throughout this article is based on the observations of many authors. Of the existing comparative cultural analyses, Northrop's *The Meeting of the East and the West* (1946/1966), Gulick's *The East and the West* (1963), Nakamura's *Ways of Thought of Eastern Peoples* (1964), Oliver's *Communication and Culture in Ancient India and China* (1971), Capra's *The Tao of Physics* (1975), and Elgin's *Voluntary Simplicity* (1981) have provided a particular influence.

Universe and Nature

One of the most fundamental ways culture conditions our existence is through explicit and implicit teachings about our relationship to the nature of the universe and to the non-human natural world. Traditional Eastern and Western perspectives diverge significantly in this basic premise. As Needham (1951) observed in his article, "Human laws and the laws of nature in China and the West," people in the West have been dominated by the view that the universe was initially created, and has since been externally controlled, by a divine power.

In this sense, the Western view of the universe is characteristically dualistic, materialistic, and lifeless. The Judaeo-Christian tradition sets God apart from this reality; having created it and set it into motion, God could then be viewed as apart from His creation. The fundamental material of the universe is thought to be elementary particles of matter that interact with one another in a predictable fashion. Furthermore, since the foundation of the universe is seen as consisting of matter, it is viewed as essentially non-living. It is seen as an inanimate machine in which humankind occupies a unique and elevated position among the sparse life-forms that exist. Assuming a relatively barren universe, it seems only rational that humans exploit the lifeless material universe (and the lesser life-forms of nature) on behalf of those who live most intensely—humankind itself.

On the other hand, the Eastern view is profoundly holistic, dynamic, and spiritual. From the Eastern perspective, the entirety of the universe is a vast, multidimensional, living organism consisting of many interrelated parts and forces. The universe is conscious and engaged in a continuous dance of creation: the cosmic pattern is viewed as self-contained and self-organizing. It unfolds itself because of its own inner necessity and not because it is "ordered" to by any external volitional power.

What exists in the universe is a manifestation of a divine life force. Beneath the surface appearance of things, an ultimate reality is continuously creating, sustaining, and infusing our worldly experience. The all-sustaining life force that instant by instant creates our manifest universe is not apart from ourselves or our worldly existence. Rather, it is continuously creating and intimately infusing every aspect of the cosmos—from its most minute details to its most grand scale features.

Thus, the Eastern view reveres the common source out of which all things arise, and at the same time recognizes that everything in this dynamic world is fluid, ever-changing, and impermanent. In Hinduism, all static forms are *maya*, that is, they exist only as illusory concepts. This idea of the impermanence of all forms is the starting point of Buddhism. The Buddha taught that "all compounded things are impermanent," and that all suffering in the world arises from our trying to cling to fixed forms—objects, people, or ideas—instead of accepting the world as it moves. This notion of the impermanence of all forms and the appreciation of the aliveness of the universe in the Eastern world view is strongly contrasted with the Western emphasis on the visible forms of physical reality and their improvement through social and material/technological progress.

Knowledge

Since the East and West have different cosmic patterns, we can expect a different approach to knowledge. In the East, because the universe is a harmonious organism, there is a lack of any dualism in the cosmic pattern as well as in epistemological patterns. The Eastern view places an emphasis on perceiving and knowing things and events holistically and synthetically, rather than analytically. Furthermore, the ultimate purpose of knowledge is to transcend the apparent contrasts and to "see" the interrelatedness and underlying unity of all things.

When the Eastern mystics tell us they experience all things and events as manifestations of a basic oneness, this does not mean they consider all things equal. They recognize the individuality of things but at the same time are aware that all differences and contrasts are relative within an all-embracing unity. The awareness that all opposites are polar, and thus a unity, is seen as one of the highest aims of knowledge. Suzuki (1968) writes, "The fundamental idea of Buddhism is to pass beyond the world of opposites, a world built up by intellectual distinctions and emotional defilements, and to realize the spiritual world of non-distinction, which involves achieving an absolute point of view" (p. 18).

Since all opposites are interdependent, their conflict can never result in the total victory of one side, but will always be a manifestation of the interplay between the two sides. In the East, therefore, a virtuous person is not one who undertakes the im-possible task of striving for the "good" and eliminating the "bad," but rather one who is able to maintain a dynamic balance between the two. Transcending the opposites, one becomes aware of the relativity and polar relationship of all opposites. One realizes that good and bad, pleasure and pain, life and death, winning and losing, light and dark, are not absolute experiences belonging to different categories, but are merely two sides of the same reality—extreme aspects of a single whole. This point has been emphasized most extensively by the Chinese sages in their symbolism of the archetypal poles, yin and yang. And the opposites cease to be opposites in the very essence of Tao. To know the Tao—the illustrious way of the universe—is the ultimate purpose of human learning.

This holistic approach to knowledge in the East emphasizes understanding concepts and the aesthetic components of things by intuition. A concept by intuition is one of complete meaning and is something immediately experienced, apprehended, and contemplated. Northrop (1946/1966) described it more accurately as the "differentiated aesthetic continuum." Within the total differentiated aesthetic continuum, there is no distinction between subjective and objective. The aesthetic continuum is a single all-embracing continuity. The aesthetic part of the self is also an essential part of the aesthetic object, whether it is a person or a flower. With respect to the immediately apprehended aesthetic nature, the person is identical with the aesthetic object; only with respect to his differentiation is the self other than the aesthetic object.

In this orientation, Taoism pursues the all-embracing, immediately experienced, emotionally moving aesthetic continuum with respect to its manifestations in the differentiated, sensed aesthetic qualities of nature. Confucianism pursues the all-embracing aesthetic continuum with respect to its manifestations in human nature and its moral implications for human society. The Taoist claim is that only by seeing the aesthetic continuity in its all-embracing-ness as ultimate and irreducible will we properly understand the meaning of the universe and nature. The Confucian claim, similarly, is that only if one takes the same standpoint, that of recognizing the all-embracing aesthetic whole to be an ultimate and irreducible part of human nature, will we have a compassionate feeling for human beings other than ourselves.

The ultimate, irreducible, and undifferentiated aesthetic continuum is the Eastern philosopher's conception of the constituted world. The differentiations within it, such as particular scenes, events, or persons, are not the irreducible atomic identities, but merely arise out of the ultimate undifferentiated reality of the aesthetic continuum. Sooner or later, they fade back into it again and thus are transitory and impermanent. When Eastern sages insist that one must become self-less, they mean that the self consists of two components: one, a differentiated, unique element, distinguishing one person from any other person; and the other, the all-embracing, aesthetically immediate, emotionally moving, compassionate, undifferentiated component. The former is temporary and transitory, and the cherishing of it, the desire for its immortality, is the source of suffering and selfishness. The part of the self that is not transitory but rather immortal is the aesthetic component, and it is identical not merely in all persons, but in all aesthetic objects throughout the universe.

While the East has concentrated its mental processes on the all-embracing, holistic, intuitive, aesthetic continuum, the Western pursuit of knowledge has been based on the doctrine of a dualistic world view. Since in the West the world and its various components came into existence through the individual creative acts of a God, the fundamental question is, how can I reach out to the external inanimate world or to people? In this question, there is a basic dichotomy between the knower and the things to be known.

Along with this epistemological dualism, the West has emphasized rationality in the pursuit of knowledge. Since the Greek philosopher Plato "discovered" reason, virtually all subsequent Western thought—the themes, the questions, and the terms—exists in essence in the writing of Plato (Wei, 1980). Even Aristotle, the great hero of all anti-Platonists, was not an exception. Although Aristotle

did not have, as Plato did, a realm of eternal essences that were "really real" and that guaranteed the primacy of reason, he was by no means inclined to deny this realm.

Thus, while the East has tended to emphasize the direct experience of oneness via intuitive concepts and contemplation, the West has viewed the faculty of the intellect as the primary instrument of worldly mastery. While thinking in the East tends to conclude in more or less vague, imprecise statements with existential flexibility, Western thinking emphasizes clear and distinct ideas by means of categorization and the linear, analytic logic of syllogism. While the Eastern view expresses its drive for growth in spiritual attainment of oneness with the universe, the Western view expresses its drive for growth in material progress and social change.

Time

Closely parallel to the differing perception of the nature of knowledge, the perception and experience of time differs significantly between Eastern and Western traditions.

Along with the immediate, undifferentiated experiencing of here and now, Eastern time orientation can be portrayed as a placid, silent pool within which ripples come and go. Historically the East has tended to view material existence as cyclical and has often characterized worldly existence with the metaphor of a wheel. The "wheel of existence" is continually turning but is not seen as going in any predetermined direction. Although individuals in the world may experience a rise or fall in their personal fortunes, the lot of the whole is felt to be fundamentally unchanging. As Northrop (1946/1966) illustrated, "the aesthetic continuum is the great mother of creation, giving birth to the ineffable beauty of the golden yellows on the mountain landscape as the sun drops low in the late afternoon, only a moment later to receive that differentiation back into itself and to put another in its place without any effort" (p. 343).

Because worldly time is not experienced as going anywhere and because in spiritual time there is nowhere to go but to eternity within the now, the future is expected to be virtually the same as the past. Recurrence in both cosmic and psychological realms is very much a part of Eastern thought. Thus, the individual's aim is not to escape from the circular movement into linear and profane time, but to become a part of the eternal through the aesthetic experience of here and now and the conscious evolution of spirituality in knowing the all-embracing, undifferentiated wholeness.

Whereas the East traditionally has perceived time as a dynamic wheel with circular movements and the "now" as a reflection of the eternal, the West has represented time either as an arrow or as a moving river that comes out of a distant place and past (not here and now) and goes into an equally distant place and future (also not here and now). In this linear view of time, history is goal-directed and gradually progressing in a certain direction, such as toward universal salvation and the second coming of Christ or, in a secular form, toward an ideal state such as boundless freedom or a classless society.

Closely corresponding to the above comparison of Eastern and Western time orientations is the recent work of anthropologist Edward Hall in his *Beyond Culture* (1976) and *The Dance of Life: The Other Dimension of Time* (1983). Hall considers Asian cultures "polychronic" and Western cultures "monochronic." The polychronic system is less inclined to adhere rigidly to time as a tangible, discrete, and linear entity; it emphasizes completion of transactions here and now, often carrying out more than one activity simultaneously. On the other hand, the monochronic system emphasizes schedules, segmentation, promptness, and standardization of human activities. The traditional Eastern orientation to time depends on the synchronization of human behavior with the rhythms of nature. The Western orientation to time depends on the synchronization of human behavior with the rhythms of clocks or machines.

Communication

The historical ideologies examined so far have made the empirical content of the East and West what they are. Eastern and Western perspectives on the universe, nature, knowledge, and time are reflected in many specific activities of individuals as they relate themselves to fellow human beings—how individuals view "self" and the group and how they use verbal and nonverbal symbols in communication.

First, the view of self and identity cultivated in the Eastern view of reality is embedded within an immutable social order. People tend to acquire their sense of identity from an affiliation with, and participation in, a virtually unchanging social order. The sense of "self" that emerges from this social context is not the strongly differentiated "existential ego" of the West, but a more weakly distinct and unchanging "social ego" as pointed out in many contemporary anthropological studies. Thus, individual members of the family tend to be more willing to submit their own self-interest to that of the family. Individuals and families are often expected to submit their views to those of the community or the state.

Also, the Eastern view accepts hierarchy in social order. In a hierarchical structure, individuals are seen as differing in status although all are equally necessary for the total system and its process. A natural result of this orientation is the emphasis on authority—the authority of the parents over the children, of the grandparents over their descendants, and of the official head of the community, the clan, and the state over all its members. Authoritarianism is a distinct feature of Eastern life, not only in government, business, and family, but also in education and beliefs. The more ancient a tradition, the greater its authority.

Furthermore, the Eastern view asserts that who we are is not limited to our physical existence. Consciousness is seen as the bridge between the finite and differentiated (our sense of uniqueness) and the infinite and undifferentiated (the experience of wholeness and eternity). With sufficient training, each person can discover that who we are is correlated with nature and the divine. All are one and the same in the sense that the divine, undifferentiated, aesthetic continuum of the universe is manifested in us in nature. Through this aesthetic connection, we and nature are no other than the Tao, Ultimate Reality, the divine life force, nirvana, God.

On the other hand, the Western view—in which God, nature, and humans are distinctly differentiated—fosters the development of autonomous individuals with strong ego identification. The dualistic world view is manifested in an individual's view of his or her relationship to other persons and nature. Interpersonal relationships, therefore, are essentially egalitarian—cooperative arrangements between two equal "partners" in which the personal needs and interests of each party are more or less equally respected, negotiated, or "compromised." While the East emphasizes submission (or conformity) of the individual to the group, the West encourages individuality and individual needs to override the group. If the group no longer serves the individual's needs, it—not the individual—must be changed. Thus, the meaning of an interpersonal relationship is decided primarily by what functions each party performs to satisfy the needs of the other. A relationship is considered healthy to the extent that it serves the expected function for all parties involved. As anthropologist Frances Hsu (1981) notes, individualism is a central theme of the Western personality, which distinguishes the Western world from the non-Western.

This functional, pragmatic interpersonal orientation of the West is contrasted with the Eastern tradition—where group membership is a "given" that goes unchallenged—in which individuals must conform to the group in the case of conflicting interest. Members of the group are encouraged to maintain harmony and to minimize competition. Individuality is discouraged while moderation, modesty, and "bending" of one's ego are praised. In some cases, individual and group achievement (in a material sense) must be forsaken to maintain group harmony.

In this social milieu, the primary source of interpersonal understanding is the unwritten and often unspoken norms, values, and ritualized mannerisms relevant to a particular interpersonal context. Rather than relying heavily on verbalized, logical expressions, the Eastern communicator "grasps" the aesthetic "essence" of the communication dynamics by observing the various nonverbal and circumstan-tial cues. Intuition rather than logical reasoning plays a central role in the Eastern interpersonal understanding of how one talks, how one addresses the other and why, under what circumstances, on what topics, in what varied styles, with what intent, and with what effect. Verbal articulation is less important than nonverbal, contextual sensitivity and appropriateness. Eastern cultures favor verbal hesitance and ambiguity to avoid disturbing or offending others (Doi, 1976; Cathcart & Cathcart, 1976). Silence is often preferred to eloquent verbalization even in expressing strong compliments or affection. Sometimes individuals are suspicious of the genuineness of excessive verbal praise or compliments since, to the Eastern view, true feelings are intuitively apparent and therefore do not need to be, nor can be, articulated. In this sense, the burden of communicating effectively is shared equally between all parties involved.

While interpersonal meaning in the Eastern perspective resides primarily in the subtle, implicit, nonverbal, contextual realm and is understood aesthetically and intuitively, the Western communicative mode is primarily a direct, explicit, verbal realm, relying heavily on logical and rational perception, thinking, and articulation. Communicators are seen as distinct individuals, expressing their individuality through verbal articulation and assertiveness. Feelings inside are not to be intuitively "grasped" and understood, but to be clearly verbalized and discussed. In this sense, the burden of communicating effectively lies primarily in the speaker.

The above characterization of communication patterns in the Eastern and the Western traditions parallels the notion of "high-context" and "low-context" communication proposed by Hall (1976). Hall's conceptualization is based on empirical studies of many cultures, and it focuses on the degree to which information is either embedded in physical context or internalized in the person communicating. In this scheme, a low-context communication—more prevalent in the West than in the East—is when most of the interpersonal information is carried in the explicit, verbalized codes.

A SYNTHESIS

So far, a number of basic dimensions of cultural *a priori* in the Eastern and the Western traditions have been examined. To recapitulate, the many differences between the two civilizations stem fundamentally from their respective premises on the reality of the universe, nature, time, and communication. Based on an organic, holistic, and cyclic perspective, the East has developed an epistemology that emphasizes direct, immediate, and aesthetic components in human nature's experience of the world. The ultimate aim of human learning is to transcend the immediate, differentiated self and to develop an integrative perception of the undifferentiated universe; that is, to be spiritually one with the universe and to find the eternal within the present moment. In this view, the present moment is a reflection of the eternal, and the eternal resides in the present moment.

On the other hand, the West, founded on the cosmology of dualism, determinism, and materialism, encourages an outlook that is rational, analytic, and indirect. History is viewed as a linear progression from the past into the future. The acquisition of knowledge is not so much for spiritual enhancement as for utilization to improve the human condition.

These different world views, in turn, have been reflected in the individual conception of the self, of others, and of the group. While the East has stressed the primacy of the group over the individual, the West has stressed the primacy of the individual over the group. Interpersonally, the Eastern concept of self is less differentiated and more deeply merged in "group ego," while the West encourages distinct and autonomous individuality. Explicit, clear, and logical verbalization has been the most salient feature in the Western communication tradition, compared to the implicit, intuitive, nonverbal messages in the East.

Thus, the mechanistic Western world view has helped to systematically describe and explain the physical phenomena we encounter daily. It has proved extremely successful in technological and scientific development. The West has also learned, however, that the mechanistic world view and the corresponding communication patterns are often inadequate for the subtle, complex phenomena of human relationship—causing alienation from self and others. The West has also learned that its dualistic distinction between humanity and nature has brought about alienation from nature. The analytical mind of the West has led to modern science and technology, but it has also resulted in knowledge that is departmentalized, specialized, fragmented, and detached from the fuller totality of reality.

The East has not experienced the alienation the West has been experiencing in recent centuries. But, at the same time, the East has not developed as much science and technology since its view of the world does not promote material and social development. It does not encourage worldly activism or promote the empowerment of individuals to fundamentally change the social and material circumstances of life. Furthermore, instead of building greater ego strength and the capacity for more self-determining behavior, the Eastern view tends to work toward ego extinction (transcendence). It also tends to encourage ego dependency and passivity since people feel locked into an unchanging social order.

It should be stressed at this point that the Western emphasis on logical, theoretical, dualistic, and analytic thinking does not suggest that it has been devoid of an intuitive, direct, purely empirical, aesthetic element. Similarly, emphasizing the Western contributions (of worldly dynamism and socio-material development) does not suggest that the East has been devoid of learning in these areas. The differences are not in diametric opposition: rather they are differences in emphasis. As a result, the range of sophistication of Western contributions to the sociomaterial process far exceeds the historical learning of the East. Conversely, the aesthetic and holistic view and self-mastery of the East offers a greater depth and range of human experience vis-à-vis other humans, the natural world, and the universe, than the West.

Thus, East and West are not competing views of reality, but are, instead, intensely complementary. It needs to be emphasized that the values, behaviors, and institutions of the West should not be substituted for their Eastern counterparts, and vice versa. The West should no more adopt the world views of the East than the East should adopt the world views of the West. Our task is not to trade one view for another—thereby repeating the excesses of the other—but to integrate. Our task is to find our human unity and simultaneously to express diversity. The purpose of evolution is not to create a homogeneous mass, but to continuously unfold a diverse yet organic whole.

COMPLEMENTARITY

To explore the possibilities of integrating the two cultural traditions in a limited space, we need to take a one-sided perspective by focusing on significant limitations in either of the two and then projecting the complementary aspects from the other. In the following discussion, then, we will look critically at possible limitations of the Western cultural orientation, and attempt to integrate the complementary Eastern cultural insights.

A growing realization of limitations in the Western world view is expressed by many writers. Using the term "extension transference," Hall (1976) points out the danger of the common intellectual maneuver in which the extensional systems—including language, logic, technology, institutions, and scheduling—are confused with or take the place of the process extended. For instance, the tendency in the West is to assume that the remedy for problems with technology should not be the attempt to minimize our reliance on technology, but the development of even more technology. Burke (1974) calls this tendency of extension transference "technologism":

There lie the developments whereby "technologism" confronts its inner contradictions, a whole new realm in which the heights of human rationality, as expressed in industrialism, readily become "solutions" that are but the source of new and aggravated problems (p. 148).

Criticisms have also been directed at the rigid scientific dogmatism that insists on the discovery of "truth" based on mechanistic, linear causality and "objectivity." In this regard, Thayer (1983) comments:

What the scientific mentality attempts to emulate, mainly, is the presumed method of laboratory science. But laboratory science predicts nothing that it does not control or that is not otherwise fully determined. . . . One cannot successfully study relatively open systems with methods that are appropriate only for closed systems. Is it possible that this is the kind of mentality that precludes its own success? (p. 88)

Similarly, Hall (1976) points out that the Western emphasis on logic as synonymous with "truth" denies that part of the human self that integrates. Hall sees logical thinking as only a small fraction of our mental capabilities, and he suggests that there are many different and legitimate ways of thinking that have tended to be less emphasized in Western cultures (p. 9).

The criticisms raised by these and other critics of Western epistemology do not deny the value of rational, inferential knowledge. Instead, they relate to the error in traditional Western philosophy and science, of regarding concepts that do not fit into its mode as not equally valid. It refers to the arrogance or over-confidence of believing that scientific knowledge is the only way to discover "truth," when, in reality, the very process of doing science requires immediate, aesthetic experience of the phenomenon under investigation. Without the immediately apprehended component, the theoretical hypotheses proposed could not be tested empirically with respect to their truth or falsity and, therefore, would lack relevance to the corresponding reality. As Einstein once stated:

Science is the attempt to make the chaotic diversity of our sense-experience correspond to a logically uniform system of thought. In this system single experiences must be correlated with the theoretic structure in such a way that the resulting coordination is complete and convincing (Northrop, 1946/1966, p. 443).

In this description of science, Einstein is careful to indicate that the relation between the theoretically postulated component and the immediately experienced aesthetic component is one of correspondence.

In fact, the wide spectrum of our everyday life activities demands both scientific and aesthetic modes of apprehension: from critical analysis to perception of wholes; from doubt and skepticism to unconditional appreciation; from abstraction to concreteness; from the general and regular to the individual and unique; from the literalism of technological terms to the power and richness of poetic language, silence, and art; from casual acquaintances to intimate personal engagement. If we limit ourselves to the traditional Western scientific mode of apprehension, and if we do not value and practice the Eastern aesthetic mode, we are limiting the essential human to only a part of the full span of life activities.

One potential benefit of incorporating the Eastern aesthetic orientation into Western life is a heightened sense of freedom. As discussed earlier, the aesthetic component of human nature is in part indeterminate, and it is this aesthetic component in us that is the basis of our freedom. We would also transcend the clock-bound worldly time to the Eternal Now, the timeless moment embedded in the center of each moment. By withdrawing into the indeterminate aesthetic component of our nature, away from the determinate, transitory circumstances, we may in part overcome the pressures of everyday events and creatively integrate them as a basis for the renewal of our life spirit. The traditional Eastern practice of meditation is designed primarily for the purpose of moving one's consciousness from the determinate to the indeterminate, freer state.

Second, the Eastern view would bring the West to a heightened awareness of the aliveness of the universe. The universe is engaged in a continuous dance of creation at each instant. Everything is intensely alive—brimming with a silent, clear energy that creates, sustains, and infuses all that exists. With the expanded perspective on time, we would increase our sensitivity to rhythms of nature such as the seasons and the cycles of birth and decay.

Third, the holistic, aesthetic component, in human nature and in the nature of all things, is a factor that pacifies us. Because of its all-embracing oneness and unity, the indeterminate aesthetic continuum also tends to make us compassionate and flexible human beings with intuitive sensitivity—not only for other humans but for all of nature's creatures. In this regard, Maslow (1971) refers to Taoistic receptivity or "let-be" as an important attribute of "self-actualizing" persons:

We may speak of this respectful attention to the matter-in-paradigm as a kind of courtesy or deference (without intrusion of the controlling will) which is akin to "taking it seriously." This amounts to treating it as an end, something per se, with its own right to be, rather than as a means to some end other than itself; i.e., as a tool for some extrinsic purpose (p. 68).

Such aesthetic perception is an instrument of intimate human meeting, a way to bridge the gap between individuals and groups. In dealing with each other aesthetically, we do not subject ourselves to a rigid scheme but do our best in each new situation, listening to the silences as well as to the words of the other, and experiencing the other person or group as a whole living entity without being biased by our own egocentric and ethnocentric demands. A similar attitude can be developed toward the physical world around us, to strengthen our determination to achieve maximum ecological and environmental integrity.

TOWARD INTERCULTURAL PERSONHOOD

The movement from a cultural to an intercultural perspective in our individual and collective consciousness presents one of the most significant and exciting challenges of our time. As Toffler (1980) convincingly documented and articulated in *The Third Wave*, there are numerous indications today that point clearly to the need for us to actively pursue a new personhood and a culture that integrates Eastern and Western world views. Toffler notes:

This new culture—oriented to change and growing diversity—attempts to integrate the new view of nature, of evolution and progress, the new, richer conceptions of time and space, and the fusion of reductionism and wholism with a new causality (p. 309).

Similarly, Gebser's "integral consciousness" (Mickunas, 1973; Feuerstein, 1987) projects an emerging mode of experiencing reality in which "rational," "mythological," and other modes of consciousness are integrated.

If we are to actively participate in this evolutionary process, the dualism inherent in our thinking process, which puts materialism against spiritualism, West against East, must be transcended. The traditional Western emphasis on the intellect and on material progress need not be viewed as "wrong" or "bad." Rather, the Western orientation is a necessary part of an evolutionary stage, out of which yet another birth of higher consciousness—an integration of East and West—might subsequently evolve. We need to acknowledge that both rational and intuitive modes of experiencing life should be cultivated fully. When we realize that both types of concepts are real, ultimate, and meaningful, we also realize that Eastern and Western cultures have given expression to something in part true. The two seemingly incompatible perspectives can be related and reconciled without contradictions in a new, higher-level, intercultural perspective—one that more closely approximates the expression of the whole truth of life.

As Jantsch (1980) observes, "Life, and especially human life, now appears as a process of self-realization" (p. 307). With an openness toward change, a willingness to revise our own cultural premises, and the enthusiasm to work it through, we are on the way to cultivating our fullest human potentialities and to contributing our share in this enormous process of civilizational change. Together, the East and the West are showing each other the way.

REFERENCES

Adler, P. (1982). "Beyond Cultural Identity: Reflections on Cultural and Multicultural Man." In L. Samovar and R. Porter (Eds.), *Intercultural Communication: A Reader*, 3rd ed. Belmont, Calif.: Wadsworth.

Burke, K. (1974). "Communication and the Human Condition." *Communication, 1*, 135–152.

Capra, F. (1975). *The Tao of Physics*. Boulder, Colo.: Shambhala.

Cathcart, D., and Cathcart, R. (1976). "Japanese Social Experience and Concept of Groups." In L. Samovar and R. Porter (Eds.), *Intercultural Communication: A Reader*, 2nd ed. Belmont, Calif.: Wadsworth.

Doi, T. (1976). "The Japanese Patterns of Communication and the Concept of Amae." In L. Samovar and R. Porter (Eds.), *Intercultural Communication: A Reader*, 2nd ed. Belmont, Calif.: Wadsworth.

Elgin, D. (1981). *Voluntary Simplicity*. New York: Bantam Books.

Feuerstein, G. (1987). *Structures of Consciousness: The Genius of Jean Gebser—An Introduction and Critique*. Lower Lake, Calif.: Integral Publishing.

Gulick, S. (1963). *The East and the West*. Rutland, Vt.: Charles E. Tuttle.

Hall, E. (1976). *Beyond Culture*. Garden City, N.Y.: Anchor Press.

Hall, E. (1983). *The Dance of Life: The Other Dimension of Time*. Garden City, N.Y.: Anchor Press.

Hsu, F. (1981). *The Challenges of the American Dream*. Belmont, Calif.: Wadsworth.

Jantsch, E. (1980). *The Self-Organizing Universe*. New York: Pergamon.

Kim, Y. (1982, May). "Becoming Intercultural and Human Development." Paper presented at the annual conference of the International Communication Association. Boston, Mass.

Kim, Y. (1988). *Communication and Cross-Cultural Adaptation*. Clevedon, England: Multilingual Matters.

Kim, Y., and Ruben, B. (1988). "Intercultural Transformation: A Systems Theory." In Y. Kim and

W. Gudykunst (Eds.), *Theories in Intercultural Communication*. Newbury Park, Calif.: Sage.

Lutzker, D. (1960). "Internationalism as a Predictor of Cooperative Behavior." *Journal of Conflict Resolution, 4*, 426–430.

Maslow, A. (1971). *The Farther Reaches of Human Nature*. New York: Viking.

Mickunas, A. (1973). "Civilizations as Structures of Consciousness." *Main Currents, 29* (5), 179–185.

Nakamura, H. (1964). *Ways of Thought of Eastern Peoples*. Honolulu: University of Hawaii Press.

Needham, J. (1951). "Human Laws and Laws of Nature in China and the West." *Journal of the History of Ideas*, XII.

Northrop, F. [(1946) 1966]. *The Meeting of the East and the West*. New York: Collier Books.

Oliver, R. (1971). *Communication and Culture in Ancient India and China*. New York: Syracuse University Press.

Suzuki, D. (1968). *The Essence of Buddhism*. Kyoto, Japan: Hozokan.

Thayer, L. (1983). "On 'Doing' Research and 'Explaining' Things." *Journal of Communication, 33* (3), 80–91.

Thompson, W. (1973). *Passages About Earth: An Exploration of the New Planetary Culture*. New York: Harper & Row.

Toffler, A. (1980). *The Third Wave*. New York: Bantam Books.

Walsh, J. (1973). *Intercultural Education in the Community of Man*. Honolulu: University of Hawaii Press.

Wei, A. (1980, March). "Cultural Variations in Perception." Paper presented at the Sixth Annual Third World Conference, Chicago, Ill.

Intercultural Education for Multicultural Societies: Critical Issues

ROSITA D. ALBERT
HARRY C. TRIANDIS

This article focuses on the need for intercultural education in multicultural societies. In the first section, we begin by presenting evidence for the notion that individuals from a given cultural group develop behavior patterns and subjective cultures (Triandis 1972) that are functional for their particular environment. We then indicate that when, due to such factors as immigration, colonization, etc., such individuals are forced to function in a different cultural environment, they are likely to experience stress, alienation, and other negative consequences.

In the second section, we propose that an important objective of education should be to prepare such individuals to function effectively in *both* their culture of origin and in their new culture. We further suggest that all children in a multicultural society should have the benefit of intercultural education. We propose that teachers, as well as pupils, should be made aware of cultural differences and should learn something about the patterns of behavior, values, and expectations of persons from other cultures. We present evidence from our own research, as well as that of other researchers, which illustrates the need for this kind of knowledge on the part of teachers.

From the *International Journal of Intercultural Relations* 9 (1985), 391–397. Reprinted by permission of the publisher and the author. Professor Albert teaches at the University of Minnesota and Professor Triandis teaches at the University of Illinois.

In the third part of the article, we present a number of objections which have been raised to intercultural education and propose some refutations based on current work.

In the fourth section, we present three approaches for teaching culture and discuss the advantages and disadvantages of each. The attributional approach (a cognitive approach) is presented in some detail because it is especially suited for use in educational settings. We cite evidence of its effectiveness from evaluation studies done by ourselves and others.

We conclude with a section on the implications of intercultural education.

ETHNICITY, BEHAVIOR, AND SUBJECTIVE CULTURE

In many countries, the population is polyethnic. This is the case in the United States, where a number of distinct groups (i.e. blacks, Native Americans, Latin Americans, to mention just a few) enjoy cultural traditions that are different from the traditions of the white, Anglo-Saxon or melting-pot-produced majority. A characteristic of any cultural group is that it has a particular way of viewing the social environment, that is, a unique subjective culture (Triandis 1972). Such subjective cultures lead members of a cultural or ethnic group[1] to behave in characteristic ways and to perceive their own behavior and the behaviors of others in a particular manner.

Personality refers to a behavior pattern characteristic of a particular individual. To the extent that ethnic groups have characteristic ways of behaving, they exhibit somewhat different distributions of behavior configurations. Thus, for example, it is widely acknowledged that Latin American individuals tend to be more (overtly) expressive than Anglo-Saxons. An ethnic group, then, may consist of individuals having characteristic behavior patterns and subjective cultures. Behavior patterns comprise patterns of abilities, habits, and predispositions to behave which emerge when individuals interact with their social environments. Subjective cultures can be viewed as consisting of norms, roles, values, and attitudes characteristic of persons in a particular

social environment. An important aspect of subjective culture is the language used by an ethnic group, since language is intimately connected with the way in which experience is interpreted and with the cognitive and affective categories which are used to conceptualize the world (Triandis 1964, 1972).

Most of the elements comprising the behavior patterns and subjective cultures of an ethnic group can be shown to be functional for the particular environment in which that cultural group has existed for a long time. For example, in the Arctic, survival requires the development of skills in hunting. Such hunting is usually done most effectively on an individual basis. Studies (e.g., Barry, Child, and Bacon 1959) of peoples who subsist through hunting and fishing (e.g., Berry 1966) have shown that members of these groups develop a highly differentiated perceptual and cognitive style (see Witkin and Berry 1975, for a review), and a personality that is characterized by independence, self-reliance, little affect, and poor interpersonal skills. On the other hand, agricultural societies such as the Temne (Berry 1966) require group action for survival. Tests administered to such groups indicate that their members develop less differentiated perceptual and cognitive styles, and their personality is characterized by much affect, interdependence, reliance on others, and good interpersonal skills. Persons with a less differentiated, or field-dependent, cognitive style are generally more skillful in interpersonally demanding occupations such as selling or entertaining, whereas persons with a highly differentiated, or field-dependent, cognitive style tend to perform well in such tasks as flying airplanes, taking aerial photographs, and doing mechanical work. Thus the ecology determines subsistence patterns, which in turn contribute to distinctive behavioral patterns.

The fact that many cultural elements are functional implies that individuals who have appropriate behavior patterns and personalities for a particular environment will fare well and will receive positive outcomes in that environment. When individuals from one culture are forced to adopt a very different cultural pattern, however, they are likely to experience high levels of stress, a reduction in positive outcomes, lower self-esteem, anomie, and general demoralization. The high rates of alcohol consumption found among Native American (Jessor, Graves, Hanson, and Jessor 1968), and the high incidence of "eco-system distrust" (distrust of people, things, and institutions in one's environment) experienced by the black ghetto unemployed (Triandis 1976) are examples of behavioral and experiential disorientation which can occur when a group is forced to exist in situations for which its culture is not appropriate.

THE NEED FOR INTERCULTURAL EDUCATION

One of the main purposes of education is to prepare an individual to function effectively in his or her environment. Viewed in this manner, education should provide skills, perspectives, and information, and should help develop attitudes which would enable pupils to obtain more positive outcomes than they would have received otherwise. Individuals who belong to an ethnic group which differs from the majority must often be able to function effectively in *two* different social environments. The degree to which such individuals will be part of each environment will, of course, vary, and will be a function of the interaction of a host of complex factors. It would seem, however, that the education of such children should ideally foster the development of skills, perspectives, and attitudes which would enable them to be effective members of both environments. A good model of how this can be done is that of a fully bilingual person. Such a person is able to switch with ease and without interference from one language to the other (Lambert 1967). His or her linguistic skills are suitable not only for one environment, but also for the other. Thus he or she is able to function linguistically in an effective manner in both environments. In a similar manner, a bicultural person should be able to interact effectively with persons from *both* cultures.

In order to enable children who differ in ethnic background from the majority to do this, it is important that educators and teachers take into account the skills, perspectives, and orientations that these children bring with them to school. Ideally, of course, this should be done for *all* children, and not just for those from a different cultural background. Thus, for example, a child who arrives in school with a field-independent orientation ideally should not be given the same curriculum as a child who arrives with a field-dependent, or field-sensitive, orientation, since for reasons discussed above, a curriculum which emphasizes exposure to many graphic materials would tend to be most helpful to the first child, but not to the second. The latter may well profit more from a curriculum which emphasizes good interpersonal relationships between teachers and students, or group learning as used by Johnson and Johnson (1983).

Ramírez and Castañeda (1974) have argued that our educational system has relied almost exclusively on the use of methods which are appropriate for persons whose cognitive and perceptual style is field-independent. Yet despite intracultural variations, many children from certain cultures (i.e., Mexican-American children) have been found to have a field-dependent or field-sensitive cognitive style. They suggest that to optimize the learning environment of these Mexican-American children, culture-matching teaching strategies, which in this case are field-sensitive strategies, should be utilized as well. Among the strategies that teachers can use, Ramírez and Castañeda mention the following: displaying expressions of approval and warmth, using personalized rewards, expressing confidence in the child's ability to succeed, giving guidance, encouraging cooperation, stressing achievement for the family, eliciting expressions of feelings from the students, emphasizing global aspects of concepts, and encouraging modeling of behaviors. Hale (1982) makes similar suggestions concerning the teaching of black children.

Schools and teachers, then, need to develop diagnostic skills which will lead to different emphases for different pupils. In addition, schools need to utilize culture-sensitization methods to make both teachers and pupils aware of cultural differences to a greater extent than they have so far. Our own research with Latin American or Hispanic pupils and Anglo-American teachers in U.S. schools (Albert 1983b, 1984a, 1984b; Albert and Adamopoulos 1976;

Albert and Triandis 1979) can be used to illustrate the importance of this.

Our objective was to find out if there were significant differences in how Latin American pupils and their Anglo teachers interpreted a wide range of common, naturally occurring school situations and behaviors. Very briefly, the procedure used was the following (see Albert 1983b for a more detailed description): Interviews with samples of teachers ($N = 70$) and pupils ($N = 150$) and detailed observations of classroom interactions were conducted to generate "critical incidents" depicting interactions between a Latin American or Hispanic[2] pupil and an American teacher.

The following is an example of a critical incident or story used in the research:

Mr. Jones was talking with a group of his students about different kinds of food. Some of the Spanish-speaking students started telling him about a dish from their native country, and Mr. Jones mentioned that he had never tasted it. The next day one of those students brought in a plate of the food they had been talking about for Mr. Jones (Albert 1984a, p. 70).

These incidents, or stories, were then presented to new samples of teachers and pupils from each ethnic group. We asked these persons to provide an interpretation of the behaviors and feelings of pupils and teachers in each of the stories. These interpretations, which were given in the respondents' own words and language, were carefully synthesized by a panel of bicultural judges into four alternative interpretations for each story.

The interpretations provided for the above incident were:
Mr. Jones thought that:

1. The student was very nice.

2. The student wanted him to know more about his country.

3. It would be interesting to try it.

4. The student should not have brought the food (Albert 1984a, p. 70).

These alternative interpretations were paired with each other for each story, and samples of Latin American teachers and pupils, and Anglo teachers and pupils, were asked to choose for each pair of interpretations the one that they preferred. These patterns of preference were then analyzed for significant differences between groups of respondents.

It was found (Albert 1983b) that there were significant differences between groups of respondents in 1,158 out of 5,922 comparisons made. This is four times the number of significant differences which could be expected by chance alone. Furthermore, there were one or more significant differences in preferences between groups of respondents in 141 out of 176 stories presented to the respondents. As expected, the greatest number of significant differences occurred between American teachers and Hispanic pupils. Some of the differences found between the two groups can be briefly summarized as follows: Latin American pupils tended to favor more personalized, individualized treatment; tended to place greater emphasis on interpersonal aspects of the situation; tended to blame the Hispanic children in the stories, rather than the teacher, for problems; expressed the view that children in several stories felt ashamed and fearful; and tended to feel that reliance on the family was extremely important. American teachers, on the other hand, tended to emphasize fairness and equality, focused more on task-related aspects rather than on interpersonal aspects of the situation, expressed the feeling that the teachers in the stories were uncomfortable with close interpersonal distances and touching, and tended to favor greater independence for the pupils. These are just some of the differences suggested by the data. There are, of course, many others, but we cannot adequately cover them here. (See Albert 1983b, 1984a, and 1984b for a detailed account of the differences found.)

A few examples may illustrate the relevance of these differences to the education of children of Latin American origin (see Albert and Triandis 1979).

The first example concerns the culturally based expectation on the part of many Hispanic children that their teachers will be as physically expressive and affectionate towards them as adults tend to be in their culture. Young Hispanic children, for example, like to cluster around the teacher's desk and touch her and kiss her goodbye. Many American teachers, being used to a different cultural pattern, are not aware of this need for touching; even if they are, they may not feel comfortable with this degree of physical closeness and may avoid these behaviors. The children, in turn, may experience the teacher's behavior as a rejection and may even come to think of their teacher as cold and distant. The Latin American teachers we have observed often reward a child who gives a correct answer with a hug or by touching him gently and with affection. (These teachers, incidentally, have reported that many Anglo kids like this, too.) Clearly here we are dealing with a cultural difference in paralinguistic behavior that has been described as well by Hall (1959) and documented by Sussman and Rosenfeld (1982).

During the interviews we conducted in the preliminary phase of the research (Albert and Triandis 1979), we were told about an instance in which a Hispanic child who did not speak much English was given a workbook and told by the teacher to work on her English lessons for a while, while the rest of the class worked in groups on a different task. The child felt not only isolated, but rejected by the teacher as well. In this particular case the teacher probably intended to help her learn English in the most effective way, but due to both a greater need for personal attention and the more communal nature of her culture, the child experienced the situation in a very negative way.

It is interesting to note that in a number of these situations the teacher is actually doing something which he or she feels is most efficient for teaching purposes (such as, for example, dealing with the class as a whole rather than with each child individually). Because of culturally based differences in expectations and interpretation of behavior, however, some of these actions turn out to have a negative impact on Hispanic children. In fact, in many situations Hispanic children do come to feel that their teacher dislikes them personally, or at least dislikes

Hispanic children. This feeling obviously has a detrimental effect on the child's motivation and is counter-productive for the teachers.

Teachers can help avoid this vicious circle by being aware of the children's culturally based expectations and by providing them, whenever possible, with the kind of personal attention that they need, or by finding other ways of dealing effectively with the problem. At the same time, of course, Hispanic children can be taught that their teachers behave as they do because they have different ways of doing things and not because they do not like them. These students can also be made aware that the teachers do not always have the time to provide individualized attention. (See Albert 1984a and 1984b for examples of one approach to sensitizing Anglo teachers to the perspectives of their Hispanic pupils and vice versa.)

Yet another perspective is provided by a situation in which white middle-class teachers interact with black ghetto children whose parents are unemployed. The parents of such children are likely to view the world with great distrust (Triandis 1976). The establishment, in particular, is distrusted and is often seen as exploitative. Consequently, persons who have "succeeded," such as teachers, are seen as exploitative agents of that establishment. Under these conditions it is not particularly surprising if the children of such parents view the teacher's behavior with considerable skepticism, if not with outright hostility.

Almost any behavior, no matter how positive, can be misinterpreted if the perceiver is strongly inclined to make hostile attributions. For example, if the teacher offers help, this could be viewed as the result of orders received from above and not really as a result of the teacher's good will. Alternatively, the teacher's behavior could be interpreted as ingratiation, the aim of which is to extract valuable information from the students. In short, given a negative perceptual framework on the part of the children, almost any action of the teacher could be seen as a hostile or, at best, a neutral behavior. Conversely, a teacher who is racially prejudiced could interpret any positive behavior of a pupil in a really negative manner. These conditions are obviously ripe for hostility and conflict, no matter how positive the behavior of the actors. In order to extricate teachers and pupils from such a vicious circle, it is necessary to break the perceiver's habit of automatically giving negative interpretations to the behavior of the other person.

The above examples suggest that intercultural education is necessary not only for students from diverse ethnic groups, but also for their teachers. In the course of interviewing teachers for our research, we found that many of these teachers failed to realize that cultural differences do exist and that they probably exert a powerful influence on their own, as well as on their pupils', behaviors. Some teachers, for example, would proffer the view that all children are alike. Others would attribute most, if not all, of the behavior patterns found among Hispanic children to their low socioeconomic status (SES). There is no question that low SES does contribute in important ways to certain behavior patterns. Yet it is also clear from our own research (where the socioeconomic status of the Hispanic pupils in our sample was the same as that of Anglo pupils), as well as from research conducted by other investigators (e.g., Díaz-Guerrero 1975), that cultural factors beyond socioeconomic status affect behavior patterns of members of a group in very important ways.

Albert (1979) has noted, in a different context, that this failure to perceive, or at any rate, to acknowledge, cultural differences has important historical, psychological, and cultural bases. She has identified a number of factors which may contribute to the relative lack of concern with cultural variables on the part of American investigators. These may well apply, perhaps in modified form, to American educators. They are the following: lack of direct experience with other cultures; a psychological need to simplify events, and hence to assume cross-cultural similarities; the realization that differences in test performance can be, and have been, used to discriminate against minority groups; an egalitarian ideology that postulates that teachers should treat every child in the same general manner; the fear of creating stereotypes; the historical experience of forging a nation out of a multitude of ethnic groups; the dominant economic and political position of the United States in the world; and ethnocentric tendencies which lead us to assume that our patterns of behavior are universal.

Teachers, then, need to develop skills which will enable them to attend to ethnic group *and* individual differences in their students, so that they can understand, and effectively reach, these students. This requires not only a variety of skills, but also flexibility and sensitivity to the cultural background of the students.

Pupils from other ethnic backgrounds need to learn a variety of skills, ideas, and principles which would enable them to function more effectively in both their own and the dominant culture. Thus an understanding of their own culture as well as of the dominant culture would seem to be vitally important for these students.

OBJECTIONS FREQUENTLY RAISED TO INTERCULTURAL EDUCATION

Having argued for the need for intercultural education, we can reasonably ask whether such education should be provided by our schools, or whether it should be left to other institutions.

For a variety of reasons, the school seems to be the most appropriate setting for intercultural education efforts. A school is often the first institution of the dominant culture which children from a minority group encounter. Their experiences in this setting are, therefore, critical to their subsequent attitudes and feelings about the dominant society. Similarly, it is often in this setting that children from the dominant culture have their first exposure to members of other ethnic and cultural groups. Schools are charged with the function of "educating" students, of teaching them about the physical and social world, as well as giving them some basic skills for functioning as members of society. Thus, while an understanding of different cultural patterns would seem critical for the minority child, it would also seem important and valuable for majority children in a multiethnic society.

A number of objections to the ideas presented here can be anticipated. Some will argue that with limited resources we cannot afford the luxury of multicultural education. The issue of cost is a complicated one, for no one knows how much money various kinds of intercultural education programs would require. Yet there is evidence that minorities drop out from school at higher rates than majority students. To cite but one example, Lucas (1971) found a 70 percent drop-out rate among Puerto Ricans in Chicago. It is well known that dropping out of school lowers a person's earning potential and may be related to higher rates of unemployment and, possibly, to higher rates of welfare payments. Thus the loss of income which results to the minority person who drops out of school, as well as society's loss of well qualified employees, and of the taxes which such employees could contribute—not to mention the human costs—should be entered into the cost equation.

In any case, there is clearly a need for making teachers aware of cultural differences through teacher in-service and pre-service training and by other means as well. Also, many of our schools already have pupils from many cultures and could utilize them as sources of information about other cultures without spending very much money. Either approach would require educational innovations and some effort on the part of teachers and administrators. It seems to us that in a society that spends over $100 billion a year on armaments that become obsolete every few years, there must be mechanisms to accomplish other kinds of goals as well. The crucial question, then, is whether we are willing to spend time, money, and above all, effort, to improve the quality of education in our society.

Another objection is centered around the argument that mainstream culture is "obviously best." This is an ethnocentric argument. As we have discussed previously, a culture produces a particular pattern of assumptions about the way the world is structured. That pattern often appears to be correct to the members of that culture, and the less information they have available concerning other patterns, the more totally correct that pattern will appear to be. Ethnocentrism (see LeVine and Campbell 1972) tends to be characteristic of persons who have been exposed to little diverse information and to child-rearing practices which did not allow them to learn about value systems which differ from those of their parents. An ethnocentric person usually considers his or her culture completely correct, better in all respects than other cultures, and obviously suitable for adoption by all others. Yet, as we have previously discussed, there is evidence that forcing members of an ethnic group to adopt the dominant cultural pattern may *not* be the best for these individuals.

Still others may see providing intercultural education as "coddling" some minorities, since in the past other ethnic groups "adjusted" without such help. The implication which underlies this argument is that such "coddling" may be unhealthy and/or unnecessary. But the discussion presented earlier suggests that for the minority child this may not be the case. In fact, the minority child needs to develop multiple skills in order to function effectively in his or her own environment and also in the environment of the majority.

The case can be made that majority children will also profit from the broad perspectives and the greater cognitive flexibility that are likely to come from intercultural education (Triandis 1976). There is already evidence that multilingual individuals are more creative than their monolingual counterparts (Segalowitz 1981). It is quite likely that *multicultural* individuals will be even more creative. Intercultural education would also probably help children develop a greater appreciation for diversity. In addition, this country is deficient in language skills (United States President's Commission on Foreign Language and International Studies 1979) and mainstream children exposed to other cultures may develop an interest in learning foreign languages.

Finally, some will argue that this is not compatible with American values. This argument is based on historical and cultural assumptions which have been alluded to above. Yet, if there is something unique about this society it is that it permits enough freedom for individuals to actualize their potential in unique ways. The imposition of a particular, limited, ethnocentric perspective limits these freedoms. Hence, it is fundamentally compatible with the American way to move toward multiculturalism and, therefore, toward intercultural education.

METHODS FOR TEACHING CULTURE IN INTERCULTURAL EDUCATION PROGRAMS

Supposing we wish to provide intercultural education in our schools, the question which arises next is how to do it. We will discuss several ways in which culture has been taught and will point out some of the advantages and disadvantages of each. A broad review of procedures which have been developed for intercultural training can be found in Brislin and Pederson (1976), Landis and Brislin (1983), and Seelye (1975). The three procedures we present below seem to be the most promising. The theoretical underpinnings of these three procedures rest on analyses of social behavior (Triandis 1975, 1977).

The first method is *experiential*. At its best it would entail having the student live in a particular culture for many years. This, however, is not a feasible way to teach a large number of students. Thus, experiential exposure to other cultures utilizing "controlled" or laboratory situations (e.g., setting up a village where trainees interact with their language teachers from the other culture over a period of months) . . . [is] used by some culture-trainers (Trifonovitch 1973). Other experiential activities which can more easily be employed by schools involve tasting foods from different countries, going to ethnic neighborhoods, and participating in relevant parades and festivals.

A second method for teaching culture is *behavioral* (David 1972). This method would entail reinforcing the individual for producing behavioral patterns which are commonly found in another culture, and discouraging behaviors which are inappropriate to that other culture. This approach would probably be most effective when what is desired is a modification of behaviors which are

primarily determined by habits. This method is time-consuming, however, since it requires that each behavior be reinforced. Furthermore, it may be contended that in settings such as schools, where persons from several cultural backgrounds interact, the aim should not be to change behaviors per se, but rather to teach individuals *about* another culture. Since the focus of this approach is changing specific behaviors (e.g., always shaking hands when meeting a person from the other culture), it does not necessarily result in increased knowledge or understanding of diverse aspects of the other culture.

A third method of teaching culture emphasizes *informational* aspects of learning. One way to provide information about another culture is to assign readings about other peoples' customs or history. This alone, however, does not usually teach a person to "see the world" from the perspective of members of the other culture. A special technique designed to do this has been recently derived from social psychological theorizing (Fiedler, Mitchell, and Triandis 1971; Heider 1958; Triandis 1975). This technique, called *attribution training*, aims to teach members of one culture to make attributions commonly made by members of another culture (Triandis 1975). Attributions are *interpretations* of behavior; that is, they are inferences about the cause of a given behavior. Thus teachers commonly make attributions about the causes of their pupils' behaviors. For example, when a pupil performs poorly on a test the teacher will tend to make attributions about the child's performance. The teacher may attribute the poor performance to the pupil's lack of ability, to lack of preparation, to his or her "laziness," to lack of time on the test, or to a myriad of other factors. Pupils similarly make attributions about the actions of their teachers. Attributions are dependent on the norms, role, affects, and consequences of actions seen to be operating in a given situation (Triandis 1975). For this reason, persons from different cultures may make different attributions to the *same* behavior.

When teachers and students come from different cultural backgrounds, they are likely to have some different expectations about what behaviors are appropriate in a given situation and, at least some of the time, they are likely to make different attributions about the same behavior. Misunderstandings can then occur which impede effective interaction between the teacher and the students. It must be noted that people are often not aware of the cause for their difficulty. Thus, for example, a Hispanic student may be doing something "perfectly normal" from his perspective when he spends some time after recess helping a friend look for his lost braces. Consequently, he may be genuinely surprised when his American teacher reacts with anger when he arrives in class ten minutes late.

Attribution training is a technique designed to teach persons from one culture to interpret events as persons from another culture do. It consists of a programmed learning approach in which a person is exposed to an instrument known in the literature as the "intercultural sensitizer" (ICS) or "culture assimilator" (Albert 1983a; Albert and Adamopoulos 1976). The assimilator is an instrument for culture learning which consists of several dozen short episodes depicting a problematic interaction between persons from one culture and persons from another culture. Each episode is followed by several alternative attributions to the behavior of one of the characters in the episode. Some of the attributions provided are those which are typically made by persons from the individual's own culture, while others are attributions commonly made by persons from the other culture. The aim of the training is to teach the individual to choose the attribution typically made by members of the other culture, and thus to expand the trainee's conception of possible attributions in that situation.

At first, the individual will have difficulty doing this, and will select attributions which are made by members of his own culture. With the aid of the feedback which is provided after each choice, the individual gradually learns to select the attributions which tend to be more typical of the members of the other culture. When the individual does this, he is given additional information about the differences between the two cultures. (See Albert 1983a for details about the process of constructing "intercultural sensitizers.")

SOME IMPLICATIONS OF INTERCULTURAL EDUCATION

Providing intercultural education is one way that schools can add flexibility and richness to each child's experience, and can teach the child that there are many ways of behaving and of perceiving the world. Such an approach could help teachers develop a new appreciation for students from diverse backgrounds, seeing their differences as resources to be explored rather than as sources of difficulty to overcome. As a result of a greater awareness of their students' backgrounds, teachers may develop new modes of teaching which may enhance their effectiveness with particular pupils.

Intercultural education could help children who belong to different ethnic groups to explore and to deal more explicitly with the difficult issue of identity, since such children would learn about their culture of origin as well as about the dominant culture of the society in which they live.

From their inception, the mission of many systems of education has been not only to provide skills and impart information, but also to provide understanding of the society in which the pupils live. Intercultural education would naturally enhance this broader mission.

NOTES

1. We will use the terms interchangeably following Glazer and Moynihan. Glazer, N., and D. P. Moynihan, (1975) "Introduction." In N. Glazer and D. P. Moynihan (eds.), *Ethnicity: Theory and Experience*. Cambridge, MA: Harvard University Press.

2. We use the terms *Latin American* and *Hispanic* interchangeably, as our samples consisted of immigrant children from Mexico, Puerto Rico, Cuba, and a number of other Latin American countries.

REFERENCES

Albert, R. D. (September 1979). "The Place of Culture in Modern Social Psychology." Paper presented at the meeting of the American Psychological Association, New York City.

Albert, R. D. (1983). "Mexican American Children in Educational Settings: Research on Children's and Teachers' Perceptions and Interpretations of Behavior." In E. E. García (ed.), *The Mexican American Child: Language, Cognition, and Social Development* (pp. 183–194). Tempe, AZ: Arizona State University.

Albert, R. D. and J. Adamopoulos. (1976). "An Attributional Approach to Culture Learning: The Culture Assimilator." *Topics in Culture Learning* 4, 53–60.

Albert, R. D. and H. C. Triandis. (1979). "Cross-Cultural Learning: A Theoretical Framework and Some Observations." In H. Trueba and C. Barnett-Mizrahi (eds.), *Bilingual Multicultural Education and the Professional: From Theory to Practice* (pp. 181–194). Rowley, MA: Newbury House.

Barry, H., I. Child, and M. Bacon. (1959). "Relation of Child Training to Sustenance Economy." *American Anthropologist* 61, 51–63.

Berry, J. W. (1966). "Temne and Eskimo Perceptual Skills." *International Journal of Psychology* 1, 207–229.

David, K. H. (1972). *Intercultural Adjustment and Application of Reinforcement Theory to Problems of Culture Shock*. Hilo, HI: Center for Cross-Cultural Training.

Díaz-Guerrero, R. (1975). *The Psychology of the Mexican*. Austin: University of Texas Press.

Hale, J. E. (1982). *Black Children: Their Roots, Culture, and Learning Styles*. Provo, UT: Brigham Young University Press.

Hall, E. T. (1959). *The Silent Language*. New York: Doubleday.

Heider, F. (1958). *The Psychology of Interpersonal Behavior*. New York: Wiley.

Jessor, R., T. D. Graves, R. G. Hanson, and S. L. Jessor. (1968). *Society, Personality, and Deviant Behavior*. New York: Holt, Rinehart & Winston.

Johnson, D. W. and R. T. Johnson. (1983). "The Socialization and Achievement Crises: Are Cooperative Learning Experiences the Solution?" In L. Bickman (ed.), *Applied Social Psychology Annual* 4 (pp. 119–164). Newbury Park, Calif.: Sage Publications.

Lambert, W. E. (1967). "The Social Psychology of Bilingualism." *Journal of Social Issues* 23, 91–109.

Landis, D. and R. Brislin. (1983). *Handbook of Intercultural Training*. New York: Pergamon Press.

LeVine, R. A. and D. T. Campbell. (1972). *Ethnocentrism: Theories of Conflict, Ethnic Attitudes, and Group Behavior*. New York: Wiley.

Lucas, I. (1971). *Puerto Rican Dropouts in Chicago: Numbers and Motivation*. Chicago: Council on Urban Education.

Ramírez, M. and A. Castañeda. (1974). *Cultural Democracy, Bicognitive Development, and Education*. New York: Academic Press.

Seelye, H. N. (1975). *Teaching Culture*. Skokie, IL: National Textbook Company, in conjunction with the American Council on the Teaching of Foreign Languages.

Segalowitz, N. (1981). "Issues in the Cross-Cultural Study of Bilingual Development." In H. C. Triandis and A. Hernon (eds.), *Handbook of Cross-Cultural Psychology* (Vol. 4) (pp. 55–92). Boston: Allyn and Bacon.

Sussman, N. M. and H. M. Rosenfeld. (1982). "Influence of Culture, Language, and Sex on Conversational Distance." *Journal of Personality and Social Psychology* 42, 66–74.

Triandis, H. C. (1964). "Cultural Influences upon Cognitive Processes." In L. Berkowitz (ed.), *Advances in Experimental Social Psychology* (pp. 1–48). New York: Academic Press.

Triandis, H. C. (1972). *The Analysis of Subjective Culture*. New York: Wiley.

Triandis, H. C. (1975). "Training, Cognitive Complexity, and Interpersonal Attitudes." In R. W. Brislin, S. Bochner, and W. Lonner (eds.), *Cross-Cultural Perspectives on Learning* (pp. 39–77). New York: Halsted/Wiley/Sage.

Triandis, H. C. (1976). *Variations of Black and White Perceptions of the Social Environment*. Champaign, IL: University of Illinois Press.

Triandis, H. C. (1977). *Interpersonal Behavior*. Monterey, CA: Brooks/Cole.

Trifonovitch, G. (1973). "On Cross-Cultural Orientation Techniques." *Topics in Culture Learning* 1, 38–47.

United States President's Commission on Language and International Studies. (1979). *Strength through Wisdom: A Critique of U.S. Capability*. Washington, DC: U.S. Government Printing Office.

Witkin, H. A. and J. W. Berry. (1975). "Psychological Differentiation in Cross-Cultural Perspectives." *Journal of Cross-Cultural Psychology* 6, 4–87.

Peace as an Ethic for Intercultural Communication[1]

DAVID W. KALE

A Ford Foundation executive with over twenty years experience in overseas travel has been quoted as saying that "most problems in cross-cultural projects come from different ideas about right and wrong." (Howell, 1981, p. 3). This executive's statement refers to two problem areas that have caused a great deal of difficulty in intercultural communication. First, many people have been in the uncomfortable position of doing something completely acceptable in their own country, while unknowingly offending the people of the culture they were visiting. This problem arose when I took a group of university students to Guyana in South America. In that warm climate, our students wore the same shorts they would have worn at home, but the Guyanese were offended by what they considered to be skimpy clothing, particularly when worn by the women. A second problem that arises in intercultural situations results when we try to get the rest of the world to live according to our culture's ideas about right and wrong. Interestingly, we get rather upset when people of another culture tell us how to behave. We like to believe that the way our culture chooses to do things is the right way and we do not appreciate people of other cultures telling us we are wrong.

Both of these problems have a bearing on ethics in intercultural communication. Discussing this topic causes stress to people of all cultures. Bonhoeffer suggests this is because we get the feeling that the basic issues of life are being addressed. When that happens, some of our most cherished beliefs may be challenged. When our cultural beliefs about right and wrong are being threatened, we feel the very foundation of our lives may be under attack (Bonhoeffer, 1965, pp. 267–268).

While such a discussion may be threatening, it must be undertaken nonetheless. With contact among people of various cultures rapidly on the rise, an increase in the number of conflicts over matters of right and wrong is inevitable. This essay addresses the ethics of intercultural communication by developing the following points: (1) a definition of communication ethics; (2) cultural relativity versus universal ethics; (3) the concept of spirit as a basis for intercultural ethics; (4) peace as the fundamental value in intercultural ethics; and (5) a code of ethics in intercultural communication.

A DEFINITION OF COMMUNICATION ETHICS

Richard Johannesen (1978, pp. 11–12) has said that we are dealing with an ethical issue in human communication when

1. People voluntarily choose a communication strategy;

2. The communication strategy is based on a value judgment;

3. The value judgment is about right and wrong in human conduct;

4. And the strategy chosen could positively or negatively affect someone else.

It is important to note in this definition that values are the basis for communication ethics. For example, we place a value on the truth and therefore it is unethical to tell a lie to another person. Without this basis in values, we have no ethical system whatsoever.

We face a major problem in our society because some people think they can decide right and wrong for themselves with no regard for what others think. Such a mindset shows that these people really don't understand ethics at all. If they did they would know that ethics are based on values, and values are determined by culture. Thus, there can be no such thing as a totally individual system of ethics. Such an approach would eventually result in the total destruction of human society (Weaver, 1971, p. 2; Hauerwas, 1983, p. 3).

Within a culture there is a continual dialogue about the things that are the most meaningful and important to the people of that culture. As a result, cultures are continually in a state of change. When cultures change, so do the values that culture holds. Thus, we must acknowledge that there is no fixed order of values that exists within a culture (Brummett, 1981, p. 293). This does not mean, however, that we are free to determine right and wrong for ourselves. It is much more accurate to say that we are shaped by the values of our culture than to say that we shape the values of our culture (Hauerwas, 1983, p. 3).

CULTURAL RELATIVISM VERSUS UNIVERSAL ETHICS

Because the values on which our ethics are built are generated by dialogue within a culture, the question must then be asked whether a person of one culture can question the conduct of a person in another culture. The concept of *cultural relativity* would suggest that the answer to this question is generally "No." Cultural relativity suggests that a culture will develop the values it deems best for the people of that culture. These values are dependent on the context in which the people of that culture go to work, raise their children, and run their societies. As such, those who are from a different context will develop a different set of cultural values and therefore have no basis on which to judge the conduct of people in any culture other than their own.

However, few would be willing to strictly follow the concept of cultural relativity. To do so would suggest that it was all right for Hitler to murder six million innocent people since the German people did nothing to stop it (Jaska and Pritchard, 1988, p. 10). At the same time, however, few are willing to support the idea that people of all cultures must abide by the same code of ethics. We know cultures develop different value systems and thus must have different ethical codes.

Both Brummett (p. 294) and Hauerwas (p. 9) have argued that because values are derived through dialogue, there is nothing wrong with attempting to persuade people of other cultures to accept our values. Before we do that, however, we must be convinced that our values are worthy and not based on limited self-interest. We must also be willing to work for genuine dialogue; too often these discussions tend to be monologues. We are generally far more willing to present the case for our own value system than we are to carefully consider the arguments for those of other cultures.

At the time of this writing, for example, people of many cultures are attempting to get the people of Brazil to stop cutting down their rain forests. As long as these persuasive efforts are based on a genuine concern for the negative effect cutting these trees is having on the global climate, there is nothing unethical about them. We must, however, also be willing to understand what is motivating the Brazilians' behavior and accept some responsibility in helping them to solve the serious economic problems their country is facing.

SPIRIT AS THE BASIS FOR ETHICAL UNIVERSALS

To develop the next point, how we are to make ethical decisions in intercultural communication, let me suggest that there is a concept on which we can base a universal code of ethics: the human spirit (Eubanks, 1980, p. 307). In the words of Eliseo Vivas,

The person deserves unqualified respect because he (or she) is not merely psyche but also spirit, and spirit is, as far as we know, the highest form of being. It is through the human spirit that the world is able to achieve cognizance of its status as creature, to perceive its character as valuable, and through human efforts to fulfill a destiny which it freely accepts (p. 235).

It is this human spirit which people of all cultures have in common that serves as a basis of belief that there are some universal values on which we can build a universal code of ethics in intercultural communication.

We have watched dramatic changes take place in the world as people in Eastern Europe and the Commonwealth of Independent States (the former Soviet Union) have attempted to improve the quality of life for themselves and their offspring. We identify with their efforts because we share a human spirit that is the same regardless of cultural background. It is this spirit that makes us people who *value* in the first place. It is from this spirit that the human derives the ability to make decisions about right and wrong, to decide what makes life worth living, and then to make life the best it can possibly be. Therefore, the guiding principle of any universal code of intercultural communication should be to protect the worth and dignity of the human spirit.

PEACE AS THE FUNDAMENTAL HUMAN VALUE

There is a strong temptation for those of us in Western democracies to identify freedom of choice as the fundamental human value. Hauerwas (pp. 9–12) has convincingly argued that freedom of choice is an unachievable goal for human endeavor. He notes that it is not possible for everyone to have freedom of choice. Some people in Czechoslovakia today want to have the country stay together as a whole while others want it to divide into two separate countries, with each being the home of a different ethnic group. It cannot be that both parties will have their choice.

A goal that is possible to achieve, however, is to direct our efforts toward creating a world where people of all cultures are living at peace with one another. This goal consists of three different levels: minimal peace, moderate peace, and optimal peace.

Minimal peace is defined as merely the absence of conflict. Two parties in conflict with each other are at minimal peace when they would be involved in violent conflict if they felt free to act out their hostile feelings. Perhaps there are U.N. peacekeeping forces restraining the two sides from fighting. Perhaps both sides know that continual fighting will bring condemnation from the rest of the world community. Whatever the reason, the peace is only superficial.

Moderate peace results when two conflicting parties are willing to compromise on the goals they want to achieve. In this case, each party has major concessions it is willing to make to reach agreement, but considerable irritation still exists with the opposing party in the conflict. Each party considers its own goals as worthy and justifiable and any of the other party's goals that conflict with its own are clearly unacceptable.

Moderate peace describes the situation that exists today between Israel and its Arab neighbors. Negotiations are proceeding in Washington between Israel and countries such as Syria, Jordan, and Egypt. The fact that these countries are at least willing to sit down at the same table and negotiate indicates that their relationship has developed beyond that of minimal peace. If those negotiations break off and hostile feelings intensify, they could be back to a relationship of minimal peace in a very short period of time.

Optimal peace exists when two parties consider each other's goals as seriously as they do their own. This does not mean that their goals do not ever conflict. The United States and Canada have a relationship that could be considered as optimal peace, yet there is considerable disagreement over the issue of whether acid rain from U.S. factories is destroying Canadian woodlands. Each side pursues its own goals in negotiations, but considers the other party's goals as worthy and deserving of serious consideration.

At the current time the Soviet republics of Armenia and Azerbaijan are locked in a bitter ethnic conflict over a territory within the republic of Azerbaijan that is populated mostly by Armenians. Because the territory is in their republic, the people of Azerbaijan say they should control it; because it is populated largely by Armenians, the Armenians say they should control it. Both groups cannot have freedom of choice in this situation, but they can live in peace if they are willing to submit to reasonable dialogue on their differences.

The concept of peace applies not only to relations between cultures and countries, but to the right of all people to live at peace with themselves and their surroundings. As such it is unethical to communicate with people in a way that does violence to their concept of themselves or to the dignity and worth of their human spirit.

A UNIVERSAL CODE OF ETHICS IN INTERCULTURAL COMMUNICATION

Before launching into the code itself, a "preamble" should first be presented based on William Howell's suggestion that the first step to being ethical in any culture is the intent to do what one knows is right (1982, p. 6). All societies set out rules of ethical conduct for people to follow based on cultural values. The foundation of ethical behavior is that people intend to do what they know is right. To choose to do something that you know to be wrong is unethical in any culture.

Principle #1 Ethical communicators address people of other cultures with the same respect that they would like to receive themselves.

It is based on this principle that I find ethnic jokes to be unethical. Some people may argue that ethnic jokes are harmless in that they are "just in fun," but no one wants to be on the receiving end of a joke in which their own culture is demeaned by people of another culture (LaFave and Mannell, 1978). Verbal and psychological abuse can damage the human spirit in the same way that physical abuse does damage to the body. Verbal and psychological violence against another person, or that person's culture, is just as unacceptable as physical violence. People of all cultures are entitled to live at peace with themselves and the cultural heritage which has had a part in shaping them. It is, therefore, unethical to use our verbal and/or nonverbal communication to demean or belittle the cultural identity of others.

Principle #2 Ethical communicators seek to describe the world as they perceive it as accurately as possible.

While in our culture we might call this telling the truth, what is perceived to be the truth can vary greatly from one culture to another. We know that reality is not something that is objectively the same for people of all cultures. Reality is socially constructed for us by our culture; we live in different perceptual worlds (Kale, 1983, pp. 31–32).

The point of this principle is that ethical communicators do not deliberately set out to deceive or mislead, especially since deception is very damaging to the ability of people of various cultures to trust each other. It is only when people of the world are able to trust one another that we will be able to live in peace. That trust is only possible when the communication that occurs between those cultures is devoid of deliberate attempts to mislead and deceive (Hauerwas, 1983, p. 15; Bok, 1978, pp. 18–33).

Principle #3 Ethical communicators encourage people of other cultures to express themselves in their uniqueness.

This principle is reflected in Article 19 of the Universal Declaration of Human Rights as adopted by the United Nations. It states:

Everyone has the right to freedom of opinion and expression; this right includes the freedom to hold opinions without interferences and to seek, receive and impart information and ideas through any media and regardless of frontiers (Babbili, 9).

In this book, *I and Thou,* Martin Buber cogently discusses the need for us to allow the uniqueness of the other to emerge if genuine dialogue is to take place.

Frequently, we place demands on people of other cultures to adopt our beliefs or values before we accept them as full partners in our dialogue.

Is it the right of the U.S. government to demand that Nicaragua elect a noncommunist government before that country is granted full partnership in the intercultural dialogue of this hemisphere? It is certainly possible that the people of that country will elect a communist government, and if they do, they are still entitled to equal status with the other governments of Central America. At the same time, we celebrate the fact that in central Europe people of several countries are finally being allowed to express themselves by throwing off the stranglehold of communist ideology imposed on them by forces outside their culture. Ethical communicators place a high value on the right of cultures to be full partners in the international dialogue, regardless of how popular or unpopular their political ideas may be. It is the height of ethnocentrism, and also unethical, to accord people of another culture equal status in the international arena only if they choose to express themselves in the same way we do.

Principle #4 Ethical communicators strive for identification with people of other cultures.

Identification is achieved when people share some principles in common, which they can do while still retaining the uniqueness of their cultural identities (Burke, 1969, p. 21). This principle suggests that ethical communicators encourage people of all cultures to understand each other, striving for unity of spirit. They do this by emphasizing the commonalities among cultural beliefs and values, rather than their differences.

At the present time we are, unfortunately, seeing an increasing number of racial incidents occurring on our college and university campuses. Many times these take the form of racist slogans appearing on the walls of campus buildings. The purpose of these actions is often to stir up racial animosity, creating wider divisions among ethnic groups. Such behavior is unethical according to this principle in that it is far more likely to lead to conflict than it is to peace.

NOTE

1. The author wishes to thank Angela Latham-Jones for her critical comments of an earlier version of this essay.

BIBLIOGRAPHY

Babbili, Anantha Sudhaker. (1983). "The Problem of International Discourse: Search for Cultural, Moral and Ethical Imperatives." Paper presented at the convention of the Association for Education in Journalism and Mass Communication, Corvales, OR.

Bok, Sissela. (1978). *Lying: Moral Choice in Public and Private Life*. N.Y.: Random House.

Bonhoeffer, Dietrich. (1965). *Ethics*. Eberhard Bethge, ed. N.Y.: Macmillan Press.

Brummett, Barry. (Fall 1981). "A Defense of Ethical Relativism as Rhetorically Grounded." *Western Journal of Speech Communication, 45*(4), 286–298.

Buber, Martin. (1965). *I and Thou*. N.Y.: Peter Smith.

Burke, Kenneth. (1969). *A Rhetoric of Motives*. Berkeley: University of California Press.

Eubanks, Ralph. (Spring 1980). "Reflections on the Moral Dimension of Communication." *Southern Speech Communication Journal, 45*(3), 240–248.

Hauerwas, Stanley. (1983). *The Peaceable Kingdom*. South Bend, IN: University of Notre Dame.

Howell, William. (1981). "Ethics of Intercultural Communication." Paper presented at the 67th convention of the Speech Communication Association. Anaheim, CA.

Howell, William. (1982). "Carrying Ethical Concepts Across Cultural Boundaries." Paper presented at the 68th convention of the Speech Communication Association, Louisville, KY.

Jaska, James, and Pritchard, Michael. (1988). *Communication Ethics: Methods of Analysis*. Belmont, CA: Wadsworth Publishing Co.

Johannesen, Richard. (1978). *Ethics in Human Communication*. Wayne, NJ: Avery Publishing Group.

Kale, David. (September 1983). "In Defense of Two Ethical Universals in Intercultural Communication." *Religious Communication Today*. Vol. 6, 28–33.

LaFave, Lawrence and Mannell, Roger. (Summer 1978). "Does Ethnic Humor Serve Prejudice?" *Journal of Communication*, 116–124.

Vivas, Eliseo. (1963). *The Moral Life and the Ethical Life*. Chicago: Henry Regnery Co.

Weaver, Richard. (1971). *Ideas Have Consequences*. Chicago: University of Chicago Press.

CONCEPTS AND QUESTIONS
FOR CHAPTER 8

1. What do you see as most necessary for the improvement of intercultural communication during the next decade?

2. How can intercultural communication be improved domestically? Internationally? Is one form more important than the other? Why?

3. Given all the complexities associated with intercultural communication, do you think there is really any hope for the future?

4. From Hatch's article on the evaluation of culture, what have you discovered that will permit you to evaluate your own culture?

5. What does Hatch mean when he differentiates between ethnocentric and humanistic values? Which are best in your opinion? Why?

6. What are the important ethical questions that communicators must ask themselves as they engage in intercultural communication?

7. What does Kim mean when she refers to a holistic approach to knowledge in the East and how does this approach differ from Western tradition?

8. Explain how Kim views Eastern and Western views of reality as complementary rather than competitive.

9. How do you believe the educational needs of a multicultural society can best be met?

10. What do Albert and Triandis suggest as the best way to achieve intercultural education?

11. Do you see a future where people of different cultures come closer together or one where they become increasingly isolated from each other? Why?

12. Why does Kale believe that ethnocentric behavior is such a serious problem in intercultural communication?

13. How can we persuade people to accept our values because they are not based on self-interest? Can there even be persuasion without self-interest?

14. Can you offer an ethical position that goes beyond the ones offered in this chapter? What is it?

15. Is it possible in this age of international contact to have a philosophy based on "live and let live"?

Epilogue

We introduced the topic of intercultural communication by pointing out both its boundaries and its territory. By looking at what intercultural communication is and is not, we were able to establish some guidelines for our investigation. In general terms, we suggested that intercultural communication occurs whenever a message sender is a member of one culture and a message receiver is of another culture. Once this broad definition was presented we were able to survey some specific refinements. We noted that culture is the sum total of the learned behaviors of a particular group and that these behaviors (attitudes, values, language, artifacts, and so forth) are transmitted from generation to generation. Differences among international, interracial, and cross-cultural communication also were examined.

Following our general introduction to intercultural communication, we focused on one of the conceptual threads woven through this book. This concept suggests that to understand intercultural communication one must realize the impact and influence of past experience. Anyone who has observed human interaction will have little trouble accepting the notion that where people come from—their cultural histories—is crucial to communication. Your prior experiences, structured by your culture, help to determine what you value, what you see, and how you behave. In short, what your culture has taught you, in both conscious and unconscious ways, will manifest during intercultural communication. Navajo Indians, for example, believe that the universe is full of dangers and that illness is a price to be paid for disorder and disharmony. These particular views are bound to be reflected in Navajo intercultural interactions. In another example, people from some cultures deem men more important than women. These people's behavior toward each sex will be influenced by this orientation. Even one's background colors what is perceived. Judgment of beauty is an example. In the United States, the slim, statuesque female represents the cultural stereotype of beauty. Yet in many Eastern European countries, a heavier, stockier body reflects the ideal. These examples—and there are countless others—point out that your culture gives the framework for your experiences and values. They, in turn, define your view of the world and dictate how you interact within the world.

Because people share cultural experiences in a symbolic manner, we explored the two most common symbol systems—verbal and nonverbal. Representing ideas and feelings by symbols is a complex and complicated procedure at best. When the dimension of culture is added to the encoding and decoding process, however, the act of sharing internal states becomes even more intricate. To help you understand this act, we sought to demonstrate the relationship between three closely related axioms: (1) language helps shape thoughts and perceptions (Whorf's linguistic relativity hypothesis), (2) diverse cultures have *different* words with *similar* meanings (foreign languages), and (3) cultures can use the *same* words with vastly *different* meanings (co-cultural use of vernacular and argot). We noted that the problems of coding systems plague actions as well as words. Even a simple hand motion can convey a host of unrelated meanings and interpretations. The hand gesture used by a hitchhiker in the United States is apt to produce a punch in the nose in Ghana. In short, the symbols used to share cultural experiences may often be subject to confusion and ambiguity.

Because communication takes place within a social context, we next explored how context affects communication and how communication differs according to the context. By viewing the issue of cultural diversity we were able to demonstrate that not only do the expected forms and patterns of communication change from context to context, but also that the expectations within a particular context change from culture to culture.

Next, we examined ideas and techniques that contribute to successful intercultural communication. We proceeded on the assumption that intercultural communication is, by its very definition and nature, an action and an overt activity. Intercultural communication is, in short, something people do to and with each other. Because of advances in technology, such as improved transportation and communication systems, all people seem to be engaging in more and more of this activity. In addition to increased communication among foreign cultures, the late 1960s and 1970s revealed that there were a number of co-communities within the boundaries of the United States. Co-cultures such as African Americans, the urban poor, the disabled, women, gays, the elderly, youth, Hispanics, and Asians wanted and demanded contact and dialogue with the main culture. Consequently, all Americans are engaging in intercultural communication at an accelerating rate. If this interaction is to be significant, and if intercultural communication is to foster increased understanding and cooperation, then potential problems must be avoided.

Finally, we extended our analysis toward the future. This is due, in part, to the fact that most intercultural interactions and meetings lie in the future. Although the success of your communication experiences may well depend on your philosophy and attitude toward intercultural communication, it will more importantly be influenced by the beliefs and attitudes you hold about members of other cultures and co-cultures. These attitudes and behaviors are deeply ingrained and influenced by racist and ethnocentric values. By this we mean that as each person acquires a culture, that person is, in both obvious and subtle ways, being taught a corresponding subjective and normative value system used to evaluate others. Many people are taught that their cultural group, whatever it may be, is superior to all others. This is one of the negative aspects of culture; it can also teach us who we must grow to hate. Richard Rogers and Oscar Hammerstein II aptly demonstrated this in their 1949 musical *South Pacific*. The lyrics of their song "You've Got to Be Carefully Taught" tell us a great deal about this cultural mechanism for creating hate:

You've got to be taught to hate and fear . . . you've got to be taught to be afraid of people whose eyes

are oddly made and people whose skin is a differ-
ent shade . . . you've got to be taught before it's too
late, before you are six or seven or eight, to hate
all the people your relatives hate; you've got to be
carefully taught.

Everyone, therefore, grows up to judge other cultures and co-cultures by his or her own learned standards. We frequently observe this when we hear people make such value expressive statements as: "Our way is the right way" or when they make reference to members of another culture or co-culture as "them" or as "those people."

The danger of such positions should be self-evident. It is indeed difficult to achieve mutual understanding if one's culture is placed in a central position of priority or worth. How foolish to assume that because one culture prays on Saturday while another worships on Sunday, one is superior to the other. Or take, for example, the cultural values of competition and winning. Because they are important values to North Americans, many assume that all cultures ought to strive to win and to be first. There are numerous cultures, however, where competition and winning are unimportant. On the contrary, cooperation and sharing are valued highly. To be guilty of racism or ethnocentrism is to doom intercultural communication to failure.

Yet each person is capable of change; but change is not simple. If intercultural exchanges are to be considered worthy of time and energy, each person must begin to realize that such change is possible and begin to accept others as equals.

Intercultural communicative behavior should not only be void of racism and ethnocentrism, it also ought to reflect an attitude of mutual respect, trust, and worth. We emphasize that intercultural communication will not be successful if, by actions or words, the communicators act superior or condescending. Every individual and every culture wants to believe it is as worthy as any other. Actions that manifest the opposite will diminish the worth and tend to stifle meaningful interaction.

The changes required are not easy. They require that we all possess a willingness to communicate, have empathy toward foreign and alien cultures, be tolerant of views that differ from our own, and develop a universalistic, relativistic approach to the universe. If we have the resolve to adopt these behaviors and attitudes and the desire to overcome racism and ethnocentrism and feelings of superiority, we can begin to know the feelings of exhilarization that come when we have made contact with someone far removed from our own sphere of experiences. Intercultural communication offers the arena for this interpersonal contact. It is our ability to change, to make adjustments in our communication habits, that gives us the potential tools to make that contact successful.

Index